To Lee and Gloria,

To grand members
of Naval Weather's Twentieth.
From the golden west.

And happy memories
of your marvelous state.

Best Wishes,

Dorothy Thomas Holland

Regards,

David B Holland, CDR, USN (RET)

THE NAVY WAS NEVER BLUE!

A Twenty-Year Chronicle of the Travels,

Travails, Opportunities and Joys of a

Naval Officer's Family

THE NAVY WAS NEVER BLUE!

FIVE FOUND IT ROSY-HUED!

By

Dorothy Thomas Holland

Miramot Publishers
Post Office Box 8663
Prairie Village, Kansas

1992

THE NAVY WAS NEVER BLUE!

Five Found It Rosy-hued!

By Dorothy Thomas Holland

Copyright © 1992 by Dorothy Thomas Holland

Published by Miramot Publishers
Post office Box 8663
Prairie Village, KS 66208

Jacket Design: Erica Fredrickson Holland

Library of Congress Catalog Card Number: 92-60050
ISBN: 1-881118-08-8

Printed in the United States of America
on acid-free paper

Dedicated to Dave

In Memory of Davie

For Lori and Bruce

Their Progeny:

Coreen, Skyler

David, Steven, Andrea

Preface

The original intent of this travel-study was to provide me, a typical Midwesterner, landlocked but with a Naval-flyer brother, an account of the unfathomable wonders of life as a dependent of a Naval officer.

With the wealth of travel and adventuring soon enhanced by three perceptive children, our family chronicle gained in perspective and volume. It also began to reflect the inordinate number of military and national crises: Korea, Bay of Pigs, Cuban Missile Crisis, President Kennedy's assassination—as well as the country's successes: the creation of the United Nations, NATO and the Advent of the Space Age.

Prompted by the arrival of the carrier U.S.S. *Independence* in the Persian Gulf in August 1990—with Dave being a "Plank Owner" of its commissioning in 1959—my "Log" assumed a topicality which I sensed might be helpful to anyone's contemplating or experiencing the unique and rewarding life of the military and subsequent adjustment to retirement. (Augmented by his splendid stint in the Navy, Dave—being young, just forty—succeeded in a second career. Now, at sixty-eight, he has launched into a third!)

Our travel was by many modes. Each destination and sojourn embraced study of the area's history, battlefields, presidencies, national contributions, literature, economy, religious and educational facilities, cuisine and disparate attractions. We investigated four corners of North American culture—from San Diego to Key West and Cuba, up the Atlantic Seaboard to Newfoundland, across the North to Alaska, down the Pacific Northwest to Monterey.

Dave's Naval career culminated with his tour in Washington, D.C., where we steeped ourselves in the gemstone of independence and riches of our national heritage. The quintessential circle was completed back to "The Heart of America," Kansas City, Missouri—to the Middle West—from whence we both emanated.

All five of us loved our grand Navy Life!
It was never "blue"—always, rosy-hued!

D.T.H.

Kenilworth, North
Prairie Village, Kansas

CONTENTS

ILLUSTRATIONS

THE NAVY WAS NEVER BLUE!

CHAPTER I

A NEW OCEAN BIMONTHLY

 Nautical Knot

There I stood ready to embrace the Navy! I had never seen an ocean nor been conveyed by a more seaworthy vessel than a Mississippi ferry but I was ready. With perfect equanimity, trembling only slightly, I faced the challenge: He stood beside me, tall, slender, tanned from California's winter sun. His hands were beautiful—long, tapering fingers, deeply bronzed, sufficiently hairy. His name was euphonious: David Bruce Holland, and his feet were enormous. There we stood, a young "jay gee" with an elfish quirk of a grin and an older maiden lady (I was already eight days his senior), joining our lives.

It was New Year's Eve of 1947. The wind was howling; the snow, whirling in a Kansas City blizzard. Guests arrived at my parents' home, formally attired. Long dresses were hoisted above tall galoshes; satin-striped trousers were tucked into high boots as the procession high-stepped down the middle of the street in wheel tracks through the swift ribbons of blowing snow. The groom's best man was late. Kenneth, Dave's brother, arrived after the fourth rendition of *Clair de Lune*—groping for the ring with one hand and pulling off his boots with the other. I tripped down the stairs wearing Mother's wedding gown of thirty years ago, of ivory slipper satin appliqued with satin braid. I met Dad at the bottom of the stairs, grateful for his strong arm and loving, comforting presence. Dave was already standing by the lemon-leaved and carnation-banked fireplace. He looked rather pale under his tan. He was not smiling, just twinkling a bit. When I stopped beside him, my legs began to tremble. Reassured by the thought of the long gown, train and veil, I composed myself. Then Dave grasped my hand in his firm, galvanic clasp and I trembled anew.

The ceremony was over and Dave kissed me, long and lingeringly. But Mother had everything well in hand. She rushed to Dave and shook his arm, "That's enough, that's enough!" Somewhat dazed, we turned to greet our friends and families.

Mother's dress was purple chiffon and velvet. It was her favorite color and somewhat of a creation: the right side was hardly begun. It had neither form nor finish, just a suggestion. She apparently had missed her last fitting and the seamstress, overzealous for her check, had carefully ironed out material and presented it for wearing. It had hung on Mother like one unending wrinkle. Something had to be done with alacrity. After repeated efforts and laudatory ingenuity, two of Mother's friends were successful: they finally got her to stand still. A few pins and hasty stitches later, Mother looked grandly presentable. "Now, Tommie, just remember to keep your right arm against your side!" Mother looked wide-eyed at me, and I, at her—and the hilarity burst! One of her favorite apothegms: "Laughter does you good like a medicine"—worked to our succor. With the first strains from the piano, the dress and intricacies of its wearing were forgotten by the few who knew and Mother, the most unself-conscious, genuine and lovable of women, went regally down the stairs to welcome her guests and preside over the festivities.

Little else I remember except we cut the cake with Dad's military sword (Dave intentionally left his in San Diego for, as he told me later, both Frank DeWitt Thomas' saber and Tommie May Lacy's wedding gown had graced a happy marriage and should do so again). When we departed, I wore beneath my fur coat, which had been full-length, a suit with skirt hem twelve inches from the floor, just topping my snow boots. A very sensible fashion for a bride of the blizzard! Dave wore a dignified blue pin-stripe suit and topcoat but no hat and the snow diamond-dusted his black curls before we got to the steps of the porch.

Traffic was not heavy that New Year's Eve. In fact, we encountered nothing in front of us as far as we could see, which sense was flirting with imagination, only globs of splattering snow which could not be erased from the windshield. We had reservations to stay at the Hotel Roubidoux in St. Joseph, Missouri, the town which had launched another trip from Missouri to California with the initiation of the Pony Express. But "express" was a hyperbolical oxymoron that night and our Holland transport gratefully skidded to a haven at the Bellerieve Hotel in mid-town Kansas City, the alternate destination which methodical, wise Dad had arranged for us.

On our first date, Dave had taken me to the Casbah Room of the Hotel Bellerieve where we had danced sambas and I had been impressed by his sophistication and grace as well as his handsome physiognomy and elegantly tailored suit. Dave had always been a marvelous dancer despite, or because of, his generous-sized "pedes." Indeed, he had rhythm and flow of all movement, not only of foot, but particularly of hand. Dave's hands could gesture, wield knife and fork, draw a map or pilot a plane with equal ease and beauty. I loved watching his hands on the wheel of the car.

Seemingly indolent and too relaxed, they flexed into taut strength or slackened to supple control with a flyer's efficiency of movement and assurance. Never hurried nor harried, never short-tempered nor impatient, Dave was as self-possessed as his hands were sure. He was a most princely human being in every attitude and behavior, in every plan and execution and I marveled at his being thus with me and contemplated my inadequacy of physical and mental attractiveness. Though I was not without self-confidence and the happy conviction that I could achieve aught that I willed, I was inwardly amazed at the undeserved perfection of my mate. I would never blatantly announce that conviction although I did allow innuendoes to escape which he modestly laughed aside with that amused, provocative twinkle in his eye. I thought of the words from a favorite hymn: "Thee will I honor; thee will I cherish; thou, my soul's glory, joy and crown."

On New Year's Day, the blizzard ceased, the sun brightened the glorious snowscape and it was Dad's birthday. I called to wish him "Happy Birthday" and to thank both of them for our memorable New Year's Eve. "Dot," said Mother, "you forgot your lipsticks!" I did not need to ask; I knew Dad would be on his way but I could not believe I had been that careless: "Wait, let me look," I urged. I lifted my dark brown suede gloves from my dark brown faille bag (both, gifts from Dave), lifted the gold crown clasp, took out a crown-embossed gold compact, a gold-edged comb in its crown case, one carefully folded white handkerchief, four folded pieces of white Kleenex, a brown coin bag with crown atop but no lipstick. With my coin bag clutched in my hand, I hurried back to the phone: "Oh, Mother; I'm so sorry, I must have left them on your dressing table. They're in a small, flat Lanvin perfume box with a clutch top." "Yes, we found them last night, Dad's already left, drive very careful-ly—it's our worst storm in years, we love you both." I laughed, relievedly; Mother and Dad were still taking care of me! And so was Dave: idly opening the coin purse, I discovered four small coins and understood the significance of the gold crowns. Dave had teased me once about my fascination with English culture and literature of the Georgian period and had now provided me with my first collectibles: four pennies, each bearing the profile of King George VI! With such wealth how could I ever be in need!

Dave was singing in the shower when Dad knocked on the door. Dad would not come in, gave me a strong hug and a kiss, my lipsticks, the *Kansas City Star* and a box tied in white ribbon with a white rose and a red. We breakfasted on our wedding cake, ate the last piece in Wichita where I had been born twenty-five years before, almost to the day, and enjoyed our first DBH dessert in San Diego with wedding-cake crumbs baked in Dave's favorite: raisin-rice pudding.

We left at noon for a planned reception in Lincoln, Nebraska, at Mother H's home. Since Dave's Mother and siblings: Mildred and husband, Dr. William H. Allaway, and four-year-old Susan; Dr. Robert E. Holland and Viola and Dr. Kenneth E. Holland and Naomi had all attended the wedding and since they were not intrepid flyer-drivers of Dave's ilk, we surmised the seven-thirty gathering might be delayed or postponed. Dad had no trouble getting to the hotel and assured me they were opening up one lane of all the major arteries and had begun the plowing of highways. "Just be sure Dave has an extra pair of chains, boots and a shovel." Dave did and we were soon driving in the brilliant January wonderland down the middle of the road, behind our own snowplow to the ASB Bridge where the plowman turned his vehicle around, waved to us and headed back south on the west lane of Oak Street.

Shortly after 2:00 P.M. we passed St. Jo where we had expected to arrive fifteen hours previously but Dave had two weeks' leave, his schedule was his own and we were enjoying each delay. Dave turned the dial to the Rose Bowl game where my alma mater, Michigan, was playing. He generously supported my eleven, was tolerant of my delighted squeals and off-key singing to the *Victors* as the Michigan score mounted. Michigan won, of course, and we won through to the Cornhusker Hotel in Lincoln with a half-hour of preparation time, apiece, before the Holland reception.

Dave left the door ajar as he shaved, for the second time that day; he was virile and handsome—even in lather and I dreaded the thought of shocking him after the reception. I would have to wash my hair and roll it up which I did every other day. Now Dave's entire family were curly-haired, with the exception of his brother Kenneth, and hair curlers were a nonentity for Mildred and Mother H. My Mother's hair was very fine, very long, it had never been cut, and had a natural loose wave, the ends of which she encouraged with a curling iron before tucking into a chignon at the nape of her neck. (I remember as a child I loved to watch the nightly ritual of Mother's "undoing her hair" to brush the long, dark mass, which reached almost to her waist, and twist it high on her head in a large flat coil for her sleeping coif.) Alas, there would be no such romantic femininity for Dave! After a beautiful reception, elaborately executed by Dave's Mother who was an accomplished hostess and culinary expert (with two such Mothers, I had much to live up to), I went back to the Cornhusker with Dave and boldly washed my hair. After taking my third bath of the day, and very leisurely, I washed my hair in the lavatory—very leisurely. It was late, I could hear no sound and I knew my new spouse was asleep. I quickly rolled up my hair, tied a matching blue chiffon scarf around it, donned my robe and opened the door. And there he sat! He didn't say a word, he didn't leave, he just grinned at me. We might both survive, after all, I decided!

We breakfasted late the next morning, my ordering baked apple and cream and Dave, French toast and sausage. Breakfast had always been my favorite meal and we lingered over it even though Dave, I discovered, was not a coffee drinker. We had only to drive to Wichita, Kansas, that day and had no other plans to accommodate. After seeing the capitol area and the University of Nebraska, Dave showed me the large three-storied white frame house where he had lived until he was twenty. It was just a block and a half from the Agricultural Campus where his father had taught. Dave slowed the car to show me the corner where he, the youngest of the family, awaited his father each late schoolday afternoon. "And then we raced home"; and we drove the path. It was a wonderful neighborhood of substantial frame and brick houses, pridefully cared for. Dave's father had died when he was sixteen but his Mother had kept the big house until Dave, the last sibling to leave, had finished two and a-half years at the University and had reported to the Navy for flight training. Then, Dave's older brothers, Robert and Kenneth, were commissioned officers in the Army; Robert, an M.D. and Kenneth, an Orthodontist, and were in Germany. Mildred had married William H. Allaway and lived in Ames, Iowa, where "Hub" was completing his Doctorate in Soil Chemistry at Iowa State University.

As we left Lincoln, driving slowly through the campus, I began to be impressed by Dave's visual acuity. He could drive his car, looking straight ahead, and see every beautiful coed on both sides of the street. Oh, the skill of the Navy flyer! Would I ever fully appreciate it? In years of flight training and flying throughout the world, in wartime and peacetime, Dave had been trained to instantaneous recognition of all objects within his peripheral, and subliminal, vision whether they were sauntering along a sidewalk or streaking with inimical intent from the clouds. And because it took no concerted effort to see, to register and to appreciate and because I knew that he knew that I knew that he enjoyed it, I refused to let him take my picture on the entire honeymoon trip! "You don't need *my* picture," I explained, "take a picture of the trees. They're wonderful trees. I've never seen anything so beautiful!" And I did love trees and even took a college course in Dendrology, so much did I love trees—but mostly, his ability to imprint his mind with pulchritudinous females was far too facile for His One not to present a mild deterrence to easy access. So we have a complete catalog of trees in every state from Missouri to California plus a shelf of the *Department of Agriculture Yearbooks* which included everything from wild clover to infectious sinusitis in turkeys—so that I could identify trees!

We stayed in a separate-unit motel in Wichita and I marveled at the complete privacy of a motel room. "Why, it's like living in your own little house!" I found. "Is there no restriction, do they rent a motel room to anyone? Would they rent to a minor? Surely there must be some limitation." Dave must have been struck by my naiveté or perhaps he was merely disinclined to discuss the ethical and legal ramifications of modern hostelry, for he shook his head "Yes" and then, "No." I looked around for literature to read on the problem while Dave made dinner reservations. I found disclaimers against any responsibility, except temporary cleanliness, and concluded that Mothers and Fathers, particularly of girls, earned their streaks of gray.

We had breakfast at the site of our first téte-à-téte dinner the night before. There was no baked apple, Dave told me—so I ordered kadota figs and cream. At each breakfast, I was served a baked apple or kadota figs. In Las Vegas, at the Flamingo Hotel, Dave deposited me in a booth and went to the desk for the newspaper, as was his wont. I finished my notes on the previous day's journey and opened the large, flamboyant menu when Dave had still not returned. When Dave slipped in beside me, I told him I would have grapefruit and raisin toast. "Why?" he wondered. "Neither apples nor figs are served," I advised him. "We'll see," and he ordered my baked apple, "and put a kadota fig on top," he smiled at the waitress. And she produced it! "How did you manage that?" I *mirated*, impressed by my handsome partner. "Easy," laughed Dave. "I don't reserve a room unless they guarantee your breakfast!"

It was probably the first time hotel reservations were made for an apple and figs—and in six different states. By the time we got to the West Coast, Dave's map was liberally covered with forbidden fruit! Each successful overnight produced an apple with hotel imprinted thereon or a fig-leaf disclaimer. With typical, nautical precision, Dave, anticipating a return from California, was charting a course which the most skilled cartographer would envy but which I hoped would not be discovered by his fellow officers—lest they read it symbolically!

We spent a week on the South Rim of the Grand Canyon and enjoyed exploring together in the warm January sunshine. I held my breath and sometimes my husband when he stood on the very edge of the outcropping boulder photographing the beauties of light and shadow below. I discovered my favorite tree was the pale, wispy west-

Figure 1. Honeymoon

ern larch, a deciduous conifer, which still displayed a few petioles of short, golden silk needles twisting in a wind-dance with every breeze. The branches were graceful and drooping, the bark reddish brown, deeply furrowed and overlapping, the cones were short and upright like a permanent plum with pointed bracts. I asked Dave what his favorite tree was. He said he wasn't fascinated by trees and he looked at me—and raised his left eyebrow! We both laughed and I felt myself blushing. "You should," he said, "you'll be sorry!"

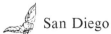 San Diego

When we arrived at Miramar Naval Air Station, San Diego, on January 12, 1948, shortly after noon, it was deliciously warm and the sky was cloudless. I wore a kelly green, long-sleeved coat dress of heavy faille and felt comfortable with the car windows down in the gentle wind. I was amazed by all of the activity: the many planes overhead, on the runways, in the hangars. Even though it was the noon hour, there was no cessation of flying. Several members of Dave's squadron came to the car to greet us as Dave pulled in front of BOQ. They had on their "greens" with gold wings above the left pocket of the blouse. They wore khaki shirts, black ties and brown shoes. In the Navy, I learned, one was either a "brown shoe," a flyer, or a "black shoe," a shipboard officer. There seemed to be a certain prestige and glamour in a brown shoe that was lacking in a black shoe. That I sensed some time later. At Miramar, of course, they were all flyers and there was a tremendous esprit de corps. Such brotherhood and loyalty were magnified in each squadron which was tightly knit with respect, devotion and genuine love. They lived together, worked together, laughed and relaxed together and depended upon each other for their very lives. It was somewhat like a college fraternity, yet there was far greater intensity and integration of personality and purpose. There was no foolishness when "on duty," rather, great fellowship.

Several of the officers wore crewcuts in contrast to Dave's appealing, short black curls. I recalled that my brother Charles, who had flown in the same squadron as Dave in Saipan, had never worn a crewcut. There was no stylization as to appearance except that their hair was short around their ears and nape of the neck; their uniforms, well-fitting, well-pressed; shoes, highly polished; their skillful hands, beautifully groomed. I had always been observant of masculine hands whether they were those of an artist, doctor or mechanic but Navy flyers seemed to have hands that set them apart. There were no short, broad, pale, hairless hands that bespoke of effeminacy and a safe, cloistered life. They were magnificent hands—creative, deft, bold. And Dave's, of course, were the most beautiful; his and brother Charles' and Dad's.

Dave was still in mufti; he had not had on a uniform for two weeks. I wondered suddenly why he had not worn dress blues for the wedding rather than formal civilian attire. I had never seen him in his dress blues nor in any uniform except summer khakis which he had worn that day in July.

Charles and Dave had flown together in the Pacific in the last stage of the war. "Our crew picked up a squadron plane (PV-2) at Kaneohe Marine Corps Air Station on Hawaii after completing crew training at Whidbey Island NAS," remarked Dave, explaining his Pacific assignment, as he showed me squadron snapshots on my Lincoln visit. "We flew to join the squadron on Saipan. That's when I met Charles. He and his squadron, while based on Tinian, had just been awarded the Air Medal for searching and discovering the six hundred survivors from the torpedoed cruiser U.S.S. *Indianapolis.*" "Yes, I remember his writing about that. What dreadful losses the country sustained in the Pacific! Why, there's Charles!" I exclaimed, as I unexpectedly discovered my "baby brother" in the handful of Dave's Saipan pictures. "With a dog!" I looked askance at Dave. "That was 'Rocket'—the squadron mascot; 'Catfish,' that is, Charles, really loved that dog!" "Catfish?" I trilled. "That's easy. His initials are 'C.F.'" "Did Rocket fly, too?" I teased. "No, but he joined in everything else—he even drank beer," Dave laughed at the recollection. "Charles

Figure 2. "Catfish" with Rocket, Squadron Mascot

flew with the skipper, CDR Frank D. Heyer. They shot skeet together, played bridge and really knew how to relax. We all had great times together—it was a close squadron." "Well, you must have performed superbly and you certainly earned your moments of levity. It's wonderful to have it all over! I'm proud of both of my Navy flyers!"

Charles became an active reserve after the war while Dave elected to stay in as an officer in the regular Navy. Dave had ferried a plane from Miramar to Memphis for O & R (Overhaul & Repair). Staying overnight in Kansas City on his way back to the coast, he had called Charles and had lunch with him. I was working as an Assistant Personnel Examiner in the City Hall, having followed in the footsteps of my older brother, Lacy D. Thomas, to the University of Michigan and the Personnel Department of the City Hall.

Lacy, just graduated from Michigan, had been in the first city government which installed the Merit System—after Hal Luhnow, in 1939 and 1940, had spearheaded the "Clean-Up" (they wore little brooms in their lapels; Mother wore hers on dress jackets) of the infamous Tom Pendergast machine. Kansas City, Missouri, soon came to be known—not for the Union Station Massacre, political corruption and racketeering and the paving of Brush Creek with Pendergast cement—but for exemplary city

Figure 3. Heyer's Air Taxi
     Service

Figure 4. Dave's Crew

Figure 5. Dave with
     Peleliu Sue

Figure 6. Ready to Roll

Figure 7. Skeet Match

Figure 8. On Line

Figure 9. Dave's Favorite
Breakfast

Figure 10. Popular Wheels

government and sane living under Mayor John B. Gage and L. P. Cookingham, City Manager.

When Lacy died in 1943, shortly after I left for Ann Arbor, having completed three years at the University of Kansas City, I vowed to continue the efforts he and Mother had made. Charles was unavailable, of course—flying in the Navy and Dad was in the war effort as a metallurgist for Pratt & Whitney. In March 1945, after being graduated from Michigan, where the male population consisted of Marines in the Japanese Language School, Med students and a few engineers, and everyone was intent upon getting through and "into the war," I took the Merit Exam for Personnel Examiner—just as Lacy had—passed it and was hired. I was privileged to work with those who knew and revered my family and were idealistically exerting themselves for effectual city management which was not notably newsworthy in the waning months of World War II and the early post-war period.

So strong was our familial commitment to continuity that, after the war ended, Charles applied for admission to the University of Michigan to achieve his Engineering Degree. He, of course, was very sanguine, with two recent graduates in the family—but it was not to be. Michigan's President, Dr. Alexander Ruthven, called Mother to explain that they did not even have room for all of their state's "G.I.s" who were clamoring for admission and that he deeply regretted having to make a negative decision, especially since Charles' credentials were outstanding and the Thomas family had been loyal patrons of the University. Charles became an active reserve in the Navy, flew monthly at Olathe Naval Air Station and continued his degree in Mechanical Engineering at the University of Kansas—to my great happiness.

I never knew why Charles, a year and a half my junior, my beloved friend and director, brought Dave to meet me July 24 of 1946. He never wanted me to know his friends, except to say "Hello"; I was certainly never to date them and, heaven forfend, that I should marry one of them! I reasoned later that perhaps Dave was just not one of Charles' select inner circle or that Dave was so obviously a much-besieged Apollo that I would have the good sense to know that he was not for me—with my so obvious limitations of which Charles reminded me daily. I was sure that he had already told Dave that I was "a fraud" and "a phony" (those words of endearment always spoken with a mischievous chuckle and pat on the back), so I continued to be bemused by the "honor" of the presentation.

I was hanging up my hat, which I always carried, never wore, having just come back from lunch, when they walked into the back office. I wore a white dress splattered with brown daisies. It was made of rayon jersey, form-fitting and quite short. I liked the dress because it was comfortable and did not wrinkle easily; but because I knew it flattered me, I always carried a huge hat clutched at my waist inasmuch as I did not like to be studied and Twelfth Street, Kansas City, was always windy. So there I stood, without my hat, and I was being roundly observed! That struck me as unfair and unmannerly though, I admitted, not unmanly. After we shook hands, and I liked his hands, I decided he was too pretty and possibly, too resolute. I ignored him, was hardly polite but he sat there, unruffled, perfectly at ease, watching me as I worked. Finally, Charles and Ensign David Bruce Holland left. As Charles told me later, Dave asked if he could call me that night, having told Charles that his plane for the coast would not leave until the next day. Charles said: "She's busy," not knowing but preferring that I would be. I was; besides, the Ensign was too assured and not in the least dismayed by my indifference which I thought I had feigned well.

The following week, I received a pleasant, short letter which was quite original: not one complimentary or flattering remark! That impressed me favorably and we corresponded awhile. The war was over and I had done my share of letter writing, so I soon desisted.

The following June (1947), Dave returned, piloting a P2V-1 from Miramar to Olathe and called for a date to which I acceded. In September, Dave wired that he had two weeks' leave and asked if I would meet his plane. I wrote that I would and he arrived commercially from California in his impeccably tailored brown herringbone suit, carrying a small portable radio and looking very dashing with a deep tan and his black hair curling crisply in the bright sun.

Dave's first leave, three months after our June date, produced an engagement; his second, in three months, a marriage. "That young man is *purposeful*!" said Mother.

Dave, when in civilian clothing, never wore a hat despite the weather. In uniform, he was never without one. Even aboard ship, I was told and soon observed, officers donned a cap when they left their stateroom or office or went to the wardroom for mess. The tables in the lounge of the wardroom would be piled with white-covered caps with differing amounts of gold braid and "scrambled eggs" (gold braid on the black visors of Commanders' caps and above). That used to amuse visiting Air Force and Army officers. The Naval officers maintained they were not in complete uniform if they sallied forth without their caps.

Caps were doffed to me, in turn, greetings and knowing glances exchanged and Dave's friends hurried off to the "O-Club" for their noon meal. "I have the neatest room in BOQ!" Dave announced, "want to come in to see it?" I thought he was jesting and wondered at the propriety of a married woman in a bachelor's quarters and said I would stay in the car. "You better come," he teased, "it's your last chance!" I shook my head, "No," laughed him away and have regretted it ever since!

Apartments, new or ancient, were impossibly scarce in post-war San Diego but Dave secured for us a new, first-floor apartment, with private beach in Queenstown Court, Mission Beach, a stone's throw from the Pacific Ocean. He advertised once in the newspaper: "Naval officer and bride, who neither smoke nor drink, have neither children nor pets, seek an apartment!" He was inundated with available apartments from which to choose. Dave wrote in his last letter to "Miss Dorothy Thomas": "Darling, I had many replies to my ad in the paper, so suffered no difficulty in finding a place to live. The apartment that I have chosen is in Mission Beach, a suburb of San Diego situated on a strand running between the ocean and the bay. It is three blocks from the beach and one block from the bay. The business district with all its stores is only a few blocks away, but it is not noisy. The apartment is very new, with a refrigerator, stove and hot water heater, tile bathroom, bedroom and living room. I chose it for its newness and its convenient closeness to the beach and stores. I hope you like it, but if you're not satisfied with every little detail we'll find another place. The address is: 830 Queenstown Street, San Diego, California." I received his wire later that day: "Reference My 14 Dec Correct Address 830 Queenstown Court Mission Beach San Diego Calif Love Dave."

What a wonderful honeymoon apartment! When we drove down the lane to Queenstown Court, my first awareness was of sound: "I'm looking over a four-leaf clover that I overlooked before. . . ." and Art Mooney's banjo hit always will be associated with our first happy domicile and idyllic days of sand, surf and sun. The small living room was fresh and immaculate with heavy pine, overstuffed furniture, coordinated drapes, golden tan tile floor and a space heater built into the wall which we needed in early mornings and evenings. There were no rugs to trap the sand and housekeeping took little time from my culinary efforts and our enjoyment of the beaches. The kitchen was long and narrow with a breakfast room overlooking the walk which led eastward to our little beach and westward to the boardwalk stretching for miles north and south along the wide sands of the Pacific Ocean. Once we walked the length of Mission Beach to the south through much of Ocean Beach but came back by trolley because Dave had night flying and afternoon shadows were beginning to elongate. When Dave flew at night, I supped on Lady Borden's vanilla ice cream and coffee, listened to every plane overhead and read until his return. I was never aware of a plane's movement in the night skies unless Dave was flying and then I heard every sputter and revving of the engines. But I did not worry, being supremely confident of his skill, I just listened—and waited for a car door to close and quick feet to come up the walk.

San Diego was the ultimate Navy town where nautical activity of fleet and air was continuous. The U.S. Naval Air Station, Miramar, was northeast of San Diego; the U.S. Naval Air Station, North Island (Coronado), was southwest; with the U.S. Naval Station, south, on the mainland and the U.S. Amphibious Base, opposite, to the west, on the Silver Strand connecting Coronado Island to the Imperial Beach, site of the U.S. Naval Communication Station. With such an overwhelming concentration of Naval personnel, protocol was emphatically observed and I was unprepared.

At Dave's behest, I later ordered a copy of *Welcome Aboard* which was not a best seller in the Midwest when we married—not being published until 1951, when I perused it with great interest. *Welcome Aboard* was the *Emily Post* of the Naval Officer's Wife and was very explicit and wonderfully dependable.

A squadron wife had alerted me that new brides were to be called upon within twenty-four hours of arrival by officers and their ladies. We were into the afternoon of the third day and I relaxed my preparedness. It was three o'clock, or fifteen hundred hours Navy diction, on a Sunday afternoon. Dave had flown most of the night, we breakfasted late, he had not shaved and we were enjoying a nap. Dave was instantly out of bed, hardly before the doorbell rang a second time—like the excellent Navy flyer he was, donning trousers and shirt and warning me: "It's the skipper!" I stepped into spectators without hose, pulled a rust-colored jersey dress with only three green buttons to secure and a wide green belt already in the loops—over my head, washed my face, brushed my hair in two sweeps and made my appearance. They were delightful! I offered them cherry-nut cake which I had baked during night flying but they had other calls to make and gracefully departed, leaving their calling cards even though my card tray had not arrived. (The officer calls on adult members of the household; his wife, only on females over fifteen.) So I was officially "welcomed aboard" San Diego!

Actually, few of the officers called upon us for most of them were "ninety-day wonders," unlike Dave. The "Academy" officers were the most strict about social decorum and they punctiliously called and expected the return courtesy within thirty days. And we were quick to accede. In fact, we were so quick that we made the first call on the Admiral, Dave's wearing his new black suit widely fretted with a fine red plaid, complete with price tag! But the Admiral would never have seen it if he hadn't lauded Dave's choice of suit. It was the turn of inspection that swung the tag from under Dave's left arm! The peacetime Navy was a jolly group and no one enjoyed a laugh at his own expense more than Dave. We were glad it was not one of Dave's extravagant, pre-nuptial, hand-tailored San Francisco suits but something that even an Admiral could afford!

There was great brotherhood in Dave's squadron and I relished the social times when wives were included. One tall, attractive officer continued to suggest to me that I go to the beach with his wife Marilyn. "She takes a peanut butter sandwich and spends the entire day at the beach. You should go with her." I thanked him but was not enticed. I loved the sun and the sand but only as long as I could prop up my head to read a book and I needed no female companion to do that. Dave had taken me to the O-Club to a dinner dance and I wore a royal blue, long-sleeved, three-quarter length, full-skirted dress with a cowl collar high in front, slightly lower in back, belted at the waist with a rhinestone and pearl clasp. My only jewelry was a beautiful rhinestone bracelet which Dave had given me and a matching comb in my hair. My high-heeled, black satin sandals had ankle straps which I discovered later Dave did not like, so that was the only time they were ever worn. I was dancing with Dave's insistent friend. "I married Marilyn for the same reason Dave married you," he averred. I stiffened in disavowal. "Just relax," he insisted, "let me lead." "I'd like a coke," I said, breaking from his hold. He walked with me to the bar. They had no coke, so I asked for a daiquiri. "You don't drink a cocktail at eight-thirty," he corrected, "what you should have is a highball." I told him to save his rules for Marilyn, that I was Dave's concern, thanked the bartender for the daiquiri and was glad to find Dave at my side. It was the only friction I ever had with one of Dave's fellow officers. They were of the same rank and so I was not

31 January 1948

Dear Mom and Pop,

It has been one glorious month now that Dorothy and I have been together. It has truly been a wonderful month.

From the very first day Dorothy has proven to be a highly capable wife. I cannot praise Dorothy too highly for her efforts to satisfy my desires. She is very resourceful in providing delectable and attractive meals. I am amazed at the way she can take foods and form them together into a dish that appears to have needed much practice and years of experience.

She is very game at trying a new dish, and I along with her, for I know that she will do a faultless job of it. What little exercise I get does not balance the amount of food I have been putting away, and I'm afraid that the weight I am gaining is in the wrong place.

Dorothy and I know that we are extremely fortunate in receiving so many lovely lifetime gifts. The silver, crystal, china and all of the other items are truly enviable treasures.

Lt (jg) David B Holland
850 Greenstown Court
San Diego 8, Calif.

SAN DIEGO
FEB 1
6 PM
1949
CALIF.

SAVE THE
IN U.S.
PAYROLL SAVINGS

Mr. and Mrs. F. O. Thomas

I wish to express my sincere
appreciation of the warm welcome
with which I was received into the
Thomas family. Dorothy is my dream
come true, and I wish to thank the
family that made this possible, for you
all spent endless hours in educating
Dorothy to be a fine woman.

Thanks ever so much for
shipping the crystal and silver in
such a careful manner. The Navy
packers could use some instruction
from you I am sure.

Thank you again for everything.

Your loving son,

Dave.

apprehensive. I was glad to learn, however, that they were not close, seldom flying together. When I told Dave I had no intention of going to the beach with Marilyn, he said: "I wouldn't want you to! She spends all of her time there and at the Officers' pool. You have nothing in common."

I joined the San Diego A.A.U.W. and the Chi Omega Alumnae and the Officers' Wives' Club which had monthly meetings and bridge luncheons. Time passed swiftly. We loved Coronado Island, that favorite Navy retirement spa, and dining at the popular hotel. La Jolla was filled with Kansas Citians but did not command our dreams. Rather, we liked the mountains and spent happy hours investigating Mt. Palomar and its magnificent observatory. What gorgeous terrain!

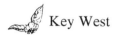 Key West

In thirteen months, we were unqualified for our apartment! But that was alright—we weren't there. For some reason, complimentary, I learned, the Navy destined Dave to be qualified in the air, under the water, on land and on sea. In ten weeks, Dave was ordered to Underwater Weapons School in Key West, Florida. They wanted him immediately. We packed only suitcases and left and each item followed us safely, including our silver flatware, jewelry and money in the dresser drawer. I soon learned to carry our silver, jewelry and favorite recipes. Not everyone was as dedicated to our survival as our altruistic landlady in San Diego, Mrs. W. B. Smith.

We had a three-day week end to drive from the southwestern extremity of the continental United States to the southeastern—and then wind westward along the Keys. Dave adroitly expedited our precipitant dart for my daytime viewing of the aqueous South and it was—splendiferous! I had never imagined there was so much water in land and circumambient to the shoreline. We swiftly saw: the Louisiana bayous, Lake Pontchartrain, the Mississippi Delta and the Gulf of Mexico. Then Dave crossed the border into the State of Mississippi, the land of Mother and Dad, and my avidity became cupidity! I wanted to invade the palatial lawns of Gulfport to gather magnolia leaves, scoop up sand on the perpetual Gulf beaches of Biloxi and look for Thomases and Lacys in every phone book.

I had "known" the aristocratic, Mississippi-Gulf resorts all my girlhood but remembered little about them since our yearly three summer months were spent, almost entirely, in Booneville, Mississippi, in the north—at Mother's home, "Five Oaks." We visited briefly at Dad's home in Verona, which was in town and smaller, yet comfortably housed us all with gracious Aunt Pauline, Uncle Ralph and loving, vigorous Grandmother Thomas.

Mama Kate and Papa Lacy's home boasted cotton fields; woods with sandy, pine-needled paths; a barn with hayloft to jump from; fig trees, pear and apple; grapevines where Charles and I had special seats to eat our grapes and green pears; peanuts in front of the corn—the former taken, hot-roasted, to the magnolia tree favored for sitting, climbing and "skinning the cat"; a garden with Mama Kate's greenhouses obscured by rose arbors, crape myrtle trees and chinaberries. We had Willie Rob to play with, Big Rob to find us a horse or let us help milk and Callie to bake sugar cookies.

Excursions were usually in the northern area, a favorite being a short drive to Corinth and across the Tennessee border to the Shiloh National Military Park where we picnicked and swam, ruminating little about the second major battle of the Civil War, April 6 and 7, 1862, where the Union's Grant and Buell had not been conclusively victorious against the Confederacy's Johnston and Beauregard—both sides' losing 10,000 men in the incredibly sanguinary two days.

The Tennessee River led us from Shiloh to Muscle Shoals, rapids, in northwestern Alabama, and the Wilson Dam, but my favorite river was the Tombigbee, a long river twisting through northeastern Mississippi throughout western Alabama. It was the area of the Tombigbee watershed which was the only part of the country never controlled by a foreign government: the Chickasaw Territory was an independent enclave ruled by Chief Tishomingo. Since it embraced the homes of both the Lacy and Thomas families, I always fantasied that Tishomingo named the beautiful River Tombigbee for the Thomas family, only vaguely accepting the Chief's friendship for Thomas Jefferson whom he championed in Indian matters. And when I learned that the Lacy-Civil War homestead was built on the banks of Mackey's Creek, the upper reaches of the Tombigbee River, the romance was heightened.

The famed Natchez Trace was not completed in the Thirties for travel from Nashville southwestward but vestiges were appreciated from Tupelo, directly south of Booneville, diagonally through marvelous wilderness passages to the Natchez bluffs of the Mississippi River. I recalled the occasional narrow tracks we stopped to walk, the scents, in the deep shade, of pine, ripening wild grapes and papaws in patches of sunlight and solitude—and wonderment about the long-ago plodders.

An ancient Indian "Path of Peace," it had been sanctioned as a post road in 1801 and later used as a wagon route to settle the Southwest. Often an escape trail for runaway slaves, it was frequented by river boatmen who guided flatboats down the Mississippi to Natchez and New Orleans and returned by the Trace, on foot or horseback, to Nashville to float downriver again.

As I "absorbed Mississippi" in our fleet passing, Dave promised to drive me down the entire Natchez Trace someday. (And he did, three years ago, after a Lacy Family-Reunion in Booneville when we toured "Five Oaks," now three, the cotton land and woods having been sold and the three-storied mansion no longer acres away from neighbors—but the house was sturdy, the stained-glass windows intact on the upper floor and the swing and cane chairs still on the porch. My treasured magnolia tree was lofty on the southeast lawn and I was permitted to break two huge white, nostalgic blossoms of heavenly fragrance! And the crescendo of rediscovery was not complete. We also saw the wonderfully preserved Lacy ancestral home! It was an unadorned frame house of two floors backed by deep woods and fronting on the river—protected by the Army Corps of Engineers, that section of the Tombigbee now a reservoir—and it was still in habitable condition! The eastern length of the house, facing the sun-rising over the river, was shaded by a porch which overhung a quaint covered well built into the southeast *L* extended from the kitchen. I went into every room: compact, low-ceilinged with fireplaces and up the dark stairs—and outside, by the big brick chimney, gathered wild sweet peas to add to my magnolia clusters. What peace and tranquillity—and brave shadows—lived in that abode of family beginning!

(Mother's cousin, Holley Patterson, our droll, oral Lacy historian, and his gracious wife, Juanita, had taken Madge Lacy Guilford and Foy, her affable husband, Dave and me to view the grand old house. We repeated the pilgrimage the next day with Jane Lacy Adcock, Honora Lacy and families and were joined by the Lacy genealogist, Maxine Lacy Martin, and Roy who lived with hospitable warmth in Booneville, in their spacious Colonial mansion. Holley and Juanita's charming modern house was in Burton. "Tombigbee River cuts through here to the Gulf," Holley gave us our bearings, "three hundred feet wide; rather than going down the Mississippi, you might go down the Tombigbee and use the Intracoastal Waterway to New Orleans." Slightly northeast of Booneville, Holley's house was built on historic Lacy land: "In this spot, the Charlie Lacy family [Papa] lived!" It was splendid! It had two columned Southern porches, both front and back, with a vast sweep of lawn which Holley maintained himself with big machinery; trees galore, including crape myrtle and fruit trees—and his own private canyon, down below. As we all gathered in Holley and Juanita's commodious family room: first cousins, second and third, and probably some "removed," I was glad—amid the anecdotes and laughter—that I could still take shorthand!)

Lacy, Charles and I had loved our Mississippi summers; Mother, and later, Mother and Lacy, drove us down in the Ford and Dad joined us the last two weeks. By that time our Lacy-Thomas family would have expanded to include Uncle Wes Lacy, Aunt Irene and Madge's having spent the last month with us at Papa's together with Aunt Beth and Jane Lacy Hughes—Uncle Shelly's joining us if his engineering schedule permitted. We wanted not for playmates. Uncle Gene Lacy and Aunt Marguerite lived in Booneville and contributed their lively girls: Martha, Katie Lou, Honora and Beth. All my cousins had gorgeous curly hair but I was the only one with brothers! And I refused to trade! Lacy and Charles even let me sew Merit Badge patches on their Scout Merit Badge sashes, their having worked on a diversity of skills during our Booneville days. How proud I was of my wonderful brothers! And of all our vast family!

The Sunday morning trek to the Booneville Baptist Church downtown was memorable: Papa in his soft white suit, black string tie and white panama, Mama Kate in a floating, pastel voile, caught at the ruffled neck with her cameo, a broad-brimmed hat atop her silvery hair, worn in a chignon like Mother's, led the Lacy entourage which strung out a block but filled in as we passed sundry Cousins' houses in town where they waited on wide, cool porches. We were half the congregation when we arrived at the Church doors—even without Uncle Gene and Aunt Marguerite's contingent, for they attended the Booneville Presbyterian Church, a block away but "fell in" for the homeward stroll. They would have early released Sally Lou, Callie's sister, to help with Sunday dinner.

Before silks and organdies were changed for cotton playclothes (Beth and Marguerite both made their girls' beautiful, delicate dresses, usually with smocking; Marguerite's having to make four—just alike; Mother and I finding Kansas City's Harzfeld's and Emery Bird's perfect for our needs); dinner was served. It generally consisted of fried chicken and it was fresh: "necks wrung" after Callie, Rob and Willie Rob and

Sally Lou and family, both of whom had cabins out back, had returned from church. There would be veal, or ham from the smokehouse, buttermilk biscuit (my cousins all drank buttermilk, and Lacy, too, but I could never fully enjoy it—though loved the patterns it made on the glass), black-eyed peas or tiny potatoes with fresh mint, sweet corn on-the-cob with freshly churned butter and apple cobbler. (Main meals were always at noon; Papa's walking home from his law office each weekday, his white suit coat on, despite the heat—just in time to cool off a few minutes before saying the blessing; his return to town by one-thirty.) After Sunday dinner, Mama Kate played her guitar or Marguerite, the piano, its being our "quiet time in the heat of the day"; we read the papers, played Rook or bridge; then, released, romped to the yard, barn or woods.

But friends were essential and often we were joined by John and Betty Reece, children of Mother's elegant lifelong friends, J. C. and Candace Stanley who epitomized gracious Southern living. Frequently the boys played tennis or rode horseback on the Stanley grounds while I assisted Betty in her girl-sized doll house—both of us hobbling, important-ly, on high-heeled, size four shoes contributed by a small-footed aunt.

And the croquet matches on Mama Kate's broad front lawn overseen by Lacy and John, the eldest two—with Charles' assistance—be-cause all the clamorous girls were hard to manage. The adults intellectual-ized on the long, wide porch about politics, law, engineering, schools, churches—but mostly, their families, while Papa smoked his pipe and warm breezes wafted its perfume with jasmine, gardenia and magnolia's.

Each vivid picture came to mind during the joyous kaleidoscope of Mississippi land and Gulf water and I thanked Dave for his thoughtfulness and patience in planning for my diurnal reminiscence. How fortunate that we, both, were dedicated to, and understanding of, familial bonds!

After Mobile Bay, Pensacola Bay and Tampa Bay, we crossed the Everglades on "Alligator Alley," scurried through Miami and being attuned to Dave's precise schedule, took time to run along the white sands of Miami Beach and dip our toes in the Atlantic Ocean! What a fanciful frolic! I had wet hand and foot in both the Pacific and Atlantic Oceans, the Gulf of Mexico—the Caribbean Sea was in our imminent plans—and I had yet to work through my trousseau!

Driving along U.S. Highway 1, the Florida Keys Overseas Highway, we marveled at the tenacity of man which could effectuate an aquatic highway, stretching one hundred sixty-four miles, mostly over water with an occasional exclamation mark of land, battered by hurricane waves, wind and unceasing traffic. It was fascinating to "fly" so low, suspended in air. When the Keys incipiently swam into view to lodge beneath our bridge-road and divide the skyey water, we were surprised at the lack of development, the look of impoverishment and the extension of the Indian culture of the Everglades: their abodes—impermanent; their occupation—fishing.

We arrived in Key West, Florida, in the early afternoon. Dave checked in at Boca Chica, Naval Air Station, Underwater Weapons School, talked to the Housing Officer who gave him an abbreviated "list" and we drove on westward into town. Dave had ascertained immediately that no Base housing was available. Stateside, an officer waited months for an MOQ assignment; in Key West, the "land" of inaccessibility, few had been built and none for TAD (Temporary Additional Duty) officers. So before we left San Diego, we knew that an emprise awaited us in Key West but never had Dave contemplated, nor I suggested, that I should return to the Midwest for six weeks. My home was where he was.

Key West was absolutely flat, totally at sea level, sandy, lushly tropical and very hot. Coconut palms grew wild, Cuban lime trees; royal poinciana, frangipani, hibiscus and oleander were all abloom with a most heady fragrance from frangipani, or perfume tree, saturating the heavy air. The blossom of the *plumeria*, smaller than a gardenia but waxy, white and fragile had overlapping petals like a large freesia. The soursop tree was not recognized by us because it looked rather like an apple tree. We discovered it was a native of the West Indies, bearing a large ovoid, spiny fruit appearing to be an elongated horse chestnut, more acid in flavor than the sweetsop and producing the most delicately flavored, rich ice cream. We also welcomed knowledge of the sapodilla which, unlike the deciduous soursop, was a tropical evergreen and a native American tree. The sapodilla had a latex which yielded chicle but the edible, russet fruit was its main appeal to us for it, too, was used in Cuban ice cream. Not as tart as the soursop, it was delectable. The ubiquitous coconut palm, producing its matchless fruit which was a drupe and the reverse of familiar stoned fruits: peach, plum, nectarine, cherry, was not neglected by the Cuban chefs and appeared in its creamy, chunky ice cream as well as in salads, pies and pilafs.

The influence and presence of Cubans was quickly apparent. Whereas the Keys close to the American mainland were inhabited by Floridian Indians and other hardy Americans, Key West which was just ninety miles from Havana was conspicuously Cuban in culture and population. Spanish was the language of conversation although English was spoken for business. But menus and shop signs were not prevalent as in Stateside and we learned to ask questions about everything; nothing being stated, all was flexible and apparently negotiable. Life was unhurried and at siesta time, it was suspended. In the intense heat of the afternoon, the island's activity was conducted at the Key West Naval Air Station and the Key West Naval Base, the only two installations with air conditioning.

Dave stopped his green Oldsmobile in front of the small, two-storied, white frame Key West Hotel and, cooled by the lazy ceiling fans in the lobby, signed for a room on the second floor.

Opposite our room, across the street, was a ramshackle, two-floored, grayed frame house which seemed never to have been painted, with glassless window frames, shutters askew and a balcony ready to tumble in the next gale. Outside the door, obscuring part of the house and overhanging the street,was an embowering, wide-arched poinciana, heavily flowered with deep flame-crimson blooms. It presented a poetic contrast between Nature's plenitude and Man's ineptitude and indolence.

Dave deposited our bags, there being no doorman, was told to leave the car out-front, and accompanied me to the dining room. Even though it was almost three o'clock and an odd time, to them, for a main meal, they prepared the specialties of Key West: green turtle steaks and Key lime pie. It was a memorable, regional repast! I was given the recipe for Key lime pie and we explored the green turtle collection before searching for an apartment.

We were directed to the Key West Green Turtle Soup Cannery, the only one in the world. Their export was similarly limited: to New York hotels. They were the largest turtles in the world and they were green. We saw huge strips of the flesh being dried for the soup cannery. Only a minuscule amount was saved fresh for steaks which were served in the contiguous, open-air restaurant and in the hotel. The turtles were very crowded in their watery compartments but their discomfort was to be short-lived since it was green turtle roundup season and the busiest days for the cannery. The mammoth shells had no commercial value, per se, and were ground. We surmised after we left the depressing scene that green turtles might soon become extinct.

Our search for housing was more uplifting. We were literally lifted into Cuban lime trees when we mounted stairs to a second- floor, screened sleeping porch with kitchen, breakfast room, dressing room and bath. Our nice American landlady provided everything, even cooking and eating utensils and bath towels as we were "without gear," as Dave expressed it in military parlance.

We drove through the entire town, noting the "Key West Mountain," an amazing two-foot bump in the road; the cemetery where all graves were above ground, the water table—being just slightly below ground level; the old Cuban cigar factories, dismantled with only shells remaining, lushly overgrown, to mark perimeters of the large masonry structures. We found one factory, not far from our tree-house apartment, which was more intact with complete walls, atop one of which Dave sighted a large molded-cement horse's head, looking outward from a cornice. The other three corners of the long, vine-covered, tree-imbedded ruin were barren, only heavy, bent iron rods indicating prior ornamentation. Dave expressed a desire for the horse's head. "Maybe we can find the owner and have him cut it down for you," I suggested, looking at the impenetrable mass of vines and wondering about snakes. "No, I want to get it myself," said Dave, firmly. "What would you do with it?" I wondered, preferring to have a cookbook and a cake pan. "I'd put it in our garden," said my dreamer, "it's just what we need!" "If you weren't accused of theft, you would be, of imbecility." "I guess I would be a little conspicuous, sitting up there with a hacksaw!" grinned Dave, looking very much like a misunderstood and underappreciated little boy. We always drove to our apartment, when coming in from the east, via Dave's Horse's Head—just to be assured that the possibility still existed. There were one or two things in life which one had an unreasonable desire for and that horse's head was one of Dave's!

We discovered Ernest Hemingway's home, a substantial frame house in a large yard secluded with tropical growth. Across the second story was a long balcony which looked out to sea. I could envision Hemingway's composing *The Old Man and the Sea* from just such a vantage point. Launched into reporting as a cub at the *Kansas City Star*, the world-surfeited writer found shelter on the Key with his third wife, Mary. It was difficult to conceive of a more isolated abode for cerebration and creative productiveness or a more soothing environment for a turbulent and impatient personality. Hemingway found peace and solace in his tropical homestead, we fervently hoped!

Our very distinguished Missourian, President Harry S. Truman, chose Key West for a home for, perhaps, the appeal of isolation and peacefulness which had magnetized Hemingway. Perhaps they were friends. They had both experienced warfare, were experts in weaponry and martial history and, no doubt, both loved fishing and the droll lore of the sport. President Truman's Summer White House was located at the Key West Naval Base on the western edge of our West Key. It was a marvelous "hideaway" for the busiest executive in the world and it was almost unnoted or, at best, casually accepted by the residents of the unhurried, unharried (no pun intended) little town of Key West, Florida.

Security at the Naval Base was not even conspicuously enhanced unless the Presidential flag was flying. The one time the President was in residence, during the Congressional spring break, Dave, who was always saluted and waved on—even when in civilian clothes—had to show his I.D. card and I, mine, and state his reason for being on the Base. The inquiry was perfunctory and swift, Dave was saluted and we proceeded on to the Officers' Club to have dinner.

Dave was not attached to the Naval Base but it was close to our apartment; we frequented the O-Club, Commissary, Ship's Service, air-conditioned movie theater. The Naval Air Station at Boca Chica, to which Dave was attached, was ten miles to the east. The Presidential plane would touch down there and President Truman would travel by limousine to the Naval Base without the least bit of fanfare for no one, except a few Naval personnel, knew of his plans. Furthermore, few would have been interested had they known. The community was a proverbial "jumping-off place," filled with non-American, non-English speaking, temporary residents who were unaware of, and therefore oblivious to, the United States Government. It was the perfect choice for a Presidential retreat: completely remote from the political milieu and constant clamor of Washington, D.C., yet still on American soil. The simple man of Midwestern culture did not believe in elaborate, extravagant arrangements for a few days of relaxation from his onerous burdens. What was good enough for his Navy men was good enough for him! And he was an old Army man!

We explored the Key from east to west and the width of it, so it was late when we returned to the hotel. The coffee shop was closed, as was the desk, and the lobby was deserted. We had enjoyed a light supper in cool comfort at the Base and savored our first soursop ice cream cone on the way back. Our only pressing need was sleep, as it had been a long day of delighted discovery. We had a slight breeze from our two windows and overhead fan and marveled at the deserted streets, there being no place to go, and the absolute quiet. The fragrance of frangipani, always exotically prominent at night, began to permeate the air as we dried from quick, cold showers and, happily wearied, turned back the sheet. From a distance, we heard the first plaintive resonance of a steel drum. Then we heard maracas blending their beat. Suddenly, a saxophone joined in mellow tone and a piano started to collect the rhythm. A Cuban lullaby! What hospitality! We had fallen in love to samba strains and we murmured appreciation. How wonderful to be in the Key West Hotel on a hot night listening to the throbbing tunes of a tropical band! It was almost 1:00 A.M. Dave went to the window, for the music seemed louder. There was dim light in an upstairs window of the ramshackle house across the street—and activity. From there, the music vibrated. Musicians came and went throughout the night; we heard no voices, no singing, just the pagan, jungle beat. We loved it for the first two hours, then aware that Dave had to "arise" early for his first day at Underwater Weapons School, we waned to disapproval. The Cubans' siestas had invigorated them to nocturnal exuberance of melodic invention and I was convinced that we were the sole occupants of the hotel or of "sleeping" quarters downtown. The streets were still deserted, all lights extinguished except the dull glow across the street but someplace, somehow—that music was not being resisted! We began to feel obligated to enjoy it, since proximity made us defenseless. The music makers polished their cha cha to a soothing cadence and we relaxed with the even, accustomed rhythm to a soporific hopefulness but then a sudden cacophony was introduced and we were compelled to attentive listening, wondering how that strain could be woven in. It was exhilarating but exhausting, as we "danced" all night. Oh, for a recorder! Our introduction to Key West could not have been more thorough—nor more distinctly redounded!

Dave's first day at Underwater Weapons School was bleary-eyed but blissfully brief with indoctrination in the morning and the afternoon at leisure. So we moved to our Cuban-lime tree house at 1417 Ashby Street, Key West. It was owned by a delightful American widow in her early seventies who had traveled widely with her husband. Key West, and that house, was the last adventuring they had enjoyed together, so she stayed and loved the repose and the happy memories. In contrast to the musicality of the hotel environs, Ashby Street was somnolent by sundown, and throughout the night, providing perfect quietude for Dave's study on our porch which occasionally received a deliciously fragrant—and sometimes cool—breeze.

I practiced cooking in the early morning hours after Dave's six-thirty departure, finding recipes in a magazine in our apartment. My first effort was a marble pound cake; my second, a yellow layer cake from a small Crisco-can label. I soon graduated to *The Pocket Cook Book*, a paperback from the food staff of *McCalls Magazine*. In a few weeks, when June 1948 dawned, it became too hot to bake or to accomplish cooking of lengthy minutes, except for breakfast. The temperature dropped, at best, two degrees during the night; humidity was excessive at all times and we wore very few clothes—Dave's pulling on his shirt and I, my dress as we hurried down our very private stairs to the car to stir up a breeze. We spent most of the evening hours at one of the O-Clubs, Key West more often as it was closer, having dinner and studying or attending a cooling movie.

I was soon aware of gossamer white flakes on the floor every morning, also on the table, in the cabinets, on the stove and around our bed. I swept them up, took my collection to the landlady for verification because Dave and I felt certain that termites were molting, and so they were. I bought only what the refrigerator could hold, including Crisco, coffee, cereal, the salt box and spices, sugar, flour and rice and kept our dishes, pans and flatware in the middle of the table, covered with another tablecloth and anchored with books. Each morning we took off the mattress before Dave left for Boca Chica and I swept off the box springs. We saw only a few of our nocturnal visitors which looked like winged ants, still crawling about on the tablecloth in the early morning unable to uncouple their wings. But they did not damage our clothing, not even the few wool suits and sweaters we had brought from San Diego's chilly evenings. Fortunately, most of our clothing, and my fur coat, had been left in our apartment in San Diego. Our wing sweeping and sawdust search became so routine that we did not feel discommoded and because the amount of our morning bonanza never varied, the location always being the same, we were far more interested than annoyed. We were told that termites would even bore through metal if it was in their path but we put little credence in that claim.

We interrupted our scientific observations to spend a week end in mid-June in Havana. It was a half-hour flight in a rickety DC-3 which routinely shuttled back and forth between the commercial airport at Key West and Havana. Most of the passengers were Cuban and when we landed, they were obviously at home and rushed off to familiar places. Havana was very large, very congested with people and oblivious of

Americans, even in the shops. We liked that anonymity and roamed far from our hotel, a white masonry structure like everything else—sparsely furnished without rugs on the floor or screens on the windows, only shutters which kept out the bugs, eyes and air—and was listed "Luxury." But it was clean and termiteless—and had a ceiling fan. The flora and aerial fauna of Havana were exactly like Key West's and the drive to and from the airport was the only time we saw extensive verdure and tropical growth. Downtown Havana was glistening white in the merciless sun, its concrete and masonry, stark and generally unfinished in appearance. To our American eye, the unpartitioned Cuban buildings were mere shells but each was inhabited and vocally bustling with businesses and tradesmen. Rather like an open-air forum, there was little formality and no urgency of movement. We walked along a broad esplanade with an occasional masonry pergola and trees on either side but there were no elegant fountains or floral plantings such as one would see in Mexico City, Los Angeles, Miami or Kansas City.

It was not a prosperous city but much money changed hands that night when we attended the Fronton where jai alai was played. Considered the fastest game in the world, it looked like total confusion to me. It was incredibly noisy, not only with the sound of the lightning-fast balls' making impact with the rackets and walls but with the shouting of bets and the clamor of little groups of spectators in heated disputation. Dave and I and very few others were seated. Most were standing, gesticulating, shouting and waving tickets, wagering being accomplished during each match, mostly by men but some women raised excited, strident voices as well. The men of Cuba uniformly wore long-sleeved, white voile overshirts with elaborate tucks and embroidered in white—to their evening jai alai match, at least. The women, very few of whom were visible at nighttime entertainment, were more plainly garbed in simple, short-sleeved dresses of dull color; they were not gaudy. The faces of the Cuban women were generally very pretty with their olive skin and black hair, yet they were short of stature and wide of girth but many of the male companions were as well. Walking leisurely back to our hotel, late that night, we felt the vitality of the Cuban culture which had seemed lacking in the daytime. Unlike Key West, most of Havana was abroad on the streets at midnight but—nowhere did we hear music as mystically compelling as that from our ramshackle samba house beside the royal poinciana tree.

The Havana Hotel was on the northwest extremity of the city overlooking the harbor and a small island upon which the Morro Castle and Fortress had been built and which Castro used in later years for political prisoners. It looked bleak and we were not enough interested to take a launch to investigate. Instead, we took another long walking tour and stopped to have pompano for lunch in an open, masonry hull of a restaurant where English was spoken. Dave and I had both studied Spanish in college, could read it but fathomed few of the Cuban idioms. We enjoyed the challenge of the Spanish-speaking shopkeepers who knew English but spoke Spanish, convinced that we understood nothing; but our food and drinking water Dave wished to discuss, in English, in the most clean, fastidious eating establishments we could find. Our fish was fresh and good and served without flair and thus compared unfavorably with Antoine's in New Orleans where we had stopped one noon in our mad dash from San Diego—a habit Dave had developed, as he had driven non-stop from San Diego to Kansas City, unknown to me, for our wedding.

At Antoine's we had luxuriated in their famous *pompano en papillote*, faultlessly served by a white-gloved, formally attired waiter who hovered at our table to tear and fold back the steaming paper bag, refresh our lemoned water, keep my coffee and the flaky biscuits, piping hot and the fruit compote, cold. It was the most extravagant and enjoyable meal of our entire "Underwater" sojourn.

We had driven late in Louisiana the night before, not finding a suitable place to stop. After 11:00 P.M., more from desperation than desire, Dave chose an old-fashioned motor court with two dingy units attached together, carports—at either end. They advertised "Vacancy" and that was the last remnant of "civilization" for many miles. Nothing better had been passed or Dave would have turned back. We were reluctant but weary and we were in the bayous where life was not easy for inhabitants—or travelers. We scorned the use of the rusty shower, laid our next day's clothes on two clean towels over the grimy chairs and Dave returned our suitcases to the car. The bed was lumpy and sagged in the middle and when Dave laughed and said, "Turn," I was glad to stay close. In the middle of the night, we awakened quickly, heard a heavy object being awkwardly dragged across the floor and heavily deposited against our thin wall. I was sure mayhem was being committed in the eerie, foggy bog. Dave said it was probably a dog. "If it was a dog, it would growl and snarl to be treated that way!" I countered, whispering. It was the lack of human voices that bothered me for that heavy, dead (and I winced at the adjective) weight had not moved itself. "I want to leave," I continued. "Alright," and Dave was whispering too, "don't turn on the light." Dave, with long experience in emergencies as a flyer, had trained me to have everything at hand and to dress in a minute in the dark. "Even in the finest hotel," he told me on our honeymoon, "you have to be prepared to leave immediately, in case of fire or other emergency. I always have my shoes at my feet with a clean sock in each and my clothes within reach." I had asked him why his shoes were contiguous to the bed with his slippers beyond which I thought reversed as were his clothes and his robe. I learned then what I had suspected on our one date: all his actions and thinking were systematic and never random. (Dave was just like my Father whom I have always revered as the most wonderfully capable, strong and gentle of men! And what excellent care both have always taken of me!)

We left swiftly and silently, Dave's carrying my make-up kit and his shaving kit. When we were in the car which he backed out without lights, we noted there was no car next door and saw no sign of "life" but sensed the situation was not salubrious. We felt we had been released from a morass and were glad to feel the dank air on our faces as we sped down the lonely highway. It was nearly 4:00 A.M. when we drove into a little Louisiana burg, parked under an elm across from the schoolhouse and slept until the sun awakened us to the splendor of a new day.

After our pompano in Havana, we investigated some of the tourist shops but limited our purchases to mahogany in which the island abounded. We chose a medium-sized fruit bowl etched with Caribbean waves, a steamship, Morro fortress and lighthouse, a palm leaf and thistles; two candle holders of mahogany, plus maracas-shaped salt-and-pepper shakers. We had to have a pair of real Cuban maracas gourds, so we would never forget our memorable music makers of Key West. On the way back to the Hotel Havana, we stopped for a thick tropical fruit drink made mostly with the swiftly blended fruit. Dave ordered banana and I, pineapple but as carefully as we looked, we could discover no producers of Cuban ice cream flavored with soursop or sapodilla. Our favorite Cuban entrepreneur had set up shop only in Key West and so, too, did we—early the next morning.

Dave reported for the final stage of the Underwater Weapons School training only to discover that he would not be there to complete it. He was ordered to the prestigious Naval War College in Newport, Rhode Island, to attend General Line School. That was the training for selected, regular Navy officers which enhanced their civilian college programs so that they were deemed comparable in preparation for Naval careers to the

U.S. Naval Academy graduates. The squadron at Miramar Naval Air Station, San Diego, would have to find another Underwater Weapons flyer and our Queenstown Court apartment, another occupant, for we were New England-bound!

The Supply Officer and his men from the Squadron packed all of our gear with the help of our landlady, Mrs. Smith, a very generous lady, who, with great delicacy and care, packed my clothes. It all arrived in perfect condition in Newport shortly after we did for we had driven, with somewhat less urgency, on quick leave to Lincoln, Nebraska, and then, Kansas City, Missouri. We would take no leave for Christmas, 1948, because Dave would be studying Naval Logistics and I, Infant Behavior. We expected to increase our family in February 1949. In Kansas City, I purchased Dick Grantley Read's *Natural Childbirth* and began my study on the trip to Newport. I was fine until we got to the Appalachians where every mile we traversed was krinkled with curves and I learned about dizziness.

We arrived at the Mayfair Hotel in Washington, D.C. It was noontime and Dr. Read had suggested in his early chapters that an expectant Mother should eat moderately but at regular times to lessen morning, or any-other-time-of-the-day—sickness. So I was willing and ready and we went to the dining room before Dave checked in at the reservation desk. But they would not seat us in the dining room!

Driving into Washington, Dave had buttoned the collar of his short-sleeved blue dress shirt and put on his tie as I held the wheel and I, in a cool black dress printed with tiny blue and rose forget-me-nots, had slipped on my black patent, high-heeled pumps, brushed my hair, powdered my nose and even pulled on my black straw hat. We deemed ourselves adequate to meet the luncheon dress code in Washington. Not so! Dave must have on a jacket.

Dave looked at me and I was getting woozier and paler by the minute and explained his dilemma to the headwaiter: "My wife is faint from heat and dizziness and I can't leave her. She should have some crackers or dry toast right away and where can I get them?" As soon as the headwaiter heard "crackers," he moved swiftly and sympathetically: "I have a jacket I reserve for our forgetful senators; I'll get it." And he ushered us in—as inconspicuously as you can seat a man, thrusting his arms into a white linen jacket three sizes too large and supporting a young woman, just beginning to wobble! I sat down, relievedly, propped up my head so I could appreciate Dave in his senatorial jacket which he wore with good humor and grace, being enviably handsome in anything, and knew I would not embarrass my adored husband who, from the first, had taken such exquisite, princely care of me!

I was immediately brought melba toast. Dave ordered bouillon, milk, hot tea and iced tea and a baked apple. After I "revived" and sampled everything, Dave enjoyed a Kansas City steak and we studied our maps and brochures of Washington. That was the only day I was ever upset and I alleviated dizziness by not drinking coffee which I had that morning at breakfast. I gave up my favorite beverage for almost a year as I could not even enjoy the aroma of coffee and afterwards, decided a "nursing Mother" should forego the stimulant.

As Dave finished his chocolate meringue pie, I mused to myself that it would be well to restrict his diet at the same time, but not to the degree, that I restricted mine. We had feasted in Key West where it became too hot to cook; in Cuba, for the novelty; at our homes because both of our Mothers were superb cooks and consequently, Dave was gaining weight. He weighed only 139 when we were married and at 5'11" was wonderfully thin but he gained thirty pounds in the first four months and now that perfect weight of 169 would have to be maintained. And I knew he would accomplish that, for he was a very disciplined man.

I thought back to our first meeting two years before in July of 1946, and our first date one year later, smiling at the recollection of our second—"date" and asking Dave if he had planned it that way. He laughed, happily, and said: "Of course!" He had flown back on leave in October 1947, and returned to Lincoln only long enough to buy a new suit and a nearly new car—a bankrupt farmer had surrendered a flashy, green, two-toned 98 Olds and Dave was the lucky purchaser and had hurried back to me in Kansas City, for what I assumed would be a routine, second date with a young officer I might see once or twice a year. But Dave had constructed a different plot for his new suit and car and told his Mother he was going to bring me back to Lincoln with him! At the parting time of our second encounter, Dave said he would like to take me back to San Diego with him, as his wife! I told him I could not go back with him then, that my parents would want to give us a formal home wedding and that I would need at least three months. (In which to change my mind, I told myself, for I was accustomed to having complete control of every situation and "this young man" was leaving me *none*.) Dave gave me exactly three months and proved that he was more forceful than I; and I discovered, surprised and somewhat indignant with myself, that I loved it!

So I did start out on a trip with him the next day in his new car, to Lincoln, four and a-half hours away. We got almost to St. Joseph, Missouri, when Dave pulled the car off the road to a little park to stop under a huge elm tree dripping golden leaves beside a bright brook. After a brief osculatory interlude, his plot continued and he produced a little box which he bade me open. "It's smaller than it should be," he apologized,

"but I bought it when I was twenty-one, as an investment for the future and it's been in the safety-deposit box." After assuring me I was the only girl who had seen it, he slipped it on my third finger, left hand. And I believed him and believed in him! Having achieved his first chapter, Dave appeared tired and admitted although he had been very comfortable in Charles' room (who was still away at KU), he had not slept much last night. So I drove awhile and Dave slept; my alternately

Figure 11. Second Encounter

looking at his handsome profile and black curls and my beautiful engagement ring flashing in the autumnal sunshine, then realizing the little brook was "my Rubicon" and there would be no backing out. How totally he trusted me—with his ring, his car, his life and I knew, suddenly, happily, that my trust in him was as great!

Figure 12. In the Holland Midst

We had a delightful visit with his distinguished family in Lincoln, his Mother and Naomi, Kenneth's wife, and Viola, Robert's wife, having cooked for days in preparation for my assured visit!

On the snowy way to our second visit in Lincoln, as man and wife, Dave posed this question to me: "If a man can rescue but one from a burning building, his wife or his mother, whom should he save?" "Why, his Mother, of course," I asserted. "Wrong!" Dave said, "I'd rescue you, of course. *You* are my prime responsibility now, both legally and morally." I felt unworthy of such protectiveness—and very humble. As both Man and Husband, Dave was nonpareil!

I experienced my first, brief glimpse of Washington that afternoon and the next morning. "We'll be back; I'll have a tour here before long," Dave promised as we headed north through Baltimore to Philadelphia. We stayed overnight in downtown Philadelphia and had time to see Independence Hall and the Liberty Bell, Carpenters' Hall, Benjamin Franklin's grave and the Betsy Ross House before leaving town and dined, luxuriously that night, on lobster thermidor at Bookbinder's, one of the finest seafood houses in the States. It was the end of an unusually long lobster season, for it was generally served fresh only in months containing an *r* in the name. I tasted Dave's cheesecake with cherry sauce, a famous Bookbinder dessert and we both vowed to eat sanely the next day.

We had early lunch at Schraft's in the Financial District of New York, watched activity on the floor of the Stock Exchange from the visitors' gallery and hurried on to Newport, arriving there in late afternoon. Dave elected to drive around through Providence, Rhode Island, rather than ferry at Jamestown on Conanicut Island in Rhode Island Sound.

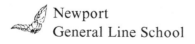 Newport
General Line School

It was such an historic state and although the smallest, being only thirty-seven miles by forty-eight miles, it had the longest name: Rhode Island and Providence Plantations. We did not stop at the capital which had been founded in 1636 by Roger Williams and was the earliest settlement in Rhode Island but drove to Providence's First Baptist Meetinghouse on College Hill which was the site where Roger Williams, in 1638, had organized the first Baptist congregation in America. Since I had taken Dave's name, he deemed it appropriate to accept my church as his and so we were married by Dr. Robert I. Wilson, minister of the First Baptist Church of Kansas City, Missouri, and erstwhile Presbyterian Dave wanted us to visit the spot where the Baptists of Rhode Island had helped to charter a state as a "lively experiment . . . in religious concernments" and a haven "for persons distressed for conscience." ("New England's 'Lively Experiment,' Rhode Island," *National Geographic*, September 1968, p. 370.) The First Baptist Meetinghouse had a wonderfully tall white New England spire, embraced by clocks on each side, small lighted stained-glass arched windows on two levels and a weather vane on the top of the needle. It was almost on an eye-level with the marble capitol dome but the Independent Man, in bronze—which was initially designed to be a likeness of Roger Williams but no authentic portrait could be found—heightened the State House to appropriate eminence. But the state's founder was not neglected and idealized monuments abounded; the most commanding and appealing, with Puritan collar, knee britches, flowing academic robe and large tablets clasped in his left arm, was found in the Roger Williams Park.

It was the lengthening of shadows that urged us on. I drove along a lonely stretch of backroad while Dave changed into summer khakis and regulation brown shoes, tied his black tie and combed his curls. He had anticipated I would "spend every minute learning about something" and had hung his uniform in the back seat of the car when we left Philadelphia. So no time was lost in our day and much to remember was gained.

Before 6:00 P.M., he had checked into General Line School in Newport, Rhode Island, received a housing list and ascertained that he would fly out of Quonset Point Naval Air Station, across Narragansett Bay, 45 minutes by motorboat, for his monthly proficiency flying: at least four hours a month, including both night flying and instrument.

Rhode Island, a surprisingly industrialized state, seemed more difficult to navigate, were one in a hurry, than even the Florida Keys, for bridges did not yet connect its insular segments to its mainland, although Jamestown on Conanicut Island, where one ferried from Newport, was connected. Eventually, a $53,000,000 Newport Bridge was completed in 1969 to connect Newport with Jamestown. It was a gorgeous white-webbed structure soaring with 400-foot towers which supported a four-lane highway 215 feet above the water allowing ships and aircraft carriers from the Newport Naval Base and Quonset Point Naval Air Station to sail grandly below. As you approached from Jamestown, you could see all of Newport mapped below and to the east, with sailboats, like miniatures from Lilliput, careening in a fairy regatta far beneath. (On a business trip in 1972, Mother, Lori and I drove back to Philadelphia and Newport with Dave and our "Little Rhody," as Mother called Lori in the first weeks—saw the land of her birth, as a young lady.)

We had reservations at the stately Viking Hotel in the center of town, across from a small park surrounding the historic arched Viking tower which looked like a round, brick gazebo. Newport was located at the southern end of the largest island, Aquidneck, which was the Indian name for Rhode Island and completed the state's 400-mile, water- scalloped coastline. Viking, Indian and Pilgrim mores seemed more prominent than English influences, yet we were in the heart of "New England."

As we awaited our New England clam chowder, made with soft-shell or long-necked clams, milk and butter and which New York-

Figure 13. Viking Tower

ers described as a "stew fit only for infants and invalids," I learned from our waiter that New York Manhattan clam chowder, made with hard-shell or quahog clams, tomatoes and water was nothing more than "a vegetable soup with a clam drawn through it." Interested in the debate at Schraft's in New York, we had sampled Manhattan chowder there and remembered it was much thinner and red with tomatoes but with lots of clams. However, when our waiter had proudly borne his steaming New England clam chowder to our table with a bowl of tiny, crisp oyster crackers, we discovered we preferred the latter. In truth, the bountiful clams with potato and a bit of onion in a rich, creamy white sauce were so satisfying and delicious that we drank every drop and I could eat nothing more. While Dave enjoyed brisket and a salad, I read to him about our remarkable new home from my lobby-acquired brochure.

"Did you know," I began, long a familiar preface to study-time, "that Rhode Island was the first state to declare its independence of England? Fully two months ahead of the other Colonies, this one state, the most geographically separated from itself—as far as I can detect—had the fortitude to declare itself independent on May 4, 1776! They still celebrate Independence Day twice a year! Can you imagine these 'men of the cloth' being the first to bear arms?" "Of course," returned Dave, "they make the best fighters. You're more fervent when you have something to fight for!" and he gallantly smiled at me. "You're right!" I exclaimed, constantly amazed by his perceptiveness. "So they protected their families, their colony, with a Bible in one hand and a rifle in the other!" "They were used to it," Dave explained, "remember, their lives were oppressed before they came here." "But not militarily, were they?" "No, generally not, but only the strong survived and dared to come here." "Yes, of course," I agreed, "and all the statues to Roger Williams, and the Independent Man are of robust, brawny might—long-haired Samsons!" "Right!" laughed my short-haired brawny warrior.

We stayed at the Viking Hotel for three days while Dave started classes at General Line School. I slept a lot; ate a cheese and raisin-bread sandwich for lunch because Dave's Mother had given us a delicious, big loaf of cheddar cheese; started Dostoyevsky's *The Brothers Karamazov* and read our literature on Newport.

Finding a second-floor apartment, within walking distance of town, which was furnished, though dark and drab—as I inferred all New England, furnished apartments would be; we had our gear delivered there and moved in.

I spent days unpacking, cleaning and lining drawers and shelves, scrubbing the stove and refrigerator and finding a place for everything when our landlady asked us to move! She had apparently overheard me make an appointment with the Base gynecologist over the downstairs-hall phone, we had none in our apartment, and asked if I was pregnant and I proudly told her I was. She said we could not live there because it would make her too nervous to have a baby around. Not even curious as to why she had not mentioned that before to a young couple, we moved the next day. She promised to return the "cleaning fee" to Dave if he would return for it the following week but then refused to do so, claiming that since we had been there a month, she had to "clean the drapes."

We found a big, bright, furnished apartment on the first floor but with kitchen-breakfast room downstairs, at 20 Berkeley Avenue, in an old mansion which had been divided into living quarters for four families. Our west apartment contained the original entrance way; the enormous, high-ceiled living room with a French loveseat in the southeast corner of the room, trellaced almost to the ceiling with a broad cornice on top and balanced by a red velveteen window seat running the entire length of the room beneath tall west windows; and the dining room, with its window seat and generous windows, which had been made into a bedroom. Our dressing room, closets and bathroom were across a hall which was occasionally used by the east-side apartment dwellers whom we, at times, heard but never saw; stairs just inside the door at the west end of the hall led upstairs. We did not encounter any of the occupants of the other apartments but assumed from their car tags that they were not "Navy." We now had "Newport atmosphere," a sun-flooded apartment for study and reading, complete privacy and a phone. Thus happily ensconced in our New England abode, we settled in for the autumn and winter.

Our old house was set far back from the street on a long lawn, quite unkempt, but displaying a cluster of hard maples in the southwest border which, by early October, was as brilliantly brush-stroked as our Key West "samba poinciana." Downtown Newport with its quaint, wooden buildings outlining one narrow, main street of eighteenth-century houses, predominantly, was "Old Town" and climbed uphill from the harbor on the west to a gentle plateau. The wonderful, old-town houses, contiguous to the street with small gardens in back, like our first residence, were occupied, well cared for and frequently identified as to date of building and original owner. Our nineteenth-century house was three or four times larger than the early Georgian homes with an unfrugal amount of yard reserved for frontal landscaping and display of the imposing structure.

Three diversely significant churches were in "Old Town": Trinity Church, with its gold crown atop a tall white spire built in 1725; the old Friends' meetinghouse, the first built on American soil, 1699; and Touro Synagogue, 1763, considered the oldest in the country. Touro Street, at the head of which was the Hebrew Cemetery (dating from 1677), was named for Isaac Touro, an early Dutch rabbi, as were the Synagogue and Touro Park where the Viking tower was located—which some historians claimed was a corn mill erected by Benedict Arnold!

The religious divergence and diverseness from Roger Williams' establishment of Baptists (known as Dissenters in England), in Providence, was due to Newport's being founded three years later, in 1639, by John Clarke, William Coddington and other Antinomians. They, believing that faith alone was necessary for salvation, had disagreed with Puritan colonists and had been forced out of the Massachusetts Bay Colony. They settled first at Portsmouth on the northern end of Aquidneck Island in 1638 and, a year later, moved to the southern point to establish Newport—which it literally and figuratively was: a new port. In 1640, Portsmouth and Newport, uniting, elected William Coddington governor and formed a government with Providence, in 1644, under a parliamentary charter, including Warwick (opposite, across Narragansett Bay, on the mainland), in 1647. Other towns, south of Warwick (which had attempted their own government, from 1651 to 1654, with Warwick), united with the islanders and obtained a liberal charter from King Charles II in 1663.

I was fascinated by the prominent names I discovered in my study of Newport history. The first newspaper was published by Benjamin Franklin's brother James in 1732, whose son James established the *Mercury* in 1758, which we read in 1948. In "Old Town," the most publicized edifice, standing at the head of Washington Square, was the Colony House or old State House which was built in 1739 and became an historic shrine where Washington, Adams, Monroe and other presidents had been entertained. Near by was the Vernon house, built in 1758, which Rochambeau occupied during the Revolution, from 1780 to 1781, to oversee the French fleet in Newport Harbor.

Amazed at the display of wealth conspicuous in some of the old homes and in their opulent furnishings, including our own (but quite apart from the famous "summer cottages" along Twenty-Mile, or Ocean, Drive), I pondered the source of the income. So I investigated at the Redwood Library which was incorporated in 1747 by the Philosophical Society founded in 1730. It occupied a building erected in 1750 and was named for Abraham Redwood, a Friend, who had contributed five hundred English pounds for books. I was intrigued to learn that vast fortunes were accumulated between 1739 and 1760 in the "Triangular Trade." That involved Newport, Rhode Island, Africa and the easternmost island in the West Indies, Barbados, which was an English colony. Newport rum was shipped from the harbor to ports in Africa where it was exchanged for slaves who were transported to the island of Barbados and traded for sugar and molasses which were brought back to Newport to be made into—more rum! By 1770, Newport's foreign trade was greater than that of New York but it was to be short-lived. Newport fell to the "Redcoats" and was occupied by the English from December 1776 until October 25, 1779. The Triangular Trade was completely destroyed, the friendly French occupied the town for two years and Newport finally functioned as an American city when it was chartered in 1784. It remained one of the capitals of Rhode Island until 1900.

Even Dave's school was historic. It lay west of Newport and north of Goat Island which was in the entrance to the harbor and just large enough to accommodate the U.S. Naval Torpedo Station out of which

Dave customarily took a motorboat, around Conanicut Island, to fly on the mainland at Quonset Point. A bit north was the U.S. Naval Base on its own little island, Coasters Harbor, where the old frigate *Constellation* was moored. Also on the island were located a training station, the U.S. Naval War College, established in 1884 as the Navy's most advanced educational institution where General Line School classes were conducted, and the Naval Hospital to which I reported once a month for prenatal care—for which I felt no need, being a "Pioneer Woman" in attitude.

The thing I had missed most in San Diego was the sight of real trees—deciduous trees—which knew the seasons, when to turn scarlet, yellow and purple and loosen their leaves. Newport had all our Midwestern verdure of properly behaved trees and autumn arrived in all its spectrum of beauty. Pyracantha berries turned deep red (only orange are produced in the Midwest) and matched the red fruit of the American holly tree, our favorite tree, we decided, but indigenous—like the fragrant boxwood—to the coasts of the Atlantic and Gulf of Mexico and the Mississippi Valley. But we vowed to have an American holly shrub in our garden next to a Cuban Horse's Head with at least two pyracanthas climbing the south side of our house with evergreen leaves and orange-berried clusters from early fall through winter. Every house had "firethorn," as New Englanders called it, as foundation plantings, trained up brick chimneys or tall yard lamps.

There was no place more hospitable to rhododendron (*rhodon*, Greek for rose and naming the state which produced them in magnificent abandon) than Rhode Island where the evergreen, in every color, was cultivated to tree-size (*dendron*, meaning tree, Gr.), much like the Southern magnolia *grandiflora*, which we, also, had placed in our "garden." Mountain laurel grew wild in all the woods together with dogwood and tulip trees, or yellow poplar, the leaves of which were shaped like tulips in profile on long pedicels, fluttering with each breeze, and crowning its height in midsummer with bright yellow 'tulip' blossoms. A marvelous tree, and deciduous, but too large for our garden.

We turned our study to kalmia *latifolia*, the mountain laurel, native to Rhode Island; Philadelphus, or mock orange; viburnum *carlesii*, Korean spice; syringa, or lilac, particularly the double-flowered French lilac from the French nursery, Lemoine's; and especially the hydrangeas. The huge heads of deep blue hydrangea *macrophylla* in the acid, eastern soil were breathtaking. We cared less for the white snowballs of the hydrangea *arborescens* but "chose" the *quercifolia*, or oak-leaf hydrangea with its very large oak leaf, growing in quite deep shade and producing long cones of white flowers turning dark rose-pink in late summer, greening in autumn as the leaves flamed red-purple and clung on long after all other shrubs and trees had layered the ground. Of great interest was the climbing hydrangea, *petiolaris*, which covered walls, trees or fences and grew to a height of forty feet and produced large, flat, lacy nosegays of showy white, sterile flowers on the outer edge surrounding small white, fertile flowers tinged with green—presenting a dramatically rich tapestry of green and white. Over-sized roses grew luxuriantly in the moist air, cool nights and sunny days. It was, indeed, a garden spot and each house, however small or large, had one.

It was not long before we discovered the Newport Creamery where ice cream cones were as rich as the Cuban soursop, sapodilla and coconut but not as memorable, yet which rewarded us in late evening after Dave had ceased his study. I was surprised that little Rhode Island was also a dairy state, the rocky terrain's inhibiting agriculture while the growth of lush grasses attracted the bovines.

The dairy cow was not the only animal of note. Across the Sakonnet River from Newport, on the eastern mainland, a memorial was erected to a chicken! The famed "Rhode Island Red" was developed near Adamsville but was no longer produced there in commercial quantity.

Each day presented a new aspect and incongruity of the remarkably distinct town. A Jazz Festival was held every year in the seemingly staid community and a week-long Folk Festival, contrasting to the annual appearance of the New York Metropolitan Opera and annual Tiffany Ball held in the Vanderbilt Marble House for a thousand socialites and sponsored by the New York jewelry firm. There was surfing by youngsters on Easton's Beach, a cove on the Atlantic where the sloping, sandy beach encouraged long, rolling combers and to the west, in Rhode Island Sound—the internationally renowned *America's* Cup yachting race had been yearly held since 1930. While the wealthy grouped at Bailey's Beach in private cabanas, "hoi polloi" tennis fans invaded the Newport Casino for national Lawn Tennis Championships. The shingled Casino was the site of the first national men's tennis championships in 1881 and later housed the National Lawn Tennis Hall of Fame.

But everything paled when compared to the palatial summer "cottages" built along Bellevue Avenue and Ocean Drive by the royalty of American finance after the Civil War, reaching a pinnacle in the "gay Nineties" and concluding in the 1920s. Newport became a symbol for extravagance and ostentation. Most of America's "baronial" families were represented: Vanderbilt, Widener, Goelet, Duke, Astor, Mills. Mrs. Stuyvesant Fish "had two ballrooms in her cottage and Forsythe Wickes, an art collector, had a Newport house—and his wife had one too" (Rhode Island, *National Geographic*, September 1968, p. 398), right next door. The three most grandiose cottages at the end of Bellevue Avenue and owned and preserved by the Preservation Society of Newport County were The Elms, an elaborate French-style mansion built for Edward J. Berwind, a Philadelphia coal merchant; William K. Vanderbilt's Marble House, gloriously aglitter with gold and marble but dwarfed by his brother's palace next door, The Breakers, built by Cornelius Vanderbilt—twice. It was a Renaissance rococo museum and was considered the most ornate private dwelling in the United States. Fire destroyed the original edifice in 1892 but Mr. Vanderbilt commissioned architect Richard Morris Hunt to design and build a new one from the ground up which was accomplished in just two years. It was the only "cottage" we paid to see and were less awed by the grandeur of silver, alabaster, marble and gilt than appalled by the waste. The view from the point, with a tremendous expanse of lawn, the roar of the breakers far below, was pleasing but the building and its furnishings were immediately forgetta-

ble. I recalled only that I would not want to pay for the maintenance of the massive iron fence which surrounded the estate. Great wealth would be a nuisance, I concluded, and heaved a happy sigh!

We ate a clam roll at the new orange and turquoise Howard Johnson's restaurant on the highway northeast from town; bought a tall Christmas tree across the street for our high, spacious living room and were ready for the snow to fall on our atmospheric first Yuletime together in New England. And the snow did fall—and Dave's engine froze! But the engine block was successfully welded before Christmas and never again were we unprepared,

Figure 14. Winter Flight Gear

automotively, for the onslaught of winter. And we were given much practice!

One of Dave's favorite themes was: "It costs only a penny more to go first class!" In the first light snow, we shopped for silver at Rough Jewelers on Bellevue Avenue, instead of going to Providence to the Gorham plant—the world's largest producer of sterling-silver products, and soon we had "no mo" pennies. We were in desperate need of eight cobalt blue salt dishes in ornate, solid silver, footed bowls, accompanied by eight gold and silver salt spoons all beautifully preserved in two royal blue, velvet-padded black boxes. Those for a dining-room table we did not have but would, and opportunity we would not long have but did. And I could not say "Nay" to a deserving man who did not have a Cuban Horse's Head; besides, we could save money in other ways!

So in January when I strode briskly along the walk in my black and white French-felt coat and was whistled at by a truck driver—I hoped I would not have a cavity! And I didn't!

And in February when I paid seventeen-fifty for five days in the Naval Hospital with my baby, I hoped I would get a refund! And I did!

On the morning of February 11, 1949, I attended a bridge foursome and luncheon with three General Line School officers' wives and after a light supper, Dave and I went to a double-feature cowboy movie in Washington Square, opposite the old State House. At 10:00 P.M., I told Dave we should not stay for the completion of the second feature but should go home to get my bag which had been packed for three weeks. It had started to snow at five when I said good-bye to the foursome's hostess and Dave reported we would be in blizzard conditions by morning. Dave alerted my doctor that the pains were five minutes apart and regular and was advised to take me in. The snow was swirling riotously when we arrived and I urged Dave to take my bag in and to go back to the apartment. I was far more concerned about him with the weather's closing in than about the baby's advent, as I had done my exercises for months, gained less than twenty pounds and was prepared for natural birth. Besides, I had secret contempt for the women who were moaning, intermittently, up and down the hall and deplored their lack of discipline; it was the woman's job to have child—with dignity. So after I was prepared and enveloped in a hospital gown and Dave was told it would probably be mid-morning before the baby arrived, he agreed to leave. Being the sole occupant of the two-bed room, I closed the door.

I slept, between intervals of cement-rolling activity, then opened the door to ask a nurse when I should summon the doctor. He came at once, saying they had forgotten I was there and asked: "How close together are your contractions?" "Every fifth foghorn," I returned. He gave me a watch which the nurse reached to him from her cavernous pocket and told me not to close the door again. I nodded, comparing my new timekeeper with the foghorns, noted that two and a-half minutes passed and that it was 7:05 A.M.

Two days earlier my obstetrician, a young bachelor which I thought odd, had volunteered that my baby would be a girl. "A girl?" I exclaimed. For nine months I had envisioned a boy baby who would look like Dave and have the initials *L.D.* for my brother Lacy DeWitt Thomas, whom Dave had known only through Charles and me. "Lacy" was my cousin Martha's eldest daughter to whom she had given the family name and in memory of her cousin Lacy, for they had been very close in Washington where Uncle Gene and Marguerite lived with their other daughters: Katie Lou, Honora and Beth.

So the night before Dave took me to the hospital, I did quick research into girls' names beginning with *L*. Turning to the back of Dave's Webster's Collegiate Dictionary, I discovered "Lorinda" which was a variation of "Laurinda" which was a derivative of "Laura" which meant "laurel" which was a symbol of victory. We liked the significance and the sound and chose "Lorinda Delle

Figure 15. Lacy DeWitt Thomas

Holland" for appropriate euphonic nomenclature. Rereading a poem which Mother had penned on a page from an old calendar book, I was sure we needed a baby girl who might be just like her "Mommy Tom":

> Just a tender half-blown rose,
> Downy head and chubby nose,
> Cherry lips that bill and coo,
> Tears as sweet as morning dew,
> Little toes so pink and warm,
> Heart that longs for Mother's arm,
> Just a babe with starlit eyes,
> Neither great, strong nor wise

But nothing dearer ever known
Than just a Baby in the Home!

In a few minutes I called to the corpsman, gave him the watch to return to the nurse and told him I was ready—and my fifth-foghorn baby began to arrive. "Now, I'm going to give you a whiff of gas at the height of the pain." I didn't want it and said it was too dry and pushed it away. The doctor spoke about a wet sponge, the cone was put over my face again and I saw Chevrolets and Oldsmobiles being moved around in the display room of McClure-Norrington, 47th & Troost, Kansas City, Missouri. "I don't need anymore," I gasped. "Alright," the doctor agreed, "roll with it; relax a moment—now PUSH!" "It's a girl," said the nurse and I thanked them for letting me "be aware of it all." "Mrs. Holland," approved the doctor, "you should have lots of babies. Some women can just do it!" He continued, "I don't even have to take a stitch!" I nodded my appreciation for the compliment thinking they were "easy words for a bachelor."

When I was returned to my room close to the office, I heard the nurse talking to someone on the phone and I knew it was Dave, so I went to sleep. When I awakened I was hungry, for I had missed breakfast but so had Lorinda. I was amazed at how tiny she was: eighteen and a-half inches long, she weighed only five pounds, four ounces. Her fingers were like little bird claws. When I got up to close the window, I carried her, blanket and all, in the palm of my left hand and when I nursed her, I feared I would suffocate her, for her little face disappeared. When I asked the doctor why she was so small, he responded: "What did you expect, a monster? That's the best size to have," and seemed personally offended. I thanked him and hurried off with Lorinda to the nursery and decided to take a shower before lunch, for Dave was due soon. When I opened the shower-room door, three new mothers greeted me and I, them. "Oh," one exclaimed, "you're the one who had such an easy time of it!" "It was just a natural birth," I returned, wondering if they were the ones I had heard in the night and of whom I had not been proud, as accurately representative of "Woman." I listened to their difficulties (they had each had a "caudal" and been uniquely affected by it), commiserated with them and when I finished my shower, I was careful to restrain my stride down the hall from too much buoyancy, for I was as exhilarated in Motherhood as I had been in expectation of it.

Dave was in the room when I returned and had seen the baby and was proud of both of us. He had called Mother who would leave for

Newport the next day and being unable to reach his Mother by phone, had sent a telegram. That message to Lincoln, Nebraska, had contrived the spelling of our dainty daughter's liquidly flowing name to "Lorinda Degle Holland." Mother H, with typical gentility and graciousness, wired congratulations and commented about the "interesting middle name" but looked quizzically at us and then, with consternation, at Lori—for two years! Mother H had told Kenneth, Robert, Mildred and Dave's Lincoln friends about Lorinda "Degle" and everyone was too embarrassed to mention it and refused to write it! Thus progressed, or regressed, the orthography of Lorinda Delle!

On the third afternoon, the heavy snow layer begemmed with sunshine, we took home our "ten-fifty" baby, receiving a refund of seven dollars for two days not stayed. Lori had lost four ounces but gained back three and was the only one of the babies who had gained. I did not realize that if she had not gained those three ounces or lost more than four, she would have been regarded as premature—that it was not the term they were carried but their weight (under five pounds) that designated "prematurity."

Mother arrived the following day, was thrilled with her first grandchild and agreed with Dave that we should move from our grandiose but inconvenient apartment. He had confided to Mother that I had slipped on one of the narrow steps, in my seventh month, which led down to the kitchen and thereafter had been apprehensive. They found a bright, clean, first-floor, all-one-level apartment in a newer section of town, totally uninteresting and away from my study haunts but excellent for baby-caring and quiet studying for Dave. So we moved for the third and last time and less than four months remained of our much-too-brief Newport extravaganza.

Lori was soon rosy and plump because I nursed her every time she awakened. Mother always heard us in the night and insisted upon changing the baby and crooning her back to sleep with Southern lullabies. As was her wont, Mother spoiled the three of us, did all of the cooking—to Dave's delight, bathed and dressed the baby, washed baby clothes and went sightseeing with avidity.

Dave took Mother to see The Breakers, Newport Tennis Casino, Touro Park and Rough Jewelers on Bellevue Avenue and the Washington Square, State House and "Old Town" along the harbor; his Naval Base, War College and the *Constellation*. On week ends, Lori and I cheerfully accompanied them to view the mansions and magnificent rocky coastline along Twenty-Mile Drive.

When Lori was three weeks old, we drove to Boston to have lunch at the fabulous Toll House Inn established by Ruth Wakefield in 1930, in an old Cape Cod house which had been built in 1709, on the outskirts of Whitman, Massachusetts. It had been, originally, a toll house where passengers paid a toll, ate a meal, and changed horses. There she had created the chocolate-chip cookie. We thought her cuisine, the finest and Mother soon agreed.

The hostess found us a table out of traffic and Dave carried Lori in her basket, pulled down the legs and pushed it into a safe corner beside me so that nothing could disturb her. Having just nursed, she would sleep for two to three hours. We turned our attention to the enticing menu and looked around at the sun-dappled room hung with philodendron and Swedish ivy in white bamboo and macramé baskets. The winter sun was flickering into Lori's basket and I asked Dave for the wicker hood, in the extra chair, to protect her eyes.

We had been so proud of ourselves to have"unearthed" a baby basket in Newport which was not a shopper's paradise unless you were in search of exotica in jewelry, silver, art objects and yachts. On Thames Street in "Old Town," we found a general dry-goods store in an old Georgian house, the upstairs of which was a storeroom overlooking the harbor. We were invited to search and Dave, with his all-seeing, quick flyer's vision, sighted Lori's basket—complete, with hood—atop a pile of boxes. It was very dusty but new. Further search disclosed an unopened box with mattress and deep-ruffled liner in blue. Mother had included wide blue satin ribbon in Dad's Christmas box, together with all conceivable types of tiny garments, buntings and blankets. Lori had been ensconced in her cozy, beribboned basket without one touch of wintry blast, for we covered the hood and basket with a wool shawl or blanket when taking her to and from the car.

We wanted everything we saw on the menu but were ultimately content with deviled crab, for Mother, served in a large crab shell on galax leaves; an avocado stuffed with fresh crab and shrimp on a bed of curly endive and water cress, for me; and, of course, lobster Thermidor buttoned up with mushrooms, in shell and on seaweed, for Dave. Mother chose a peach melba salad; Dave, a pear macaroon and we were each served hot pecan-rum biscuits. Dessert was a Mary Ann for Mother: a dimple of sponge cake, the hollow filled with hot chocolate sauce, a ball of pink peppermint-stick ice cream crowned with almond cream—which we all sampled, that being all we could manage—together with my Concord grape sherbet and Dave's lemon pie with six-inch meringue! What a beautiful, luscious meal and memory! Lori remained blissfully asleep the entire time, and while Dave bought *Toll House Recipes* for Mother, Mother H and me, containing recipes for the delectable dishes we had just enjoyed, the hostess peeked into the basket to be sure we really had a baby in there.

How wonderfully our daughter traveled! And more was planned. We were driving through Boston to Wellesley College so that Mother could visit the Robert Browning Room in the Wellesley Library where she, as a past president and active member of the Kansas City Browning Society, had been granted permission to see and read the Browning Love Letters which had been purchased by the college for $90,000 some years before. As we awaited the librarian with the love letters, we examined the massive, dark oaken door, displayed against a high, broad, red velvet drapery, lighted softly overhead, from Elizabeth Barrett's father's house: 50 Wimpole Street, London. It was that front door from which Elizabeth Barrett, taking only her little dog Flush and maid Wilson, had eloped with Robert Browning on September 19, 1846, to live in Italy and never again be spoken to, or of, by her wealthy father who had forbad her marriage.

The Browning Love Letters were surprisingly small: the envelopes of Robert's letters measuring three and a-half inches by two inches were addressed in legible, unadorned script to "Miss Barrett, 50 Wimpole St." and postmarked New Cross, canceled with a circled 67 over a one-penny stamp of a woman in profile, probably Victoria, but it looked Grecian; the back center was sealed with five-eights of an inch of initialed wax and dated with only the year "1845," readable. The letter paper of Robert Browning's first to Miss Barrett was three and a-half inches by five inches, his handwriting comparably small but facilely decipherable:

New Cross, Hatcham, Surrey.
(Post-mark, January 10, 1845.)

I Love your verses with all my heart, dear Miss Barrett,—and this is no off-hand complimentary letter that I shall write,—whatever else, no prompt matter-of-course recognition of your genius, and there a graceful and natural end of the thing. Since the day last week when I first read your poems, I quite laugh to remember how I have been turning and turning again in my mind what I should be able to tell you of their effect upon me, for in the first flush of delight I thought I would this once get out of my habit of purely passive enjoyment, when I do really enjoy , and thoroughly justify my admiration—perhaps even, as a loyal fellow-craftsman should, try and find fault and do you some little good to be proud of hereafter!—but nothing comes of it all—so into me has it gone, and part of me has it become, this great living poetry of yours, not a flower of which but took root and grew—Oh, how different that is from lying to be dried and pressed flat, and prized highly, and put in a book with a proper account at top and bottom, and shut up and put away . . and the book called a "Flora," besides! After all, I need not give up the thought of doing that, too, in time; because even now, talking with whoever is worthy, I can give a reason for my faith in one and another excellence, the fresh strange music, the affluent language, the exquisite pathos and true new brave thought; but in this addressing myself to you—your own self, and for the first time, my feeling rises altogether. I do, as I say, love these books with all my heart—and I love you too. Do you know I was once not very far from seeing—really seeing you? Mr. Kenyon said to me one morning "Would you like to see Miss Barrett?" then he went to announce me,—then he returned . . you were too unwell, and now it is years ago, and I feel as at some untoward passage in my travels, as if I had been close, so close, to some world's-wonder in chapel or crypt, only a screen to push and I might have entered, but there was some slight, so it now seems, slight and just sufficient bar to admission, and the half-opened door shut, and I went home my thousands of miles, and the sight was never to be?

Well these Poems were to be, and this true thankful joy and pride with which I feel myself,

Yours ever faithfully,

Robert Browning

Miss Barrett,
50 Wimpole St.
R. Browning.

(After they were married and their correspondence ceased, for they were never separated, Robert Browning numbered their letters consecutively on the backs of the envelopes and placed them, side by side, in an inlaid box into which they fit perfectly. There were over five hundred letters which Browning, having destroyed all other correspondence, gave to his son, Robert Barrett Browning, shortly before his death in 1889, saying, "There they are, do with them as you please when I am dead and gone!" [*The*

Letters of Robert Browning and Elizabeth Barrett Barrett, 1845-1846, I, Note.] Almost ten years later Robert Barrett, an artist who married a wealthy young American socialite, decided they should be published.)

Elizabeth Barrett's calligraphy was less easily read, though it was somewhat larger and more widely spaced. Her envelope measured four and an-eighth by one and five-eights inches and was addressed to "Robert Browning, Esq., New Cross, Hatcham, Surrey," postmarked G¹ Marylebone with a canceled one-penny stamp; the back center bearing a neat four-eights of an inch wax seal with "EBB" imprinted therein and dated by the post office. Her thin writing paper measured four inches by five and a-half inches and she responded to Robert Browning's letter, immediately:

50 Wimpole Street: Jan. 11, 1845.

I thank you, dear Mr. Browning, from the bottom of my heart. You meant to give me pleasure by your letter—and even if the object had not been answered, I ought still to thank you. But it is thoroughly answered. Such a letter from such a hand! Sympathy is dear—very dear to me: but the sympathy of a poet, and such a poet, is the quintessence of sympathy to me! Will you take back my gratitude for it?—agreeing, too, that of all the commerce done in the world, from Tyre to Carthage, the exchange of sympathy for gratitude is the most princely thing!

For the rest you draw me on with your kindness. It is difficult to get rid of people when you once have given them too much pleasure—-*that* is a fact, and we will not stop for the moral of it. What I was going to say—after a little natural hesitation—is, that if ever you emerge without inconvenient effort from your "passive state," and will *tell* me of such faults as rise to the surface and strike you as important in my poems, (for of course, I do not think of troubling you with criticism in detail) you will confer a lasting obligation on me, and one which I shall value so much, that I covet it at a distance. I do not pretend to any extraordinary meekness under criticism and it is possible enough that I might not be altogether obedient to yours. But with my high respect for your power in your Art and for your experience as an artist, it would be quite impossible for me to hear a general observation of yours on what appear to you my master-faults, without being the better for it hereafter in some way. I ask for only a sentence or two of general observation—and I do not ask even for *that,* so as to tease you—but in the humble, low voice, which is so excellent a thing in women—particularly when they go a-begging! The most frequent general criticism I receive, is, I think, upon the style "if I *would* but change my style"! But *that* is an objection (isn't it?) to the writer bodily? Buffon says, and every sincere writer must feel, that "Le style c'est l'homme;" a fact, however, scarcely calculated to lessen the objection with certain critics.

Is it indeed true that I was so near to the pleasure and honour of making your acquaintance? and can it be true that you look back upon the lost opportunity with any regret? *But*—you know—if you had entered the "crypt," you might have caught cold, or been tired to death, and *wished* yourself "a thousand miles off;" which would have been worse than travelling them. It is not my interest, however, to put such thoughts in your head about its being "all for the best;" and I would rather hope (as I do) that what I lost by one chance I may recover by some future one. Winters shut me up as they do dormouse's eyes; in the spring, *we shall see*: and I am so much better that I seem turning round to the outward world again. And in the meantime I have learnt to know your voice, not merely from the poetry but from the kindness in it. Mr. Kenyon often speaks of you—dear Mr. Kenyon!—who most unspeakably, or only speakably with tears in my eyes,—has been my friend and helper, and my book's friend and helper! critic and sympathiser, true friend of all hours! You know him well enough, I think, to understand that I must be grateful to him.

I am writing too much,—and notwithstanding that I am writing too much, I will write of one thing more. I will say that I am your debtor, not only for this cordial letter and for all the pleasure which came with it, but in other ways, and those the highest: and I will say that while I live to follow this divine art of poetry, in proportion to my love for it and my devotion to it, I must be a devout admirer and student of your works. This is in my heart to say to you—and I say it.

And, for the rest, I am proud to remain
Your obliged and faithful
Elizabeth B. Barrett.
Robert Browning, Esq.
New Cross, Hatcham, Surrey.

(I laughed to discover as I read with Dave—being graciously permitted to do so by the librarian—that Robert Browning had been as unconcerned with middle names as Dave who had asked me to marry him and then asked, "By the way, what is your middle name?") This excerpt from Elizabeth's letter of Tuesday, September 16, 1846, four days after their secret marriage at the Marylebone Church:

Would you put it this way . . At such a church, by such a minister, Robert Browning Esquire, of New Cross, author of "Paracelsus," to Elizabeth Barrett, eldest daughter of Edward Moulton Barrett Esquire of Wimpole Street. Would you put it so? I do not understand really, . . and whether you should be specified as the author of "Paracelsus" . . but for *me*, it ought be, I think, simply as I have written it. Oh, and I forgot to tell you that what we did on Saturday is quite *invalid*, so that you may give me up now if you like—it isn't too late. You gave me a wrong name—*Moulton* is no Christian name of mine. Moulton Barrett is our family name; Elizabeth Barrett, my Christian name—Behold and see! . . (Her maiden name was Elizabeth Barrett Barrett.)

And the last Love Letter: E. B. B. to R. B.

> Friday Night.
> (Post-mark, September 19, 1846.)

At from half-past three to four, then—four will not, I suppose, be too late. I will not write more—I *cannot*. By to-morrow at this time, I shall have *you* only, to love me—my beloved!

You *only*! As if one said *God only*. And we shall have *Him* beside, I pray of Him.

I shall send to your address at New Cross your Hanmer's poems—and the two dear books you gave me, which I do not like to leave here and am afraid of hurting by taking them with me. Will you ask *our* Sister to put the parcel into a drawer, so as to keep it for us?

Your letters to me I take with me, let the "ounces" cry out aloud, ever so. I *tried* to leave them, and I could not. That is, they would not be left: it was not my fault—I will not be scolded.

Is this my last letter to you, ever dearest? Oh—if I loved you less . . a little, little less.

Why I should tell you that our marriage was invalid, or ought to be; and that you should by no means come for me to-morrow. It is dreadful . . dreadful . . to have to give pain here by a voluntary act—for the first time in my life.

Remind your mother and father of me affectionately and gratefully—and your sister too! Would she think it too bold of me to say *our* Sister, if she had heard it on the last page?

Do you pray for me to-night, Robert? Pray for me, and love me, that I may have courage, feeling both—

> Your own
> Ba.

The boxes are *safely sent*. Wilson has been perfect to me. And *I* . . calling her "timid," and afraid of her timidity! I begin to think that none are so bold as the timid, when they are fairly roused.

The most famous and eloquent love sonnets written by Elizabeth during this period, *The Sonnets From the Portuguese*, were not given to Robert Browning until the summer of 1849, nearly three years after their marriage when they were living in Bagni di Lucca. There were forty-four sonnets; the forty-third was probably the most famous sonnet ever written. Browning explained in a letter to Julia Wedgwood (a niece of Charles Darwin) the discrepancy in time between completion and presentation of the sonnets:

> Yes, that was a strange, heavy crown, that wreath of Sonnets, put on me one morning unawares, three years after it had been twined,—all this delay, because I happened early to say something against putting one's loves into verse: then again, I said something else on the other side, one evening at Lucca,—and next morning she said hesitatingly "Do you know I once wrote some poems about you?"—and then—"There they are, if you care to see them,"—and there was the little Book I have here—with the last Sonnet dated two days before our marriage. How I see the gesture, and hear the tones,—and, for the matter of that, see the window at which I was standing, with the tall mimosa in front, and little Church-court to the right. (*Sonnets From the Portuguese 1845-6*, Introduction, p. vii.)

> How do I love thee? Let me count the ways.
> I love thee to the depth and breadth and height
> My soul can reach, when feeling out of sight
> For the ends of Being and ideal Grace.
> I love thee to the level of every day's
> Most quiet need, by sun and candlelight.
> I love thee freely, as men strive for Right;
> I love thee purely, as they turn from Praise.
> I love thee with the passion put to use
> In my old griefs, and with my childhood's faith.
> I love thee with a love I seemed to lose
> With my lost saints,—I love thee with the breath,
> Smiles, tears, of all my life!—and, if God choose,
> I shall but love thee better after death. Sonnet XLIII.

Elizabeth Barrett, who first refused to marry Robert Browning in her determination not to burden the brilliant young poet with an ailing wife, was so restored to life by Browning's exuberant strength and love that she eloped with him to Italy. Elizabeth was forty and Browning, thirty-four and they lived fifteen blissfully happy years; productive—each continuing to write poetry—entranced with Robert's namesake, Robert Wiedemann Barrett Browning, born in 1849. Most of their years together were spent in Florence in the Casa Guidi where she died in 1861; he was forty-nine and, though lionized—with Robert Browning Societies springing up around the world—remained faithful to her memory and never remarried. He returned to England to educate his son who bore the name Robert Browning which his father and grandfather had been named but died in Venice on a visit to his son, December 12, 1889. He was buried in Westminster Abbey and it was suggested that Elizabeth Barrett Browning's body should be removed from Florence to be placed beside him but their son demurred.

I had "been reared" on Browning by Mother, long a devotee of the poet, who had been similarly influenced by her Mother's avid studying, teaching, writing and lecturing in Browning and the Victorians. I discovered, early, that Mother wrote in all of her books and found on the title page of *Elements of Ethics* (which she studied at Blue Mountain College after her engagement to Dad and his departure, after Mississippi A.&M. graduation, to the Philippines for military duty), a typical appreciation for the epigrammatic Browning: "The little more and how much it is, / The little less and world's away" (Paraphrase from Robert Browning's "By the Fireside"). I rarely opened a book of hers, from that day to this, without discovering at least one quotation from Robert Browning. It seemed appropriate that the poet, with a four-generational respect for his family name, should imprint our fourth-generation of "scholars" with his aura of poetical brilliance! We left Wellesley College with Mother's quoting from "Pippa Passes":

> The year's at the Spring,
> The day's at the Morn,
> God's in his Heaven,
> All's Right with the World!

Dave and I and Lori, agreed! Returning home, to Pinard Cottage #3, Annadale Road, after the long, invigorating day, Dave studied and

Mother and I planned our next literary excursion. She would soon be leaving and Boston was so rich in literature, especially in American Transcendentalism and the Brook Farm Experiment that men and women of letters and ideas had made it their capital, their seat of literary and political liberalism—and she could not see it all.

Dave decided for us and the next week end we drove to Concord to Nathaniel Hawthorne's Old Manse where he had lived the first four years of his married life. Hawthorne had been educated at Bowdoin College in Maine where he was a classmate of Longfellow and Franklin Pierce and had joined, briefly, the Brook Farm literati before his marriage, thus the Old Manse soon became a center for savants.

Mosses From an Old Manse was one of Mother's annotated books I had long been acquainted with. It was a description of the wonderful old house, sketches, essays and short stories—including the highly symbolic, Puritan classic, "Young Goodman Brown." But the Old Manse not only inspired creative genius in Hawthorne, it accommodated Emerson as well who wrote his famous essay "Nature" in the rear of the house. As Hawthorne had chosen the room for his own efforts, with approbation he described it as "the most delightful little nook of a study that ever offered its snug seclusion to a scholar" ("The Old Manse," p. 2). It was from a window, facing northward, in the little room that the clergyman, the Manse had always belonged to the village minister, "stood watching the outbreak of a long and deadly struggle between two nations. He saw the irregular array of his parishioners on the farther side of the river, and the glittering line of the British on the hither bank; he awaited in an agony of suspense the rattle of the musketry. It came, and there needed but a gentle wind to sweep the battle-smoke around this quiet house" (p. 3). The historic old house stood on the brink of the Concord, "the river of peace and quietness—for it is certainly the most unexcitable and sluggish stream that ever loitered imperceptibly toward its eternity the sea." And a short distance from the house:

> Here we are at the point where the river was crossed by the old bridge, the possession of which was the immediate object of the contest. On the hither side grow two or three elms, throwing a wide circumference of shade, but which must have been planted at some period within the three-score years and ten that have passed since the battle day. . . . The stream has here about the breadth of twenty strokes of a swimmer's arm—a space not too wide when the bullets were whistling across. Old people

who dwell hereabouts will point out the very spots on the western bank where our countrymen fell down and died, and on this side of the river an obelisk of granite has grown up from the soil that was fertilized with British blood. The monument—not more than twenty feet in height—is such as it befitted the inhabitants of a village to erect in illustration of a matter of local interest, rather than what was suitable to commemorate an epoch of national history. (p. 5.)

At the Old Manse, which was set back in shadows quite a distance from the wide road, we were struck by the historicity it represented and the intellectual splendor of those who had frequented it. There was a solitude and a silence, almost reverential, which nothing could disturb. One long paragraph in Hawthorne's essay, "The Old Manse," was definitive of the atmosphere:

Many strangers come in the summer-time to view the battle-ground. For my own part, I have never found my imagination much excited by this or any other scene of historic celebrity, nor would the placid margin of the river have lost any of its charm for me had men never fought and died there. There is a wilder (sic) interest in the tract of land—perhaps a hundred yards in breadth—which extends between the battle-field and the northern face of our Old Manse, with its contiguous avenue and orchard. Here, in some unknown age before the white man came, stood an Indian village convenient to the river whence its inhabitants must have drawn so large a part of their subsistence. The site is identified by the spear and arrow-heads, the chisels, and other implements of war, labor and the chase which the plow turns up from the soil. You see a splinter of stone half hidden beneath a sod. It looks like nothing worthy of note; but if you have faith enough to pick it up, behold! a relic. Thoreau, who has a strange faculty of finding what the Indians have left behind them, first set me on the search, and I afterward enriched myself with some very perfect specimens so rudely wrought that it seemed almost as if chance had fashioned them. Their great charm consists in this rudeness and in the individuality of each article, so different from the productions of civilized machinery, which shapes everything on one pattern. There is exquisite delight, too, in picking up for one's self an arrow-head that was dropped centuries ago and has never been handled since, and which we thus receive directly from the hand of the red hunter who purposed to shoot it at his game or at an enemy. Such an incident builds up again the Indian village and its encircling forest, and recalls to life the painted chiefs and warriors, the squaws at their household toil and the children sporting among the wigwams, while the little wind-rocked papoose swings from the branch of a tree. It can hardly be told whether it is a joy or a pain, after such a momentary vision, to gaze around in the broad daylight of reality and see stone fences, white houses, potato-fields and men doggedly hoeing in their shirt-sleeves and home-spun pantaloons. But this is nonsense. The Old Manse is better than 1,000 wigwams. (pp.7-8.)

Ralph Waldo Emerson was the mentor of the young American Transcendentalists who subscribed to his doctrine of self-reliance and individualism without undue dependence upon government, religion and material possessions. Most of them had been educated as gentlemen and lived so, except for the experimental community in West Roxbury, Massachusetts—Brook Farm—where the artificial in life was obviated by a combination of manual labor and mental productiveness which was to achieve a salutary society; and Thoreau's sojourn of about two years at Walden Pond. There he built a cabin on land owned by Emerson, planted a garden, hunted, fished and swam and wrote painstaking records of scientific observations as well as his famous meditative entries in his *Journal*, in fourteen volumes, for which he constructed a wooden box into which they fit with typical exactitude.

Henry David Thoreau was born in Concord in 1817 and was graduated from Harvard College as was his father-figure Emerson in whose household he lived for a while, teaching and laboring with his hands. It was natural for Thoreau to absorb from Emerson, the high priest of "Self-Reliance"—a vehemently independent self-sufficiency. In fact, he exceeded the teaching of Emerson and wrote *Civil Disobedience* in 1849, which became the handbook of demonstrators against government throughout the world in the twentieth century. But for the Thomas and Holland families, Thoreau's *Walden*, or *Life in the Woods*, another omnipresent, childhood book, was his paramount contribution to a good life; rather, a magnificent one. Thoughts from *Walden, Volume II*, "Where I Lived, And What I Lived For" have always had appeal:

When first I took up my abode in the woods, that is, began to spend my nights as well as days there, which, by accident, was on Independence Day, or the fourth of July, 1845, my house was not finished for winter, but was merely a defence against the rain, without plastering or chimney, the walls being of rough, weather-stained boards, with wide chinks, which made it cool at night. . . . The winds which passed over my dwelling were such as sweep over the ridges of mountains, bearing the broken strains, or celestial parts only, of terrestrial music. The morning wind forever blows, the poem of creation is uninterrupted; but few are the ears that hear it. Olympus is but the outside of the earth everywhere. . . The only house I had been the owner of before, if I except a boat, was a tent, which I used occasionally when making excursions in the summer, . . . With this more substantial shelter about me, I had made some progress toward settling in the world. This frame, so slightly clad, was a sort of crystallization around me, and reacted on the builder. It was suggestive somewhat as a picture in outlines. I did not need to go outdoors to take the air, for the atmosphere within had lost none of its freshness. . . . I found myself suddenly neighbor to the birds; not by having imprisoned one, but having caged myself near them. I was not only nearer to some of those which commonly frequent the garden and the orchard, but to those wilder and more thrilling songsters of the forest which never, or rarely, serenade a villager,—the wood-thrush, the veery, the scarlet tanager, the field-sparrow, the whippoorwill, and many others.

I was seated by the shore of a small pond, about a mile and a half south of the village of Concord and somewhat higher than it, in the midst of an extensive wood between that town and Lincoln, and about two miles south of that our only field known to fame, Concord Battle Ground; but I was so low in the woods that the opposite shore, half a mile off, like the rest, covered with wood, was my most distant horizon. For the first week, whenever I looked out on the pond it impressed me like a tarn high up on the side of a mountain, its bottom far above the surface of other lakes, and, as the sun arose, I saw it throwing off its nightly clothing of mist, and here and there, by degrees, its soft ripples or its smooth reflecting surface was revealed, while the mists, like ghosts, were stealthily withdrawing in every direction into the woods, as at the breaking up of some nocturnal conventicle. The very dew seemed to hang upon the trees later into the day than usual, as on the sides of mountains. (*The Romantic Triumph*, pp. 262-263.)

(Thoreau was so rich in figurative language that I traditionally included the last paragraph and other selections on final exams in Advanced-Placement English when I taught at Shawnee Mission South High School. His poetic prose abounded in litotes, metonymy and synecdoche and, occasionally, when he was droll, an apophasis.)

All memorable events, I should say, transpire in morning time and in a morning atmosphere. The Vedas say, "All intelligences awake with the morning." Poetry and art, and the fairest and most memorable of the actions of men, date from such an hour. All poets and heroes, like Memnon, are the children of Aurora, and emit their music at sunrise. To him whose elastic and rigorous thought keeps pace with the sun, the day is a perpetual morning. It matters not what the clocks say or the attitudes and labors of men. Morning is when I am awake and there is a dawn in me. Moral reform is the effort to throw off sleep. Why is it that men give so poor an account of their day if they have not been slumbering? They are not such poor calculators. If they had not been overcome with drowsiness, they would have performed something. The millions are awake enough for physical labor; but only one in a million is awake enough for effective intellectual exertion, only one in a hundred millions to a poetic or divine life. To be awake is to be alive. I have never yet met a man who was quite awake. How could I have looked him in the face?

I went to the woods because I wished to live deliberately, to front only the essential facts of life, and see if I could not learn what it had to teach, and not, when I came to die, discover that I had not lived. . . . I wanted to live deep and suck out all the marrow of life, to live so sturdily and Spartan-like as to put to rout all that was not life, to cut a broad swath and shave close, to drive life into a corner, and reduce it to its lowest terms, and, if it proved to me mean, why then to get the whole and genuine meanness of it, and publish its meanness to the world; or if it were sublime, to know it by experience, and be able to give a true account of it in my next excursion. . . . Our life is frittered away by detail. . . . Why should we live with such hurry and waste of life? We are determined to be starved before we are hungry. Men say that a stitch in time saves nine, and so they take a thousand stitches to-day to save nine tomorrow.

Time is but the stream I go a-fishing in. I drink at it; but while I drink I see the sandy bottom and detect how shallow it is. Its thin current slides away, but eternity remains. I would drink deeper; fish in the sky, whose bottom is pebbly with stars. I cannot count one. I know not the first letter of the alphabet. I have always been regretting that I was not as wise as the day I was born. The intellect is a cleaver; it discerns and rifts its way into the secret of things. I do not wish to be any more busy with my hands than is necessary. My head is hands and feet. I feel all my best faculties concentrated in it. (pp. 265-268.)

And from *Civil Disobedience*: I have paid no poll-tax for six years. I was put into a jail once on this account, for one night; and, as I stood considering the walls of solid stone, two or three feet thick, the door of wood and iron, a foot thick, and the iron grating which strained the light, I could not help being struck with the foolishness of that institution which treated me as if I were mere flesh and blood and bones, to be locked up. I wondered that it should have concluded at length that this was the best use it could put me to, and never thought to avail itself of my services in some way. I saw that, if there was a wall of stone between me and my townsmen, there was a still more difficult one to climb or break through before they could get to be as free as I was. I did not for a moment feel confined, and the walls seemed a great waste of stone and mortar. I felt as if I alone of all my townsmen had paid my tax. They plainly did not know how to treat me, but behaved like persons who are underbred. In every threat and in every compliment there was a blunder; for they thought that my chief desire was to stand the other side of that stone wall. I could not but smile to see how industriously they locked the door on my meditations, which followed them out again without let or hindrance, and *they* were really all that was dangerous. As they could not reach me, they had resolved to punish my body; just as boys, if they cannot come at some person against whom they have a spite, will abuse his dog. I saw that the State was half-witted, that it was timid as a lone woman with her silver spoons, and that it did not know its friends from its foes, and I lost all my remaining respect for it, and pitied it.

Thus the State never intentionally confronts a man's sense, intellectual or moral, but only his body, his senses. It is not armed with superior wit or honesty, but with superior physical strength. I was not born to be forced. I will breathe after my own fashion. Let us see who is the strongest. What force has a multitude? They only can force me who obey a higher law than I. (pp. 257-258.)

(Thoreau had refused to let the good-hearted jailor, Sam Staples, pay his tax for him but without his knowledge or permission, his Aunt Maria paid the poll-tax and he was summarily released.)

We found Walden Pond serene and beautiful and touched only by a swimming concession on the extreme eastern end of the lake. Thoreau's beloved woods, hills and rills and pond had been preserved without one building to mar its pristine wilderness, only a marker which indicated the site of his hand-wrought, rough-hewn cabin and his favorite path to the shore. Thoreau, who had been an athlete and exceptional swimmer all his youth, ironically died of consumption in Concord, May 6, 1862. He had loved but not married and all the pronominal references to his love in his *Journal* were changed in later years to the masculine gender. As a man of letters, Thoreau was more successful with Nature than with Man, for, much like his friend Walt Whitman, he was too original and unconventional to satisfy his highly educated, but conventional, contemporaries. But historians and scholars honored the genius of Thoreau as most typifying the soil and spirit of New England, together with the skeptical and earthbound brilliance of Nathaniel Hawthorne.

In the domain of science, Thoreau's contributions were never questioned: he was successful as a naturalist, ornithologist, dendrologist and limnologist. (It was interesting that our Midwestern nephew, Rick Holland, Robert and Viola's youngest son, encountered the observations of Thoreau for he achieved a Ph.D. in Limnology and currently does research for the U.S. Government on the Platte River in Nebraska.) Thoreau was triumphant as an ecologist, studying long before ecology—the relation of plant, bird and animal to its environment, including the relation of each to man—was a major part of natural science. As he wrote in *Walden, Volume II:* "I am monarch of all I *survey,* / My right there is none to dispute" (p. 261). Lacy had always read Thoreau with great approbation and I came to identify the two in many ways.

A book could be written about each hour we spent in Concord; it was the richest spot in the world for literary and historic mining. We drove reluctantly away from Walden Pond north to the home of Bronson Alcott, one of the founders of the *Dial* magazine to which all the Transcendentalists contributed and participant in the Brook Farm and Fruitlands communal experiments. His educational and philosophic achievements were overshadowed by the fame of his daughter, Louisa May Alcott, who wrote *Little Women* and *Little Men.* The Alcott home was a modest frame, rambling bungalow and offered a bronze plaque for our inspection.

We drove to the center of town which was the proper location, literally and symbolically, for the decorous, prosperous-looking, two-story white frame house, beautifully kept and built for the "Sage of Concord," Ralph Waldo Emerson. He had lived for a while in the Old Manse which had been built for his grandfather, Rev. William Emerson, in 1765, but after marriage moved to the substantial white house where he spent the remainder of his impressive, highly influential life. Hawthorne, in "The Old Manse," best described the hero worship attendant upon Emerson:

> These hobgoblins of flesh and blood were attracted thither by the widespread influence of a great original thinker who had his earthly abode at the opposite extremity of our village. His mind acted upon

other minds of a certain constitution with wonderful magnetism, and drew many men upon long pilgrimages to speak with him face to face. Young visionaries to whom just so much of insight had been imparted as to make life all a labyrinth around them, came to seek the clew (sic) that should guide them out of their self-involved bewilderment. Gray-headed theorists, whose systems at first air had finally imprisoned them in an iron frame-work, traveled painfully to his door, not to ask deliverance, but to invite the free spirit into their own thraldom. People that had lighted on a new thought, or a thought that they fancied new, came to Emerson, as the finder of a glittering gem hastens to a lapidary to ascertain its quality and value. Uncertain, troubled, earnest wanderers through the mid-night of the moral world, beheld his intellectual fire as a beacon burning on a hill-top, and, climbing the difficult ascent, looked forth into the surrounding obscurity more hopefully than hitherto. The light revealed objects unseen before—mountains, gleaming lakes, glimpses of a creation among chaos—but also, as was unavoidable, it attracted bats and owls and the whole host of night-birds, which flapped their dusky wings against the gazer's eyes, and sometimes were mistaken for fowls of angelic feather. Such delusions always hover nigh whenever a beacon-fire of truth is kindled.

For myself, there had been epochs of my life when I, too, might have asked of this prophet, the master-word that should solve the riddle of the universe; but now, being happy, I felt as if there were no question to be put, and therefore, admired Emerson as a poet of deep beauty and austere tenderness, but sought nothing from him as a philosopher. It was good, nevertheless, to meet him in the wood-paths, or sometimes in our avenue, with that pure, intellectual gleam diffused about his presence, like the garment of a shining one; and he so quiet, so simple, so without pretension; encountering each man alive as if expecting to receive more than he could impart. (pp. 23-24.)

One of the earliest theses which Mother imparted to me was the Emersonian concept that life was "a circle of compensation," and, many a time, I reflected upon and benefited from that metaphor of optimism. Mother won honors in college for her explication and dramatic presentation of passages from Emerson's essay on *Compensation*; those passages she marked "This" and underlined in her text:

Polarity, or action and reaction, we meet in every part of nature; in darkness and light; in heat and cold; in the ebb and flow of waters; in male and female; in the inspiration and expiration of plants and animals;

in the systole and diastole of the heart; in the undulations of fluids and of sound; in the centrifugal and centripetal gravity; in electricity, galvanism, and chemical affinity. Superinduce magnetism at one end of a needle, the opposite magnetism takes place at the other end. If the south attracts, the north repels. To empty here, you must condense there. An inevitable dualism bisects nature, so that each thing is a half, and suggests another thing to make it whole; as, spirit, matter; man, woman; subjective, objective; in, out; upper, under; motion, rest; yea, nay.

Whilst the world is thus dual, so is every one of its parts. The entire system of things gets represented in every particle. There is somewhat that resembles the ebb and flow of the sea, day and night, man and woman, in a single needle of the pine, in a kernel of corn, in each individual of every animal tribe. The reaction, so grand in the elements, is repeated within these small boundaries. For example, in the animal kingdom the physiologist has observed that <u>no creatures are favorites, but a certain compensation balances every gift and every defect.</u> (Underlining—Mother's.) A surplusage given to one part is paid out of a reduction from another. . . . (pp. 84-85.)

And this paragraph had appeal to Mother from "Spiritual Laws," the other essay in the slender, Blue Mountain College, Mississippi, textbook:

Human character does evermore publish itself. It will not be concealed. It hates darkness—it rushes into light. The most fugitive deed and word, the mere air of doing a thing, the intimated purpose, expresses character. If you act you show character; if you sit still you show it; if you sleep, you show it. You think because you have spoken nothing when others spoke, and have given no opinion on the times, on the church, on slavery, on the college, on parties and persons, that your verdict is still expected with curiosity as a reserved wisdom. Far otherwise; your silence answers very loud. You have no oracle to utter, and your fellow-men have learned that you cannot help them; for oracles speak. Doth not wisdom cry and understanding put forth her voice?

Other paragraphs from "Compensation" were provocative and intrigued Mother to marginal questions:

The league between virtue and nature engages all things to assume a hostile front to vice. The beautiful laws and substances of the world persecute and whip the traitor. He finds that things are arranged for truth and benefit, but there is no den in the wide world to hide a rogue. Commit a crime, and the earth is made of glass. There is no such thing as concealment. Commit a crime, and it seems as if a coat of snow fell on the ground, such as reveals in the woods the track of every partridge and fox and squirrel and mole. You cannot recall the spoken word, you cannot wipe out the foot-track, you cannot draw up the ladder, so as to leave no inlet or clew. Always some damning circumstance transpires. The laws and substances of nature, water, snow, wind, gravitation, become penalties to the thief.

On the other hand the law holds with equal sureness for all right action. Love, and you shall be loved. (Underlining—Mother's.) All love is mathematically just, as much as the two sides of an algebraic equation. The good man has absolute good, which like fire turns everything to its own nature, so that you cannot do him any harm; but as the royal armies sent against Napoleon, when he approached cast down their colors and from enemies became friends, so do disasters of all kinds, as sickness, offense, poverty, prove benefactors.

> "Winds blow and waters roll
> Strength to the brave and power and deity,
> Yet in themselves are nothing."

The good are befriended even by weakness and defect. As no man had ever a point of pride that was not injurious to him, so no man had ever a defect that was not somewhere made useful to him. (Underlining—Mother's.) The stag in the fable admired his horns and blamed his feet, but when the hunter came, his feet saved him, and afterwards, caught in the thicket, his horns destroyed him. Every man in his lifetime needs to thank his faults. As no man thoroughly understands a truth until first he has contended against it, so no man has a thorough acquaintance with the hindrances or talents of men until he has suffered from the one and seen the triumph of the other over his own want of the same. Has he a defect of temper that unfits him to live in society? Thereby he is driven to entertain himself alone and acquire habits of self-help; and thus, like the wounded oyster, he mends his shell with pearl.

Our strength grows out of our weakness. (pp. 99-101.)

It was time to leave Concord but I asked to see the Old Manse and Minuteman Bridge again. Dave drove us slowly past the Alcott home which had been called the Orchard House and had accommodated in an adjoining building, Bronson Alcott's Concord Summer School of Philosophy and Literature, which he established long after his Utopian Fruitlands experiment in Harvard, Massachusetts. Alas, that innovative, hard-working scholar was less well-known than the Concord grape which was first grown in the historic village.

Dave stopped briefly at the Old Manse, preserved as a museum and the only one of the three we had been privileged to enter and parked close to the bridge over the Concord River where Emerson's *Concord Hymn* had been sung July 4, 1837, on completion of the battle monument:

> By the rude bridge that arched the flood,
> Their flag to April's breeze unfurled,
> Here once the embattled farmers stood
> And fired the shot heard round the world.
>
> The foe long since in silence slept;
> Alike the conqueror silent sleeps;
> And Time the ruined bridge has swept
> Down the dark stream which seaward creeps.
>
> On this green bank, by the soft stream,
> We set to-day a votive stone;
> That memory may their deed redeem,
> When, like our sires, our sons are gone.
>
> Spirit, that made those heroes dare
> To die, and leave their children free,
> Bid Time and Nature gently spare
> The shaft we raise to them and thee.

Across the lazy stream from the granite obelisk, which marked the spot where the first British soldiers fell, stood the magnificent bronze Minuteman to honor the American colonists—the "embattled farmers" and villagers, our first Revolutionary soldiers.

It was late when we returned home but I was sure "our littlest scholar, little Rhody," from Mother's lexicon, had absorbed every lesson of our exhilarating day and was as edified as we three. Lori, newly seasoned traveler, had been perfectly behaved on her second literary jaunt. She had slept blissfully most of the day; we had planned our meals and viewings around her needs which had been so easily satisfied. What a joy she was! *She* was our *greatest* study!

When Mother was satisfied as to our lullabies (I sang no recognizable notes but the effect was startling and diverting); our baby-bathing techniques; our mastery of *Frog Went A-Courtin'*; and had approved of a mature baby sitter so that I could leave, if necessary, for three hours at a time and had baked a large, deep-dish apple cobbler, flouring a pork roast, with vegetables, ready to be popped into the oven—she felt comfortable about leaving her first grandchild, Lorinda Delle. Mother had been with us for three weeks and had made parenthood seem natural and facile to both Dave and me as it had always been to Dad and to her. She had written to Dad every day and he, to her and their devotion was beautiful to behold precisely because they were each so self-actualizing, so self-sufficing that the awareness of interdependence was the greatest affirmation of love and strength. Mother simply said when she was content with our efficiency: "Now—I need to be home," and we knew it was so.

Dave continued to enjoy his classes at General Line School and studied assiduously every night during the week. After he had logged adequate flight time at Quonset Point, his week ends were free. When Lori was one month old, in mid-March, no snow being forecast for New England, we set out for Burlington, Vermont, on Lake Champlain which Dave had wanted me to see. The summer before, on August 30, 1948, a hurricane had worked its way up the East Coast and all the Navy planes at Quonset Point had to be evacuated. The municipal airport at Burlington, Vermont, was selected as a safe haven. Dave and a fellow classmate flew out a P2V-2, being the only pilots "checked out" in the twin-engine plane with tricycle landing gear, an ASW (Anti-Submarine Warfare) aircraft. They returned VFR (Visual Flight Rules) on the third day after the hurricane had moved out to sea and all of Newport had mopped up. But he had spent two days in Burlington and wanted me to enjoy its picturesque beauty before he left Line School.

We drove to the eastern mainland of Rhode Island through Tiverton and North Tiverton and across the Massachusetts border to Fall River, an old mill town on the Taunton River and northwest on Highway 195, skirting Providence to Pawtucket, Rhode Island. I had been reading about the factory system in America and its origin at the Old Slater Mill in Pawtucket on the Blackstone River. It had all started because a boy from Derbyshire, England, had a retentive memory.

Samuel Slater had arrived in the United States, in 1789, as a farm worker. As a lad in England, he had learned the art of spinning cotton fibers on water-powered machines, the design of which was a close-guarded secret giving England a monopoly in textiles. In fact, the construction design was so closely protected that no mechanic of the Richard Arkwright machine was permitted to leave England. Samuel Slater wrote from his home, offering help in the development of the machine, without blueprints, to Moses Brown who with his three brothers, John, Joseph and Nicholas, had dominated trade and contributed to the wealth and distinction of Rhode Island before and long after, the Revolution. (They were committed to the Baptist religion and education, and Rhode Island College, the seventh in the colonies, was founded at Warren in 1764, and encouraged by the Brown brothers, moved to Providence in 1770, changing its name, in 1804, to Brown University in honor of Nicholas Jr. Lori's cousin, John Holland, who was three weeks' her senior, later began college as a Freshman at Brown. Not anticipating that happy eventuality, we bypassed Brown University until years later when our "one" had become three "Navy brats.")

"Farm worker" Samuel Slater, financed by Moses (note the wonderful Biblical *nomina*) Brown, successfully duplicated the Arkwright machine and, in 1790—built completely from memory—the wheels of America's first water-powered spinning machine began to turn. By the 1920's, spinning and weaving occupied three-fifths of the manufacturing labor force in the state. America's Industrial Revolution had been launched in the Old Slater Mill in 1793, and I needed to see it so I could understand, in part, "Lori's State's" contribution to the country. And I was not disappointed.

The red and white frame building of three stories and many tall windows had a gazebo-like fenced cupola on the end of the peaked, *L*-shaped roof. The picture-book factory, reflected back from the Blackstone River, was as graphically distinctive as its history. Samuel Slater's mill had been made into a museum, steam power's having supplanted water power and electricity's having replaced both. The textile industry no longer dominated in Rhode Island: most mills had moved to the South in the early and mid-Forties in search of cheaper electric power and labor.

Dave stayed in the car with Lori, sleeping happily in her hooded basket in the back seat. Dave had anchored the basket with the front legs down on the floor so that it would not tip over and so that I could reach her out easily at hunger time without opening the door and letting in cold air. Although it was sunny, the wind was high and the air, colder even than the Blizzard Day a month before—so I stayed only long enough to get literature and glimpse the earliest spinning, weaving and knitting machines and, fortunately, had no interest in the modern. I was not a knitter, having knit one sweater in high school—a "jiffy knit" which took me two unquick years and produced a neckline as broad as a tent-flap. Knitting, I wisely concluded, was not a talent of mine. How glad I was for there were so many books I "needed to read!" (Dave always laughed when he heard *that* expression and said I got both the phrase and proclivity from Mother and he was right—and I was grateful!)

Contemplating my preference for books to knitting, I thought of my favorite book, *Of Time and The River* by Thomas Wolfe and appreciated anew the quest which had sent him from North Carolina, where he had been born and educated, to Harvard and New England—and discovery. His novel, written in 1935, three yours before his short life ended at the age of thirty-eight, exploded with his insatiable thirst to know and his ebullient absorption with New England. "Dave," as the highway signs announced Boston, "may we drive through the Market and see Faneuil Hall; we don't need to stop. Listen to this." And I read from *Of Time and The River.* (I had brought just two books: Wolfe and Robert Frost's *Collected Poems.*)

His hunger and thirst had been immense: he was caught up for the first time in the midst of the Faustian web—there was no food that could feed him, no drink that could quench his thirst. Like an insatiate and maddened animal he roamed the streets, trying to draw up mercy from the cobblestones, solace and wisdom from a million sights and faces, or he prowled through endless shelves of high-piled books, tortured by everything he could not see and could not know, and growing blind, weary, and desperate from what he read and saw. He wanted to know all, have all, be all—to be one and many, to have the whole riddle of this vast and swarming earth as legible, as tangible in his hand as a coin of minted gold.

Suddenly spring came, and he felt at once exultant certainty and joy. Outside his uncle's dirty window he could see the edge of Faneuil Hall, and hear the swarming and abundant activity of the markets. The deep roar of the markets reached them across the singing and lyrical air, and he drank into his lungs a thousand proud, potent, and mysterious odors which came to him like the breath of certainty, like the proof of magic, and like the revelation that all confusion had been banished—the world that he longed for won, the word that he sought for spoken, the hunger that devoured him fed and ended. And the markets, swarming with richness, joy, and abundance, thronged below him like a living evidence of fulfillment. For it seemed to him that nowhere more than here was the passionate enigma of New England felt: New England, with its harsh and stony soil, and its tragic and lonely beauty; its desolate rocky coasts and its swarming fisheries, the white, piled, frozen bleakness of its winters with the magnificent jewelry of stars, the dark firwoods, and the warm little white houses at which it is impossible to look without thinking of groaning bins, hung bacon, hard cider, succulent bastings and love's warm white, and opulent flesh.

We drove slowly through the Boston Market, paused with traffic in front of Faneuil Hall, a many-windowed, two-storied, red brick building looking more like a meetinghouse for public forum, which it was, than a market, which it was on the ground floor. Nothing had changed in the fourteen years since Thomas Wolfe described it: "Right and left, around the central market, the old buildings stretched down to the harbor and the smell of ships: this was built-on land, in old days ships were anchored where these cobbles were, but the warehouses were also old—they had the musty, mellow, blackened air and smell of the 'seventies,' they looked like Victorian prints, they reeked of ancient ledgers, of 'counting houses,' of proud monied merchants, and the soft-spoken rumble of victorias."

And then Wolfe explained the sobriety and sternness of New Englanders:

> Perhaps the thing that really makes New England wonderful is this sense of joy, this intuition of brooding and magic fulfillment that hovers like a delicate presence in the air of one of these days. Perhaps the answer is simple: perhaps it is only that this soft and sudden spring, with its darts and flicks of evanescent joy, its sprite-like presence that is only half-believed, its sound that is the sound of something lost and elfin and half-dreamed, half-heard, seems wonderful after the grim frozen tenacity of the winter, the beautiful and terrible desolation, the assault of the frost and ice on living flesh which resists it finally as it would resist the cruel battering of a brute antagonist, so that the tart, stingy speech, the tight gestures, the withdrawn and suspicious air, the thin lips, red pointed noses and hard prying eyes of these people are really the actions of those who, having to defend themselves harshly against nature, harshly defend themselves against all the world.

I promised to read aloud just two more paragraphs from Book II, "Young Faustus," having read from Chapter XIII; I began XIV:

> He had spells and rhymes of magic numbers which would enable him, he thought, to read all of the million books in the great library. This was a furious obsession with him all the time. And there were other spells and rhymes which would enable him to know the lives of fifty million people, to visit every country in the world, to know a hundred languages, possess 10,000 lovely women, and yet have one he loved and honored above all, who would be true and beautiful and faithful to him.
>
> And by the all-resuming magic of these spells he would go everywhere on earth, while keeping one place to return to; and while driven mad with thirst and hunger to have everything, he would be peacefully content with almost nothing; and while wanting to be famous, honored, celebrated man, he would live obscurely, decently, and well, with one true love forever. In short, he would have the whole cake of the world, and eat it, too—have adventures, labors, joys, and triumphs that would exhaust the energies of ten thousand men, and yet have spells and charms for all of it, and was sure that with these charms and spells and sorceries, all of it was his.
>
> He would rush out of the great library into the street, and take the subway into Boston.

Dave turned around so that I could see Faneuil Hall and its sturdy cupola at a distance, then slowly, the heavy traffic and market vehicles prevented any other speed, drove again by "The Cradle of Liberty," as it was popularly called. He found Highway 93 and we headed northwest to Derry, New Hampshire. Robert Frost had retired from teaching at Dartmouth where he had attended his first year of college; Harvard, where he had finished; Amherst, Michigan and Yale, where he had also taught; and was writing and farming near Derry.

We had no interest in discovering Robert Frost's farm, for all of New England was synonymous with his name. He had been born in California and represented the strong, moral value system of men and women of "the soil" and of good conscience throughout the country. I always felt he was a national poet laureate in tone and attitude and universality and should have been so appointed rather than the casual system of state-appointed poet laureates, should the state be interested in such. We were soon in his Derry terrain and every farm and rocky pasture had a stone fence and clumps of birches and I was sure we had seen him with his luxuriant white mane, wielding a shovel to remove "A Patch of Old Snow." Seeing the white-barked, graceful trunks and branches of birch trees, some still iced and thinly layered with snow, I felt compelled to read my favorite Robert Frost poem, "Birches," to Dave because I knew he would identify with the "swinger of birches":

When I see birches bend to left and right
Across the lines of straighter darker trees,
I like to think some boy's been swinging them,
But swinging doesn't bend them down to stay
As ice-storms do. Often you must have seen them
Loaded with ice a sunny winter morning
After a rain. They click upon themselves
As the breeze rises, and turn many-colored
As the stir cracks and crazes their enamel.
Soon the sun's warmth makes them shed crystal shells
Shattering and avalanching on the snow-crust—
Such heaps of broken glass to sweep away
You'd think the inner dome of heaven had fallen.
They are dragged to the withered bracken by the load,
And they seem not to break; though once they are bowed
So low for long, they never right themselves:
You may see their trunks arching in the woods
Years afterwards, trailing their leaves on the ground
Like girls on hands and knees that throw their hair
Before them over their heads to dry in the sun.
But I was going to say when Truth broke in
With all her matter-of-fact about the ice-storm
I should prefer to have some boy bend them
As he went out and in to fetch the cows—
Some boy too far from town to learn baseball,
Whose only play was what he found himself,
Summer or winter, and could play alone.
One by one he subdued his father's trees
By riding them down over and over again
Until he took the stiffness out of them,
And not one but hung limp, not one was left
For him to conquer. He learned all there was
To learn about not launching out too soon
And so not carrying the tree away
Clear to the ground. He always kept his poise

To the top branches, climbing carefully
With the same pains you use to fill a cup
Up to the brim, and even above the brim.
Then he flung outward, feet first, with a swish,
Kicking his way down through the air to the ground.
So was I once myself a swinger of birches.
And so I dream of going back to be.
It's when I'm weary of considerations,
And life is too much like a pathless wood
Where your face burns and tickles with the cobwebs
Broken across it, and one eye is weeping
From a twig's having lashed across it open.
I'd like to get away from earth awhile
And then come back to it and begin over.
May no fate willfully misunderstand me
And half grant what I wish and snatch me away
Not to return. Earth's the right place for love:
I don't know where it's likely to go better.
I'd like to go by climbing a birch tree,
And climb black branches up a snow-white trunk
Toward heaven, till the tree could bear no more,
But dipped its top and set me down again.
That would be good both going and coming back.
One could do worse than be a swinger of birches.

What a glorious winter's drive: the roads were clear; the snow, deep and clean; the houses, trees, church spires and hills, exquisitely mantled. We expatiated with Frostian delight. Dave could not have chosen a more gorgeous week end for adventuring in the snow-clad White and Green Mountains.

After we passed the busy towns of Manchester and Concord, New Hampshire, heading north, cars with skis and poles atop began to swoop around us—impatient with mere sight-seers. We continued to edge through Alpine-resort areas of rustic log buildings and lodges hugging the road with slopes in the distance. Wide avenues divided the snowy timberland on high and ski lifts dangled from dimly visible wires. Activity was frenetic at roadside as if it was the last snow of the winter, as perhaps it was, or because they were late arrivals who dared not squander the mid-afternoon sunshine by remaining earthbound.

We spent the night in a backwoodsy hotel in the famous White Mountains of New Hampshire and arrived early the next morning at The Flume, near Whaleback Mountain, about which I was well-informed because Dave had remembered it from a boyhood visit with his family. While I stayed in the car with Lori, Dave pulled on boots and a heavy parka, even putting a knit hat in his pocket and trudged forth through the undisturbed snow to reconnoiter the deserted natural wonder. I nursed Lori in the brilliant morning sunshine, shading her eyes with her bonnet, changed her and was explaining to her what I understood The Flume to be, when Dave returned—red-cheeked and beaming. "It's just the way I remembered!" he enthused, "I went clear to the top! But don't you try it," he cautioned, "it's too icy. I've drawn a map. Go just where I've indicated. And hang onto the railing the entire way. There are patches of snow with ice underneath but you'll be fine. Just take your time and follow the map." He took off his heavy coat and boots and reached for Lori, "Let me hold her awhile." I put on my heavy "Michigan-football" coat, boots, scarf, hat and gloves and, map in hand, approached The Flume. Ascending a long flight of wide steps, I turned and there was the amazing spectacle: as far up as my eye could see were waterfalls' cascading at different levels from the mountainside. I started up the steps, which were steep, careful to keep my hand on the rail and following Dave's way when the stairs divided. The steps narrowed, being cut out of the mountain which was identified as Mount Flume, naturally enough, and Flume Brook it was, leaping on the other side of me from a craggy wall with ledges of snow exhibiting the white bark of birch clumps and heavy leafless vines which looked like wild grape and twisted like wisteria. How beautiful it was in the snow! I could envision its splendor in the spring. I walked through a grotto with moss, brown on the walls, and upward on wooden steps. There was not much protection from a misstep but no one to compete for the railing. When I got to the landing Dave had marked: "Stop Here," I looked up and was glad I could go down! I could understand how he remembered: it was phantasmagorical and frightening enough to impress even a young boy's daring mind. I descended very carefully, saw the car far below at one turn to an iced ledge, wanted to wave but did not think I could afford to, being more aware of the height and treacherous footing, going down than coming up. But it was a breathtaking phenomenon and an experience, not forgettable, and I knew we would bring Lori when she could remember.

Dave had another boyhood memory to appease and verify and drove from The Flume in Franconia Notch State Park to Crawford Notch State Park, sixteen miles to the northeast, to Mt. Washington, the highest point in New Hampshire, an elevation of 6,288 feet which could be reached by Cog Railroad! His boy's memory of exploring the White Mountains had been unflawed by time thus far, so I knew another and maybe, even "better," challenge awaited me. What was my boy-man getting me into? But after all, wasn't I a trained Camp Fire Girl? Hadn't I earned my Wohelo Badge? Wasn't I a tomboy and a swinger of Mississippi grape-vines? Ah, yes, wasn't I, also, a new Mother—for whom protection would be provided. What glorious beauty surrounded us! New Hampshire's White Mountains in late winter: birch and craggy oak, fir, pine and hemlock in the snow, in the sun. I wondered why the whole country wasn't crowding into the superb scene.

Alas, the Cog Railroad was closed for the winter! But Dave had not even planned to go up, not even to see the National Weather Observatory on top because there was not enough time. He intended to be in Burlington, Vermont, by nightfall so that we could drive through the Green Mountains and see the maple-syrup terrain in daylight. We had a quick lunch in the lodge at the base of Mt. Washington, briefly inspected the Railroad with its open coal-car-like vehicle and engine which backed, almost sheer, up the mountain, and I knew we would return, in force, another day.

Dave drove back to Franconia Notch, to the north and west of it, for there was a third vision he had to recapture but one which could be achieved from the car, in passing. We were heading to "The Great Stone Face" which Nathaniel Hawthorne had immortalized in his short story of the same name. The Old Man of the Mountain, a huge profile of natural stone carved by the elements on the outcropping of Cannon Mountain, was visible at a strategic stopoff some distance from the range. I had prepared for the viewing at home and produced my notes on Hawthorne's "Passages From the American Note-Books—Materials for Fictions": "'1839. The semblance of a human face to be formed on the side of a mountain, or in the fracture of a small stone, by a *lusus naturae*. The face is an object of curiosity for years or centuries, and by and by a boy is born, whose features gradually assume the aspect of that portrait. At some critical juncture, the resemblance is found to be perfect. A prophecy may be connected.' And that's all there is to his aperçu," I remarked.

"From those four sentences, Hawthorne produced a long short story," I told Dave. "Can you imagine anyone being *that* prolix?" I marveled. "Yes," Dave chuckled and nodded, not bothering to divert its direction from me. "Touché!" I acknowledged, after a moment of reflection. Dave had stopped the car at the vantage point and we could actually see a prominent profile. "Now listen to this and see if you think 'The Great Stone Face' is really the Old Man of the Mountain," and I read from page two of Hawthorne's short story in his collection, *Twice-Told Tales.*

The Great Stone Face, then, was a work of Nature in her mood of majestic playfulness, formed on the perpendicular side of a mountain by some immense rocks, which had been thrown together in such a position as, when viewed at a proper distance, precisely to resemble the features of the human countenance. It seemed as if an enormous giant, or a Titan, had sculptured his own likeness on the precipice. There was the broad arch of the forehead, a hundred feet in height; the nose, with its long bridge; and the vast lips, which, if they could have spoken, would have rolled their thunder accents from one end of the valley to the other. True, it is, that if the spectator approached too near, he lost the outline of the gigantic visage, and could discern only a heap of ponderous and gigantic rocks, piled in chaotic ruin one upon another. Retracing his steps, however, the wondrous features would again be seen; and the farther he withdrew from them, the more like a human face, with all its original divinity intact, did they appear; until, as it grew dim in the distance, with the clouds and glorified vapor of the mountains clustering about it, the Great Stone Face seemed positively to be alive.

Dave agreed that Hawthorne had described the Old Man of the Mountain and recalled that one had to be at just the right spot for discovery of a face and demonstrated by driving forward a few yards, losing the profile, and backing slowly to bring it once more into focus. "Imagine riding out to this lonely wilderness on horseback or in a bouncing buggy to study a face on a mountain! Would one travel that far to hear a philosophy expounded, a sermon preached or to view a portrait painted by man? Why do legends command so much time and attention?" I queried. "Because they're flexible," Dave quickly asseverated. "They can be tailored to need." "Yes," I agreed, "they can be used for identification of self, self-magnification—even self-exculpation. That's exactly right!

Dave, you're omniscient!" And I patted him on the knee, "How'd I ever get you?" "Just lucky!" he chortled.

Dave found Highway 302, paralleled the Lower Ammonoosuc River to a covered bridge at Bath, which we stopped briefly to examine, and crossed the Connecticut River at Woodsville into the state of Vermont, the "Green Mountain State." And it was beautiful! The verdure was the same: birches, beeches, pines and firs. The mountains were similar with ski slopes, high serpentine streams, rustic lodges at road level, and lakes, glistening everywhere. We passed by granite quarries at Barre and saw the capitol at Montpelier but the most picturesque scenes were along the winding roads between extensive groves of huge sugar maple trees with intermittent buckets hanging about two feet above the snow, with a shed of rough construction, here and there in the woods—from which smoke squeezed, sometimes from a chimney, sometimes from the roof itself. We stopped to buy a heavy pitcher of brown crockery filled with maple syrup to send to Papa Lacy who had recently joined the Thomas domicile in Kansas City; cans of syrup for Mother and Dad and Mother H, and one for us with a round of sharp, white Vermont cheddar cheese. Now we could proceed onward, Burlington—next, having dispatched our "touch of New England" to the Midwest.

Burlington, on Lake Champlain, was a lovely small city, very clean, modern, sparkling with wide streets and twentieth-century residences and buildings—far more Midwestern in appearance and bustle than the quaint, atmospheric towns of eastern New England. It had a special warmth for us, a beauty and graciousness that encouraged approval and I was as charmed by it as Dave had been. The streets were so wide downtown that it even had diagonal parking in front of the hotel! Dave pulled in, gently, because I was holding a well-bundled Lori who had just awakened, its being her "tea time," opened the door and helped me out and reached for Lori. For some reason, the transfer of Lori from my arms to Dave's was very awkward and confused as if we had never exchanged an infant before in our entire month of glorious parenthood. We made several assays, but four hands interfered rather than helped with our precious little bundle. I looked up and laughed, wondering if people, several of whom had stopped to watch with concern and amusement—suspected us of kidnapping. Finally, Dave suggested: "Don't *give* her to me, just hold her—and I'll *take* her." And I did, and he did, and it was *so* simple!

Shortly after we had solved the enigma of the Great Stone Face and Dave was hard at study in Newport, Lori and I, watching for the first robin; Dave's new orders arrived. He was to report in late June 1949, to the Naval Air Training Command, Pensacola, Florida. Whether he groaned inwardly, I never knew for he accepted each tour with equanimity and enthusiasm as a forwarding of his career as a permanent Naval Officer. I inferred he would be a Flight Instructor and I had heard flyers' wives bemoan that duty when it fell to their husbands, which vociferousness I thought both disloyal and inappropriate.

Indeed, I chided a friend, over the bridge table, for speaking with too much specificity and pejoration of her flyer's assignment. And he, and Dave, agreed. "But," she argued, "*I'm* not in the Navy. I can say what I wish!" "True," I admitted, "but your attitude influences your husband and he reflects your displeasure. He has to *know* every time he climbs into his plane that his wife is swollen with pride and glories in the dignity of his job—of mastering such a complicated mass of machinery, of serving his country. *You* are the mechanic of his mind and emotions." Since Dave always asserted and proved: "We're first—gentlemen; then, officers; then, flyers"; wives, I was convinced, had to reflect commensurate decorum!

Dave and I never discussed his actual flying. I did not know the how, the where, the why of it and was convinced I should not—that I should look at him with stars in my eyes and tell him how wonderful he was, how proud of him, I was. And if, occasionally, in the camaraderie of a party, I heard Dave and friends, teasing and laughing about a flight—I savored the gem. It was usually years later before I heard of an incident, if I heard at all—for Dave was totally without braggadocio, a trait which many pilots, particularly fighter pilots, exuded. Being without self-deception and the accompanying verbalization needed to reinforce it, he was an honest, dispassionate appraiser of his own limitations and an appreciator of his multitudinous abilities without the compulsion to herald the latter or the need to demonstrate them. Consequently, Dave was a decisive, exuberantly self-confident, yet modestly quiet, happy man—ergo, an outstanding flyer! A friend asked me once: "Is Dave always that happy?" I, happily, nodded: "Yes!"

Dave had chosen Korea for the topic of his paper for General Line School and I had been permitted the role of researcher. He subscribed to a weekly Korean newspaper published in Seoul and printed in English. Entitled the *Light of the Universe*, it was not a hyperbolical claim. In my research, I discovered that Korea (which had been annexed by Japan in 1910) had a legendary history dating from 2333 B.C., and had been dominated by Chinese dynasties and Buddhism but the language had been homogeneous throughout the peninsula and literature, art and science had been encouraged. Buddhist monks controlled the government until Mongols invaded Korea in 1231 A.D. The Korean General Yi defeated the Mongols in 1364 and brought "Light" to his country by deposing the last Wang ruler and establishing his own dynasty in 1392, which held sway until the Japanese annexation. Under the Yi dynasty, Korea enlightened the world intellectually and culturally; Buddhism was curbed and monastery lands surrendered to the people. Fifty years before Gutenberg's famous invention, Korea was printing Chinese characters in movable type, in 1403! The world's first college of literature was established in 1420 and first phonetic alphabet, the "Onmun," developed in 1443!

Korea was divided at the 38th parallel in August 1945, for the temporary expedient of accepting surrender of Japanese troops. The United States was to accept surrender of Japanese forces south of the 38th parallel, and Russia, north of the 38th. It was anticipated that Korea would soon become a free and independent country in accordance with the Cairo declaration of 1943, signed by Generalissimo Chiang Kai-shek, Prime Minister Winston Churchill and President Franklin D. Roosevelt. That declaration was reaffirmed again, in 1945, by the Potsdam agreement with President Harry S. Truman, Prime Minister Clement Attlee, who replaced Winston Churchill in late July, and U.S.S.R.'s Joseph Stalin.

By June 1949, the first week, Dave's paper on Korea was completed and submitted as the last of the 50,000 U.S. Occupation Troops withdrew from south of the 38th parallel, having begun their withdrawal on August 15, 1948, when the government of the Republic of Korea was formed—and Dave had initiated the writing of his didactic, topical paper. For ten months he had plotted the outcome and direction of the first democratic election in the history of Korea, which was held May 10, 1948. The outcome was immediately apparent and I remember Dave's concern when we heard the news in Key West: only South Korea voted in the first democratic election because the Soviets refused to let the North Koreans participate! Thus the trouble began and we both had followed it closely, but not hopefully, for a year. Ironically, the undemocratic North Korean government, "elected" under Communist supervision which barred United Nations' observation teams, proclaimed itself the Democratic People's Republic of Korea!

General Line School had concluded, Naval scholars were praised and honored in a ceremony at the War College and we left Newport, as soon as Dave changed from dress "whites" to mufti, with our own three-and-a-half-month-old trophy. It had been a thrilling, ten-month anchorage in Newport, Rhode Island. We two had come, naive and empty-handed, to the smallest state and left—enlightened and enriched with the greatest gift of all: Lorinda Delle Holland!

Dave's leave of three weeks passed swiftly in Lincoln, where we compared babies—Kenneth and Naomi's John being slightly older than Lori, and in Kansas City, where Mother and Dad cuddled Lori with brother Charles' help while Dave and I shopped for furniture at Duff and Repp's. Lori was outgrowing her baby basket and had to have new, high-quality furniture of demure design, not cavorting with chicks and ducks and bears.

We found a heavy, unusual, pearl-gray Storkline crib with solid head and footboards, delicately garlanded with pastel blossoms, and an oversized matching chifforobe. We chose a blue upholstered highchair; a playpen of sturdy wood and a youth bed, both in Storkline aqua. Since we did not intend our new daughter to be contaminated by old furniture, we completed selection of a houseful: a French Provincial, fruitwood bedroom suite for us; a Duncan Fyfe dining-room suite of mahogany with a junior-sized table and six chairs. The capacious buffet would accommodate our twelve place settings of Lenox "Belvedere" china and Blue Willow (both given us by Mother H and "the Hollands"); an Italian Blue Bird demitasse set from Mother (demitasse spoons purchased and engraved at Rough Jewelers, Newport); our Watson "Lotus" silver flatware from Mother and Dad (the first place setting chosen by my U. of Michigan chum, Naomi Esther Shapiro, with an Old English, lower case *h* engraved on it at Saks Fifth Avenue, New York, her card saying: "This is the closest thing to hand-wrought silver on the market today. From West Attleboro, Mass. You can't return *this*, Love, Nicky."); Finnish "Karhula" crystal, short, heavy-balled stems for frequent packing and silver serving pieces. Our living-room selection consisted of a blue-gray, seven-foot Simmons duofold couch which opened parallel into a double bed and one red velveteen occasional chair. Since my linen-filled cedar chest and other wedding items were at Mother and Dad's, we had our new furniture delivered there to be packed and transported to Pensacola.

Lori was dedicated Sunday, June 12, 1949, by Dr. Robert I. Wilson, at the First Baptist Church, Linwood and Park, Kansas City, Missouri, with proud parents and grandparents, overjoyed. It was a delight to be back in the Midwest again for no place was more wonderful, even in hot weather! Charles was an engineer at Butler Manufacturing Company and, with limited time for flying, was in the Naval Air Inactive Reserves. How wonderful to be in the expanded-family midst: with Beth, Mother's sister and Papa, the baby on his knees! Dave and I relished being spoiled by all!

On June 19th, Dave drove to Pensacola and reported in at the Naval Air Training Command, the "Annapolis of the Air," the world's largest air-training facility, teaching everything from ground school to carrier-deck takeoff and landing. They even trained their own doctors, Aviation Medicine being taught at the Naval Hospital on Base. Dave was to have a six-week Ground School Refresher Course and Lori and I thoughtfully stayed with Mother and Dad for the month of July, so he could have four weeks of uninterrupted concentration. I did not believe he wanted that much but two grandparents were sure that he did. Indeed, it had been a hardship: when the Grandmother did not live across the street—which Dad said should have been a national law! Lori and I loved being with Mama Tom and Grampy Frank, with photographer Uncle Charles—able to use up his old film from Saipan and Tinian days of yore, with Beth and Papa. No four-month-old cherub ever had more loving attention and adoration!

Figure 16. Lori—Conferring with Epaminondas

CHAPTER II

PROFICIENCY IN PENSACOLA

Lori and I left for Pensacola the first of August. Mother and Dad put us on the train at the Union Station, Dad's having a word and a tip for our Pullman porter. We had a very comfortable bedroom for the day-and-night trip, a perfect arrangement for a nursing mother—my three meals being served in the room. Dave had arranged to meet our train in Flomaton, Alabama, Saturday morning rather than await our change of trains to Pensacola. And it was so typically helpful of him to come aboard to carry off Lori and see to our luggage. Everyone had been kind who knew of our presence, and few did, for Lori had not cried once. She was an exceptionally good baby; of course, she was an exceptional baby!

It had been our first separation, except for overnights, and we were elated to be together again. Dave was amazed at the growth and development of his five-and-a-half-month-old Lori! "I'm glad she hasn't forgotten me," he smiled. He was anxious to show us our new home, a very small cottage, he had written, which was being completely refinished, floors and all, and painted. It would be ready in a week and he had wired Mother to have our furniture shipped. In the meantime, he had rented a furnished, downstairs apartment in town.

We drove through an unscenic terrain of scrub and yellow pine in northwestern Florida and I asked Dave the source of the heavy, acrid, yellowish smoke which so filled the air we were forced to roll up the windows. "Paper mills," he explained, "they're processing wood pulp. It's the chief industry throughout this entire area." "Good heavens!" I remonstrated, "is Pensacola permeated with this odor?" "No, no," he laughed, "we're seventy-five miles north of Pensacola. You'll have fresh Bay breezes there: Pensacola Bay on the south, Escambia Bay on the east." I was vastly relieved. My reading in the *Encyclopædia Britannica* at Mother's, added to the impression gained when we drove through Pensacola enroute from San Diego to Key West, convinced me that I would find a strange eclecticism of cultures and living styles in a town which, like Topsy, had grown without a grand design. I had read that paper, chemicals, lumber, cottonseed oil and fertilizers, in addition to excelsior, sails, naval stores and small boats predominated but I did not anticipate the olfactory sense would be assailed (no pun planned), first. We were soon out of the wood-pulp area, with its huge black smokestacks and mountains of sawdust, into softer scenes. And I loved it all—even the paper in-the-making—because we were together again and I was home!

Dave drove first to our house—our doll's house! It was perfect for our needs and just half a block from the Navy Boulevard and a mile from the U.S. Naval Air Station, slightly north of the north arm of Bayou Grande. Number "8" was the only digit over the door of our cunning, white frame cottage: 8 West Jackson Avenue, Warrington, Florida (now 8 Winthrop Avenue). The owner lived next door in a substantial brick house which he had just built, having outgrown his bungalow—refinishing the latter for a rental property and anxious to entrust its care to a young Naval flyer and small family. It was set back from the sandy road; the yard had a few tufts of Bermuda grass and a wire fence and did not clamor for attention, there not being one shrub, vine or even a perennial flower. But that was perfectly acceptable because we were growing our own!

The front door opened into a small living room with a sizable space heater ending the east side over which a three-ledged mantel had been built to accommodate, I ecstatically judged, at least a hundred books. As if that was not thrill enough—at the west end of our paneled room, which glistened with newly varnished hardwood floors, was a small screened porch—not much larger than Lori's new playpen—to catch the south and western sunbeams! What a consummately successful house hunter was Dave! I was ebullient with joy!

I arranged all of our furniture: the long couch would go in front of the windows on the south (there were new venetian blinds at all windows); an end table with shelf to house a dozen books and lamp, just inside the door; a floor lamp, at the west end. An 8 X 12' Deltox fiber mat in a royal blue tweed would be on the bright new floor and the pedestal dining-room table with four blue-striped damask chairs, opposite the couch with ample room to open it up for a double "guest bed," or when closed, Lori's playpen could be opened. The red velveteen occasional chair would be placed on the east side of the room and would be the first object viewable when coming into the house. Our bedroom, at the front, with windows on south and east, would have a fiber mat (the same size, as was Lori's), double bed against the west wall, dressing table and mirror on the southeast balanced with chest of drawers and bachelor mirror and brass lamp, with parchment shade and movable arm, for Dave to cinch his tie at eye-level, and cedar chest by the south window. My French Provincial night stand, with drawer and cabinet for books, and lamp, on the left side of the bed—for I always read in bed while Dave studied at a table—and a dining-room chair on his side. Lori's room would find her crib by the east window, the long buffet on the east wall which would be inconspicuous because Lori's room was wood-paneled as was the entire little house, with the exception of the large kitchen and bath. Her chifforobe would fit the south wall with a dining-room arm chair, for nursing, and the youth bed on the west.

The kitchen had a refrigerator and range both of which looked clean but I was anxious to sterilize; ample cabinet space and counters; a pantry area by the back door where I could put a folding, drying rack and room for a breakfast table and chairs, two, which were the only additional furniture pieces we needed to buy. There was no basement, which was always a rarity in Florida, so Dave's cruise box; my wooden book box which Dad had built for me to take to Michigan with a screwed-down lid, enabling me to unpack and repack it with my lady's screw driver; and large, flat, indestructible steamer trunk which had taken Dad to military duty in the Philippines in 1912, Lacy to the University of Michigan in 1937 and me, in '43—had to be stacked to the ceiling in the pantry-storage room.

The back yard was similar to the front, almost grassless and plant-free and fenced, with a long wire clothesline across the north which I rarely used. (One of my sisters-in-law asked when we were in Lincoln if I had to wash clothes often. "Oh no," I said, "just three times a day." And I was not being facetious. It was routine and simple to wash my dishes three times a day and then, while I was at the sink, to put on rubber gloves and with the very hottest water I could draw, to wash out the baby clothes used since the previous meal or overnight and hang them, a step or two away, on the drying rack by the back door. We had a diaper service and I found no need, or space, for a washing machine and Dave had all of his laundry and cleaning done at the Base, just as in bachelor days.) Since even the bathroom, like the kitchen, was sizable for a small dwelling and afforded room for a "potty" chair, diaper pail and hamper, there was not one thing lacking to our comfort—except our furniture. That arrived, intact, after a delay of ten days, on Lori's sixth-month birthday.

How happy we were to see the big van pull in front of our little house, for Lori had completely outgrown her baby basket and her entertainment: one rattle, one pair of beads. If Mama Tom had not searched the gift shop at the Union Station to discover and christen a stocking doll for Lori's constant companion and confidante, life would have been bleak. But then "Mehitable Sophira Jones, the First" had sat up straight and communicated with big brown, embroidered eyes, all of her secrets, to—Lori and was almost like having her Mama Tom to whisper to—until I lost the sunny "Mehitable Sophira Jones"! But she had her

Figure 17. Confidantes

picture taken with Lori August 14, 1949, as soon as we had unpacked the playpen pad and could let them both sit to converse in the afternoon shade in the front yard and Lori's eyes were as big and round and brown as Mehitable's! I sent an SOS to Mother and Dad and I knew a relative would soon be on her way.

Our furniture was in place, books unpacked and filling the three-sided mantel, the card tray placed on the end table by the front door, draperies hung, our forty-eight hours up—and we were ready for Navy callers. I baked a cake (which was always refused but which I always wanted to offer), unpacked enough china for dessert and coffee, left the rest in barrels in Lori's room where the buffet had been placed, arranged Lori's chifforobe and set up her playpen on the screened porch and we both enjoyed a respite in the breeze. Lori rediscovered "Beautiful Helen," a rubberized pull-doll; "Epaminondas," the pink squeeze dog (Mama Tom's names, of course); "Neptune," the fish; Grampy Frank's fist-sized, recently harvested gourds and The Duck. I alternately read a book—and watched and marveled at Lori and thought: if Mother were here, she would exclaim: "The world is so full of a number of things, I am sure we should all be as happy as Kings!"

And we were! Life flowed smoothly in our doll-house kingdom and effortlessly, there being no yard to maintain and very little within—except our universe! A more facile course of "Home-Tending for a Small Family" could not have been compiled. We had complete privacy and quietness on an unfrequented side road, with a non-interfering, non-gregarious landlord for neighbor on the west (ideal should a need arise); a very small church, attended sparsely on Sundays, across the broad road; a wooded, unbuilt lot to the east. Except for initial Navy callers and invited guests, we lived in poetic isolation and wanted for nothing. We sought no friendships and were, undoubtedly, selfish but the world seemed forgiving of new parents. We gloried in our togetherness—dazzled by our daughter—but were content and motivated in the hours apart. And we knew there would be many periods of prolonged separation but never discussed it—confident of self and each other. Every hour together was treasured and any departure, reluctant and important—even the brevity of mundane grocery-shopping. And it was positive as well!

Lori and I always accompanied Dave to the door, whenever he left, to kiss him and be kissed good-bye (a habit Dave and I have yet to overcome). One morning as he backed out of the driveway and flashed farewell, his ring glittering in the day's first sunray, I thought of how tacit our relationship had been from its inception, how little we had discussed, how much we had intuited and known. Rings, for example: I had never liked the appearance of a narrow gold band on a man's large hand nor the concept, which expressed to me, more tenuousness than tenacity—as if metal fettered. We had never alluded to the practice, popularized by the swift marriages and uncertainties of World War II, but neither of us had endorsed the device. I gave Dave, on his twenty-fifth birthday, a heavy gold ring with an oval onyx as glistening and black as his hair—a piece of jewelry to be worn at whim—on either shapely hand. Material manifestations, patently displayed or publicly verbalized devotion, vociferously proclaimed, were subterfuges which never ceased to provoke laughter. I was reminded, in the presence of any such artificer of deception, of the adage of the dinner party: "The more he extolled his honor, the faster they counted their spoons!" And I further applied, from Mother's copious, axiomatic collection: "What you *are* thunders so loudly, I can't hear what you *say* you are!"

Mother wrote to Lori the first of September:

Dearest Lori, Mother and Dad, Well Mehitable Sophira Jones is not losted any more for she sits now on the table making goo-goo eyes at me as I write! Only since it is fall she has donned an outfit of white with deep red trimmings—all of the yellow Mehitable's having flown like the yellow drifting leaves. This white and red one was the last one to be found in the big old Union Station where you turned your head back to look up and all around at its vastness. (They sold all of the 2nd shipment.) We drove down from church this morning feeling sure she would hide away somewhere and wait for us. So many woolly dogs were out no wonder she hid . . . anyway, Mehitable will be on her way to your playpen and bed soon as "Pop" gets time to pack her up and send her on the way. Sorry we have been so long. This letter, too, is to tell you how we love your last pictures and what a darling baby girl you are anyway. Everyone just raves about these jolly Kodak pictures. They want to know whoever made such professional-looking pictures—so clear and such lovely poses. We knew your Daddy made them and we all congratulate him. You do not need a professional photographer to take your picture. You are growing so rapidly and are just the most perfect seven-months-old we ever saw. Keep smiling! We are so proud of you. Everyone says "how like Dave." Charles says "she's like Sis with her pug nose." Others who do not know Dave say "how like Charles." So evidently you are a general mixture. But we think that your Daddy has a pretty strong claim on you! Anyway don't you disturb your pretty head about being like anyone but Lori as *you* are a great credit to both sides of the house for sure! Now a few words to Mother. . . .

October was a momentous month for Lori! She became eight months old and received this letter from Mama Tom: "Dearest 'One-Tooth' and Family, How proud we are of you and your latest achievement, that of growing a tooth without Mother and Daddy knowing about it and worrying about your discomfort. Well, we think you are about the smartest little lady we know of anywhere! . . ." Lori had just graduated from nursing to drinking whole milk from a cup and her tooth had erupted, unannounced, and now she was walking in her playpen and we had just bought her first shoes, at eight-and-a-half months! Was that not inordinate precocity!

Dave discovered an Aerology Instructor was needed in Ground School at Whiting Field, located in Milton, Florida, and part of the enormous network of the Pensacola Naval Air Training Command. He applied for and received appointment to Whiting. It meant an hour's drive each morning and evening but he was pleased, its being one of his areas of interest and expertise. Advanced flight in SNJs (single-engine with tandem seats) was taught at Whiting; presently, Dave would be in an SNJ just for his own flight time. Instructing in Aerology at Whiting would encourage him to apply for Postgraduate School in Aerology held in Monterey, California. The Navy had marvelous schools and Dave was a scholar and the sky was unlimited!

We had Lori's picture made, with her one tooth barely visible in her bright smile, the deep dimple very prominent in her left cheek, her large brown eyes—luminous and atwinkle, with arched, quizzical eyebrows—just like her Daddy's, at her inimitable age of eight months. The discerning photographer said: "She's a beautiful baby!" and admired the dainty, round silver frame which her Grandaunt Beth had given her for precisely such distinction. And it was true that wherever we went, Lori attracted attention and elicited laudative comment, for she was not only beautiful (modestly admitted by not-reluctant parents), she bubbled with smiles and gurgles of happiness.

Next to the photographer's studio in Warrington, we found a lamp which we thought belonged on our dainty darling's chifforobe: an old-fashioned girl, demure in an "Alice blue gown" with white pantaloons, holding a nosegay with a reticule on her left arm, wearing a sunbonnet with flowers atop her long curls. The lampshade was tufted with white chenille and edged with tiny, balled braid and, in Alice-blue to match the bouffant dress, was a perky-tailed bluebird, in his ceramic splendor—sitting on high. Thus Lori's room was appropriately complete with a bluebird to reflect her happiness and to oversee her activity.

Indeed, Lori's bluebird led us to other discoveries and we found just the right lamp for the living-room end table: a heavy, creamy white with della Robbia cherubs a-dance on Wedgewood blue. For the dining-room table where Dave studied and planned, a grape lamp (to condition him not to hunger for chocolate!) with gold fruit on the white base and white grapes on the gold shade. In the efficacy of the power of that suggestion, I had some dubiety but Dave liked the lamp. We also bought the swivel-arm lamp of brass and crystal-ball base for Dave's tie maneuvering and hair brushing—with his silver brush and comb, my wedding token from Jaccards.

We were surprisingly comfortable in our Florida abode during the heat of August and September and early October. It cooled at night in Pensacola, unlike Key West, and with the front and back doors open, as well as the screened-porch door, with windows wide and Lori in the north room which had been designed for a dining room and had two doors, we were not in need of fans.

What our yard lacked in verdure, it compensated with trees. There was a large, double-trunked pin oak in the front on the southeast which shielded the house and car, with many oaks, in the lot to our east; also,

Figure 18. Doll's House

Figure 19. In Their Whites

southwest, smaller oaks to shade the screened porch where Lori spent much of her playtime.

Summer stayed long in our Southern realm, Dave's wearing dress whites on September 25, for Inspection at Whiting Field and my proudly taking his picture with Lori in her "whites" in front of our petite white house.

It was still warm in the sunny November days when Mother H came to try our new duofold. She refused our bedroom which we thought would have been much more comfortable and vowed she liked sleeping on the Simmons couch. Mother H was a grand traveler and enjoyed visiting us but had not done so when we were in Newport because her Mother, Grandmother Zimmerman, had been living with her then.

When we left Newport for Lincoln, we visited Grandmother Zimmerman at Aunt Nora's in Winnetka, Illinois, on Chicago's fashionable North Shore, Grandmother's having just moved to her younger daughter's home for that year's stay. Nora was an elegant, sophisticated, highly successful professional woman who had studied medicine in Vienna, Austria, Grandmother's keeping house for her there and supervising her efforts which was probably not necessary, for Nora, although beautiful and feminine, was totally committed to medicine and would never be distracted—not even by marriage. While her older sister Susan, Mother H, had married a professor and had four children, Nora had studied medicine, interned and begun her practice in Chicago as an Ear, Nose and Throat Specialist. An earlier attempt at marriage had failed and she was married to John V. Johansen, an engineer who had invented the pineapple-cutting machine, a roofing machine and other lucrative mechanisms, in especial, the hydromatic gearshift.

Nora visited with me in the sumptuous guest room while I nursed Lori, shortly before dinner was announced. I complimented Nora on her remarkable achievement of having ascended to the top of Man's world and in such a competitive city as Chicago to become Dr. Nora Brodboll, symbolically using her maiden name. I eulogized courageous, career-minded women who soared to success, thinking, too, of her close friend, Mignon G. Eberhart, the famous mystery writer. I careened on in loquacious applause until my all-seeing, new-Mother's eyes noticed tears in hers as I tendered her my baby to hold. Quickly desisting, I told her how beautiful the room was and unpacked a dress for dinner, inwardly aware that professional recognition and wealth were not quintessential to every life.

We went down to early dinner in the sun-brightened but air-conditioned solarium surrounded on three sides by velvety grass and floral borders. Grandmother Zimmerman, as Nora laughingly explained, would be in later: "She fired the cook, as she always does—just as soon as she comes home—and she's cooking herself. So please start!" John's "man," over whom Grandmother Zimmerman had never been granted jurisdiction, served the fruit compote filled, of course, with precision-sliced and cubed fresh pineapple—strawberries, mangoes, nectarines and blueberries. Grandmother joined us for her roast chicken, au gratin potatoes, carrots and peas. "John hates fancy food," she began and John, who was not garrulous, nodded. "Now, I boiled extra potatoes," resumed Grandmother, "and in the morning, all I have to do is to slice them and fry them with ham, for breakfast. I *make* them *both* eat a good breakfast. I don't think Nora ever stops for lunch." Hot rolls were passed, tempting and fragrant but I had to decline. "I bake enough for three meals and freeze them," Grandmother instructed. She was in her late eighties and her energy seemed inexhaustible. She *made* John and Dave eat cake!

Grandmother Zimmerman and I had become immediate friends, Dave being her favorite grandchild, when he took me home to meet his family in the fall of 1947. We talked politics, current events, sports and family like two sorority sisters. And she knew everything! I was overwhelmed when, the following year, she gave me the handknit bedspread she had labored on for years. It was the most gorgeous thing I had ever seen! I was glad she proffered it to me in the presence of Mother H so that the three of us could discuss the giving of it, rather, to Mildred, Naomi, Viola or Nora—someone more deserving and less new to the family. "No! Dorothy," they reacted, in duet. And Mother H explained that they had already discussed it and the decision had been made. And that was not all! Grandmother Zimmerman then produced a silver, square box and removed a layer of cotton to take out an enormous cameo brooch. It was absolutely exquisite! "Dorothy, I want you to have this," and Grandmother put it in my hand. "I bought this in Budapest, Austria-Hungary, when Nora and I were traveling." It was a handsome Greek warrior in profile, his visor raised from a helmet entwined with laurel leaves, with a winged, long-tailed lizard protecting the crown. The warrior's features were duplicated on the visor, every curling tendril of hair to his shoulder and vein in the leaves were sharply etched. Behind the creamy white cameo, the shell was a rosy coral. It was mounted in wide gold and edged with ornate, gold filigree looped at the top so that it could be worn as a lavaliere but it was so big and heavy, I feared it would hit something and be damaged and always wore it as a brooch on my finest blouses and dresses.

I also was given two quilts Grandmother Zimmerman had made, one with beautiful, bright red tulips with long green stems and leaves; the other, huge sprays of orange, rust and red-blended poppies with buds and blooms in various stages of opening—accurate foliage in shaded greens, all on a white background finished with a scalloped band of leaf green. And then she gave me her cedar chest to house my resplendent treasures wrought by her loving, talented hands! How much Lori and I had to aspire to, surrounded as we were by brilliant, creative Holland, Thomas, Brodboll and Lacy women!

Mother H was the enantiomorph, the mirror-image, of her Mother in capability, interests and accomplishments. Susan Marea was eleven years older than Nora whom she must have influenced with her pioneering spirit of courageous independence, as she later influenced her own children. ("Strong women produce strong progeny," Charles used to say of Mother. "Their children give up *or*—they learn to excel. They are survivors!")

Mother H had majored in Music at Wesleyan University in Lincoln, Nebraska, taught braille in the School For The Blind at Nebraska City and *homesteaded*, alone, in Winner, South Dakota, where she supported herself by teaching in an Indian School. She was a totally intrepid woman and nothing was beyond her in the grand adventure which she made of life. As soon as I met her, I comprehended why Dave was at once modest and self-assured in his competence and undeterredly independent in his thought and action.

Dave's brothers had "gone Army"; Dave "went Navy." "He was always that way!" Mildred laughed, at a family assembly, putting her arm around her youngest brother. "When Dave was two and a half and we were visiting Grandmother and Grandfather Zimmerman in Chicago, he decided he'd rather be at home. And off he started! It took the family, friends, neighbors and police the rest of the day to find him—and a kind Chicagoan, miles from Grandmother's, who called the police to report a determined little boy, all alone on Asbury, carrying his sand bucket and shovel and walking as hard as he could go—due south!" Mildred shook an admonishing finger at her little brother, "How you worried us!" And then she hugged him. "Dave was always decisive," she told me, "he knew exactly what he wanted and didn't deviate after he got it. Remember our Canadian trip?" turning to Dave. "Robert, Kenneth and I chose red

Hudson Bay blankets with white, yellow and black stripes but *you* wanted the white; and then we all wanted that one and you wouldn't trade! And I bet you still have it!" Dave, heartily laughing about the childhood acquisition, nodded affirmatively and I acknowledged I had just put a new yellow binding on it, our favorite and warmest blanket. "But the worst thing," Mildred continued, "he kept records! Every cent he saved or earned went into a little black book. To make more, he would substitute for Robert, take his paper route, as well as his own, and keep the accounts neatly separated—he probably charged Robert a banking fee! Then, when we needed to borrow money from Dave—even if it was Dad—he charged us interest!" We all laughed to tearfulness and I affirmed he was still methodical but that his frugality was moribund. "His assertiveness is undiminished, though," I added, as we bantered our helplessly convulsed boy.

Voilà! Dave had *always* been different! I had never conjectured about it because I had found it appealing—and his idiosyncrasies had helped balance mine. Dave was special and I had always liked the extra attention he demanded: the egg in his milk shake at Winstead's in the culminating hours of our date; his iced tea, strong, filled with eight ice cubes—then, the lemon and the mint; his fruit at the bottom of his cereal, to keep it from becoming soggy; his toast broiled on both sides, buttered and quickly rebroiled before the butter bubbled; coat hangers and clothes facing the same direction; shoetrees for each pair of shoes, military and civilian—they weighed more than my books! But each penchant was logical and he was never critical if plump blueberries accidentally topped his rice crispies; if his toast, occasionally, was like mine—buttered first and broiled on one side only; or if one of my dresses coquettishly confronted his dress blues! Being acclimated to Dad's military preciseness and habitual neatness, it was not difficult to accustom myself to Dave's. Indeed, it was an element of our elective affinity. Weren't all of my shoes stuffed and wrapped with tissue paper and then boxed? And handbags and hats as well—and labeled as to color, material and season? My sweaters were carefully rolled and scarves nicely folded and layered with sachets. But when it came to the linen closet, I was creatively abandoned, militating against picayunish order and refusing to stand inspection, were it ever announced.

And it never was, for my wonderfully subtle Dave was the propounder of diplomacy: he never said, "Do it this way" or even, "*Do* it!" It was invariably: "I usually do it this way," followed by a demonstration.

I was entirely free to do as I deemed best. I wondered often if his father had possessed that delicacy of tact and gentleness; my father always had—and Dave was so like Dad.

Dave's father must have had many noble qualities to have won such a wife and managed such an "All-American Family"! I wished I could have known him! Robert Ellsworth Holland of Sugar Run, Pennsylvania, had wooed and won the beautiful, adventuresome Susan Marea Brodboll and established his family in the three-story house at 4217 Starr Street in Lincoln (where Dave grew to young manhood), teaching at the University of Nebraska, Agricultural College from which he had been graduated. He had joined the FarmHouse Fraternity, noted for its scholarship and non-Greek name, and been honored as one of the Fraternity's "Builders of Men." Personally "building" three when a young professor, Robert Holland had influenced his sons and his daughter to perpetuate his predilection for studiousness and leadership. Kenneth and Dave had joined and benefited from FarmHouse Fraternity but had diverted far from agriculture and community service with the onset of World War II.

Dave benefited in yet another way from his father's talents. Half-humorously, Dave credited his poise and stage presence (he gave a graduation oration on soil erosion entitled "Seven Inches to Starvation" which did not immediately put his classmates to sleep and began with: "As a Nebraska farmer and his wife were sitting on their porch one summer evening, watching the Kansas farms go by. . . .") to his father. "When Dad was Supervisor of County Agents, he was host of a radio program every weekday at noon. They discussed everything, although agriculture was the emphasis." Even Dave's interest in music, somewhat less polished a display, reminded him of early paternal association: "The theme song was *Corn Silk* and I used to pick it out on the piano." "Did you ever play it on your clarinet?" I teased. "No," Dave smirked, "I wasn't very accomplished; I played second clarinet because I couldn't play the chromatic scale at the try-outs. But I only played with the band between halves at the football games because I was Student Manager during the game—didn't weigh enough to play—except for basketball." (He still has his "M" letter, somewhere, for Jackson High—which has elaborate reunions every year for every class which attended the small high school composed, almost exclusively, of Ag-College Professors' progeny. We attend when Dave's class of '40 is host, buoyed by Marian Linch and John Bottorff at their historic Linch-Bottorff home, to suspire and fay in nostalgia: the old school, the teams, the teachers, the old neighborhood, the Dads and families and the extraordinary closeness and success of the offspring.)

It was not until after Dave's father died that Mother H sold her homesteaded land to the state of South Dakota for the gravel concentrated there, kept the big house in Lincoln and turned to Dietetics (which she had also studied in college), successively, at the Baptist Memorial Hospital, the Y.M.C.A. and the Y.W.C.A. She gave up her violin, having given lessons in that for some years (an appreciative granddaughter, Joanie, has the instrument and a great granddaughter is now playing violin in college), to enjoy her less practice-demanding piano and organ. But her greatest joy was in being with her family and it was a thrill for us to have her in our first "real home."

Mother H brought me a thick, blank-paged cookbook which her Presbyterian Church had devised and I began the transfer of only my choicest recipes into that special book which I thenceforth carried in my suitcase at each move. Every year at Christmastime, Mother H had gathered her requested and new Yuletide recipes and printed them in a festive, little book with a cover of her own decoration and sent them to family and friends. I told her how, our first Christmas alone in Newport, we had made divinity from Mother's recipe; fudge, from her published "book" and Spritz cookies from mine, using the cookie press I had requested for Christmas when I was twelve years old. (We had sent a big box to Mother, Dad, Charles and Papa but none to Mother H who had cookie-candy experts in Mildred—home for the holidays, Naomi and Viola.) I asked her about the marble slab that she used in fondant-making and which Dave had recommended the December before as we had labored in our basement kitchen. Having made divinity with Mother but never fondant, I had persuaded Dave we could succeed with the former and had compromised on the latter by pulling taffy. My candy lover had also wanted to make English toffee, pour it out on that marble slab, smooth melted chocolate over the top and sprinkle it with chopped pecans and then break it, when hard, with a candy hammer. I decided I would not demur if he wanted to "go home" every Christmas.

It was November 1949, and we were planning just that happiness with Mother H. For the most part, we stayed close to Pensacola during her three-week visit, as she wanted just to be with us and to see the Navy Installations; the Blue Angels fly; have some red snapper which, being an expert in cuisine, she knew abounded chiefly in Pensacola waters and, if time permitted, go to the Bellingrath Gardens in Mobile, Alabama. I had made reservations for two A.A.U.W. luncheons: Bridge and Current Affairs, had accepted one dinner invitation for the four of us and planned to have eight for dinner and two tables of bridge.

I took great pride in my developing culinary skills, and I had the most challenging exemplars to attempt to equal in Mother, Mother H and Grandmother Zimmerman, and loved having Mother H's approval of my efforts. I had to rise very early in the morning, however, to prevent her from doing all of the work. Inasmuch as it was her vacation-time, I felt she should not "have to" cook. I also felt I was efficient at management and wanted her to see that her youngest son was being well cared for. She was a perfect Mother-in-law and never, over many happy years, offered one word of criticism, as her acceptance of Lorinda "Degle" could attest.

For our bridge dinner, Mother H was "chief cook and bottle washer," since we had promised our two tables that they would enjoy a Lincoln-Nesque rarity: "Yum Yums," the first confection I ate with Dave in his town when he took me home to meet his family. Although we were going to have dinner at Mother H's, Dave insisted on taking me to the "Yum Yum Hut" for their specialty; in fact, their only offering: barbecued ground round on a hot bun. So we ate one for late lunch and it was as delicious as claimed. And soon I had the recipe in my new cookbook, "Mother's Version," and she was preparing vast quantities, for our guests, of the slowly bubbled spicy sauce, the browned ground round stirred in and, when cooled, mounded in the center of rich, yeasty dough (Mildred's recipe) and allowed to expand to six-inch, flat "pasties" to be baked in a hot oven at serving time. And that was almost all we had for dinner, except much merriment and praise! I had fixed a Waldorf salad with dates and Missouri black walnuts and peach melba for dessert, making vanilla ice cream but having to buy the raspberry sauce.

That was the night Dave announced that when he retired from the Navy, he thought we might build a house on the timberland he thought he might buy at just three dollars an acre; John Sands interrupted and said: "No, Dave, go in with me, let's buy a satsuma grove!" I filed the tree dream with the Key West Horse's Head but for years, Dave told me how much his timberland would have been worth if he had bought it when he had wanted to, in 1949. Then he would laugh and I, too, for we both knew our wealth was already great—and immeasurable!

We took Mother H to the Pensacola Naval Air Station which included the historic Ft. Barrancas, the old Spanish fort built on the Big Lagoon, "barranca," meaning deep ravine, which had been converted into the U.S. Naval Hospital, the native brick facade completely preserved. We took her early on a morning of her last week end when the Blue Angels were scheduled to take off from their field at the western extremity of the Base, bundled up Lori and walked to the end of the boardwalk on Barrancas Beach. Six Blue Angels took off in formation, climbing straight up, over the Lagoon and Gulf of Mexico, to perform their daring, thrilling precision maneuvers for huge crowds, most of whom had gathered on Santa Rosa Island. There on the uncrowded beach, we could only see the takeoff—at very close range—and the amazingly swift ascent, and hear the mighty roar of their engines to which Lori, like the seasoned Navy flyer's "brat" she was, had long ago grown accustomed.

Early the next morning, Sunday (the Blue Angels traditionally performed two days in a row to accommodate crowds), Dave drove us across the Pensacola Bay Bridge to Pensacola Beach on the long, narrow Santa Rosa Island with Ft. Pickens on the west and Ft. McRae, on the east. The latter had been the site of a town built by Spain in 1723 but destroyed by a hurricane in 1754, forcing survivors back to the mainland to the present location of Pensacola proper. Pensacola Bay had probably been visited by Ponce de Leon in 1513, with De Soto's establishing a base of supplies near by, in 1540. Pensacola was taken for France in 1718, changed hands from Spain to France to Spain until it was ceded, with the Floridas, to Great Britain in 1763 and made the capital of West Florida, when most of the Spanish populace left for Mexico and Cuba. During the Revolutionary War, English loyalists from the northern colonies came to the Florida port and remained until the town was captured by the Spanish governor of New Orleans. Since trade had remained in the hands of English merchants, the War of 1812 found the British operating out of Pensacola but they were repulsed in 1814 by General Andrew Jackson, as they attempted to take formal possession. In 1818, General Jackson, his patience at an end, captured Pensacola from the Spanish, convinced that the Spanish had encouraged the Seminole Indians to attack the Americans. It was 1821 before Florida was transferred to the United States and Jackson established the present city limits of Pensacola. In 1824, it became a city and was selected as the site of a federal navy yard. Another conflict, prior to the April outbreak of the Civil War, eventuated in January 1861, when the Confederate state government seized the Federal Naval Yard but Ft. Pickens was held by the Union and the Confederates evacuated the city on May 8, 1862.

Driving south on the Pensacola Bay Bridge over the strategic waters, Pensacola Bay on the west, Escambia Bay, east—for which nations had fought during four centuries, we arrived at the first isthmus and city of Gulf Breeze. Dave stayed on Highway 98 and did not slow down, our objective being to watch the Blue Angels perform, but promised to turn east with the highway, on the way back, to the Naval Live Oaks Reservation—a tree plantation established by John Quincy Adams in 1829. (Whenever a "tree" was involved, whether it was buying a grove or seeing an ancient stand, Dave ogled me and laughed at his pseudo-dendrologist!) Taking Highway 399 to the Bob Sikes Bridge, he turned west from Pensacola Beach Boulevard, or 399, toward Ft. Pickens which was at the western tip of Santa Rosa Island and once held the legendary Indian warrior Geronimo, captive. Dave drove a short distance along the Gulf Islands National Seashore with its scenic seascapes of sand; the Gulf of Mexico on the south, Pensacola Bay on the north and both visible with just a turn of the head.

Returning to Pensacola Beach, to the east and contiguous to the Gulf Seashore, he found space for four in a beach restaurant, overlooking the Gulf of Mexico, which boasted a glass roof and front with viewing-deck beyond. We had a leisurely breakfast, its being still two hours before the Blue Angels' Aerial Performance; Lori, sitting very properly in a highchair and enjoying scrambled eggs and applesauce—with her one new tooth.

The restaurant was soon overflowing with hungry spectators. We moved outside to the deck, enjoying a cloudless November Sunday and resort warmth, Dave's showing us which way to look for the first sight of the famed Blue Angels—since we could see them before hearing their thunder. And it was not long before Dave, holding Lori in her white sweater, leggings and hat who was holding Mehitable Sophira Jones, II, pointed aloft to the west and the Blue Angels flashed overhead trailing smoky ribbons of red, white and blue to twist, turn, soar and roar in the most miraculous, simultaneous, gasp-provoking maneuvers which enthralled us for half an hour—and then they were gone. In the sudden silence, we mere mortals walked to our car and began the terrestrial trip by slow automobile back to Pensacola where the Blue Angels had landed even before Dave had unlocked the car doors. As often as I saw them, it was always with breath-held ambivalence: amazed by their skill and training, I wondered why such talented young life had to be so risked.

With the weather predicted to be mild and dry on Thanksgiving Day, the four of us decided to forego turkey-roasting and attendant savory endeavors to drive to Bellingrath Gardens, southwest of Mobile, Alabama, about an hour away. We wished we could have approached the mansion, atop tall flights of wide, native-stone steps leading to the water's edge, by boat—anchoring at the grotto with its exotic waterfall, alight with bowers of pastel impatiens, ferns and cascading clematis. Huge stone urns of vivid yellow allamandas outlined the tiers of ascending steps and one expected to see Queen Titania, Puck and the entire fairy court grace the descent from on high. Giant hibiscus still bloomed in the formal gardens along brick walks leading to the mansion with tea roses in the orange, red and yellow splendor of fall. Red and yellow amaranthus, summer poinsettia, looking like oriental lanterns glowing from flickering wicks, brightened the brick paths; true-blue plumbago, nestling underneath, edged both sides with alternating fans of liriope and delicate stems of grape-clustered blue. Buds were heavy on camellias and azaleas and I hoped we could return in March but the crimson crape myrtle soon convinced me there was no loss of glory. There was too much to see for long musing in any spot but I had to sit under a Southern magnolia *grandiflora* to make a few notes, while Dave, Lori and Mother H wound down to the Japanese garden with lagoon, curved bridge to walk across and black swans to follow in their stately glide. It was a lovely quick visit to a paradisiacal garden which could never be adequately seen—its beauty, seasonal and ever varietal. Our own young beauty was somnolent and ready to nestle with Mehitable on the back seat.

Mother H left the next morning early with Dave who drove her to the airport for a breakfast flight to Omaha, Nebraska, where Kenneth would meet her on the Thanksgiving week end. We had made plans to be in Lincoln the day after Christmas, staying until New Year's Eve afternoon, so that we could celebrate our wedding anniversary in Kansas City and New Year's Day with Dad on his birthday. Mother H would have Mildred and Hub, plus the Lincoln entourage and five grandchildren and she had graciously suggested that we should spend Christmas Day with Mother and Dad who had long ago invited us to be with them "for 'a feast of reason and flow of soul' and some other feasting, too, perhaps."

Lori discovered Midwestern winter and held her first snowflakes on a mittened hand. We had a perfectly picturesque and symbolic family-Christmas Day in Kansas City with Mother and Dad, Charles, Papa and Beth and ten-month-old Lori, the center of the festival. Lori was overwhelmed with packages from her five Holland cousins, one great grandmother, a great grandfather, two grandmothers, a grandfather, a grandaunt, three aunts and four uncles—all of whom played Santa, Mrs. Claus and the Elves, to her delight, in forty-eight busy hours.

Lori ate mashed potatoes and peas with her first taste of succulent turkey and dressing, for she now had nearly four teeth! Dave observed Dad's skilled carving of the twenty-two-pound, flawlessly cooked turkey, its browned skin, unruptured on breast and leg, displayed enticingly on an enormous, heirloom Lacy platter, surrounded by sweet potatoes fluffed in orange shells, wedges of pomegranate and sprigs of parsley. Dave and I had studied each step of the bird's preparation from the washing of it and draining, by Dad because of the heaviness, the salting of breast and neck cavities by Mother, Dad's having turned the turkey, on a four-sided cookie tin, first on its breast for easy access to the neck, then to its back. The turning was repeated for Mother to loosely press in the sage-and-corn-bread dressing, pungent with thyme, onion and cubed, toasted white bread, sprinkled with poultry seasoning and moistened with giblet broth, butter and an egg. The entire bird was rubbed with softened butter, salted and expertly trussed with sterilized white string around legs and pignut, the wings tied together, loosely across the breast. Mother mounded dressing on the wings to keep them moist and in the depression of the tied legs, with a raisin-stuffed cored apple securing the dressing-filled breast. The turkey was transferred to a rack with handles in a large, open roaster and completely covered with an oleo-moistened cheesecloth, a metal pie tin laid over the neck. It was roasted approximately four and a-half hours at 325°F. and usually not basted until time to remove the cheesecloth which was then saturated with hot turkey broth to loosen it. Turkey roasting, garnishing and carving would doubtless take more than one lesson but we had fared well with Mother's explicit and illustrated written instructions to our Newport underground kitchen and now we were refurbishing knowledge with the masters.

During dinner, Mother mischievously asked: "Dave, would you like one or two more peas?" We all laughed, for Dave was a now-notorious pea-eater. When seated at the dining-room table midway through our pre-nuptial dinner, which Mother had served at home the night before our wedding, Dave suddenly disappeared from sight—engrossed with the carpet under the table. I was wearing a dark rose velveteen basque with a long, voluminous taffeta skirt which I felt being lifted carefully from the floor. "What's wrong? Dave, are you alright?" Mother appealed. Dave let go of my skirt and triumphantly straightened up: "I found the pea I dropped!" he exulted, producing same, and not finding a pea-recovery dish on the table, he put it carefully on the edge of his plate. Mother, lachrymose with laughter, recovered speech: "Dave, you're marvelous! You remind me of the wealthy old woman's dinner guest who ate the bug with his lettuce leaf. But I don't have a million dollars to leave *you!*" "You're giving me *more* than that!" rejoined the gallant Dave, clasping my hand. Dr. Wilson, who laughed more heartily than I thought a minister could, told the tale, according to Mother's first letter to "Mrs. David B. Holland," of Dave's wayward legume—at Dad's birthday dinner party given by the Wilsons, January first, the night after our unforgettable blizzard-wedding.

Our Christmas dinner culminated with Dad's ambrosial bowl of fresh, frosty deliciousness which he had learned to prepare in the Philippines. Several days before Christmas, Dad sawed, opened, peeled and grated three coconuts, having first drained the milk from their "eyes." Sitting at the breakfast-room table, he worked hours to grate the meat, leaving tiny lumps—too small to hold—for children, small or large, to share. (Three days after Christmas, Mother baked me a fresh coconut birthday cake. Oh, the lusciousness of those special, lovingly prepared delicacies!) One-fourth-inch cubes, you could measure with them, of orange flesh and juicy pineapple were next prepared by Dad, mixed at serving time with lightly sweetened whipped cream and the snowy, fragrant coconut, reposited in a cut-glass bowl and garnished with stemmed cherries and sprigs of mint to be served by Mother, at the table, of course, in Dad's finely sawed, coconut-shell bowls. And then the companion treat, thinly sliced, rich, dark fruitcake on a crystal plate bordered in matching cathedral-window colors, was passed. It, too, like their lives, was a combined effort and success!

A few days before we left for Pensacola, Hal and Ila Luhnow came to see Lori. Hal Luhnow was one of Mother's close friends, having worked with her in the Junior Department of the First Baptist Church as her song leader and classroom teacher during the twenty-seven years she was Superintendent; she, in turn, assisting him in the early '40s to remove the last vestiges of the Pendergast machine. Hal Luhnow was the nephew of William Volker, Kansas City's great philanthropist who had given the land for the University of Kansas City (now the University of Missouri at Kansas City), among other endowments, and in other cities: Wayne University in Detroit, for example; Kansas State University at Manhattan,

Kansas—but who had lived with great personal frugality. Never owning a car, he took the streetcar to work, his lunch in a brown paper sack.

Hal Luhnow had become President of the Volker Enterprises when Mr. Volker died and, although a multi-millionaire, lived almost as simply and without ostentation, as had his uncle. Ila Luhnow, together with Mother's two best friends from Mississippi girlhood to the end of their lives: Charlene Schultz (Mrs. Arthur Schultz, Booneville), and Candace Stanley (Mrs. J. C. Stanley, Booneville), signified elegant, languid ladyhood in contrast to Mother's energetic savoir-faire and intellectually vital refinement.

Mother had taken Papa to the doctor's and I was to plan for demitasse and a sundae to be served with Mother's fruitcake which Hal always expected, and requested, to be served. I made my vanilla ice cream and chose canned blueberries for a topping. Mother was somewhat aghast when she returned: "Dot, *canned* blueberries? Why Ila has never even *seen* a canned blueberry!" And she was right. But Ila graciously commented that they were very good and that she would never have thought of serving them, with a tone of genuine appreciation for an opportunity to appraise a unique fruity form.

Beth visited with Ila who had two married daughters, both in California, having gone to college at Stanford and told of her Jane, living in St. Louis with new husband, Billy Jo Adcock—famed for football at Vanderbilt, beginning his career as a young executive at Monsanto. The men: Dad, Dave, Charles, Hal and Papa (Mother and I were listening to both groups) were discussing Korea and North Korea's latest incursion across the 38th parallel which the South Korean and U. N. forces had not easily handled. The U.S. was in the process of procuring a stronger "U.N. force" to assist. Hal was saying it would then all be over very quickly. I politely disagreed; I referred to Hanson W. Baldwin, Military Expert of the *New York Times.* "We could never win in Korea. It is not the type of war, should it come, that America could fight to victory." I became a bit vehement: "We won't bomb women and children to root out North Koreans." Charles took immediate umbrage: "You don't know anything about it. Let the men handle it." And I could understand the disgust that any man, especially a young flyer who had just experienced war in the Pacific, would feel but I reminded him, quietly, that I had studied the Korean situation for a year and a half and that our subscription to the Korean paper from Seoul had just expired. My concern had not been assuaged and I knew I did not need to tell him why. I would continue to read all I could discover in the *Sunday New York Times*, especially the "News of the Week in Review," the *Kansas City Sunday Star* which Dad had sent me every week in Ann Arbor and thereafter, *Time* magazine and *U.S.News & World Report*, plus editorials which Mother mailed in her almost daily letters. She and I preferred to be informed!

I informed Mother when I said good-bye that she would be Grandmother to two in July!

Dave and I did only a modicum of entertaining in Pensacola. He always had paperwork at night and I had gotten in the habit of reading in the bedroom, as I nursed Lori, and was engrossed in the *Pepys' Diary*, having found the complete edition, in nine volumes, in Newport, and in studying for my monthly Current-Affairs group in A.A.U.W. Besides, it was our "baby tour"! We were so awed and delighted by Lori's daily development that we felt no need for other companionship. Since Dave's Base at Whiting was an hour away, we limited social functions there and I did not even attend the Officers' Wives' Club but stayed in Pensacola for the Chi O's and University Women. Lori and I went to the Naval Hospital at Barrancas, the Naval Air Station—just minutes away, for shots and checkups.

One of my best friends insisted upon being taken out to dinner, without children, once a week, by her husband. Our favorite evening "out" was to take Lori with us to a drive-in movie on a warm night, stopping first for a barbecued beef with a superb white sauce and chocolate milk, for Dave, in a frosted glass at the White Hut on Navy Boulevard. They also barbecued whole chickens, which Lori loved to watch turn slowly on small rotisseries—the huge beef rumps turning too imperceptibly, with no distinguishable parts, to interest her. I was never successful at duplicating the white barbecue sauce. It was comparable in excellence, though with polarity of appearance and taste, to the Yum Yum Hut's. Oh, the savory offerings of those little huts! Dave, loyally, said he preferred his own little "Holland Hut"! That was a fortunate conviction for we were soon far from the others which, sad to realize, later ceased to exist, except in accurate, appreciative nostalgia where successes never waned.

Dave drove with four other flyers to Whiting Field each working day, rising at 5:30 A.M. on his driving day and 6:00 A.M. on the other four. Only once did we awaken to an insistent 7:00 o'clock call: the pounding on the front door and the staccato ringing of the bell, to remind me that I had not set the alarm the night before. Lori, too, was still "slug-a-bug" and she was generally conversing with Mehitable and

Epaminondas by six, at the latest. We were just relieved it was not "Dave's day" to drive. But everything was laid out, as was his wont, and while he leapt into shirt, trousers, socks and shoes, I put a graham-cracker packet in one pocket of his "greens" and an apple and napkin in the other and he exited in five minutes, shaving kit and tie, in hand, and even bussed me in passing! But we preferred our more leisurely routine of breakfast at six or, usually, six-thirty, Lori and Dave's eating their scrambled eggs, crisp bacon or sausage, together, juice and milk and water—he was insistent upon water with every meal, and all day long, a valuable training instilled in me by Dad from early childhood—while I fixed his lunch because he preferred being a "brown-bagger" to taking time for lunch at the O-Club. Then, with Lori at work in her sunny room next to the kitchen, I had my eggs, kept hot in the double boiler, and having given up coffee for the rest of the year, read the paper that much more quickly, washed the dishes, her few clothes and we were ready for *our* day.

By early January, we needed heat from the oil-burning space heater in the living room the first hour or two of the morning and in the evening, our little house's warming rapidly and evenly. We were never uncomfortable. By Lori's first birthday, which we celebrated with a miniature angelfood and lightly sweetened pineapple-cream-sauce cake—just large enough for one pink candle, she had produced enough curly wisps of hair to cover her head and at thirteen months, had curls to her eyebrows and nape of her neck. We were glad that she was, finally, hirsute, looking like her Daddy's daughter, and warm. Mother H had crocheted her a white wool sacque and bonnet, edged in pink, which was exactly the warmth needed from March through Easter, when Lori scorned both the bunny rabbit and his chocolate eggs, to play with the jelly beans. Too soon did she learn they were edible!

Summer arrived in May with June's finding us on the white sands of Pensacola Bay most week ends along a deserted stretch of beach, tourists' preferring to populate Pensacola Beach on the Gulf of Mexico. Lori loved the water and Dave was a strong swimmer, as was I—if I wasn't too indolent. Dad used to call me "a beach swimmer!" Of course, too, I floated on my back and that was all I was inclined to do.

The warm days brought heat to the Korean crisis as well. On June 25, 1950, without warning or provocation, armed forces from North Korea invaded South Korea in strength, penetrating considerably south of the 38th parallel. We had only five hundred advisors with the South Korean Army and they were, literally, that. But the United Nations' Security

Council met in the afternoon in New York; the Soviet's representative being, strangely, absent. That same day, President Truman ordered United States Naval and Air forces to give "cover and support" to the South Korean Army. He soon appointed General Douglas MacArthur as Commander in Chief of the United Nations' forces in Korea. (I knew when I paid my $8.75, for five days, on July 14, 1950, to the U.S. Naval Hospital, Pensacola Naval Air Station, that it would be a boy because, statistically, more boy babies are born when a nation is at war. Therefore, we had a boy's name ready and did not have to use Dave's dictionary!)

What a happy flurry of activity there was in Kansas City! On June 30, 1950, Charles Francis Thomas and Barbara Nadine Spear were married by Dr. Robert I. Wilson, in an informal ceremony in The Upper Room at the First Baptist Church. Just the immediate families were privileged to kiss the happy, young couple who would establish their first domicile in Kansas City. We were not invited, for no one felt it advisable for my last anticipatory month, but there was the rare extension of two Lacys: Beth and Papa to augment the delighted Thomas and Spear celebrants.

Dave took me to the hospital very early, in the dark, on the morning of July 25, 1950. The baby was soon adawning and I was introduced to the duty doctor, a Flight Surgeon, who was delivering his second baby but the nurse knew what he was doing—or should have been. He was a friendly man and let me function, naturally. While the baby was deliberating, we discussed the differences between an optometrist, an ophthalmologist, an optician and an oculist. At one point, the nurse back to my right said: "Doctor!" sharply, and in a theatrical aside to the nurse on my left: "Well, I could see it clear back here!" The alerted doctor soon gasped, "Oops—right in the ear!" And the nurse, needlessly: "It's a boy!" And I laughed joyously at my self-proclaiming offspring: Bruce Thomas Holland had arrived—Old World, take notice! And when I thought of his little "tucum"—I laughed again, for I had always thought "tucum" a synonym for the male wherewithal because Mother used to allude to: "Baby Charles' little 'tucum'" and when Dave and I had driven through Tucumcari, New Mexico, on our honeymoon, I had expostulated, indignantly: "Oh, what a *vulgar* name. There it is again!" and Dave had looked at me as if I had lost my last bit of wit but wasn't too surprised, for we already had been married three days. (I didn't realize that Mother had devised a metaphor out of the first two syllables of that unvulgar, delightful town of Tucumcari when Dad drove her through it, shortly after baby Lacy was born in Albuquerque. It was months before I confessed my ignorance to Dave—or even discovered it was not universally interchangeable, a term, male physiology not being among my tomes of erudition; sisterhood, if diffusion *was* confused, should have been diploma enough. At any rate, Webster had never delimited the Thomas lexicon and my risibility increased with my suddenly remembered ridiculousness!)

"Macho" Bruce was born at 7:06 A.M., weighed six pounds, six ounces, had my generous proboscis, very little face, which was red, and lots of long, black hair, looking very much as Mother had described my initiation—and he and I were still chortling with glee at his *joie de vivre*! I had missed my breakfast—my babies' arriving with the dayspring—but presently, I was rewarded with toast and tea; then Bruce, the corpsman's making a feather with two fingers at the back of Bruce's black head as he tendered me my papoose. "Well, at least I didn't whoop down the hall," defended he. "I wish you had," I exulted, "isn't he *wonderful*!" Bruce was a pound and two ounces larger than Lori had been and looked positively robust and he was vigorously hungry.

Dave came soon after the corpsman returned for Bruce and said what every new Mother wanted to hear: "I *think* he'll be alright." I felt too exalted to remark, verbally, his seeming hesitancy but decided when I got home I would read him *Tristram Shandy*'s chapter on Noses which I had not thought to bring, having only Dostoyevsky's *The Brothers Karamazov* which I took to the hospital for each advent deeming it mandatory reading, and rereading, for new parents. But in the next moment, Dave was jubilant: "I got to hold him and he didn't cry! He's healthy, has a beautiful mouth and the nurse said he wouldn't be red in a day or two." And I knew that "Tristram" would stay on the shelf. Dave laughed uproariously when I told him about the baby's virility and accuracy, at birth. We agreed that he should be circumcised as soon as feasible and that I would stay the full five days for that reason and because I had promised Mother I would—she, unable to come since Papa was not well and Beth was moving to Gulfport, Mississippi.

I missed Lori greatly but knew I would not see her until Sunday, inasmuch as the Navy did not encourage children under five to visit hospitals, especially since polio was rampant nationwide. At seventeen months of age, she had never been in a nursery or even played much with children other than her cousins and those of close friends, my being a cautious Mother and fastidious about Lori's immediate environment. But Lori was now a "big sister" and was ready to love and help care for baby Bruce. She was "potty trained"; spoke in loquacious syntax; sat at our table and daintily savored the same foods; put up her toys and knew where to find clean clothes in the lower drawers of her chifforobe. And Dave had taken a week's leave and Lori, busily, helped him keep house. Although we had a very fine neighborhood grandmother who loved baby-sitting with our mature daughter, I wanted Dave to hurry back home. He told me how elated all three parents were and Charles, too, who had called Mother early every morning from work to inquire about "news from Sis." Charles had become very attached to Lori during our month's visit in July of '49 and had insisted her new crib be set up by Dad and him in his room, so that I could "get some rest" at night. And, indeed, whenever she awakened—which was rare—I knew he would pat her back to sleep and love doing it, thus I slept soundly on the daybed in Mother's big room, the "girls' dorm," for Beth was there, too. Therefore, Charles was not averse to our producing another sweetheart like Lori but was overjoyed to welcome a Thomas nephew named Bruce.

We were home by mid-morning on Sunday; I, thrilled to kiss and hug Lori and she, to welcome us both but, especially, baby brother. She was completely intrigued by that diminution of humanity, never having seen mortal so minute, except in her picture books, and was totally unthreatened by his presence. Bruce was as fascinated by Lori when we all four were on the couch, Dave's laying the baby brother on Lori's proffered lap. I was, never once, apprehensive when Lori "watched over" Bruce. She had never cared for dolls or fantasied that she was "a little mother" or formed an attachment to one toy, not even Mehitable Sophira Jones, II, or a blanket—which my reading in child psychology led me to believe was inevitable, and felt no compulsion to mother, to master or to possess her baby brother. Lori had always been very mature, very cerebral and very literal-minded with a scientific curiosity about the actual but with no penchant for the make-believe.

While Dave watched Lori at play on her sun porch and Bruce, in his basket in the breezy doorway and read the Sunday paper, I retired to the kitchen to fix braised pork chops and sweet potatoes for dinner and while they baked, a coconut cream pie for which Dave had hungered and a fresh pineapple and cottage cheese salad I had looked forward to. In celebration of our homecoming, we opened one of our last cans of asparagus which Dave had helped his Mother can on his leaves to Lincoln before our nuptials. They had gone to the community canning facility and, with typical Holland proficiency, had produced thirty cans a season, three years in a row, for the families' pantries. I had never tasted such delicious asparagus, even fresh, before or since. (One other expertise of Mother H's which we were never able to approximate by commercial purchase was the home-dilling of pickles! In fact, I never sampled one of her pickles but Dave searched the globe, literally, for just *a* pickle which was comparable to his Mother's. In desperation, Bruce grew up quickly, and knowing what he had to do to *preserve* his wandering father's sanity—planted cucumbers, planted dill, brewed his own brine, or vice versa, and presented his parent with a quart of the most marvelously pickled, dilled and coddled fruit achievable by the pertinacity of progeny! None of us, thereinafter, heard another word about dill pickles—Holland-style!)

My aunt, Mary Beth Lacy Hughes, whose middle name had inspired mine, arrived in Gulfport, August 2, 1950, having lived with Mother and Dad for sixteen months, to start life anew in Mississippi, at the age of forty-nine—completing the circle back to the land of her birth. Mother and Beth were polar opposites, very much like Dave's Mother and younger sister Nora—both sibling sets separated by a decade of age. Mother was the most individualistic human being I ever knew. With no categorical identification possible, I had always conceived of her as an epitome of the Edwardian Gibson Girl in appearance, dress, education and refinement but an insatiable intellectual and an avant-garde creative genius who was never a "feminist" because she made no distinction between male and female ability and achievement. She was never angry, never without complete poise and composure—always in charge of herself *and* the situation, whatever it was, wherever it be, whomever it involved. Beth, also intellectually endowed and beautiful, in a most striking manner, possessed an anger and impatience which typified the "liberated woman," the "Flapper," and, indeed, she did cut her hair and go off to New York, to Columbia University, for both degrees. She smoked and enjoyed having a cocktail; Mother, of course, approving of neither, verbalized objection to both, as an older sister's responsibility. Beth was dismayed by the sad termination of her marriage which, for several years, vitiated her respect for men.

She and I had dinner downtown together in July of '49 and she told me how restorative it had been to be with Mother and Dad, of whom she said: "They saved my life!" She told me that Dad "was a prince," and that she had been so glad to know Charles—how fine he was, and that she had known and loved Lacy, that he used to visit them often in Findlay, Ohio, on week ends from Ann Arbor. "You're blessed with wonderful men in your family—and Dave is a dear!" (Mother wrote that Beth had been so happy when Bruce Thomas Holland had been born "to carry on the family tradition!") But a tinge of cynicism remained: "Life is a stage," Beth said, "'Hamlet' was right. We're all actors, playing a role. You're playing a role, I'm playing a role; we're not ourselves." "You mean," I queried, "I'm not what I think I am, I'm not what you think I am; I am what *I* think *you* think I am?" "Exactly!" Beth nodded. We talked about the study of literature for awhile, how important books had been to the Lacys and the Thomases, discussed Anthony Trollope's *Barchester Towers* which I had just read and Robert Browning, Beth's having joined the Kansas City Browning Society which she enjoyed attending with Mother.

Bruce soon lost his Indian hairdo, it seemed to dissolve in the bath water, his cheeks filled out and he became positively handsome. He was a joy and an excitement to care for but both Dad and Charles enjoined us not to get too excited but "to rest on our laurels!"

There were no laurels in Pensacola but we relaxed under the spreading mimosa, or "silk tree," in riotous bloom, pale pink to orange, the fruiting wild grapevines and the ubiquitous live oak or we played in the sand and dabbled in the water at the beach. We were on Pensacola Bay August 26, 1950, Bruce, a month and a day old, shaded by the hood on his basket, stayed with me on the sand while Lori and Dave explored a weathered tree trunk wedged on the water's edge. She dug for a while with her little shovel and filled her bucket but soon decided the trunk was better as a lookout seat than a bay-going barge. It was a beautiful day and serenely calm as we looked

Figure 20. Lori Looks to Sea

far across the water to the horizon of the town. In the Midwest we would have been bemoaning the end of summer but we knew we had at least another month of beach weather in Florida.

But in two days the beaches were deserted and so were we! On August 28, 1950, Navy hurricane hunters, flying into the eye of the storm, tracked its movement and direction and alerted the Naval Air Station to evacuate planes and take carriers out to sea. Dave called from Whiting, said the Navy was evacuating families to brick buildings farther inland but that he had agreed to let Charlie pick us up in half an hour to stay in his brick house which was safely remote from bays and bayous. Charlie was the Supply Officer and not a flyer and one of the few close Navy friends we ever had who did not fly. He was soon at the door in his new "three-hole" Buick. We heard planes revving up at the Pensacola Base and I knew Dave was already airborne in an SNJ, for he was leaving as soon as he hung up. "Where's Dave heading?" Charlie wondered. "Memphis," I replied, "and he thinks he'll be gone several days. It's slow moving but should hit here tonight." Charlie put the baby basket in the car, came back for our suitcase and Lori as I finished filling the tub and sink with water, having refrigerated two gallons and covered every available panful, on the table. "I'll share my water if it gets bad," I promised. I closed all the venetian blinds, drew the living-room drapes, got a raincoat-hat-and-boot-packed bag (for both Lori and me, a parka for Bruce) slung it with my shoulder bag, picked up Bruce, asleep on the couch, and locked our little frame house which I hoped to see again.

I had a pork loin roast I was planning to cook and jumbo artichokes but Charlie wouldn't let me bring a thing, "unless you've got some Yum Yums!" he grinned. We had a delicious dinner of baked ham, candied yams and peas, lettuce and tomato salad, prepared in quantity, for those foods could survive without refrigeration if power was lost. After we put the children to bed, and I had much help since they had no little ones, we played three-handed bridge and—listened. The rain was torrential but the hurricane did not hit until almost three in the morning.

In the interim, I admired Charlie and Helen's "retirement home" which they had designed themselves. It was all-brick and even had hurricane shutters which Charlie had secured on the outside of the low, rambling ranch-style house; it, also, afforded a garage for his Buick. Naval officers, and others, too, I was sure, frequently chose their "retirement town" early in their careers, bought choice land close to Naval facilities and built their permanent residences, lived in them as long and as often as they could (sometimes for two tours, if they were lucky), then rented them to fellow officers until they had completed their "twenty years." That efficient scheme did not appeal to us inasmuch as we did not intend to retire to a Navy town and when we built or bought a permanent house, we hoped to be continuous, rather than, continual—occupants.

The late August afternoon and night was our easiest hurricane, nestled as we were in a snug, solidly built and shuttered house, sufficiently inland. I was only sleepily aware of the eye's passing after about twenty minutes of intense calm, of windless quiet for the hurricane's gathering force to strike again, from the opposite direction. How grateful we were to our friends! Dave wondered, feeling keenly the irony of having to abandon his role of protector for his family, how we could ever repay, or even adequately articulate appreciation for, their generous helpfulness.

Charlie brought us home the next morning after breakfast, although he thought we should stay longer as it was raining heavily and the winds were still high but the hurricane had veered to the east and I was anxious to be where I could make ready for Dave's return. Dave called almost immediately. It would be at least two more days before his return unless the predicted high winds, which he did not foresee happening, suddenly subsided. He pondered again what we could do for Charlie and Helen. "Don't worry," I persuaded, "I've invited them to Yum-Yum bridge and I'm going to surprise them with a dozen to take home for their freezer." He laughed and appeared somewhat mollified. Dave's prognostication about Hurricane Edna was accurate, her movement was barely perceptible all day, small boat warnings were still posted and winds, unabated. Finally, she headed north and dissipated over land on the fourth day, and early on the fifth day, September 1, Lori alerted me to the happy sounds of planes overhead. By mid-morning, Dave had landed at Whiting Field and announced that he would be in the mood for roast pork at dinner time and wondered if I would like apple-black walnut crunch for dessert! I told him nothing could be finer and that he had been much missed, and Lori told him, too.

September was a beautiful month of flawless weather and we had uninterrupted week ends to explore beaches and late flora. The tourists had departed, thus the natives and the Navy were in control of the terrain but interest and concern began to focus on Korea. Since Pensacola was a training command and flight school, there was no direct movement from Pensacola to Korea but we were soon aware of squadrons and friends leaving from the West Coast. One of Charles' close friends, Charlie Peterson, was called up as an Active Naval Air Reserve and ordered to report to California; Charles, as an Inactive Reserve, felt unthreatened.

Dave, having been in Pensacola fifteen months, expected new orders by the first of 1951. He had applied for Postgraduate School in Aerology for a future tour but anticipated an overseas billet when his next orders were cut. No discussion would ameliorate his next assignment, for it was not in our hands, so we did not dwell upon possibilities. We enjoyed our little family in the warm harvest sunshine and Lori posed for photographer Dave beneath the wild grapevines in a pale pink, organdy pinafore, a pink sunsuit and a red-ruffled rhumba romper. Bruce, sweetly aslumber and always agreeable when wide-eyed, preferred not to participate in, or interfere with, Lori's Fashion Show—Clothier and Sponsor, Mommy Tom.

Figure 21. Lori Under the Grapevines

Bruce was exactly five months old, Christmas Day which we spent with Mother, Dad and Papa in Kansas City, Charles and Barbara's adding to the family circle and all of us missing Beth, who spent Christmas with Jane and Billy Jo Adcock in St. Louis. As usual, we drove to Lincoln the day after Christmas so we could match the growth and development of cousins and have Holland picture sessions, all brothers being inordinately fond of photography. Then back to K. C. again for New Year's Eve which we celebrated with Charles and Barbara, our radiant young lovers, at Mother and Dad's who were entertaining their "Dozen Club" for dinner and bridge and the annual birthday bussing of Dad by the ladies, at midnight. Our extra table left, however,

Figure 22. 1950 Christmas Foursome

to watch the New Year in—at Charles and Barbara's apartment, so cozy and convenient. We had a joyous, busy visit, Dave's announcing in both towns that he would be Alaska-bound in early February 1951, but that the children and I would be with Mother and Dad in Kansas City, at least, for a number of months.

When Dave had received orders to Kodiak, Alaska, he learned there would be at least a year's wait for Base housing and applied immediately for MOQ (Married Officers' Quarters), to shorten the wait as much as possible. Real estate was not a flourishing business in the little fishing-cannery town of Kodiak, most residents' building their own, shacks and quonset huts, in vogue. Naval personnel were, therefore, *strongly* urged not to bring families until Base housing was assigned; nor to attempt driving up the "Alcan" Highway which was only euphemistically so designated, its being a logger's trail of deep mud ruts, occasional stretches of gravel, bridges uncertain—due to the permafrost and lack of upkeep—and no place to stop: not to sleep, nor to eat, buy gas and tires, and, most dissuading of all, there was no facility for car repair, nor a towing service. Even if you had no personal gear in your car, added the Navy, it would be impossible to carry enough new tires and gasoline, not to mention food and water, to complete the trip.

And Dave had just bought a new car, dreaming, I guess, of the Alcan, which Dad and he had managed to conceal in the garage until the morning of Christmas Day, when Dad, taking me by the arm, confided: "Sis, Dave needs you in the garage." I bundled up and unsuspecting, thinking of all the paraphernalia we traveled with, opened the door to help and there leaned Dave, against the hood of a shiny, black, four-door, huge red-beribboned Pontiac, grinning mischievously at my "hoodwinking!" He apologized for its being black (which neither he nor Dad would ever choose) and a Pontiac but that was the only car Dad's favorite dealer had available on short notice and Dave felt it was mandatory to take a new, trouble-free car to Alaska. I told him it was "be-utiful" and very sporty-looking with white side-walled tires and red upholstery. When we got back in the house, Dad had a hearty chuckle at my still-apparent surprise and approved Dave's decision: "That will be a fine car for rugged Alaska!" I hugged my beloved Dad and thanked him for his advice and help, knowing that his sagacity and counsel were greater than Solomon's—to my ears.

We tested the snow-ruggedness of our new vehicle when we left Pensacola, February 1, 1951, saying good-bye to our little white cottage and summery sojourn for the wintry vicissitudes of Northland exploration. And it was not long before the North came South with canoes, light boats, aquaplanes and water skis strapped to car roofs—with swirling snow and sleet's lashing in their wake. They scurried like Innocence, demon-pricked with pitchforks, and we laughed at the ludicrous picture of Summer's attempting to outrun Winter but our laughter was swiftly attenuated by the discovery that the snow, suddenly large-flaked and heavy, was beginning to stick to fence-posts and make black and white ski-paths on the highway—and we were only in Alabama!

Whether the Southern-going Northern cars or the Northern-going cars from the South were more lugubrious became quickly moot, for it looked as if the entire Southern universe would soon be captured and bound by unfamiliar snow. I asked Dave if he should stop at a station and have his chains put on. "They probably wouldn't know how. I should do it myself." But when we got to Meridian, Mississippi, and saw a bustling filling-station with a garage, I inveigled him to stop. In the warm garage, the young man seemed to know what chains were used for but when he elevated the car on his grease-rack, took air out of the back tires before he secured the chains, my dubitation was similar to Dave's. He replaced the air in the tires, let the car down, much to Lori's amusement, and it was all done in minutes. Dave inspected the chains, saw that the ends were anchored but he questioned the tightness of the right chain. Dave filled the gas tank, thanked and paid the helpful young man and off we went into the flurry of white, having been reassured that the one link in the right chain which had kinked a bit when tightened on the tire would "flatten right away."

A bit beyond Booneville, Mother's town, an "eighteen-wheeler" was jackknifed across the road with a very narrow space between the front of the ponderous vehicle and deep gully. Dave, with his flyer's vision which measured with unfailing accuracy, distances large or small, said he could go around, the trucker agreed and Dave did. The Mississippi State Trooper, up ahead, where a truck was in the ditch, advised Dave to find a motel. "It's a widespread storm; roads will be impassable by night." Dave thanked him but we were impelled to go on, for we surely would be snowbound for days if we stopped. Dave reasoned that if we could get through a short stretch of Tennessee and Arkansas, the road crews would be out in Missouri. At any rate, motels began to post "No Vacancy" signs and, after a refreshing, hot meal in Corinth, Mississippi, we proceeded to drive nonstop to Kansas City, taking two-hour shifts at the wheel.

The right chain broke in Arkansas and clanged against the underside of the fender, awakening Lori and prompting Dave: "I *knew* I should have put them on myself! And that was my new pair." I evinced guilt and offered to help. He discovered a crossroads, pulled on his boots, coat and hat and found mine in the trunk. I gave Lori a little box of raisins and explained we'd have the chain fixed in a few minutes. "Will you bring me a snowball?" she requested. Dave laughed at the opportunism of the female and I unscrewed the cup from the thermos and received the flashlight from my good-natured, resourceful spouse. Dave deftly mended the chain with a short, strong piece of wire and his pliers while I "helped" by holding the flashlight. He replaced the pliers and flashlight in the trunk and pelted me with snowballs. It was warranted and I called: "Touché," but reciprocated while he stooped, defenseless, to pack a snowball for Lori. Lori tasted her snowball, planted a few raisins in it, ate them and by that time Bruce was awake, ready for his nocturnal nourishment. It was very easy to travel with a nursing baby, a mature young child, and a skillful, gallant, forgiving husband!

It was after three in the morning of February 3, 1951, when Dave eased through the heavy snow of Dad's driveway to park under the porte-cochere. "Just throw a blanket over me; I'll sleep here!" he instructed, with relieved comicality. Dad had roused, turned on garage, porch and house lights, dressed and come to our assistance while we were putting sweaters, coats and hats on slumberous babies. Mother was downstairs in a robe and was overjoyed to see us, and a day early! "We thought you wouldn't even try to come through this! We're so thankful you're safe and sound and that you are *here!*" And then, in an undertone, she added: "Papa isn't a bit well," and there was urgency in her voice. "Leave everything here until morning. The beds are all ready: the crib has been scrubbed and made up in your bedroom; Lori is to have the daybed in my room. You're exhausted," and she kissed us again, took Lori by the hand. "Now go to bed!" And we went.

Papa Lacy died that night and Dave and I realized, sadly, that our tacit determination to continue that long, hazardous trip had been intuitive. We had just finished dessert when Mother slipped from the table, "I just want to go to check Papa again." She had been up twice during dinner and had come right back, so we continued our visiting with Dad, Charles and Barbara and were unconcernedly laughing at Dave's description of our snowy escape when we heard a sudden pounding on the floor above. Mother had called but we had not heard, so she rocked the night stand back and forth, heavily, to get our attention. Dad, Dave and Charles were up the stairs, immediately. Lori was already in bed, as it was after nine and Bruce would not awaken for another hour. I followed

Charles, with Barbara, and when we got to the door, I knew Papa was gone. I heard Dad asking quietly: "Do you want the dimes now?" Mother was very composed and replied, "Yes, please, they're on the dresser; let Charles call the ambulance. He passed away peacefully and I think he knew his loved ones were here!" And when we were all together, later: "Now, don't be mournful, any of you. He wouldn't have wanted that. He was ninety-two, wasn't that wonderful! Papa had such a long, productive life. We'll all miss him; poor Mr. Blair will just be lost—we'll have to help *him*."

Mr. Blair had been Papa's best friend in Kansas City. A neighbor of Mother and Dad's, Mr. Blair was about thirty years younger than Papa and was blind. Retiring some years before Papa came to Kansas City, he lived with his daughter and family. The two friends had, daily, taken long walks together; the near-sightless leading the blind, for Papa had cataracts in both eyes but he could read street signs, because of his height, by standing directly beneath them. A gentlemanly credo and a lack of vision were their only common bonds. Mr. Blair was a short Northerner which Papa, a tall Southerner, could do nothing about. But Mr. Blair was also, and ill-advisedly in Papa's opinion, a Republican and Papa intended to mitigate, if not completely correct, such "short-sightedness"! So their perambulations, when disputatious—for Papa discovered Mr. Blair to be "an avatar of Republicanism"—frequently took them far from home and, more than once, a kind neighbor or friend drove them back, with courtly "thank-yous" from both, to Papa's front porch, or called in a lookout report to Mother. Papa succeeded in one reformation, however: at the age of ninety, he quit smoking his pipe which he had enjoyed his entire adult life because he "resented the fact that it might have become a habit"! And he challenged Mr. Blair, an inveterate cigarette smoker, to give up *his* habit and helped him do it, filling the pockets of his walking coat with sour lemondrops and peppermints—which drenched the smoke but might not have quenched the politics.

The next morning at breakfast, I appreciated, anew, what Mother's allusion to the Emersonian "circle of compensation" symbolized—and she elucidated further: "Just think of it. Here was Papa, born on the *25th* of the month, November, almost a hundred years ago, in 1858, bearing a middle name for *his* Mother's family, Charles Riddle Lacy, and I'm taking him back home to his beloved South, to his Mississippi soil. And up from the South, hours before Papa's passing, struggling through Booneville in a rare snowstorm"—and Mother turned to Dave and smiled: "I'll bet it wasn't as bad as your wedding night! (A negative nod and positive chuckle.) Here comes precious baby Bruce, born on the *25th* of the month, with the middle name of Thomas and he's going to be a gentleman and a scholar and lover of *all* people—just like Papa!"

Mother left by train early the next morning for Booneville, Dad's putting her on the Pullman and seeing that everything was in order. Uncle Wes and Gene would meet her train and Beth would arrive later from Gulfport. Mother had planned the service from Kansas City but there were many people to see, in addition to friends and relatives, for he had lived a long, distinguished life in Booneville as an educator, lawyer, judge and state senator. The big, old house was suddenly empty in Kansas City: Dad drove on to Des Moines, Iowa, on a delayed business trip and Dave, Lori, Bruce and I left at the same time for Lincoln.

We stayed with Mother H a week, always amazed at her energy and enthusiasm after working all day at the "Y." We played bridge most evenings with Kenneth and Naomi, one of the daughters-in-law, usually sitting out. Mother H and Dave always won when they played together which Naomi and I encouraged—but how they laughed! Naomi was a consummately gentle and loving Mother; she had infinite patience and generosity of time and strength. I deemed her archetypical as a wife and as a woman. I had the greatest admiration for Naomi and, sometimes, must have embarrassed her when I adulated her before the family with my fervent verbosity, but everyone always concurred. She was the matrix, with Kenneth's constant assistance, of the ever-conglutinating Holland family, for it was through her home's wide portals that we flowed and adhered—ofttimes forgetful of the hours and the days of her unflagging "duty."

Robert and Viola, when living in Grand Island, Nebraska, invited us to visit them, a bit farther westward, which we were delighted to do. Our sessions there were not with cards but with ideas, facts and opinions—into the night, ad infinitum! We drank coffee, except for Dave, and talked. Robert was less opinionated about politics than some of the conservative Nebraskans and Viola—as patient and loving as Naomi and an unsatiated political student—was reflective, objective and read widely, both sides' arguments, before choosing a candidate but I was usually the sole avowed Democrat at any meeting of Hollands—until later, when Lori and one or two of her cousins became "cerebral"—and I thrived on such disputatiousness! Robert was our marvelous anecdotist, psychiatrist and genealogist and, usually, we just listened, asked questions and benefited prodigiously!

We returned to Kansas City. Mother had just a few days' respite from family cares but she welcomed us joyfully and was anxious to spoil all of us, especially Dave, during his few remaining days in the States. He left on February 19, 1951, for Seattle, Washington, and typically drove too long: 843.2 miles in 14.9 hours to Roswell, New Mexico, feeling lonesome for Lori when he saw windmills "Go 'round and 'round." He missed "Bruce peeking out of his basket at me with his 'million-dollar smile.'" I was asked to send some of his calling cards to his Kodiak address: Box No. 30, Navy 127, c/o PM, Seattle, Washington. And I did so at once for Dave had warned me that mail would be slow, both ways.

And, indeed, it was an understatement to define mail as "slow." My first letter from Kodiak arrived on March 11, having been written the day Dave arrived, February 28, but not postmarked in Seattle until March 9. He had a nine-hour flight from McChord AFB in a four-engine R5D with bucket seats instead of plush but improvised for the night flight with cushions, pillows and blankets and slept awhile. He had wanted to fly during the day but upon discovering the flight would be over clouds most of the way, he took the earlier plane. He was distressed to discover that he was on the housing list very near the bottom. "The worst part about it is that LCDR's go to the top of the list . . . Some j.g. (Dave's rank) who has been here 6 months started with #27 and now is #34. The housing in town is reported to be terrible, but I am going to start looking. I'll get you up here one way or another." He was assigned to the Air Department of the Kodiak Naval Station; reported that the winter had been mild there and that he had received a nice welcome at the O-Club when he was introduced to the crowd playing Bingo and he won $7.50 for the children's savings account! I was entrusted with the banking at Park National in Kansas City, which was where our account remained, until some years after Dave's retirement. It was convenient to go weekly or monthly with Dad who went methodically once a week.

I shopped for heavy clothing for the children and me, although not much was available. Mother baby-sat and rushed me off to Emery, Bird, Thayer and Harzfeld's downtown, the morning after Dave left. I was fortunate to find essentially everything I needed at Emery Bird's: a dark green and red nylon snowsuit with hat for Lori, quilted and heavy; two corduroy dresses for me, both alike, one in dark rust, the other, green; a forest green corduroy suit and forest green storm coat, very long, with a big mouton collar and revers and a matching green beret. Mother and I had already found a dark brown wool, double-breasted Little-Lord-Fauntleroy coat, billed flyer's hat with a strap under the chin and leggings with long zippers at Harzfeld's when we shopped for Alaska, briefly at Christmastime. I was so grateful for that discovery in December, since everything on the racks was for Bunnytime and it was only February; warm clothing for little boys was almost nonexistent. Remembering how the Luhnows had shopped at Harzfeld's in November for summer clothing to wear in Hawaii at Christmas, I requested winter pants, shirts and sweaters, boy's size 2, and when I told them I was going to Alaska, they were not only helpful—but sympathetic! I bought high, waterproof boots for the three of us, always two sizes too large for the children, and low-heeled travel shoes in dark red for me to match the hand-tooled Mexican bag with shoulder strap from Ann Skoog, one of Mother's dearest friends who had—when I was a child—taken me "under her wing" and joined in helping to equip me for expeditious travel with two little ones.

Everyone who learned of my anticipated excursion to hibernal Alaska looked at me with immediate interest, patted me pityingly and commended my courage! At first, I murmured demurral. In a few days, however, the predictable iteration of the patterned response became such an amusing tool that I contrived to use it with complete strangers: on the streetcar to and from town, sharing a table at Wolferman's. I was surprised at the genuine fascination felt for the remote territory and the lack of knowledge evidenced. I took a private poll and found that most would not object to Alaska's becoming our 49th state, primarily reasoning it to be a defense against Russia—but they unanimously and emphatically, did not want to live there!

I began our series of inoculations for overseas in April, even though housing news from Dave was still bleak. The Dispensary at the Olathe Naval Air Station took good care of us. Routine "DPT" shots were continued for Bruce; boosters for Lori and me, polio shots and a smallpox vaccination. I felt somewhat redundant when they vaccinated me again even though I had an ugly scar on my upper left arm to display. "But this one will be little and pretty!" the persuasive corpsman promised. Dave had taken all of his shots and vaccination in a week's time in Seattle and thoughtfully urged us to start in April, hoping we'd be with him by summer.

Easter was mild and sunny and the Bunny Rabbit hid eggs in the back yard for Lori and Bruce, with Daddy Frank's assistance. Charles and Barbara, in handsome spring suits, came for the hunt; Uncle Charles' taking pictures of Lori's frolicking in the dainty aqua coat and bonnet Mommy Tom had selected, beribboned basket in hand, while Bruce propelled his "kiddy-car" in unpredictable and sudden directions. We all went to church together and Lori sat with us in the balcony, Bruce's taking a nap in the nursery. Lori wanted to be up high so that she could look down to where she had "taken my flower" the week before in Mother's Palm Sunday procession and program with children and choirs, flora and palms. Lori was intrigued with the huge lighting fixtures, ceiling and stained-glass windows and panoramic view from the balcony. It was the first time she had stayed with us for the sermon and she was appropriately contemplative. Mother's leg-of-lamb luncheon was, as always—"meltingly delicious," borrowing Mama Kate's metaphorical depiction. It was a happy day for the children with Mother and Dad, Barbara and Charles' compensating for their Daddy's absence.

Figure 23. Stand-Ins for Dave: Mother, Charles, Dad

The month of May started eventfully when Bruce rode down the basement stairs in his kiddy-car, *very* quickly, but without a scratch or a bruise! Since it demolished "Blue Ducky," riding lookout on his suction-cup perch, we vowed to make the hallway, as well as the basement entrance, off limits for Bronco Bruce. Dad had opened the gate at the top of the stairs just long enough to pick up a brief case at the bottom and when his back was turned, Bruce careened through the breakfast room, into the hall, turned the corner, and *flew* to the bottom. The flight was a bit bumpy and Bruce and Blue Ducky landed in a nose-dive on two front wheels as Clown catapulted to safety under the ironing board; but Daddy Frank was there immediately to release the pilot, so astonished by the suddenness of it all—that he didn't have much time to cry. Bruce was *quick*! There had been no doubt about that from the first.

In recompense for Bruce's flawed "solo," Dave's next letter announced we would be flying to him in Alaska in June! Oh, happy, happy news! He had ordered our furniture shipped from Pensacola where it had been in storage and hoped it would arrive in mid-June. At any rate, we were to come ahead and he would check out a crib for Bruce and bed for Lori and card table and chairs, bedding and dishes. We would sleep on permanent box springs because the upper room of the two-room, spruce log cabin he had just rented had been built around them, the stairs being too narrow to accommodate their removal. Mr. MacDonald, landlord and owner of the fish-freezing and Stateside shipping company, assured Dave he would be happy to borrow our new box springs for his personal use in suitable exchange for his inextricable set, thereby not charging us storage rent—for where would we put an extra set of box springs? But Dave and I were both eager to assent to the sophistic Mr. MacDonald's suggestion, since he had a house to rent boasting of two rooms—one of which was known to be even larger than a double bed!

Dad took me early the next morning to the Union Station and Municipal Airport to get tickets and Dave called that night to learn our schedule and announce he had just made LT (Senior Grade)!

CHAPTER III

WE LIVED AT "SHANGRILOG," KODIAK, ALASKA

We were off to Alaska in a hatbox! It was June 1951. I was traveling from Kansas City with Lori, twenty-eight months old and Bruce, ten months old, to join Dave in Kodiak, Alaska; I had packed all of the clothing we would need for the trip in a cardboard hatbox. We were to be comfortably clothed from the summertime warmth of Kansas City through Seattle's rain to Alaska's chilled clime. I always had prided myself on the compactness of my packing. For our northernmost trip, I knew I had accomplished a feat which was remarkable.

In addition to the hatbox, our luggage was comprised of a carry-all containing Bruce's diapers, a plastic laundry bag for soiled diapers, a pullman case and a make-up kit. I had to carry only three articles: Bruce, a handbag and a diaper bag. The latter was filled with a gallimaufry of baby food, raw carrots, raisins, balloons, apples, crackers, clothes pins, Christmas cards and *A Child's Garden of Verses.*

By 8:00 P.M., Sunday, June 17, 1951, we were ready for our 9:30 P.M. train to Seattle. To ease the tension and for an equivocal leave-taking, we drove through the Country Club and Plaza Districts and then to the Union Station. Mother and Dad, Charles and Barbara escorted us to the train and established us in our bedroom compartment at 9:15 P.M.

We were scarcely alone after tearful, restrained farewells when the porter rang: "Your mother wants to see you at the platform." I clutched up my handbag, Bruce and Lori and stumbled to the gate on the platform. The train was beginning to move and Mother was running alongside it calling to me. She said something about my luggage but I could not hear her. She called again and then I heard, with painful clarity: "Your hatbox! Dot, we forgot your hatbox!"

We were off to Alaska with all of the clothing we did not need—with none which we did!

When we descended the train in Seattle the next night, we were warmly, if oddly, dressed. I had opened the pullman case and gratefully pulled out wraps for all of us. Bruce was dressed in a pair of dainty, blue overalls, an engulfing gray playcoat of Lori's and a white silk, beribboned cap which fit perfectly to the top of his ears. Lori was wearing a pair of dark brown, carrot-streaked overalls which she had worn since she left Kansas City—offset, or set off, by an aqua forget-me-not embroidered coat with a matching bonnet which was tied at one side of her chin in a sprightly bow. I looked fairly normal, but as colorful as the spectrum, in a bright green suit, a dark green beret, a yellow coat, red shoes and my red shoulder bag.

It was 11:00 P.M. when we reached the station. Our plane was to leave at 12:15 A.M. I had one hour and fifteen minutes to locate and pick up our reservations and take a taxi to Boeing Field which was half-an-hour's distance from town.

As soon as the three of us were arranged in a telephone booth, I dialed Seneca 0383 as indicated by the wire which confirmed our flight reservations to Kodiak. At Seneca 0383, I was told to call Cherry 4500. I called Cherry 4500 and received no answer. Frantically, I again called Seneca 0383. I was not calm and I was not polite. Consequently, the young woman remembered that a message had been left for Mrs. David B. Holland: "If you call Prospect 7677, Miss Wilson will talk to you about your reservations." Running out of nickels and patience, I dialed Prospect 7677 with a quivering forefinger. The phone rang—and rang—and rang—and rang. I sat there in stupefaction, the telephone clutched in my hand, wondering what to do next. It was 11:15 P.M. I had exactly one hour to find our tickets, make the half-hour trip to the airport and board our plane to Alaska. I decided to start over and to call Seneca 0383 again. As I reached up to put the phone back on the hook, I heard, faintly: "Hello?" "HELLO!" I shouted. "This is Mrs. David B. Holland." "Who?" I knew at once that it was not Miss Wilson. "No, this is Miss Wilson's mother. My daughter isn't at home." "Isn't at HOME? But this is Mrs. David B. Holland." I hastened to explain my predicament. "Can you locate my tickets?" I begged. "I think they're at the office," Mrs. Wilson volunteered. "At the OFFICE? But the office told me to contact your daughter." "Well, my daughter has gone to a party but she should be home by 1:00." "ONE?" Each remark amplified my anguish. "But my plane leaves at 12:15! Can't you help me?" I was almost in tears. "Oh! That's the flight to Kodiak!" Mrs. Wilson was wide-awake now. "I think that's been canceled till tomorrow morning." Recovering slowly from the happy shock, I realized that Mrs. Wilson was still talking: "I said, where will you be staying?" "But are you sure it's canceled?" I insisted. "That's what I'm telling you. I'll have my daughter phone you. Where will you be in half an hour?" "Oh! Well, I'll be at the Olympic." (Thanks to Dad, I had made hotel reservations in Seattle for just such an emergency.) "Now, you won't forget to have her call me?" Assured that she would not,

I hung up and hugged my weary children to me as we hurried to the taxi stand.

At the Olympic Hotel, I waited interminable minutes in line at the desk. There was a convention in town. Finally, the bellhop took us to our room. It was the most remote room in the hotel. Halfway down the hall, I could hear the telephone ringing. It was Miss Wilson! Our tickets! Would he never open that door! But the telephone was still ringing. The door was opened and I had the phone clutched in my trembling hand. With just enough strength for one more effort, I gasped: "Miss Wilson?" "Yes, this is Miss Wilson." It was the most soothing statement I had ever heard. Miss Wilson had everything under control and Seattle was suddenly wonderful. I learned that the flight had been canceled until 8:00 A.M. the next morning, Wednesday, July 20. A limousine would pick us up at 7:00 A.M. in front of the Olympic to take us to Boeing Field. There I could pick up our tickets.

We were too relieved and too weary to be disappointed that we would awaken the next morning in Seattle instead of Kodiak, Alaska.

The next morning, I had an inchoate realization of the casualness of Alaska and everything connected with it. Time was insignificant! The limousine from the airline did not arrive at 7:00 A.M. It did not arrive at 7:15, nor at 7:20. At 7:20 A.M., the children and I took the regularly scheduled bus from the hotel to Boeing Field. We got there a few minutes before 8:00 A.M. and I began to reenact my frantic efforts of the night before to locate our tickets.

In a small room crowded with dark-skinned men who, I thought, must be prosperous Eskimos, there were a number of plainly marked airline booths. There was no sign of a PNA (Pacific Northern Airlines) representative and no one seemed to have even heard of PNA. The only person I could beseech to help me was a sympathetic janitor. He agreed to go to the hangar to see if a plane with the bold letters P-N-A was ready to take off. In the meantime, I called Seneca 0383 (I shall never forget that number) but there was no answer. The janitor learned no more than I. So we waited—and hoped. I found an unoccupied bench and deposited the children and our paraphernalia. There was not a woman in the room. I noted only two or three white men. They were young and appeared to be college students. In a few minutes, I called Seneca 0383 again and learned that Miss Wilson was on her way. And by 8:30 A.M., she arrived!

We finally left Seattle in record time. We were only two hours off schedule! At 9:45 A.M., we made our trek from the waiting room to the plane which was far more substantial than I had dared to expect. It was a DC-4. By 10:00 A.M., we were in the air. Lori and Bruce were asleep by the time the plane pierced the clouds and I relaxed in the deep seat with Bruce in my arms and Lori at my side.

I looked about me at the black-haired, dark-skinned men who had preceded us into the plane. They were quiet, well-mannered men, neatly dressed. There were no other women in the flight with the exception of the stewardesses. Three young men whom I had correctly assumed to be college boys were going to Kodiak to work in the salmon-canning factories for the summer. As I learned later, the men were enroute to Kodiak for the same purpose. They were Filipinos who had been hired for the summer by the Kodiak salmon canneries. Their homes were in San Francisco. Each year, the canneries paid their expenses to and from Kodiak, and Alaska was no new adventure for most of them.

An attractive and refined young Filipino from the University of San Francisco sat in the single seat next to our double seat. His name was "Alex." He was born in Manila but had lived most of his life in Honolulu and San Francisco. Alex was the greatest help with the children. He trotty-horsed them, played peep-eye, read to them and held Bruce while I enjoyed a light snack at noontime and drank revivifying hot coffee.

At 5:45 P.M., Pacific daylight-saving time, 2:45 P.M., Alaska standard time, we were over Kodiak. The ceiling was dangerously low and we continued two hundred miles northeastward to Anchorage, on the mainland of Alaska. (I learned the next day from Dave that if our plane had taken off just one and a-half hours late instead of two hours late, it could have landed at Kodiak. The field was open all day until 2:15 P.M.)

Our plane landed at the Air Force's Elmendorf Field outside of Anchorage after a one-and-a-half-hour's flight from Kodiak. An airline limousine drove the children and me, and the stewardesses, to a cafeteria on the base where we relished our first real meal of the day. We were served a hearty meal of roast beef and gravy, mashed potatoes, creamed corn, bread, fresh milk and coffee. I noticed for the first time Alaska's ubiquitous canned milk which was placed on each table, a hole punctured in the top.

After a brief while, we returned to the waiting room hoping to continue on to Kodiak that afternoon. I turned my watch back to 6:00 P.M., Alaska standard time, although we were sleepy enough for 9:00 P.M. which my watch had registered. Alex joined us and Lori, who had grown attached to him by that time, climbed on his knee. She was soon the center of interest as she sat there with Alex. She dimpled as he whispered something, her bright curls and fair skin emphasizing his dark face and hair. Lori wound Alex's wrist watch and then leaned over to wind "Mommy's watch." Passengers awaiting the Fairbanks flight watched us with more alarm than approval.

At 7:00 P.M., the ticket agent informed us that due to Kodiak's continued low ceiling, our flight had been canceled until 8:00 A.M. the next morning. After hearing the ticket agent's unshocking news, the children and I put on our light coats and hats which would have been uncomfortable in Anchorage's mid-seventy temperature, except for a cool drizzle. Alex carried our bags outside. He helped us into the airline limousine and waved good-bye, to the apparent relief of many, still watching from the waiting room.

Elmendorf Air Force Base was about three miles from the city of Anchorage. As we drove along the busy highway to town, we noted with approbation that the trees looked like trees at home, that the road was paved, the cars many and new. We even saw a train which, surprisingly, was very modern-looking. It was emblazoned with the identification: "The Alaskan Railroad." Lori "oh"ed about the train and the driver, who had been pointing out noteworthy buildings and locations, told her: "Take a good look at that train because you won't see any where *you're* going." He pointed to a building under construction. "That's the Providence Memorial Hospital they're putting over there. It's run by the Alaskan Native Service." "You mean that's for Eskimos throughout Alaska?" I asked him. "Eskimos and Aleuts," the driver explained. "Most of 'em have TB, and they didn't have a place big enough to take care of 'em." I asked him who Aleuts were. "You'll see a lot of 'em." He was willing with advice: "But don't get close to them. Some of 'em are awful dirty." I asked him from where they came. "They come from the Aleutian Islands," the driver informed me. "The Japs drove them out when they invaded Attu and Dutch Harbor and we've still got them. They won't go back."

We were on the outskirts of Anchorage. Two buildings loomed tall in the skyline and I asked what they were. "Those are new apartment buildings. The largest buildings in town," I was proudly informed. "They're each fourteen stories high! Haven't finished them yet and I don't know who's gonna live in them. Rents start at $150 and that's just for one bedroom." He shook his head. "I can't see it."

I was as curious about our driver as about Anchorage. I asked him how long he had been in Anchorage, where his home was and why he liked

Alaska. He told me he had been in Anchorage seven years. "Haven't been 'Outside' in all that time. Haven't been any place except to Fairbanks a couple times." His home had been in Seattle and he liked Alaska "because you've got freedom here. You can do anything you want to and nobody cares. It's got it all over the States." I was to hear that explanation of preference for Alaska, in slightly different phraseology, from each person of whom I inquired.

By some magic, the ticket agent at Elmendorf had secured a room for the children and me at the Anchorage Hotel. Hotel accommodations in Anchorage were as precious as gold. A stewardess on our plane had told me of her experience. Arriving in Anchorage for the first time, she went to the hotel where she had made reservations two months in advance. "And what do you think happened?' she asked me. "They told me I was twentieth on the list!" We were, indeed, grateful for our room in one of Anchorage's best hotels. It proved to be a clean, comfortable room with three single beds, a desk, a chest of drawers and a telephone. We not only had a private bathroom but the bathroom contained a tub! That bathtub was the last we were to enjoy until we returned to the States a year and a half later.

The next morning at 7:30 A.M., we were ready to leave the Anchorage Hotel for Elmendorf which was used by the commercial airlines. We had rested well in our comfortable room despite the daylight which most of the night framed a shade too short and too narrow for the window. I had sent a wire to Mother and Dad through the Army Signal Corps (there was no Western Union in Alaska) and one to Dave. Neither message could be delivered until the next morning. I knew Mother and Dad would be relieved to know that we were someplace in Alaska. It did not occur to me that Dave, as Air Clearance Officer of the Kodiak Naval Station, had been following our plane's movements since it left Seattle and knew before I did that it diverted to Anchorage.

There was no coffee shop at the hotel. We had walked a block through the drizzle to a juke-box cafe which had been open all night. Feeling an urgency for haste, I had ordered only toast and milk. The children relished their milk poured from half-pint bottles, marked "Homogenized, Grade A." I wrapped the dry toast in a napkin, stuck it in my cavernous bag, paid the normal-looking, blonde waitress and hurried with my adaptable children back to the hotel.

I waited in vain for the airline limousine which was to pick us up at 7:30. I was experiencing again the frustration of the previous morning in

Seattle. Efforts to call the waiting room at Elmendorf were futile—the telephone to the Air Force Base was out of order. My sole thought was that the plane had changed its schedule and left without us. We were the only ones at the hotel; the Filipinos had been taken to barracks on the base. At twenty minutes to eight, I was able to get a cab which deposited us at the door of the waiting room at eight o'clock.

No one was in the waiting room except a strange ticket agent. Fearfully, I asked about the 8:00 A.M. flight to Kodiak. The ticket agent looked uncomprehending but deigned to inquire of someone in the back room. I listened—then breathed! The flight was delayed until 10:00 A.M.

We sat down to wait in the empty room. Lori and Bruce shared their last apple. Then Bruce was ready for sleep; Lori, for investigation.

Within the next half-hour, a few people came in but none for our flight. Time was passing slowly. I watched a man and woman come through the door. The woman was carrying a baby which appeared to be no more than three or four months old. Three handsome, well-groomed young boys followed them. The mother came over to sit on our bench. We smiled about our mutual interests and soon were chatting. She introduced her husband and young sons. The baby, she told me happily, was a girl. That meeting was to be the most stimulating and inspiring contact of my eighteen months in Alaska. Their name was Stump and they lived on Lake Iliamna ("Lake of Volcanoes") which was on the mainland near Bristol Bay, one of the richest fishing areas in Alaska. They had come to Alaska from Oregon eight years earlier on a vacation. While there, they had felt a penchant to do missionary work and soon returned to live among the natives on isolated Lake Iliamna. They impressed me as being more than ordinarily intelligent. They were cognizant and concerned about national and world affairs, not mentally isolated by their life in the wilderness. The Stumps had been in Anchorage three months, having traveled to Anchorage by dog sled and bush plane the first of April, a month before the baby was born. They were taking back two sled dogs, books, clothing and food staples as well as a precious daughter. A teen-aged Eskimo girl, named Yanonas, was going home with them for the summer. She was a student at the University of Alaska at Fairbanks. An extremely attractive girl, she bore few traces of her clan and spoke English without an accent. In a three-hour conversation with the Stumps (our plane was late in taking off as was theirs), I learned of such things as sled dogs, mukluks, parkas, shoe-pacs—about life, generally, in the wilderness of Alaska.

Black bear, they told me, was better to eat than brown bear because the latter fed principally on fish, the former on berries. When I looked awed at the thought of eating bear, Mrs. Stump laughed and reminded me: "There are no butchers where we live, you know." They smoked salmon for their eight sled dogs each of which consumed two salmon a day. Enough had to be smoked during the short summer to last throughout the winter. They shot elk, reindeer, moose and caribou for their own needs. "Reindeer is the best eating," Mr. Stump told me, "but they're getting hard to find. We even eat porcupine," he continued, very amused at my wonderment. I asked how he got rid of the needles. "We just split the skin on the belly and roll it back; just like rolling up dust in a rug."

I was curious about what sort of clothing they wore in the wintertime. Mrs. Stump laughed at that. "Mostly things from Sears," she told me. The entire family obviously found me more of a curiosity than I, them. "But, don't you wear fur clothing like the Eskimos?" I was disbelieving. "The only thing made of fur we own are mukluks. The natives in our village make them out of land otter," Mrs. Stump explained. Half-hidden by the coffee counter, with her husband and sons grouped in front of her, Mrs. Stump was nursing the baby. I did not have to inquire if formulas were used for babes in the woods!

Mr. Stump, I learned, had built a one-room log cabin the first summer at Lake Iliamna. He had added slowly to it each summer. He had just added a fourth room to their home before they left for Anchorage. I wondered how they heated their cabin and was told that they used oil flown in by bush pilots.

But I still wanted to know what they wore when it was cold. "Well, we wear parkas most of the winter," Mr. Stump began. "Are they lined with fur?" I asked eagerly. I did not intend to get that close, vicariously, to the Eskimos without learning about their fur clothing. But Mr. Stump disappointed me. "No," he said, "our parkas are lined with alpaca and they're very warm. We wear shoe-pacs if it's not cold but if it gets colder than twenty below, we wear our mukluks."

I wanted to know, explicitly, what shoe-pacs and mukluks were. Shoe-pacs, I was told, resembled a regular boot. The top was of leather and laced in the same fashion as a boot. But the shoe part of the boot was made of rubber. That allowed the foot to breathe and flex more easily than an all-leather boot thus diminishing the danger of frozen feet. I could think of nothing colder than rubber shoes on ice and snow but accepted Mr. Stump's word (and later my husband's) when he said they were comfortable in zero to twenty-below-zero weather worn over two or three pairs of woolen stockings. The mukluks sounded more sensible. But I discovered they were worn very infrequently. They were made of fur, generally land otter or caribou; the sole, of whaleskin. They were not close-fitting and binding like a boot. (Dave bought several pairs of mukluks at Nome. They resembled nothing I could think of except the long, wide, red felt stockings which the children hung at the fireplace once each year. Of course, mukluks were not red but they were heelless and had a rounded toe and flared slightly at the top like a Santa Claus boot. Some extended to just below the knee; others, to the calf. They were held on the foot by a leather thong wrapped once or twice around the ankle. It was never difficult to determine the authenticity of a pair of mukluks. All one had to do was—sniff! Mukluks, dolls and fur goods the Eskimos made for their own use and for sale were extremely odoriferous.)

When our flight to Kodiak was announced at 11:45 A.M., I, reluctantly, bid the Stumps good-bye. It had been a stimulating and profitable morning. I thought about the Stumps as we lifted from the runway and headed for Kodiak. Their life in the wilderness was brave and unselfish. But it appeared infinitely safe and serene compared to many disturbed lives throughout the world.

In one and a-half hours, our plane settled on terra firma. We, at last, had arrived at the Kodiak Naval Station on Women's Bay. I had anticipated the flight from Seattle to Kodiak with slightly more trepidation than I suffered with approaching Motherhood. But, like the latter, the flight proved to be painless—particularly in retrospect.

When the plane had cleared of the Filipinos, I arose, slung the straps of my bags over my left shoulder and balanced Bruce on top of the bags. Alex, carrying Lori, had been one of the first out of the plane. When Bruce and I were at the head of the steps, I looked down and saw Dave! Dave had never been more handsome as he smiled up at us, Lori held tightly in his arms. And I had never been more happy to see him! After joyous greetings, we made our way to Alex to thank him and visit a few minutes.

The first impression I had of Kodiak was the magnificence of the mountains. Even as the plane was turning around at the end of the runway to taxi to the offloading ramp, I was captivated by the brilliant green of the mountains which loomed up around us, grandly enclosing the landing strips on three sides. Richer than emerald, the green had a translucent quality as if the mountains were reflecting color from their cores. I wondered at the apathy of my fellow passengers. To me, every direction was glorious and awesome! Alaska! The fact that I was a Midwesterner on a happy mission perhaps explained my rapture.

As Dave led us to the car, he expounded upon the mountains. "There's Old Woman, Lori and Bruce," pointing to the mountains north of the runway. "Old Woman is supposed to watch over ships coming through St. Paul Harbor—that's where the Kodiak docks are located—into Women's Bay." "Well, she watched over us, too!" I applauded. "Didn't we come in over Women's Bay?" Dave affirmed that we had. "Now look straight ahead," pointing to an abruptly rising mountain at the end of our runway. "That's Barometer; see how the runway slopes uphill?" "That's terrible," I sympathized. "Why don't they make the contractor flatten it out?" "It was intentional!" Dave laughed. "When planes come in fast, it helps slow them down on their run-out—otherwise, they'd crash into Barometer." "Good heavens!" I exclaimed, "is this the only place you can land?" Nodding affirmatively, Dave chuckled, "It gets worse!" Pointing south, "That's Pyramid. See that sharp peak up there? Pilots' taking a waveoff have to bank sharply to the left to avoid Barometer—and then there's Pyramid!" "My goodness, Dave—all this beauty is treacherous! Have you had to take a waveoff?" "Not yet—we practice it in all weather; it's not that bad!" "You mean such impediments are routine?" Dave grinned: "Sometime I might tell you about Dutch Harbor on Unilaska in the Aleutians, Juneau, Nome, Barter Island—but look over there at those tennis courts!" And I knew the most lengthy and graphic description I'd ever heard about his flying had been—terminated.

I was surprised to see tennis courts marked off in revetments which had been blasted out of the mountains. I mused aloud at the corries. It was the twenty-first of June and I was chilly in a suit, a coat and a hat. I asked Dave if the courts were ever used. He said: "Of course, the station has a team which enters the All-Alaskan tournament each year. They do pretty well, too!" I concluded that people in Alaska, at least in Kodiak, must lead fairly normal lives, after all—once landed, that is.

It was good to see the car again. Dave's black Pontiac still looked new, beneath the layer of volcanic ash. Inside, it even smelled new.

As we drove slowly around the Base (I wanted to see everything) and then along the cliff road to town, I marveled, excitedly, at the beauty of Alaska. The mountains, the lakes, the spruce trees, the wild flowers and the cascades of melting snow were ineffably beautiful. The road to town high on a cliff was bordered by mountains on the north, the sky and water on the south. Perched on the side of the mountain, we looked down upon docks, boats, floating canneries, channel lights, buoys, islands covered with spruce trees—and far out into the Gulf of Alaska.

As we approached the town of Kodiak, I saw that houses were built on the mountain's precipice. What perfect lookouts they afforded for wives of fishermen awaiting their husbands' return! As we wound closer to Kodiak, I noted that the business section was concentrated into a small, sea-level area. Knolls lined with houses led down to the crowded point of land which dipped into the bay like a thirsty tongue. We passed a filling station, a few dusty houses and a Shore Patrol office.

"Well, this is it!" Dave announced. "This is Kodiak, Alaska!" And I thought it was wonderful. It was exhilarating just to be in Alaska. I was like an ingénue in my eagerness to learn everything, at once, about Kodiak.

Main Street was three blocks long and the only paved street in Kodiak. "Is this the street everyone makes so much fun of?" I wanted to know. Dave laughed: "They say Main Street is 'about as straight as the path of a cow looking for four-leaf clovers.'" I was soon convinced. Every few hundred feet, Main Street right-angled and disappeared from view. Traffic moved like a snail along the two-lane street which was constricted from both sides by narrow, frontier-styled buildings and the latest in parking meters. Atop a small hill overlooking Kodiak Proper (population 1,700) was a cocoa brown, two-story building identified by clean, white letters: "Kodiak Hotel." Fanning out below the hotel was a bank, several barber shops, a grocery store, a motion-picture theater, two drug stores, several souvenir shops, a jewelry shop, three garages, an airlines office, an Elks Club, two department stores which sold everything from baking powder to fishing boats—and nineteen bars. On the perimeter of the shopping area was a hospital, a schoolhouse, a laundry, two bakeries and a telephone company. Balancing the hotel were two buildings on a hill across town: The City Hall and the United States Jail. The latter appeared to be the most respectable and substantial building in town. Below the jail was the fire station.

We turned from Main Street onto Mission Road. It was an incredibly poor road, deeply rutted and gouged with holes. "Oh, what is that?" I pointed to an odd-looking church. It was like a white frame church one would see in New England except for the top which resembled a mosque. Dave was prepared to tell me all about it. "That's the Russian Greek Orthodox Church. I understand that the cupola and the bell tower, it's on the ground next to the church, are the originals from Baranov's time. You know that Kodiak is the oldest town in Alaska, don't you?"

I nodded. I had read about Kodiak in the Chamber of Commerce folder Dave sent and the *Encyclopædia Britannica* from which Mother had copied the complete description of Kodiak when Dave received his orders (to Alaska) in Pensacola.

(Kodiak, located on St. Paul Harbor near the northeast corner of Kodiak Island—"The Sunshine Isle of the North Pacific"—was the "oldest town and newest city" in Alaska. The summer climate was mild with temperatures often reaching eighty degrees. Winter temperatures seldom dropped below zero; the average winter temperatures were between thirty and forty degrees. Annual precipitation was about sixty inches.

(The town of Kodiak was founded in 1791 by Aleksandr Baranov, a Russian trader and colonist. During the next decade, Kodiak was the training center and capital of the Russian Empire in the North Pacific. After 1800, when Baranov shifted Russian headquarters to Sitka on the mainland, Kodiak was little more than a fishing village.

(During World War II, a Naval Base was constructed on Women's Bay which had been the site of a cattle ranch. Kodiak became a boom town of construction workers and military personnel and was still in the boom stage after a brief lull following the close of the war.)

On a hill in the residential area overlooking Kodiak was an attractive, newly constructed church. It, too, was white frame as were the majority of church buildings both in town and on the Base. "And which church is that?" I asked. "You'll never guess," responded Dave. "It must be the Baptist Church!" And he nodded in mock amazement.

Kodiak had four churches: Roman Catholic, Russian Greek Orthodox, Community Baptist and Church of God. The Naval Chapel was non-denominational; Jewish, Catholic and Protestant Chaplains conducted services.

On the waterfront road below us was the Kodiak Electric Association and the cold storage plant; the latter, Dave told me, was owned by our landlord, Mr. MacDonald. Dave slowed the car. He pointed to a long, flat building the ground floor of which was built below the level of Mission Road. "That's Sear's Construction Company. He owns everything in town. See that sign!" I saw a dirty, cardboard sign in the window which looked as if it had been there for years. It bore two words: "No Vacancy."

Whenever Dave slowed down for a passing car or to make an abrupt turn, I pointed to the nearest "house." "Is *that* it?" When he shook his head, I would ask: "Does it *look* like that?" When he said, "No," I felt great relief. The only houses I had seen were painfully untidy and ramshackle. There were skid shacks; some were being lived in, others were just burned shells. There were rotting houses which leaned menacingly over the road like old barns. One wooden house, clinging precariously to a hillside, hung a third of the way over the road six feet below. Someone apparently had tried to move it but had a change of mind—literally, in midair. Tauntingly, it appeared to be one of Kodiak's better houses. Although Dave had sent an explicit description and drawing of our "log cabin on the beach," I was becoming more and more wary as we drove farther down Mission Road.

Dave finally turned from Mission Road and eased the car down a steep glade which leveled off into a muddy rut. A small store with a large sign proclaiming: "Fosters" was at the end of the narrow, grooved lane. Dave drove straight towards "Fosters," turned sharply in front of the store and we bumped into the woods. As Dave twisted the car through the spruce trees—it was the roughest landing we'd had—I looked about. To the right of our slow progress was a skid shack patched with tar paper and odd boards. To the left was a house partly concealed by the wreck of a float plane. Oil barrels overflowed the yard with household debris. I looked, hopefully, the other way. There, neath the splendid evergreens, reposed—an old truck. Its wheels and engine were gone, the doors hung open and the windows were broken. I clutched Dave's sleeve. "Dave, where are you taking us?" "You'll see," was his unconsoling reply. He stopped the car deep in the woods; I could see nothing—but trees. "Let's get out," he prompted, "we're here!" I lifted Bruce out of the car and followed Dave and Lori down the hill. All I could see was an oval of water through an aperture in the opaque grove. Then I stopped and pointed in horror: "Dave, is *that* it?" To the right of the path was a small, crumbling building. The door, which stood open, was several feet from the ground. There were no steps. I could see two windows both of which were covered with cardboard. Dave, too, had stopped. When I turned beseechingly, he just laughed and waved for us to come on. I went. I thought nothing could be as uninhabitable as that.

And then I saw it! "Oh, Dave, is that it?" I thought I had never seen anything more beautiful. A log cabin overlooked the water from a slope of mature conifers.

I saw the back of the cabin first, its slanting green roof just a few feet above the level of the hill. A broad stone chimney extended high above the roof. Our log cottage was set into a terrace, green with moss and fern, prolific with wild flowers beneath the spruce trees. All about us were luxuriantly leaved shrubs bearing delicate pink blooms. Dave told me they were salmonberry bushes.

Figure 24. Our Path to the Gulf of Alaska

He pointed out high and low-bush cranberries, blueberry bushes, and in the garden—rhubarb and strawberries!

A brief stone path led around to the front of the cabin, the facade of which was almost entirely of glass. Peering inside, I saw hardwood floors, a modern sink-cabinet, an oil stove and a huge fireplace. We *found* Shangrilog! Lori's alert two-year-old speech had contracted Shangrila Lodge, the original name of the cabin, to more apt "Shangrilog."

The view was magnificent! Several hundred feet from the

Figure 25. "Shangrilog"

door of "Shangrilog" was the Gulf of Alaska. Beyond, was an amphitheater of islands with cliffs obscured by an untouched wealth of spruce trees.

The darkness of the spruce islands made a stage for snow-touched mountains, fanciful clouds, the brilliant summer sun. The islands, less than a mile's distance across the water, made a perfect half arc with the cabin, the center. Dave identified the islands for us. Woody Island at the extreme left was the only island which was populated. A radio station was maintained there for the direction of air traffic to and from the Naval Station. Bird Island was off center to the left. I observed that first evening, and each subsequent evening, how apropos "Bird" was for the island. At dusk, the gregarious "seagulls" gathered on the island giving its rocky beach the appearance of restless white sand. Directly across from us was Holliday Island, remarkable for the celestial symmetry of its piney forest. Crooked Island was distinguished merely because it was crooked. Near Island, at our extreme right, completed the half circle; at the mouth of St. Paul Harbor, its channel light and bell were to be my sole comfort and proximity to civilization, on many nights when Dave was away.

The cabin was completely constructed of peeled spruce logs both outside and inside. As our landlord, Mr. MacDonald, explained the night after we arrived, the cabin was begun in the winter and the pale logs which formed the walls almost to the ceiling were winter logs. The double row of dark brown logs just below the ceiling as well as the ceiling beams were summer logs, the cabin's having been completed in the summer. Both the winter and summer logs had been peeled then scraped irregularly to leave streaks of tan and brown against the lightness of the denuded wood. The contrast was bucolic and attractive.

Dave opened the door of Shangrilog. We went expectantly inside—and shivered. I put Bruce on a chair and wrapped my coat around him. Then Lori and I attempted to lay a fire while Dave lighted the oil stove. I looked around at our living room-dining room-breakfast room-kitchen. In the center of the room was a card table with four chairs which Dave said he borrowed from one of his friends. That was to serve as our dining table for three months. A large cardboard box contained blankets, cooking utensils, dishes and silverware. Those Dave had secured from the Welfare Department on the Base, a function of which was to aid families until the arrival of their household gear. Another box contained groceries. In it were several quarts of milk frozen in paper cartons, fresh airborne eggs, fresh tomatoes, oranges, plums, grapes, lettuce, apples, carrots and avocados. I had been told by friends in Pensacola who had just returned from a tour in Kodiak: "You'll do well to get a dried-up cabbage." So I was overwhelmed by the bounty.

Beneath the staircase was the powder room. For a log cabin, it was luxurious. Dignified by a white door splashed with red geranium decalcomanias, it had aqua walls, two shelves and a mirror.

I asked Dave what was upstairs. "Not much," he admitted, "why don't you go and look." Lori and I went up the stairs. They were very steep and painted a dark, burgundy red. There was a curtained closet at the head of the stairs beneath the eaves. A large hot-water tank was at the side of the door leading to the bedroom. The bedroom was of average size. Furniture space was lessened, however, by a shower cabinet, lavatory and the pipe from the stove which was boxed off with plywood. At the far end of the room was another curtained closet.

Our bedroom was temporarily supplied with a Welfare crib for Bruce, a rollaway bed borrowed for Lori and, in the middle of the room, that promised, permanent set of box springs! When Mr. MacDonald completed the bedroom—attractive with plywood walls of aqua and woodwork of gray—he had, indeed, built the room around the box springs. The door was too shallow and the windows too narrow for the box springs to be removed. (When our furniture arrived, we effected the agreed-upon trade. I wondered if he was bedless when his cabin was vacant.)

Several days after our arrival, Mr. MacDonald brought us a platform rocker. For the next three months, we took turns sitting in it. Having noted my difficulties with Bruce, ambulating at ten months, Mr. MacDonald also brought a playpen. It was not *exactly* a playpen but it served the purpose. "This is a halibut box," Mr. MacDonald explained, pointing to a long, high box. "Some frozen halibut came in it but I thought it would be better than nothing." It was. And for the next three months Bruce smelled more like a fish than a baby!

Our rent was $120 a month for the two-room, unfurnished log cabin. The oil stove, with its door propped up by a piece of wood braced against the sink-cabinet, heated the two rooms and also served for cooking purposes. There was neither a refrigerator nor window box in the cabin.

We learned that it was Mr. MacDonald's intention to sell us a refrigerator—and a washing machine—and a deep freeze. He was not only in the real estate and cold storage business, he also sold refrigerators, washing machines, radios and other electrical appliances.

Even though refrigerators were difficult to obtain in Kodiak, Dave, happy to pay high rent to have his family, adamantly refused to buy anything from Mr. MacDonald. After a few days of dashing out into the summer rain to retrieve soaking sacks of fruit, meat and vegetables, eggs and butter which we had cached under the leaky eaves, we began to search in town for a refrigerator. At Knudsen's, where you could buy a chocolate soda or a nickelodeon, we found—actually—a small 7 cu. foot Admiral refrigerator hidden behind stacks of corrugated boxes. It was a lucky find for our small "kitchen."

In addition to the rent, we had a few utility bills to pay. Oil for the stove averaged $25 a month; electricity, $15 a month and the telephone bill, when we were privileged to pay it, $7.50 a month. Our expenses for each month that we lived in the atmospheric log cabin were $160. From March 1952 (the telephone month), until we moved aboard the Base in June 1952, our expenses were $167.25 a month.

Our water had but one virtue. In a town of exorbitant prices, it cost us nothing—and it was worth nothing. Our water was drawn by an electric motor from a "well" a considerable distance behind the cabin. The "well" proved to be a shallow pool of dingy water which had in it a collection of spruce needles, spruce cones, salmonberry leaves, sticks and tin cans. It provided a convenient watering and wading place for dogs and little boys. We found the source of our well water by following a path of rust-colored rocks into the woods where we discovered a tiny stream. Mr. MacDonald had assured us of the safeness of our water because it continually ran in and out of the well. "Ran," we thought an overstatement; it did not even trickle, it seeped! The brilliant burnt orange color of the water, he explained by the presence of volcanic ash. "But it's nothing to worry about," comforted Mr. MacDonald who was ill two-thirds of the time, "*we* drank it for four years. All you have to do is toss a cup of Clorox in it every now and then."

Drinkable water was our greatest concern the entire time we were at Shangrilog. Weil's disease, which was an Asiatic disease affecting one much like yellow jaundice—also prevalent in the area—was attributed to diseased rats and contaminated water, both of which we had. The cases of Weil's disease grew to epidemic proportions. It could not be controlled due to inadequate sanitation standards and the inexplicable apathy of the residents of Kodiak, particularly the owners of rental property.

Three wives of Coast Guard officers who lived near us in the woods, on the other side of Foster's, were hospitalized with Weil's disease for a month on the Base, then sent to the States for three-to-six-months' recuperation.

Because of the prevalence of Weil's disease, we used our well water with caution and restraint. Reluctantly, we used it to wash dishes, to wash clothes, for the shower and to boil eggs. Dave, in a vain effort to purify the water, put chlorine bleach so frequently in the well and I used such strong detergents that the skin on my hands split and opened in cracks until it bled. I resorted to rubber gloves; each pair lasted almost two weeks. Dave lessened the bleach content and then our well water was even more ruinous on hair, skin, clothing—and disposition.

After three or four washings, wool socks and sweaters rotted in holes and tears. Bristles fell out of hair brushes, tooth brushes and bottle brushes. In the rusty water, the children's white clothing became unsightly. I would have minded less if it had become a flaming orange which, at least, was positive. Instead, the children's once-white garments turned an insipid shade of pale toast. It was a constant surprise to me that the children emerged from their baths (in the sink) with their skin, not the hue of an Indian, but in a fair state.

In desperation, Dave carried all of our drinking water from the Base in a galvanized five-gallon can with a tight lid (a new garbage pail) which we used for every purpose from brushing our teeth to watering the sweet potato plant.

None of us minded the lack of furniture during those busy, summer days. I, particularly, was uncomplaining—housekeeping had never been so simple! Ours was a perpetual picnic both inside—and outside.

We had a favorite flat stretch in the spruce forest a short drive from Shangrilog; an easy walk along an old logger's road to a quaking aspen

Figure 26. Picnicking

Figure 27. **Studying Abandoned
Dwelling**

Figure 28. **Searching for Gold**

under which Dave placed Bruce in an orange crate as I removed our few essentials for cooking. Fascinated by the chiaroscuro of aspen-leaf shadows dappling the sunny ground, Bruce was content with scientific observation if Lori brought rocks to study from the shallow, limpid stream and leaf planes to fly into the breeze—and I cooked quickly enough. Our spot had all requisites of affordable dining: the cold rivulet to chill our cokes in, a broken beaver dam with lodged twigs, sticks and branches of fire-building dryness, loose soil and pebbles for quenching of coals—and prandial entertainment by Nature before, during and after. We reserved the quaking aspen and merry brook for week-end noontimes.

Bright evening hours were spent discovering the mysteries of the woods behind our cabin and the beach in front of it. We scoured the moss-floored spruce woods for red salmonberries and found yellow violets hidden beneath the low bushes. I made jelly out of the salmonberries which were almost purple when fully ripe. It was a beautiful ruby red to look at, tart and delicious to taste. Above the beach in the tall, lush grasses, Lori and Bruce picked tremendous dandelions, oversized white and red clover blossoms. They found perfume flowers, shooting stars and buttercups. On the beach which abounded with barnacles, seaweed, swarms of black gnats and mosquitoes; we found pools of minuscule Irish Lords, butter clams in the sand and myriads of pulsating insects beneath each rock. Dave pulled starfish out of the water to show to the children. We saw an occasional porpoise, the ever-present "seagulls," a few ducks and our first raven. The latter winging overhead made a sound as nerve-jangling as a saw on steel.

We watched the continual, varied activity on the water. Through-out the day until late evening (in mid-summer we read without artificial light until 11:00 P.M.), we watched the boats as they passed into view. We noted all types of watercraft: canoes, native skiffs, row boats, outboard motor boats, fishing vessels, Navy patrol boats, floating canneries, Alaska Steamship Company's freight and passenger ships, the Admiral's launch and Alf Madsen's luxurious hunting yacht, the *Kodiak Bear.*

We watched all of those and recorded such names as: *Ketovia, Blackfish, Ketchikan Duchess, Seamount, Juno* (from Juneau), *Janguar, Wawona, Widgion, Barracuda, Blue Pacific, Yaquina, Eskimo, Cape Uyak, Totem, Porpoise, Denali, Attu, Whale, Popeye III, Yarsh, Black Prince, Kaguyak, Afognak, Sea Lion, Aleutian, Menshikof, Marmot,* and the inevitable *Bonnie Mae and Santa Maria.* With the aid of Dave's binoculars, we recorded the names of several hundred boats which regularly passed our cabin during the summer months.

The children's favorite boat was the *Sunrise* which belonged to the Kodiak Cannery fleet on the other side of the island. It was painted a shocking fire-engine red!

I was intrigued with an antiquated halibut boat, the *Pioneer*, which announced its coming far in advance of its arrival with a distinct and pitiful spluttering. I was particularly aware of its passing in the early morning hours between 3:00 and 4:00 A.M. when, due to its antiquity or the captain's eagerness for halibut, it chugged out to sea in the day's first sunrays. In contrast to the sleek, fishing boats announced only by a swish of water against their hulls, the *Pioneer* sounded mechanically uncertain. But it was still able, in its fashion. It reminded me of a grandmother who tediously beat egg whites with a fork rather than acknowledge the modern way.

For one of the fishing boats, I felt kinship. It was not surprising why—it was named the "Dorothy." The *Dorothy* was, without doubt, the dingiest craft on the water. It was not only old, but what pained me more, it was unkempt. One beautiful, sunlit Saturday as I was prosaically engaged in scrubbing the floor, Dave watched the *Dorothy* pass and mused audibly: "Why, there goes *Dorothy*!" I gasped—then ruffled and speechless—I hurried to the powder room. Plying lipstick and powder with injured haste, I vowed that one Dorothy, at least, should have a bright face!

We could set our clocks by the Woody Island boat which passed each day at 8:10 A.M., 12:10 P.M. and 4:10 P.M. on the short trip across the bay to Woody Island. In fifteen minutes, it passed into view again on the way back to the D & A (Donnelley and Acheson Department Store) dock. It made the three trips in all weather. Frequently, it was the only boat on the water the entire day. We always hurried to the window to see it. The children learned to recognize the American flag by watching the Woody Island boat pass our Shangrilog.

With a landing strip for seaplanes and float planes in view of our windows, we were able to watch Alaska's famed bush pilots in action. Bush pilots were indispensable to Alaska. Not only did they afford sight-seers panoramic views of Alaska, they carried mail, food and clothing to remote islands and isolated native villages. They were revered for their mercy missions, particularly in areas where the Navy-Coast Guard Search and Rescue Service was not available. In the case of childbirth, sudden illness, exposure and distress at sea; Alaskan weather was never too miserable for bush pilots to respond.

That summer of 1951 we experienced, with epicurean savor, the seafood of the cold Alaskan waters. Fresh fish was far more delectable than frozen fish but we discovered the most delicious of all was smoked fish, especially smoked salmon. Halibut, which made its appearance before any of the salmon runs started, was a treat to us. To our knowledge, it was the first time we had eaten fresh, Kodiak halibut. We relished it baked and pan-broiled but preferred it filleted, cut in one-inch squares, dipped in a batter of flour, milk, baking powder and salt and fried crisply in deep fat. We ate Dolly Varden trout, rainbow trout, grayling, whiting, humpback salmon, sockeye salmon (red salmon, Alaska's choicest) and silver salmon which was the last salmon to run.

We ate so much fresh salmon that we became tired of it before the season was over. We ate it baked, broiled, fried, creamed, in salads, souffles and mousses. But we never tired of smoked salmon. There were several ways to smoke salmon, none of which we tried—we bought ours at the cannery. LT Bob Matmiller, who lived in the Belle Flats housing area on the Base, built a small shed and smoked thirty or forty salmon at a time burning alder boughs in an oil drum, continually, for seven days. Housewives smoked a few salmon together, by bathing them in liquid smoke and putting them in the oven overnight with the heat as low as possible and the oven door, wide open. One ingenious man smoked his salmon on the living room floor beneath five electric fans, repeatedly applying liquid smoke for five days. Smoked salmon provided our favorite canapé and hors d'oeuvre in Kodiak. As a canapé, we simply served a long flake of it on a saltine. For an hors d'oeuvre, we wrapped a sliver of smoked salmon around a piece of gherkin spread with cream cheese and pierced it with a toothpick.

In addition to the fresh and smoked fish, we consumed several bucketfuls of butter clams, in New England clam chowder, and ate a few dungeness and tanner crabs in salads. But, to us, the most delicious of the Alaskan shellfish was the king crab. Its meat was less stringy than the dungeness having somewhat the texture of lobster meat. A tremendous crab, the largest ever caught (by the fishing boat *Juno*—not far from Kodiak Island) weighed twenty-five pounds and three-quarter ounces. One average-sized crab, ten to thirteen pounds, lasted us the entire week. The first night, we would eat in our fingers, the large chunks of meat, shaken from the legs, which we dipped in butter. The next two nights, we relished deviled crab stuffed in the crab shell which was purple when the crab was alive, brilliant red after it was boiled. The shell would easily hold two quarts of crabmeat. The fourth and fifth nights, we enjoyed crab à la Mornay which was flaked crabmeat baked in a rich cheese sauce.

Figure 29. Crab on the Rocks—Igneous

A salad usually followed which we liked with diced avocado and a Russian dressing. The last bit of the king crab was used in crab à la King.

It was our wont, during those first months in Kodiak, to look for beaver in the beaver ponds which were numerous in the Cliff Point, Chiniak and Pasagshak areas.

Figure 30. Beaver Construction

It was an excitement to the children, as well as to us, to see the beaver's streak in his private pool as he swam with only his nose protruding. Lori had her picture captured atop a large beaver dam and as she pointed to a tree which the beavers had gnawed to the toppling

Figure 31. Unfinished Job

stage. She was not appreciative at the time, questioning the pointing, but we felt compelled to make the record—for her future geography classes!

We sighted sea lions from the cliff at Fort Abercrombie. At Cape Chiniak, we watched the white-hooded and white-tailed bald eagles in their curious, limp-winged flight. It was sporting, and lucrative, to shoot the eagles. A pair of feet sent to Juneau was rewarded with a bounty of two dollars!

The picking of wild flowers consumed many happy summer hours. Cliff Point proved most prolific in the varieties of Alaskan wild flowers. We found brown-eyed Susans, black lilies, fireweed, shooting stars, monkey-flowers, wild celery, lupine, and roses, wild sweet peas, wild geraniums, cat-tails and pastel fleabanes, wild iris, buttercups, blue forget-me-nots (the forget-me-not was the

Figure 32. In the Cotton Patch

official flower of the Territory), Alaskan cotton, cinquefoils, clovers, yellow violets, marsh marigold, arrowheads, perfume flowers, paint brushes, and many others we were unable to identify.

The wild flower we particularly liked was one of a deep, bluish-purple color. It looked like a garish, overgrown lily-of-the-valley. We called it the "tinkle bell" for the inelegant reason that we would never have found it if Lori had not asked to stop so she could "tinkle" at a distance from the lonely roadside. We discovered that it was a bellflower but we always referred to it as "Lori's tinkle bell."

The most abundant flowering plant was the wild celery which bloomed in profusion throughout the spring month of June. It was known also as the poison weed or blister weed because the juice from its thick stalk could seriously blister and burn the skin. It grew to a height of four or five feet and spotted the mountain and hillsides with its course, white blooms. Except for its broad, deeply notched leaf, it could have been mistaken for wild carrot or Queen-Anne's-lace.

The last week of July, the fireweed flowered. It sent its rose-pink blooms up a tall, narrow-leaved stalk until mid-September. As the lowest blossoms dropped from the stalk, long red fingers pointed to tight green buds at the pinnacle. Winter was heralded when the last buds had opened, bloomed and dropped in the wake of the prodding red fingers.

There were no snakes in Alaska! Salmonberry gathering, wild-flower picking, meanderings along the wooded ocean cliffs and other outdoor excursions were, therefore, delightfully carefree. But, on the other hand, it seemed that Kodiak boasted at least sixteen varieties of mosquitoes! They swarmed about our cabin in the woods in unbelievable quantity. In order to get the children comfortably to the car, we bathed their arms, legs, necks and faces with "6-12" mosquito repellent. And then we swept a path with flailing arms so that only a minimum would fly into the children's faces. Mr. MacDonald was comforting. "These are the worst mosquitoes I've ever seen. They won't be this bad next year." Next year, we were confident that a few of us would be gone!

Kodiak's houses afforded little protection against mosquitoes. Most of the houses had no screens on the windows and doors. Our cabin, of course, had no screens. In fact, only two windows could be opened. There were two windows upstairs which could be opened, partially, from the top. We had the choice of being victimized by the mosquitoes or the heat. Strangely, we were unable to purchase in town either mosquito-netting or screens. We compromised with cheesecloth which Dave folded several times, stretched on wooden frames and nailed over the upstairs windows. From then on, we had no mosquitoes—and very little air.

One moonlit night in early July, Dave brought Lori downstairs to see the moon. She looked through the front door over the light-streaked water and exclaimed ecstatically: "Daddy, we have the moon in our yard!" It seemed that we did. The moon, low and pale behind a rosy-blue haze of the late sunset, sped a sparkling path to our front door for the fairies to dance upon. It was an entrancing sight. Later, after Bruce had been brought down to see the moon and then both children had been tucked again in bed, we took kodachrome pictures from our darkened house. In a very short time, the moon reeled in its shimmering ribbon of elfin yellow and dipped behind the mountains, and the sky and the water were dark.

On another night in July, shortly after 2:00 A.M., we were awakened by a frightful pounding on the door. Terrified, sensing that no living being but a bear would venture into the woods at night, I leapt from the box springs. Stumbling down the room to turn on the light at the head of the stairs, I groped for the chain, pulled it and found myself in the closet—at the opposite end of the room. Dave was up and halfway down the stairs before I could disengage myself from the closet curtains. "Come back!" I screeched. "Dave, come back. It might be a bear!" He laughed, a little shakily, I thought, and went on down the stairs. The pounding continued—and then, as I sank back on the box springs, weak-kneed—I heard a man's voice: "Dave, it's Max. We've got a SAR! Get out there as soon as you can."

Thus I was initiated into SAR (Search and Rescue) summons in the middle of the night. From then on, I ceased to be frightened—more than a little, when we were unceremoniously awakened in the dark hours of the night.

On the last day of July, Dave flew to Point Barrow (that was his fourth trip) in a PBY to take part in a Naval expedition at the"Top of the World."

He was scheduled to leave for Point Barrow at 7:00 A.M. on Sunday morning. Shortly before 3:00 A.M., we were awakened by an accustomed pounding on the front door. Dave flung on his robe and hurried down the stairs mumbling: "It's a SAR." It was, of course. A woman in Cold Bay, on the Alaskan peninsula, had acute appendicitis and needed emergency aid. Dave was to leave immediately. The hop to Cold Bay, then on to Anchorage where the woman would be treated and back to Kodiak took eight hours. When he returned at 1:00 P.M., the children and I met his plane and drove home to the cabin for a quick lunch. Dave, the other pilot and crew had decided to fly on to Point Barrow that afternoon. They could at least get as far as Nome.

At 3:00 P.M., the yellow-tailed PBY lifted from the end of the runway and left Kodiak. The children and I watched until it was a dark spot in the cloudless sky and then it was gone. With its disappearance, we were lonely, and the drive back to town on the beautiful Sunday afternoon was a solemn one. Everybody was out in the sunshine. We were driving back to our cabin in the still woods and Dave was flying to what seemed like the end of the world.

The next morning, distress presented itself. There were many makeshift appliances in our cabin of which the commode was the most impossible and unworkable. In lieu of the magic handle, a doubled string, stiff and rust-colored, dangled beneath the lid of the cabinet. That morning, as I pulled the string that lifted the valve which was to flood the cabinet with water, the string pulled off in my hand. There was not even a trickle of water in the cabinet—just a threat of it in my eyes. After minutes of frustration, I remembered and tried to imitate Dave's repeated demonstrations. I lifted the cabinet lid with my left hand, pushed the bulb down with my right, seated the plunger in its hole, then switched the weight of the lid to my right hand and groped to find the valve upon which the string had been tied. By the time both of my arms were orange up to the elbows, I discovered the valve. I pulled up on the valve with two fingers of my left hand reinforced by my right hand on my left wrist. That was both painful and futile. I was more enraged than discouraged and vowed, strongly, to fix it. From the conglomeration of the we-might-need-it-sometime drawer (in the sink cabinet), I snatched a small piece of string and leapt back to the powder room before the balancing lid could crash to the floor. I pushed the short string under the arm of the bulb and around the only groove I could feel in the valve. Then I tied my best Camp Fire Girl knot. Squeezing my eyes tightly shut and hoping fervently that when I pulled up on the string the valve would come up, I pulled. And the valve came up! And after I "hit the pump," Dave's in-shower plea, the water rushed in! At last, I felt that I was conquering Alaska.

On August 4, the first Saturday after Dave left, we awakened to a cold house. Imagine being cold on August 4! The kerosene stove had been on all night but the wind had found each cracked log and had boomed into our empty house. The rain, too, had found entrance but there being nothing to get wet but a floor which needed it, I turned my concern to the lack of warmth.

I looked skeptically at the fireplace wondering if my tender pieces of kindling would afford as much comfort as cheer. The rain had soaked the logs piled against the house but there were a few twigs left in the fireplace from our indoor picnic of the day before. With the twigs and the kindling, I laid a fire I was glad Dave could not see. Lori cautioned me not to burn her marshmallow sticks. They were among the odd burnable objects in the wood box which I was tossing indiscriminately into the fireplace. The fire blazed up almost too soon. It was comforting even though tears prevented visual appreciation. For some reason, the fire smoked; in fact, it rolled out enough smoke to signal all the Indians in Alaska!

We huddled at the opposite end of the room where there was neither smoke nor warmth and, on that day, I was happy to admit defeat. I doused the fire, put sweaters on the children and worked feverishly to cook our delayed breakfast. By the time the smoke had cleared, we were warm, satiated and I, convinced of one thing: the man should be the master of the house—at least the plumber and the fire-builder.

Dave returned from Point Barrow the middle of August. He was laden with trophies. From Point Barrow, he brought Eskimo dolls, more "odiferous" than artful; mukluks of the same caliber; a walrus tusk; long-haired strainers, black, from a whalebone whale's mouth— which had strained out plankton, plus small shrimp for the toothless whale's simple nourishment; and three beautiful, black boats of gradated size fashioned exclusively of black whalebone, known as baleen, by talented

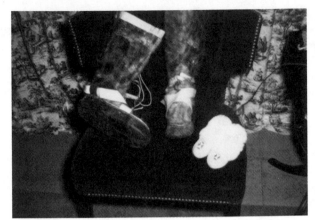

Figure 33. Caribou Mukluks and Rabbit Moccasins

Eskimo artists. At Nome (where bananas were seventy-five cents a pound), Dave acquired eighteen gold nuggets and four pounds of reindeer steak. The latter, I looked upon with unrestrained approval.

I listened, enravished, to Dave's talk about Point Barrow, the "Land of the Midnight Sun," where one hundred and twenty flowering plants were found on the Arctic tundra by botanists attending the Arctic Research Laboratory and the migration of songbirds was studied by visiting ornithologists. I would not have believed that Point Barrow had either flowers *or* songbirds. I was further astonished to learn that Point Barrow, at the top of the world, was less cold than Fairbanks in central Alaska. Fairbanks had recorded sixty-six degrees below zero; Point Barrow, only forty degrees below zero. I asked Dave if any of the Eskimos could speak English. Dave said: "Of course. The postmaster is married to an Eskimo woman who's a college graduate!" Flossie, the Eskimo with a degree, taught school in the village of Barrow (distinguished from Point Barrow which was solely a Navy installation) which all the Eskimo children attended to learn English, reading, writing and arithmetic. When Dave returned home after his last trip to Point Barrow, in August 1952, he told me that the village of Barrow was building a new school. "And it's already a room too small!" he added. "There are five to twelve children in the average Eskimo family. By the way, 'Eskimo' is Danish; they call themselves *inuit*."

Dave took many kodachrome pictures of the Eskimos. Those of particular interest depicted the Eskimos' diet. One picture showed ducks "ripening" on racks out-of-doors. According to Dave: "The Eskimos let the ducks ripen for about a month, then when they're ready to eat them, they pull off the skin and feathers and toss the ducks in a pot just—to warm." I was appalled! "You mean, they don't even clean them?" "Of course not," Dave raised his eyebrows at my igno-

Figure 34. "Top of the World" from a PBY, Pt. Barrow Quonsets

rance. "To the Eskimos, entrails are a delicacy." Beneath the ducks on the rack were a dozen or more small stakes arranged in an oval on the ground. I asked Dave what they were. He explained that a sealskin was being stretched on the ground between the stakes. To the left of the sealskin was a dark object which looked like a large football. That, Dave told me, was the body of a small seal; the Eskimos would probably store it in an ice cellar after it had matured.

Another picture showed six or seven walrus heads on the ground, their long tusks still intact. "When they find an evenly matched pair, they leave the tusks connected to the skull and sell them. See these dark things in the oil drums?" Dave continued. "They're hunks of walrus meat. They let them weather until they're completely black and as tough as leather. The Eskimos got a lot of walrus this summer because the ice was close to shore. Much of the time, it was just five miles out." (Walrus were killed, with guns, on the ice floe.) At the upper right corner of the picture was a road lined with oil drums. I, of course, wondered why they were there. "That's to outline the road when it's covered with snow," Dave explained.

"The Eskimos never throw away an oil drum. They have thousands of them which they use for every conceivable purpose."

A littered area of small tents which Dave said was the Eskimos' summer camp was pictured in another slide. "They leave their winter houses and live in tents in the summertime. They say they get too hot in their winter houses even though summer temperatures average only about forty-five." (The Eskimos' winter homes, for the most part, were sturdy, conventional, twin-story houses of wood painted a dark green or brown, or a green with white. "They look very much like Stateside houses," Dave elaborated.)

Figure 35. Eskimo Summer Camp

I noted from the slides that the Eskimo women wore cotton parkas with fur-lined hoods. Those summer parkas, Dave told me, were made from Sears' finest cotton prints. "Every Eskimo family has the latest Sears' catalogue. They had so many they didn't need that the post office was lined with them." The women's parkas were apparently all made from the same pattern. They were long, worn below the knees, hanging lower in back than in front. Each parka had a deep flounce at the bottom.

Figure 36. Barrow Winter Homes

The only dissimilarity was in the material. Some of the parkas were plaid, others striped or floral but all were bright red, green, purple and blue.

Most of the Eskimos, both men and women, were wearing mukluks even though the younger men were dressed exclusively in Sears' slacks, jackets and caps.

The most interesting thing Dave saw, and took pictures of—on his trip to Point Barrow was the excavation of a sod house conducted by Dr. Clark, an archaeologist from Cornell. Dr. Clark estimated the sod house to be one thousand years old! In it, he found a whale skeleton, various hunting and fishing implements and

Figure 37. One-Thousand-Year-Old Sod House

a section filled with layers of meat which had been preserved in a frozen state for a thousand years, a dish of left-over meat tucked in—between layers.

A short distance from Point Barrow was a memorial to Will Rogers and Wiley Post who were killed in Wiley Post's light plane on a lagoon fifteen miles south of Point Barrow, August 15, 1935.

Dave returned from Point Barrow just in time to witness Kodiak's most important event since Lord Baranov's advent: A Rodeo! A Wild West show, prominently billed as the first rodeo ever held in the Alaskan Territory, was presented at Kodiak to launch the cancer-fund crusade. It drew a crowd of six hundred and ninety-three! Cattlemen and farmers flew to Kodiak from the Matanuska Valley on the mainland. Many spectators came from Anchorage and even from Fairbanks to witness the un-Alaskan spectacle. The cowboys were heralded as authentic although an Alaskan cowboy was difficult to envision, there being few cows in Alaska and fewer horses. The rodeo events were typically rigorous and colorful: saddle-bronc riding, wild-cow riding, calf roping and a quarter-mile race. Cowgirls also participated! I was amused by the names of the horses used in the bronc-riding event. Typical were: Yukon Mare, Fish and Wildlife, Rose of Kalsin Bay, Payday, Willawa (Williwaws were Alaskan winds), Flesh Red, Klondike Kate, Sam McGee, Mission Road Mauler, Gold

Stream, Dangerous Dan, Juvenile Delinquent, Kobuck Maiden, Injun Sign, Jack McCord and Hillbilly!

The last days of August, when the fireweed was still climbing its long stalk, we spent many evenings watching silver salmon spawn in the rocky, low, saltant streams. We watched in fascination as the salmon struggled in the clear water which in many places was too shallow to cover the fins on their backs. Striving to lay their eggs in rocky nests in the sand, they struggled to protect them. It

Figure 38. Fireweed's Last Ascent

was not an appealing sight for the exhausted salmon were bruised and torn by the rocks and their attackers until great streaks and holes of torn flesh mottled their gray skin with white. Frequently, a salmon would be pushed up the sharp bank by the spawning jam to die there and be devoured by the screaming "seagulls."

The glaucous gull, the cry of which sounded like a child's wail of pain, was incongruously beautiful in appearance with luxuriant white plumage. The largest of the gulls, the glaucous was indigenous to Alaska, breeding on Arctic coasts of the Bering Sea south to Bristol Bay islands and Kodiak Island on Shelikof Strait. Bird Island, opposite our cabin, was completely inundated by the "seagulls" which we closely observed on our beach each time we fed them and through Dave's powerful binoculars, on theirs—when they flocked for the evening and took wing in the morning. Often Dave summoned Lori and Bruce to watch aerial acrobats floating in the updrafts as the gulls performed between islands in effortless, spectacular glides. But at the salmon-spawning streams, the beauty and grace of the glaucous gulls was obliterated—and we turned away. Not content to claim as booty the salmon already dead, gulls attacked egg-layers in the roiling water, ceasing their frenetic pecking only long enough to emit horrendous screeches of triumph in unearned victory.

On our peaceful, ever-changing beach in the waning days of summer, the children were Dryads to their flora-and-fauna subjects, including the post salmon-run gulls and seemed to lack—nothing. One bright morning, three children ran hallooing down our fast path, jumping the walk ledge, to almost stumble over Bruce and Lori gathering pebbles to secure their shooting-star garden.

Startled by the sudden encounter, one newcomer recovered speech: "Can we play?" Lori, self-contained and garrulous, usually, looked at the trio appraisingly and remained—mute. Unseen, by a shaded boulder where I was piling driftwood, I called out: "Hello, children!" The threesome, two boys and a girl, all considerably older than my two, jumped, squealed and scrambled back up the path and out of sight. Lori looked disapprovingly in my direction. "I wanted to play!" she protested. "Then why didn't you say 'hello' and invite them to stay?" I inquired. "My mouth wouldn't talk," Lori explained. I laughed at her accuracy but she did not.

The night before, Dave and I had returned late from a formal dinner-dance at the O-Club. Knowing we would be away many hours, Dave had brought in a mature and trusted Yeoman from his office to stay with the children whom I had fed early and tucked in before Dave and the young sailor arrived. Lori and Bruce were aware that a baby sitter, new to them but personally selected by their Daddy, would keep watch in our absence; that it would be too late for a younger sitter to be away from home. "You'll probably be asleep before he comes," I told them. "His name is Yeoman Mike and he's big and strong—has a little brother and sister back home. He'll take good care of you." I added, after kissing them good night: "He'll be quiet and won't disturb you with the radio; he's studying for an exam."

And the Yeoman *was* quiet—and so were the children.

Upon our return, Mike gathered his books and notes, as Dave prepared to drive him back to the Base, and gave us his report: "They didn't make a sound! Once, at eleven, your daughter came down the stairs, looked me over thoroughly but didn't say a word. She went straight to the cabinet and took down a baby-food jar in each hand, looked me over again and walked back upstairs and went to bed." He laughed: "I don't know if she approved of me or disapproved but she let me know who was in control! And without a word!"

As Lori, Bruce and I walked up from the beach for lunch, I realized with a jolt that it was Lori's control and emotional maturity which my selfish enjoyment of our scenic isolation could exacerbate. I could insulate my children into veritable "babes in the woods"—socially, by their very adaptability and my own preference for privacy.

The next day, no baby sitter came down the path at one for my weekly trek to the Commissary and Ship's Service. Nor the next day, when I attended the Officer's Wives' Bridge Club and signed up for the Discussion Group and the children were welcomed into the Rose-Pink Nursery, not far from the Little Red Schoolhouse. When I left them, Bruce was remonstrating tearfully at the change of nap-time locale but Lori took him by the hand and led him to the blocks in a big box—almost halibut-size. Mrs. Storms whispered, as she pushed me gently, "Go, quickly." And I did.

Thus did summer end and "school" begin.

By the first of September, top blooms on the fireweeds were fugacious. Dry needles began to sift from the dark spruce branches and winter was being announced. The air was brisk and, frequently, we had a fire in the fireplace. I unpacked our winter coats and wrote Mother to have my fur coat sent from storage at Emery Bird's. But when the sun was bright and the "trees quiet," as Lori observed, a suit was still comfortable in the afternoons and early evenings.

Mr. MacDonald warned away our hopes of a mild fall: "You go to bed the last day of September and when you wake up, it's winter. There'll be ice on all the ponds." (It snowed October 5.)

By late September, there was but a paucity of green leaves on the cottonwood trees—Kodiak's other tree. Yellow leaves clung feebly, then twirled to the ground—to be watchfully accumulated by the children. The mountains mantled themselves in a patchwork of browning grasses and ever-green spruce clumps. Water was high in the salmon streams from excessive fall rains and the spawning salmon had disappeared, leaving the parasitic gulls forlorn on the banks. The red elderberries, the last vestige of summer vividness, topped stark brown branches which, short days ago, were rich with foliage. Nightfall was at six o'clock. The long Alaskan nights were soon to engulf us.

During the summer months and the days before the snow fell, we had collected driftwood on the beach for the fireplace. Dave sawed it in proper lengths and stacked it beneath a shelter he built against the lee side of the cabin. He sawed down dead spruce saplings in the proximity of the cabin and cut up a larger spruce tree which a williwaw had torn from the ground. It seemed to me that we had a tremendous amount of wood but Dave was not satisfied that it would last throughout the winter. Further, we had lately discovered that a driftwood fire, which was unmatched in beauty dancing in red, yellow, blue, green and purple, burned slowly with an insatiable need for kindling.

One afternoon in the fall, as we were driving along the road to Spruce Cape, "Bruce" Cape as Lori called it, we discovered that spruce trees—their limbs lush with green needles and spruce cones—had been felled all along the road. It seemed implausible that they would be widening the little-traveled road. I asked Dave why they were cutting down so many beautiful trees. He recalled that a telephone line was being run out to Spruce Cape. I looked sadly at the spruce trees. It seemed tragic to cut them when so many lay uprooted in the thinning groves. Their roots' insecure grasp in Kodiak's distressingly shallow soil had been insufficient against the impetus of the wind. Dave stopped the car briefly and I got out to pull clusters of the spruce's miniature cones from the boughs for the children and to examine moss-covered mounds on the topmost branches. Those mounds of green moss were called "bunny bears." Volcanic ash sifted thickly on the limbs of the spruce trees during the 1912 eruption of Mt. Katmai which was northwest of Kodiak Island on the mainland of Alaska. (Not far from Mt. Katmai was Aniakchak, the largest active volcano in the world.) The ash from Mt. Katmai's eruption not only sifted on the lofty forest, it covered the entire island of Kodiak to a height of four feet. The volcanic ash which was not blown from the spruce trees remained humped on the limbs to nurture a heavy growth of luxurious green moss shaped like a prone teddy bear or a resting rabbit.

Farther down the road we noted several teams of men plying their long saws. On our way back, they were still at work and Dave stopped to talk to them. As we drove on homeward, Dave said that one of the men promised to sell him a load of the smallest trees for the fireplace.

And in a few days the "Holland Sawmill" was established! The man to whom Dave had talked not only brought one load of trees, he brought two—of the most tremendous spruce trees they had felled. He was in the act of depositing a third load—in the only spot where Dave could back the car to get out of the woods—when Dave, coming home from work, apprehended him. After a horrified glimpse, Dave asserted that two loads would be enough. He asked the man how much the loads were but the accommodating gentleman shook his head, said: "Nothing," and thanked Dave! It appeared that his sole concern was where to put all those trees.

Dave borrowed an electric chain saw from the Base and sawed as many of the reasonably sized trees into back logs as he was able to unearth. When Dave had returned the saw, he shook his head, skeptically: "Mr. MacDonald will probably sue me. Why, there are enough spruce trees up there to build *another* Shangrilog!"

Our furniture finally arrived the first of October. How happy we were to see it being rolled and dragged down the hill. Everything was progressing nicely until the movers took the children's chifforobe upstairs. It got stuck on the third step between the ceiling beam and the side of the narrow stairs. They tried three times and three ways to get it up the stairs. It was impossible. I had visions of a bedroom in a living room and wondered why I had felt crowded with "just two rooms." Fortunately, our movers were resourceful! One suggested ripping out the pipe which was a drain for the lavatory and shower and substituted for a stair railing. Another volunteered that the bedroom furniture should be lifted through an upstairs bedroom window which was approximately twelve feet from the ground. The latter plan was adopted and a bedroom window on the northeast side of the house was selected. It was a wide window supported at the top of both sides by chains. The chains were easily removed and the window lifted from its frame. I held my breath as the first piece of furniture, the chifforobe, was lifted bodily by two men on the ground to another prone on the roof held by a fourth who leaned far out of the window frame.

I ran from upstairs to outside to help push and from outside up the stairs to help pull. Despite my efforts, they got the chifforobe through the window. I unloaded the cedar chest in the living room and the two ground men carried it around to the back of the house assuring me: "This will be a lot easier." Assuming they did not want my help, I hurried upstairs anyway—just to suggest. My suggestions must have been excellent because they got the cedar chest through without a bit of trouble! After a few more lifts and pulls, all of the bedroom furniture was upstairs and the window, back in place.

All of our furniture, clothing, china and glassware arrived in good condition except a French Provincial chest of drawers which did not even arrive. Dave and the Supply Officers searched frantically for it, traced it from its point of origin to Seattle and from Seattle to Kodiak and then gave it up as lost. After I concluded that I would never see it again, I realized that it was my favorite piece of furniture—the one I least wanted to lose.

To our happy surprise and relief, it was brought down the hill one day in late October. It had been delivered to someone else by mistake.

With all of our gear miraculously intact, we were comfortable and content at Shangrilog.

For months before our furniture arrived, in fact, as soon as I had inspected the cabin, I had made—and discarded—diagrams for the arrangement of our furniture. By the time it had been shoved and hauled into our cabin, I wondered why a hermitage required furnishings. We placed Deltox fiber rugs on the living room and bedroom floors which provided perfect sieves for the volcanic ash. The fifteen-foot picture window, which was divided in the middle by a heavy spruce beam, was brightened with plastic drapes of red and white provincial print which hung in five wide sheaths. The drapes could be pulled completely across the window to conceal the night and to retard the rain and to substitute as a windsock.

Opposite the picture window was the buffet, the dining-room extension table and the children's play corner which consisted of a toy chest the size of a steamer trunk, two chairs, table, a red wagon and a plastic pony. Our red velveteen occasional chair provided a note of inharmonious formality in the rusticity. The davenport and two end tables completed the room in a room. It was still home and we could learn to be civilized again.

Entrance into the kitchen was announced by the linoleum which covered the floor in front of the sink, around the stove, under the breakfast-room table, in front of the refrigerator and under the door into the powder room. A tall, wide cabinet which Dave fashioned of packing cases and painted mahogany brown separated the breakfast table, chairs, Bruce's highchair, the refrigerator and apartment washer from the dining-room area.

Our bedroom was even more cozily overfurnished than the downstairs room. The bedroom contained a complete double bed, dressing table and bench, cedar chest, the dilatory chest of drawers, youth bed, chifforobe, crib and the "T"-chair—plus the shower cabinet, boxed stove pipe and lavatory.

It would be a long time before I forgot the first night we enjoyed the luxury of our own furniture in the cabin. With a mattress on the box springs and legs beneath it, our bed was so high off the floor, I dreamed that I was sleeping in a box in a tree and could not get out or down. I awakened in a profuse perspiration suffering from claustrophobia and a fear of far ground!

There was benefit for the busy housewife-mother in a combined kitchen-living room. With a screech and a leap, I was usually able to thwart the children in their inventive, oft-destructive play. With a glance, I could apprehend their curling the bristles of a plastic broom in the fireplace or "helping with the groceries" by sampling every apple in the sack and looking for chickens in the eggs. We were as surprised as they that the eggs yielded no chickens—eggs had quite a bite in them by the time they arrived in Alaska!

We had maintained a running stretch for Lori and Bruce down the middle of each room. Upstairs, with good aim, they could run from the top of the stairs between the beds into a doorless closet. Downstairs, the children could run in a considerably wider swath between the davenport and dining-room table from the fireplace to the kitchen sink.

To illustrate the spaciousness of our furnished abode, we could accommodate two tables of bridge in our living room and one in the kitchen. Of course, no one could stand up until everyone voted to rise but we were pleased with the achievement.

The town of Kodiak was no less interesting than its natural environment. It was an inimitable town embodying more of the old than the new. A phlegmatic fishing village, its houses were casual to the extent of being disreputable. Without tracks, there was no wrong side to live on. It was peaceful, with no coveting of a neighbor's property.

Buildings which should have afforded but temporary occupancy were lived in permanently by a great part of Kodiak's residents. There were skid shacks, quonset huts, trailers, one and two-room cabins, cellars and partially patched, burned-out houses. (Kodiak had an alarming number of fires due to an almost exclusive use of oil stoves.) Rooming houses shielded a considerable number of the community's citizens. The largest of the rooming houses, a log-walled mansion built by the Russians in 1785, had been declared unfit for occupancy but was still occupied. The trim, two-story Kodiak Hotel provided room for fishermen and big-game hunters from the States, visiting politicians and any others who could afford it.

Everyone in Kodiak dabbled in real estate. You could rent a house or an apartment, in the unlikely event that one was available, from the garbage collector (one of Kodiak's more affluent members) to the city physician. Mr. MacDonald, for instance, rented his Shangrila Lodge, three apartments above his cold-storage plant and had just opened a trailer camp to accommodate eighty-five trailers. Next year, he "might build a few houses. I like to keep my money working for me," he, frequently, told us. (He did keep his money: he was two thousand dollars in arrears for back taxes which he paid immediately, in cash, when the city threatened to auction his property.) Our neighbor, who owned Foster's Grocery Store which his wife operated while he worked as a carpenter at the Base, was building houses on Mission Road in his "spare time."

Throughout Alaska, construction costs were two and a half times greater than in the States. Labor was comparably high. Consequently, everyone who could effectively wield a hammer did his own work. It was a strenuous schedule to work during the daytime to make enough money so that you might build an apartment or house during the week ends and evenings. If one completed a house or apartment in a year, they had accomplished a near-miracle. I vouched that Kodiak had more unfinished houses than any town its size in the world. Yet most of them were inhabited in makeshift fashion by desperate Navy families and Civil Service workers.

LT. Gene Silliman, a friend of ours from Pensacola days, who arrived in Kodiak the last of January 1952 (he inherited Shangrilog, June 1), began an immediate search for housing. After his first frustrating efforts, he had a comment to make: "There aren't even garages in Kodiak—someone is living in all of them!" But he laughed about it and continued his search.

It was a strange thing that the people who complained most about Alaska's inadequate housing were those individuals who did not live in Alaska. Those who did made the best of a less-than-ideal situation and looked upon being in Alaska as a lark, particularly if they were members of the Armed Forces, experiencing Alaska temporarily. Civilians, who made their homes in Kodiak, either improved their housing situation or became inured to it which in the end afforded the same peace.

The group which was conspicuously concerned with the deplorable housing in Alaska were quick-trip politicos. Observing that Alaska was adequately newsworthy as a defense area and future state, they championed the Territory vociferously and squaring their shoulders declared that they were going back to the States to make "recommendations." Thus "A-la-as-ka," a contraction of the Aleut name meaning "the great country," was intermittently rediscovered, valued and championed—and then forgotten.

Kodiak had an amazing number of taxi cabs for the size of its population. Such was explained by the fact that aviation was essential to

Kodiak's economy. Kodiak had no airport and incoming and outgoing airplane passengers had to commute to and from the Naval Base five miles from town.

The road from town to the Base was a treacherous one. It was a narrow, tortuous road of volcanic ash, hewn from a mountainside. An occasional guide post, a mound of rocks and, closer to the Base, a line of steel cable were precautions against a five-hundred-foot precipitance into the bay. During the snow-free months, there was the danger of cascading rock from the mountain face. In the winter, one was concerned with sliding ice and snow—and with just staying on the road.

Kodiakians put chains on their cars with the first snow and left them on throughout the winter regardless of weather conditions. Whether you were driving on snowy or clear roads, the roads were rutted and guttered to a comparable degree so that tires suffered little with chains on when the roads were temporarily free of snow.

There were two bus companies in Kodiak. The Kodiak Transit Company operated from town to the Naval Base. The Shopper was driven from the end of Mission Road to the edge of town. Fares on the Shopper, which took children to school, were ten cents for children, twenty-five cents for adults. It was owned and usually driven by a woman, Tenora Rockney, who had her finger in many community pies. Her son assisted, just with the driving.

Kodiak had one dime store, the Kodiak Variety Store, but it was short-lived. The city physician raised the rent and the dime store withdrew from the premises. The building later housed the Kodiak USO, the first USO to be established overseas since "the close of the war."

The City of Kodiak had a mayor, six councilmen, a city attorney, a chief of police, a deputy marshal and a fire chief. There was one physician and one dentist. There were enough dental demands for two dentists and too much work for one physician but not enough for two. There was one bank and one insurance company and a two-man telephone company notorious for its ineptness and inebriation. There was one hospital, the Griffin Memorial Hospital, which cared for the townspeople and all emergency cases brought by SAR planes from near and remote islands. The hospital was staffed with five Gray Nuns and Kodiak's sole physician.

What the town lacked in the way of services to its citizens, the Naval Base frequently supplied. Most civilian families seemed to have one member who worked on the Base; thus making the Base's facilities available to its dependents.

Dave had remarked, the first time we drove through Kodiak, a very joyous day in June 1951—that the town lacked one important facility: a laundromat. He claimed, then, that if we had enough money we could invest in a laundromat and make a quick fortune. We were soon to sense that in Alaska, due to high transportation costs, it took nearly a fortune to make a fortune.

We were surprised to learn that the dark-skinned, slant-eyed natives we saw in town were not Eskimos but Aleuts. The Aleuts, as the airline-limousine driver in Anchorage had told me, came from the islands in the Aleutian Chain which the Japanese infiltrated during the war. After the Japanese were repelled from the rocky, treeless Aleutian Islands, a great number of the Aleuts remained in Kodiak to make their livelihood by fishing. Others migrated to Anchorage, Fairbanks and smaller towns on the mainland. Aleuts had been described by John Driscoll in *War Discovers Alaska* as "sawed-off Indians with slant eyes." He wrote that they had an admixture of Oriental blood and were cousins of the Eskimo. But, Mr. Driscoll reminded us, Aleuts were "as 100% American as anybody from Georgia or Arkansas. They have broad tastes ranging from baseball and sealing to Bing Crosby and blue foxes."

We understood there was only one Eskimo in town: an elderly Eskimo woman whom we never saw.

The Eskimo mood was reflected by a ditty entitled, *"When the Ice Worms Nest Again"* which was invariably announced as Kodiak's National Anthem. (It was claimed alike by all Alaskan towns.) According to the song, the hero and heroine were wed in mukluks:

> In the land of the pale blue snow
> Where it's 99 below.

During the wedding feast of seal oil and blubber:

> All the polar bears will dance their arms around us
> And the walrus will click his teeth in joy
>
> In the shadow of the pole
> I will clap her to my soul
> When the ice worms nest again.

Ice worms were described by Robert W. Service, the Arctic-lore specialist, as being six inches long with gray backs, bilious blue bellies and bulbous red eyes. They survived by masticating each other's tails and nested only in ice which was below the freezing point!

Kodiak was the subject of various artistic temperaments, especially among servicemen. Stanzas from *"Kodiak—The New"* by Jack Schmidt typified the talent:

> Here in the land of the Midnight Sun
> Where a man goes nuts and thinks it's fun,
> Days and miles off the beaten track
> Lies this isle of Kodiak.
>
> Nestled here in cool green hills
> Whose sight alone this mortal thrills:
> Its beauty has a far-flung fame—
> Even the bear has earned his name.
>
> Big and tough this bear has grown,
> Wherever man lives, this chap is known.
> But tho' his name this isle has graced,
> He's just a great big panty-waist.
>
> Compared to life in Kodiak
> He'll have to take the seat in back.
> For life in Kody's twice as tough
> As that big bear out in the rough.
>
> Now, in the "States" where I've lived long,
> Life's made of women, wine and song.
> But here in Kody—you get your laugh
> With "hooch"—a klootch and phonograph.
>
> So tho' it seems a lonesome battle,
> Someday it's back to old Seattle
> And Kodiak will be to me
> A happy, Rowdy memory.

Kodiak boasted one newspaper which was on sale for ten cents each Saturday. It brought us "News of America's Last Frontier" offering such tidbits as: "A new neon sign has been installed above the marquee at Tony's." "Mrs. Bob Small is working in the grocery department at Donnelley and Acheson." "The *MIRROR* office and composing room floor received its pre-spring scrubbing and swabbing Wednesday as melting snow and ice water flowed into the back door and was pushed out the front by members of the staff."

The bank was the most interesting place in town. It had a small collection of Eskimo implements and art work which I studied time and again as I waited in line. Of greater fascination were the large, upright, stuffed bears which were placed immediately within the door of the bank, one on either side.

I shall never forget my horror when I saw my first Kodiak bear cub. It was a Saturday morning in the fall of '51. I was rushing to the bank at ten minutes of twelve to buy a bond for the children. As I hurried through the door, I stood aside for several people to pass who were likewise in a hurry. As I moved to stand in line, my hair caught on an obstruction in the small, crowded bank. I turned, a bit impatiently, to free it. To my horror, I was looking at the sharp, curled claws of a monstrous bear upon which my hair was tangled. I stood there open-mouthed knowing that the bear was stuffed yet too captivated to move. Some kind woman, undoubtedly accustomed to that initiation of the unsuspecting, untangled my hair and patted me on the shoulder. Embarrassed, I glanced around the room but no one had even noticed. If they had, they recovered before I did. When I left the bank at noon, still hurrying, I turned to look back through the window. The bear was not terrifying, after all! It was merely a Kodiak cub five or six feet in height.

Prices were high in Kodiak. In November, we had our first pound of Folgers Coffee which was a great treat. The Commissary Store at the Base did not carry Folgers and we had been using odd brands as well as Navy-Issue coffee. Dave forgot to get coffee one day when we were having guests for dinner and stopped at Kraft's, a sell-all department store, to buy a pound. He discovered that they had Folgers and brought it home like the rarest treasure. The pound was priced at one dollar and five cents.

Lettuce was fifty cents a head in town whether it was of good quality or poor quality and, generally, it was the latter. Oranges were one dollar and twenty cents a dozen, the same price as airborne eggs. Fresh milk was sixty-five cents a quart including bottle deposit. Frozen milk was thirty-five cents a quart. Canned homogenized milk was fifty cents a quart.

The last of November, I made a special trip to town to buy a few yams which the Commissary did not have at the time. I bought six large yams for which I paid one dollar and seventy-five cents. The man in front of me at the check-out counter bought two quarts of fresh milk and a small loaf of wheat bread for one dollar and eighty cents.

Fresh produce was not only expensive in Alaska, it was scarce. I copied an ad from the *Anchorage Daily News* which we received whenever PNA could break through to Kodiak. On August 9, Joe's Quality Market in Anchorage announced in a half-page ad of broad black letters: "PRODUCE SALE." Great delicacies were boasted: "Avocados, cantaloupes, celery, corn, watermelon, honeydews, peaches, plums, bananas, peppers, pears, tomatoes, cucumbers, lettuce." No prices were listed because no one cared about the prices. They were only interested in the fact that the phenomenal sale would last Thursday, Friday and Saturday!

Ironically, with the exception of king crab, you generally could not buy fish in Kodiak. Most acceptable hauls of fish caught either on hooks or in traps were canned or frozen and sent to the States. If you wanted fish, you caught it or were given it. If a cannery was at the city dock during the fishing season, you might buy a small quantity there. Canned Alaskan red sockeye salmon was ninety cents a can. It was caught and canned in Alaska, labeled in the States and returned to Alaska for sale.

If you wanted an Alaskan fur coat, you trapped the animals yourself. You might buy skins, of questionable quality, from an independent trapper. Choice skins were sent to furriers in the States, mainly to St. Louis. If your heart was set on a beaver coat, you had to be a resident of Kodiak three years before you could trap beaver. Land otters were long ago extinct and seals, carefully guarded on the isolated Pribiloff Islands. In Kodiak, you might buy a rabbit parka for several hundred dollars. It would probably have a Seattle label. If you wanted a brown, Kodiak, bearskin trophy, you took to the wilds—provided you had resided in Kodiak one year. If not, the hunting license was fifty dollars and you had to be accompanied by a trained guide. The best trained guide in Kodiak would take you in his sleek yacht, the *Kodiak Bear*, and guarantee a Kodiak bear for the nominal fee of two thousand dollars!

Throughout Alaska, fresh milk was a precious commodity. It was obtainable at exorbitant prices and the quality was uncertain. One paid too much in town for fresh milk which was later banned from sale because of the dairy's questionable sterilization of the milk bottles. We never bought town milk, having been warned early.

For the first ten months in Kodiak, we drank frozen milk which the Commissary sold for eighteen cents a quart. It was processed by Seattle's Alpine Dairy and was very palatable unless it had been thawed in transit and then refrozen. Its only disadvantage was the time consumed in preparing it for drinking. If allowed to thaw in the carton, it had the lumpy, watery appearance of sour milk. If heated to below the boiling point, then strained, it was as digestible as any milk in the States.

In the spring of '52, a new type of milk was presented to the Alaskan housewife. Darigold concentrated milk appeared at the Commissary. One quart of Darigold, which sold for sixty cents, would make three quarts of milk. Preparing Darigold was simple: add two quarts of cold water to one quart of concentrated milk. It was simple, that is, for everyone but us. But Alaska and facileness—we philosophically decided—were not compatible. Dave now had to carry twice as much drinking water from the Base so that we could mix our milk.

Less than a month after the Darigold concentrated milk appeared at the Commissary, the frozen milk contract was canceled and the Darigold milk was arriving from the States, frozen. After thawing a carton of Darigold which had not been processed for freezing, the milk was as thick and gritty as clogged salt. Heating helped but the butter fat was contained in such thick lumps that smooth, palatable milk was impossible to obtain from frozen Darigold. I heated, beat, diluted and strained, but to no avail. Frozen, concentrated milk was not usable except for baking purposes.

We next experimented with Med-O-Milk which was canned, homogenized milk advertised as "natural milk from healthy cows." It was neither condensed nor evaporated and no preservatives had been added yet it could be kept in its three-quart tin at room temperature until opened. In town, Med-O-Milk was one dollar and fifty cents a can; at the Commissary, it was ninety cents. It had a tinny, unnaturally rich flavor but we drank it eagerly after our experiences with frozen Darigold. But Med-O-Milk, we immediately discovered, also had a disadvantage: it was heavy to carry down the hill.

Fortunately, after a few weeks, Darigold concentrated milk began to arrive at the Commissary in its original liquid state. We used it happily and successfully from then on until we left Kodiak for "Outside" in December 1952.

The lack of fresh milk in Kodiak was not due to an insufficiency of grazing land. In fact, Kodiak Island was considered to be exceptionally adaptable to dairy and beef cattle. The luxuriance of grasses, long from melting snow and spring rains, lushly green from sun into the night, afforded excellent pastureland for cattle. Kodiak's winters were mild enough for cattle to graze throughout the year. But for a number of considerations, of which we could only speculate, cattle were inconspicuous in the Kodiak area. We were inclined to believe that for aesthetic as well as pecuniary reasons, cattle, in large numbers, were purposely excluded from the island.

The Kodiak bear, the largest carnivorous animal in the world, inhabited the western part of the island in declining numbers. The fear seemed to exist that cattle in quantity would eventually push the Kodiak bear from the island. Not only were Kodiakians interested in preserving Kodiak Island as a shrine for the bear, they were also interested in preserving the bear as a target for hunters.

When we first arrived in Kodiak, the used-car market was excellent. Due to the high cost of transportation, it was almost prohibitive to buy a new car in Kodiak. The only people who were willing to sell a good used car were Navy and Marine personnel who brought their cars to Alaska at government expense. They found that they could sell their cars to residents of Kodiak for as much or more than the original price. Few cars, with the exception of the latest models, were worth taking back to the States after eighteen to twenty-four months over Kodiak's deplorable roads. With both parties thus eager for a transaction, a car could be advertised and sold on the same day.

In less than a year, we observed the overcrowding of the used-car market. Where a year before, the Naval Station and the streets of Kodiak had been filled with new cars—jeeps and jalopies were taking their place. Now jeeps were the most practical mode of transportation for the Alaskan terrain, but the value of cars ten to fifteen years old was disputable. In the summertime, they had difficulty making the steep grades to the fishing and sightseeing areas. In the winter, they were hard to heat and harder to start. In the case of mechanical failure, cars could be repaired in town at one of the three garages. The charges were not prohibitive but the waiting lists were. The garage at the Naval Station did little more than grease cars, sell and repair tires. Too many of the latest arrivals in Kodiak had "gotten the word": old cars will take the beating and sell well. We noticed that many old cars sat out the winter and that many were never sold but loaded back on the ship for the States.

We discovered that there were two legal holidays observed in the Territory which were not observed in the States. One was Alaska Day which was celebrated each October 18, in observance of the unfurling of the Stars and Stripes over Alaska on October 18, 1867. On that day, the Russian eagle gave place to the American. Seward's Day was recognized on March 30 to mark the anniversary of the signing of the treaty arranged by President Andrew Johnson's Secretary of State, William Henry Seward, by which Russia ceded Alaska to the United States on March 30, 1867, for $7,200,000. (Each season, the Alaskan fishing industry earned over twelve times the purchase price.)

Kodiak did not lack for entertainment. During the summer, fishing was the paramount activity, professionally and socially. Every stream, lake and bridge revealed the camaraderie of fishermen. Fishing craft of varying dimensions and degrees of prosperity passed continuously night and day. Picnickers were everywhere, along rocky beaches and lucid salmon streams. A few hardy individuals swam in sheltered coves. Suntans were universal. The long hours of daylight delayed everyone's bedtime. In early fall, the fishing season ended officially with a Salmon Derby. Prizes were awarded in town and at each of the clubs on the Base. We attended the Fishermen's Ball at the O-Club where hip boots, levis and plaid shirts predominated.

In the winter, bowling and basketball were the chief divertissements both for the townspeople and the Base personnel. The Kodiak firemen's bowling team pitted themselves against the cab drivers; the bartenders against the policemen. Dave played basketball on the Base's "Old Stars" team. They lost regularly to the Kodiak High School. After such an excellent workout (so claimed the "Old Stars"), the Kodiak High School team won the All-Alaska high school championship. There was always the local cinema to attend. There was one in town which was formerly managed by that versatile gentleman, Mr. MacDonald. We never attended the Kodiak movie, preferring to drive to the Base to the O-Club or the Alsec (Alaskan Sector) theater, before it burned the first of January.

For the outdoorsmen, there was skiing at the Ski Chalet on the Anton Larsen Bay Road and ice-skating on all the ponds. For the adventurous, there was wild-game hunting.

Socially, the town was also active. I noted meetings posted for the Masons, the Elks, the VFW, the Rotary Club, the Grandmothers' Club,

Business and Professional Women and the Kodiak Garden Club. (We never could find the garden.)

We were to find that the water situation was not our only problem; we faced one almost as serious: the scarcity of baby sitters. An experienced baby sitter was almost impossible to find and discouragingly expensive when found. Every young boy and girl who could be trusted to their own devices for a few hours were in the baby-sitting "profession." The age ranges and rates were established:

9 to 13 years of age	$ .35 per hour
13 to 17 years of age	.50 per hour
17 and older	1.00 per hour

Our baby sitters averaged fourteen years of age. We found them adept at puzzle-fitting, paper-doll cutting, the making of intricate designs with a hammer-and-nail set and artistic coloring of the children's coloring books—every page. They taught the children tumbling on the bed, teetering on the night stand and balancing on the davenport back, all of which the children demonstrated with gleeful pride.

Our most mature and satisfactory baby sitter was Roger MacDonald, our landlord's son. Roger was "almost sixteen"; too young to date and too old to stay at home. Roger was wonderful with the children—he was a stamp collector! Toys and stunts bored him. When we discovered what a jewel we had in our own back yard, we booked him in September for Christmas night, New Year's Eve and the Spring Formal.

Soon after our furniture arrived, and we began to live in a fairly Stateside manner, we requested the Kodiak Telephone Company to install a telephone in our cabin. We had been warned that the telephone company was short of instruments and that we, probably, would not get one.

Dave, however, was able to check out a telephone at the Base in view of the fact that it was difficult to contact him for emergency flights without one. It was a thrill to have a telephone again, even one which was not connected. Home seemed near for the first time and we anticipated talking across the ocean as well as across town.

When Dave stopped at the telephone company to tell them that he had a telephone and would appreciate their hooking it up as soon as possible, he was informed that there was also a shortage of lines and poles. I was highly amused at the reputed shortage of telephone poles—we were surrounded by them! The manager, an ill-respected dipsomaniac, was apparently unimpressed when Dave explained that he could supply both the telephone and the telephone poles. "But it's the wire!" he told Dave. "*That's* our greatest shortage." Yet he offered a nuance of hope: "Wait until the next boat comes in."

The first of November, after many boats, Dave and a neighbor, LTJG Bob Long, climbed a mountain on the Base in search of telephone wire which the Navy had abandoned and they were given permission to cut and use. Their first attempt in the midst of a spirited Alaskan rainfall was futile. The next day, a Sunday, was bright and they set out on their mountain climb with a roughly assembled drum on which to wind the wire. They were gone the entire morning and Lori and I were becoming excited about the joy of having a telephone when Dave and Bob returned—cold, hungry, dispirited. They could find no wire. The next week end, they made another attempt. It, too, was unrewarding. The following week end, heavy snow covered the mountain. Consequent to wirelessness, we spent a phoneless winter.

Dave came home late Monday afternoon, November 19, 1951, looking very tired and, I thought, hungry. I asked him if he was as hungry as a bear. He laughed and said that he certainly was. I laughed too: "Well, that's just what we're having!" We ate our first black-bear steaks that night and thought them, delicious. They were similar to a beefsteak with a slight gamey taste which we found very agreeable. Later, we enjoyed moose steaks which were even less gamey than the bear steaks. The reindeer steaks, which Dave had brought from Nome on his return from Point Barrow, were, in our estimation, the most delectable of all.

There were a number of intrepid individuals who actually hunted Alaskan wild game. One of our Navy friends and neighbors, LT Sam Jensen, who supplied us with the black bear and moose steaks, and whose wife had driven up the Alcan Highway with three young children and a dog, hunted on the Kenai Peninsula, one hundred and fifty miles northeast of Kodiak. He successfully hunted elk, caribou, black bear and moose and, on the western end of Kodiak Island, the brown, or Kodiak, bear.

Black bears, which were very small in comparison to Kodiak bears, fed mainly on berries. The Kodiak bears' diet was chiefly fish. For that reason, brown bearmeat was seldom eaten; whereas, the black bear was an important item in the Alaskan diet as I had learned earlier from the Stumps.

Kodiak had a diversity of birds. In addition to the glaucous gulls, magpies, bald eagles and ravens, there were puffins (often called sea parrots due to their parrot-like bills), teals, cormorants, ducks, ptarmigan and geese.

Neither Dave nor I had the proclivity to hunt wild animals but we became proficient as trappers, at least Dave did. Dave was the trap-setter and I, the goad: I reminded him of the constant threat to the children's health and safety and to our own. Living as we did deep in the woods, we were not immune to ravages of the woods. For months, we matched wits and were outmatched by a particularly elusive animal but we remained undaunted and fiercely determined. Dave's nightly chore was to drag out a large trap and to set it. After it was placed in a position which we hoped some night would prove strategic, we retired to lay awake, listening. Each wind-pushed spruce cone alerted us. Once, in exasperation, I suggested that we purchase a gun and, in turn, stand watch downstairs. Dave laughed and told me, rather like a man, that my myopic aim was bad at best; if frightened, I would be more of a threat than the wily animals themselves. He also reminded me that I did not know how to shoot a gun.

So—we continued to experiment with every type of bait from peanut butter to pumpkin pie. A family of enormous rats frequented our living room, nightly. They brought their cousins, aunts and uncles to sample everything from Dad's prize gourds to the kitchen curtains. They knocked dishes out of the curtained pantry cabinet and gnawed holes in the babies' bibs. They chewed the top out of Dave's baseball cap and manifested an insatiable craving for pie crust and peppermint-stick candy. But the most disconcerting characteristic of those foot-long rats was that they scorned cheese, despite its degree of pungency.

We felt as frustrated as the residents of Hamelin before the appearance of the Pied Piper. The rats were not only noisome and a nuisance, they were the main carriers of Weil's disease which was still at epidemic heights. It was rather frightening to be warned that Weil's disease was fifty per cent fatal. We were unwilling to use rat poison for fear the children would find it before the rats. Nor was it feasible to buy a cat or a dog to catch the rats as cats and dogs were likewise carriers of Weil's disease.

The solution, when we discovered it, was supremely simple. I learned to put everything in the refrigerator—hearkening back to Key West's termites—that I could squeeze in: bread, cakes, pies, flour, sugar, carrots, onions, dry cereals and crackers; also, mustard, pickles, olives, honey, molasses and anything else in bottles and jars that had been opened. What I could not fit into the refrigerator, I put in boxes and tied securely and placed in a small wooden cabinet. I was scrupulously careful to keep the floor free of crumbs and to shake out all crumbs from bread wrappers before burning them in the fireplace. After taking such simple precautions, we were immediately freed of the menace of the rats.

Each time Mr. MacDonald dropped in, we enjoyed a lengthy monologue about the corrupt mayor (who sued Mr. MacDonald for defamatory remarks) and the merits of an oil stove. He once suggested to me: "That oil stove has spoiled you for electric stoves. You'll really miss it!" I opened my mouth; I was aghast—but speechless. He accepted that as silent approval. On subsequent visits, when Mr. MacDonald presaged my longing for the oil stove, I just nodded. I had learned long before that he demanded as desirable tenants, not only a family with pre-school-aged, non-destructive children but also—appreciation. But my thoughts did not inhibit wishes for that worthy oil stove to achieve early desuetude.

There were, however, to give Mr. MacDonald some credit as a sage, a number of advantages to an oil stove besides the cooking of food and the heating of a house. The prime advantage, for me, was the fact that I had hot coffee throughout my waking hours. After I made the coffee in an inexpensive, aluminum dripolator, I merely moved it from the left side of the stove to the right where it stayed steaming hot as long as there was a drop in the pot. An electric coffeemaker was as out of place in Alaska as a Cadillac convertible. We found that an oil stove made excellent grilled sandwiches in the area over the oven, proximate to the direct heat. Pancakes made on an oil stove—a clean one—were unexcelled. And like most users of oil stoves, we ate hearty breakfasts supplied from a sourdough crock and a slab of bacon.

A sourdough (which named those experienced in Alaskan existence, the hunter, the prospector: the Sourdough) was a pancake made with the usual ingredients plus yeast and sour milk. The batter was allowed to ripen for at least forty-eight hours before pancakes were made. It was never depleted. After each breakfast or supper of the delicious pancakes, the sourdough crock was replenished. For best results, and to prevent a lava-like overflow, sourdoughs should be eaten at least every other day. To start a sourdough crock, Alaskan cooks advised you to obtain a "starter" from someone who had a well-ripened batter. We preferred to start our own, however. Having been warned that only a container made of crockery would make a suitable receptacle for sourdough, we purchased a large cookie jar and had surprising success with our batter. There were a few unhappy experiences when I forgot to feed the crock or when we became satiated with sourdoughs and did not eat them for days and days. When confronted with an overflowing crock, I was as frantic as the *Sorcerer's Apprentice* when he forgot the magic word. Without a magic word, but with a reluctance for more pasty efflux, I finally stopped the flood by emptying the crock after three months and twice as many pounds.

The advantages of an oil stove did not offset the fact that an oil stove was about as demanding as a newborn babe. You had to keep it almost as clean for fear that it would explode and burn down the house. There were times when Mr. MacDonald dropped in for a visit—just to see if we were still alive. After a polite interval, he would pull out a piece of Kleenex from our ever-accessible box and wipe lint from the back of the stove. Gently, he would remind me that I should wipe it frequently because it might catch on fire, particularly where the stove leaked steady drops of oil into a wire-suspended soup can. That stove was our constant concern. Several times a day, I cleaned the top of the stove, the cooking surface, with heavily waxed bread papers. When rubbed quickly over the top of the stove, the wax on the bread paper softened and absorbed most of the grease spots. For more thorough cleaning, I scraped the stove top with a porous brick—which procedure liberally powdered the floor as well as the stove. It developed that the stove top was polished only when I was in the mood to wet mop the floor, which was not every day.

The thorough stove-cleaning job was Dave's. At least once a month, on a day warm enough to surrender our heat, the inside of the stove had to be cleaned. After the stove had cooled for several hours, Dave would begin his grimy job. Rolling his sleeves well above his elbows, he rubbed his arms with water and caked them with a soapless detergent. As a result, the soot could be washed off more easily at the end of the chore. Dave lifted out the cooled clinkers with his hands after removing the plate from the fire compartment. Then he lifted up the large oven plate and scraped and scooped the soot with Lori's sand shovel. At the bottom of the stove was a drawer which concealed a small opening. Into this, Dave poked an instrument that looked like a miniature hoe and raked out the last of the soot. The amount of clinkers and soot Dave cleaned from the stove always amazed us. Every month, there was enough to fill a bushel basket.

But cleaning the inside of the stove was not the most nimbus-producing act—that was the cleaning of the chimney. It was a simple matter for Dave to climb up on the roof and shake a car chain tied on the end of a long rope down the stove chimney, but it was not so simple to catch the soot which flowed forth. To prevent the soot from cascading into the stove, Dave blocked the chimney entrance to the stove with a long piece of cardboard down which the soot tumbled into a large box with a smaller box catching the overflow from the large box and the floor catching the overflow from the smaller box. The unrewarding thing about cleaning a stove chimney was that there was no end to the amount of soot which could be shaken down. It was like licking the cake bowl—as long as you had the will to lick there was always just a little bit more, the simile slightly more positive than the task.

At length, Dave would descend from the roof to survey, with uncontained amusement, our gray room. After a few scrubbings, we were able to blend the soot into the floor, fairly evenly. If we were careful not to disturb the curtains or to walk up and down the stairs too heavily and to tiptoe around the stove, only a *slight* sprinkling of soot peppered our food.

By late November the sun rose, at 9:30 A.M., directly opposite the house from the southeast. It climbed in a quick arc over the islands to set, at 3:00 P.M., behind the mountains in the southwest. So short was the path of the sun that with a slight shift of my eyes, without turning my head, I could see where the sun rose and where it set.

Winter arrived in Kodiak the last week of November when we had our first real snow. There had been a light snowfall the first week of October but it had not even capped the mountains. It had melted quickly and left the mountains and the land, brown and bleak. We welcomed the November snow. The children were fascinated and watched, delightedly, as the flakes fell. It was new and thrilling to them. Bruce was too young to remember the last winter's snow in Kansas City and Lori was only vaguely reminded of icicles and Jack Frost's paintings. Summer in Kodiak had been beautiful but winter was glorious. Few sights were as entrancing as spruce trees in the snow. When the dark green boughs of the spruce trees in our front yard—and in every direction we looked—were first sifted with snow and then bejeweled by the sun, the picture was one of breathtaking radiance.

With the November snow, we donned our warmest clothing. From our Kansas City purchases, Lori wore her two-piece, all-nylon snowsuit and Bruce, his all-wool legging outfit. With those, their tall rubber boots and snug mittens, they were warm during Kodiak's coldest days. Dave protected himself against the wind and penetrating cold with a parka, fur-lined gloves and Arctics. The latter resembled the old-fashioned, high, black rubber boots which buckled up the front. Parkas were readily accepted as the most practical coat and headgear for Alaskan winter. The Base issued them to all personnel and for a time, many of the officers' wives found it fashionable to appear in their husbands' rough-looking, khaki parkas at informal functions.

I was comfortable throughout the unbelievably brief winter in my full-length storm coat made of water-repellant zelan and lined with alpaca. The large mouton collar and revers were guard against the sharp wind; the snug-fitting beret, worn without compliance with high fashion, kept my head warm. High, rubber boots which reached to the hem of my storm coat assured me fairly dry passage through the snow drifts from cabin to car.

I thought it hilarious that when Dave flew to Point Barrow, in the wintertime, he wore clothing which was one or two sizes too large. Dave was a droll sight when he had on his oversized, blanket-lined khaki trousers, held up by suspenders (belts were never worn in extremely cold weather) and gaping in kangaroo fashion both front and back and on each side. He looked like the choice nominee for Hobo King at KCU. The seemingly absurd practice was to allow air to circulate through the clothing to prevent its freezing to the body. I began to understand why Eskimos were not stylish!

Most of Kodiak's houses were not built to withstand winter weather. They abounded with cracks and drafty, unfinished rooms. For that reason, plus the lack of central heating, Kodiak's houses were very difficult to heat. Generally, the oil cook stove was the only heating device whether the house had one or two stories. A Navy acquaintance of ours lived in a two-story log house in an isolated area far from the city limits. Although he had four children, he shared the average-sized, two-story house with two other families. There was no electricity in the house. Our acquaintance claimed that to heat the poorly constructed house and illuminate it with oil lanterns, two hundred gallons of oil were consumed each week.

An Army Sergeant who was a veteran of Alaskan winters, having served with the Alaskan Communication System for many years, made a comparison: "I'll have to go back to Nome where it's really cold to get warm again." In Nome, the winter temperatures frequently dropped to thirty degrees below zero. The Sergeant was complaining more about Kodiak's houses than about its damp air and chilling wind. "The houses in Nome," SGT Smith pridefully informed me, "are built for winter comfort with good insulation and double storm panes on all windows and doors."

LT George Jewell, a Texan, who cared little for Kodiak's weather and less for its housing, lived in an apartment above the Idle Hour Bar. It was a nice apartment with a large living room which had an oil space heater, a kitchen equipped with an electric refrigerator and an electric stove and a fair-sized bedroom with closets built in two walls from floor to ceiling. But it was cold up there! George told us just how cold it was: "Why, it gets so cold in our apartment, the refrigerator goes crazy. It's colder outside of the refrigerator than it is inside!" He yearned for his tight little house in Houston where warmth was assured by a flick of the thermostat. "Those closets," George continued, "are wonderful in summer but I hate to open them in winter. The carpenter didn't put any ceilings on them. When I open the door, the wind nearly knocks me over. Why, it's like going up on deck in a 50-knot gale!"

Our house had a few idiosyncrasies, too. The cabin itself was atmospheric both figuratively and literally. We had so much atmosphere in the house that the door curtains billowed like a skirt in the breeze. On the picture window, the plastic drapes breathed steadily with the wind and the waves. Our closet upstairs, the drapes of which puffed out like the old bag of wind himself, was accurately refrigerated for the storage of frozen milk. According to Mr. MacDonald, all that was wonderful. He assured us, with a big grin: "A little ventilation is good for you." And we *liked* ventilation but we found ourselves growing colder and colder as we watched the dance of the drapes.

We finally solved the problem of the cracks, at least around the front door which, in the winter, we were able to open in slightly less than ten minutes. All we had to do was to pull away a tarpaulin-draped drying rack, unhook a string rug hung from top to bottom of the door and dislodge the society section of the *Sunday Star* and the drama section of the *New York Times*—which, folded in thick lengths, perfectly filled out the door. Bits of newspaper, prodded into smaller cracks, hindered the wind at the bottom and sides of our air-conditioning door.

That door, in all weather, was the obverse perversity of our cabin. Its ailment was a singular backwardness: it was easy to get into from the outside but almost impossible to open from the inside where, with a great display of strength and a wrenched back, it could be opened almost a third of the way. As recompense for the awkwardness of pulling it open, the door had two locks to keep it closed. One locked with a key which dangled from a long leather thong; the other, with a bolt. Throughout the time that Dave was in Point Barrow, I locked the door securely with the bolt lock which looked much the sturdier of the two locks. It was rather alarming to be deep in the woods with two babies, no telephone, the nearest neighbor—a recluse, and I was grateful for the heavy, substantial-looking lock. When Dave returned from Point Barrow, I learned to my consternation and chagrin that the substantial-looking lock locked nothing! There was no support in front of the lock. But neither was there an assuring degree of protection when the door was locked with the key—it could be pushed open half an inch. For eleven months, I lived in unceasing fear of a bear's first huff! But the back door presented no threat: it was sealed shut, being lodged against the forest slope. Only driving rain and melting snow found entrance.

It got cold in our cabin that first winter in Kodiak. There were times when we went to the Alsec, the Base movie, for the sole purpose of warming our toes. But it was far less cold in Kodiak than in most places in Alaska. According to LT Leonard ("just-call-me-soupy") Campbell, the northernmost part of Alaska got so cold that the white men never shaved: "They just broke off their whiskers and pounded them into the wall for coat hooks."

"Project Oakum" was started at Shangrilog the last of November. We became aware of daylight and wind streaming through cracks in the cement between the logs of our cabin and undertook the tedious task of filling each crack with oakum. Soon, we knew every crack in the house; there was a multitude of them and our job seemed endless. Nail files were our chief tools for most of the cracks were as hair-fine as a knife's edge, yet they admitted a sharp stream of frigid air. Oakum had the disagreeable odor of hot tar, plus the acridity of wet varnish—at least it reminded me of that combination which was the most head-splitting I could describe. At the completion of our oakum project (I finally finished it in Dave's absence), we experienced less the sensation of increased warmth than one of near-asphyxia. But daylight winked at us through the cracks no more and the wind no longer perceptibly stirred the sweet-potato vine.

During the stormy days, the closest the children got to nature was when they dug loose rocks out of Mr. MacDonald's hearth. During the rainy season, they furthered the effect of being outdoors by catching drips of rain on the windowsill in hollow blocks, tin cups, coffee cans and canned milk tins—all of which we saved for defense. A favorite game of the children's was "let's play oakum." Dave and I would find bits of

Kleenex and the *Sunday Star* prodded into deserving cracks as high as their little fingers could reach.

Our record player was a boon to all of us. In Alaska, a record player (always called a phonograph) was not a luxury. It was more of a necessity than a radio which brought you Easter in July and Christmas on George Washington's birthday. The record player, plus a varied collection of books (from *Mother Goose* to *The Caine Mutiny* and *Pepys' Diary*), was our chief reliance for happy hours during the wearisome winter nights. Our record repertoire consisted of everything from Tex Williams' *Hey, Good Lookin'* to Rachmaninoff's *Rhapsody on a Theme of Paganini.* The children listened enraptured to *Bugs Bunny, Alice-in-Wonderland, Tom Thumb, Rudolph, the Red-Nosed Reindeer* and *It Came Upon the Midnight Clear.*

Throughout the fall days, we continued to have fresh fruits and vegetables from the Commissary. It was true that there were days when the Commissary had nothing, not even an onion. But when MATS (Military Air Transport Service) came in, we enjoyed every delicacy: honeydew melons, fresh broccoli, bell peppers, acorn squash, cranberries, bananas, delicious apples, tokay grapes, finger grapes, celery, lettuce, oranges, Brussels sprouts, carrots, yams, Irish potatoes, crenshaw melons, casaba melons, persian melons—and artichokes! Later, a further food luxury was added: we bought mangoes!

By the first of December, the spruce woods were filling with ax-bearing hunters of Christmas trees. Ironically, it was difficult to find a suitable Christmas tree in the miles and miles of spruce woods. A perfect Christmas tree had to be small and it had to stand alone to be symmetrical. Many times, in the week before Christmas, we sighted a tree from the road which we thought would make a beautiful Christmas tree. As we approached through the woods for closer inspection, the tree seemed to grow suddenly in height. If a tree happened to be the proper height, we discovered it was either too sparse or unsymmetrical. We wondered how the Navy had been able to cut so many trees so quickly to send to Adak where nothing but tall grasses grew.

At length, on a Saturday afternoon after a morning of unrewarding search, Dave parked the car on the edge of the frozen road; with the children in hand, we began a trek deep into the woods. There was little snow on the slope which we descended, weaving along a narrow trail through salmonberry brambles and scratchy spruce boughs. In the dale below, snow covered icy patches of a marsh. I was cautiously following

Dave and Lori across the ice, having lifted tortoise-paced Bruce in my arms, when I looked down and saw a tremendous track in the snow. I was horrified! I looked again and saw another track. They pointed in the direction we were going. A Kodiak bear was in the woods! (Insensately, Kodiak had instilled in me a consciousness of that renowned inhabitant.) I screamed to Dave who was at the edge of a spruce grove. He was lifting Lori over a low fence. "Dave, come back! There's a bear in there." His response was not reassuring: "What?" I shouted again. Dave picked up Lori and hurried to me. "Those tracks. Look!" and I pointed to the right of me, to the tracks. "Oh, hurry!" I was panicky. I turned around, frantically, and there to my left, were more huge tracks. I began to run up the hill with Bruce, pulling Lori by the hand. As I ran, I called to Dave to: "Hurry, hurry!" When I got to the top of the hill, I looked around for Dave. He was standing just where we had left him and he was laughing! In fact, I had never seen him laugh so hard. He motioned for us to come back. "NO!" I told him and ran on toward the car. "Come on back," he shouted, "I want to show you something." And he was still laughing. I locked Lori and Bruce in the car and went, hesitantly, down the hill. "You're funny," Dave told me. "You're like Winnie the Pooh tracking Woozles. Look!" and he walked through the snow. "See the Bear Tracks!" My relief was between tears and laughter as I looked down at the tracks which Dave's size-twelve brogans were making in the snow.

We found our Christmas tree not far from the "bear tracks." Dave sawed down a moderately small spruce tree. When it had fallen, he measured the tree from the top down and sawed off several lengths of firewood leaving the beautifully plumed top for our Christmas tree. He cut boughs for the mantel from the freshly sawed logs while Lori, Bruce and I picked bright red berries which clung to dingy, brown shrubs. The return through the woods, dragging our tree, logs and boughs and grooving icy slides uphill and down—and the trip home were, happily, uneventful. After a warm supper, we proudly put up the tree with Lori and Bruce's supervising the arrangement of each bright bulb and ornament.

The morning before Christmas, we awakened to find a token scattering of snow on the ground. We had had no blanketing snow for several weeks but hoped our Alaskan Christmas would be a white one. Ironically, it was not. By mid-morning of the day before Christmas, when we drove to the Base to call our parents in the snowbound Midwest, the light snow had melted. No snow fell that night nor the next morning. Christmas Day was warm and bright.

After we had talked to Mother and Dad in Kansas City and Dave's Mother in Lincoln, Nebraska—how wonderful to hear their voices—we drove back through town, past our turnoff into the woods, on down Mission Road to the Kodiak Baptist Mission.

The most impressive thing to me about Kodiak, probably because I had heard of it from childhood, was the Kodiak Baptist Mission. It was at the end of Mission Road, to which it gave its name, built upon a hill in a heavily wooded area of spruce trees which overlooked a lake. The Kodiak Baptist Mission supported sixty orphaned and under-privileged native children and, in turn, was supported by Baptist Churches throughout the States (one of which was the First Baptist Church of Kansas City, Missouri). The children were housed in three large, attractive white cottages of wood construction. A fourth cottage was at Ouzinkie on Spruce Island, a short distance from Kodiak Island. Activities were coordinated between the cottages by the *Evangel*, a colporteur boat, which made trips from Kodiak to Ouzinkie. In addition to the trip to Ouzinkie, the *Evangel* took food, clothing and medicine to other isolated villages thus completing the cycle of ministry of the Kodiak Baptist Mission.

Lori and Bruce wanted to take a Yule token to six-year-old Louise Cohen, one of the Aleut orphans whom the Women's Society of the First Baptist Church had "adopted." We discovered that, a short time before, she had been legally adopted by Kodiak's Deputy Marshal Dizney. In Alaska, it was not uncommon for those of Anglo-Saxon blood to adopt native children.

Although Louise was not there, we were invited to stay for a visit. Everyone was involved in pre-Christmas chores. We observed most teen-aged girls were engrossed in house-cleaning and cooking. I smelled bread baking in the oven; a large turkey (courtesy of the Elks) was defrosting on the drainboard. There was a lovely, big tree in the living room which probably had been cut from the back yard. A few pretty packages were already beneath it.

Christmas was a busy time at the Mission. We were told of the many gifts which had been received from Baptist Churches and individuals in the States. They were systematically recorded so that each organization and individual could be written a note of thanks. Each year more gifts of new toys, new books and new clothing arrived than the Mission felt it needed. (The Mission was proud of the fact that no child received a used article at Christmastime.) Except for the perishable delicacies, such things as: oranges, tomatoes, bacon and fresh eggs—the extra articles were unwrapped, the contents recorded and filed, then rewrapped, labeled and carefully stored until the next Christmas.

After a pleasant chat with the gracious woman, whose name I did not record, we were taken on a tour of the cottage. Downstairs, were three large rooms: a living room, dining room and kitchen. Upstairs, were a library and study room, a large bathroom and eight bedrooms—some with bunk beds, others with twin beds. The rooms were comfortable-looking and the furniture, in good condition.

After our tour of the main cottage, Lori and Bruce put their packages under the tree and we left, wishing them all a "Merry Christmas." As we got in the car, Dave asked: "Don't you want to invite some of them to Christmas dinner?" I told him: "No! Their dinner will be better than ours, we aren't having turkey." (At Thanksgiving, we had cooked a turkey in our oil stove. It was a luscious golden brown on the outside and inside, as pink as a strawberry. We had neglected to clean the stove and the heat was absorbed less by the turkey than by the soot and clinkers.)

Driving down the hill to Mission Road, we saw that many of the younger children from the Mission were skating on the frozen lake. We stopped to watch them in their white skates, snowsuits, mittens and bright stocking caps. They were warm and happy and having a wonderful time.

On Christmas Eve, the fragrance of spruce from the Christmas tree and the burning logs filling the room, the children hung their stockings. They then placed nine carrots (we had saved them for weeks) on the hearth for Santa's reindeer and Rudolph. After the children were "tucked all snug in their beds," Dave gathered up their carrots. One of the carrots, he grated coarsely and scattered in tiny mounds on the hearth. To the children on Christmas morn, Dave would suggest that Santa had slid down the chimney leaving nine cold, hungry reindeer atop the roof. But the miniature reindeer must have smelled the carrots and must have slid down the chimney, too, to nibble them—right on the hearth!

On Christmas morning when we came downstairs, each of us—wide-eyed; not a trace of the carrots could be found. Dave's realism had gotten carried away! Santa's reindeer might have nibbled on the carrots but the Northland's fat Uncle Rat had gobbled them all up!

January 22 brought us a violent snowstorm attributive, I immediately claimed, to California's astounding blizzard! The snow blew from the southeast in horizontal thickness. A quarter of a mile away, Holliday

Island was invisible. I heard, but could not see, a boat which passed close to shore. The spruce trees in the front yard were concealed by a snow blanket so opaque that I could not even see out of the window. As Lori observed: "It's hurrying! The snow's hurrying against the windows." The snowflakes were tremendous. They swirled and bounced against the windows like popcorn which was ready to be buttered.

The storm dissipated in less than two hours. When Woody Island was visible again, its dark spruce trees were dull and gray with splotched snow. But below the evergreens, the evenly whitened beach was without flaw.

We awakened the next morning in a mythical winter wonderland. The lowest boughs of the spruce trees were held to the ground by heavy snow which had fallen during the night. Verdant branches hung "to earthward," as had the Robert Frost birches, beneath their heavy white cloaks. The scene reminded me of one of Mother's cherished metaphors: "Every spruce, fir and

Figure 39. Snowbound Shangrilog

hemlock is robed in ermine too dear for an Earl!" It was one of the most complete "snowbounds" we had ever seen. I waited anxiously until Dave could get home at noontime to photograph the wintry splendor lest the snow-laden boughs release their loads to stretch skyward again.

The children and I were encasing ourselves in snow outfits when Dave arrived. He had, already, taken a few pictures of the breathtakingly beautiful scenes as he struggled down the path through fourteen inches of snow. Lori, in quilted green and red snowsuit and red boots, looking like one of Santa's helpers, tumbled out into the snow after Dave. I struggled with Bruce to get him zipped and buttoned into his brown leggings and brown Frosty boots. I put on my storm coat, which had received very little wear, my beret and rubber boots. Dave had on his parka and Arctics, wearing both for the first time in Kodiak that winter.

We played with the children, posed them in the snow and inspected their week-old Frosty I and Frosty II. All snow men were naturally known as "Frosty" who, according to the children's favorite record, *Frosty, the Snowman*, came to life one day to wander over the hills of snow. Frosty I, in the back yard, had that same inclination to wander. He was a robust and jubilant snow man, laughing up at the children's windows with his eyes, nose and wide mouth of "Bruce" cones. But when he was aged seven, he became as restless as his namesake and seemed bent upon wandering far over the hill on which he perched, very precariously, for he leaned like a bow, arms outreaching; his once-cheery face, downcast at the snow.

Figure 40. "Where's the Path?"

Frosty II, now, was of a different bend. Snow lord of the side yard, for a week, he had peered through the kitchen window at the children as they ate their meals facing him. He was a spry, dapper snow man with his arms folded

Figure 41. Sun-Loving Frosty II

across a three-button vest. Bruce loved him the best. His inclination was more ethereal than earthly. He looked up at the sky, so constantly, that he arced in a back bend until his aging head almost touched the snowy ground. He could see out of just one eye but he promised to look sunward as long as he existed for, at the end of the ninth day, he was flat on his back.

The snow was fresh and flavescent in sunshine. The children made first tracks around both Frostys and beneath the arched spruce branches. Then Lori remembered her "bird seeds" when Bruce and I turned houseward. Lori had been taught by Mommy Tom that if she saved cantaloupe seeds in the summer and tossed them on the snow, the redbirds would never leave. Lori had found no redbirds in Kodiak but there was no dearth of gulls and ravens which never left anyhow. We ate as many cantaloupes as the Commissary would allow, two to a purchaser—and filled every small bottle and jar with cantaloupe seeds. Later, at Lori's insistence, we saved seeds from acorn squash. She felt certain the glaucous gulls could handle them. Remembering how they could handle a large salmon, we concurred. By late fall, Lori had collected enough "bird seeds" to

Figure 42. Time for a "Bruce" Fire and Lori's Bird Seeds

provide longevity for many a salmon. She and Bruce tossed seeds on the snow by handfuls. But not a bird pecked at a seed, not even a rat or a squirrel. When the snow melted, I swept the seeds from the walk, but with each snow, there was a new dispersal of seeds. Lori and Bruce might have failed to nourish the birds but they sowed Alaska's biggest cantaloupe and squash crop!

During the last of January, the day brightened by eight o'clock. Faint beams came briefly through the east window; stronger beams through the front door which faced southeast. Our days were noticeably longer: the sky was not dark until 5:00 P.M. We welcomed the normal winter sunlight.

If one secured a telephone in Kodiak within two or three months after their request, they were exceptionally fortunate. Six months had passed before the telephone company even acknowledged that we desired a telephone. One blustery morning, the last week of January, to my amazement and ebullient delight, the telephone manager's assistant knocked on our door. He was "just seeking information." Our conversation was succinct: "Now, Mrs. Holland," Mr. Gelinas began, "have you got the telephone?" "Yes!" I said eagerly, pointing to it. "We've had it for months." "And do you have the telephone wire?" "Oh, yes, we have that too." (Dave had obtained the wire from the Communications Department on the Base.) Mr. Gelinas said thank you, that was all he wanted to know and good-bye. In parting, he observed that it was too windy to put up the telephone wire that day but he promised he would be back soon.

I was surprised, for the second time that day, when Mr. Gelinas returned shortly after noon. It was still windy but it must have occurred to him that the wind outside would not prevent him from installing the instrument inside. In a brief time, he had hooked up the telephone, running a short wire through the window frame and attaching a shiny, oblong box to the outside of the house. We chatted amicably and he appeared to be more in the mood for work. He thought he would put up "just a bit" of the wire which had to be strung from the road almost a thousand feet away and through a circuitous path in the woods to our cabin. His intentions were excellent but he discovered one obstacle: he needed help!

Early the next morning, Mr. Gelinas reappeared and put up the wire with facility—and no help. Civilization seemed miraculously near! "But," he told me sadly, after he had climbed down from the last spruce tree, "you'll have to wait until Monday to get a phone number. They're awfully busy down there." And we waited until Monday. In fact, we waited *eight* Mondays before they were un-busy enough to assign us a telephone number.

In March of 1951, a month after Dave arrived in Kodiak, the Navy's Operation Ski Jump was launched from Point Barrow. The experiment determined the feasibility of landing aircraft—from jets to six-motored bombers—on the Arctic ice floe from the coast at Point Barrow to the North Pole. A ten-man survey team, which included two Woods Hole oceanographers, flew from Quonset Point, Rhode Island, in an R4D flying laboratory. They dubbed their flying lab: "The Thing." "The Thing" was ski-equipped and specially winterized for Arctic flying.

Dave was copilot of the PBY sent from Kodiak to act as SAR escort for the flying laboratory on its flights over the Arctic. His descriptions of the operations and the frozen Arctic were chilling—my double-entendre, intended. Dave told of how difficult it was to land on the ice. The entire area was completely white with ice and snow. Accurate depth perception was almost impossible. Unless a lead could be found where the ice had recently refrozen to provide a smooth surface, the ice was deceptively rough. It was the practice of the PBY to remain in the air to cover the R4D's landing. The R4D, piloted by LCDR Edward M. Ward, circled over the ice to find the best landing strip, then tested the strength of the ice by a touch-and-go landing. That left tracks in the snow (the R4D landed on skis if there was snow on the ice) which the PBY checked from the air for cracks caused by thin ice. If the ice appeared firm enough, the PBY signaled the fifteen-ton Flying Lab to land, and then circled overhead as oceanographers, from the Lab, cut a hole in the ice with a seven-foot chain saw. If the ice was sufficiently thick, LCDR

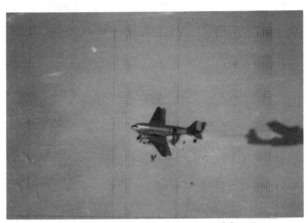

Figure 43. PBY Circling "The Thing"

Ward cut his engines and the PBY was signaled to return to Point Barrow.

As soon as a plane landed on the Arctic ice, engine covers were placed over the engines. A plane could sit for two hours in forty-below-zero cold with engine covers on, without needing pre-heating for a takeoff. If they remained idle longer than two hours, engines had to be heated for an hour and a half before they could even be started. Dave stressed how difficult it was to maintain the planes in such extremely cold weather. Mechanics combated the impossibility of turning small screws with their gloves on and the danger of their skins' sticking to the metal without gloves. They solved that problem by heating the engine parts on oil stoves in a quonset hut where all the equipment needed during the expedition and the spare plane parts were stored to prevent freezing.

The Woods Hole oceanographers made probings in the ice field by detonating dynamite, the short waves of which they measured to record ocean depths of two miles. They estimated that other Arctic areas had depths of three miles or more. The scientists were able to determine the salinity of the Arctic water and ice and discovered that the water was comparatively warm. Temperatures were recorded as high as thirty-one degrees Fahrenheit. Shrimp proved to be the sole marine life.

In March of '52, on the anniversary of Operation Ski Jump, Operation Ski Jump II was begun. The experiment was again conducted by the R4D Flying Lab, "The Thing," accompanied by two P2V Neptunes from Quonset Point, Rhode Island—instead of the PBY from Kodiak which accompanied "The Thing" in 1951. Operation Ski Jump II, which was primarily oceanographic as it was the prior year, made landings on a floating ice island sixty miles from the North Pole. The floating ice island, which was about the size of Guam, was known as T-3. Popularly, it was known as "Fletcher's Ice Island"—or just "Fletcher's Island"—named for the Air Force Colonel who established a four-man observation station on the island on March 19, 1952. (It was still maintained at our departure from Alaska and welcomed planes, which flew several times a week over the Pole, with strains from *When the Ice Worms Nest Again.*)

Early in April, both of the P2V Neptunes landed successfully on the ice island but the remainder of the experiment was beset with ill luck. "The Thing" had to be abandoned when its left landing gear collapsed on takeoff from the ice floe, 410 miles from the North Pole. The Flying Lab and its crew were stranded 779 miles above the rim of North America, the plane damaged so extensively that it could not be repaired. The oceanographic phase of Operation Ski Jump II was thus abruptly ended.

When LT Frank Brink, Public Information Officer for the Seventeenth Naval District at Kodiak, made a flight to the ice island (in one of the Neptunes) and saw the abandoned Flying Lab below, he radioed the figurative comment: "The crippled-bird appearance of the former Flying Laboratory intoned to the passing twenty-four men the foreboding thought that this great arid and calm desert was not an easy conquest." The Neptune in which LT Brink was flying was also destined for misfortune. It had landed on "Fletcher's Island" and was enroute to the North Pole when it lost an engine. The Neptune was forced to turn back from the North Pole goal and land on T-3 where the crew and passengers were evacuated later by a C-47 from Thule, Greenland. The second P2V, which had lost an engine earlier but had feathered it and had flown back to

Kodiak for repair, continued on over the North Pole and to Greenland before returning to Point Barrow. That flight was the height of Operation Ski Jump II's success.

It was interesting to learn that while on the Polar cap, the stranded Flying Lab party saw Polar bear tracks but no bears. The only animal they saw was an Arctic fox which, they reported, evidently had never seen a human being and showed no fear. They took its picture before they shot it. I wondered why the picture had not sufficed.

The last week of March, a man dressed in the fashion of a lumberjack, wearing a red plaid shirt and high leather boots, rapped on the door. "I'm from the telephone company," he announced. I was elated—even if he was "just checking" on the existence of the telephone and the wire. I jerked open the door the full three feet and invited him in, with an: "Oh, how wonderful!" He proceeded, without a word, to make a few adjustments and in a few minutes, I heard a single, sharp ring. "Well, you're in business now!" he told me. I thanked him profusely and we chatted a short while. He was George Cushing, brother of the telephone company's manager, Ed Cushing. George Cushing had been working on the Base but had just resigned to work for his brother. It was he who had organized the telephone company four years before; he was apparently trying to put it back into operation. He was very pleasant and completely sober.

Our telephone worked perfectly—for six days. On the morning that Dave was to leave for San Diego to take down an R4D, he lifted up the receiver to check with Aerology on the weather. He was filing to fly VFR and the point of destination as well as departure had to be favorable: ceiling at one thousand feet; visibility, three miles. Dave put the receiver abruptly back in the cradle. "The phone's dead. The cable must be broken." "Oh, no!" I could not believe it and as a woman was prone to do, I lifted up the receiver as if my touch would be magic. But the telephone *was* dead.

After the children and I had taken Dave to the Base and had watched the long, silver plane take off and diminish to a dot in the clear sky, I stopped at Kodiak's telephone company. As Dave had presaged, the cable on Mission Road had broken. Forty-three telephones were out of order. By mid-morning of the next day—obviously they had more than one customer to lose—our telephone was back in order. It was a comfort to me, isolated from the Base by distance and icy roads, to have a telephone which actually worked. As Dave and LT Max Roushman filed each flight plan, I was able to follow their long flight to North Island, San Diego, via phone calls from the Duty Officer at the Tower.

The first morning Dave was back from San Diego to his Air Clearance desk in the Tower, he called me. The telephone rang once and I picked it up eagerly. My ear was punished with deafening static. I listened a few seconds—with the telephone held at arm's length. Then I hung it up hoping the static would clear the next time it rang. It rang immediately. I lifted the receiver again and shouted: "HELLO!" I heard Dave say: "Dorothy?" and nothing more. In a few minutes the telephone rang again. The static was less severe and I called: "Dave? Hello, Dave?" A man's voice—not Dave's—said: "This is the telephone company. Can you hear me?" I told him I could, almost. The telephone rang once more. I waited; and it was Dave. I heard him well enough, intermittently, to learn that he was leaving the next day for a three-day SAR Conference at Elmendorf. It was not good news, for Dave had been home one day from the States and was standing duty for the next twenty-four hours but he told me he would get home before he left for Elmendorf—long enough to have lunch and pack. I was grateful for any sight of Dave and for any message via our temperamental telephone.

In a few hours, George Cushing came to inspect our telephone wire. He informed me that the wire should not have been put up because it was indoor wire. It was not heavy or strong enough to withstand the williwaws, the snow and the ice. "The wire is soaked," Mr. Cushing reported, after a brief inspection of it. "That's why you have all the static. I don't think I can do a thing about it." I asked him if he could put up heavier wire. He said they did not have a bit of wire. I despaired of ever using the phone again but expressed the hope: "Maybe it will work when the line dries." Mr. Cushing nodded, without conviction, and said he would look around to see what he could do. The children observed, wonderingly, as he climbed a spruce tree with his cleated boots and buckled a heavy strap, which hung from his waist, around the spruce trunk.

He worked for an hour, climbing the spruce trees, cutting the wire and splicing it. He pulled the ladder from the back of the house, always kept in place by the upstairs windows—in case of fire, and climbed up on the roof to work there for awhile. At length, he came in and remarked that he had found three breaks. Unscrewing the bottom of the telephone, he worked a few minutes, then dialed three numbers. The phone rang, he listened, hung up and dialed again. The phone rang again and he listened briefly. "Well, I guess you're all set." I thanked him for coming so promptly (it had taken six months the first time, then two months, now three hours) and he replied: "That's my business. Call again if you need any help." I was sure I would not—but in two days, he was back again!

The newest caprice in communication was intriguing. I could call out but no one could call me because the bell would not ring! The problem: Mr. Cushing had left a wire dangling in the little box on the outside of the house.

Without the practiced virtue of patience, life in Alaska would have been intolerable—for in Alaska, you waited! You waited for a telephone to be installed, for a number to be assigned, for the telephone to be repaired. But you began to wait long before that. You began to wait even before you got to Alaska—for the plane, long-delayed, which took you there. And once in Alaska, you waited for ships and planes with news from home, food and clothing. You waited on the weather, for the fog and low stratus clouds to lift so your pilot-husband could return from his stranded flight. You waited for water to drink which must be carried from the Base. You waited for the frozen milk to thaw so the children could eat their cereal. You waited for the low tide so you could dispose of your garbage. You waited for the rain to cease so you could dry your dripping clothes which hung on a wire stretched between spruce trees. You waited for the electric motor to push on to draw water from the well so your dishes could be washed and the commode cabinet filled. In the late afternoon, you waited for a car door to slam two hundred yards up the hill which heralded your husband's arrival. Frequently, the car door did not slam and you were still waiting—until a fellow officer came with news of an emergency hop.

The quality of patience never had been well defined in my demeanor until my arrival in Alaska. But from that time, I learned to relax with at least superficial calm, to expect no one until one came, to accept nothing as being until I was able to see it, hold it or hear it. In effect, I "didn't sweat it," the Kodiakians' earthy motto for sane, unhurried, unflurried existence which one heard from the moment of arrival.

May was an eventful month for us. It was in May that Dave received notice that he had been assigned quarters on the Base in Belle Flats. The quarters would be ready for occupancy June 1. After almost a year in Kodiak, we were getting housing on the Base. Dave's name had been on the officers' housing list since February 28, 1951, and it took *only* until June 1, 1952, to be assigned, even though forty-two new officers' quarters had been constructed in the meantime.

It was not without reluctance that we thought of leaving Shangrilog. I knew we surely would have stayed if it had not been for the increasing threat of Weil's disease which was alarming everyone in the town of Kodiak. I thought of the quiescent woods, the privacy of our cabin, the beauty of Chiniak Bay and the Gulf of Alaska—we had spent a countless number of happy hours, just watching the water—and we hated to leave. But when I discovered the apartment in Navy Belle Flats not only had white water in every faucet, an electric stove, even heat in each room and real rugs on the floor, my misgiving was soon decrescent. Dave

Figure 44. Belle Flats Invites Bruce and Lori

and I reached consensus: "Let's take it!" And the children discovered swings!

An event of even greater excitement occurred on May 6, shortly after 10:00 P.M. We were driving home from the O-Club (we had taken the children to see *Jack and the Beanstalk*), when we saw the Northern Lights! Flaring up behind Devil's Prongs, a low mountain range north of the Base, were vertical streaks of light. There was a wispy quality about the lights which made them appear to be illuminated streams of smoke. They disappeared than reappeared at evenly spaced intervals across the horizon, moving in a pattern from east to west. The lights were not yellow, pink and green as I would have expected to see but white lights which—tritely—resembled moving rows of Rexall beacons. The traditional colors of the aurora borealis were perhaps dissipated by the moon which was bright in the southwest sky. We were thrilled to see the Northern Lights and watched intently for half an hour until the last beam had faded from the sky above Devil's Prongs.

The first Sunday in May, we made a spring excursion to the woods of Cliff Point to watch the beavers. As we rounded a sharp turn on the Cliff Point road, Dave stopped the car suddenly: "The road's out!" It looked to me as if a bridge had been washed away but Dave assured me that no bridge had been there. The melting snows and early rains had washed away the easily eroded road of volcanic ash. Dave parked the car at the side of the road and we pulled on our boots to start a long walk to the beaver ponds. The snow was surprisingly deep in the sheltered valley and we walked slowly. We found budding pussy willows and gathered a handful of the grayest twigs. Lori, who had gone ahead to do her own investigating, stooped down to look at something and then exclaimed, excitedly: "Oh, look! Here's a baby Bruce cone." There, deep in the snow, encased in the bottom of a crystalline tube, was a tiny cone, no bigger than the tip of Lori's little finger. It must have dropped on the snow from the leafless tree overhead and gradually melted a well to the ground. Lori pulled off her mittens and dug out the fragile cone with her fingers. She discovered others as we walked along and insisted upon digging out each embedded cone which she stuffed in her pocket or held tightly in her hand. We stopped frequently to listen to the chorus of dripping grasses or to admire a clump of bright moss. Lori and Bruce found a beaver skeleton in the road and pointed with delight to a waterfall far below. We found no beavers in one pond, only wild ducks. They took flight as we approached. The beaver pond which had been a favorite of ours was nothing more than a wet bowl of rusty ground—the beaver dam was broken. We turned and walked back to the car, with less invigilation because we were beginning to be very cold; but Lori still stopped to extract gently from the snow, the pretty little cones.

Dave remarked that Lori's face looked unusually red. I said that it was just red from the wind and by the time we got to the car, Lori's face was not red at all—it was merely pink and so were the blisters. Lori's face was covered with blisters which, it took us a while to conclude, must have been caused by the pretty little cones. We emptied the cones from her hands and pockets, put her mittens back on and begged her not to touch her face. Dave drove home as quickly as was feasible on the slushy roads but by the time we were home, Lori's blisters had disappeared.

The first thing I did when we got in the house was to look through Dave's thick book labeled *TREES—Yearbook of Agriculture, 1949* which identified the cones as hemlock. Alaska abounded in western hemlock and Lori had been the first to discover it!

One day in mid-May, as we were packing to move to the Base, Lori brought an old *Life* magazine to me which she had been "reading." She pointed to the Coca Cola ad on the back cover where a minute milk bottle could be seen partially hidden in a refrigerator behind a coke bottle. "Mama," she puzzled, "why can't we have milk with paper on the top?" I explained to her that milk of that kind was scarce in Alaska but that when we returned to the States we would have "milk with paper on the top" delivered to our door—every other day!

After eleven months in Alaska, there were many things which we missed—in addition to fresh milk. We missed Home in general. Specifically, we missed the children's Grandparents. And we missed such "silly" things as the rumblings of a distant train. I thought with nostalgia of trains I had heard at home and could almost hear again—their lonely whistles' reverberating through the night. We missed the thud of the morning paper on the porch (we missed a porch) and the sound of the mailman's opening the mail box. The brisk click of hurrying heels on the sidewalk, we did not hear. Our eroded path of volcanic ash was followed noiselessly by Dave, except on icy days when he was heralded by Lori: "Daddy's home!" as the clang and bang against the back of the cabin announced the water can and Dave had broken their slide. (But if the weather was good, Ronnie, the *Anchorage Daily News* carrier, came down the path four or five days a week!) We missed current radio programs; particularly, the fifteen-minute news which poor transoceanic reception so frequently precluded.

But there were two things which we did not miss: the busy city streets and the confining yards. We loved the somnifacient woods which secluded our cabin on three sides and the bay, to the front, with its slow, quiet activity—our enchanted thoroughfare which was always a source of fascination, instruction and entertainment to us.

Some days, the bay was calm with a vitreous translucency. The stilled water, stretched tautly from shore to shore and pinned beneath the rocky beaches, reflected in a sculpture the peaked spruce trees of Holliday Island. At intervals, the lucid bay was animated by frolicking silver salmon which leaped in high bright arcs—or small fishing craft which left narrow traces that rippled and widened to the shores. But the water was not always calm. There were days of tempestuousness when the bay was as precisely peaked as the meringue on a pie. And other days—sinuate, pulsating white caps and violent swells were pulled and pushed by the Aeolian williwaws. When the williwaws reached one hundred knots, they lifted vast sheet after sheet of salt spray from the bay so that it appeared to be snowing from the water to the sky.

Williwaws, a noteworthy Alaskan phenomenon, were capricious winds of hurricane velocity (seventy-five knots) which suddenly changed direction and intensity. In hurricane areas in the States, when winds of definitive velocity approached, planes were evacuated, families moved from low waterfront areas to brick buildings inland, as we were in Pensacola. Windows were boarded up and objects which could not be moved into houses and garages were secured to the ground. Every precaution was taken; everyone remained indoors. In Kodiak, the williwaws came suddenly, without warning. They were frequent but of short duration. Kodiakians regarded them with supreme casualness and went about their tasks as usual. Mainstreet was as congested as on a summer's day; pedestrians dodged flying boards and debris with the insouciance of experience. They seemed more amused than alarmed when a gust knocked them down. Occasionally, a chimney blew off a skid shack or a car door was torn loose but damage, in general, was negligible.

One calm, bright spring day became as mercurial as a williwaw for Dave's routine SAR flight (if such could ever be) north of Kodiak across the Gulf of Alaska, east of Homer. Dave, flying copilot in a PBY with a Chief Petty Officer as pilot, took an Ordnanceman 1C to the Coast Guard Station at Seward on Resurrection Bay. The Ordnanceman had been summoned to inspect a mine reportedly washed ashore on the beach of a near-by island. We heard about the vicissitudinous weather.

Dave described the condition of Resurrection Bay for Lori, Bruce and me after pointing it out on our large study map. "A stalled-out warm front lay along the coast. As we approached the coast, the ceiling and visibility kept decreasing and decreasing. At fifty feet above the water, we lowered our wing-tip floats and following our radarman's guidance headed toward the bay entrance. When the ceiling dropped to near-zero, we 'landed' on the water"—and both Dave and Lori laughed together at the oxymoron. "And then what happened?" I urged, realizing the rareness of my opportunity. "We taxied on into Seward," Dave resumed. "But why didn't you land on land?" Lori was puzzled. "There's no landing strip on land at Seward—too many mountains; besides, we couldn't have seen it at all; just lucky there weren't any boats out. We had to fly VFR because there were no instrument navigational aids we could use, no radio beacon to home in on." Dave laughed again: "We called it VFR: Victor Fox Radar! We had to set down on water when the ceiling and visibility were almost zero-zero and taxi seven miles—but the water was fairly calm with the low clouds. But we got to the Coast Guard ramp, taxied up on the apron and discharged our passenger."

I was cautious not to seem too concerned but ventured a: "Goodness! Then did you wait for the ceiling to lift?" "No, we went in for a brief visit, about fifteen minutes—when we noticed the wind picking up. The Chief and I grabbed our crew and dashed to the plane. By the time all five of us had gotten up through the bubble and forward, the winds were about fifty knots. As we taxied out for takeoff the waves were five feet high with spray splashing across the windshield. The wind and waves bounced, banged and jarred the plane so much the Chief and I, both, could hardly hold the wheel. That was the roughest takeoff I ever had in a float plane! But—we finally got up enough speed. Midway back to Kodiak, with just sixty-five miles to go, we came out from under the front and flew VFR in fair weather." "What happened to the mine?" I wondered. "It wasn't one," Dave declared. "It was only a buoy. But we had to check it out."

Our bay was kinder than Resurrection Bay.

During the days of May when we were preparing to leave Shangri-log, we noted another mood of the bay. Those were days when diffident zephyrs stirred the bay to gentle motion. Shallow waves which coruscated with a sprinkling of sunlight led Lori to exclaim: "Look at the little stars in the water! They're winking. Oh! they're candles. They're candle stars!" We noted the signs of incipient spring on the bay and all around us.

Above the beach, Lori found her first dandelion and cowslip—and perfume flower. "Doesn't that smell good!" I appreciated. "Mama, can't you say 'fragrant'?" corrected my three-year-old daughter, indignant at my underestimation of her vocabulary. Turning her attentiveness then to the beach—the tide's being out—Lori took Bruce by

Figure 45. Boat Launching, Gulf of Alaska

the hand to the water's edge and they floated their spring fleet which had wintered in the wood box.

Fresh green tufts of grass splotched the drabness of our yard. The spruce trees were still a dull green but sharp dry needles showered from the branches as spring winds readied the boughs for new buds. And in a few weeks, as June approached, the spruce trees became tipped with pale green. Like soft green paint brushes daubed with brown, they burst from confinement into timid color. The exquisite rainbow hues of the first wild flowers modified the evenness of green on the hills and mountains. The lavender lupine, pastel sweet peas and yellow violets heralded the vernal brilliance. Fragile ferns formed vertical webs on the umbrageous, forested slopes. Snowcapped mountains reached the summit of beauty as they pulled their verdant tapestries from the munificent lushness of the valleys to the pale peaks.

We had thrilled to the kaleidoscope of indescribable beauty of our first Alaskan summer, fall and winter; then, we reveled in the glories of Alaskan spring!

We prepared to leave Shangrilog, feeling that such happy days should be treasured and content in the knowledge that, with the opening of our "log," we would share again the joyous days at Shangrilog, Kodiak, Alaska.

Home would be MOQ, Belle Flats, Kodiak Naval Station—a beautiful flat off of Women's Bay, fluttering with cottonwoods and aspen trees and bounded by the low mountains, and most wondrous of all—a playmate across the hall!

We would be glad to have Dave flying south of the Arctic Circle (66.67 degrees North latitude), from Kotzebue on the Baldwin Peninsula in the Kotzebue Sound, to the Mainland of Alaska—Nome, Fairbanks, Anchorage and Juneau—and to Adak on the western extremity of the Aleutian Chain. But he had one last trip to the top.

And Dave sent greetings from Barex '52, "Top of the World," Pt. Barrow, Alaska, to Mother and Dad on August 12, 1952, where the annual resupply of Pt. Barrow by ship was underway. Barrow Expedition— "Barrel," as Dave dubbed it—required ice reconnaissance flights due to the unpredictable movement and shifts of Arctic ice. And night was approaching: the sun would set there, on September 21, for six months of darkness, having already shone its twenty-four hours of daylight on June 22 to illuminate the unceasing preparations for its departure.

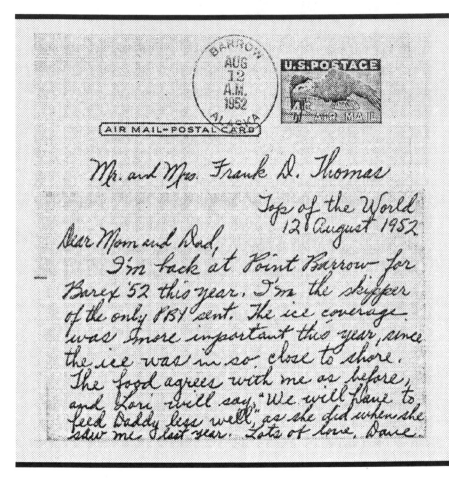

Mr. and Mrs. Frank D. Thomas
Top of the World
12 August 1952

Dear Mom and Dad,

I'm back at Point Barrow for Barex '52 this year. I'm the skipper of the only PBM sent. The ice coverage was more important this year, since the ice was in so close to shore. The food agrees with me as before, and Lori will say, "We will have to feed Daddy legs well," as she did when she saw me last year. Lots of love, Dave

CHAPTER IV

ATOP A HILL IN MONTEREY

We were heading home to the States! Dave drove the car to the MSTS (Military Sea Transport Service) dock on December 18, 1952, for loading; our furniture and gear would follow later. We bundled up Lori and Bruce early the next morning and after a delicious breakfast of ham and eggs, biscuit and gravy, Texas style, Bob and Jeanne Wright and Puckish son—the children's favorite playmate—drove us to the MSTS ship and we set sail for Whittier, across the Gulf of Alaska, on the mainland. We stayed on deck to wave to Jeanne, Danny and Bob, our dear friends and neighbors. Bob, an avid fisherman, had kept us supplied, when we moved aboard the Base, with sockeye salmon and Alaskan king crab, fresh and smoked. Danny, their adopted son, liked fishing at the age of four and always accompanied Bob whom he, uncannily, mirrored in his round-faced, impish appearance and unrestrained, Huck Finn behavior. They were, all three, a most lovable, carefree, unpredictable family. We would miss them, Belle Flats and Alaska—and we would never forget!

The Alaskan skies had become gray by the time we docked at Whittier in mid-afternoon for more loading of military families. Lori and Bruce became engrossed in the study of the huge cranes which lifted cars into the hold which we watched from the windy deck, Dave's explaining that our car had been lifted in just that manner the day before at the Kodiak dock. We watched until we heard the first-dinner gong, then hurried to our stateroom—comfortable with four bunks, two chairs, bath with shower—doffed our coats, washed hands and faces and arrived at the first sitting to which all families with small children had been assigned. Lori and Bruce had discovered the "fenced tables" at lunchtime and laughed again at the barriers which they couldn't imagine the necessity for, the ship being motionless and the sea being calm for their first two meals aboard. We had been given dramamine to have on hand in case of motion sickness but we felt we would be fine. And we were, until I lifted my head too suddenly as I sat on the bottom bunk helping Bruce tie his shoes—Dave's warning to keep my head down, ringing in my ears and transferring to my head with a blinding thud as I misjudged the distance. I recovered shortly, although Dave told me years later: "You haven't been the same since!" but implied no seriousness by his guffaw.

We went down the ladder to the wardroom for a pre-bedtime snack. Lori wondered if she would ever see the Rose-Pink Nursery again: "Because that's my favorite color!" "I liked it, too," claimed Bruce. We became nostalgic and we hadn't even left Alaska; we were still docked at Whittier. I recalled the first few times I had taken the children to the rosy-toned nursery. I had left Bruce in tears and picked him up in tears. "While you were in Point Barrow for two weeks that first August," I told Dave, "a wonderful thing happened at the Rose-Pink Nursery!" "Tell me!" Dave encouraged. "Mrs. Storms greeted me with the wish that she could have taken a picture of my children for me." And I hugged them both. "I love Mrs. Storms," Lori smiled. "I do, too," chimed Bruce. "I know you do," I continued, "and she loves you both." I patted Bruce on the head and Lori climbed onto Dave's knee. "Do you remember that special day last year when you had been sitting together watching children go down the little slide—as you must have watched each time I left you—when you, Bruce, suddenly got up and climbed the steps of the slide and slid down! Mrs. Storms said she rushed to the bottom to catch you but you didn't tumble off, just stood up and ran around to climb the steps again. By that time, Lori, you responded to Bruce's boyish boldness and you slid too. Wasn't that a victory!" I squeezed them again and looked at Dave. "When I went to get them, they were both on the steps of the tiny slide and I saw them both lift their arms and go down without being aware of me—behind the curtained door. From that day, Bruce *wanted* to go to the nursery and Lori asked if I had written to Mommy Tom about their slide. Patting a soft cheek of each, "And now you're both so big and accomplished!" "Rough and tumble Alaskans—all four!" laughed Dave. "We're regular old sourdoughs!"

We left Whittier, pulling anchor from Prince William Sound, shortly after the first-breakfast sitting, on December 20, 1952, and said good-bye to the Territory of Alaska (which did not become our 49th state for seven more years, in 1959). Hurrying back to our stateroom for coats, snow-suits, boots, gloves and hats, we got on deck in time to see the ship cast off and the last of the heavy ropes whipped from the coils on the dock. We waved good-bye to mainland Alaska and soon saw it no more, for we were not sailing the Inside Passage but navigating in a straight line down the Pacific Ocean to San Francisco. (The children were excellent sailors and we prided ourselves on being the only family to make every meal—thanks to Dave's salutary management.)

December winds were strong and the swells high on the second day out but Dave insisted we have a 7-Up twice a day and get plenty of fresh air. It continued to snow and both water and sky grayed together into a vast, impenetrable dullness. We walked a lot amidships, snacked, played bridge while the children dealt out cards and said "pass" at their little table, joined all passengers on deck for a life-preserver, lifeboat drill and took an afternoon nap. We had showers before dinner and with proper nautical frugality: Dave and Bruce together, wetting down, turning off the shower to lather, then on again—quickly to rinse. Lori and I followed, repetitively. We dressed in Sunday attire for dinner at six bells.

A delicious mutton soup was served which tasted rather like Campbell's Scotch Broth but with less barley and more vegetables. Alaska had made devoted soup-lovers of us all and the children waited for theirs to cool and then we all sampled it together when Dave was served. "Is yours too hot?" I asked Lori. "No," she considered, "it's just like *The Three Bears*." "Oh," I queried, "you mean it tastes like the Baby Bear's soup?" "No," she returned with her precise word choice, "it's *like* the Baby Bear's soup: it's not too hot, it's not too cold—it's *just right!*" Lori's bear soup reminded Bruce of his favorite Mother Goose Rhyme which also was very topical for the season of the year. "*Little Jack Horner,*" he began, "sat in a corner, eating his Christmas pie, he put in his thumb and pulled out a—" and Bruce cocked his head to look up at Lori who began to giggle on cue—"*grape!*" Bruce laughed so hard when he switched purple fruits that he nearly tumbled out of his chair. That night when bedtime Mother Goose held sway, Bruce had a rational question about another rhyme he recited verbatim with one change: "*Wee Willie Winkie,*" Bruce had our attention, "runs through the town, upstairs and downstairs in his gown-night." And Bruce consistently refused to use an illogical juxtaposition just to contrive a rhyme. Since a gown is worn at night, he insisted: "Why isn't it a gown-night?" Thus, independence and poetic license began to run rampant in the Holland lineage and ever might!

We docked in San Francisco at the U.S. Naval Station, MSTS at Oakland, the afternoon of December 22, and waited for the offloading of our car, Dave's making reservations at a motel in Frisco, deeming it more expeditious to start at 5:00 A.M. on the morrow rather than drive late at night. We wanted to get the children home to Kansas City before Christmas morning. There were two days left and one night but snow was predicted throughout the Midwest and we anticipated encountering it even on the southern route; yet, elatedly, we fancied driving through on *real* highways, any amount of Stateside snow. "O frabjous day! Callooh! Callay!" And I "chortled" in my joy with *Jabberwocky*—for we were Homeward-bound!

Dave had orders to report to the U.S. Naval Postgraduate School, Monterey, California, for Aerology School, February 1, 1953. He had a month's leave before returning to the West Coast to begin his intensive course. So it would be a study mode for us again for which we all had a natural propensity. Dave felt housing would not be difficult to obtain but that I would probably prefer to stay with Mother and Dad until the furniture arrived.

Although we had been out almost every day in Alaska and picnicked until late August along the shallow mountain stream at our quaking aspen, we knew the mild clime of California would be relished.

I was glad, however, that I had kept a log of our Alaskan adventure for the children to enjoy again, later, and had sent the typed copy to Mother and Dad for their perusal and safekeeping. Since they, with considerable financial sacrifice, had provided for my literary education in the finest of schools, the University of Kansas City and the University of Michigan, and personally directed me with their own erudition and writing proclivities—it was natural and facile for me to share our experiences with them. It took only a little discipline and I had been born of consummately disciplined parents!

We left San Francisco at five the next morning for our December 23 dash to Kansas City and encountered snow in Arizona. We seemed always to trail snowstorms in our wake, whether driving from Kansas City to California or from California to Kansas City—or from Florida to Kansas City. Dave laughed about it, too: "We provide our own blizzard of activity wherever we go, but no one can claim we're not well-trained!" By the time we got to New Mexico, the children, awakening from naps, thought we'd taken them back to Alaska! But we protested we were making progress and promised to get them to Mommy Tom and Daddy Frank's before Santa arrived.

And we did—just barely, pulling into the snow-hidden driveway, marked only by the fireplug on the street edge and the supporting beams of the porte-cochère, at 5:00 A.M., Christmas Day, 1952! We had been driving twenty-four hours and the big, rose-pink (Lori's "favorite color") stucco house, with Dad's maroon shutters and trim, glowed under the street light, emanating the warmth and love from within. Never had it been more beautiful than on such a significant, snowy morn. The world was pristine and pure and we were bringing our babies Home!

Dave bundled up Lori and, carrying her, made a path up the steps to the porch to give the door chimes staccato taps announcing our safe arrival to Dad who would be up and dressed and starting breakfast in the kitchen. I followed with Bruce, still asleep, jingled Mother's brass bells on the fluffy, fragrant door greens to herald *our* approach and saw Mother at the top of the stairs. Laying Bruce on the loveseat in the living room, I hurried to the stairs to greet Mother who was halfway down as I started up. "Merry Christmas, Merry Christmas," Mother sang, then stepping on her trailing robe—stumbled: "Catch me, Sis!" and I was there, throwing my arms and flapping shoulder bag around her in my best Alaskan bear hug, grateful that she had called to me, for I was moving aside to let her pass. My red bag thumped down the steps, strap broken. "Wasn't that awful?" Mother sighed. "You've carried that bag thousands of miles!" "But it helped break your fall!" I exclaimed, "no better purpose could it serve! Oh! it's wonderful to be home!" And I turned to hug, fervently, and kiss—beaming Dad. "Welcome home, Sis! We're grateful for your safe trip!" and he turned to the hall closet for coat, hat and boots, telling Dave, "I'll unload the car; you and Sis go on up to bed." Dave carried Bruce, still sleeping, upstairs; Mother's following with Lori. "I'll undress them and tuck them in before they fully awaken. You sleep as long as you can. We won't have dinner until three. Shut your door and sleep the sleep of the blessed!" and she kissed us again.

We awakened at noon and after lovely, long, hot baths, went down for breakfast. Mother and Dad greeted us with hugs, Dad's chuckling at Dave's pink cheeks and still-damp curls. "Was that the first bath you've had in eighteen months, Dave?" Dave could only nod, laughing so hard at Dad's drollery, he couldn't speak, while Mother admonished them both. "Hush, you two! The children are still asleep."

We sat down, still weak with laughter, to Dad's Christmas grapefruit, always with a cherry, and salt-rising toast which I had not smelled nor tasted for eighteen months. And that was joy enough for me but there was another. "Look, Dot," and Mother handed me the Feature Section of the *Kansas City Star*, Sunday, December 14, 1952, and there were Lori and Bruce on the front page smiling in an Alaskan cotton patch! "I took it to the *Star* this fall," Mother was saying, "the editor said it was way too long, even too long for the *Saturday Evening Post* but that he would look at it if I wanted to leave it. Then he read it and called soon

FEATURES

THE KANSAS

KANSAS CITY, SUNDA

I JOINED MY HUSBAND FOR A NEW HOME IN ALASKA

THE LOG HOUSE in its he "Shangri-La."

Living in Kodiak With Two Small Children Presented Unusual Housekeeping Problems for a Kansas City Young Mother— Few Actual Hardships on a New Frontier Where a Near-by Air Force Base Yielded Items of Comfort—A Log House in the Woods Was Their "Shangri-La."

Hundreds of young wives all over America have been permitted to join their husbands in strange places of foreign lands to set up housekeeping and make family life for our men of the armed services. This is the story of one of them, Mrs. David B. Holland, the former Miss Dorothy Thomas of Kansas City. Her story, written for The Star, tells of experiences keeping house and rearing two small children in Kodiak, Alaska.

BY DOROTHY THOMAS HOLLAND

KODIAK, ALASKA—My two babies and I were off to Alaska with a hatbox!

From Kansas City I was to travel with my two children, Lori, 28 months old, and Bruce, 10 months old, to join my husband in Kodiak. I had packed all of the clothing we would need for the trip in a cardboard hatbox. We were to be comfortably clothed from the summertime warmth of Kansas City through Seattle's rain to Alaska's chilled clime. I always had prided myself on the compactness of my packing. This time I knew I had accomplished a feat which was remarkable.

In addition to the hatbox, our luggage consisted of a carry-all containing Bruce's diapers, a plastic laundry bag for soiled diapers, a pullman case and a make-up kit. I had to carry only three articles: Bruce, a handbag and a diaper bag. The latter was filled with baby food, raw carrots, raisins, balloons, apples, crackers, clothespins, Christmas cards and "A Child's Garden of Verses."

Left in June, 1951.

By 8 o'clock that eventful Sunday night, June 17, 1951, we were ready for our 9:30 train to Seattle. We drove from our home at 25 East Sixty-eighth street terrace to the Union Station. Mother and dad, my brother, Charles, and his wife, Barbara, escorted us to the train and we were ensconced in our bedroom compartment at 9:15 o'clock.

We were scarcely alone after tearful, restrained farewells when the porter told me, "Your mother wants to see you at the platform." I clutched up my

Seattle for just such an emergency.)

I hung up and hugged my weary children to me as we hurried to the taxi stand.

At the Olympic hotel, I waited in line at the desk. Finally, the bellhop took us to our room. Halfway down the hall, I could

STRANGE CROP in Alaska. Lori and Bruce play in a cotton patch.

hear the telephone ringing. Was it Miss Wilson? Would he never open that door?

At last I had the phone clutched in my trembling hand. With just enough strength for one more effort, I gasped: "Miss Wilson?"

"Yes, this is Miss Wilson."

It was the most soothing statement I had ever heard.

Back at the telephone again, I called that familiar Seneca 0383. This time I learned Miss Wilson was on the way with our tickets. She finally arrived.

Next morning we climbed aboard our DC-4 plane and were asleep by the time the plane had covered a few miles and I re-

plane the first of April, a month before the baby was born. In a 3-hour conversation with the Stumps, I learned of such things as sled dogs, mukluks, parkas, shoe-pacs—about life, generally, in the wilderness of Alaska.

Black bear, they told me, was better to eat than brown bear because the latter fed principally on fish, the former on berries. When I looked awed at the thought of eating bear, Mrs. Stump laughed and reminded me: "There are no butchers where we live, you know." They smoked salmon for their eight sled dogs, each of which consumed two salmon a day. Enough had to be smoked during the short summer to last throughout the winter. They shot elk, reindeer, moose and caribou for their own needs. "Reindeer is the best eating," Mr. Stump told me, "but they're getting hard to find. We even eat porcupine," he continued, very amused at my wonderment. I asked how he got rid of the needles. "We just split the skin on the belly and roll it back; just like rolling up dust in a rug."

Parkas and Mukluks.

I was curious about clothing they wore in the wintertime. Mrs. Stump laughed at that. "Mostly mail order things," she told me. "But don't you wear fur clothing like the Eskimos?" I inquired. "The only thing made of fur we own are mukluks. The natives in our village make them out of land otter," Mrs. Stump explained. "We wear parkas most of the winter, not lined with fur, but lined with warm alpaca. We wear shoe-pacs if it's not cold but if it gets colder than 20 below, we wear our mukluks."

I wanted to know what shoe-pacs and mukluks were. Shoe-pacs, I was told, resembled a

the mountains were reflecting color from their cores.

As Dave led us to the car, I was surprised to see tennis courts marked off in revetments which had been blasted out of the mountains.

It was June 1 and I was chilly in a suit, a coat and a hat. I asked Dave if the courts were ever used. He said: "Of course, the station has a team which enters the All-Alaskan tournament each year. They do pretty well, too!" I concluded that people in Alaska, at least in Kodiak, must lead fairly normal lives after all.

It was good to see the car again. Dave had brought up a new Pontiac in February. And it still looked new, beneath the layer of volcanic ash. Inside, it even smelled new. As we drove slowly around the base (I wanted to see everything) and then along the cliff road to town, I marveled at the beauty of Alaska. The mountains, the lakes, the spruce trees, the wild flowers and the cascades of melting snow were ineffably beautiful. The road, high on a cliff, was bordered by mountains on the north, the sky and water on the south. Perched on the side of the mountain, one looked down upon docks, boats, floating canneries, channel lights, buoys, islands covered with spruce trees—and far out into the Gulf of Alaska.

As we approached the town of Kodiak, I saw that houses were built on the side of the mountain and the business section was concentrated into a small, sea-level area. Hills lined with houses led down to this crowded point of land which dipped into the bay like a thirsty tongue. Main street was three blocks

Figure 46. Kansas City Star, 14 December 1952

4 C   THE KANSAS CITY STAR, SU

FAMILY CHRISTMAS IN ALASKA
CENTERED AROUND NATIVE TREE

BY DOROTHY THOMAS HOLLAND.

WINTER in Kodiak is glorious. Few sights are as entrancing as spruce trees in the snow. When the dark green boughs of the spruce trees are first sifted with snow and then bejeweled by the sun, the picture is one of breathtaking radiance. We had our first real snow the last week of November which fascinated the children who watched, delighted-ly, as the flakes fell. But the real blizzard came in January.

The snow blew from the southeast in horizontal thickness. A quarter of a mile away, the islands in the bay were invisible. I heard, but could not see, a boat which passed close to shore. The spruce trees in the front yard were concealed by a snow blanket so thick that I could not even see out of the window. As Lori observed: "It's hurrying! The snow's hurrying against the windows." The snowflakes were tremendous. They swirled and bounced against the windows like popcorn which was ready to be buttered.

We awakened the next morning in a veritable winter wonderland. The lowest boughs of the spruce trees were held to the ground by heavy snow which had fallen during the night. The branches dipped "to earthward," like Robert Frost's birches, beneath their heavy white cloaks. The scene reminded me of one of mother's favored quotations: "Every spruce, fir and hemlock is robed in ermine too dear for an earl." It was one of the most complete "Snowbounds" we had ever seen.

Seeds for the Birds.

There was fourteen inches of snow on the path, Dave told me after he had trudged through it. All of us went outside. Lori, in her green and red snowsuit with red boots, looking like one of Santa's helpers, tumbled in the snow after Dave. I struggled with Bruce to get him zipped and buttoned into his brown legging outfit and his boots. I put on my storm coat, which had received very little wear, my beret and rubber boots. Dave had on his parka and Arctics, wearing both for the first time that winter. We made two snowmen and put out seeds for the birds. The snow was fresh and beautiful in the woods.

That was the sort of snow we had hoped to have for Christmas. But it was not to be:

At the Start of Decorating, a Young Kansas City Wife, Her Husband and Children, Went to the Woods and Cut Down a Spruce—Setting in Deep Snow Is Perfect for Santa—Children Leave Carrots for Rudolph—Fright From "Kodiak Bear."

height. If a tree happened to be the proper height, we discovered it was too sparse.

At length, on a Saturday afternoon, Dave parked the car on the edge of the frozen road and, with the children, we began a trek into the woods. There was no snow on the slope which we descended, weaving along a narrow trail through salmonberry brambles and scratchy spruce boughs. In the dale below, snow covered icy patches of a marsh. I was cautiously following Dave and Lori across the ice, having lifted tortoise-paced Bruce in my arms, when I looked down and saw a tremendous track in the snow. I was horrified! I looked again and saw another track. They pointed in the direction we were

not far from the "bear tracks." Dave sawed down a moderately small spruce tree. When it had fallen, he measured the tree from the top down and sawed off several lengths of firewood, leaving the beautifully plumed top for our Christmas tree. He cut boughs for the mantel from the freshly-sawed logs while Lori, Bruce and I picked bright red berries. At home after a warm supper, we proudly put up the tree with Lori and Bruce supervising the arrangement of each bright bulb and ornament.

On Christmas eve, with the fragrance of spruce from the Christmas tree and the burning logs filling the room, the children hung their stockings. They then placed nine carrots (we

HOME FOR AMERICANS is a rear view of "Shangri-La" [

breeze. Our closet upstairs was accurately refrigerated for the storage of frozen milk. We finally solved the problem of the cracks by taking pages of the Sunday Kansas City Star and stuffing them into the apertures. There was a multitude of cracks and our job seemed endless. Nail files were our chief tools, for most of the cracks were knife edge thin, yet admitted a sharp stream of frigid air. Even the children helped. Dave and I would find bits of Kleenex and the Sunday Star prodded into deserving cracks as high as their little fingers could reach.

LAND OF CHRISTMAS TREES . . . WHEN MR. AND MRS. DAVID HOLLAND WANTED A CHRISTMAS TREE FOR THEIR CHILDREN, THEY CUT ONE FROM THE FOREST NEAR BY. THIS VIEW LOOKS OUT OVER CHINIAK BAY IN THE GULF OF ALASKA.

Figure 47. Kansas City Star, 21 December 1952

and said they would like to do it in two installments. Then when he heard you were coming home for Christmas, he was just thrilled! 'We'll wait and run it then,' he said, 'the two Sundays right before Christmas!' Aren't you pleased?" she laughed. "Look, they gave you the whole front page!" And she opened it out and there was my article, heavily excerpted, but well presented with pictures of the children and Shangrilog which they had construed to "Shangri-La" and identified as near an "Air Force" base but the lead-in was good and concluded with the statement that I was a daughter "of Mr. and Mrs. Frank D. Thomas," a former student of Paseo High School and the University of Kansas City. It was entitled "I Joined My Husband For A New Home In Alaska." Under the title was a brief synopsis and then the article, with its familiar verbiage—with elisions here and there—filled the rest of the page. The *Star* for Sunday, December 21, 1952, announced in the lead-in: "This story about Christmas in Kodiak, Alaska, is the second and concluding installment in a series written for The *Star* by Dorothy Thomas Holland, daughter of Mr. and Mrs. Frank D. Thomas," and showed the Plaza Lights at the bottom of the article.

If I had thought of publication, that was the disposition I would have chosen, I realized, for it had given so much pleasure to Mother and Dad already—and to their friends, I soon learned, who had been so interested and concerned in every aspect of our Alaskan sojourn. So it was a doubly joyous return to the States because so many shared it with our lucky, little family! And, of course, Santa had left many, special enchantments while we slept after our arrival back in the Heart of the United States of America!

We made our traditional post-Christmas visit to Lincoln, the children's having such happy playtime with Kenneth and Robert's youngsters, there being three of each older brothers' progeny. We gathered at Ken and Naomi's. They had moved while we were in Kodiak to a lovely, large, white Colonial house and Ken was in partnership with the town's most successful orthodontist. Robert was practicing general medicine in Grand Island and Mildred and Hub and their three had moved to Washington, D.C., where Hub was a Soil Scientist at the Beltsville Experimental Laboratory, Department of Agriculture, after finishing his PhD. in Soil Chemistry at Iowa State. Our family group was incomplete due to the fact that Mildred, Hub, Susan, Nancy and Bill had elected to stay on the East Coast. Living in Silver Spring, Maryland, their Yuletime in the Midwest would be limited.

Figure 48. The Hollands: Viola, Dorothy with Bruce, Robert
with Patti, Ken with Johnny, Naomi with Jane, Mother H,
Joanie, Kenny, Lori

Figure 49. The Allaways: Nancy,
Mildred, Hub, Bill, Susan

Grandmother Zimmerman was living with Mother H, having moved back to Lincoln when Nora died, not quite fifty years of age, after surgery some months earlier for breast cancer, in the summer of 1950. It had seemed so needless and ironic for Nora, living and working in the medical world, to die of cancer! But she told Mother H she had never worried about herself: "I knew one in our generation would die, Susan, but I always thought it would be you." And Mother H had never worried about herself for Mothers who nursed their babies rarely developed breast cancer, she told us. Nora, of course, had never had children although she had married three times.

We had a strangely parallel loss in the Lacy family, too. Beth Lacy Hughes died in her sleep, at the age of fifty, in Gulfport, Mississippi, September 1951. (Each of the older sisters lived into their nineties: Susan Holland, 92; Mother, 93.) And once again, Mother had to make the sad trip to Booneville, having just taken Papa in February of the same year. Mother always felt heartache had contributed to Beth's shortened life and I always surmised that Nora's life, without children, had been very deprived.

Dave left in mid-January 1953, for Monterey, California, anxious to find us a house before his school started in February. Lori, Bruce and I stayed three weeks longer with Mother and Dad who settled us in our bedroom compartment on February 5, glad that our visit had been over a month long but conscious of the brevity, nonetheless. Those long separations from their grandbabies were always so difficult and heartrending for them, yet they never dwelt upon the loss of proximity but upon the fulfillment of reunion. I could not have been a Navy Wife without their constant love and protection and wisdom. Mother and Dad were our Anchor, our mainstay throughout fifteen years of adventuring forth and returning to the undiminished fires of their strength and their devotion. How noble were they!

Dave met our train in Castroville, California (artichoke land), twenty miles northeast of Monterey, Saturday morning, February 7. He was so handsome when he popped his head in the door and swooped up Lori and Bruce who both rejoiced: "Daddy!" and kissed him soundly! He leaned over and greeted me, too! "Want to see our house?" Dave suggested. "Our furniture will be delivered early Monday morning and we should buy a stove today." But the children wanted to tell their Daddy first about the train and how they had walked through "lots of doors" before they could eat. At breakfast, they wondered where the snow "had gone" because it had covered the ground in Colorado at bedtime. It was cool and overcast as we left the train in "sunny" California (no clouds for us) but dry underfoot. "Where will you fly?" I suddenly wondered. "Municipal Airport, Monterey," Dave said. "They have SNBs (a twin engine) and a PBY which I fly so the Aerology students can practice weather observation through two large bay windows in the after-fuselage." 'Twill be easier than Alaska, I hoped to myself.

Dave left our luggage at our week-end motel in Pacific Grove on Monterey Bay. "Oh, look at the funny trees!" exclaimed Lori, pointing to the wind-swept cypresses, their contorted shapes resembling storm-straining women—their hair pulled perpendicular to their bodies, bent with exertion. Lori was intrigued, as were we all.

The Monterey Cypress was the remnant of a prehistoric forest of evergreen conifers which had stretched geologic ages ago, in great quantity, forty miles westward from the California coast into the Pacific Ocean bed. The survivors of the ancient trees were limited to the Monterey Peninsula. Many of the cypresses, remote from ocean winds, produced gnarled yet symmetrical arms of shadowy green but the trees which appealed to us were twisted and bent defensively—defiantly withstanding the unpacific gales.

Dave promised to take us to the Point Lobos Reserve near Carmel to study the world's largest grove of Monterey cypresses. "Lori and Bruce, did you know my Aunt Mayble Holland painted cypresses like these, at Capistrano? I just remembered that!" Dave laughed. "Is that where the swallows go?" Lori asked. "Yes! and we'll go there, too!" "Doesn't Mother H have that painting in her dining room?" I thought. "She does," Dave nodded, "and Mayble wants us to have it when we get settled." "Oh, that's wonderful! Were you *her* favorite too?" A modest grin.

We heard foghorns and felt immediately at home. We were never far from the sea, in our Navy life, and we loved it—with all its sounds, activities and mysteries. Dave and Bruce were watching California gulls gliding in slow dips and sweeps in the updrafts. "I've got crumbs," remembered Bruce, and pulled on my red shoulder bag for his breakfast toast. So we crossed the street and walked along the cement esplanade of the deserted public beach while Bruce fed the squawking gulls with unbuttered toast from the diner, giving a handful of crumbs to Lori and to his Daddy, too.

We drove across the Spanish-style town of Monterey with its low, sprawling, white stucco buildings, arched walkways with baskets of tuberous begonias and ivy geraniums, the foliage trailing healthy green leaves and a few tight buds on the geraniums beginning to show color.

Monterey was not a Navy town. An old town with many adobe homes still sturdy, it had been the capital of California under both Spain and Mexico until the U.S. occupation of 1846. The seat of military government, it was the commercial and financial center of alta California.

There was more Army than Navy in Monterey; Fort Ord, U.S. Army, was the closest base. A presidio, founded by the Spanish in 1770, was home to the U.S. Army Language School. The oldest remaining military establishment west of the Rocky Mountains, it boasted another distinction: The Presidio marked the landing site of Sebastián Vizcaíno, the Spanish explorer who discovered Monterey Bay in 1602, the town and the bay named for the viceroy of New Spain.

Monterey continued as the capital until 1850, when California was admitted to statehood; its importance had waned, however, after gold was discovered in 1848, San Francisco's becoming ascendant.

Being close to the sea and the soil of Salinas Valley, Monterey was famed for fishing and the canning industry. A distinguished native of Salinas and resident of Monterey, John Steinbeck reflected that milieu in *Cannery Row.* He represented, too, the writers and artists who found inspiration in the quaint old community of ocean and bay, wooded hills, sudden vales, sheltered chasms, chaparrals and peaks—for privacy and aesthetic achievement.

We had much to discover about our new home terrane.

Dave drove us through the Postgraduate School grounds, elaborate with landscaping, to his classroom building which had been the fashionable Del Monte Hotel before the Navy had acquired it. It was across from the Del Monte Golf Course and Country Club which was still privately owned. Driving slowly around the Golf Course, east and a bit south, Dave wound us up into the hills of spreading live oak trees—evergreens resembling American holly—interspersed with pine and deciduous oak, still bare but beginning to swell at each node. It was a very circuitous road and one which could never be traversed with speed. We were twisting in our ascent to Del Monte Heights when Dave finally slowed the car on the top and entered a cul-de-sac which overlooked a Spanish mission far below.

Pausing to point down at the mission, Dave quizzed me to be sure I had studied a bit. "Know anything about the old Spanish missions—or shall *I* tell?" he quirked. "Actually I do because *Ramona* was one of my favorite books." He waved *that* away. "Alright! There were twenty-one," I dutifully recited, "from San Diego to Sonoma, built by the Franciscan friars a day's walk apart to civilize and convert the Indians—and sailors too!" I reminded him. "The mission here, San Carlos, was established by Fra Junipero Serra (I remember the name by thinking of junipers in the Sierras), who was father of the entire project and soon moved San Carlos to Carmello Valley." Bruce laughed, "Sounds like candy." "That's probably why they shortened it to Carmel Valley," his Dad agreed. "And that's where Fra Junipero is buried," I concluded.

"Good!" Dave applauded. and pointed across the road as he curved around the cul-de-sac. "There's our house! 1336 Castro Court," to happy squeals of approval.

Dave drove downhill on the curved, gravel driveway, stopping at the foot of the cement steps which led up to a large cement terrace nestled in, and overflowing from, the *U*-shaped back of the redwood-planked house. One Dutch door led to the dining room with kitchen at the front of the house, overlooking the mission. A second Dutch door led to the bedroom hall, connecting the children's room on the north, at the front of the house, and ours on the south, with a large, long bathroom in between. The third terrace door led to the guest room which could not be entered from the house and was built over the garage but was contiguous and perpendicular to our south bedroom. It was a large room but only partially finished and we used it for our storeroom.

The living room overlooked the mission in the valley to the north and the terrace on the south where a fire-place and man-tel were high-lighted by two large windows. The dining room extended to the east edge of the terrace and framing it were two, right-angled picture windows to

Figure 50. In the Woods Again

catch the first beams of the sun and exhibit the woods which sloped down from the house on three sides, dropping precipitously to a deep cavern and highway far below. Our closest neighbor was a block away to the east and from our rocky, wooded eminence, we would likely see more deer than people. Looking from our sylvan peak across the wide canyon, south, a comparable height of rock, oak and pine sheltered the home of Shirley Temple and second husband, Charles Black, whose family controlled the Pacific Gas and Electric Company.

Our curiosity about "Hollywood personages" was undeveloped and we never turned our car in that direction. If Grandmother Thomas had been alive (she died November 27, 1943, aged 91), I would have made an effort, at least written a letter, explaining our proximate precipice and describing the scrapbook Grandmother kept of an adored little Shirley's career. I treasured the large, meticulously arranged scrapbook, for it was a spectrum of Dad's Mother's wide interests and embraced patriotism, politics, religion, love of children in all ages, Victorian picture cards and stylistic art, poetry, Shirley Temple, articles about Grandmother's prestigious family in Mississippi and her favorite Presidents. As it was, we never saw a home of a "famous star" nor a back lot of a studio; our interests lay—almost everywhere else.

The children had tried both stairs of the terrace, before Dave had unlocked the dining-room door, and swung on the black iron railings outlining the wonderfully large, cement terrace and steep steps. They wanted to examine the Dutch door. "Oh, it's a children's door!" squealed Lori, and Dave accommodated his enthralled offspring by opening just the bottom half and we all stooped under while the children's-door discoverers ran in and out and in and then discovered their other door, in the bedroom hall. So Dave half-opened that—for Lori and Bruce and enjoined them not to run in the house nor to go off of the terrace. The house had beautiful hardwood floors throughout, still covered with protective runners, for we were to be the first occupants.

With his usual serendipity in finding us suitable housing, Dave had encountered a Navy LT who had just completed his retirement house while in Postgraduate School but had been ordered to the East Coast, leaving his wife behind to rent their "dream house" to a personally selected Naval Officer. And she chose Dave—naturally!

It was a charming house. The living room and dining room were paneled in redwood which had been brushed with white and quickly wiped off, leaving a softened rosy glow to the room. The hall and bedrooms were in knotty pine with two large closets in each bedroom and a built-in vanity recessed between the closets in our bedroom, the hall's boasting deep shelves with wide doors and long linen drawers, beneath. The children's room had been painted in blue with the wet paint rubbed into the knots and rings in the pine panels and then wiped off, after it had been under-coated and wiped in white. Their closet doors and the entire hall and cabinets had been treated in the same manner, producing a most surreal mosaic—like a high summer sky swirled with an occasional white smoke of cloud, shadowed and underlined in blue. Our room was aqua over white, the knotty pine's giving the same effect of a summer's sky but with a reflection of verdure. The bathroom had long counters and cabinets below, with concealed fixtures for a washer and dryer which I did not care to have. Dave had bought me a little portable washing machine in Kodiak which had an attached ringer to collapse and fold into the top when not in use, with an aluminum lid which became the clothes-catching tray when anchored behind the roller. It had a hose attachment which fitted onto a sink faucet and it was exactly the machine for me because I still did no linens or clothes for Dave, except his socks which he felt laundries were hard on with his size often difficult to replace. We measured for a gas stove and felt our small Alaskan-bought refrigerator would suffice. The water and gas had been turned on and the phones would arrive Monday morning. We decided to buy wool rugs for the living room and dining area and two club chairs for the north window-space; ten panels of drapes which I intended to leave open, for we were completely isolated; one floor lamp and one large picture of trees. I suggested acacias, redwoods or something indigenous.

We bought an inexpensive gas stove; good quality gray rugs, twisted and looped, a 12 X 15'and a 7 X 9', so that the new hardwood floors could show; had two expensive, oversized club chairs with loose pillows made up in a dull gold, geometric frieze; bought framed smoketrees to go over the gray couch-duofold and we were ready to accept our furniture and gear on Monday and occupy our Monterey-hilltop house. We needed only drapes and a floor lamp and since we had no formal Navy calls to receive or make, all Naval officers' arriving at the same time and many of the instructors being civilian, I deferred drape selection until the furniture and new chairs were in place.

Luxuriating in hot baths, the children's still considering a bathtub a novelty after eighteen months of showers, they "swam" awhile at the motel and napped while Dave and I dressed for dinner.

Dave introduced us at the O-Club where there were many young families gathering for dinner with movies or cartoons to follow. Most of the officers were in civilian clothes, except for duty officers, only wearing their uniforms to class on duty days and when they were scheduled to fly. When not in mufti, Dave wore his winter greens to school which I preferred to any other service uniform, probably because only flyers wore them. They were actually a dull olive shade with a slightly bloused and belted back; similarly cut, were his flyer's grays, in a lighter, mid-season weight. He would wear summer khakis and dress whites again which he had not donned for almost two years, having worn just his greens, grays and dress blues in Kodiak. And Dave had enjoyed not wearing whites which were laundered and heavily starched and stiff as boards, with a high collar—but how splendidly he affected them with his deep tan and black hair. Alas, he had probably outgrown his Pensacola whites or they had yellowed from disuse.

And I reminded him at dinner, "Dave, you better try on your whites as soon as we unearth them. You might have to go to the tailor shop." "White what?" Lori requested clarification and Bruce said: "Why do you want a tail?" Dave laughed at our alert listeners and explained that a "tail-or" cuts out clothes and sews them and that we were talking about his white uniform which he might need to replace: "have a new one made," he quickly added. And we both laughed at our imprecise diction and were glad that our children asked *precise* questions, rather than just "why?" It made *us* easier to teach! We enjoyed cartoons until bedtime, then took our little ones back to the Pacific Grove motel for they had spent a very long, first day in Monterey.

Sunday, after a late breakfast, we went to the house in the warm February sunshine. The children were dressed and booted to investigate the forest terrain with Dave and gather firewood while I washed and lined the kitchen shelves and drawers, the hall cabinets, closets and dressing table and readied the bathroom.

The children rushed in with pine cones and sturdy sticks ready to build a future fire, Dave's following with logs to report that all the firewood we could burn was on the south slope where trees had been felled from the housesite and driveway. "We forgot to get a grate, screen and fire tools," Dave told Lori and Bruce, "but I think our old ones from Alaska will hold up for a while. Be sure to keep those out," he turned to me. "By this time tomorrow, our furniture will be here," I joyfully anticipated, "and you may have my bucket now for your firewood." The children laid their gatherings on the hearth and disappeared under the door, Bruce—hugging the bucket.

I caught them the next trip, made them wash their hands and we sat on the steps in the glorious California sunshine and ate our apples. "We need porch furniture," Dave observed. "Yes, maybe willow but not redwood," I suggested, "it's too expensive." "Right," Dave concurred, "it might be years before we'd use it again."

"There are so many unanticipated expenses every time we move," I contemplated; "you're at the top of the heap with flight pay but how do Line Officers survive? And NCO's, and sailors with their families?" "Black shoes live less well than we—if they live on their Navy pay," Dave explained, "of course, if they're Submariners, they get extra-hazardous pay. That's comparable to flight pay. And I've known some Chiefs who not only saved their money, they made it with investments and their wives usually worked. Sailors have their families with them when base housing is available and they *need* their families. They get into trouble without them: go AWOL, drink, run up debts; then it costs the Navy time and money to straighten them out. That's why most base housing is for married enlisted men. It makes for a happier, more efficient personnel and is cheaper, in the long run. Then there's always housing for Senior Officers: Captains and Admirals, who operate the base. But it's a good life," and he squeezed my hand. "Yes," I amplified, "it's wonderful! I wouldn't trade it for any other. Just think what the children have experienced already, at such tender ages! They're so mature, so resourceful, and so disciplined, self-disciplined, as well as, obedient. Viola was just amazed at them—that they would stay in their room and be quiet until we all went downstairs together as a family, at your Mother's. Their cousins were noisy and fretful, clamoring for special attention and refusing to stay quietly in their rooms, much less their beds. They could never be Navy brats," I opined, looking proudly at ours.

The children came in to get cleaned up and change their clothes, as did Dave and I, and then we drove to Carmel-by-the-Sea for Sunday dinner. "This is a favorite Navy retirement town," said Dave, "especially for Senior Officers. Real estate is very expensive, there's so little of it," and he gestured toward the hilly streets, crowded with closely set houses which sloped upward from the sandy, forested beach like a populous amphitheater. There was a very limited, level section of elaborate shops and small restaurants. It was an elegant, exclusive little town which did not invite tourism, there being few facilities, but in which its permanent residents took pride. "Carmel Valley is another retirement spot," Dave added. "You can have land and horses there but it's being discovered by tourists."

After dinner in a quaint, little, white-cottage restaurant, we put boots over the children's Sunday shoes, Dave and I changed ours, and we walked along the sandy beach, cypress trees' growing almost to the edge of the Pacific Ocean. We soon were on rocky bluffs and the water became inaccessible. The entire California coastal area was unlike Gulf of Mexico and Atlantic Ocean beaches with their fine white sands, firm, smooth surfaces over which a car could drive to the lapping waves. There was dissimilitude, as well, to the Gulf of Alaska beaches—darkened with volcanic rock and brightened with spruce groves' bordering to the tides. Yet the Pacific Ocean's turgescent roughness, belying its name, visible in crumbling boulders and crooked trees, had a contorted, provocative beauty, a lineal appeal. No wonder so many painters lived near.

We drove through Pebble Beach Golf Course and Country Club, one of the most exclusive and famous courses in the world where the annual Bing Crosby Golf Tournament was held. It was a magnificent setting: a rocky prominence jutting out into the Pacific, lush greens outlined by twisted cypresses and exotic grouping of tropical trees. Dave commented he would be content to play at Del Monte—should he ever have the time. I was not a golfer, cared little for it as a spectacle and understood it, not at all.

Monday was a dry, sunny day and we were early abroad to receive our furniture. We had brought most of our luggage the day before so as not to delay Dave's departure for school and were armed with graham crackers, peanut butter, apples, raisins, fruit juice and instant coffee, plus paper plates, cups, a paring knife, wash cloths, towels, liquid soap and cleanser. The children sat on the steps of the hall door in the morning sun, with two little boxes of raisins apiece, to observe the unloading of the big van by three men. I had asked the movers to uncrate on the terrace and after placing the furniture, to bring into the house only boxes marked: *toys, linens, kitchen, every-day dishes, lamps and coat hangers.* All else I wanted placed in the guest room-storeroom and asked if they would loosen, but leave on, the lids of the barrels and crates. They were very pleasant and set up the children's room first, placing Lori's bed on the east wall (all determined the first day), Bruce's youth bed on the west, chifforobe—northeast corner; table, chairs and toy chest underneath the north windows. The back closet had been chosen for their toy closet because it had shelves on either side of the clothes rod and two shelves on top. The toy cartons were soon produced and I returned to the kitchen amidst trills of delight as Lori and Bruce discovered old favorites and I could hear indices of which shelves were for her, for him and "in between." And I knew she would be fair; they had always been good friends—besides, Bruce would insist upon it. He was sweet, gentle and generous but he could defend his own. There was reinforcement, but also—territorial assertiveness, in a little boy which a big sister, especially a perceptive one, as was Lori, was first to acknowledge.

Everything went smoothly: the refrigerator worked, was placed and washed, the stove and phones installed and the movers were backing out of the driveway by early afternoon. The beds had been set up and the box springs, which Mr. MacDonald had said he intended to use, looked surprisingly fresh, so I had those laid. I had located the cake tins and had washed and stored those with mixing bowls, measuring cups and double boiler, for next day Lori would be four years old! I got my cookbook from my suitcase and listed my needs for her pineapple parfait cake, having found the pink birthday candles in the box of taped spices. Lori had requested: leg of lamb, baked sweet potatoes, artichokes, which she and Bruce had been introduced to at Mother and Dad's and saw growing in the fields at Castroville as we arrived, and banana jello salad, her Daddy's favorite. What a joy to be getting ready to cook again—a Stateside birthday dinner!

We had late lunch on the terrace, Lori and Bruce's carrying their little red chairs and I, the table which they set with paper plates, napkins and cups while I quartered apples and spread peanut butter on crisp graham crackers which we soon discovered did not stay that way in California. I learned to store crackers and cereal boxes in the side compartment of the gas stove which always stayed warm from the pilot light's abundant heat. Repairmen could not lessen the heat loss nor further turn down the pilot light and the gas company said it was safe, so our cheap stove functioned as a crisper, as well as a cooker. And it cooked quickly and evenly and I exulted in the novelty of not having to alertly turn baking-roasting items every few minutes to avoid burning on one side and leaving raw on the other—a caprice of an Alaskan kerosene stove. We had an electric stove in MOQ, Belle Flats, which I then preferred but gas was proving its worth in Monterey. And what I had—became what I benefited from and learned about and life continued to be grand and our abode, idyllic—whatever or wherever it was.

We sat without sweaters in the California sun and it was February 10! In Alaska, at Shangrilog, the snow would be knee-deep! "When we build our dream house," I told the children as we finished our apples and juice, "we'll have a terrace, maybe not as large as this, but with a southeast exposure protected by the house so that we can enjoy the winter sunshine." "Can we have flowers?" Lori asked. "And pine cones?" Bruce requested. "Oh, yes!" I promised. "Now, let's make up your beds and you can have a nap before Daddy comes home. Then you can unpack more of your toys and I'll put some on the top shelves." Their big toy cartons were sturdy and I intended to save them for reuse, in the storeroom together with barrels, book and linen boxes, for we would be packing again in eighteen months—three semesters.

The third day, February 13, 1953, we received a letter, our first to 1336 Castro Court, Monterey, California. It was from Mommy Tom:

Home Feb. 11, 1953.

Greetings one and all on Lori's 4th birthday! We are thinking of you and wishing we could share some of the joys of the day with you. She is such an adorable four year old and a regular young lady. Tell her she has meant so much of beauty, joy and happiness to all of us since that day 4 years ago in Newport, R. Island when she first opened her beautiful brown eyes in this big old world. We love her and expect her to continue to grow in loveliness and grace every day! Hug and kiss her for us and dear ole Brucie too, he is so precious and altogether lovable and so rightly a toughie as little boys should be! We were so delighted to get your card this morn written Sunday and the house sounds most picturesque and attractive. We trust you have a stove and some heat by now and beds to sleep on. Know you are very happy to be all together. Take your time about getting straightened up and do not overwork.

Dad is still in with a cold. He went to Post Office with a box of things this morn. One other box had to be sent by express as it was too big for Parcel Post. It was the toys and overalls. Will send the silver set and fur coat later on.

Trust Lori got her little cards, the books etc. Barbara sent a pkg. too. Am due at the church to meet Jack McCoy, director of Music. First time I have been out since you left. Will write more fully later. Much love and many, many hugs and kisses to Lori with the Most Happy Returns of the Day.

We love you all and are *so* lonesome.

Devotedly, Mommy Tom and Daddy Frank

In March, calla lilies popped up and fuchsias set bud along the north foundation of the house. But, alas, only two calla lilies bloomed and the California fuchsias, dark red and purple, were nipped in the bud. But not by sly Jack Frost! Nocturnal gourmets, the deer, had discovered the delicacies. No abundance of salt licks prevented their preference. To be in California and not be able to grow fuchsias! Lori, Bruce, and I tried hiding some on the east foundation, shaded by shasta daisies but with ill success. So Dave screwed hooks in the east overhang of the terrace on either side of the hall door and we hung two baskets of fuchsias, one with enormous hybrids of red with purple sepals, the other all pink and two more hooks for tuberous begonias.

We drove to the Watsonville area, known for orchids, but more famous for begonias to choose from the latter. I had never viewed such greenhouse plethora of gorgeous blooms! It was breathtaking and bewildering but the children, never at a loss, made suggestions and sped selection. We chose an amazingly large, double salmon bloom which cascaded from a sphagnum-moss-filled wire basket and another basket of double blood-red hanging begonias—Dave's favorite. I could not resist a single yellow upright begonia, as large as a camellia, which I wanted for our willow table—knowing I would have to bring it in every night. I thanked the deer for forcing us to hang our blooms for they were much more graceful and floriferous than the standards.

We had planted sweet pea seed in February, on Lori's birthday, to climb up the stair posts and they had begun their ascent in late March. It was apparent that the deer avoided the shasta daisies because of their extremely acrid odoriferousness in contrast to the fragrant callas, which they could not resist. The LT's wife had set out the shastas so I could not remove them, although African daisies would have been more dramatic and less offensive. Actually, she had told Dave we could do as we liked but I did not like to negate her happy efforts in her own yard.

A man selling willow furniture had come to our door in late February and I had selected a settee, two chairs and a table of his peeled willow furniture which we could enjoy and leave when we moved, for they were not a great investment. I discovered, as we perpetuated an out-of-doors existence on the terrace, that I even enjoyed ironing for the first time! I put my dampened bags of little shirts, dresses, napkins and my blouses on the willow table and set up ironing shop in the balmy, piney breeze and listened to the birds' warbling while my own birds napped in their room. Oh, what a beautiful spot!

And it remained so until I discovered, after Dave had warned me to be careful, that I *was* allergic to poison oak. As a child, poison ivy had been my greatest nemesis but I had not encountered it for years and thought that poison oak was less virulent. Whenever I tried to outwit the deer, thinking I had discovered a flower they would not savor, I got poison oak. Wherever I dug, it was in the soil. I wore gloves and long sleeves and I continued to get the blistering rash but the children and Dave did not. And *that* was of paramount importance; I could easily desist from attempting to garden in the yard; and I did.

Dave continued to enjoy classes and thrive on Aerology at Postgraduate School. We made strong friendships in Monterey but entertained infrequently, for every school night and most week ends were reserved for study.

One officer and wife we saw often inasmuch as Dave was checking him out in the PBY and they lived on Dave's route to school. Bob Born flew Lighter-than-Air (Airships) but had switched back to Heavier-than-Air (Airplanes). Bob and his wife, Mary June, were intellectuals and non-party-goers and our rapport with them was immediate. Bob developed a debilitating virus which made him too weak to go to school but the Navy doctors, administrators and faculty granted him permission to finish the first semester at home. Dave volunteered to take notes for Bob and to go over the material with him, their having the same course, and be lesson-courier. On light-work nights, every few weeks, we joined them for dinner and bridge and when Bob was stronger, he and Mary June came to our hilltop. They were both Easterners, from Pennsylvania, and were avid students of current affairs and we had felicitous evenings together.

Dave Minton and Marydee were two of the dearest friends we had in the Navy. Dave and Dave flew together and were in school together and were totally unlike in appearance and habit. Dave Minton was not a prototypic Navy flyer, at a glance. He was overweight and cared little for the straightness of his tie or the set of his cap. But he was brilliant and could do everything, whether it was play the piano or solve a complicated problem in calculus—and he was generous. He helped so many fellow students get through the course that his own grades suffered and his gentle wife and his friends could do nothing to change his altruism. Nor did his habits help. He took a nap every night from eight until ten, despite the accumulation of his own unfinished work. But he was so gifted that he

𝔐𝔬𝔫𝔱𝔢𝔯𝔢𝔶 𝔓𝔢𝔫𝔦𝔫𝔰𝔲𝔩𝔞 𝔥𝔢𝔯𝔞𝔩𝔡
Thursday, February 5, 1953. 9

A STORMY COURSE FOR THE NAVY

Weathermen Trained at Monterey's Postgraduate School

By BILL COONEY

We're having a lot of weather these days.

That's nothing startling, because we've always had weather, and we always will. The important thing is what kind of weather we're having and what kind we're going to have.

Being able to predict mother nature's operations weather-wise is the immediate goal of the 84 officers enrolled in the basic course of Aerology at the Naval Postgraduate School.

The last graduating class had only 28 men. The reason for the fourfold increase in enrollment is the Navy's greatly increased fleet requirements for trained aerologists.

STUDY BEHAVIOR

Aerology itself is the science of meteorology which places special accent on the behavior and effects of the upper atmosphere in the development of storms and other weather phenomena.

A Navy aerologist first of all must be throroughly familiar with all phases of fleet, amphibious and aircraft operations. During this course he learns the effect atmosphere and ocean phenomena will have on these operations; whether the weather will help or hinder their success.

While at the school here, these officers will receive a thorough groundwork in mathematics and the physical sciences. They will become familiar with the most advanced methods of predicting and analyzing weather, and the proper techniques of communication, instrumentation and observation.

Lt. W. S. Houston Jr. (center), aerology instructor, demonstrates the preparation of a radiosonde transmitter, parachute and baloon assembly to two students. Measurement of high altitude pressure, temperature and humidity are transmitted by this assembly to the radiosonde receiver. Students art Lt. David B. Holland (left) and Lt. To Shen of the Chinese Nationalist Navy.

Figure 51. Monterey Peninsula Herald, 5 February 1953

survived and Dave and Dave were assigned to continue their weather expertise together in Newfoundland. The Daves were alike, however, in one important respect: their character. They were honorable and even-tempered, laughed readily at themselves and were never angry; they were undaunted by life and loved the Navy. Marydee and I used to marvel at our wonderful husbands! Dave Minton was from Forest City, Missouri, and we vowed that we would see them often after retirement because they and we were determined to return to the Midwest.

Jack and Joy Hinkleman were special friends in Monterey and again in Washington, D.C. Jack was slightly older than Dave and a rank ahead of him and was especially talented in mathematics, both applied and theoretical. He was a flyer, too, and his red-haired wife was appropriately named Joy. We became more close during Dave and Jack's Washington tours—barbecuing chicken in their back yard, one of their specialties; offering seafood from our kitchen. There was always good bridge after "Navy talk." We found Jack and Joy both occupied and happy when we visited them in Boulder, Colorado, in 1968, with our three children; theirs, numbering four. Jack was with the prestigious National Atmospheric Research Lab and had retired from the Navy. Joy had designed their distinctive hillside house and was a realtor as well. It was a pleasure to find them unchanged—as if we had parted but days before.

And then there was Colin Armstrong, a bachelor flyer, who was an artist—at least, Dave viewed his weather maps with as much verbal appreciation as I viewed, a tree! Dave explained exactly what Colin did: "He drew a 500-millibar, upper-air map which showed the wind velocity and direction and drew the jet stream, which has winds of 50 knots or greater, in the form of a tube or tunnel with the strongest winds at the center, of course. It was always a work of art. I wish I had saved one! He could show how the jet stream," and Dave demonstrated with his graceful hands, "changed altitude and direction—both vertically and horizontally. It would dip here and rise there." Dave thought a moment. "He may have done it on the 300-mb map, also; 30,000-foot altitude is shown there." "Was it unconscious artistry or was he trained?" I wondered. "I'm not sure," Dave pondered, "I think he was trained. But it was, certainly, a hobby." Well, I thought, I needed to learn about art while in an art-famous environment.

In April, I discovered Florence Lockwood, a portrait artist, whose studio was in her home in Carmel-by-the-Sea. I called her and asked if she would paint my children's portraits: Lori, almost four and a half and

Bruce, almost three. "They're younger than I like to paint and I'm awfully busy. I've just had a show and I'm behind in my schedule," Miss Lockwood was not at all encouraging. "May I bring them to see you?" I politely asked, convinced from my research, that she was the outstanding portrait artist of California. "Yes, but I don't think it will do you any good," she added. I thanked her and she gave me five minutes "to run in" the following week. I *knew* she would want to paint my children.

I dressed Lori in a short-sleeved, watermelon-pink cotton dress which Mother had given her for Christmas. It had a small white collar with just a hint of apple-green showing in a narrow velveteen bow. Her golden brown curls were pulled straight back from her forehead with a dress-matching, inch-wide grosgrain ribbon looped widely across the top back of her head but visible, slightly, from the front—both loops and ends. Bruce wore a white shirt with turned-back collar and a soft yellow, long-sleeved wool sweater with a V-neck, contrasting with his dark brown eyes and dark brown hair which I did not attempt to part but brushed to a sheen.

We arrived a bit early in Carmel which was, essentially, an artists' colony and followed Dave's map to Florence Lockwood's dark frame house, the south end of which was the studio, apparently, because it was mostly glass. I knocked on the door five minutes before our appointment, thinking an assistant, or someone, would let us come in to wait but the door was opened by a short, gentle-faced woman, middle-aged, in a floral smock with her graying brown hair tucked up in a chignon. She was smiling and unhurriedly held open the screen but before she said a word, greetings were screeched from a distance: "Come in, come in! Wanna cracker, wanna cracker!" The children laughed delightedly: "Is she named Polly?" asked Lori. "Of course," admitted Miss Lockwood. "And you are Lori. Hello, Bruce!" She graciously ushered us in to meet Polly and I was surprised she had remembered their names. The children felt immediately at home; so much so, I was quick to remind them: "Now, don't touch a thing and do just as Miss Lockwood requests."

They took off their spring coats and hats, both—Navy blue, "nautical" and double-breasted with gold buttons which Miss Lockwood noted as she hung them up, Bruce's giving me his cap to hold and Lori, her beret. "You have beautiful children, Mrs. Holland." "Thank you," I laughed, "but they look like their Daddy." "No," Miss Lockwood corrected, "Bruce is like you." "Why, thank you!" I beamed. She motioned me to sit down and took Lori and Bruce by the hand, back to see Polly and to talk quietly to them, when the bird desisted. They took a turn of the room, Miss Lockwood's commenting to them about objects they pointed to or portraits lining two walls and returned to where I was observing, too.

"I'd like to paint them," Miss Lockwood smiled, "in these outfits. I've never painted this color before," and she fluffed Lori's puffed sleeve. "What is it?" I asked. "I call it a rose-melon," Miss Lockwood cocked her head, studying Lori a moment longer. "It's my favorite color," glowed Lori, "Mommy Tom gave it to me for Christmas!" "And she gave me my sweater," and Bruce held out the waist ribbing. "Well, your Grandmother has excellent taste. Where does she live?" "With Daddy Frank," returned Bruce. "In Kansas City," appended Lori. And we were all laughing by that time, even the bird. "You may both go and talk to Polly a few minutes," Miss Lockwood directed. "But don't put your fingers or faces near her cage. I'm the only one she takes food from and she hates to be teased. She'll ask for crackers but she doesn't even like them." "What *does* she like?" the children chorused. "Special parrot food." And I was relieved, for I could see the plans forming in Lori and Bruce's fertile brains.

"Your children are very mature for their ages, and intelligent, but a half-hour sitting is generally all, even older children, can manage." "Mine can do more," I promised. Miss Lockwood looked toward Lori and Bruce's standing well back from the cage, arms at their sides and talking animatedly to Polly who was rehearsing her entire vocabulary for her rapt audience. "Yes, I think so, too," nodded Miss Lockwood. "Let's try one hour, every other day. I'll do Lori first. I never thought I'd be this excited about little children"—more to herself than to me. "I'll start next week," and she turned to me, "if that's agreeable to you." "Oh, that's wonderful!" I exclaimed. "But I don't want to crowd your schedule." "No, I really want to do them now—they change so rapidly." She took down the coats and called the children.

"I do my own frames, build and finish them myself. They're expensive but I don't want my portraits ruined with a cheap frame. I'd like to do antiqued ones," after I had vigorously nodded agreement, "white underlay, rubbed with gold and shadow colors from their clothing." And she showed me several framed portraits, then one of her daughter at ten with the exquisite frame she had just described. "Oh, that's perfect!" I enthused. "Will they look just like that?" "Pretty much," said Miss Lockwood (really Mrs. Lockwood) "but I'll probably let more white show. Pam was a lot older than your children. Now when was Lori four?" and she got out a small spiral from her smock pocket. "And Bruce will be three—" taking down ages, full names, as well as Dave's, phone number and address. "May I leave you a check?" I asked. "No, not today," she shook her head, "this is the part I hate. I'll paint a few days, then you can sign an agreement."

We talked about size, Miss Lockwood's recommending a 17 X 21" with a two-inch frame. And liners were pointed out to me. "I don't have one here, but a one-inch dark rose velvet would be dramatic. You don't have to decide that today. We'll know when we get into it. You might prefer just a natural linen."

The children pulled on their hats, asked if they might go back to say good-bye to Polly who was screeching against her abruptly curtailed admiration. Miss Lockwood, nodding, went with them: "I sometimes threaten to hood her cage when she gets too obstreperous. Tell Lori and Bruce good-bye, Polly!" "Good-bye, good-bye," obeyed Polly, and for good measure: "Wanna cracker!" and our "five minutes" had grown into an hour and the children had made two exciting new friends!

We returned the next Monday morning for Lori's ten o'clock sitting; she, equipped with a small box of peanuts in shell and two little boxes of raisins. "Now don't eat them until Miss Lockwood says you may and, remember, give nothing to Polly! You don't want her to get sick; she has to have special parrot food." "I'll remember," said Lori. "Polly's my friend!" Miss Lockwood met us at the door. "Do you want us to stay or shall we come back?" I inquired. "You and Bruce come back in an hour." "May I see Polly, then?" Bruce requested. "Of course," smiled his friend, "come in now, too." And Bruce rushed in: "'Ori," he commanded his sister, "teach Polly my name!" said, "Hi, Polly, Hi, Polly," and rushed out again.

Bruce and I went shopping for an hour. "When it's warmer," I suggested, "We'll bring your bucket and shovel and we'll go to the beach." "We can go now," Bruce offered. "It's a little brisk today and the beach isn't much fun when it's blowing sand." "Alright," agreed Bruce and we parked the car and started for the candle shop.

At the corner, a woman passed us, striding briskly down the slight hill. I was looking at Bruce and saying to myself: I recognize those ankles! and looking up, I recognized the Admiral's wife from Kodiak! I couldn't remember her first name and "knew" her too well to call: "Mrs.—" By the time she turned into the gift shop in mid-hill, I had decided to wait and ask Dave her name, remembering that the Admiral had retired to Carmel-by-the-Sea, a few months before we left Alaska. We had liked both of them but she had come back to the States early to choose their retirement home and I had not seen her for almost a year. Well, I would see her again, I concluded, for our portrait-painting would probably take months.

I chose two tall, hand-dipped white candles on which were imposed: wax-molded red roses, green stem and leaves, for the buffet, to pick up the red in our red, black, white and gold geometric-patterned drapes and the red velveteen occasional chair. Dave's favorite flower was a red rose and those would have to suffice while deer and poison oak precluded my rose-gardening. But the sweet peas were in bud and the hanging fuchsias and begonias had been glorious with every-other-day spraying and watering. Bruce and I looked at the shelves and tables of candles, from all over the world, as well as the handmade creations of the shop owner, walked slowly around the block and drove back to Miss Lockwood's. Lori was still in her chair and Miss Lockwood was ecstatic: "Lori's just a darling and we've gotten so much done; those raisins were a wonderful idea. She was *so* good!" I looked around Lori's chair for dropped peanut shells. "I didn't eat them; let's give them to Brucie. Bruc-cie, Bruc-cie," Lori belatedly remembered Bruce's injunction and called to Polly who wouldn't even enunciate her own name; but she responded: "Wanna cracker, wanna cracker" which, I was glad she didn't.

"I'm doing the children in pastels; I can work more quickly," explained Miss Lockwood. "I hope that's alright." "Oh, of course," I applauded, "I'm learning so much!" "I'm doing charcoal sketches first. I think I'll just put in Lori's *left* dimple with just a hint of the right which her hair will shadow. I like her straight forward, don't you?" as she showed me her initial sketch. "Look at her cocked right eyebrow. Isn't that perfect!" and she tipped up Lori's smiling face. "You should see her Daddy's!" I laughed. "They're exactly alike!" "I want to," enthused Miss Lockwood. "Can you bring him tomorrow night at seven? Just to run in?" "Yes, indeed," I was enthusiastic too, "and he'll want to give you a check." "Alright," agreed our completely untemperamental, gracious artist. "Good-bye, Lori and Bruce; bring Daddy tomorrow night!"

Dave, of course, was delighted with the wonderful Florence Lockwood and she, with him. He still had on his greens, since the children and I had met him at the O-Club for early dinner and driven straight from the campus. When he took off his cap and she saw his black curls and handsome physiognomy, she clapped her hands like a little girl and giggled: "I got it right. The eyebrow!" She hugged Lori, "You're certainly your Daddy's darling!" "And Mommy's, too?" worried Lori. "Oh, of course," laughed Miss Lockwood. "You belong equally to both of them and so does Bruce. They wouldn't trade you for a million!" "For *how* much?" and Miss Lockwood, realizing she wasn't dealing with an ordinary child, but a masterful logician, surrendered Lori to me and showed Dave the first sketch. He loved the rough likeness and laughed at the raised eyebrow, admired and approved of the antiqued frame. Bruce and Lori entertained Polly while Dave asked to sign the agreement and I wandered about scrutinizing liners and wondering if the old rose velvet would detract from the children and I concluded it would. She had none on her walls but I envisioned it as more appropriate for a young woman's portrait in an oval, Victorian frame. I asked Miss Lockwood and Dave: "Don't you think the natural linen liner would be better for the children than the old rose? They won't need any enhancement." "Yes," Miss Lockwood acceded, "I've thought that, too. Let's use the natural linen. LT Holland, do you agree?" And Dave did. It was a cordial meeting and we went happily home, savoring our first experience in the artists' world. "Let's see 'Peter Pan' again," said Lori. "We've got a Polly now," added Bruce.

Mother ushered in our California summer with her jubilant letter:

Home Thursday, May 1st.

Dearest Family,

"It's May-time, it's May-time! And all the world is bright and love is in the sunshine and the golden stars of night." "Awake and call me early, call me early, Mother dear, For tomorrow I will be Queen of all the Year!" Tell Lori that's what she is, "Queen of all the Year" and Bruce is the "Prince Charming!" It's a lovely fresh May morning. Once I knew a story about "Did you ever *feel* a May morning?" It's like *feeling* the blossom of a *yellow primrose*, all dewy before the sun comes out with its golden mop to dry up the dew! etc. I've forgotten all of those younger-day whimsies!

Have been out doing the more prosaic task of grubbing up chick weed with my fingers after last night's shower; it is easy to pull up. The ole chick weed is just taking all of the lawns in K. C. I hear people tell about the weed eradicators' killing the grass instead of the weeds so I do not know anything better than to pull them up before seeding. Well, the world is in such a chaotic state I think the *real things* are growing *life*: children, the soil and the enduring verities in which we can find solace and comfort. But the world has gone thro' many such crises and part of it has survived—so I guess it will this May day. The strikes are the main issues here—steel and oil but I believe both will be settled soon. Dad says he won't drive any distance out of town until the oil situation eases as gasoline supplies are somewhat limited, of course, for a few days, tho' some companies are not striking. . . .

I wrote Mother that we were "growing life" and our "verity" would arrive with the autumnal colors in late October.

Life was beautiful and placid on our Monterey hilltop.

I agreed with Mother about world conditions. Eisenhower, who had taken over the reins of government from Truman—having dramatically journeyed to Korea as the President-elect in fulfillment of his pledge—was not finding a swift solution to the Korean impasse. It was ironic that another General—also with Presidential ambition—had been thwarted by Korea: General MacArthur, commander of the Korean War, had been fired in April 1951 by President Truman, who, as Commander in Chief, would not brook disobedience to his orders. Dwight Eisenhower, as renowned as a war hero, though less flamboyant than his peer, was a valiant leader and widely supported as President. His convoluted syntax, however, made him, at times, excruciating to listen to or read. I knew too many brilliant and articulate officers, thinking immodestly of my own, to attribute his limitations with the English language to his "military background," especially since General Douglas MacArthur had "faded away" with such elegant, eloquent, poetical diction.

I thought back to Hanson W. Baldwin's prediction that Korean unification would never be won in a war. That was three years before and our young men were still embroiled in America's most frustrating debacle which, apparently, never would be settled by brute strength. Our American youth had been decimated, Korea and its populace had been devastated—"the light of the universe," extinguished. History might never justify our involvement by designating Korea anything more than a "United Nations" fiasco and our fine young men—the sacrifice for a grandiloquent "world order" which, per se, was a squalid oxymoron. There was no extrication in sight from the Korean morass. Even so, the country was sanguine about the popular Eisenhower's campaign promises and mollified by his avuncular personage.

June provided a magnificent international spectacle. England's young Elizabeth Alexandra Mary, of the Royal House of Windsor, heiress presumptive from the age of eleven, had ascended to the throne of the

United Kingdom of Great Britain and Northern Ireland, and become Head of the Commonwealth, and Defender of the Faith, on the sixth of February 1952, at the sudden death of her father, King George VI. She was to be crowned in Westminster Abbey June 2, 1953.

I was particularly interested in Elizabeth's "career" for her married life had paralleled mine! Elizabeth (her first name; my middle, Beth) had married a distant cousin, LT Philip Mountbatten, Royal Navy, formerly Prince Philip of Greece, in Westminster Abbey on November 20, 1947, a month before I had married my Navy LT (junior grade). A son, Charles Philip Arthur George, was born at Buckingham Palace on November 14, 1948, three months before Lori was born, February 11, 1949. And Princess Elizabeth gave birth to Anne Elizabeth Alice Louise in her official residence at Clarence House on August 15, 1950, three weeks after our Bruce was born, July 25, 1950. (Interested in onomastics and feeling four "forenames" redundant, that every newborn deserved a last name, I was glad when Elizabeth II announced in 1960 that *her* descendants would have a surname: Mountbatten-Windsor, except those titled: prince or princess. The name Windsor had designated the British royal house since 1917; Mountbatten was the surname of Prince Philip's mother, Alice, who had married Prince Andrew of Greece.) So I had followed Elizabeth's marital career with considerable interest and had enjoyed the articles Mother sent me in Kodiak when Princess Elizabeth and the Duke of Edinburgh had visited President Truman in October 1951, at the White House. After Christmas in England, Mother's articles informed me, the Princess and Duke had left for a tour of Australia and New Zealand, January 31, 1952, but they got only to their Forest Lodge in Sagana, an exotic wedding gift from the natives of Kenya, when they were summoned home by the unexpected death of King George.

Princess Elizabeth, summarily a monarch, flew back immediately to London and on February 8, 1952, delivered an emotional speech to the accession Privy Council accepting "this heavy task that has been laid upon me so early in my life." She was twenty-six years old. The first three months of Elizabeth's reign had been passed in seclusion at Clarence House because it was a period of full mourning for George VI. It was summer before she moved to Buckingham Palace to assume the routine duties of the sovereign.

When we returned to the States at the end of 1952, Elizabeth had just carried out her first ceremonial duty, the opening of Parliament and the reading of a speech by the Prime Minister. I considered that task of reading a speech someone else had written, demeaning. If I were a queen, that would be the first tradition I would rescind!

Joy Hinkleman invited the children and me and several others to watch the 2:00 P.M. delayed telecast from Westminster Abbey, June 2, 1953. Lori remembered seeing television once at Charles and Barbara's but Bruce had not been with us as we completed a quick trip to town to pick up the spring coat Mother had chosen for Lori's fourth birthday. Television was a novelty to Dave and me, too, but we had enough ambivalence about the merits of it to even consider purchasing a set. But that telecast from London, delayed and condensed as it was, convinced me of the potential educational advantage of such an instrument.

It was absolutely marvelous to witness, belatedly, of course, the historic coronation of Queen Elizabeth II by the Archbishop of Canterbury. How could she, I wondered, physically sustain that ponderous crown and still sit upright and unbowed on what appeared to be, and my study had revealed, indeed was, a very uncomfortable, stiff throne! (Of heavy oak, it had been built around a rock! England's Edward I had stolen Scotland's Stone of Scone upon which their monarchs had been crowned for centuries and surrounded "the stone of destiny" with *his* throne in 1300. Scottish zealots reappropriated the stone in 1950, returning it to Scotland, but it was shortly recovered and restored to Westminster Abbey where the weighty throne was readied for Elizabeth II's coronation, moved close to the altar and covered with cloth of gold.)

I thought how, as a girl, Princess Elizabeth had been trained to regal poise and had recited all of her lessons, standing, correctly erect with weight on both feet because, as a Queen, hours of standing at ceremonial functions would be demanded of her. Elizabeth Alexandra Mary performed flawlessly at her coronation, imperiled by the heavy royal robe weighting down her shoulders and on her head, the cumbersome, ornately jeweled crown—fashioned for Queen Victoria in 1838 and containing gems worn by Edward, the Confessor; the Black Prince, Edward III's eldest son; and Elizabeth I. Her arms must have become leaden as she held the regalia of a sovereign: the orb in her left hand; the scepter, in her right. But her husband was the first person to kneel and do her homage and that must have strengthened her resolve, as well as her back.

The telecast was a bit fuzzy at times but it was a grand experience. The children were very good but soon elected to play in the fenced yard, three Mothers and I taking turn at supervising; Joy, expectant, but having no children. We all returned for the actual settling of the crown, however, and even the children were impressed to stillness, especially when Elizabeth II stood up and walked safely down the steps in all of her royal adornment, displaying her ceremonial gown; jewelled hands and wrists, sparkling as she trailed the legendary velvet and ermine cape. It was an unforgettable, but wearying, afternoon! I was glad I was an American Naval wife with limited minions—and not a Queen!

It did not take the children long to discover that they "needed" a parrot. "We know all about parrots," Lori began. "We ask Polly," Bruce continued. "We've seen 'Peter Pan' twice and we read our *All About Birds*," reinforced Lori, persuasively. "But you're forgetting, children, Daddy is here to study—that is his job. Do you think it would be fair to him to have a babbling bird?" (He already had two vociferous females.) "Well, . . . " Lori pondered. "Maybe we could get a *dumb* parrot," Bruce suggested. "Remember, we will be here just one more year. Do you really want a pet you'd have to leave behind?" "Yes!" both were emphatic. Time, for children, was always *now*. It was a perfect place for a pet, one that could run and play with our active duo, and we had the unfinished room with windows and screens for ideal sleeping quarters.

"Would you like a cat?" I hoped. I heard Dave putting the car up and was glad he could participate in the momentous decision. "But cats eat birds," Bruce demurred. "But *kittens* don't," Lori came to our succor. "Oh, I love kittens," helped Dave. "When I was a little boy, we had a kitten and I got to take care of it!" "And we had a cat," I recalled. "She was black and white and her name was 'Puss.'" "In-Boots?" finished Bruce. "Yes, that's right, but we just called her 'Puss' or 'Pussy.' You'd think of a better name, I'm sure. What would *you* like to name a cat?" "I'd call her 'Betsy'—that's almost like *best*," offered Lori. "Yes, 'Betsy,'" approved Bruce, "can we go now?" I looked appealingly to Dave—it was only 4:30. "They *wanted* a parrot," I whispered. "Oh!" he grinned, raising his famous eyebrow. "I'll take them now." So the phone book was searched; two calls were made; Dave promised to come back with just one kitten, no puppies, birds, turtles or fish and I prepared dinner, somewhat uncertainly, for I had three children abroad—in pet stores.

Amazingly, they were back within the hour—with just one little animal: an adorable, tawny gold, fluffy kitten which Bruce was carrying, an enraptured expression on his face. Lori, beaming, was carrying a wicker basket with a pillow in the bottom and Dave, as elated as the other three, held a large sack. "Aren't you glad we called her Betsy?" prompted Lori. "She's the best pet in the whole world, isn't she, Bruce?" "Mommy, get the milk," Bruce was too busy to applaud, "I get to sleep with her!" "It's a warm night, Bruce," Dave restrained, "Betsy needs to sleep in her own bed and you need to sleep in yours. She's so small she might get tangled up in your sheet or you might roll over on her in your sleep." "That's a poem!" Lori giggled. "We'll talk about rules at dinner," Dave promised. "And read the Cat Book—after dinner," I hoped.

The following weeks, we emphasized Nursery Rhymes, stories and books about the care of, and responsibility for, human babies and how they must be handled gently by older brothers and sisters and loved and taught. Lori had never been a doll-player, a charcoal-colored French poodle had been a sometime favorite but neither she nor Bruce had ever developed an attachment for an inanimate object. But they felt compassion and affinity for every living creature and we sensed it was, after all, a very timely and wholesome experience—to have Betsy. There was, usually, wisdom in the demands of a child!

It was soon Bruce's turn to sit for Florence Lockwood. As Lori had suggested, the peanuts in shell and box and boxed raisins were both helpful to keep him sedentary and occupied. Miss Lockwood was soon calling Bruce her "little peanut" and commended his behavior as she, of course, had Lori's. I loved the early stages of both portraits and thought I'd like to stop her there but the next strokes were even more marvelous! She let me view, and the children too, each day's progress and it was fascinating to watch the perfecting of a personality. "A smile becomes an affectation over the years," she said, "it almost diminishes intelligence." So she painted Lori with just the vestige of a smile, pensive and quizzical with the perfectly, and typically, arched right eyebrow, the left dimple—prominent. Bruce was being painted, eyes straight-looking, missing nothing, mouth slightly upturned as if he was suppressing laughter as he thought of a succinct, profound pun he was trying not to hurl at Polly. Miss Lockwood's work with the children soared beyond our hopes. She was a perspicacious psychologist whose hand could illuminate and transfer her understanding. She elucidated knowledge of our children, in their pristine personas, for all time!

The portraits were finished by the end of June and we said reluctant good-byes to Florence Lockwood and to Polly. Dave had a week's leave between semesters and Mother H had been invited to travel with us to Yosemite and Sequoia National Parks. We made our usual early morning start, Dave's having taken Betsy, who was becoming a beautiful Persian, to the vets the night before. I sat in the back seat with Lori and Bruce, behind Dave so that I could rest my head in the corner, if the need arose, and the children, upon me but I felt innervated and exuberant.

It was a welcome respite from study for Dave and we were making him struggle with bags and road maps and crowded highways, but he loved it and was always relaxed when he drove; he enjoyed having his Mother in the front seat to navigate and polish his sunglasses. Lori and Bruce took turns at their window but Bruce soon put his pillow in my lap and Lori put hers, on Bruce. It was the height of the park season and Dave stopped short of Yosemite, driving eight miles north and east of Mariposa to Midpines where we discovered rustic cabins and lodge with an attractive and clean restaurant, twenty-three miles from Yosemite. Dave reserved a two-bedroom cabin for two nights and we drove on to the Park. Traffic slowly passed through the gates; every car had questions to ask and, in turn, was given a pamphlet—which answered all the questions—and a map, as fees were paid. It was a warm, sun-shot June afternoon with swaths of deep shade from cliffs, pines and redwoods.

The children were wearing cotton plaid suspender pants, the matching jackets folded in the back window, short-sleeved shirts and sturdy brown playshoes. I wore a smoky-blue, roomy sailor dress which buttoned down the front, in a size 14, which Mother had sent, tucking a perky red handkerchief in the breast pocket. Finishing my fifth month, I probably would not need a maternity dress until the eighth but had included a cool, gray and white-striped seersucker, with a low, square neck, double-breasted and tying in back. I did not like elasticized maternity dresses and that one was a favorite because I had worn it much for Bruce's summer advent. I thought of my "little firecracker's arrival," head pillowed on my lap, and laughed to myself as I smoothed his hair and brushed a curl out of Lori's eyes. What perfect progeny we had, what joys we had experienced—and soon there would be another—and more!

We had taken Highway 140 at Merced, 67 miles west of Yosemite, which led into the Arch Rock Entrance of Yosemite Valley—carved eons ago by the Merced River. The children were in the famous Sierra Nevadas but were unawed, at first, because they thought snow—which they saw all year in Alaska—belonged on all mountains. But when Dave parked the car and took Lori and Bruce in hand to view El Capitan, rising 3,600 feet from the pine and fir floor, they thought it was a pretty impressive rock. There was enough granite in that bald and stern facade to fashion three Rocks of Gibraltar, I had read in the *National Geographic*.

Dave drove from the Valley floor to an overlook and provided us a glorious panorama with El Capitan on the left; Bridalveil Fall, with its misty plume, cataracting the last of May's melting snows; triple-crowned Cathedral Rocks—on the right; and Half-Dome, towering like a halved Jefferson Memorial on the distant horizon, in center-view. Driving toward Glacier Point, which was almost as high as El Capitan and had paved roads for easy access, I read to my captive hearers that Yosemite Park had been named for grizzly bear, the Indian name being "Uzumati," but no grizzlies, unhappily, were left in the park. Seeing the children's worried expressions and pending distressed questions, I quickly added: "But there are lots of black bear and we'll see some, and mule deer and their pretty, little spotted fawns." "Like our deer?" asked Lori, which we had never seen, our nocturnal curiosity, not well-developed. "Yes, I'm sure they are cousins." Glacier Point was 3,250 feet above Yosemite Valley and offered a spectacular view of Yosemite Falls, the highest in North America, plunging 2,425 feet, in a roaring cascade from the granite heights.

During dinner at the Glacier Point Hotel, where Dave checked to see if there had been any room cancellations—in vain; we discussed whether we should wait until 9:00 P.M. for the fire-fall, burning fir-bark embers pushed from beside the observation ledge at Glacier Point and visible from Camp Curry in the Valley below or drive on to the Wawona Tree in Mariposa Grove—through which we could drive our car! It was called "Yosemite's living tunnel" and had been cut through the base of a *Sequoia gigantea* in 1881 for stagecoach traffic. (The giant redwoods had been named *Sequoia* for the Cherokee Indian who had given his tribe an alphabet. The coast redwoods had been found by Spaniards in 1769 and *Sequoia* became their genus. Yosemite's Big Trees had been discovered by Joseph R. Walker in 1833 and in 1852, named 'Wellingtonia' by an English botanist in honor of the British general. Patriotic naturalists wanted an American name and were overjoyed when scientists decided the Yosemite Big Tree actually belonged to the coast redwood's genus, *Sequoia*.)

We decided on the Wawona tree, prompted, no doubt, by my strange identification with trees and because we thought the children might remember it longer, and they would have to remember it, for photography-light was dimming. It was over twenty miles away on a slow, winding road to the southern end of the Park but we encountered no traffic in our direction; everyone was going to Camp Curry to witness the fire-fall! I secretly reasoned, we could do both.

Deep dusk had lowered when we got to the tree and drove through, twice. It was absolutely amazing that the tree, the trunk of which had been hollowed out to accommodate the equivalency of a bus, was still living. The cocoa-brown, deeply fissured bark was about two feet thick and, like asbestos, it was fire-resistant. Hearts of all *Sequoia giganteas* were dead, only the sapwood—inner bark and outer rings—were alive, carrying water and food. It was too dark to take pictures but Dave backed through the second time so that the car lights illuminated the "living tunnel" and angled our lights at some distance from "Wawona" for a last glimpse. From that point on, I urged Dave to haste since there was no traffic, but whispering it to him since my law-abiding children were wide-awake and I was shocking Mother H by my wild, capricious demands. But it was a futile recommendation, as I knew, for Dave would not speed (flyer's instinct does not admit rule-breaking), even if one could in a mountainous forest; moreover, we were low on gas and he planned to stop at the midway station. "Besides," Mother H reminded me, kindly but judiciously, "we voted, you remember, *not* to see the fire-fall." But Dave still tried, reasonably, and when we pulled into the Camp Curry parking lot, we could smell the fir smoke and see it in white ribbons drifting from Glacier Point. The fire-fall was discontinued some years later and the Wawona Tree fenced off from vehicular traffic but not until we had driven through again, before leaving P.G. School, with all of our Holland progeny.

We scouted Yosemite more leisurely the next day, after a good night's rest at Midpines and a hearty breakfast. The children were surprised that such enormous trees as the redwoods and sequoias had very minute cones, about the size of a small grape. They found piñon nuts, fir cones of all sizes and recognized manzanita shrubs growing on sunny slopes. Florence Lockwood had several floral arrangements in her studio built around the white, multi-twigged and twisted manzanita branches which art shops sold for exorbitant prices. Knowing little about life not spent in woods, Lori and Bruce were not tempted to take fruits of the forest back to ours, so we silently acknowledged the National Park signs to resist temptation and enjoyed unburdened discovery.

Close to lunch time, we fortuitously happened upon a small log store where we bought cheese, ham slices, two tomatoes, bread, lettuce, mustard, mayonnaise and apples, washed our hands in a stream—the tomatoes, lettuce and apples, in our drinking water from the thermos jug and had a picnic in the filtered shade of a *Sequoia*, sitting on the sandy, soft-needled, fragrant floor. Walking woody paths, at high elevation, and kicking through the forest groves on our own exploration, had made us ravenous—and appreciative of the thoughtfully placed store.

The following day, we took Highway 41, south of Mariposa to Fresno and southeast on Highway 180 to Kings Canyon and Sequoia National Parks. We wanted to walk through the Giant Forest in the Sequoia National Park and see the General Sherman tree, the most massive of living things, with a 272-foot trunk, 37 feet in diameter, and towering as high as the Capitol dome in Washington. It was over 3,500 years of age and had once been a seed the size of an oat flake, its seed-holding cone not much larger than a muscat raisin from Fresno's San Joaquin Valley. We drove back to Kings Canyon National Park, to Grant Grove, one of the two parks' many groves of *Sequoia gigantea*, to compare the second-largest *Sequoia*, the General Grant tree, to the General Sherman tree. The General Grant tree was designated a National Shrine honoring Americans killed in war. What an overwhelming and humbling stroll it was! Then, placards reminded us that the Giant Forest and Grant Grove had to be saved, from the desecration of *man*, by such naturalists as John Muir and Theodore Roosevelt. The two parks protected thousands of the ancient *Sequoia giganteas*, native to only a small zone, 4,000 to 8,000 feet in the western Sierra Nevada Range. We were amazed by all we had seen and ready to return to and protect—our own little wooded, private park where the children could run with Betsy, pick up and keep their favorite pine cones, and maybe, see their own deer.

July passed swiftly and Bruce became three years old on the 25th. Two days later, the Korean Armistice was finally signed; there had been no winners and one entire country had been wasted. (It was announced on November 21, 1991, that the last American troop withdrawal, scheduled for 1993 to 1995, had been delayed.) But the sun shone brightly in California; the sweet peas were fructiferous; and Dave's second semester was underway. The three-year caterpillars were devouring the live-oak foliage in the front yard which was the only place I walked in safety from the poison oak; Betsy, daily, had to be de-ticked—Dave's turning the hard, black insects counterclockwise with tweezers; but the begonias and fuchsias still dripped beautiful blooms.

One late summer Saturday, a shiny, *slithy* villain entered our lofty Eden and I sent Dave out armed with flight gloves and boots and sundry weapons to attack the only snake the children had encountered. They thought it "pretty and nice" but it looked enormous and deadly to me, and I insisted herpetological research would have to wait; defense must begin at once. We had never a snake to worry about in Alaska and I insisted upon a pregnant Mother's rights: rid me of snake-worry and Dave, reluctantly—telling me it was a harmless garter snake, he felt sure—did. And it was, I guess, though it looked almost like a bull snake and I felt more justified when I alluded to it as such. But it *was* huge and the children never found another.

Autumn arrived and soon, pumpkin-time and I went twice to Fort Ord Army Base Hospital with false labor pains. It was embarrassing to confirm it was my third but the Base was half-an-hour's distance and the pains came conveniently when Dave was home and the doctor had stated, "Don't wait, just come!" So we didn't and I did. The third time, there were no pains. The water broke at five in the morning of November 3, 1953. I alerted Dave who dressed with unbored alacrity and summoned Lori and Bruce who awakened less quickly. But, with practiced skill, they pulled slipper socks over their sleepers, pushed arms and heads into coats and hats laid out on their red table and were perfect in their timing, having drilled every other night—in the middle—for the past six. They each carried a pillow and I, a quilt, for the children, somnambulating through the procedure, would resume their night's rest. Dave escorted us out the front door, where there was only one step, and we were efficiently on our way—again.

But on 3 November, arriving shortly after 5:40 A.M., I stayed. The baby arrived at 6:30 A.M. and was very polite: they had to announce his sex! David Bruce Holland, Jr., looked exactly like Dave, weighed seven pounds, two ounces and was twenty inches in length. "And he's just in time for breakfast," laughed Dr. Andresen, letting me look at my beautiful boy at a distance but my nearsighted vision saw all the squirming health and vigor and I heard the first cry and the whole world was rosy with the sunrise! How wonderful! Two Holland scions and one Dutch princess—to hold the fort and rule the realm!

Driving over to Fort Ord, Dave had chuckled: "You always have your babies when I'm in school!" "Of course," I laughed, "you're home every night. It would take a hurricane or an earthquake to escape!" Dave had called ahead and the corpsman took my bag inside the door; I had sent Dave and the children back home. "When you see me again, in a few days," I told the children, "our new baby will have come!" "Will new parents come, too?" requested Bruce, not willing to surrender his. "No," I considered, barely suppressing my smile, "Mommy Tom is coming and we won't need anyone else." "You and Lori will then have Mommy and me,

Mommy Tom and Baby, . . ."—"And Betsy," interrupted Lori. "Yes," understood Bruce, "and Daddy Frank and Grammy Sue!" I hugged them all and went, happily, with the familiar, very patient corpsman.

To become a Mother was the most exhilarating of life's experiences. I was elated, again! Dave had a namesake, in his grand image, and the children, a little brother to love, protect and train to their precocity. I could have run to my room! But they wheeled me, prosaically, to the sun porch; it had been a busy few days, one corpsman apologized, but I could have my choice of four beds. I chose the southeast corner overlooking a slope of lawn, the sun's lighting the lowest branches of cypress and pine—and they brought me breakfast. It was Tuesday and Dave was probably already on the way to school, taking the children to the campus nursery. Knowing he would have called Mother H and Mother, who would be making joyous plans to come, I slept briefly and then they brought in my beautiful black-haired, dimple-cheeked cherub. My little Davie—just like my big! and, oh! he was hungry.

Dave came, beaming broadly, at noon—he had a free hour after lunch—had seen his little replication; our Mothers and Dad were thrilled and the children, excitedly going to the nursery, were anxious for Mommy Tom to arrive. I told Dave not to come in the evenings but to put the children to bed early for their days would be long and napless, to relax and study. He planned to take them to the O-Club for dinner, if I really didn't want him to come back, studying at school until five-thirty. Wednesday night they had children's cartoons at seven and he would study until six and surprise them. "Do not come tomorrow," I urged. "Yes, I want to," Dave stated, "I'll eat lunch here and, maybe, even study a few minutes."

Mother wired her arrival schedule the next morning. It was addressed to: "Lieut David B. Horuynd (I wondered how many misunderstandings, and wars, had been created via telegraphy) Leaving tonight Union Pacific Arrive Monterey 6 57 Friday Evening Congratulations to Dot Love Mother" Mother's train was on time and Dave brought her straight from the station to see the baby, staying in the car with Lori and Bruce. She was ecstatically proud of us all and wished Dad could see Baby Davie—he so loved tiny tots—but she knew Dave would take lots of pictures.

I paid our bill early the next morning, making out my check to: U. S. Army Hospital, Fort Ord, California, 7 November 1953, for $7.00—the receipt stating 4 days @ $1.75. Mother bundled Davie into his hooded blue bunting while I put *The Brothers Karamazov*, a card with Davie's precious little footprints, a blue-bordered card proclaiming: "Holland, Baby Boy" and statistics, and sundry cards and telegrams into my bag, which Mother insisted upon carrying—handing me Davie, and we hurried to the waiting room to join Dave, Lori and Bruce.

What a happy family we were! At home, the children showed Davie their cowboy hats, guns and scarves, and Betsy—"from a distance, only," Mommy Tom said, and I busied myself in the kitchen, suddenly enthusiastic about baking pumpkin pies, one of Dave's favorites. Mother loved our hilltop home, as had Mother H, and thought the portraits were marvelous. "It's too bad you'll leave before Davie is old enough for Miss Lockwood. Maybe you'll let our neighbor, Dwight Roberts, do him. He spends his winters in Arizona. When will you be back from Newfoundland, Dave?" "Probably, January of '56," thought Dave. "I'll introduce you when you come home in June," Mother said, "you've seen him, I'm sure. His wife is tall and blonde and beautiful, they have one grown son; they're very prominent, socially, with the young sophisticates. I like him very much and she is really, quite stunning. They used to come over to visit with Papa and me—and Beth, on the front porch, when Dad would be out of town. Beth was very impressed with both of them." "Davie would be the right age," I mused, "I'd want him younger than Bruce; he was three, lacking a month. Davie would be twenty-six, almost twenty-seven months old." "I'll ask Grace Jenkins what his reputation is," Mother continued—then laughed: "he's an excellent literary critic—he loved your Alaskan article, Sis!"

The next week, I heard Lori tell Mother, with great sobriety and in

Figure 52. Appraisal Time

her best judgmental mien: "I've seen that dress before, Mommy Tom—but that's alright!" Mother was so tickled, she laughed until it was almost a pain; Lori dimpled and tried to soothe a suddenly indignant Davie, while Bruce solemnly scrutinized the provokingly innocent dress. I almost became hysterical with hilarity, clutched my aching sides and had to sit down—because never before, nor since, was Lori, or I, "fashion's slave." Her closest sartorial encounter had come when she and Bruce had been invited to participate in a fashion show given for the Officers' Wives' Club by a Monterey clothier who reasoned, correctly, that adoring Mothers would buy all the frocks and suits their adorable children had modeled—and Lori had looked adorable in the red, white-striped dress with white collar and natty navy bow and matching red slippers.

Bruce had worn a summer shorts set with contrasting hat and carried an inner-tube animal but refused to entertain the acceptability of *any* of his attire and said "no more" to the whole venture.

Lori soon wore her outfit again when she and Bruce appeared on a children's

Figure 53. One-Time Model

television show, having been recommended as both attractive in appearance and loquacious in verbal exchange by some one of their secret admirers. I wondered what we'd have to buy as I sat with the other Mothers behind the glass enclosure where we could see but not be heard. They gave Lori a big baby doll and she shook her head, not smiling, not showing her dimples: "I'd like the Shirley Temple doll, please," she announced, and I was audibly aghast. I thought my non-doll-lover would ask for the microscope. Bruce was given a red fire truck with an attached hose and then they both smiled. Lori told me as we drove home that girls were to be given *only* dolls and she was making the best of an unpleasing situation.

Week-end jaunts became the mode while Mother remained in Monterey. We showed her the California Salad Bowl in Salinas Valley; artichoke fields in Castroville; and the begonia nurseries, at Watsonville; went by the Luhnows at Burlingame (Mother knew they would still be in Hawaii but left a note with the housekeeper); spent an afternoon at Stanford in Palo Alto; had seafood in Fisherman's Wharf, San Francisco and on to see the coastal redwoods, northwest of San Francisco at the Muir Woods National Monument. We bought redwood burl compotes for Mother and Mother H, Mother's finding a quaint redwood-bark shaggy doll for Lori to scientifically examine. The entire doll was made of redwood with flat seeds for eyes, the tiny redwood cones painted silver, for buttons, brushed shreds of bark for the fluffy hair and a thin twist of fiber for the belt, tied in a bow, at the waist. She wasn't a pretty girl and looked

rather like a fireplace broom but Lori preferred her to Shirley Temple and put her beside Mehitable Sophira Jones II, on the shelf over her bed. Bruce was awarded a redwood truck and logs to go on his shelf and he could unstrap the logs and wash them off, outside, with his red fire truck. Dave and I indulged in a large redwood burl vase with fascinating grain, rubbed and polished to a marvelous sheen.

Mother stayed until Davie was five weeks' old and acclimated to his older brother and sister who were eager to begin *their* training. It had been a wonderfully helpful visit. Mother convinced us not to exhaust ourselves with a Christmas trip to Kansas City, especially since

Figure 54. First Cowboy Lesson: Unheeded

Dave would be studying for his second semester exams. We concurred and knew it would be wise for him to have uninterrupted study over the holidays.

We enjoyed a mild, sunny Christmas in Monterey with a beautiful tree from California woods and green boughs and huge sugar cones on the mantel which Lori, Bruce and Dave had found in the hilly terrain north of San Francisco and gathered for all the families in the Midwest to share.

Lori and Bruce hung their stockings from the mantel, placing Davie's, which Mommy Tom had just sent, in the middle and reminding Dave not to build a fire "because that's Santa Claus's only way, without snow!"

Figure 55. "Stockings Were Hung. . . ."

Dave read them "The Night Before Christmas"and then we tucked each of them snuggling to bed—whilst visions of California's dates, figs, almonds, oranges and plenitude put them sweetly to sleep.

Figure 56. "'Twas the Night Before. . . ."

Shortly after Christmas, the Luhnows, returning from their Hawaiian trip, came to see Davie, sorry to have just missed Mother. It was gracious of them to come and we told them all the news of Kansas City and Mother, Dad, Charles and Barbara.

Davie was plump and handsome and prompted a categorical syllogism in logic when I nursed him, which had been prompted by their Daddy, of course; Lori and Bruce's chanting: "Cows give milk, Mother gives milk; therefore, Mother is a! . . ." But I still loved them all!

By Lori's fifth birthday, a very warm February 11, 1954, the sweet peas—the fat, black seeds of which the children had planted for me along the terrace in November— regaled us with a fragrant nebula of bloom. I cut her commemorative bouquet from each step of the terrace where the

Figure 57. Petticoat of Sweet-peas

Figure 58.   Five-Year-Old Curls

children's healthy vines twisted long-stemmed flowers to the top of Dave's tautly tied cords. As Lori dressed for her second pineapple-parfait cake in Monterey, I gave her "a lapful of posies"—which Dave could not resist recording.

Our favorite springtime entertainment was driving the half-hour's distance to Salinas to a drive-in movie after early supper at home. Salinas Valley, one of the most flourishing truck-farming areas of the world, had been popularized by John Steinbeck's depression-era novel, *Grapes of Wrath*, to which the prosperous land of the Fifties bore no resemblance. The children enjoyed the cartoons which were presented first and then ate their raisins. I thought of the little boy I had seen in the Commissary, sitting in his basket seat, the Mother's saying: "Johnny, do you think you'll ever learn to like raisins?" "Yes," said Johnny, "but not to eat!" Mother and I both laughed; "Make that boy, a politician!" I urged. After the cartoon segment, our threesome slept; Davie, up front, on my lap.

I thought back to our first drive-in movie, in Pensacola; Bruce, just a month old, had cried and cried, and I had just nursed him and knew it was not hunger and he had just been changed. Dave, always the solver of mysteries and finder of missing items, discovered that Bruce's toe was twisted in the fringe of his baby shawl. After that, I was aware of baby toes and baby shawls' incompatibility and stockinged the first when using the latter.

We enjoyed shopping for children's essentials in Salinas, too, the Ship's Service on campus being without a children's department. Mother supplied Lori, Bruce and Davie with most everything because it delighted her, and Dad, to do so. I had learned to order playclothes from Sears when we resided in Alaska and Salinas was the closest store. At the end of May, we were returning a pair of shoes to Sears which we had bought for Bruce. It was the last time he would try on only the left shoe! The clerk had neatly wrapped and fitted two brown boy's shoes in the box, each a different size. As we entered the Sears store, I was carrying Davie, who was eight months old, almost, and had just taken a step or two but loved to stand alone and be a big boy, like his brother. I put him down at the top of the escalator but held his hand, as we awaited our turn. Suddenly, the escalator stopped moving and startled expressions flooded faces, which seemed turned back toward me, and then people pushed and hurried to get off under their own locomotion. Dave, behind me, wisely asked Bruce what was wrong and a woman rushed to find the manager. Bruce leaned over; "Davie," he said, "punch the button again," laughing so hard I thought he had originated the magic. But he hadn't, and Davie knew exactly what to do and we sailed on down on escalator power; my trying to look innocent, or stern, or both. Dave stayed back to examine the temptation and discovered the button—just at Davie's eye level but too low for Bruce's. Both boys looked yearningly in that direction, each time we went to Sears, just twice more luckily—but we were looking too!

Dave's eighteen-month tour at the Naval Postgraduate School had been very demanding with seventeen hours of class work a week and two hours of outside study for each hour spent in class. Being a flyer, additional hours were necessitated for flight proficiency but there were no month-long, or week-long, or even overnight absences. It had been an unknown joy to have Dave with us every night, uninterruptedly, without even a SAR summons! How we loved being secluded with Dave on our hilltop in the still woods! And how good the children and I were!

Lori, Bruce, Davie and I offered few distractions to Dave's study—each of us inclined to varying degrees of individual, quiet activity and investigation. We had no television; records were played in children-hours and radios, at early news time. No car turned into our cul-de-sac; no street light broke the darkness; no noise, the silence. An occasional melic whispering of wind tunes through oak or pine brushed the ear—and often soothed too successfully our struggling scholar. Indeed, Dave's only threat to monastic scholarship was the succumbing to slumber in the benevolent solitude.

But Dave was successful as were eighty other regular line officers, four Waves, a Chinese Naval officer from Formosa and LT To Shen of the Chinese Nationalist Navy.

I was interested in the variety of the new assignments. Many were naturally related to Naval aviation, both afloat and ashore. Flyers, in my estimation, were all pseudo-meteorologists, conversant as they were with cloud heights, wind velocity, visibility, turbulence, icing. Of course, highly trained weathermen were needed with the increased speed and range of aircraft and ships, the emphasis upon jets and their dependence upon upper altitude data.

Some of the graduates were assigned to fleet units to provide specialized services; others to the forecasting of weather for amphibious landing operations; or to Fleet Weather Centers throughout the world. I was fascinated by the responsibilities involved in predicting weather for aircraft weather reconnaissance squadrons—the hurricane-hunters. They looked forward to finding and flying into the eye of tropical storms, typhoons and hurricanes. Once in the center, accurate position and tracking records had to be made and sent to fleet and shore establishments, civilian population and military, alike, relying upon their accuracy.

CDR C. D. Good, head of the P. G. School, told his students he had confidence in their ability to cope with the present and future meteorological demands. He referred to puzzles in ballistics, atomic warfare, radar propagation, sound propagation in the ocean, microseismic storm-tracking techniques and micrometeorological forecasts related to effectiveness of smoke screen as affected by near-surface conditions.

It was a very impressive Naval Institution and we were proud of our nearly graduated Meteorologist!

Dave and Dave Minton, both Newfoundland-bound, had finished their papers on their new billets, delivered their lectures, presented with slides of weather parameters—which my Dave had prepared, and were accorded high marks. It had been a wonderful, Dave-productive tour.

We said good-bye to California and on our last week end, drove north to Children's Fairyland, Oakland, where at the "Old woman, who lived in a shoe"—which Lori and Bruce climbed through, my holding Davie; a woman approached me and said: "That's not your baby, is it?" So, I handed Dave, Davie and she smiled, not really intending to report me for baby-napping. But Florence Lockwood had said *Bruce* was mine! I took *him* by the hand and we all hurried back home. While I baked brownies, Dave gave away Betsy and three kittens. The packers came June 2, and Dave graduated at noon June 3, 1954. I kept out one book inscribed by Dad in the world's most beautiful calligraphy: Rachel Carson's *The Sea Around Us*. It would soon be so again.

CHAPTER V

ADVENTURES IN NEWFOUNDLAND

The situation was provocatively familiar. Once again, I was traveling to the Far North to join Dave. Three years before, in the summer, I had made a similar trip with Lori and Bruce. Then, we had flown westward to Kodiak, Alaska. Now, we were eastbound to the U.S. Naval Station, Argentia, Newfoundland, Canada. Located on Placentia Bay, Argentia was on the rugged, indented southern coast of Newfoundland.

When we had departed for Alaska on a warm summer night in June 1951, Lori was two and a-half years old and Bruce, a babe of ten months. Now, it was August 1954. Lori was almost six and Bruce had just passed his fourth birthday. Once again, I was traveling with a ten-month-old baby boy; this time, David Jr. When we had left Seattle's Boeing Field for Alaska, I was the sole woman passenger in a planeful of Filipinos destined for work in the Alaskan salmon canneries. Leaving the Naval Air Station at Patuxent River, Maryland, I was waved aboard first, being the only dependent among Naval enlisted men and officers, all Newfoundland-bound.

How natural it seemed to be flying over an ocean again: east o'er the Atlantic, to join Dave. After our return from Alaska, we had delighted in Dave's eighteen-month tour at Monterey, California. We had explored the diverse beauties of California and had enjoyed its fruits, its vegetables and its dime stores—three of the accustomed things we had missed most in Kodiak. Surfeited with a year and a half of civilization, we were prepared and almost eager for another overseas tour.

The children and I were strapped in our seats. Bruce, in the seat adjoining mine; Lori, in front of us. I held Davie on my lap, the safety belt fastened around both of us. He was intrigued with the heavy buckle on the belt and played with it as we were airborne. I felt supremely comfortable and relaxed in the knowledge that I was aboard a Navy R5D. With loyalty typical of a Navy flyer, Dave had delayed our flight to assure us space aboard a Navy plane. The families of two other officers, ordered with Dave from Monterey to Argentia, arrived several days prior to our arrival. They arrived in an Air Force plane. To that mode of transportation, Dave would not agree and we were perfectly happy to proceed alone via Navy air.

Shortly after takeoff, the children were asleep, having arisen early after a short night's sleep in a small, hot room. We had stayed overnight in the transients' quarters at Patuxent River. Loosening the safety belt around Davie, I settled him more comfortably and thought about the preparations we had made for Dave's tour in Newfoundland. The children had all had typhoid, tetanus and smallpox boosters as had Dave and I. Photostatic copies of birth certificates had been secured for each of us, in case Canadian visas were necessary. Dave and I had duly drawn up our wills, signed them before witnesses and left sealed copies with Mother and Dad in Kansas City.

When we were in the air over the Atlantic Ocean, I had the poignant realization that we were leaving the States and home for an indeterminate overseas tour. I had a different feeling about going to Newfoundland, a foreign land, than I experienced enroute to Alaska. Alaska harbored Americans almost exclusively and was, in reality, an extension of the States. Newfoundland, I knew, would provide a new challenge, a new stimulation and I felt ill-equipped in my knowledge of the place.

I recalled how we had made a trip to the Monterey Public Library as soon as Dave's orders to Argentia had arrived. There, to our disbelief, we discovered but two books on Newfoundland. One was a dismal account of the economic solvency of the island. The other, entitled *Newfoundland Holiday*, was a gazetteer for tourists. In the latter, I found a paragraph about Placentia which we knew was the most likely area for off-Base housing. In the paragraph, I discovered the name of a Newfoundland woman who had provided shelter for the author one night, affording him "all of the conveniences one might reasonably expect."

With elation at the sudden wealth, I wrote to "Mrs. Cahill" wondering if she truly existed. Hoping that she did, I inquired at length about housing, drinking water and schools—in that order. Within two weeks, my stamped, self-addressed envelope was returned and I felt I had a friend in Newfoundland! Mrs. Cahill was very gracious and wrote me that there was one house which could be rented in Placentia and that it had been leased for six months. She apologized for having no room in her own home for a large family but suggested several persons whom I might contact.

There was an estimated eight-months' wait for Base housing and I was determined to join Dave if adequate housing was obtainable. To sit and wait was not my proclivity. I corresponded with Mrs. Cahill for two months. Each letter from her brought a hint for my search but with the admonition that the housing of the Placentia-Jerseyside-Dunville-South-east Arm area would not have the conveniences I would desire with three small children.

Somewhat discouraged, I wrote to the Secretary of the Tourist Development Center in St. John's which was also mentioned in *Newfound-land Holiday.* I would have been happy to live in St. John's, which was ninety miles from the Base, with Dave's commuting on the week ends. But housing was desperate there, also, due to the large number of Americans attached to Pepperrell Air Force Base on the outskirts of St. John's. I even advertised, in two of St. John's daily newspapers, for an apartment and wrote to numerous boardinghouses. Those efforts were rewarded by two responses: a bill from each newspaper.

It was through Mrs. Cahill that I eventually learned of the Orcan apartment house in Placentia to which American service personnel had entrée. I wired immediately to the manager of the Orcan who placed our name on the waiting list. In two months, Dave was given the key to Apartment Number 7 at the Orcan and we were on our way to join him.

There were two things I knew definitely about Newfoundland. (I confess I was ignorant of both before our trip to the library but then I had done little thinking about Newfoundland before the spring of '54.) First, I knew that the word "Newfoundland" was pronounced with the accent on the last syllable, "land" being given full emphasis as if it stood alone. I felt supremely cosmopolitan with that important bit of knowledge. Further, I knew that St. John's, Newfoundland, was the oldest city in North America. What visions of romance and antiquity I conjured about St. John's!

I reflected, with amusement, how to everyone that convenience and politeness allowed, I had mentioned our going to Newfoundland for a lengthy stay. And then I noted their reactions—much as I had before starting off for Alaska. Many thought it perfectly wonderful that *I* (not they) could go to Newfoundland wherever *that* was. Others were vociferously sympathetic. Very few were envious. I was delighted to be going and thoroughly enjoyed planning and preparing for our trip and observing the fluxion of vicarious pleasure and dismay. Those who involuntarily shuddered did so more at the thought of flying from Kansas City to Newfoundland than of spending a year and a half in the strange land. But we were flying Navy! And Navy flyers were the most select, best trained, most disciplined and skilled flyers in the world!

I thought, too, of the fervor with which sales personnel had outfitted us for bleak, frigid existence in the Northland. Grim-faced, they had pulled forth garments which would have provoked guffaws from even the most timorous tenderfoot. They had accepted the explanation of our going to Newfoundland with a sense of personal challenge and had shook a vocal fist at that foreign, assumed-to-be arrogant, inhospitable land.

Yes, our preparations for Newfoundland had provoked and resummoned all attitudes and responses experienced—Alaska-bound. It was all very familiar and festal—for Alaska had been a grand holiday.

The entire trip, from Kansas City by plane to Washington; from Patuxent River, Maryland, to Argentia, Newfoundland, was fluid and flawless. Mildred and Hub had met our plane in Washington, D. C., and taken us home with them to Silver Spring, Maryland, for the night, delivering us to the Patuxent River Naval Air Station the next night for the early morning flight to Argentia.

The children behaved admirably. Thanks to the Navy, they had been seasoned travelers from infancy, having traveled by road and rail, air and sea, in all weather.

The flight from Patuxent River to Argentia was accomplished in slightly less than seven hours. Everyone aboard was wonderful to us. I was particularly grateful to the enlisted men who entertained the children, fed them and made room on their bucket seats for the children to stretch out and sleep. The Wave stewardess was also of great help.

Approaching Argentia, we encountered unusual weather which I had not been advised to expect. It was not raining! In fact, there was a glorious, fulgent moon overhead as our Navy pilot settled the R5D expertly on the runway at the Argentia Naval Station in Argentia, Newfoundland, Canada.

Looking at my watch, I noted that it was exactly 8:00 P.M., Stateside time. The children were struggling with their safety belts as we were officially welcomed to the Argentia Naval Station. As soon as the perfunctory, yet pleasant, military greeting was over, Lori and Bruce, halfway into their spring coats and hats, began to squeal and point: "There's Daddy! Mama, there's Daddy!" Realizing that any tall, handsome man with black, curly hair and a tender smile could be mistaken for their Daddy, I said: "Yes, that's fine. Put your coats on." One does not just stroll aboard a Navy transport to greet friends and family, I reasoned to myself, as I buttoned Davie's coat and secured his hat. Looking back, I was shocked to find that it *was* Dave. In answer to my quizzical expression, Dave laughed: "They *let* me." He kissed us all and hurried us into our wraps and toward the steps. We were all talking excitedly, only Davie was poised—his Daddy was holding him again. Then, we were standing in the door of the plane breathing fresh air.

It had been so hot when we left the States and comfortably warm during the flight that we were unprepared for the frigidness of the Newfoundland wind. It was impossible to believe that the month was August. What, I wondered, would March be like! Slowing our descent from the plane, the impeditive wind seemed to be holding us in appraisal before accepting us on Newfoundland soil.

In a few minutes we were inside the Air Transport Office and getting warm again. Dave, with Davie, went to the desk to check us in while Lori and Bruce tried all the empty seats, drank water again and again and, quickly, limbered their limbs. I studied the map of Newfoundland on the wall and the various photographs of aircraft and scenes of the snowy North. The wall clock indicated that it was 10:00 P.M., Newfoundland daylight-saving time. I was reminded that it was long past the children's bedtime but sleep seemed far from their inclinations. I glanced at my watch and was startled to discover that it was eight-thirty, eastern. An hour's difference in time, I could understand; one hour and a-half's difference seemed aberrant. When Dave came from the desk announcing that the bags had not been brought from the plane, I asked him about the puzzling time difference. He explained, simply, that Newfoundland was midway between time zones.

Our bags arrived. While Dave put them in the car, with the children's rompish help, I again thanked the men who had been of such great assistance to us on the flight. Dave came over to thank them, too, and to shake hands as the children said their good-byes.

Lori and Bruce, laughing to have the car again, gleefully took their places in back. I held a sleepy Davie and Dave started off—bumping us over a ragged road through primeval woods to Placentia, an hour's distance from the Base.

Placentia, the old French capital of Newfoundland, when English rivalry was in flower, was to be our home for the next eight months. To arrive in Placentia, one must either go the long way by car around Southeast Arm, an indentation in the coastline resembling a giant's prodding arm, or the short way via small boat. That night, not desirous of a boat trip, we drove around Southeast Arm to Placentia, laden as we were with baggage and anxious to see everything along the way.

Although the children had spent most of their remembered lives in the woods: in Alaska's spruce woods, the pine and live oak woods of California—they were magnetized by each stream, pebble and bough. So, late as it was, Dave stopped beside the first stream. Lori and Bruce scrambled happily from the car: "May we throw some

Figure 59. Dave, on French Cannon Remnants Overlooking Placentia

rocks?" In the brightness of the moonlight, the children gathered and tossed their handful of pebbles and helped Davie toss a few and, as of old, received instruction from their Daddy in the art of skipping stones. After the children were deposited once again in the car, we drove slowly along the ungraded, forest-shadowed road toward our Newfoundland home. Dave and I talked little; we were just happy to be together again. But the children were garrulous, had many questions to ask and wondered how far it was "to Mommy Tom and Daddy Frank's in Kansas City."

After nearly an hour's drive, we came abruptly down from the uniplanar woods, with its freshness of spruce and fir, its glistening of streams and ponds, to a narrow depth of rocky land projecting in the sea. "This is Placentia," Dave announced. "*This* is Placentia?" I repeated, never having thought to ask Mrs. Cahill or Dave what trees grew in Placentia. Dave nodded admission. Moonlight usually touched with kindness all in its domain but the moonlight of that August night did not diminish the starkness of the "land." Placentia was nothing more than a bleak strip of treeless rock!

Figure 60. Our Treeless Home

On either side of the road, where one might see trees, shrubs, grass or soil or even sand, were boulders, rocks, pebbles. They were of the same slick, rounded contour, varying in size and color, smoothed by centuries of washing, disgorged upon the land for further centuries of uselessness. And I pondered the valuelessness of a rock and wondered at the people who must live in Placentia a lifetime, tolerating the land's infertility and invariability.

Dave proceeded selectively on a wriggling route over the rocky beach. And then, there were houses binding the road on both sides. They appeared to be exclusively of frame construction, modestly dingy, as grayed and weathered as the beach. But light streaked from windows and doors and I felt, inexplicably, that the people and scenes within would belie my first impression of Placentia.

Dave made many turns from one narrow, rocky lane to another and I wondered if I would ever find my way alone through that congested village. Then we turned into an alley. It was superior to any of the roads we had thus traversed. Dave pointed to a rusted, bulbless marquee: "Orcan," stopped the car and told us we were home. Home was a one-time motion picture theater which had been converted into eight apartments and was bounded on the east by a narrow stretch of water which Dave referred to as "the gut."

I was pleasantly surprised by the modernity, if not the commodiousness, of our apartment. Its arrangement left something to be desired, however, the front door's opening into the entrance to the bathroom but, mainly, it was warm with baseboard heat in every room—all four, neatly in a row. Next to the bathroom was the kitchen with an unusual amount of shelf and cabinet space. It was one of the choice kitchens in town because it did not have an oil stove. In fact, it contained a very modern electric stove and a large electric refrigerator, both American-made. For whatever inconvenience we would have to endure, in our isolation from the Base, I felt those two objects would recompense.

A small room, which opened out of the kitchen, cleverly done with dark green on three walls and the ceiling, dark red on the one-windowed wall—appeared to be the living-dining room. I was audibly thrilled at the sight of a chrome dinette set, a well-used studio couch, one chair which was odd, indeed, and a strange fixture with four drawers which Dave labeled a buffet. "I bought it all from the departing officer," laughed Dave. Our bedroom afforded room for a bed, an oversized youth bed, snugly against two walls, and a dresser.

The children's room was the most wonderful of all. It contained miniature bunk beds for Lori and Bruce, Davie's crib, sent from Monterey storage, a chifforobe, both of my cedar chests, a night stand, large closet area and an automatic clothes dryer! The latter, plus a lavish amount of French perfume, was my "welcome-to-Placentia" token from Dave.

Having strewn the apartment with objects of travel from the door to the master bedroom, we were forced to retrace our excited steps to find articles for retirement. Coming once again into the kitchen, we realized that we were hungry and found the refrigerator and cabinets fully stocked by our thoughtful Dave—even to fresh fruit and frozen lobsters! We drank appreciatively of the cold water which Dave had boiled and placed in the refrigerator. The children each enjoyed a glass of milk: "mechanical cow" milk as we learned to call it. That was powdered milk, whipped to a fury by the Navy and made palatable when icy cold. There was no fresh milk available in Placentia unless one chose to drink the unpasteurized milk sold by the local dairy which was concentrated in three cows behind the Bank of Canada.

Our apartment was on the second floor, facing north and overlooking the village's main road, alongside the gut, which was nameless as far as I could determine. The house immediately next to us, into whose yard we looked, was the most prosperous in town. It glistened with fresh white paint, boasted two red brick chimneys and a bright blue door with a brass knocker. Moreover, there was grass in the yard, several minute deciduous saplings and rose bushes! Enclosing the yard was a white picket fence with a gate of the same bright blue. That was the doctor's house. Patently, he was the most distinguished, most revered and best-sustained citizen in town. The doctor, we learned, was a native of St. John's, Newfoundland, who had been sent by the Canadian Board of Health to the outpost of Placentia. He directed the hospital which was operated by Catholic nuns and, with his assistant, cared for the ten thousand inhabitants of Placentia and neighboring villages. The doctor was married to an attractive English woman whom he met in London during the war while he was serving with the Newfoundland Army. She was an outdoorswoman and kept a horse, a cow, five sheep and two dogs within the limited confines of the yard. All of the doctor's family, including the "Newfie" housekeeper, were friendly—and distinctive with their English and French-English accents. Lori and Bruce made friends with Annie, seven, and Jimmy, three, the doctor's two younger children. His twelve-year-old son, whom we never met, was at school in London.

Although the doctor's family was Protestant, Annie attended a Catholic school. It was the only school in the village just as the Catholic church was the only church. Yet if one were to go a few miles' distance to a neighboring village, it would be discovered that its church was Anglican and its school, Anglican. We inquired about the peculiarity and learned that when Newfoundland was developed, settlement took place according to religious affiliation (much as our colonies had evolved) so that each village was predominantly one of the three chief denominations: Roman Catholic, Anglican, United Church.

It was the complaint of some that the schools of Newfoundland were still denominational. Since earliest times, they had been built and controlled by the churches of the several religions. In past years, certain Protestant denominations had united to establish "amalgamated schools," but there seemed to be no strong trend away from the system of denominational education.

Proximate to the doctor's house was the Bank of Canada which was directed by Jim O'Brien, a distinguished Newfoundlander with whose attractive wife I frequently played bridge. We paid our monthly rent to the bank which, in turn, forwarded it to the owner of the Orcan in St. John's. Our rent was paid in either American or Canadian money. The Canadian rate of exchange varied from day to day, fluctuating generally from one to four cents on the American dollar. Newfoundland currency had become obsolete on April 1, 1949, when Newfoundland formally became the tenth province of the Dominion of Canada. Newfoundland coins became a popular collector's item among service personnel. We, too, gathered a minute sample of "Newfie" money.

There had been much speculation as to why Newfoundland desired and accepted confederacy with Canada. Several of my Newfoundland friends expressed disappointment over the union with Canada and confessed their hope that union with the States might have been possible. Actually, it was an inevitable choice.

Newfoundland, which was Britain's oldest colony (discovered by John Cabot, a Venetian navigator in the service of England, in 1497), was granted self-government in 1832, and in 1855, with Labrador as a possession, it became the Dominion of Newfoundland but unfortunately, self-government was relinquished in 1933, amid the general world depression. During World War II, Newfoundland experienced a wave of prosperity. Naval and other military bases were built on the island by the United States and Canada, pouring into the pockets of Newfoundland working men and women, hundreds of millions of dollars. Prices of fish products soared and Newfoundland became a self-supporting unit of the British Empire. At the end of the war, England again considered the question of self-government for the island. A petition signed by a considerable number of Newfoundland voters requested that union with Canada also be considered. In a referendum held in June 1948, union with Canada did not receive a majority. One month later, however, it was voted for favorably.

If Newfoundland had accepted self-government, they could have expected no further aid from England. Confronted again by the specter of poverty, Newfoundland would have been forced to seek aid from Canada. It appeared better to accept confederation with Canada when Newfoundland could secure favorable terms than to go later as a suppliant. There, too, was the strong inducement of social security, of family allowances and old-age pensions. And so England's oldest colony, created in 1497, lost its identity as a separate unit of the British Commonwealth of Nations, in 1949.

It was wonderful to be together again in our own family unit. And we squandered no opportunities to enrich our understanding of Placentia, Argentia and environs. Dave augmented our enthusiasm with creative plans for excursions and needed accessories.

First, we voyaged by boat to Jerseyside to a dark, elements-battered store elevated on stilts and warmed on most days with a pot-bellied stove. It was a treasure-trove and supplied not only such piscatorial needs as fishing poles and tackle and Newfie boots—heavy, black, tall, rubber, pull-on boots with thick wraparound soles, we even found a miniature pair for Davie—but also, luxuries in ceramic pots with attached saucers and raised grape leaves for my philodendron. I bought the last three: a pair of yellow and one of green—and acquired a flower garden in two tea cups: red rambler roses and pink morning glories, which were identical to those abloom on the doctor's fence, on our side—an Edenic display we watched appreciatively and rather possessively.

And then we took to the forests, not thick, lofty and gradually sloped like Alaska's, but suddenly rising from the sea—with all the latter's enchantments. Attenuant in places where boulders outcropped and soil did not cling, the woods were deeply greened by spruce and fir and splotched with early fall yellow by birch stand. Clean, shallow streams, we found (not oranged by volcanic ash), frequently squirming with fish; then work began. And when Lori, Bruce and Davie's voices were still, which

Dave sometimes signaled for, we listened to the melody of the stream's breaking over rocks, the perpetual wind's tones and moans, and the grating wings of the herring gulls in sudden, noisy departure.

We found, by car, on a rutted, mud, logging road, small ponds floating with lily pads, the lilies' blooming in yellow profusion, which had a particular appeal for Lori. She insisted that she be allowed to pick a water lily. In answer to Dave's explanation that it would wither as soon as it was picked, Lori persisted: "I don't care. I want one. I've seen them advertised and I've seen froggies sitting on them but I've never picked one. Now I want you, please, to stop!" And so Lori plucked a Newfoundland water lily—that is, Bruce, in his new Newfie boots, waded in and grasped it for her.

Ever observant, our naturalist Bruce returned with another specimen typical of the island. He had found a small, yellow berry floating at the edge of Lori's lily pad, about the size of a fresh blueberry, which we were able to identify as a baked-apple, an edible cloudberry or north-temperate raspberry. Finding more baked-apples growing on the edge of the pond, we picked several handfuls which we sampled at home. We found that they *did* taste like baked apples—baked without sugar. Later gatherings produced an excellent, tart jam, despite the enormity of the seeds, which we enjoyed on our Sunday-morning waffles.

We spent most of the first month of our eighteen-month visit in Newfoundland studying the island's tapestry of trees and flora which ennobled the granite rock. A geologic extension of the Acadian Forest established on Precambrian rock (some of the world's oldest, our books divulged) of the Canadian shield, Newfoundland was a disjointed part of the northeast coast of North America, which stretched south to Massachusetts and embraced shorelines and waterways westward to the St. Lawrence River and eastward to the Grand Banks. Having been weighted down by glaciers during four ice ages and then inundated, the "new-found land" was referred to as a "drowned coast" with its land depressed and its sea level raised. Instead of river valleys, bays and fjords abounded; instead of mountains, towering and unmenaced, telluric hilltops became islands in the melting glaciers and invading waters.

Placentia, severed, barren, bereft of even primitive vegetation, was our rock-solid launch from which we clambered upward into primordial-seeming hills, the verdure of which was new—for geologic age. The familiar spruce, both black and white, and sometimes gnarled and stunted of growth, intermingled with balsam fir and gave some ground to deciduous birch, alder, tamarack (a North American larch) and an occasional evergreen juniper. Hemlock, frequently invasive and in a grove by itself, was both avoidable and a reminder to Lori not to pick up any of its pretty little cones lest they be from the poison hemlock she discovered in Kodiak.

And, as in Alaska, there were multitudinous wild flowers, but in clumps rather than carpets, during the short summer months: buttercups, field daisies, thistles and fireweed being the most prolific. We found, too, butter and eggs, evening primroses, spider flowers, clover, wild roses, asters, forget-me-nots, wild iris and penstemons. Blueberries grew in great abundance. We enjoyed many a sumptuous breakfast and supper of blueberry pancakes made with fresh blueberries the children gathered near the wood's edge. Frozen blueberries, interestingly, were the only agricultural product exported from Newfoundland.

I tried to think of what wild fruit we had in the States which Newfoundland did not have. One day I asked a friend, Helen Bitsack, the charming Newfoundland wife of an American civilian, if she had ever heard of persimmons and papaws. "No," she admitted, "have you ever heard of marshberries and partridge berries?" "I concede!" I laughed and we returned to our bridge game.

No historical allusion to Newfoundland failed to conjoin fishing and dogs. The "Grand Banks" of Newfoundland was probably the most famous fishing site in the world. Influenced by the icy Labrador Current from the north and the warm Gulf Stream from the south, a dramatic food chain, from plankton to whales, had developed. Newfoundland fishermen and fishermen from numerous other countries had fished there for centuries. But we learned, alas, upon inquiry, that the great fleets of "bankers," or line-fishing fleets, had almost disappeared. Canada and Portugal seemed to be the only countries which continually used them. Replacing them were fleets of otter trawlers, most of them operating from European bases. But Newfoundlanders continued to fish in the "Grand Banks" with their own trawler fleet and had become an important producer for the frozen-fillet trade.

When we inquired into and discussed the lore of Newfoundland, there was association, as well, of the large, black-haired Newfoundland dog, indispensable to the many sheepherders on the island. There, too, we were disappointed; very few purebred Newfoundlands were left. We saw not one during our entire stay.

Codfishing predominated in Newfoundland, although herring, salmon and lobster fishing were also important. Caplin, a minute fish which swarmed into shore in inexhaustible quantity during the warmth of the summer, was a chief bait for codfishing. Codfishing was known as "inshore" fishing which took place in the narrow belt of coastal waters along the entire coast of Newfoundland. That type of fishing was unique. Huge quantities of fish were caught within a short range of the shore usually in small, open "trap boats" so-called because the fish were caught in cod-traps. A cod-trap was a large net strung with cork floats along the outer edge. Many a day during the fishing season, we would see the cod-traps spread to dry along Placentia's main road.

Much of the cod hooked or netted in the St. John's area was sun-cured for export to Spain, Portugal, Italy and Greece. And we drove the bumpy road to the outskirts of the capital city to see that ancient process.

Even in the modern age, there was no financial security for the codfisherman. A good year, as in 1954, when the cod were "eating the rocks," a Newfie expression which meant the fish were so plentiful they were swarming inshore in search of food, might be financially disastrous. Even if the catch were large, we were informed—by the ever-patient Newfoundlanders, much of the fish might be lost due to the method of curing. Codfish was cured in the sun much as it was done in the sixteenth century. The fishermen split the freshly caught cod, removed the heads, backbones and guts, then salted the fish and stacked them in "stores" or warehouses. When the weather was sunny, we could see men, women and children "make fish"—that is, spread the salted cod on wooden platforms called "flakes" to dry in the sun. If the summer was rainy and foggy, as it had been the year before, in 1953, the fish spoiled before it could be dried and a massive catch would be less profitable than a normal catch.

Being an insular people, Newfoundlanders naturally ate a great quantity of fish. They ate parts of the fish which we did not. Vi Densmore, vivacious wife of an outstanding civilian engineer—both of whom forsook California for Newfoundland—related a conversation: "I was talking to a Newfoundland woman about fish. She asked me if I had ever eaten—fish heads! 'Good heaven's no!' I told her and decided I'd go talk to someone else. But my curiosity was too great; I just had to ask her: 'What do you do with the eyes?' '*Pop* 'em,' she said, looking at me as if I was the most ignorant woman she'd ever seen. 'You pop 'em,' she repeated, 'same as you do with rabbit heads.'"

Important to Newfoundland's economy were the seal hunt and the whale fishery. The former we learned little about since sealing was conducted on the Arctic ice floes. Dave observed numerous herds of seal when he flew over the Arctic wastes to Narssarssuaq, Søndrestrøm and Thule, Greenland, but did not witness a seal hunt. But, at least, we would return to the States with a souvenir of Newfoundland seal: a paperweight shaped like a seal and made of natural sealskin. In addition, I was the happy possessor of a midnight-blue baby seal cape which Dave bought from St. John's famous furrier, Ewings, in a showing at the O-Club. It was one of the loveliest pieces of fur I had ever seen. Still, I demurred at Dave's extravagance. "But I never buy you *anything*!" was my generous mate's rejoinder. I looked askance at him and both Marydee and Dave Minton hooted with laughter at Dave's dissembled innocence!

One of my friends, Phyl Morrison, American wife of a top civilian on the Base, told me about shopping for a full-length sealskin coat. A very petite woman, it was just not the coat for her. "Dot, it would have fit the two of us. It was down to my ankles, cuffs so I couldn't bend my elbows. I turned to my husband: 'Dear, this is not glamorous!' I looked like the animal itself in that one."

We learned more about the whale fishery which was conducted in the Chapel Arms, New Harbor and Old Shop area, just northeast of Argentia at the head of Trinity Bay. The whaling was carried on by the Arctic Fishery Products Limited at South Dildo. That was the least attractive community we had ever visited—at least as far as the olfactory sense was concerned. The Arctic Fishery operated two whaling boats which navigated approximately thirty miles out to sea to take large whales up to seventy feet in length. Those enormous mammals were baleen whales (from which our black Eskimo boats were made), or whalebone whales, the elastic, hornlike plate in the upper jaw, the baleen, stripped into stays for milady's "garment."

In early summer, another type of whale was harpooned, the mink whale, which varied from twenty to thirty feet in length. From that whale, choice cuts of edible meat were taken. They were called "Arctic steaks," and were similar, we were told, to beefsteak. The other cuts from the mink whale, as well as the meat from most types of whales, were sold to local mink ranches and exported to fur farms in the United States and Canada.

In his northern flights, between St. John's and Thule, in the Davis Strait, Dave spotted herds of beluga, small, white whales, eight to ten feet in length. Called "the sea canary" because of its stridulous trilling sound, the beluga was a member of the dolphin family but looked more like a whale than a porpoise and was considered a sturgeon when Russian fishing fleets took it in the more southernly Black and Caspian Seas for its roe, or caviar. Dave also had observed schools of beluga, which frequented most northern waters, in the Bering Strait when on ice reconnaissance flights in Alaska.

The only whale drive we were permitted to witness was that of the pothead whale, a much smaller whale than the baleen or even the mink. Using squid as bait and aluminum pots and pans as noise makers, the whale boats, together with the small fishing boats, herded the whales into narrow bays. There they were harpooned and towed, at low tide, upon slanting wooden platforms. The water reddened and widened slowly with the blood of the dying whales; the sand of the beach became dubonnet and we did not linger long to watch the gory scene. I did not learn how the pothead whale was used but understood entire villages were dependent upon its abundance.

Newfoundland was called "The Sportsman's Paradise." The tourist trade was developing rapidly and might, one day, be a chief source of revenue for the island. Even in the mid-Fifties, during the summer months, it was almost impossible to rent a tourist cabin or a room in St. John's or in any village where hunting and fishing areas were accessible. The many lakes on the island had an abundance of trout species. The rivers proliferated in salmon and sea trout, the salmon rivers being considered among the best in the world. In the unsettled interior, large caribou herds roamed at will. Moose, which were earlier imported and thrived, were plentiful, for the hunters. The chief game birds were the wild duck and the willow grouse, which Newfoundlanders referred to as a partridge. Tuna fishing in the coastal waters attracted many fishermen in the last months of summer.

As Naomi Melewicz, wife of the Commanding Officer of the Fleet Weather Central, commented: "If you aren't a fisherman when you come up here, you are when you go back!" And Dave and the children were

Figure 61. Newfie Boots and Fishermen

caught up in the furor of fishing. With their rods and reels and favorite boots, Lori and Bruce (I kept Davie away from fishhooks) spent many hours in the streams and along rock-strewn ponds, fighting the mosquitoes and hooking an occasional trout.

We were all tormented by the minute black flies which Newfound-landers called mosquitoes. Those tiny flies, or mosquitoes, seemed to bite off pieces of the skin. The children's heads and faces bled copiously, particularly at the hairline, in and behind the ears—whenever they played outdoors. Before each playtime, we would saturate the children's heads, faces, arms and hands with mosquito repellent. Then we dressed them in blue jeans, Newfie boots over heavy socks, long-sleeved jackets and close-fitting hats. That precaution was rewarded with unsuccess. When the children came in for lunch, an apple, or a cowboy gun, their faces and necks would be trickling with blood. Neither wind, sun, chilled air nor rain diminished the mosquitoes. It was ironic that on many of Newfound-land's perfect summer days when the sun was brilliant and the temperature in the high sixties, the children had to play indoors. It was not only ironic, it was exhausting!

Lori became a schoolgirl—a seafaring schoolgirl—that special autumn we spent in Placentia. To get to her Kindergarten class at the Base school in Argentia, she had to cross the small strip of water known inelegantly but definitively as "the gut." The gut separated Townside Placentia, where we lived, from Jerseyside Placentia where Dave kept the car parked to drive to and from the Base every third day, sparing his vehicle and shar-ing, as did two other Navy Orcaners.

We were conveyed across the gut by a small boat known, of course, as the gut-boat. The gut-boat was an open boat with a

Figure 62. Jerseyside, The Gut, Townside

small enclosure protecting the gasoline engine. There were narrow benches along either side which were used primarily to step upon when entering or leaving the gut-boat. Everyone elected to stand despite the height of the waves or the drenching of the spray and, if one enjoyed standing in a roller coaster, adaptation to the gut-boat was effortless.

At Jerseyside, a school bus met the children to creep up a narrow, steep road overhanging the water far below and offering no barrier to an icy death except the nerve of the driver. Since the Newfoundlanders at the helm of boat and bus were both respectful of the sea and road and were steady-handed, I learned to accept the gut and the nightmarish road with consummate calm and soon feared neither. Of course, from the first gut-boat-bus familiarization, Dave and the children had thought both—a lark.

There were three Kindergarten-aged children living at the Orcan plus assorted other ages whom we did not trust to supervise the five-year-olds. Each morning, one of the three Kindergarten Mothers accompanied the littlest lambs onto the gut-boat, crossed the gut with them and put them aboard the school bus. Then the same Mother met the school bus at noontime in Jerseyside and brought them back across the gut. It would have been simpler to have taught the Kindergarten class at the Orcan. There were many days when I did just that and tutored my own. Those were the days when the children and Mother missed the gut-boat, or made the gut-boat and missed the bus, or just could not get to the gut because of high winds, or the flood tide submersed the road.

There were many stories connected with the gut-boat. The episode, for instance, of the Naval officer—an inmate of the Orcan—who stepped from the gut-boat, both arms clutching bags of groceries, to take a Chaplinesque plunge into the icy gut. He reappeared, seconds later, still clutching his bags of groceries. (There must have been oranges at the Base Commissary—one hung on to those for dear life.) And the tale of the little girl enroute to Kindergarten class who accidentally tossed her nickel overboard and forgot to let go. And there was the fable of the sailor's midnight crossing, via horseback, in the wake of the gut-boat's last eve.

You had almost a fifty-fifty chance of getting safely out of the gut-boat. If you did not fall out of the boat itself which had no handrails or other debarking aids, you slipped from the slimy moss steps of the dock, bared for your hazard by the low tide. During high tide, the gut-boat put into the side of the dock where there were no steps. A long-legged man could bound with enviable ease from the gut-boat to the top of the dock. Women had to be pulled from above and hoisted from below. When no able male passengers were aboard, the predicament was great. Fortunately, the most robust and least timid of the gut-boat operators was usually on duty during times of stress.

One had not fully exploited the caprices of the gut-boat (and Dave and I had) if they had never crossed at night, in formal attire, during a thunderstorm, when the tide was high.

For fourteen years, since the building of the Naval Base at Argentia, the gut-boat had chugged back and forth, unfailingly, bailing water, which passengers perfunctorily did, if the day was damp. It had hoarded its dimes and nickels against ineluctable retirement and had supported half a dozen Newfie families in its days of grace. And the end came.

In November of 1954, the gut-boat was retired from operation by the long-heralded appearance of a ferry, the *Ambrose Shea*, which could accommodate six cars and at least four times more passengers than the gut-boat.

The *Ambrose Shea* was officially launched the first week of October, the ceremony being attended by

Figure 63.   Gut-Boat's Last Crossing; Ferry in Dock

Premier Smallwood, Hon. E. S. Spencer, Minister of Public Works, and Hon. Gregory Power, Minister of Finance, plus the commanding officers of the Army, Navy and Air Force forces in Argentia. The ceremony itself lost most of its excitement to the presence of four red-coated Royal Canadian Mounties with whom Lori and Bruce were privileged to have their pictures taken. That day remained one of the high points of our children's stay in Newfoundland.

I believed most of us, especially "the Americans," as we were called, were secretly sad to see the gutboat cease operation. Crossing on it was neither convenient nor pleasant but it was a tradition. Living in Placentia became less of a pure

Figure 64. Mounties and Admirers

novelty and negative distinction. Our source of amused derision was gone. Life was rendered simple and easy without the fluctuant trip by gut-boat. It was like living on the Outside—almost.

By the second week of October, roses were still blooming in the doctor's yard—Bruce picked a nice bouquet for me with three-year-old Jimmy's help—and the weather was mild and sunny. But within a few days, the first snow fell. We sent Lori to school, via the *Ambrose Shea*, warmly togged in a snowsuit, boots and mittens with a long, wool scarf wrapped about her face and neck as protection against the lashing, horizontal snow. Snow never *fell* in Newfoundland, it blew faceward, parallel to terra. Our first snow melted within a few days but the wind, powerful and horizontal throughout the year, did not abate and winter welcomed us.

Our apartment, which overlooked the gut, being separated from it by the road and a low spruce-log fence, gave view to a rugged spruce island, a stone's throw across the gut, which was inhabited only by goats and sheep. From its rocky beach, the gregarious herring gulls launched their flight, with awkward perpendicularity, in the updrafts of the wind. Untouched by the woodman's ax, unmarred by building or shed it was as fresh and beautiful as our Shangrilog islands, as singular in the snow.

One Saturday we sighted a boat beached in its cove, a long black sloop with black sails. We five envisaged eye-

Figure 65. The Orcan-Gut Group

patched pirates, or rum smugglers, or at least, rapparees, stealthily mounting the top of the island to conceal their contraband in a rocky cave. By the time we each were coated and booted for a snowy pirate search, the enigmatic sloop became elusive and sailed around the back of the island and disappeared. We never sighted it again but we continued to talk about that sloop: outré in its sleek blackness, an eerie enlargement of our Alaskan whalebone souvenirs, out of harmony with watercraft of Placentia

Bay, its Navy ships, whalers, native skiffs—and connected it forever to our raptly watched, romanticized mystery isle.

There were few safe places for the children to play in the area of the Orcan. But it was not satisfactory to keep them in all day, especially when the fire extinguisher bounced from its clamps and foamed, with saponaceous swiftness, under our door each time the latter was opened hurriedly without a firm, precautionary hold.

Lori was surprised, one day, by the sudden sudsy outpouring when no one was there to help right the tank, anchor the hose and hold back the foam. She was able to straighten the heavy extinguisher and close the door but the irrepressible bubbles boiled under and rolled, wave on wave, to greet us as we sloshed our way up the steps to help stem the tide.

Bruce, of course, had little difficulty keeping occupied whether he was in or out-of-doors. It was always a question of which environment I should protect. His tally for the first month, out, in Placentia: two mops and a bucket in the gut, one broken window in the Orcan. He also managed to be kicked over the back fence by an irate bull and to fall into the gut. Fortunately, it was low tide and his plunge was witnessed.

Lori, studious until *meridies*, was no less energetic and was scarcely more cautious than her adored coherer. Together, Lori and Bruce visited some local hens to test the fruit of their labor and were belabored, in turn, by the henhouse owner. Never had they returned home more swiftly! Screaming with mortification, they demanded fifty cents apiece "to buy some eggs"—and safe conduct as far as the henhouse.

What creative play the fire extinguisher, the gut, mosquitoes and rain did not restrict, the snow and wind intermittently did. On Thanksgiving Day, we awakened to a heavy snow and Jack Frost's etchings upon each windowpane. Our Placentia Christmas of 1954 was not white but such lack was compensated for by a white Easter when Storm Condition One was imposed upon the Base and there was no traffic movement, except pedestrian, for two days. We were overjoyed that weatherman Dave was stranded at home for the holiday blizzard and that the Bunny's eggs were not hidden by snowdrifts but lamplighted within. But as any Newfoundlander would tell you, it was unusual weather—and we agreed as we pulled on our sou'westers and searched snowmounds for the car.

We had no real inconvenience the entire time we lived at the Orcan. Once or twice the electricity went off during high wind or a snowstorm and temporarily we had no heat, no hot water, no refrigeration and no means of cooking. Dave could not cross the gut because the lowering and lifting of the ferry ramps were accomplished electrically. And so we ate peanut butter and jelly sandwiches while Dave drove the slow road around Southeast Arm, lighted our candles and did calisthenics until bedtime. But it was a routine, always short-lived.

Water was our only problem. The Base Medical Department warned against drinking the Placentia water without boiling it for two minutes. "What is the danger of the water?" I asked Dave, while I put another pan of water on to boil. "Dysentery," Dave replied. "And deepness!" Lori added.

Everyone felt the same concern about drinking water. Mary Bloomfield, a neighbor at the Orcan and the wife of a Naval officer assigned to Argentia with Dave, once told me: "Dot, I started to knock on your door to borrow some ice cubes, then I realized that you just *don't* borrow ice cubes in Placentia."

The classic of all water stories concerned an officer and his water bottle, which Dave related with risible appreciation. At the end of the working day, when the officer had gone to the departmental "reefer" to get his bottle of water, he had been confronted by an extremely irritated Newfoundlander: "Don't take my bottle!" the Newfie accused. "But this is *my* water bottle," and the officer grasped it quickly, shielding it with both arms. "I bring this thing from Placentia every day to fill it with *good* water." Realizing he had made a mistake, the Newfie backed away: "Well, just be careful and don't take *my* bottle! I bring that water all the way from Placentia—can't stand the Base water!"

I indulged in very few social activities the eight months we resided at the Orcan. Transportation was difficult but with a few of my valiant neighbors, I did try to attend the monthly luncheons and bridge parties at the Officers' Club. Infrequently, I held a bridge luncheon at the Orcan inviting friends from the Base, graduates of Placentia, or Newfoundland wives of American civilians, neither being in trepidation of the gut or the poor roads. Dave and I ventured forth at night, leaving the children with a Newfie baby sitter, seldom more than twice a month. We did not feel comfortable in leaving the children in Placentia, as we feared fire among the closely set wooden houses, the majority of them heated with oil stoves.

Placentia had a shamefully insufficient fire department. Shortly after our arrival, a two-story house burned to the ground killing an American serviceman and his infant son trapped in an upstairs apartment. The hoses of the local fire truck were twisted and punctured with holes; fire equipment from the Base was an hour away. Had there been a high wind which there miraculously was not, the entire village would have been threatened.

Since we were to spend so much of our time in our Placentia apartment, I determined to make it as attractive and cozy as possible. I launched upon a scheme to paint the entire apartment. I had always wanted a pink kitchen so I proceeded to paint the kitchen camellia pink, in its entirety. Finding the kitchen so perfect in its pinkness, I painted all the woodwork and all the doors, camellia pink. The living room walls and ceilings, I painted a light gray. Although it was difficult to put gray over dark green and red walls, it took three coats, I was determined to have lightness in a room where not one ray of sunshine penetrated. To economize on paint and turpentine cans, I painted the children's room gray; our bedroom, Wedgewood blue and the bathroom, Wedgewood blue. Our apartment was so small that one room would be stacked to the ceiling with furniture from the other room and there was no room for anything, especially us. But I felt pride in my achievement as I finished each space and I got painting out of my system—if not out of my hair, never mastering the technique as I lavished prematurely gray paint on the dark green ceiling.

Dave went to Washington, D. C., the last of January of '55, for two months' temporary duty. Before he left, he attempted to secure housing for us on the Base (he had been number one on the three-bedroom housing list for months) and was encouraged to think that we would be given temporary Base housing shortly after he left. I assured him we would be alright at the Orcan, feeling anything else was too much to hope for. It was.

Dave flew to Washington early one Sunday morning. It was sunny and beautiful and there was no snow upon the ground. I told Dave as we drove onto the ferry, enroute to the Base: "See, Dave, this beautiful day presages a bright and happy time for you and for the children and me. I have never seen Placentia more appealing and the gut more calm." And it *was* beautiful, all day long.

Monday found us sequestered in Placentia in the midst of a violent snowstorm. By Tuesday afternoon, the village was being dug out and Lori was looking forward to going to school again. Wednesday morning, Lori awakened bright and early—with the measles. She had high fever for days, ate nothing at all and lost a considerable amount of weight. I missed her joyous talk, her ebullience about school. I was elated and both the boys were, too, when she sat up briefly, after almost a week and asked for crackers and milk.

Bruce and Davie had behaved with becoming restraint while their Daddy was gone and Lori was sick. They were quiet and almost obedient. What wonderfully cooperative boys I had! And every day I exulted in the realization that my careful training had been effective. There swelled kindness and tenderness in both of their big hearts and I was proud of my two sons. The very next day, after Lori sat up—they both had the measles!

Time passed rapidly during five weeks of measles. That left only three without and then Dave would be home but Lori's hair would have grown some. Lori's long curls, not brushed or rag-tied during the height of her feverish weakness, had tangled and matted and I had wielded reluctant scissors against the luxuriant mass. Lori, habitually mature and dignified, had not demurred—and patted *my* hand consolingly.

During the children's days of lassitude, I became the best Old Maid shark in Newfoundland. I also mastered the ditties of all the children's records and was most effective with "*Rudolph the Red-Nosed Reindeer,*" their former favorite.

Of one thing I was glad: Lori, Bruce and Davie had all been sick while Dave was gone. I had felt perfectly self-sufficient to care for them and completely content to do so. I did have wonderful help from friends, of course. One neighbor-friend in particular, Marydee, brought groceries and mail from the Base and dropped in frequently for coffee and laughter. By the time Dave returned from Washington, I knew the value of unselfish friendship.

April dawned and Dave was home again. At least, he had been home. He was in Thule, Greenland, and other northern points, having been assigned additional duties as Ice Reconnaissance Officer for military operations centering around U.S. and Canadian bases in the Arctic.

Dave's military career in Newfoundland had been an odd one. A Naval flyer, he had been ordered to Argentia as an Aerological Forecaster and then became CTU (Commander Task Unit), Arctic ice reconnaissance. But, with typical sanguinity, he enjoyed his latest assignment; it was more than a mundane routine. He and his men were pioneering in a new field and it presented a worthy challenge. I knew little about his work and was able to ask less. Most of his activities and those of the men under him were classified as "Confidential" but I speculated from my reading of the *Kansas City Star, New York Times* and *Time* that his ice flights were connected to the resupply of the DEW (Distant Early Warning) Line.

I had been a Navy wife long enough to know when not to ask questions and did not. Even so, I was chastised verbally by a fellow officer of Dave's when I checked Dave's ETA (Estimated Time of Arrival), Argentia, found it was delayed again and commented that I suspected Dave would be away from home most of the time. "You don't know a thing about it," he told me. And he was absolutely correct.

We saw our first robin April 11, hopping on the light snow in the doctor's yard where baby lambs were frolicking. On April 16, we had our last spring blizzard. Dave was still in the Far North where I hoped the weather was more benign. And once again the children and I were inhibited in Placentia (as if Placentia wasn't inhibitor enough) by the heavy, wet snowflakes, graupel and windstorm, but that time, the children exhibited nothing—not even the mumps. And when the road was plowed by a horse and board, the children rode a Newfie sleigh pulled by the same fat, white dobbin and friendly drayman.

In late April, Dave returned to Argentia, bringing his usual souvenirs. Appropriately, he brought Danish silver bracelets from Søndrestrøm, Greenland, for Lori and me; cuff links, for the

Figure 66. Newfie Transport

boys. Greenland was a possession of Denmark and U. S. bases in Greenland, such as Thule and Narssarssuaq, were leased from the Danish government. Greenland, according to Dave's reports, was a bleak, frigid, fjorded land abounding with glaciers and mountains and covered with an ice cap—and rarely green. Movement at the Thule Air Force Base was by underground passage and Dave had seldom ventured outside—except to board his plane.

Dave returned with yet another trophy which he had purchased at the Hudson Bay Company in Frobisher Bay, Northwest Territories, Canada. "Guess what else I brought you," Dave teased, after we had stowed his flight gear in the car. He still had on his Arctic anti-exposure suit with its deep fur hood and attached boots designed and insulated to withstand subzero temperatures. "We're just glad to have *you*," I told him. "But what else did you bring?" seeing how pleased he was. "You'll never guess," he laughed, "so-o-o, I'll tell you. I brought you . . . a rock!" "A *rock*!" I shrieked. "You brought me a rock to have in rock-bound Placentia?" "But it's not the kind of rock you think!" We were both laughing, uncontrollably. "Good heavens, I hope not!" And when I could speak again: "A rock!" I mumbled, "he brought me a rock, all the way from the Arctic—to *admire* here in Placentia!" I turned to the children, but they hadn't even heeded. They were heads-down on the back seat focusing, speechlessly, on their packets of Danish coins and stamps.

When we got home, we all clamored to see that remarkable rock which Dave had carried on his back over three miles of ice and snow, his fellow shoppers' leaving suddenly when they saw the size of it. It was unveiled, at last, and there before us was a monstrous soapstone about a foot and a half long carved by the Eskimos into the shape of a walrus! It had tusks of ivory and was realistic to the point of having an ivory harpoon thrust into its side. It *was* an interesting souvenir and I told Dave, both of us still laughing, I thought it was wonderful—if you liked rocks. And, of course, we all did! (And I still laugh when I see it. It sits beside me, by the hearth, as I write—a bit battered, Davie's having hammered out the harpoon with his first hammer set and practiced the Holland hobby of rock-hounding, on the flippers.)

Dave was not able to observe the Canadian Eskimos at first hand but one of his ice observers, Jim Brooks, spent many months in the Arctic and brought back his observations of the Eskimo settlement in Resolute Bay, Northwest Territories. Jim's many tales about the Eskimos were both humorous and respectful. We learned that a Royal Canadian Mountie was custodian of the Eskimos at Resolute and that a concerted effort was made by the Canadian government to concentrate the Eskimos into a good game area in hopes of making them self-supporting. In a good hunting season, it was not unusual for an Eskimo to accumulate several thousand dollars trapping Arctic white fox and polar bear. (The Canadian Eskimo, or "*inuits*," as Alaskan Eskimos, as well, referred to themselves, had negotiated with the Canadian Government in Ottawa since 1976 to take political control of the eastern two-thirds of the Northwest Territories which included northern Hudson Bay, east to Baffin Island bordered by Davis Strait and Baffin Bay, land north of the Arctic Circle through Resolute Bay to include Ellesmere Island, southwestward through Victoria

Island to Great Bear Lake, then slicing southeastward along the Northern Limit of Wooded Country to the northwest corner of Manitoba. In December of 1991, the largest land claim ever granted to native claimants was agreed upon for the Inuits of Canada: a 770,000 square-mile territory to be known as Nunavut, "Our Land." The Canadian Parliament, plebiscites to be held in the Northwest Territories and the Nunavut areas, would vote final approval—it has been predicted.)

I was intrigued to learn that the Canadian Eskimos' families were small (far smaller than Newfoundland families), that their homes and persons were extremely clean. They were religious people, either Anglican or Roman Catholic, and had a Christian marriage. "And they're young looking," Jim said. "I met one Eskimo girl who was twenty-two. She looked like she was twelve years old!"

He described the igloos which the Eskimos built when there was enough ice and snow. The stoves used in the igloos were nothing more than a soapstone grooved down the center with seal oil poured over dried moss which was then ignited. The soapstone stove served both as illumination and as a means of cooking. "It might take them two hours to boil a pot of water," Jim Brooks said, "but what's two hours to an Eskimo!"

Telling us about the Eskimos' traits, Jim commented, smiling at the thought: "They never buy one of anything. If they need a flint, they buy the whole card full. They buy boxes and boxes of cough drops. Now what would an Eskimo want with a cough drop! Tea is their biggest item. They drink it by the hour—on the hour.

"The Hudson Bay Company," Jim continued, "is the biggest thing in the Arctic. They have their own money—a metal disk with denominations stamped on it. To the Eskimo, it's the *best* money."

With Dave, home from Thule, we finally moved aboard the Base on the first of May 1955. After eight months across the gut, we were ready for it but knew we would miss the doctor's yard, the ferry and friendly Placentians and our mystery island. "How do you like living on the Base?" I asked LT Al Ristan, a former resident of off-Base housing. "How do I like living!" was his vehement reply.

But all was not easy when we were finally in Base quarters. The Navy had just taken over McAndrew Air Force Base adjoining the Argentia Naval Station and had ordered new furniture for all of the quarters which were refinished before being assigned. (The Air Force had moved its furniture to Pepperrell Air Force Base in St. John's.) We were assigned one of those quarters, a very commodious two-story, three-bedroom apartment.

For the next six months, we received lovely new furniture, a piece at a time and just in time for our second Newfoundland Thanksgiving dinner, we received a table!

For the first five weeks of Base living, we had nothing except the beds and dinette set we moved in from Placentia. As LT Hogue, a Coast Guard officer, in the same predicament, aptly commented: "You either eat or you go to sleep."

But for Davie, Base existence was not dichotomous; he was more resourceful. Davie discovered eyebrow tweezers fit perfectly in electrical outlets—but melted there and would not come out. His eighteen-month-old fingers discovered how to let go quickly! Turning back to his hammer and established, trustworthy skills, he kept his tricycle in perfect running order and helped as we drag-mopped all of our splendiferous and rugless, hardwood floors—which soon had two chairs!

Figure 67. Davie's Base Transportation

In our lovely, newly painted apartment, I, particularly, appreciated the professional freshness. We had neither a stove nor a refrigerator but how good that unboiled water tasted! In lieu of a refrigerator, we used a new garbage can in which Dave had carried water from the Base to Placentia, after the *Ambrose Shea* arrived and he could drive to the Orcan. Placed under the eaves by the back steps, our refrigerator not only held a surprising quantity of milk, eggs, butter, cheese and frozen meat, it also afforded me a chance to test the weather before sending the children into it. But, for weeks, I waged a continual battle with neighbor children, the dogs—and the garbage collectors. With both an In and Out can, aural and visual surveillance were unceasing and good memory helped as well. For cooking, we used a borrowed two-burner hot plate. One of the burners worked perfectly, if you struck it sharply enough.

Such adjusting as we made, plus eight months in Placentia, not at the plush Orcan, and a demolished car, led one of our friends to exclaim with exasperation: "This place has been against us since the day we arrived and it will be against us until the day we *Leave*!"

But not everyone disliked Argentia. As one of the squadron flyers, "Bush" (he had a bright red mustache), told his buddies: "Now don't make up your mind you're not going to *like* Newfoundland—you may *hate* it!"

Perhaps Dave and I had a finer sense of humor, or sense of the ridiculous, because we suffered not at all, and enjoyed every—inconvenient moment of it. And the children thrived!

CDR Frank Melewicz, Dave's commanding officer, made an appreciative comment about Argentia as we were having dinner at a poorly attended party. "One good thing about these outposts," he laughed, "you can always find a seat!"

The month of May was our rainy month. June, July and August were just like May. But it did not rain *every* day. Some days were merely foggy and some of the foggy days were days of light fog and other foggy days were days of heavy fog. It was plain to see, when one could, that our summer weather was extremely variable.

Our apartment, though, was drip-free and gave us as much light as there was, both east and west with two floors of windows; in addition, there was much space for the children: a large bedroom for Bruce and Davie, and for Lori—her own estate for the first time in her life.

Occasionally, we had sunshine during the summer months. As Marydee told me, with a bemused expression on her face: "The sun came out and I went to get my sunglasses. By the time I found them, I didn't need them!" She had been overjoyed to see the sunshine, hoping that it would produce her flyer-husband, then LCDR, Dave Minton. "I'll be back in an hour," he had told her, three days before—and had flown to Torbay, half an hour away.

The children loved living on the Base. They had many playmates and a wonderful place to play, for behind our quarters was a limitless expanse of spruce and fir woods. Lori and Bruce picked raspberries and blueberries on the hillsides and found "gold" in a little stream which, trickling into a waterfall, flowed beyond our back driveway, several yards above the wooden stairs leading to their discovery slope. They played with Davie in the knee-high banks of buttercups and field daisies and, all three, enjoyed normalcy, being away from the hazards and restrictions of the gut.

I recalled a typical summer day when Bruce rushed through the back door with muddy boots on his feet and a huge brown bag in his hand. He hurried by me, in the kitchen, with a rapturous countenance and busy

thoughts. "Bruce," I called to him, "what have you in the bag?" "Strawberries, Mama. Fix me a strawberry pie!" And he was out the door again.
After wet mopping his path, I went to the refrigerator, into which he had
hurriedly thrust the sack, to examine his "strawberries." In the bottom of
the tall sack were a few red berries thoroughly crushed and ready for the
pie. They were about as big as timid peas and bore no resemblance to
strawberries except in redness. I was unable to identify them, for the next
time I opened the refrigerator, both sack and berries had met another fate.
And so had the mud-tracks! Bruce had remembered to leave his boots on
the boot rug. How I loved those Newfie boots! They pulled off and on *so*
easily and helped us retain sheen on our floors and newness in our
furniture.

President Eisenhower attended a conference in Geneva in July with
Great Britain, France and Soviet Russia—the first meeting of the major
powers since Potsdam in 1945. Hopes were high for a thaw in the Cold
War, a rather urgent need with the hydrogen bomb's having superseded the
atomic bomb in both "superpower" countries. Since Stalin's death in
March of 1953, Premier Bulganin and Khrushchev appeared conciliatory
but the spirit of peace was short-lived and the nuclear incubus clutched
tighter. The alignment remained: NATO countries, including West
Germany in 1955, with the Warsaw Pact of 1955 in opposition (Albania,
Bulgaria, Czechoslovakia, East Germany, Hungary, Poland, Rumania,
U.S.S.R.). Agreement could not even be reached to create an all-German
government. But further talks were scheduled.

SEATO, Southeastern Asia Treaty Organization, founded in
September 1954 in Manila as a defense against Communist China included
the United States, Great Britain, France, Australia, New Zealand, the
Philippines, Thailand and Pakistan. Inadequate truces in Korea and
Indo-China did not ameliorate relations with the Chinese Communists
whom the U.S. refused to recognize. In turn, they increased pressure upon
the Nationalist Government of Chiang Kai-shek, which we supported, in
its exile on Formosa. After President Eisenhower withdrew the U. S.
Seventh Fleet from the Formosa Straits which President Truman had
ordered there to enforce the neutrality of the area, the Chinese Communists proceeded to bomb the Nationalist-held islands of Quemoy and
Matsu.

But in Argentia, our children played happily throughout the
summer. Davie toddled about in the flirting sunshine, fighting the nipping
mosquitoes, unconcernedly, as he had no memory of mosquitoless summer

play. All of the neighborhood children looked as if they had chronic cases of drippy measles but it seemed to bother no one, except the Mothers who had to wash the splattered, repellent-reeking, combat clothes.

Once in a while I attempted to cover a particularly large loss of skin with a band-aid to keep the scab on, especially on Davie whose little digits were more investigatory than his siblings'. But I was never successful until I discovered children's adhesive strips with star shapes, new moons, circles, hearts and blue, red, green and yellow animals. A late August morn, loosening a wound at hair-washing time, I doctored it and asked Davie to select a bravery-signifying symbol. He chose a green, his favorite color, pony and went obediently in for nap time.

When Davie reappeared, during spirited bidding of my bridge foursome, coming downstairs all dressed with shoes and socks in hand, his green pony still in place on his face—together with all the other cats, dogs, ducks, stars and moons; my startled friends wavered between consoling or reporting me—until they saw bandages on Davie's shirt-tail and shoes.

Ship's Service was unprepared for the sudden run on band-aids but Barbara, inquiring as to the children's Christmas wants, resupplied our star-stuck animal advertisement with a dozen boxes.

Dave declared the Chapel and the O-Club, off limits.

In September, Bruce became a proud member of the morning Kindergarten class and Lori, now one of the "older children," spent a full day in First Grade. Hurrah! hurray! There was no gut to cross! The Base school was in full sight at the top of a hill less than a block away!

When our older two went off to school, all was not dull and quiet at home because Davie, almost two, had been well tutored by his brother Bruce in the mischievous but winning ways of little boys. His mornings were busy with me and he loved to help with selections at the Commissary and Ship's Service—even without his band-aids. But, only when Bruce returned, did the day's real adventure begin.

Soon Halloween was at hand and on the occasion arrived a special treat: the children's grandmother from Lincoln, Nebraska, "Grammy Sue," as Lori and Bruce called her; "Gammy Goo," Davie claimed. Dave's mother traveled by plane from Omaha to Boston and by ship from Boston to Argentia to spend an extended vacation in a land she had merely known as a steppingstone to Europe. She visited us almost two months, until Christmas Day, when her ship left the harbor at three in the afternoon, a month before our own departure. Dave's Newfoundland tour was a more memorable one because we were able to share it with our family.

During Mother H's visit, we made excursions to many neighboring villages, taking her, of course, to see Placentia. We made several trips by car to St. John's to shop and just to spend the day in North America's oldest city. One of the first places we would visit in St. John's—after we had enjoyed a typical luncheon of codfish cakes and apple turnovers with golden sauce—was Nonia's, a knit-goods shop located in the modern Newfoundland Hotel. All of the goods, which ranged from baby garments to two-piece suits, were handknit. Yarns of the finest English mohair, together with patterns, were distributed to fishermen's wives living in remote villages on every coast of Newfoundland. Their finished work was returned to Nonia's (Newfoundland Outport Nurses Industrial Association) where it was sold at very reasonable prices. It was exquisite work and I was soon regretful that I acquired so little of it, buying only a shawl and a throw for Mother.

In department stores and gift shops along famed Water Street (where most of the women wore gorgeous fur coats of seal, muskrat, beaver and mink), we purchased cups of English bone china (Mother H collected cups from her world traveling); Irish linen tablecloths; children's books published in England; in especial, Beatrix Potter's *The Tale of Peter Rabbit, The Tale of Mrs. Tiggy-Winkle* and *Epaminondas and the Eggs* (one of Mother's favorites) by Constance Egan; and a lovely gray muskrat cape which Mother H could not resist and bought for Nebraska's clime.

By Christmastime, Argentia was beautiful with a deep snow. We drove into the fairy-perfect woods a week before Christmas to cut our tree of balsam fir. Ornamented on the top branches with small cones, it filled our apartment with Christmasy fragrance and nostalgia. It seemed redundant to deck the tree with ornaments and tinsel—it was effective in its fresh fullness, as it stood, or just with blue lights—but the children wanted to decorate it as the trees at school had been treated and they knew precisely what was needed.

On Christmas Eve afternoon, we took a drive through the undisturbed snow of Southeast Arm to Placentia and circled around to Fox Harbor, a secluded village of pastoral beauty. It was a scene such as poets rhapsodized of: sheep in the snowy dales, children skating on the ponds, a horse-drawn sled racing from the top of the hill to the bottom to stop at a white-spired church. The spruce trees, lavishly sifted with snow, gave softness and purity to every vista. Mother H, surveying it all with wonder, said it looked "as you would expect Christmas to look." We drove slowly homeward through the snowy lane, filled with the celestial quietness and beauty of Newfoundland and the significance of the season.

Curving along the thin Fox Harbor road on Placentia Bay, the car practically in the water, Lori called: "Stop, Daddy! Those are *pancakes*! And *lily pads*! And I can touch one!" Well schooled in ice formations, as were we all, Lori, once again, "had seen pictures of lily pads" and pancakes but never touched one. Not dressed for ice reconnaissance, Lori still insisted Dave drag a pancake from the Bay so that she could feel it, with frigid fingers. Gritting her teeth and shivering, her discovery was touched and then recorded with Dave's ever-present camera.

In our warm quarters, Lori matched her pancakes and lily pads to technical descriptions in Dave's *Glossary of Meteorology* and glowed like Christabel Columbus! And Dave got out his slides of ice in its myriad forms and we

Figure 68. Shivering Lori—With Her Pancake

enjoyed a Christmas Eve showing which was pleasant to Mother H_and all—to be so cozy within and to have the Bears so far away!

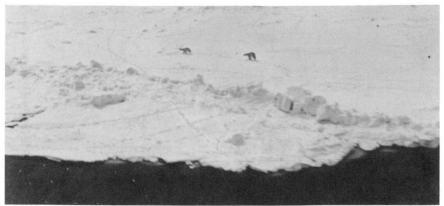

Figure 69. Hummocked Ice Between Shore Lead and Polar Bears

Figure 70. Grease Ice, Cake Ice, Brash and Growlers

Figure 71. Arched Iceberg Off Narssarssuaq

Figure 72. Shadow on the Brash

Figure 73. Bergy Bits Locked in Winter Ice

The last showed a PV on the runway at Argentia with an Arctic-garbed Ice Observer's having con- "fronted" the ice, from the plastic nose cone.

The end of our Newfoundland stay was drawing close and we were anticipating departure with regret. Dave had received his orders to report to Oceana,

Figure 74. Ice-Recon Plane. Anti-Exposure Suit

Virginia Beach, Virginia, and we were preparing to leave Argentia by ship the last of January. The children, who were excited about seeing *Davy Crockett* for the first time, and I would be at home with Mother and Dad until Easter. We were all anxious to be on a highway, although I feared the traffic and speed would terrify us.

For a year and a half, we had driven a maximum of twenty miles an hour except for the three times we had taken trips to St. John's when we must have sped to nearly thirty-five miles an hour! Driving on the Base was restricted to twenty miles an hour and off-Base driving was similarly restricted—if one desired survival.

We had never encountered more challenging roads. Built of dirt and gravel and eroded by rain, wind and melting snow, the roads, particularly the road from the gut to the Base, were filled with an infinitude of holes: wide ones, deep ones, long, short, shallow holes. As the schoolchildren chanted to the adroitly swerving bus driver: "Miss one and you'll get a dozen!" The roads in the Placentia-Southeast Arm area were infrequently repaired by hand labor. The road grader generally used consisted of a wooden scraper which was dragged by a horse, the scraper heavier and longer than Placentia's "snowplow." That inutile procedure did not leave the roads in perfect condition. Indeed, it did little to relieve vertical motion. Heavy snowfalls, alone, provided the fastest forward movement. Dave always carried two spare tires, even for a short run off Base, and frequently used them both. But the Newfoundland roads were a minor discommodity after we moved aboard the Base where facilities and maintenance were Stateside and one left its paved roads, sidewalks and grassy lawns—only for backwoodsy recreation.

If one were not happy to travel by car, plane, ship or ferry, they might travel via the "Newfie Bullet" as the train was indulgently known. The "Newfie Bullet" was a remarkable thing. A narrow-gauge, doll-like train, it could travel almost five hundred miles, across the top of the island from St. John's to Port-Aux-Basques, in twenty-four hours! "On long trips," Phyl Morrison reflected, "they use both a steam and a diesel engine and, believe me, there is no harmony between the two. You no sooner pick yourself up off the floor, than you're down again!" "It goes about twenty miles an hour," Naomi Melewicz laughed, "when it goes." But like the gut with the amusing stories surrounding it, the Newfie Bullet was part of the color and distinctness of Newfoundland.

We were leaving Newfoundland feeling that we had learned something about a land new to us. It was not an insignificant island, we discovered. In fact, many history-making events had taken place in Newfoundland. The first successful transatlantic cable was landed at Heart's Content, Trinity Bay, in 1866. At St. John's, Marconi received the first wireless signal across the Atlantic, in 1901. The first air-crossing of the Atlantic was made from St. John's that same year of 1901, by Alcock and Brown. In 1941, a famous meeting occurred aboard ship in Placentia Bay, off the coast of Argentia. There, Winston Churchill and Franklin D. Roosevelt met to frame the Atlantic Charter.

More important to us than the historical significance of Newfoundland were the warmth and generosity of its people. We once read a banal account of Newfoundland citizenry as an ill-educated and poorly nourished lot, subsisting mainly on fish and cabbage; drinking Newfie "screech" (rum) in enormous quantities; dancing the Newfie stomp, a curious dance akin to neither jitterbugging nor square dancing; speaking a *lingua franca.* We found no verification of such effete depictions.

While it was true that the culture of Newfoundlanders, generally, was provincial—a fact true of most insular peoples—some of the most educated, sophisticated yet charming people we had ever known were Newfoundlanders. Without exception, all whom we met extended a hospitality which was proverbial. I often wondered if we could be as gracious to those who were uninvited to our land.

And so we parted from our Newfoundland and American friends in Argentia feeling we would meet, at another time, our military friends and knowing in our hearts that if the opportunity were presented, we would journey again to Newfoundland.

CHAPTER VI

FROM THE BEACH, TO THE LAKE, TO THE "BIG POND"

 Virginia Beach

We left Argentia, Newfoundland, January 26, 1956, by Coast Guard Cutter, having had the traditional farewell party for Dave at the O-Club where he was given an elaborate table lighter with the map of Newfoundland embossed thereon, showing Argentia; St. John's, the capital; Gander, one of Dave's favorite destinations, which was also an international stopover for transatlantic flights; St. Anthony, the northernmost tip; Corner Brook, to the far west and Stephenville, slightly southwest, with its U.S. Air Force facility. The children accompanied us for the dinner, the trivial, titivated gifts from Dave's fellow officers and the clever after-dinner speeches—at which all Navy flyers were adept from training and practice.

When we were aboard the Cutter, the Admiral came for a last good-bye and the Mintons, too, who would not return to the States for another month. Typically, we were traveling in stormy weather but our zeal was undiminished, for the thoughts of the Midwest and Oceana and Stateside home fires were ascendant.

As soon as we put out to sea in Placentia Bay, it was very rough and raw with Newfoundland wind's issuing congé and prodding us onward. We avoided the deck except for morning fire drills, life-preserver and lifeboat instruction. Toastily amidships, Lori, Bruce and Davie loved the tempestuous Atlantic. They could sit on a couch in the wardroom and slide across the room, without putting feet to floor, and back again. And single chairs twisted dizzily around, scooting in unpredictable courses and bouncing against bulkheads. When Dave and I added weight to a chair or couch there was a slight slowing of the slide but the seas were in flexuous control. From our embarking, Newfoundland's Aeolian might and the Atlantic's fierceness auspicated a successfully swift and exciting voyage. We were not disappointed by our initiation into wintertime North Atlantic passage.

On January 28, we arrived in Brooklyn, New York, U.S.A. I had not hit my head even slightly, and once again, we were the only family to make every meal. Proud of our familial sturdiness and nautical adaptability, that boast pleased us. And I soon forgot that for the next two weeks, I walked aslant, leaning to starboard on a sloping, heaving deck, still hearing the ship creak and feeling it bump down every step, after teetering interminably on top of each white-capped landing. By the third week, the decaying waves, the swells, only slightly influenced my gait and the floors had ceased to move with each stride. But I had not been dizzy aboard ship; our reputation had remained intact!

It was a day after we docked before the car was offloaded at the Brooklyn Naval Base, so we enjoyed a night and half day in New York but spent most of the time tracking down one of Dave's cruise boxes which, after many phone calls, was discovered to have been unloaded in Stephenville when we had stopped to take on Air Force dependents.

Starting on our merry way to Kansas City, we smoked most of it, for Dave had permitted a helpful filling-station attendant to put a high-detergent oil in the car which he promised would "really clean it out," and it did. The cleanest white smoke trailed behind us, all the way home!

The day after we arrived in Kansas City, February 1, 1956, Dave took our addicted black Pontiac with the sporty red upholstery (which had guzzled a quart of oil every two hundred miles from East to Midwest) to Dad's favorite Oldsmobile dealer, and bought a two-tone blue 98 Olds. That sturdy black car had served us without one failure in two cold Northern climes but now we were ready for warmer tones and smoother byways.

Everyone was well in the Thomas and Holland households in Kansas City and Lincoln. Charles and Barbara had moved to Peoria, Illinois, where Luanne Elizabeth Thomas had been the perfect Christmas gift, December 25, 1954; Mommy Tom and Daddy Frank's having four "out-of-pocket" grandchildren at that advent. But I intended to stay until after Easter and they would have three to love and spoil for two months.

Dwight Roberts, Kansas City's much sought-after portrait painter and neighbor to Mother and Dad, had been apprised of our schedule and came over to meet us, especially Davie, who was just twenty-seven months old and the very image of his dashing Daddy with curly black hair, long, luminous brown eyes and dimples. Dwight Roberts said some very flattering words about Mother and Dad and volunteered his services to paint Davie. We showed him the reproductions of Lori and Bruce; he was impressed with Florence Lockwood's work and had admired the children's portraits several times, which Mother had hung in the living room in the fall of '53. He laughed about the parrot, said Davie would just have to be bored at *his* sittings, but approved of peanuts in shell and raisins in little boxes. I had thought of a rust-bronze, double-breasted corduroy suit and a white, turn-back-collared shirt and sought Mr. Roberts' opinion, holding the jacket up to Davie, who dutifully stood still, as I asked: "Would that blend suitably with Bruce's yellow sweater and Lori's rose-melon dress?" Mr. Roberts averred that it would and asked if we would like to start sitting in two days; he had saved time for us in February. His studio was at 39th and Main and the Country Club streetcar stopped right in front, he thoughtfully suggested.

Dave drove us for the first two sittings and we selected a beautiful hand-carved oval, wood frame, deepening to a gracefully curved rectangle, its 21 X 24.5" dimensions washed lightly in white, the knife strokes creating a mosaic of the natural wood, a tawny tessellation, a shade lighter than Davie's soft nutmeg suit. Mr. Roberts was painting Davie in oils, with a slight smile so that both dimples showed in his full-front portrait. His black hair, brushed—at Davie's insistence—like his brother Bruce's, without a part, showed no curl and he was altogether, a very manly little boy, with cherubic pink cheeks and dimpling mouth. We were delighted with the product of Dwight Roberts' consummate skill and appreciative of his friendship for Mother and Dad, knowing that portrait painters did not prefer to paint frisky angels, however mature and raisin-hungry. But Davie *was* good for I sat in the waiting room, reading my *Time* and it was so quiet, without a parrot, I wondered how painting could be accomplished. Davie was an excellent subject, Dwight Roberts told me, in a very gracious aside. And I was proud and pleased, for I knew that his respect for Mother and Dad had prompted his exception-making to paint Davie.

Dave departed on February 15, 1956, for Oceana Naval Air Station, Virginia Beach, Virginia, not taking a full-month's leave because we were houseless again. He soon discovered that Norfolk, site of the world's largest Naval Base, a short distance from Virginia Beach, had an inadequacy of choice housing; that Virginia Beach was totally without houses for sale as every one was rented, with rates tripling during the winter; that Oceana Base's environs offered nothing we would consider and decided we should build.

He liked the new houses being built around Lake Smith, a reservoir for Norfolk which protected it from public usage, and bought a choice lot on the west side—just a few minutes' drive from the Little Creek Amphibious Base and equidistant between the Norfolk Naval Base and Oceana Naval Air Station.

Our home would take six months to build, Dave reported, so he rented us a garage apartment on the Beach which we could have April first until ours was completed.   Virginia Beach was expensive, even though winter rates would have ceased, but he thought we would all enjoy the sun-living after the dull skies and Newfoundland cold.   There was a public school near by so that Lori could finish her last two months in First Grade and a private school (there were no public kindergartens in Virginia) for Bruce.   A private bus service would take them to their respective schools.

When Dave called for our final approval, it seemed like a wonderful plan and he was very enthusiastic about building his own house.

It proved to be a wise decision for we were to live in our Lake Smith house almost five years, far longer than we had lived anyplace before.

We had a busy visit in Kansas City.   Mother began rehearsals for Palm Sunday at the end of February, Easter's being early.   (I was always bemused when I thought how that most Christian of all celebrations was still based upon a pagan formula: Easter would arrive on the first Sunday, after the first full moon, after the vernal equinox.   How ironic that no date ever had been established for the celebration of the supreme sacrifice; it was as if man was ill-equipped to fathom his own humanness.)

First Baptist Church, at Linwood and Park, was home to Mother and Dad at that time of the year for rehearsals with Powell Weaver, the famous organist-composer, the choirs, Dr. Wilson, teachers, Mothers, "wing-aways," custodians, and florists at Mohr's (who grew potted palms just so Mother could use them on Palm Sunday).   It was an especial time for the children: Lori, Bruce, and Davie would participate in the Palm Sunday processions; Lori, for the second time.

All three children had been dedicated by Dr. Robert I. Wilson and although they, as infants, had been unaware, the Church had never forgotten or lost touch with them.   Lori had been dedicated Sunday, June 12, 1949, after Dave's Newport tour; Bruce, at the Christmas Service, December 24, 1950, shortly before Dave left for Alaska; and Davie, June 13, 1954, prior to Dave's Newfoundland departure.

Palm Sunday's ritual was as grand as ever and Mother and Dad, escorting three beaming children, joined me in the balcony, in the family pew.   "Weren't they precious?" Mother leaned over to whisper.   "Yes," I nodded and wrote on my bulletin: "The service was never more beautiful! Thank you!"   We watched the Children's Baptismal Service, having described what our children would see and elicited their questions, on the half-hour drive to the Church.   There were many youngsters to be baptized on the most important day in the Church-calendar and our three watched it all, wide-eyed and without a question.

It was two o'clock before we sat down to leg of lamb, cooked slowly all morning and browned until it looked "meltingly delicious," laughed Mother, quoting her Mother—or "larrapin' good," I added, quoting my Mother. Dad said the blessing and carved the lamb quickly for the children were ready for post-prandial naps, after a very long and memorable morning, but hungry enough to stay awake for their favorite roast and candied sweet potatoes.

Lori went off happily to First Grade at Border Star Elementary, just a few blocks east, the second of three different schools she would enjoy in 1955-56. Dave and I had enrolled Bruce in Kindergarten there, but for some reason, Bruce had refused to stay. I had tried taking him the next two days but with the same negative results. It was not until we were in Virginia Beach in April that I discovered Bruce would not be left by his Mother but would ride the bus, eagerly, with Lori, from home and enjoy every moment of his schoolday. He was reluctant for his Daddy to leave him, as well. Kindergarten had become just too mobile for Bruce and he was afraid his parents would forget at which school, in which city, in which state, in which country they had deposited him! Lori loved each school, the last two, especially, since her teachers and classmates were intrigued about Newfoundland. And then they discovered that she had lived in Alaska, too!

Davie and I continued with the portrait-sitting. The ground was still sere in March but there was no snow and it was balmy. We walked westward, the few blocks to Wornall Road, for the ever-adventuresome streetcar ride, Davie's sitting by the window and exclaiming, gleefully, each time the streetcar stopped and he saw arriving and departing heads bounce into view, well below his. He loved the bustling metropolis. Occasionally, he would point to a billboard, as he did to commercials during *Davy Crockett*, and exclaim: "Me want that!" Then a little lecture in pronominal usage would ensue and Davie queried, logically, why, if he was a "me" at the end of the sentence, he had to be an "I," at the beginning? It *was* confusing, I admitted, and Davie remained unready to submit to traditional illogic—just as Bruce had refused to accept, unchanged, Nursery Rhymes. All three children were problem-solvers at early ages, inheriting their Daddy Frank's and their own Daddy's mathematical brilliance, and never asked if the analysis they were charting was correct but argued why the other construct was flagrant and wrong. We encouraged independence of thought and were grateful they were not cut to a pattern but were self-paradigms.

It was a summery April when the children and I arrived in Norfolk. Dave met our plane and took us to see our lake lot and foundation which was beginning to assume the shape of a two-story Town and Country house. In a few months, it would be brick all around the first floor, white siding and Colonial blue shutters on the second with deep cobalt, or Colonial blue, doors leading to the living-room's hallway on the north and family-room's south entrance, both directly below the slightly overhung second story. The brick garage was attached to the north, and the back of the house was all glass with a cathedral-ceilinged living room and dining room's overlooking the lake, a louvered door giving access to the patio and brick barbecue, which extended from the chimney at the northeast corner. The back yard was very deep, stretching to the lake top which was edged with tall, slender ailanthus trees of willow-like foliage. There were a few large swamp white oak trees on the slope but our view of the lake from the house was, generally, unrestricted.

Dave escorted us to the lakeshore and told the children: "You are *never* to swim in the lake. It is against the law; only boats are permitted. This is a city reservoir which in times of low rainfall provides water for Norfolk. Look how deep it is. It drops straight off; it's way over *my* head. *Never* get in the water. Do you understand?"

Dave reminded them that they would have almost the entire summer on Virginia Beach and that when we moved, we would be just five minutes from a swimming beach, at Little Creek Amphibious Base. "As a matter of fact," he remembered, "swimming classes start there, in two weeks, and I've signed you all up!" "Oh, boy!" enthused Bruce, and let out a whoop. "May we skip rocks?" Lori asked, remembering how her Daddy had trained them to that skill in Alaska and Newfoundland. "Me, too?" insisted Davie, who probably had forgotten, but would not be excluded. "Of course," laughed his Dad, "and you're first." So we now had our own rock-skipping course and plenty of missiles on the slope. Detecting poison ivy on one of the oaks, I moved, searchingly, back up to the "yard" and planned my flower beds and placement of shrubs.

The long terrace extended in front of the living room-dining room with space for planting Exbury and Hino azaleas beneath the kitchen windows on the east and roses along the southern foundation, flanking the kitchen, bathroom and laundry room. I asked Dave to extend the walk from the garage, contiguous to and edging the western front of the house, swinging widely from the house on the south and east to connect with the terrace and from the northern end of the terrace to the back garage door.

I then had protected flower beds on the south and east and the children could ride and drive their vehicles completely around the house, through the garage and up and down the long driveway without being tempted by the street.

We were only one lot away from a cul-de-sac and our street, Sunrise Drive, would be restricted to traffic eventually, but houses were going up quickly with heavy trucks everywhere and I wanted our motoring minions to be delimitated, within sight, but unthwarted.   "And gardenias will be planted completely across the front of the house, bordering the walk, with three Betty Prior shrub roses—they look like huge, flat, deep pink dogwood blooms—edging the circular extension from the driveway, so that there is plenty of room to get in and out of cars. Remember your favorite saying: `It costs just a penny more to go first-class!'" And I waggled my finger at him. "Oh yes," I pursued my plan, "let's put four white, wrought-iron trellaces, spaced evenly, to connect the overhang to the edge of the walk. That will provide a nice background for my gardenias and I promise not to grow vines on them," remembering Key West and knowing we were in termite country. "I'll plant just one clematis, a Ramona, which is blue, of course, and it will grow on the northwest corner of the brick garage."

Dave agreed to everything, so I continued: "And then we should have a blue picket fence with wide boards—I don't like the narrow New England slats for such a big yard—around the back yard, connected to the back southeast corner of the kitchen, following the perimeter of the lot to the top of the lake and back to the northeast end of the garage. I'd like a wide gate, at the walk by the kitchen and another at the lake top, both with strong latches on the outside, so that children—Davie's size—playing in the back yard, cannot open the gates. We can put a swing, slide, et al, at the northeast corner of the back yard and only one tree, for the children to have a little shade—maybe a weeping willow, although hurricanes take those up first, but they grow quickly—at the southeast." "Is that all?" laughed my amused spouse. "Well," I rejoined, "you've given me two months to study your diagrams and pictures, so I estimate I have room for thirty camellias, mostly *japonica* but a few *sasanquas* inside and outside of the fence, north and northeast of the garage. This is excellent, acid soil for gardenias, azaleas and camellias. Won't it be wonderful! And do you realize we can also grow the dark red crape myrtles? I want three in the southwest edge of our front yard." Dave acquiesced: since he had chosen the lot and house, some of which I could still change, if I wished; I certainly should plan the yard. Actually, he had consulted with me, by phone and letter, every step of the planning and my "yard" was a mere suggestion.

We did effectuate it, at proper planting times, within a year, however, placing the gardenias, large balled plants, in August, when the yard was sodded. I flooded them twice a day with water and we had blooms in the house every day until frost. The gardenias, or cape jessamine, as Mother and Mama Kate called them—were a very hardy, resilient Southern shrub. Dormant roses from Jackson and Perkins were planted in November and sweet peas, in jumbo seed, along the outside of the fence, from the house to the front gate, no more than eight feet, for sweet peas produced prodigious blooms and then, vines became unsightly. We began to select *sasanqua* camellias in November for I wanted to see them in bloom but chose mostly the large, exotic, later-blooming *japonicas*, both singles and doubles, in March, April and the first two weeks of May.

The children loved being at the beach house, which was just a sandy mound away from the Atlantic Ocean. Dave and I were pleased, too, and found the halcyon beach and modus vivendi not a difficult adjustment. We spent few hours indoors.

Our two-story garage was very comfortable

Figure 75. Atlantic Yard; Garage-Tipped Dune

and casual with its simple furnishings, plus our dishes, utensils and linens from Newfoundland which Dave, with traditional thoughtfulness, had unpacked before our arrival. Our furniture and gear would remain in storage until our house was completed and the only items we had brought from Newfoundland: one small bedroom set, a dryer, my little portable washing machine, trunk and cruise boxes, the latter having just been brought from Dave's BOQ, were commingled into our beached garage. It proved to be quite capacious with a living room, large kitchen with table and chairs and storage space, downstairs; upstairs, three small bedrooms, a full bath with both tub and shower and even a small sun deck outside our south bedroom where I read while the children napped. There were no rugs on the planked floors, except for the soft cotton rugs I put by each bed, nondescript curtains and sturdy blinds. There was a shower attached to the house, by the front door, for de-sanding arms, legs, and feet but to little effect because Davie—to whom sand was the greatest marvel in the world, having experienced only rock, snow and ice—was supplied sand, inside, by Bruce.

We collected all of Bruce's sundry, sandy containers and poured them into a sizable plastic play box, so that rain or shine—Davie played in the beach. But when Bruce, Lori and Davie tried to import their sand crabs, for "a rainy day," I demurred. I didn't even associate with them on the beach and always wondered at the children's galvanized interest and pursuit.

When Lori, Bruce and Davie were not frolicking in the water, practicing their new strokes or paddling on inner tubes, they spent hours digging for sand crabs and collecting them in buckets of ocean water. They discovered crabs died in the potable water from the house but Atlantic water kept them frisky overnight. After their scientific curiosities were assuaged and they ceased carrying them back and forth, they dug holes in the sand a few feet from the

Figure 76. Sand-Crabbing Trio

ocean's edge, each late afternoon, and poured their playmates, home.

By the first of June, the children were brown as dried rose petals. They had enjoyed their Virginia Beach schools, Bruce's coming home on the bus at noon to have lunch with Davie and me, nap and go to the beach and, every other afternoon, swim in beginners' classes at Little Creek with Lori, who returned from school shortly after two.

As soon as school was over for the summer, I drove them to the Norfolk campus, College of William and Mary, for morning classes, indoors, in intermediate swimming. While Bruce swam from nine to ten, I taught Lori "phonics" and Bruce studied reading from ten until eleven, while Lori took her lesson in the pool.

The "look-say" method was currently in vogue in Virginia. I thought it was ludicrous to teach a phonetic alphabet without reference to the phonemes and phonetic symbols upon which it was built; in fact, I deemed it impossible. Proper emphasis upon orthoëpy had been supplanted by easy memorization. My determination to have authentic readers in my children transcended the concern generated by the best-selling *Why Johnny Can't Read* and I bought an old phonics (at that time a 'verboten' noun) textbook in bright red with an Indian (representing the short *i* sound) etched in black on the cover and taught my two older children how to read correctly. I was an ogre about the education of children and scoffed at the "new methodology."

Make learning "fun," teachers were apparently being told and, *voilà*, Johnny will become brilliant—if he's happy enough. Even Davie, collecting treasures in his sand bucket and alternately, studying his alphabet and number flash cards, correctly recited the sounds of the short vowels and wanted to read "the Indian book," too. (Children, I well knew, did not mind studying if it was productive and logical; it was adults, frustrated by their own limitations, who announced that learning must be made "easy and fun for children"; the latter, generally overshadowing the aptitude and perceptiveness of those "teaching" them.)

I was not timid about taking care of my own and knew I was the type of parent whom a weak teacher would deplore and fear, for I would do my own teaching—without pretense. In fact, when Davie was old enough to go to school, they might find me there too!

Oceana Naval Air Station was five miles south, slightly west, of our beach garage. Since we lived in a civilian neighborhood, if I needed the car, I awakened the children and we drove with Dave to the Base in the early-morning sunshine. The children loved the ride for they not only got to see their uniformed Daddy saluted by the Marine guard at the gate, a salute which he briskly returned, but their favorite "bump" was on the, usually deserted, at that hour, road to the back gate. When there was no car in sight on the straight stretch of county road, a mile northeast of the back gate, Dave would accelerate a bit and we would "fly" over the slight rise in the road which dipped beyond. The sudden drop would always take the children's breath away and they would squeal delightedly. It didn't produce a roller-coaster effect on the way back, so after they kissed their Daddy and saw the planes for the second time, they lay down to somnolence and I drove back, in complete silence, planning our day.

The children and I would pick Dave up at five but we were seldom successful "bumpers," on the way, for we couldn't fly if we had to brake for traffic ahead; besides, sailors were notorious speedsters (except flyers) and I always drove with special wariness at Base-exit time. As a matter of fact, so many accidents had occurred on highways in the Virginia Beach area, involving Naval personnel, that a hideously smashed car was displayed, and too frequently changed, just inside the gate with signs urging caution and sobriety.

I was always proud of Dave, for not only did he not drink, except for a highball, occasionally, at a mandatory cocktail or dinner party—even then he usually drank a coke—but he was ready to go home when we arrived. I didn't have to go to the O-Club to extricate him from "happy-hour" socializing. Dave, also, drove expertly, within the speed limits, and never needed to "show off," in a car, in a plane—or in any situation. Indeed, he was a perfect husband and father and set only positive, laudable examples!

Dave was the Meteorological Officer attached to the Operations Department at Oceana Naval Air Station which served various squadrons of carrier-based planes and Fentress, the Gunnery and Bombing Range, twenty miles south, an area where the carrier jets and props practiced landings and takeoffs, as well as bombing and strafing runs. The Operations Department kept a helicopter, to fly to Fentress and to the carriers, and a jet but most of their planes were SNB's and R4D's, Dave's flying the latter two. It was a busy, multifarious Base for Virginia Beach had excellent weather for flying—and forecasting.

One morning, early, as we drove with Dave to Oceana so that I could check the rebuilding of the fireplace—Dave had discovered that it was crooked and asked the builder to remove it and rebuild it—we stopped at a traffic light in Virginia Beach, long enough for Bruce to observe busy insects hovering over the flower bed. "Look, Davie," he alerted his brother, pointing to the monardas, nicotianas, and weigelas, "the bees are getting nectar. Mommy, can we plant those?" "Yes, we can. Thank you for discovering them." "If it weren't for bees," Bruce postulated, "the whole world would be juice!"

 Lake Smith, Norfolk

Bruce helped me plant his bee-attracting monarda (bee-balms), in the front of the azalea bed, six red ones, the following week. We planted two red weigela shrubs on the northwest corner of the garage but deferred planting nicotiana (tobacco flower) seeds, since the highly fragrant plant was an annual, until the springtime. They would go, with the monardas, in the sunny front of the southeast azalea garden. I had completely overlooked the hummingbird-bee-and-butterfly-attracting fragrances and botanically structured, tubular shapes for nectar extraction of those three blooms, so important for every garden where there were three, scientifically soaring offspring and a sympathetic soil.

Figure 77. Space for Bruce's Bee-Balms

It was the middle of August and we finally were occupying our own new house on Lake Smith, 6300 Sunrise Drive, Norfolk (later changed to Virginia Beach), 2, Virginia.

Our furniture, rugs and drapes had fit in beautifully in the living room-dining room with its cathedral ceiling

Figure 78. 6300 Sunrise Drive

accommodating wrought-iron-railinged hardwood stairs to a wide landing and hall, stretching in front of the three bedrooms and bath. We had only a paucity of furniture, mostly toys, in the family room so had journeyed to High Point, North Carolina, a major furniture-manufacturing center, to order a long, sectional couch which could be made into twin beds, choosing a heavy textured blue-gray nylon for it; a large club chair with ottoman to be upholstered in a blue and white linen in a provincial floral pattern; a round, black breakfast table, with dried, pressed fronds of Christmas and ostrich ferns laminated in a circular border, amid hair-fine streaks of gold ribbon interspersed throughout the top and laminated within. We ordered five chairs, seats upholstered in black vinyl shot with gold thread; and a large, blue nylon tweed, foam-backed rug for the family room which was in stock and was sent first, the kitchen chairs soon following.

In two months all had arrived and our domicile was completely functional. We even added a washing machine to accompany the dryer in the laundry room, which became a great boon with my three naturalists. They could enter the family room door, discard muddy clothes, wash a bit in the bathroom, don clean clothes and go on about their adventuring—or even come into the living room to greet my bridge players.

A few weeks after our move to Sunrise Drive, Dave made LCDR and was pic- tured in the September 7, 1956, *Virgin- ian-Pilot*, Nor- folk's daily newspaper, being congratu- lated by his skipper, CAPT H. H. Hale, together with recently pro- moted CDR C. M. Scott, the guided-missile officer, and Base medical

Figure 79. Up the Ladder

officer, CAPT J.M. Jacoby (MC). Dave was described by the *Virginian-Pilot* as the "station aerologist," which was the original designation by the Navy, later changed to the civilian terminology: "meteorologist." The *Oceana Jet Observer* of September 14, 1956, published at USNAS Oceana, Virginia Beach, captioned the picture "Up the Ladder" with LTJG H. L. Cassani (not pictured) making LT grade the next day.

Dave, CDR Scott and CAPT Jacoby were hosts of the traditional cocktail-buffet, "wetting-down" party (new stripes were "wet down" with appropriate libation) given for their fellow officers and wives at the swank, new Oceana O-Club, where they were recipients of the customary good-humored anecdotes, nonsense gifts and impromptu speech-making—and reciprocated in kind.

It was a socially active base; we attended many formal dinner dances and entertained often at home. Two of our close friends, LCDR Charlie ("I'm a 'good ole boy' from Mississippi") King and Katie, his aristocratic wife, also a Mississippian, dining with us for the first time, discovered that our china, Belvedere by Lenox, would increase their twelve places to twenty-four and Katie asked to borrow them: "Oh, I'm just dying to give a real dinner party," she exclaimed. "At home," in her lovely Mississippi tones, soft, musical—almost as mellifluous as Mother's and I could deny her, nothing—"I'd borrow Mother's or my sister's, we all had 'Belvedere'." "You also had big houses and Negroes," Charlie chuckled. Katie clapped her hands, her diamonds brilliant in the candlelight: "I'm going to give a party! Will you come?" "Of course," Dave teased, "where our dishes go, we go." "But I'm going to mark mine," I said, "I'm sentimental. I'll put a piece of red tape on the bottom of each piece." I shook my finger at Katie, "You tell your girl I want all of mine back; I'm going to check them," I laughed. "You better," Charlie drawled, "y'all better. . . ."

I enrolled Lori in Second Grade at Bayside Elementary School, Bayside, Virginia, four blocks from the Lake, and Bruce in First Grade—their fourth school since the year began. Davie and I studied, gardened and played together while the rest of the family, for the first time, were away all day.

Dave drove to Oceana in twenty to twenty-five minutes and on Commissary, A.A.U.W., Girl Scout, O-Wives' luncheon, or bridge-luncheon days; Charlie King picked him up or Davie and I drove with him, depositing Lori and Bruce at school. When I went to the Commissary at Little Creek Amphibious Base, five minutes away, Davie generally wanted to play at the Commissary Nursery because he saw some of his "school friends" from Sunday School there.

The children had started Sunday School at Little Creek, while Dave and I attended Protestant Chapel, as soon as we moved to Virginia Beach. It was a joy to have an accessible Church-affiliation again; Newfoundland's weather, "the gut," and Catholicism—Placentia's only established religion—precluding regular attendance. At Argentia Naval Base, we had attended Chapel and Sunday School the last few months after we moved aboard. We were soon thriving in family, church, school and community normalcy.

Almost the entire Lake neighborhood was Navy, officers' building west and north of the Lake Smith Reservoir, while enlisted personnel rented houses of more modest proportions between our half circle of the Lake and Bayside Elementary. Our immediate neighbors, to the south, Al and Pauline Jacobson, who owned an advertising company and were childless and read six or seven books, apiece, a week, were the only civilians in the Lake lineup. They lived in a ranch-style house with a screened porch fronting the ailanthus-bordered water and were delightful neighbors and wonderful cooks. North of us was the Haselton family; Bob was a Submariner and took all of us "down" for lunch one day, including Mother H. There were three Haselton siblings and north of them, four young Platz's, their Daddy attached to a Cruiser. A "non-com," CPO Warren Olney and Virginia, who was my assistant Girl Scout leader and little curly-headed Karen, lived next to LT Platz. Southwest of us, opposite the cul-de-sac and immediately west of the Jacobson's, CDR Frank Melewicz, Dave's superior in Argentia, Newfoundland, had built for his wife Naomi and beautiful daughter, Melanie.

We had a most congenial neighborhood and the children played together with good judgment and genuine amicability. Dave and I played bridge with the parents, excepting the Melewicz and Jacobson couples, who did not play, preferring conversation and "Navy talk" in the first instance; books and current affairs, in the latter.

Soon after Katie's lovely formal buffet and a week before Christmas, Dave and Charlie had a harrowing flight back from Washington, D. C., in an SNB from the Base. It was just a routine flight to take an officer to D.C. Their prop plane made it up VFR (Visual Flight Rules) in an hour and fifteen minutes. Dave filed his return flight plan in Washington, VFR, collected Charlie and headed to the plane for takeoff but the Tower called him back: "You'll have to file an IFR plan; weather's closing in." Dave went back (Charlie told me this; Dave never narrated), scrapped the VFR flight plan and filed for IFR (Instrument Flight Rules) and returned to his plane. By the time he had checked his instruments, revved up his engines, and been cleared by the Tower for takeoff, the weather had closed in at Oceana. (Charlie told me he was glad he was flying with Dave!) They encountered such turbulence, after a clear, smooth flight less than two hours before, that most of their prolonged return to Oceana was up and down, "like being on a broken elevator, dropping suddenly, bumping, bumping, then shooting up again." Washington, D.C., and immediate environs, was known for its unpredictable, sudden, severe turbulence. The Exec's wife had just been killed in a commercial crash, enroute from D.C. to Norfolk; we were still trying to recover from that tragedy. Finally, after long minutes without radio contact, Oceana's GCA (Ground Control Approach with radar) locked in on Dave's plane and he was talked down to a skilled landing; and all was well, after the wind, the rain and Mother Nature, roaring louder than the radio, had challenged man's ability to fly—both blind and deaf. Dave should have experienced a feeling of mental empire after that flight but I surmised he did not; he would have given the GCA crew all the credit—but Charlie King did not.

Christmas of 1956 reunited us again with our Nebraskans and Missourians, our traveling first to Lincoln for pre-Yule celebration and home to Kansas City for Christmas Day; our wedding anniversary and New Year's Eve and Dad's birthday; the Rose Parade on television and the Rose Bowl game (which Dave and I did not attend until the Eighties and planned to take the five grandbabies and parents in the late Nineties—when some would be old enough, and others, young enough, to remember).

In 1957, we designated most week ends for studying the

Figure 80. Mother H, Joan, Ken, Lori, Bruce, Patti, Johnny, Bobby, Davie, Jane

Officer's Yule Not So Cool This Year

By NANCY BENJAMIN
Star Staff Writer

After two Christmas holidays spent in frigid Newfoundland, Lt. Comdr. David Holland and his family can expect more moderate temperatures for this Yuletide season.

The Navy aerological officer, now stationed at Virginia Beach, Va., was in Lincoln recently visiting his mother, Mrs. Susan M. Holland, and his brother, Dr. Kenneth E. Holland, and family.

After the visit, Lt. Comdr. Holland and his family went to Kansas City, Mo., to spend Christmas Day with Mrs. Holland's parents.

Last Christmas the Hollands—including the children, Bruce, David Jr. and Lori—cut their own fir tree and spent the day sledding.

Checked Ice Conditions

The Hollands lived at Argentia AFB, Newfoundland for 18 months where Holland served as ice Reconnaissance Officer for the Fleet Weather Central, checking on ice conditions in the northermost regions of the globe.

The Navy officer called the ice work "challenging" because of its importance and adventure in flying over uncharted territory—often being the only plane ever to have crossed the region.

The work of this group was to chart the ice floes and advise ways for supply ships to reach the remote bases near the polar regions.

Flying a two-engined F-2V Neptune, the men were able to chart ice features and size, and even determine the age of the floes by their color.

Magaznes and store catalogues were sometimes dropped to isolated villages where residents were out of contact with the rest of the world. Many of the settlements depended on dog sleds for supplies, received mail deliveries as rarely

as twice a year and kept contact by radio.

The move to Oceana Naval Air Station at Virginia Beach last January meant an abrupt change in climate and living conditions for the Hollands.

As aerological o f f i c e r, Lt. Cmdr. Holland is now more interested in the movement of tropical storms than in ice floes.

He now checks the local and cross-country weather conditions for air flights and to warn authorities of any necessity of plane evacuation.

Holland isa former University of Nebraska student. He joined the Navy in 1943 and received his B. S. degree in aerology at the U.S. Naval Post-graduate School, Monterey, Calif.

The officer has also served at posts in Saipan; Kodiac, Alaska; San Diego, Calif.; Newport, R. I., and Pensacola, Fla.

Quite A Difference

Christmas in the Midwest is going to be a change for Lt. Comdr. David Holland and his son, David Jr., after the Holland family spent the last two Christmas seasons in Newfoundland. Lt. Cmdr. Holland, his wife, Dorothy, and children, Bruce, Lori and David, spent several days in Lincoln visiting Holland's mother, and brother, Dr. Kenneth E. Holland, before traveling to Kansas City to spend Christmas with Mrs. Holland's parents. (Star Photo.)

Figure 81. Dave and Davie Meet the Press, Lincoln Star

Figure 82.   Davie, Daddy Frank, Mommy Tom, Lori, Bruce

Figure 83. Christmas Eve, Kansas City

Figure 84. Stockings Hung with Care

rich historicity of the Chesapeake Bay country which included both Virginia and Maryland. The Chesapeake, deriving its name from the Indian word meaning "Great Shellfish Bay," was a shallow inland sea—the largest estuary on the Atlantic Coast: 195 miles from the mouth of the Bay, almost due north, to the Susquehanna River. With forty-eight rivers and over one hundred branches plus countless creeks meandering into it, the Chesapeake Bay had been described by a cartographer as looking "like the deck plan of an octopus." The Bay cut both states in twain, creating the Eastern Shore between the Chesapeake and the Atlantic Ocean where the Shore people, of old English stock, lived quaintly with their own customs and speechways. Beyond the Eastern Shore, the Atlantic Ocean formed the Chincoteague Bay, creating Chincoteague Island, Virginia, where one of Lori's school chums had a summer home and invited Lori to attend the annual wild-horse roundup on the contiguous island, Assateague Island, Maryland. We deemed our Second Grader too young to adventure with horses, especially wild ones which were invariably given away upon capture, and credited Terry Hamer's friendship as origin of Lori's determination to own her "favorite animal, sometime" (realized between her second and third degrees when she was teaching school).

Our first investigation began at Cape Henry on the northern point of Virginia Beach between the Atlantic and the Bay and a short distance from our beach house. A granite cross marked the first landing of the first English colonists to come to the New World with Captain John Smith in the *Sarah Constant, Goodspeed* and *Discovery*, in 1607. They sailed into Hampton Roads, where the battle of the later ironclads March 9, 1862, revolutionized naval warfare. The Confederates had captured the Federal *Merrimac* during the Civil War, renamed it *Virginia* and rebuilt it, fitting it with iron plating. The Union's *Monitor*, a raft-like boat, armored, with two guns in a turret which swiveled, fired for hours, almost point-blank; the *Merrimac's* ten fixed guns' returning the fire, but neither boat could be sunk. (I heard all about the remarkable battle the first week I taught in the Virginia schools. A precocious second grader gave a speech about the *Merrimac* and the "Thermometer"!)

From Hampton Roads, Captain Smith sailed his three little English ships into the James River where the first permanent English settlement in the New World was established at Jamestown, May 13, 1607. It took us three hours by car to make the trip which they had started April 26, from Cape Henry, consuming almost three weeks. The children were amused by slowness of sailing but when they saw, and boarded, the brightly painted,

duplicated *Sarah Constant, Goodspeed* and *Discovery* docked at Jamestown, they pondered how the fragile-looking craft could cross a river,
much less an ocean. "I'm glad we didn't sail in one from Newfoundland!"
Lori exclaimed. "He can't even stand up," observed Bruce, pointing to a
seventeenth-century English "sailor" who stooped low to go between decks.
"I can," demonstrated Davie. And that was just the size of the Jamestown
ships.

We discovered later when aboard the *Constellation* in Newport and
the *Constitution* in Baltimore that even those large ships precluded upright
stature between decks, except for Davie, of course, personal space and
comfort sacrificed for supplies, incredible amounts of coiled ropes, plus
cannons, munitions and barrels. Hammocks were slung and unslung in
airless quarters, which we wondered how anyone could survive. We
marveled at the courage and tenacity of crews and passengers in those
ancient vessels and applauded their fabulistic achievements.

Of the original colony at Jamestown, only foundations remained
and a rebuilt church maintained by the National Park Service but, near by,
the State of Virginia had reconstructed a palisaded James Fort showing
how the colonists lived in thatched houses and tried to survive disease,
starvation and tomahawks. Jamestown had been burned in 1676, during
Bacon's Rebellion, a revolt against class tyranny among the colonists led
by Nathaniel Bacon, a century before the colonists revolted against the
English hierarchy in the American Revolution. Undaunted survivors
rebuilt the town. It was finally abandoned in 1699, after a second fire and
continued pestilence in the low-lying terrain which had been inhospitable,
from the first, for the birthplace of a nation. Inhabitants moved to
Williamsburg and on upriver on both sides of the James to found tidewater
plantations, grow tobacco, build mansions and plant elaborate boxwood
gardens.

The children were most intrigued with the Jamestown glass blowing
which duplicated the seventeenth-century recipe and procedure, producing
a rough, heavy, green, almost opaque, glass after it was heated in an
igloo-shaped oven to its viscid state, blown in ballooning shapes on long
tubes, cut with shears and immersed in water to harden. We bought a
sample of the lime-green glass, a thick coaster impressed with a lower-case
j, so the children could compare it with twentieth-century glass products.
We walked back through the original site, imagining more accurately what
the township of one hundred and four English colonists had looked like,

and paused awhile at the very small stone church, reconstructed, where the Indian Princess Pocahontas married the English John Rolfe in 1614.

Williamsburg, capital of Virginia from 1699 until 1780, when legislators moved to Richmond to escape the British warships, was probably America's first planned community being "laid out regularly in lots . . . sufficient each for a house and garden and . . . affords a free passage for the air which is grateful in violent hot weather." (*National Geographic*, "Williamsburg, City For All Seasons," December 1968, p. 818.) Houses were built closely together on the edge of broad avenues with gardens at the back surrounding kitchens and storehouses with flowers, trees, vegetables and herbs and often, a formal English boxwood garden and rose arbors. Most of the public buildings were built of red brick, English Georgian in architecture and furnishings; the residences, shops and taverns of frame construction.

The historic town had died and nearly decayed when the Reverend W. A. R. Goodwin of Bruton Parish Church persuaded John D. Rockefeller, Jr., to restore and preserve it in 1927, at a cost of $79,000,000 to the Rockefellers over a period of forty-one years.

We visited the Capitol building with its rounded attached towers and round windows, the right wing of which was the House of Burgesses where Patrick Henry had protested the Stamp Act of 1765. Imposed by the British Cabinet to tax stamps used on legal documents, ships' clearance papers, newspapers and pamphlets, it was to be paid in silver—a very rare metal in America. The Colonists had furiously refused and in the Stamp Act Congress of 1765, Patrick Henry had urged—"If this be treason, make the most of it" ("Williamsburg," p. 812). Politics had been learned in the House of Burgesses by George Washington, Thomas Jefferson and James Madison.

After visiting a few shops exhibiting works of a silversmith; weaver (all as they were accomplished in the eighteenth century); printer; bootmaker; blacksmith; gunsmith—where Davie bought a miniature brass cannon; wig maker and sand caster; we had lunch at the King's Arms where enormous napkins were tied around our necks and we enjoyed our first taste of hot, delicate Sally Lunn bread with our oysters, Welsh rabbit and mutton chops.

Most of the shops were on the main Duke of Gloucester Street as was the famous Raleigh where the colonial statesmen met for pipes, dinner and momentous discussions in the white frame Tavern with sleeping quarters above to accommodate them for the night, three to a bed. The part of the Raleigh Tavern the children found most interesting was the bakery in a separate building at the back where gingerbread cookies, baking on the hour, filled the air with irresistible aroma and provided our dessert, the children's standing in line for the huge, hot, spicy cookies.

We found a solid brass, very heavy, mortar and pestle at the chemist's shop for Bruce's home experiments; from the forge, an iron, wood-burning stove, in doll-sized proportions, was purchased by Lori, just like the gingerbread-baking stove at the Raleigh Tavern Bakery. I bought a small volume at the bookbinders entitled *The Williamsburg Art of Cookery* by Mrs. Helen Bullock which the preface told me was "The first American Book on the Art of Cookery, The Compleat Housewife, or Accomplish'd Gentlewoman's Companion . . . printed in the Year 1742, by William Parks in Williamsburg in Virginia." Dave bought silver quill charms for Lori's charm bracelet and mine and two small pewter porringers for raisins and Virginia peanuts.

We walked swiftly through the Governor's Palace, impressed by the spacious ballroom, elaborate wall sconces, artistic dried-flower arrangements; the boys' approving most of the lion and unicorn atop the pillars of the front gate. We drove to the College of William and Mary at the western end of the Duke of Gloucester Street with the venerable Wren Building, modeled by Sir Christopher Wren, English architect, the oldest academic structure still in use in the country and the centerpiece of the handsome brick buildings where Thomas Jefferson, John Marshall (Chief Justice of the Supreme Court, 1801-35, influential interpreter of the U.S. Constitution), James Monroe, Benjamin Harrison, John Tyler had distinguished themselves as scholars in the nation's second oldest college. In 1693, James Blair was a fiery minister from Scotland with an equally fiery wife, English Sarah Harrison, who, in 1687, when asked if she would "love, cherish and obey" her husband, responded emphatically: "No obey." After the third reading of the vows and the third "NO OBEY," the disbelieving Reverend Blair gave in but Sarah never did! (David Hackett Fischer, *Albion's Seed*, 1989, p. 295.) A Virginia commissary of the bishop of London, the hard-working Dr. Blair obtained a charter from King William III and Queen Mary II to found with William Randolph's assistance the liberal arts College of William and Mary. George Wythe, tutor to Jefferson, joined the faculty and established the first School of Law in the colonies. The Honor System was founded at William and Mary as well as Phi Beta Kappa, the honorary scholastic society, in 1776.

Harvard University, Cambridge, Massachusetts, was founded in 1636 and named Harvard College in 1639 for its first benefactor, John Harvard, an English minister, a Nonconformist (a member of a Protestant denomination dissenting from the Church of England, principally: Baptists, Congregationalists, Methodists, Presbyterians, Quakers and Unitarians), who contributed £780 and 260 books to the wilderness "college." After 1869, the organizational scope of Harvard was that of a university but the "college" with its liberal, cultural training of undergraduates remained the focus of Harvard University.

Jamestown, on the James River bank, was the beginning of the Colonial National Historical Parkway. Williamsburg, almost at midpoint, connected Jamestown on the southwest to Yorktown, on the York River and southeast, where the British surrendered under Cornwallis in the culminating battle of the American Revolutionary War, October 19, 1781.

The Yorktown Battlefield prompted the children's zest to see more battlefields and so we began the backward study of the American Revolution, beginning at the end—at Moore House, Yorktown, Virginia, where the aristocratic General George Washington accepted surrender of British forces from his English equivalent, Lord Cornwallis; and ended at the beginning with the Minutemen at the Concord Bridge and Lexington and Bunker Hill, in Boston, Massachusetts.

As we surveyed the backward movement of the War for Independence, the American Revolution, we observed the progression of the Nation's capital from the temporary capital in Annapolis, Maryland, where General Washington resigned his commission at the State House, December 23, 1783, to New York City, to a permanent site designed for the capital in the newly created District of Columbia, the land being ceded by the States of Virginia and Maryland.

While the remarkable new city was built, the Government resided in Philadelphia until (Washington's words): "The first Monday in December, 1800, the seat of the government of the United States shall, by virtue of this act, be transferred" to a district "not exceeding ten miles square, to be located . . . on the river Potomac." (*The White House, An Historic Guide*, p. 9.) The newly formed Republic, developing spasmodically, had never had a central Governmental seat but each of the colonies had their own capitals.

In the Virginian capital at Williamsburg, the Continental Congress was proposed May 27, 1774, a few days before the act closing the port of Boston was to go into effect on June 1, 1774. The colonies agreed to form a colonial congress and to send delegates to meet in Philadelphia on September 5, 1774, in the first meeting of the Continental Congress to consult upon their "present unhappy State." The Continental Congress brought the new Nation into being and governed it from the voting of Independence in 1776, until it elected John Hanson the "first President of the United States" under the Articles of Confederation, in 1781. President John Hanson died in 1783, and the States were without a President until George Washington was elected under the Constitution of the United States, in 1789. (We were fascinated by our visit to the birthplace of John Hanson, a modest replica of his home at Mulberry Grove, Maryland, on the bank of the Potomac where he was born in 1721, an American Revolutionary leader whom history accorded a few bathetic words. By contrast, Washington's birthplace, due south across the Potomac in Wakefield, Virginia, was a National Monument, the mansion where he was born February 22, 1732, having been authentically reconstructed in its idyllic, pristine site beautifully maintained by the Government.)

Neither the Government nor the President functioned in Washington until 1800, when our second President, John Adams, supervised movement of offices in June and took up residence with Abigail, November 1, 1800, in an unfinished White House, designed and built by Irish architect James Hoban. Hoban built the "President's House" in a Georgian style but added an American eagle in the north pediment with the typical Georgian hipped roof, balustrade and alternating window arches.

It was unfortunate that George Washington lived in none of the President's Houses, three having been designed and built for him in New York, in Philadelphia and Washington, District of Columbia. He was, apparently, happier without too many trappings of office and retired to his beloved Mount Vernon at the end of his second term as President in 1797, where he lived two years as a Virginia gentleman-farmer, dying December 14, 1799. He had exhausted himself for his country, having served for forty-four years, since 1755, when he was appointed Commander in Chief of the Virginian troops during the French and Indian War and named Commander in Chief of the new U. S. Army in 1798, a year after he retired from the Presidency.

The most elegant home of the famous Virginians was the ancestral home of Robert E. Lee at Stratford, just a short distance east of Washington's Wakefield, on the shore of the Potomac where he was born January 19, 1807. It was a very large, graceful Georgian mansion with sweeping, semicircular stairways from the second floor of the stately white stories which fronted a long, grassy mall, the Potomac at the back, framed in wooded slopes.

Driving north and west and crossing the Rappahannock River at Port Conway, we arrived at Port Royal, the birthplace of James Madison, our fourth President, born March 16, 1751. The Virginia estate to which he retired in 1817—he died June 28, 1836—was named Montpelier.

The most interesting and most imposing home of the Virginia Presidents was Thomas Jefferson's Monticello, Italian for "beautiful mountain," which he designed and built in the heights above Charlottesville and the University of Virginia, the construction of which he watched from a cement terrace with a telescope of his own specifications. Jefferson's epitaph, which he wrote, stated that he was the founder of the University of Virginia, an achievement of which he was the most proud; the author of the Virginia Bill of Rights for Religious Freedom and the Declaration of Independence; he made no mention of having been our third president, serving from 1801 to 1809. He retired in 1809 to Monticello and lived there, busily, until his death, July 4, 1826.

The children were particularly intrigued with the eight-day clock which Jefferson had invented, the weights being cannon balls which dropped slowly from the top of the wall on the first floor through round openings in the ground flooring into the basement below where Negro servants pulled them up to the top, every eight days. A writing desk with a swivel arm could be pulled across the bed, Jefferson's invention for facilitating his writing at which he was constantly employed, being a lawyer, eloquent statesman, President, inventor, gourmet cook and an exacting gardener. The furnishings were rich and discrete; most were of his design and construction. We laughed at his short, narrow bed, a Jeffersonian original, and were informed that most of the Virginia gentry slept in a semi-upright posture. There was a magnificent approach to Monticello with a long amplitude of lawn bordered with formal flower beds of annuals and perennials and wide walks, the domed and columned mansion splendid in the background.

South and east of Monticello was Oakhill, near Leesburg, the retirement home of James Monroe, fifth President—serving from 1817 to 1825. Monroe had been born in Westmoreland County, not far from the birthplaces of George Washington and Robert E. Lee on April 28, 1758, but the house had not been preserved. He lived at Oakhill from 1825 to 1830, when he moved to New York City to live with his daughter; he died in New York July 4, 1831. The Oakhill home was almost overwhelmed by the glorious English boxwood shrubs which shaded the front walk to the house and encircled it with the most delicious, fresh pungency. The house had been designed by Monroe's close friend, Thomas Jefferson (nota bene: both died on the Fourth of July), who had been Monroe's mentor, preceding him to the College of William and Mary and the Virginia House of Burgesses and to the Presidency.

West of Charlottesville and slightly north was Staunton, Virginia, the birthplace of (Thomas) Woodrow Wilson, the twenty-eighth President serving from 1913 to 1921 but afflicted with a paralytic stroke in 1919; his second wife, Edith Bolling Galt, whom he married December 18, 1915, after his first wife died in 1914, serving in his stead—the remainder of his second term. Woodrow Wilson was the eighth President from the State of Virginia, born December 28, 1856, in Staunton and dying in Washington, D.C., February 3, 1924. A distinguished scholar, he had been graduated from Princeton University and later became its president. The natal house was Victorian in appearance, built close to the street in front, with porches on each story at the back, overlooking a lovely, formal Southern garden.

A short distance northeast of Charlottesville was the town of Barboursville, Virginia, where Zachary Taylor, our twelfth President was born November 24, 1784. Elected as a military hero, General Taylor had defeated Mexican General Santa Anna at the Battle of Buena Vista and secured victory in the Mexican War. The family moved the year following Zachary's birth to a plantation near Louisville, Kentucky, where he was educated by tutors and later entered the U.S. Army as a First Lieutenant. Probably because he lived just a year in Virginia and survived just a year of his presidency, from 1849 to July 9, 1850, there was no monument in Virginia to his fame as an Indian fighter and to his brief Presidency.

More short-lived than President Taylor was our ninth President, William Henry Harrison, born on the banks of the James River, as it wound west from Jamestown, at Berkeley, in Charles City County, Virginia, February 8, 1773. He was elected in 1840, campaigning successfully on the slogan: "Tippecanoe and Tyler too," the former term's applying to the Battle of Tippecanoe, November 7, 1811, where he, General Harrison, defeated Shawnee chief Tecumseh and Tyler's referring to his running mate, John Tyler. President Harrison was inaugurated March 4, 1841, and, while delivering the longest inaugural address on record in which he promised not to run for a second term, became so thoroughly chilled he developed pneumonia and "served" only a month; John Tyler's becoming the tenth President and serving the full term.

John Tyler's family home was Sherwood Forest to which he retired in 1845, having been born at the estate near Charles City, Virginia, March 29, 1790. In 1861, in February, he was chairman of a peace convention which attempted to avert the Civil War but later, at a Virginia convention, voted in favor of secession. He died January 18, 1862, in Richmond, Virginia, without taking his seat in the Confederate House.

We visited Mount Vernon on the upper reaches of the Potomac, last in our Virginia Presidential peregrination and I would have bartered it, immediately, for Washington's birth home at Wakefield on the lower Potomac, the Edenic setting of woods and river's providing a seclusion and appeal that distinguished it from the grandeur of the Mount Vernon setting on a bluff high above the Potomac. The white Georgian house had been built on 475 acres by Washington's half brother, Lawrence, in 1743, and named for British Admiral Edward Vernon under whom Lawrence had served in the Royal Navy. Washington inherited it in 1754, and added the second story, improving the house and developing the land until the outbreak of the Revolutionary War.

Mount Vernon was long but narrow, only thirty feet wide, the width of a room, which was compensated for by the wonderful columned verandah tiled with flagstones along the entire eastern front of the mansion and picturesquely secured to the grassy eminence overlooking the Potomac River, 125 feet below.

The daily work on "The Mansion House Farm," as Washington called his estate, was accomplished in the many outbuildings: the butler's pantry, the kitchen, the spinning house, the storehouse, the smokehouse, wash house and coach house. Lori and I liked strolling the flower garden with the precisely clipped boxwood and the herb garden near the kitchen but when the boys announced Dave was taking them down the south slope to Washington's Tomb, Lori ran off and I followed her lead. We had to see that hallowed shrine because all vessels of the U.S. Navy, when passing Washington's Tomb, lowered their flag to half-staff and tolled a bell, while the crew stood at attention.

Virginia's colleges were almost as celebrated as its statesmen, the University of Virginia being the most noteworthy for us because it was not only founded by Thomas Jefferson, in 1819, the beautiful buildings were also designed by him, some of them looking very much like Monticello with its classic dome and columns. (Jefferson had sent in a design for the

"President's House," anonymously, during the colony-wide contest, with the Jeffersonian dome, a lofty feature.) I could envision Jefferson, on the site at Charlottesville as his scholastic and architectural dream took form and then, at Monticello watching through his telescope, the fruition of his ambitious, unselfish plan.

We walked through the campus and beautiful walled gardens, read placards, took many pictures and had lunch at Howard Johnson's because it boasted that the "Raven Room" was downstairs; the actual table still in the cellar tavern where Edgar Allan Poe had held court, and written a bit, in 1826, his one year at the University of Virginia and the last half year of Jefferson's life. I wondered if the two had ever met; they were both geniuses of the pen but antithetical in nature and discipline, leaving a polarity of gifts to mankind: "The Fall of the House of Usher," "The Raven," versus "The Declaration of Independence."

We drove southwest from Charlottesville to Lexington to visit Washington and Lee University, a private school established in 1749 as the Augusta Academy, changed to Washington Academy in 1798 to honor a $50,000 gift from George Washington and renamed Washington and Lee in 1871, as tribute to Robert E. Lee, school president from 1865 to 1870. The children liked Washington and Lee best, especially its unique brick, serpentine walls enclosing the Colonial campus (where Susan Allaway's future husband, Lash Larue, Harvard Law School, would teach). From V.M.I. (Virginia Military Institute, founded in 1839 in Lexington), we drove on to Randolph-Macon Woman's College (1893), near Lynchburg, about which I had long heard because some of Mother's girlhood friends, and one of mine, had gone there from Booneville, Mississippi. We rewarded the boys by driving quickly to Appomattox, a short distance east on Highway 460 to the National Historical Park and Court House where General Robert E. Lee had surrendered the Confederate Army, April 9, 1865, to General Ulysses S. Grant, ending the Civil War. The two most devastating wars of the young Nation had begun in other states but had terminated in Virginia with noble Virginians participating: General George Washington, in the first, and then, General Robert E. Lee in the second surrender; their families, neighbors and friends.

Our three never tired of battlefields, nor did Dave, so we energetically continued our study at the Richmond National Battlefield Park in Hanover County where our Lacy ancestor, Thomas Lacy, had been given a land grant in 1680, after helping the English capture "Blackbeard, the Pirate," Captain Edward Teach.

Richmond, the capital of the Confederate States of America, had been abandoned April 2, 1865, on the urgent advice of General Lee. The President of the Confederacy, Jefferson Davis, with his cabinet, archives and treasury, grimly withdrew via the Richmond and Danville Railroad southwest 150 miles to Danville, Virginia, where General Robert E. Lee was to join them. But one week later, on Palm Sunday, General Lee surrendered at the village Court House in Appomattox.

That same week, on Good Friday, April 14, at Ford's Theatre in Washington, D.C., President Abraham Lincoln was assassinated by John Wilkes Booth, an American actor. Lincoln was carried across the street to a small house where he died the next morning, the bullet never detected because he lay on a metal bed. Andrew Johnson was sworn in as President, the seventeenth, on April 15, 1865.

John Wilkes Booth, a Confederate sympathizer, had plotted with several conspirators at the home of Mary E. Surratts, Prince Georges County, Maryland—a few miles southeast of Washington, D.C., to assassinate the chief officers of the Government. William Henry Seward, Secretary of State and architect of the Alaskan Purchase in 1867, was fired at several times through the windows of his home but survived. When Booth, after shooting Lincoln in the back of the head, jumped from the President's box to the stage, he broke his leg and sought treatment from Dr. Samuel A. Mudd, to whom he was unknown. Dr. Mudd was sent to Ft. Jefferson on Dry Tortugas to be imprisoned for life but was pardoned in 1869 by President Johnson after saving the lives of yellow fever victims. Booth was shot in a barn, twelve days after he shot Lincoln, in Bowling Green, Virginia; three conspirators were hanged on Capitol Hill, together with the only woman ever to be hanged by the United States: Mary E. Surratts, owner of the boardinghouse where the plotters met. (In the twentieth century, the state of Maryland pleaded her innocence in Congress and has petitioned to have her name cleared, innumerable times.)

Mother H's visit to our Virginia establishment in September of 1957 coincided with a State visit by Queen Elizabeth and Prince Philip to Williamsburg and Washington, D.C. Dave, on leave, took Mother H to Williamsburg on a sunny, warm morning to see the Queen and Prince ride down Duke of Gloucester Street in an open, horse-drawn carriage accompanied by Winthrop Rockefeller, head of the Williamsburg Foundation. The children, Lori and Bruce, were in school which I thought more important than seeing a queen; besides, Dave and Mother H had promised to bring back gingerbread cookies from the Raleigh Tavern. The children were satiated with Williamsburg, except for the cookies, and looked forward to going down in LCDR Haselton's submarine for lunch the day after the Queen's visit.   Our priorities immutably favored gastronomy.

A submarine was certainly an adventure for Mother H, the children and me.   Just squeezing down the narrow, circular ladder and wedging ourselves through tight passages and low hatches to see the engines, torpedo tubes and "fish," as they called the torpedo shells, required special contorting and realignment.   We were led to see the Operations Room and instructed in how to look through the periscope (the children constructed one when they got home—out of Christmas-paper rolls, the long cardboard cores which always served for such essential engineering).   The wardroom, little more than a circular booth, accommodated all the "boat's" officers.

I was always amused by the appellation "boat."   A submarine was not a ship but a boat; a sailboat was not a boat but a ship; the PBY was not a plane but a P-boat, as were all seaplanes with pontoons; and lighter-than-air planes were ships, never aircraft even though they were driven by props, propellers, through the air but, nevertheless, they were not flying boats—those were airplanes—they were simply—airships.   At least the term for helicopter was metaphorically sensible: it was an "eggbeater."

We five landlubbers squished together in the booth for one o'clock luncheon, our host and neighbor, Bob Haselton, precariously perched on the outer edge with Dave opposite and enjoyed a delicious meal with dessert, a foolish decision, all served expertly by an immaculate and deft Stewards Mate.

By the time we smelled air again, I had become claustrophobic and we had not even submerged but the semblance had been impelling.   I was glad Dave had chosen to fly a plane, or a boat, rather than sail a boat, or a submarine, and concluded that all Submariners deserved their extra-hazardous pay.

Before we left, as I was breathing delicious air at the top of the ladder, Bob called Lori and me to come back down the hatch; Bruce and Davie had asked to see how quickly the hatch could be secured and its heavy iron enclosure clamped into place.   It was amazing to see the dexterity and speed with which that unwieldy-looking "lid" (my term) was secured, airtight and watertight; I just hoped they were as swift and sure with the reverse motion. And, of course, they were. Our Navy! Our wonderful American Navy!

It was an unforgettable day and the boys, Bruce and Davie only, were ready to sign on, just to man the periscope and close the hatch, I suspected. I was proud of both Dave and Bob in their hazardous careers of dedication but relieved that Lori, at least, was planning to dig in the earth, for fossils of land creatures.

Mother H loved our lake house and the Norfolk-Virginia Beach area but could not stay long as she was expected at Mildred and Hub's in Washington, D.C. where Hub was ascending at the Experimental Lab in Beltsville, Maryland. The schools in Silver Spring, Maryland, Montgomery County, still ranked at the pinnacle of public schools nationwide, probably attributable to the wealth of the county and the presence of international embassies and residences of high-government officials, scientists and lobbyists.

We gave Mother H a tour of the World's Largest Naval Compound, driving from Norfolk Naval Base, under Hampton Roads through the tunnel, which the children ever delighted in; to Hampton, northwest across the Intercoastal Waterway; southwest to Newport News, by itself one of the world's largest shipyards, producing both warships and ocean liners; south and east on Highway 17 from the Newport News Bridge to the Portsmouth Naval Shipyard, a foremost builder of the Navy's fighting ships; completing the awesome circle at the Norfolk Naval Air Station, contiguous to the Norfolk Naval Base.

Since Mother H only had time for the area tunnel-tour and not Jefferson's cannon balls and telescope (the children wanted to show her their favorites), we fixed a Jeffersonian meal and pretended we were at Monticello, slowly baking, after having scraped the heavy black-pepper coating from the rind and simmering—an old Virginia ham which we had detoured a few miles north, crossing the Newport News Bridge, to buy at Virginia's famous ham-curers in Smithfield. The ham had been cured two years and was half the thickness of a sugar-cured ham, the water's having evaporated and the fat's having shrunk. The meat was a dark burgundy in color with a strong, rich flavor. It had been cured with coarsely crushed black peppercorns and smoked with hickory chips just as in Jefferson and Washington's smokehouses.

My research had unearthed two of Thomas Jefferson's favorite recipes and I served them both with the dinner of baked old Virginia ham: broccoli-rice casserole with mushrooms and very sharp cheddar cheese; for dessert, a chocolate-cookie base (I used "oreos") baked with butter, covered with butter-brickle ice cream (Jefferson was the popularizer of ice cream in the Colonies having learned how to make it when he was ambassador to France, 1785-1789), spread with Jefferson's rich, buttery chocolate sauce and sprinkled with Virginia pecans and frozen. We even ate by flickering candlelight after Dave carved thin slices of old ham with the silver Holland heirloom set Mother H presented to her youngest's family of dining sophisticates.

Shortly after Mother H's departure, *Sputnik I* was launched October 4, 1957, by the Russians. The world's first artificial satellite was a metal ball just twenty-three inches in diameter but it circled the earth in 1 hour 36.2 minutes and The Space Age had begun. *Sputnik II* was launched November 3, and carried the first living organism: a dog named Laika.

Christmas of 1957 was spent at home on the Lake, the children content to cut their own tree as they had in New-foundland's wondrous woods (Lori dimly re-membered Alaskan tree-felling) and so we pre-pared for "Christmas of yore" in the green land of Virginia. *Frosty, the Snowman* and *Rudolph* were rediscovered in the record box, California sugar cones were un-wrapped for the mantel and designated pine woods south of the Base at Oceana were invaded by determined lumber-jacks, each in Newfie boots—which were be-ginning to pinch. A perfect, lonely Christmas

Figure 85. Three "Stockings Were Hung. . . ."

Figure 86. "'Twas the Night Before. . . ." in 1957

tree, revealed in warm sunshine, was discovered, measured to twelve feet and ceremoniously sawed by Lori and Bruce, in turn, after their Daddy made the first deep cut and Davie grooved a bit with his little saw. How proudly were the lights and decorations hung! And stockings, too, at the pine-boughed mantel, Davie—boosted by his little red chair. Lori and Davie named and arranged carrots for Rudolph and his followers while Bruce constructed a peanut butter and jelly sandwich and remembered the glass of milk—which Santa would find helpful. After Dave rendered "'Twas-the-Night-Before" tradition to his attentive, still wide-eyed, listeners, we kissed them all soundly and escorted them up the stairs to sweet and innocent dreams.

The new month of 1958 promised to be memorable for the United States' Space Exploration. It was January 31, 1958, when we launched our first satellite: *Explorer I* soared, almost four months after *Sputnik I*, but it discovered the inner (Van Allen) radiation belt. That success was followed by *Vanguard I* on March 17, which contained two transmitters, one of which operated on solar power.

The children were enthralled by all the fantastical activity and began their own atomic study. By Father's Day, June 15, 1958, one could witness the knowledgeable results. Lori made her Father a "happy-little-atomic-explosion" card with the inscription: "This little explosion will be your friend on Father's Day to wish you many happy wishes. Love, Lori." Bruce's greeting included a satellite, a flying saucer and a Nike missile. Davie saluted his Father with a rocket of mystical, Martian design.

And Dave received another greeting and launch-off a few days later. He was ordered to report aboard the Navy's U.S.S *Independence*, the world's largest carrier being completed at the Brooklyn Naval Shipyard, New York, her keel having been laid in July 1955, with commissioning to take place in January 1959. Since he was to report aboard in December, and would be at home only on week ends, commuting from New York; we decided to condense our remaining study of the area into his two weeks' leave the last of July, for his time at home the next two years would be very limited.

It was an honor to be chosen as a Plank Officer for the mightiest ship in the United States Navy which exercised great care in selecting its officers to commission and launch a new ship. Dave would be the *Independence*'s first Aerology Officer, reporting aboard early to oversee the completion of his office, the placement of the complex instruments, the ordering of supplies for the anticipated long periods at sea, the important familiarization with other offices and departments, officers and personnel. By the time of the first Builders' Sea Trial when it unhinged and flattened its vast mast to pass under the Brooklyn Bridge, it would be home to 3,500 officers and men, two thousand of whom were in training at Newport, Rhode Island's Fleet Training Center—the largest group they had ever seen—as Dave reported aboard. All personnel would be given a piece of the ship; the Officers—a plank of the original oak timber in the form of a large, finished frame displaying the U.S.S. *Independence*, CVA-62 (Carrier, Heavier-than-air, Attack) mightily afloat in the green Atlantic.

We began our pre-Independence jaunt on the northern end of North Carolina's Outer Banks, a thin strip of land and islands, stretching from Virginia Beach south along Currituck Sound, southeast, separating Roanoke Sound from the Atlantic and curving southwest along Pamlico Sound to Cape Lookout at the southern tip of Core Sound—the top half designated as Cape Hatteras National Seashore, and the lower, Cape Lookout National Seashore (Proposed).

We were interested in the windy, lonely lifesaving station at Kitty Hawk where an airplane was launched, sailed and brought to earth, first, under perfect control. It was piloted by Orville Wright who, with his brother Wilbur, had experimented and labored—with their sister Katherine's encouragement and income from teaching and nursing and their minister-father's assistance and large library—for eight years in their small bicycle shop in Dayton, Ohio. They had read about the air-gliding machines of Germany's Otto Lilienthal who was killed in 1896, when his engine-driven air glider descended too rapidly and crashed. The Wright Brothers' efforts were tireless, ingenious and undaunted. They developed a heavier-than-air machine which weighed 750 pounds, including Orville's weight and was propelled by a four-cylinder petrol motor of twelve horsepower. They made four flights on a high, very windy hill December 17, 1903; the longest flight by Orville lasted fifty-nine seconds with a speed of thirty miles an hour. (The airplane was exhibited at the Science Museum at South Kensington, London, for twenty years. Finally, on the forty-fifth anniversary of the remarkable flight, December 17, 1948, it was formally installed in the Smithsonian Institution, Washington, D.C.)

On down the Outer Banks south of Kitty Hawk and Kill Devil Hills where the Wright Brothers' National Memorial was located, we stopped south of Nags Head, North Carolina, to inspect the legendary birthplace of Virginia Dare, the first English child born in the New World. John White, one of Sir Walter Raleigh's colonists, made three voyages from

England to what they called "Virginia," in 1585, 1587 and 1590. On the second he became governor of the settlement on Roanoke Island, across the Roanoke Sound from Nags Head, leaving his daughter and granddaughter, reluctantly, to sail back to England for supplies. When he returned to the New World three years later, the "Lost Colony" had disappeared, the only evidence of human habitation was the single word "Croatoan" carved on a tree. No trace was ever discovered but theories and fables abounded.

Croatoan was the name of an Indian tribe which had inhabited the Outer Banks in the sixteenth century but we were heading to study modern Indians at the Cherokee Reservation southwest of Asheville, North Carolina, at the edge of the Great Smoky Mountains. We spent the night at Durham so that we could visit Duke University where Susan Allaway was to be a freshman in the fall semester.

The Blue Ridge Parkway, one of the most beautiful drives in the country which Dave picked up east of Asheville, led us to the Cherokee Indian Reservation, and Davie's inchoate fascination for his native "brother." Most Indian tribes had been moved by the United States Government to Oklahoma and westward but the Cherokees had fled into the Smokies to escape the West in 1838, and there remained three thousand Eastern Cherokees supporting themselves in dignity, mostly through the tourist trade, at the Reservation east of the Great Smoky Mountains National Park.

We enjoyed observing eagle dances, pottery making, the stringing and drying of green beans for winter—called "leather britches," blowgun demonstrations and basket-making with flat strips of willow colored with natural dyes. I bought a flat, slightly curved, yellow and tan basket for my cut camellias and gardenias at the elaborate gift shop where prices and quality were both high. The children surprisingly wanted no souvenirs, they just wanted to ride the Indian ponies again. After lunch in the outdoor restaurant, they rerode the ponies and then spent the next hour observing canoe-building procedures—closely. After a tree was felled, it was allowed to dry and then hollowed out by fire to fashion a dugout canoe; a specified area burned by a small, controlled fire, then smoothed with a hatchet—the last two processes demonstrated to our captivated threesome. We had a number of large, fallen trees around Lake Smith, for ailanthus trees and willows were shallow-rooted and short-lived and I could see plans promulgated in the intensity of observation, the nods and glances exchanged. "No!" I said, just arriving from the basket weaving demonstration, "dugouts will have to wait a few years." "Until you're older," added Dave, "and I'm home to supervise. Let's go see the melon patch, maybe they'll sell us some seed." "And we can plant Indian corn," suggested Bruce. "I'm going to plant gourds like Daddy Frank's," decided Lori. "He plants tomatoes and sunflowers, too," remembered Davie, "and we can have *watermelons!*"

After checking the fructifying, twining, bean-poled farm plot, we went back to the gift shop. No seed of any kind was available which we thought a peculiar oversight—and Bruce called that to their attention. And so we bought decorative Indian-corn ears in husks: purple, red, yellow, and tan. "Will it grow those colors?" Bruce asked one of the good-natured Cherokee girls we had just insulted. She smiled, beautiful in her fringed and beaded Indian dress. "Yes," he was told, "it's grown just for the colors; it's too tough to eat." And I could see Bruce lose interest in planting Indian corn (which remained safely ornamental on the living-room hearth until needed for geese and ducks).

We drove through the Great Smoky Mountains where North Carolina met Tennessee, through the greatest mountain mass east of the Rockies, to Clingman's Dome, 6642 feet, the highest point in the Appalachian Mountains, on the Tennessee border. We stopped to see Rainbow Falls, on Highway 29 out of the Indian Reservation, and found at the height of the peaks, red spruce, fir and mountain ash with other trees of the North: hemlocks, maples, oaks and rhododendrons—most of them, at least, thirty feet tall. Tennessee's mountain resort, Gatlinburg, where Dave had made reservation weeks before, was fashionable and decorous.

Leaving the beautiful little town early the next morning, after savory country sausage, eggs and pancakes with pecan syrup, we began the descent through beech and basswood, magnolias, mountain laurel and sweet gums—stopping once to watch three black bears, a mother and two cubs, beside the road. In the distance were mountain peaks of graduated elevation, clouds' misting their tops and drifting in streaks around them. "Look!" exclaimed Dave, "I'd like a picture of that!" But there was no place to pull off the road and cars were close behind and approaching. So we watched the deep purple-blue of the mountains' merging with the diaphanous clouds and the pronounced azure haze's mantling the horizon. "It's blue smoke!" exclaimed Lori. "Yes," agreed Dave. "That's how the Great Smokies got their name. How I wish I could get a shot!" "We'll all have to remember it. It's too ephemeral to capture, don't you think?" I asked. "Probably," said Dave. "But I wish I could try!" And the Great

Smoky Mountain horizon that was never photographed became a Horse's-Head memory and was alluded to with regret, by Dave, and remembered longer, by all, as a consequence.

We wanted to see Oak Ridge, the U.S. Atomic Energy establishment west of Knoxville but it was off limits and Dave, wisely, did not mention it to the children. We talked instead of our next destination: The Hermitage, home of Andrew Jackson and Rachel, northeast of Nashville. It was a large estate with a splendid Southern Colonial house constructed with balconies and columns and many outbuildings; the carriage house, and main house shaded by magnificent American holly trees, oaks and magnolias. I had never seen holly trees with such spread and enormity. The children spent a long time in the museum, the erstwhile carriage house—there were so many war mementoes of the seventh President, who served from 1829 to 1837, having been a hero of the War of 1812.

General Jackson, "Old Hickory," had been my favorite President from childhood when I had become intrigued by his fierce independence, pragmatism, military exploits and gallant championing of his wife, Rachel Donelson Robards, whom he married in August 1791, and remarried January 17, 1794, upon learning that her divorce from her first husband was not final until 1793. He was cast in the mold of an Horatio Alger self-made hero. Born March 15, 1767, in Waxhaw settlement, South Carolina, he joined the militia in his state at the age of thirteen to fight in the Revolutionary War, read law and was admitted to the bar in North Carolina and married Rachel. By the age of thirty-one he had been a soldier, lawyer, U.S. Congressman, U.S. Senator and Tennessee judge. At thirty-nine, Andrew Jackson defended his wife's honor in a duel and killed her maligner.

After defeating the British in 1815, in the Battle of New Orleans, General Jackson drove the Seminoles out of the Florida Territory and became provisional governor. While serving in the U.S. Senate again, 1823-25, he opposed John Quincy Adams, Henry Clay and William Crawford for the presidency and won the most votes but no candidate had a majority and the House of Representatives chose John Quincy Adams. Jackson won a sweeping Presidential victory four years later, 1828, and a second term and was the only President to ever pay off the National Debt. Retiring to his Hermitage in 1837, he lived there until his death at the age of seventy-eight, June 8, 1845. Alas, Andrew Jackson and his beloved Rachel had no children.

In later excursions we visited Lincoln's adult home in Springfield, Illinois, where the museum of the sixteenth President's (1861-65) memorabilia was chiefly commercial; the Ford Theatre and house across the street in Washington, D.C., and his magnificent monument as well as replicas of his Emancipation Proclamation; and in Gettysburg, Pennsylvania, the site of his Gettysburg Address delivered November 19, 1863, at the dedication of the Soldiers' National Cemetery.

Next, was Theodore Roosevelt, twenty-sixth President, 1901-09, sworn in September 14, 1901, after the assassination of President William McKinley at the Pan-American Exposition, Buffalo, New York. Theodore had been a very sickly child but a courageous one and grew up to be a naturalist (eventually responsible for the National Park system), big-game hunter, gentleman-scholar, soldier—Colonel in the "Rough Riders," leading the charge up Kettle Hill in the battle of San Juan, Spanish-American War and Davie's special Hero. So we visited Roosevelt's estate at Oyster Bay, New York, Sagamore Hill, where he died ten years after leaving the Presidency, January 6, 1919; born October 27, 1858, New York City; graduated from Harvard; historian-author of forty books.

We finished our Presidential tours by visiting Franklin D. Roosevelt's estate and birthplace, Hyde Park, New York, where he was born January 30, 1882, and served as our thirty-second President from 1933 to April 12, 1945. His death occurred at Warm Springs, Georgia, the Summer White House. The house was elegant despite the ramps built in 1921, after the athletic Roosevelt was stricken with polio, never to walk again. It had been presided over by his Mother, assisted by his Wife, Anna Eleanor Roosevelt (a fifth cousin and a niece of Theodore Roosevelt), and their large, active family. His love for the sea was visible throughout the home, estate and Presidential Library which had such an historically important and immense collection, we were awed—just being within its doors. Franklin D. Roosevelt was buried in the Rose Garden at Hyde Park.

Harry S. Truman, thirty-third President from 1945-53, succeeded Roosevelt on April 12, 1945, an underestimated Missourian born in Lamar, May 8, 1884—the modest home of his origin in contrast to Roosevelt's Hyde Park; Kansas City Law School not quite as distinguished as Harvard and Columbia University Law but productive, in both instances—home and education, of a President as great, often contended, as Franklin D. Roosevelt. Harry Truman, physically slight without even a middle name (he chose *S.* himself which signified nothing—until he imbued it with singularity), became the fabric of a folk hero. An avid historian and student of military tactics, as well as an unostentatious, outspoken Midwesterner, he supervised the building and functioning of his Presidential Library in Independence, Missouri, which housed evidence of a most chaotic world which Mr. Truman had the intrepidity and wisdom to lead. He died in Kansas City, December 26, 1972, at the venerable age of eighty-eight and was buried in the garden of his Library in Independence, Missouri, the "Show-Me" State, which he did—to the world.

Dave's time was growing short and he wanted to help with house and yard maintenance before going aboard the *Independence*, so we spent little time in the beautiful blue-grass region of Kentucky, choosing Mammoth Cave National Park in central Kentucky, which was honeycombed with hundreds of miles of caves where sinkholes had replaced creeks and allowed basins of water to slowly dissolve the layers of limestone beneath—for our Kentucky study. And it *was* mammoth although only 150 miles of passages, waterways and caves were explored and accessible by boat, elevator and stairs. But that was an overwhelming sufficiency since we had only half a day and wanted to see just a chamber of stalactites curtaining the ceiling and stalagmites formed on the floor by the drip of calcareous water to create fanciful "icicles" and columns of calcium carbonate—pictures of which the children had seen in Daddy Frank's geology books but had never "discovered." With that sighting achieved, Dave drove us back to Virginia through the Shenandoah National Park and on to Washington, D.C. to visit Hub's Experimental Lab in Beltsville, Maryland, which would have taken weeks to see and forever to comprehend.

I wanted to check the latest hybrid of the magnolia, a fossil tree, the *Magnolia grandiflora* being a primitive angiosperm from the Cretaceous and Tertiary periods, 135 million years ago, to find a cross to survive Midwestern clime. (My only success—later: Dr. Brian Thomas and his beauteous Louisiana rarity, Nurse-Wife Karen, sent a gloriously fragrant, glossy-foliaged blossom, by Barbara, from their Atlanta home!)

Hub took Dave and the children to observe what different colored lights did to growth and flowering habits of both vegetables and flowers and the growing of vegetables by hydroponics, soilless culture, in anticipation of gardening in space. Hub told the children where to buy Hyponics, a commercial chemical additive to water, so that they could begin their experiments in hydroponics and took us home with him for delicious dining with Mildred and the Allaway children.

Early the next morning we went to the Smithsonian, "the red museum," as Davie called it, to see the "Spirit of St. Louis," flown by Lindberg, and the Wright Brothers' plane and drove home via the Naval Air Test Center at Patuxent River, Maryland, to which Hub and Mildred had driven us for our separate flights to Newfoundland—Dave's requiring two: one for him, one for his brief case which he had left in the back seat of Mildred's car.

The children had not seen any of the Navy's experimental planes when Hub and Mildred brought us for our flight in the summer of 1954, and would not have remembered them if they had, so we took time to complete the flight circle begun at Kitty Hawk, North Carolina, with the first power-driven plane—that flight measured in seconds—to the latest sound-barrier-breaking jet which could be refueled in midair. And there was a history lesson as well: the Naval Air Test Center was located in St. Mary's County, first settled by English colonists in 1634, led by Leonard Calvert, brother of Cecil Calvert, Lord Baltimore, to whom a proprietary charter had been granted by King Charles I of England. The colony founded was named in honor of Charles' Queen, Henrietta Maria: "Terra Maria," or in English—Maryland. St. Mary's City, on the banks of the St. Mary's River, became Maryland's first capital in 1676, until 1694, when it was moved north on the Chesapeake Bay to the mouth of the Severn River, to Annapolis. The land between the St. Mary's and the river named by the Patuxent Indians on which the Navy tested its experimental planes, about two thousand acres, had been presented to Father Andrew White, English missionary, by the friendly Mattaponi or Mattapient Indians.

As we drove home to Bayside, we talked of the history of the wondrous bay land, airplanes and friendly Indians who had probably welcomed the first Europeans as guests. Even Powhatan, chief of the Powhatan Indians and father of Pocahontas, whom legend described as bloodthirsty and bent upon slaying Captain John Smith until twelve-year-old Pocahontas intervened, had been chronicled as offering hospitality, a tribal ethic, to Captain Smith: "Come not thus with your gunnes and swords, to invade as foes. . . . What will it availe you to take that perforce you may quietly have with love, or to destroy them that provide your food? . . ." attested to by Stan Steiner's *The New Indians*, one of Davie and Bruce's later references, (p. 76).

I enrolled Davie in private (there being no public) Kindergarten in Baylake Pines Elementary, owned by an Air Force Officer's wife in a fashionable community. I was impressed because she tested all children before admitting them; Davie tested out at 166 I. Q. and was studying his flash cards and books so that he would "be prepared." Bruce would be in Third and had already won summer track competitions and was co-captain of his team. Lori was to be in Fourth Grade at Bay-side Elementary and

Figure 87. Fleet Co-Captain

would go off with Bruce to school which would soon be upon us. I would drive Davie to school and pick him up at noon and then he would help me with the Girl Scouts and Cub Scouts and since I would soon lose my Chapel partner, I had volunteered to teach Davie's Sunday School class at the Little Creek Amphibious Base and, like my own Mother, I seemed to be permanent room mother for Lori and Bruce's classes and Davie was chief assistant there, too.

Charles, Barbara, Luanne and Brian delighted us with a visit in late summer. Charles, a busy young executive with Butler Manu-facturing Company, had time for only an abbreviated visit so the children played fast and hard in the fenced-in yard, for young Brian Lacy's security, and listened

Figure 88. Quiet Time: Luanne, Bruce, Davie, Lori

to records in the heat of the afternoon while the junior member slept.

When Dave packed his cruise boxes, he asked for two books of my recommendation. I gave him *Plato* and *The Practical Cogitator*. (The latter, he described later as being "very cogitating" but despite his amused, slight disparagement, he supplied from it, occasional topical quotations for the *Independence*'s daily newspaper and radio station. *Plato* was read in the Med after he finished his correspondence courses for promo-

Figure 89. Brian's Future M.D. Smile

tion to CDR.) Dave requested a family address book and asked if I had remembered to include Brian's birth date and I promised to check.

But we had a while before his departure and I had an agenda—overly long, as usual.

As we were scraping the fence preparatory to putting on a white undercoat and a blue finish, Dave suggested that a white fence would be nice and much quicker. "No, I want it blue again," I asserted. "But why do you always have to be different?" "I just don't like to be like everybody else. . . ." I started to explain. "Yes," Dave chuckled, "and have time on your hands!"

But I did not *seek* busyness and deemed myself the most indolent person in the world who looked longingly at the Jacobson's screened porch, a time or two, where they sat—books in hand, for hours; I wondered what *that* would be like. I did not find out immediately, for the children needed pets; that was second on my list.

As we drove, with great excitement, to the pet shop, the children determined what type of pet they wanted and we helped them: they could have a white, tan or black rabbit, as long as they were all the same sex. Then Lori made the reasonable suggestion that she would prefer a guinea pig. Bruce, always ready to enhance a project, looked mischievously at Davie and asked: "Well, Lori, why don't you just get a plain pig?"

Davie named his all-black rabbit "Nibbles"; "Happy" was the name of Bruce's white rabbit with a black nose; Lori named her brown and white guinea pig "Rose Petal." Life was blissful with our new pets until, one day, Lori decided Rose Petal was lonesome. We made another trip to the pet shop before Dave left for the Ship, having determined with supreme intelligence—the sex of Rose Petal.

Figure 90. Davie, "Happy" and Bruce

The new guinea pig was especially pretty with markings of tan, black and white. It didn't live long enough to be named, however, for the next day, next-door neighbor, Polly Haselton, stuffed *her*, we had felt assured, into a discarded rain gauge which the children played with in the sandbox.

The funeral service beneath the wild black cherry tree beyond the fence, which selected friends attended, was a quietly woeful affair; it was the children's first experience with the death of a pet. Polly, responsible for the demise, was very remorseful and volunteered to sing. The children bowed their heads and Polly, bravely, taking a deep breath, sang the *Brownie Smile Song!*

It's admittedly difficult to determine the sex of a guinea pig, and we hadn't—except in one. Rose Petal kept getting fatter every day. Davie postulated she was eating too much grass; Lori and Bruce concurred and even cut down on her carrot consumption. And she wasn't being very loving: she kept nipping at Happy and Nibbles who learned, without even any training, to jump over the fence. In fact, untutored as they were, they not only jumped over the fence of their pink hutch, they also squeezed through the blue pickets of the big fence. Oh, what frantic chases developed! Happy finally escaped, merrily, to the woods to live but Nibbles would jump back inside the hutch fence, eat his meals there and then retire to the garage. But soon there were little Rose Petals, here, there—and everywhere.

Bruce, the butterfly enthusiast, having planted adequately and successfully, butterfly-attracting blossoms, next needed a butterfly net. That was third on our list. And we found one after much searching, and he became very proficient. Two days before Dave left, Bruce caught three fish. And we thought he was just supplying for spring!

The day before Dave left, I had six tables of luncheon-bridge.

The morning started in typical fashion. Bruce insisted upon making carbon dioxide before breakfast; Davie couldn't find the book he was reading—something about keeping goldfish healthy and he wouldn't read any other. I handed him rules of duplicate bridge and he grumbled refusal; it was even the same color and the same size. Dave had a button missing from the pocket of his khaki shirt and had packed the others. I sent Bruce upstairs to get Davie to find which shoe he had dumped the buttons into. Davie was nowhere to be found but we emptied all the shoes in his closet and found pennies, marbles, "I'm a 4 year-old" button, screws, caps, string, stamps, pop beads, four erasers, colored popcorn and a miniature harmonica—but not one button. I facetiously suggested to Dave that he wear one of his new, initialed, reversible handkerchiefs in that pocket. Just as I was about to be chastised for my levity, Lori held forth a damp khaki button. She had found it beneath a rock in the turtle bowl. "I didn't have any colored pebbles," explained Davie, when we found *him*, "and the turtles didn't know the difference!"

Davie awakened us early Sunday morning, the day of Dave's departure with LT Al Shine and CDR Paul Haas for the Brooklyn Naval Shipyard to report aboard the U.S.S. *Independence*, CVA-62. "Daddy, when are they going to have Children's Day?" "Children's Day?" his Daddy repeated. "You mean like Mother's Day?" "Yes," said Davie, patiently, "when are they going to have Children's Day?" "Davie," I had to tell him, although I had not been asked, "*every* day is Children's Day!"

"The child is father of the man!" At last, I knew what that meant! When in college, my professor had scorned my analysis of Alexander Pope's famous suggestion in his "Essay on Man," later used by Wordsworth in "Intimations of Immortality from Recollections of Early Childhood." My analysis then was symbolic of the origin of man, redolent of umbrageous meaning and ethereal connotations. Now, I was firmly assured that Pope meant naught but that the child was lord and master of the man: his will, we struggled to achieve; his whim became a dire necessity to be fulfilled. Occasionally, a lamentably weak "No" would emanate from our lips, not because we wished to utter a negative or a remonstrance but just to see if such word was still retained in our enervated, parental vocabulary. *But* though the child was, literally, the governor because of his dependence upon and faith in—the man, he invited perimeters, rules and paradigms graphically distinguishing "you may" from "you may not," "you should" from "you should not," antipodal "good" from "bad" and rewarded us with swift comprehension and emulation when rules were fair and lucid; and patterns, honorable. It was a wonderful, inextricable, convoluted whole: child and man, each fulfilling both roles, interdependently. What greater joy in life than to be a parent watching over a child watching over man!

I hugged Davie, nuzzling him under his right ear, kissing his rounded cheek, noisily: "What makes you so smart!" "You and Daddy," he replied, modestly. "No, not I!" and I kissed him again, "you're far ahead of *me*!" I resigned. And Bruce came in to be kissed and praised, and Lori, too.

We all got up happily on Dave's last day at home, for a while, had a quick breakfast and went to Sunday School and Chapel.

Returning from Little Creek at noon, we opened the door to the welcoming aroma of braised beef and vegetables. While I thickened the gravy and set the table, Lori served the salad, poured the milk and water and joined the boys who had taken their bag of shaved carrots, lettuce, celery and raisins to feed the menagerie.

Dave came down the stairs with his suitcase, brief case, dress blues on a hanger, cap under his arm, wearing civilian travel clothes and black uniform shoes; the latter to expedite changing into uniform before reporting in. "I just talked to Paul; he wants to leave at two," Dave informed me, depositing his bags on the couch by the family-room door. "We'll be back Friday night about nine. Can you survive until then?" with cocked eyebrow and a grin. "It'll be hard," I laughed.

We sat down to an unhurried Sunday dinner, Dave's saying the blessing and the children, theirs. Dave carved the roast, with his usual expertness, while Lori, Bruce and Davie gave their daily livestock bulletin: Nibbles was living in the lawn chair behind the extra tires in the garage but still eating out; Happy was gone for good, although Bruce found him once when he was fishing and almost netted him; Rose Petal was indifferent to her offspring, over which Lori had appointed Bruce, guardian, but she was more loving and didn't nip any more. Dave reiterated the children's special chores for the week, kissed them good-bye and announced that he was leaving me in "good hands"! CDR Paul Haas knocked on the door at 2:00 P.M. and we knew it would be a busy, short week until Dave's return.

Dave commuted every week end until the *Independence* was commissioned 10 January 1959, and then his schedule became erratic with

Builders' Sea Trials, Acceptance Checks and the final completion of the Brooklyn Yard's work. The Ship was anchored in Hampton Roads, Norfolk, by mid-April to take on supplies and ammunition at the Norfolk Naval Base pier after the channel was deepened sufficiently for the vast heavy-attack Carrier to dock. While anchored out, Dave stayed aboard one day in every three but came in by launch whenever he was at liberty.

Dave had the duty when they docked in mid-afternoon but, after school, the children and I drove to the pier to watch the giant slowly glide to dockside. It took four tugboats to get her in: one at the bow, one at the stern and at port and starboard and the Mighty "I" was finally in her home port, securely berthed. The gangplank was quickly maneuvered into place, a huge *L*-shaped contraption which paralleled the ship to a platform, then turned for a lofty ascent directly to the hangar deck. We did not ascend because Dave had Command Duty and we preferred to see the Ship under his guidance but the children got to hear the Bosun shrilly pipe a visiting Admiral aboard and Dave, as CDO, was there to salute and brief him. After the Admiral left, Dave waved to us and disappeared but we were going aboard Sunday, after Church, for our first inspection and dinner in the Wardroom and a movie.

The children were impressed with their Daddy's large, double stateroom which was convenient both to his office and his meteorological instruments and the bridge to which he hastened to brief the Captain, in person, when there was an impending weather change or flying was in progress. His hours were so unpredictable, being always on call when aboard, that no fellow officer had been assigned to share his quarters. (Bruce and Davie were beneficiaries because Dave invited them to be his guests for the day-and-night Family Cruise when the Ship returned from the Shakedown Cruise.) Dave took us up to see the bridge with the big wheel which steered the Carrier; the compass directly in front of it; the Navigator's office to the side; the Operation Officer's small desk which was manned constantly when planes were flying. The bridge was in the superstructure with the Admiral's bridge immediately above—occupied only when the Admiral was aboard; the Skipper, always a flyer on a carrier, responsible for conning—steering—the ship. That first visit was brief; it was almost 1300 hours, at which time dinner would be served, and we went down several ladders and decks rather hurriedly.

In the Wardroom, the children watched white dress caps with varying amounts of "scrambled eggs" beginning to cover a table near the door as their owners came in for Sunday dinner. Dave reminded the children, who were becoming increasingly tickled by the mounding of the headgear, that an officer in the Navy was not in complete uniform if he did not have his cap with him at all times. "Did you ever get the wrong one?" chuckled Bruce. "Not yet," laughed his Dad, "you automatically look for your name." "What if you have the same name?" posed Davie. "Then you'd have to underline one or use a distinguishing symbol," said Dave. "Who types the labels?" wondered Lori. "The Tailor Shop," replied patient Dave, nodding as the Steward located our placecards on one of the long tables. It was a delicious meal served formally from the left by efficient Mess Boys who handled gleaming silver platters and bowls with pleasant helpfulness but the children each manipulated serving spoon and fork without mishap. Lori, unused to such immediate, individual attention to her gustative needs, was a bit dismayed by the discovery that whenever she took a sip or two of water, her goblet would be refilled by a watchful Mess Boy. She finished the luscious meal, being well-trained and not weight-worried—every bite. "But," she sighed and finally admitted to her host-Daddy, "I don't believe I can finish my water!"

The U.S.S. *Independence*, CVA-62 left Norfolk April 23, 1959, for the Caribbean and eight weeks of Shakedown Training under the U.S. Fleet Training Command, Guantanamo Bay, Cuba, to return July 1, or 1 July 1959—as the Navy penned it, at 1400 hours.

While Dave was in "Gitmo," Davie finished Kindergarten at Baylake Pines Elementary. He so delighted in his school, and I, too, that I signed him up for First Grade, inasmuch as he was too young for public school First Grade. Mrs. Bosserman, owner-principal, complimented me on my Davie and asked if I would consider teaching High School English and Latin next fall and added that she would love to have Lori and Bruce too: "They're too bright for public school; they belong here where all the children are accelerated." I agreed to her two proposals, enrolling Lori in Fifth Grade and Bruce in Fourth but did not respond to her comment because I had substituted for her the last two weeks of school and had been pleased with both program and attitude but had no knowledge of the Public School System, except as a Room Mother and P.T.A. member. She was decidedly pleased to have a Latin teacher (hard to find) and three precocious Navy "brats" and laughingly commented that she hoped my husband wouldn't conclude that the Air Force had overwhelmed the Navy! It was well-known that Navy flyers considered their planes and training superior to the Air Force's and rather blatantly denigrated, but generally with good humor, their Air Force counterparts. She told me to bring Lori and Bruce in any afternoon to be tested, that she did not want their public school records; my contract would be signed the first of August, with faculty meetings to begin August 22.

Our busy summer began. We had bought a piano—fourth item on our pre-*Independence* list—and Lori was taking lessons at home from a local Bayside lady, the piano placed on the north wall of the living room with a special heating attachment to prevent warping in the sea clime. Bruce was busy with Cubs, and teaching Davie every thing he knew—and invented.

The month of June, I was director of the Girl Scout Day Camp, Camp Linkhorn, in Virginia Beach, which kept the four of us from home from daybreak until dusk; Bruce and Davie being my indispensable assistants.

Our theme was Weather because of an outdated barometer—and rain gauges that needed to be appreciated by other than guinea pigs and one of Dave's Aerographer's Mates at Oceana, an artist whom I "commissioned" to paint in his hours of off-duty enterprises, a composite of weather myths. I used Volume I of *Pictured Knowledge*, 1923 edition, to explain what I wanted and he produced a large wall hanging for camp headquarters with reproductions for each Girl Scout leader.

At the upper right, in a burst of sunlight was Apollo, Greek and Roman sun god, driving four white horses and thrusting forth sunrays which were being obscured by black clouds hurled by the ram-drawn thundering chariot of the battle-attired Norse god of thunder, Thor. The battle cape of nimbus clouds billowing behind him, Thor protected himself from his own lightning bolts with a huge shield, breastplate and winged helmet while the god of winds, Aeolus, and a wind sprite blew gales in opposing directions to force ships against the light-towered cliffs, flatten the proboscis of the Sphinx through the centuries and create desert storms, simoons, which pelted the camels and drivers with stinging sand and pitted the mighty pyramids. In a tall tree, lower right, Father Robin made an umbrella of his wings to shelter the mother robin and baby birds in their nest while, beneath the protecting tree, a frog called in his weather readings to a wise astrologer in a tall cone-shaped hat embellished with stars and a waning moon.

Standing on a stool behind the enormous weather map (both the high stool and tall cap were later used derisively to chide boys who had not done their lessons); the weatherman-astrologer plotted the winds as reported by three other frogs, always concerned about rain, one sitting on the globe at "the top of the world," Point Barrow, a second carrying a ruler to measure gradients and a third, wearing spectacles, conferring off the Yucatan Peninsula with frog number one. The astrologer, with a long pointer, indicated on the weather map the origin of the famous Galveston Hurricane of 1900.

(Benjamin Franklin had plotted the earliest weather maps, showing the same wind could blow in two opposite directions at the same time. He proved with the help of friends in different parts of the country who noted the direction of the wind at a given hour on a given day that, after all the wind directions were charted, they formed a circle. The wind movement was likened to a man and woman waltzing across a room—turning round and round and moving forward at the same time.)

Two weather-wise ducks read the Chinese barometer and rain gauge and one kept a trained eye on the weather vane to report wind direction and the anemometer which obviously indicated adequate wind velocity for the duck's wings were extended and he was ready to carry his report aloft.

Lori and the other Girl Scouts seemed enthusiastic about the weather project and gathered daily statistics and drew their own weather maps for their meteorological notebooks.

We had combined our study of weather with Dendrology, of course, and read tree "rings" to determine years of ample rainfall compared to evidence of deprivation—there being many fallen trees in the sandy woods together with evergreens which were just developing their new cones and "candles" to measure and analyze.

And that led to the class on the mythology of trees; the laurel's aura, a favorite with the girls because the nymph Daphne escaped the amorous god Apollo (one of their weather "men") by being transformed into a laurel tree, *Laurus nobilis*. The boys preferred the legend of the mulberry, genus *Morus*, or the "mitten tree," and found proof in the woods of a god's providing, upon supplication of a poor, cold, starving family, fruit to eat and mittens to wear—on the right hand, on the left hand, a mitten to fit either hand, possessing two thumbs, and a mitten for baby, thumbless. And the meteorological-dendrological concepts led to experiments with tree products to protect *against* weather; much fiber from the raffia palm (imported) was used to fashion sunshades and rain hats. Ad infinitum—we learned. How swiftly June sped!

It was the last Saturday in June, the 27th, and I did not have to arise at dawn; only two more days of camp and Dave would be home. What a wonderful world! I smiled and slept again. I was awakened, suddenly, by children's voices beneath my window. Who on earth would let their children out—so early in the morning to awaken their neighbors? I turned over to look at the clock. Only seven! I rolled out the screen to look, saw nothing but heard low murmurs and hammers by the front door—they were either breaking up the walk or taking bricks out of the foundation. "Please go back home," I called in exasperation, "it's only 7:00 o'clock!" "Hi, Mommy," chorused Davie and Bruce. "Good heavens!" I ejaculated, "what are you doing out there?" "We're splitting geodes," answered Bruce, matter-of-factly. Geodes? What are geodes? Nothing alive, at least—no longer. Feigning intelligence, I asked: "Why?" "Crystals!" they cried, not offended by my ignorance. "Oh! Well, come in and I'll call Lori." "She's already out," I was informed. "Catching skinks," Bruce added. Skinks? What are skinks? Will I ever catch up? I wondered, sleepily. "Well, come in and I'll fix your breakfast." "I've already cooked it!" called Davie—jubilantly. And that got me downstairs in a hurry.

The boys, having broken their fast with Davie's pop-tarts in the toaster, cheerios, milk and juice, found no crystals in their round rocks but Lori ran in triumphantly from the Lake with a handful of skink. "Look," she exclaimed, in ecstasy, as she caressed an ugly, little lizard, "it's a five-lined skink and they're rare!" And she showed us five cobalt blue lines that ran from the creature's head to the top of its swishing tail and, looking closely and imaginatively, I did see beauty in its form and coloration. "You can have my turtle bowl," offered Davie. "Better tie a lid on it," suggested Bruce. "You hold him," Lori said, generously proffering her trophy to her brothers, "I'm going to ventilate a plastic shoe box; he needs to run." So last week's leaf collection from Girl Scout camp was dumped and three heads pondered *All About Reptiles* and Rose Petal and family and Nibbles had competition.

As we drove Wednesday, July 1, to the Norfolk Naval Base, shortly after lunch, the ETA still 1400 hours, I thought of the first letter I had received from Dave from Guantanamo Bay. It had been written the night of the first day of flight operations, an exciting but nervous time for all aboard. The weather had been cooperative and Dave, after briefing the Skipper, had moved to a walkway along the superstructure halfway between the conning bridge—which he had just left—and the air-control tower to watch the first takeoffs from the *Independence*. The walkway was filled with officers when Dave arrived and all happily applauded the first catapulting: an A4D light-weight attack plane. When the second plane was maneuvered onto the catapult, an F8U heavy-photo-recon plane, Dave had a premonition of disaster and darted from the crowded walkway, raced down the ladder to the bridge, fearing that the Catapult Officer had set the catapult steam pressure for an F8U <u>fighter</u> which was lighter than the F8U photo-recon plane. But he was too late! The photo-recon lifted off and plunged straight down into the sea; neither pilot nor plane could be recovered. It was human error on the part of the Catapult Officer who knew the order of planes in the launching sequence, each pilot being totally dependent upon *him*—also a flyer—to determine the exact amount of pressure to put on the catapult based upon the weight of the plane and the speed of the wind over the flight deck (normally, 35 knots). So theirs would be a sad homecoming. (In several months, a steam pressure gauge was mounted on the side of the flight deck so that the pilot himself could read the setting and approve it before being launched by the Catapult Officer.)

Dave did not have the duty after the Carrier was brought in by the

Figure 91. Manning the Rails

tugboats—the children loved that part because *Tuffy, the Tugboat* had always been one of their favorites—berthed and tied, at 1715 hours. Dave was one of the first down the gangplank and we captured him! And for the next year he was ours, almost every night!

Dave had surprises from the West Indies for all of us: hand-tooled and painted miniature leather boots and satchels, fully zipped, for concealing small treasures, medals and coins from Guantanamo Bay, as well as an impressive trophy from the children's archetypical pirate island—Hispaniola. "We know all about that," Davie asserted and Lori and Bruce joined in to talk of Robert Louis Stevenson's *Treasure Island*, Captain Smollett's ship the *Hispaniola*; Jim Hawkins' listening in the apple barrel; one-legged pirate Long John Silver and his parrot, Captain Flint, screeching: "pieces of eight, pieces of eight!" "And don't forget Ben Gunn, the looney one," added Bruce, who liked to rhyme. But Dave's souvenir was from a far older source and he asked Lori to get her map he'd sent from Gitmo.

On the R and R scouting party, Dave had flown from the Carrier to Ciudad Trujillo, Dominican Republic, to ascertain the port's suitability for the crew's week-end shore leave. Christopher Columbus' discovery of the eons proved to be acceptable harborage for the *Independence* and the Carrier put into port.

Dave described the ancient capital city, Ciudad Trujillo: "It's mostly cement, like Havana, being in the hurricane belt. General Trujillo has done a lot to modernize but he's not very popular; his dictatorship's in trouble. We were a little apprehensive about shore leave; but it went well. Columbus is buried there, you know." Which we didn't. (Rafael Trujillo's thirty-one-year dictatorship [1930-1961] ended two years later when he was assassinated and the capital was renamed Santo Domingo, for the patron saint of Columbus' father, where Christopher Columbus was supposedly buried—in the Cathedral of Santo Domingo. The romance continued into 1992, the quincentennial year of Columbus' discovery of America. The explorer, born in Genoa, Italy, circa 1451, under the patronage of Ferdinand V and Isabella of Spain, sailed westward to reach the Orient on August 3, 1492, with three ships under his command: the *Pinta*, the *Nina* and his flagship, the *Santa Maria*. In October 1492, Columbus apparently reached the north coast of Hispaniola and due to the loss of the *Santa Maria* had to leave forty of his men on the island; thus creating the first European settlement in the New World. Santo Domingo, south, on the Caribbean Sea [named for the fierce defenders of the Antilles

Islands, the Carib Indians], became the oldest city, founded in the name of Spain, in the Western Hemisphere. The Dominican Republic comprised the eastern, mountainous two-thirds of Hispaniola; with French-colonized Haiti, the western one-third. The five hundredth year since Columbus' discovery had produced an elaborate new monument in Santo Domingo in the name of Christopher Columbus but island harmony did not extend to Haiti where oppressed "boat people" fled to the United States.)

Needing a lasting monument of Ciudad Trujillo and its historic wealth, Dave chose a handsome, solid mahogany coffee table intricately bordered in a hand-carved garland of lance-shaped, vein-etched, mahogany leaflets. Ingenious hinging permitted compact collapsing of the two aprons into a portable, boxable, stateroom-storable table from the indigenous tropical tree, the West Indies mahogany.

July was a perfect month, most of which the children and I spent at the Officers' Pool, Little Creek Amphibious Base, in the mornings where Bruce and Lori were in Advanced Swimming classes and Davie, five years old, in the Beginners' class; Dave, being the expert, joined us on the week ends to check their progress at the O-Pool or took us to the beach at Little Creek.

The Amphibious Base was abloom with oleander and mimosa and magnolia; the camellias did not like the heat and the tree wisterias had ceased to drip purple but the crape myrtles were beginning to open in crimson, pink, white and lavender. Our yard produced two Indian baskets full of gardenias a day, all as perfect as the first one I bloomed, but I seldom picked more than six for the living room since our bedrooms were above the gardenia row, the spicy fragrance—nocturnally heady—filling our open-windowed rooms with exoticness. Our deep crimson crape myrtles were showing lacy color but our roses which loved the sun and moist air—were under attack.

Figure 92. First Gardenia

The year of the Japanese beetle arrived and roses were their pièce de résistance; they plagued us every other year, always when our blooms were robust. The chemical which controlled them spotted the roses and foliage and left a sticky residue on the ground so I appointed my three naturalists

Figure 93. Irresistible Roses

to de-beetle the roses daily and they each filled a tall peanut-butter jar with the black, hard-shelled, peanut-sized destroyers. Weekly, Dave burned the mound out behind the fence and I boasted the cleanest roses on the Lake.

With the long growing season in Virginia Beach-Norfolk, our yard had reached maturity in 1959; the acid-loving plants: gardenias, azaleas, camellias and crape myrtles being further enriched by the pine needles we gathered in the woods of Virginia Beach each autumn. The Bermuda-grass lawn grew lushly but it took almost three hours to cut and trim both sides of the fence in the back yard; when I had it to do, I was not too particular about the fence and wished the boys would grow big in a hurry. Oh, it was nice to have my gardener back in summertime!

The first of August, I enrolled in William and Mary, Norfolk Campus, for the Fall semester night school, to get

Figure 94. Camellia japonica

six hours of Methodology in the Education Department, so that I would be accredited to teach—as if any Mother needed other than that school to learn to convey what she knew, and to admit what she didn't, or become as astute as the child and remedy ignorance with a question. But Norfolk was a militarily impacted area and needed teachers and I could not contribute three demanding pupils without making an effort in their behalf; besides, I was selfish and did not welcome eight months of just bridge with *Independence* O-Wives when the Ship was in the Med.

Then I went to the Baylake Pines Elementary School office to sign my contract. Mrs. Bosserman was glad to see me, glanced at my degree and transcript from the University of Michigan, approved it quickly and than asked if I would cut my shoulder-length hair. "You mean, short, like yours?" She smiled, modestly, lightly caressing her perfect hair, "Yes, the faculty and I think it would be less distracting."

I went home, cut my hair, washed it and returned. "How do you like my hair?" turning slowly for her scrutiny. "Oh, you're lovely!" she beamed. "Now, let's sign the contract." I declined. She was unbelieving! "But why did you cut your hair?" "It wasn't important," I told her and withdrew my three children from her unimportant school.

I signed a contract to teach at Bayside Elementary from which I had not yet withdrawn Lori and Bruce and we all went off happily together the first day of school, depositing Davie at another private First Grade which was elated to get him and which he loved from the beginning: they served pear pie for lunch!

The new principal at Bayside Elementary, Mrs. Parkerson, having taught Lori in Third Grade and knowing Bruce's ability, permitted me to teach Bruce in an Accelerated Fourth Grade which I combined with a regular-track Fifth. It was a sensible scheme for much of my material was the same for both grades except in group and individual programs. It was a time of felicitous, family pedagogy because Davie, arriving after lunch, was permitted to sit in the back row and "audit" Fourth Grade. All was serene until, in the springtime, I assigned Bruce to schoolground "Clean-up Committee." He inferred that unlittering the grounds meant picking up stray cats. The entire class vociferously insisted he should "get to" take them home. That inexact but effective verbal produced one cat for Bruce: "Patches." I didn't know three-colored cats were female! Bruce did.

It was easy and natural for all of us (except Dave—the usual student) to teach and learn together in school at Bayside Elementary. Dave drove Davie to his First Grade in Norfolk each morning and the school van brought him to Bayside after lunch. Bruce, Lori and I walked the six blocks to school or rode in the bus which obligingly stopped for us at the driveway if the weather was inclement. Most of the time we walked and I felt like the "Pied Piper of Hamelin," my childhood's favorite Robert Browning poem of perambulation (which I had found under the Christmas tree at 5119 Brooklyn Avenue, Kansas City, together with three other miniature volumes nested in a box, forming the nucleus of my library, at age seven). Lori and Bruce's friends "fell in" along the way, and some of my pupils—my attempting, with brisk strides to keep well ahead lest I looked less like a Mother, teacher and friend and more like a peripatetic martinet—or worse, a teacher soliciting approval and beseeching popularity. Since my own could not curry educative favor from me, I "distanced" myself from their friends—many of whom I was teaching; others, who continued to play at our house. But children were wise and they intuited, obviating the need for verbalization, that there was a difference between their friend's Mother and their Teacher.

One of the wisest was Bruce's best friend, next to Davie, of course, Charles Schoenfeld, who had been in the familial comradeship for three years and lived at the northwest turn of Sunrise Drive, his father a black shoe LCDR stationed at the Naval Base. Bruce and Charles always finished class work well ahead of their peers and moved on to special assignments or assisted me if "tutors" were needed. They were both modest and quiet in class—they were so busy—but rapscallions at recess and when they got home, where Charles was usually awaiting us, sitting by the front door, when we arrived. I channeled their energy for my Cub Den, as well.

Lori's "best" friend, Terry Hamer, was in my Fifth Grade and walked home with us on Girl Scout-meeting afternoons and down two houses to Ginny Olney's, my generous friend, who had taken over the Scout Troop when I started to teach school.

Teaching proceeded smoothly and enjoyably and I went two nights a week to my William and Mary postgraduate course in Human Growth and Development conveniently presented at the Princess Anne High School close by, the Professor's instructing us in Football and Knitting, as he fondled a long hair on the top of his nose and alluding, occasionally, to Child Psychology. But I dutifully and interestedly perused the text, wrote an excellent paper and helped him keep the discussion going, when it wasn't about knit and purl, and felt I had earned my "A." Midway in the last month, he asked who would volunteer to take the "C." "I have to give one," we were told, "William and Mary grade on the curve." I surveyed the room, surmised that most of my classmates were dependent upon their income from teaching and I was taking the course for certification only, so—I waived my pride and waved my hand. "I can't give it to *you*, Mrs.

Holland," he had the grace to respond. "I'll find me a goat." We all laughed; I doubted that he would bother. He didn't.

The next semester I was tempted to sign up for graduate credit, just to protect my grade, but resisted the hypocrisy since I did not want a Masters in that field. Indeed, I generally scoffed at courses in "Education" but wanted acknowledgment for what I earned. Second semester produced fewer stories and much more grade; the poor man was no longer hirsute on the proboscis and seemed depressed. He *had* been interesting and knew his Psychology—when not distracted.

Mother and Dad came to visit us in late October, encountering a light snow in the Shenandoahs which "sugared" the autumn foliage. "Children, can you imagine these," Mother exhibited her sweet gum, black gum, yellow poplar and maple leaves of burgundy, red, orange, yellow, green and gold, "encased in ice and sugared on the edges with fine snow and hoarfrost and then, the sun came out! It was the most breathtaking sight; we drove through a jeweled forest! Oh, how we wished for all of you!" And then Dad came in with their luggage and we all kissed and hugged and said, "Hello." Lori showed them her leaf collection and notebook from Girl Scout camp, explaining how she had dried and pressed them facilely, at the same time: pressing them, with supervision, between sheets of waxed paper with a hot iron, the label of identification and location ironed in at the bottom of the sheet. After they admired those and were taken out to see the menagerie and pile of geodes which weren't but might have been—Daddy Frank's promising the boys and Lori, too—his geological pick and tools when they were a little older, we gave them a quick tour of the house and planned our brief week end together.

They were on their way to Washington, D.C., to visit Gene and Marguerite and Katie Lou; Honora and Martha were married and living with their families in Florida—but Beth was in D.C., with her six children and husband, FBI Agent, Thomas Keane. (Tom Keane was honored by J. Edgar Hoover in 1972 shortly before the latter's death. J[ohn] Edgar Hoover, born in 1895, had directed the Federal Bureau of Investigation forty-eight years, since 1924.) Tom had invited Mother and Dad for a special tour of the facilities while he was still on duty in the District. Since Gene and Marguerite, who had been working in the crowded, bustling Capital during the war years and now, thoroughly wearied of it, were planning to move back South—Mother and Dad decided upon a quick trip, Dad never eager to be long away from his business.

Figure 95. Beth Lacy Keane, Family, and J. Edgar Hoover

After an abbreviated run through the Naval Base (the *Independence* was, unfortunately, in dry dock), Oceana and Virginia Beach, Davie wanted to show Mommy Tom where he went to Sunday School at Little Creek Amphibious Base and Bruce and Lori wanted them to see where "the frogmen train" in the special area marked "Off Limits," viewable only from a distance; we returned home, baked a Smithfield ham and spent two days visiting and learning what the children were learning—in school and otherwise.

At Halloween we reversed the "trick-or-treat" procedure. Wearing the costumes they had worn to the room parties at school, the children set out in the early evening, carrying boxes of orange-pumpkin dough-nuts—Mother had sent me the recipe—frosted in orange or chocolate butter cream, to immediate neighbors and friends on the block, then hurried to "man the door" with their Daddy, giving out nutritious apples. Fortunately, the children *preferred* being at home to witness the coming of their friends and classmates because Dave and I did not approve of the concept or practice of "trick-or-treat." We thought it not only unimaginative but unhealthy—I, especially, who restricted their sugar intake and looked askance at chewing gum, sugar-coated cereal and all candy, except peppermint stick at Christmastime—and preferred home parties and the conveying, rather than the soliciting, of favors. Our children and friends actually learned how to "bob for apples," pin the tail on the black cat and carve—only the older Boy and Girl Scouts—jack-o'-lanterns.

The leafless ailanthus trees pictorially silhouetted the Lake and early sunset-reflecting clouds and the year subsided into November with only a few days of negative progress—when the children's toes popped through their sleepers or Dave's nautically knotted socks in my sewing basket exceeded those in his top chest drawer or when Nibbles ate the azalea buds or Polly went a-berrying among my Chinese holly. But I always managed it well, if Dave was at home,

Figure 96. Ailanthus Sentinels on Lake Smith

and took an early after-dinner bath in a full tub of reddening hot water, languishing long and imagining the activity below with supreme detachment. Dave would manage to dictate a few spelling words to Bruce, play Uncle Wiggily with Davie and later, watch the latest exploits of Pluto on *Disneyland.* As I luxuriously splashed in steamy isolation, I envisioned the scene I must soon behold. The playroom floor would be covered with a sprinkling of pennies and marbles sowed by Davie's hand; the davenport slip cover would be draped onto the rug, with books and papers askew and oversized blocks, strategically strewn, would complete the hazard.

As I knotted my robe, I would call majestically from the top of the stairs: "You have exactly five minutes to 'pick up' the room" (that, as much for Dave's benefit, as the children's). "If the room isn't cleaned up in five minutes, none of you will see *Sea Hunt*"—the most villainous threat I could pronounce because the children imagined those exciting amphibious escapades to be exactly what the "frogmen are doing at Little Creek!" In five minutes, I would saunter down and find the room looking not too disjointed, with innocence smirking from every face, looking about the way it would when I hired a fifty-cent baby sitter.

The year ended swiftly for us in Kansas City as Dave and I and the children celebrated Christmas with Mother and Dad, Charles, Barbara, Luanne—a Yule birthday girl—and brother, Brian Lacy, a rarity of balmy April. We observed my thirty-seventh birthday, December 28, with the traditional, ineffably luscious Mommy Tom-Daddy Frank fresh coconut cake; our twelfth wedding anniversary on New Year's Eve and Dad's seventieth birthday on New Year's Day; the Rose Parade; incomparable turkey tetrazzini à la Thomas; the Rose Bowl and Orange Bowl—happy fare for the New Year of growth and discovery.

We visited briefly again at Eastertime, in the Midwest, Dave's taking his last leave of the year before eight months in the Med. He recorded our rare summer presence in Kansas City with a billfold-sized picture of Mother and Dad, Lori, Bruce, Davie and me in front of "the big pink house," as the children always called it.

Figure 97. Big Pink House

Then back to Lake Smith where the fifth and sixth months flew in a twinkling and we had our last barbecued steaks with Dave as chef and sweet Bruce's hand was burned as he held the platter for his Daddy and a steak was misplaced. But first aid was immediate, ice water and unguentine, and Bruce was very brave and insisted it was his fault and not his Dad's who was

Figure 98. Med Correspondents

miserable-looking and chided himself for his carelessness.

But Bruce's hand was healing nicely when the Ship left 13 July 1960 for Mock-Ship Exercises off the East Coast and Lori's foot was less sore, as well. When a carpenter was repairing our fence, he borrowed our garden fork and drove it so deeply in the ground that the handle came out. Lori was attempting to lodge the handle back into the fork when the latter slipped and went into her instep, quite deeply and close to a tendon. Being minutes away from Little Creek Dispensary was a help and the young man went with us to carry Lori into the Emergency Room; there had been surprisingly little bleeding and we had packed it with ice and wrapped it with sheet strips.

Neither Lori nor Bruce had shed a tear when injured. How fortunate we were to have sturdy, unhysterical children. Their only complaint was that they could not go swimming.

Dave wrote from the Ship with instructions for Bruce, almost recovered, to cut wood from the old chairs (which we had tried to leave in Monterey but the Navy had stored them and they had held up in Norfolk three years) to the proper size; Lori was to get out the nails and Davie, stack the wood neatly on the north side of the barbecue but not obstructing the fireplace trap which Bruce was further empowered to clean out. Then Bruce and Davie were to sweep the gravel out of the front gutter and dump it at the base of trees, out back of the Whiteford's—who wanted it for some reason; "Bruce knows where it goes," Dave wrote; I was just to remind him. I was authorized to call Mr. Gifford, our contractor, and to get a diagram of the septic-tank location and the run-off drainage system. As a reward, I could select several more books for the Med Cruise—in the direction I "wanted him edified!"—after the septic tank had had its every-two-years' cleaning. Oh, yes, Davie was to put on more weight and learn to swim with his head under water because we were going camping and fishing next summer and he would have to be a strong swimmer so that more than two could fish from the same boat—which logic I did not understand but I was sure Davie would know the implications thereof.

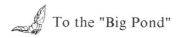 To the "Big Pond"

The *Independence* returned Dave to us briefly in mid-July until 27 July 1960. They bade fervent farewell and sailed for the Mediterranean

Sea. Dave left us hale and hardy, if not hearty; Bruce's hand was not a bit scarred and Lori could wear her shoes on both feet and Davie was practicing underwater work in the bathtub. And we had almost a month to swim again at the O-Pool and beach before school started. And school was much on my mind as I reviewed the year just completed: it had been successful for all of us—Bruce had been challenged and kept busy, Davie had enjoyed both of his schools and Lori, whose classroom was next to ours, had benefited, too.

I had taken my class to NATO Headquarters May 17, 1960, in Norfolk, one of my Navy-brat-pupil's father's arranging our 7:00 A.M. visit on Norway's National Day to witness the flag-raising ceremony.

Figure 99. L, B and D and Class at NATO

Fifteen flagpoles were arranged in a semicircle in front of the North Atlantic Treaty Organization Headquarters compound, the American flag in the center which went up briskly at 7:00 A.M. (Dave was always critical of the way flags at sporting events and other civilian activities were raised: slowly, usually in time to the *Star Spangled Banner* which was incorrect and egregious. The American flag—which all military men, women, Boy Scouts and Girl Scouts knew—was to be raised "briskly" and lowered slowly.) Norway's flag was raised second, on the country's National Day, and then the other thirteen flags were raised simultaneously and briskly.

Immediately after the ceremony, my class formed their own semi-four-tiered circle, with Lori and Bruce in the center back and Davie's kneeling in center front with my shorter students and their picture was taken.

We had a special tour and learned the significance of NATO: it was a defense coalition formed by twelve nations of North America and Western Europe on April 4, 1949. The charter members were: the United States, Canada, Belgium, Denmark, France (which withdrew in 1966), Great Britain, Iceland, Italy, Luxembourg, the Netherlands, Norway, and Portugal. Greece and Turkey were admitted in 1952; West Germany became the fifteenth member in 1955. The organization was a collective defense against threats from the Soviet Union and its Communist satellites and a reaffirmation of the members' faith in the United Nations. My students collected greetings and signatures in the many different languages and an abundance of literature, maps and miniature flags and we all arrived back at school, half an hour early.

I visited in the hall before class with Lori's Fifth-Grade teacher and asked her observations about Lori and Sixth Grade next year. "Oh, she should do very well," she enthused, "she's making straight A's!" "Have you ever looked at her test scores?" I inquired. She nodded, "There was something about them," her brow furrowed with uncertainty. "Of course," I said, "Lori's 99+ across the board, both V. and N." "How did you know?" clutching her gradebook to her chest. "All of my children have been privately tested." (Thanks to Mrs. Bosserman; I wouldn't have done it otherwise.) She opened her gradebook, "You're right! I knew she was either very high or surprisingly low. I really thought she was low in math—an over-achiever." I didn't ask how she could justify "straight A's" and low ability. "Lori should *not* be in Sixth Grade next year," I advised her. Her eyes opened wide: "Oh, we have *never* skipped anybody at Bayside!" "Why don't *you* recommend that Lori be skipped to Seventh," I suggested. "*Request* that she be tested. Mrs. Parkerson, who has taught Lori and sparkles every time Lori's name is mentioned, would commend your 'perceptiveness.'" "I think I will," she glowed, "thank you for calling it to my attention." I shouldn't have had to, I said to myself, but smiled at her comprehension, unlocked my door and opened it wide for my enthusiastic youngsters, bubbling over with NATO knowledge, flourishing foreign calligraphy and behaving with their normal effervescence.

The first week of August, Lori breezed through her Seventh-Grade-Placement Exam and was enrolled in an accelerated Seventh Grade at Bayside taught by a demanding, middle-aged woman who was unafraid of her bright students and of whom I, unrestrainedly approved—to my family. Davie was accepted into accelerated Second Grade, although Bayside normally discounted private school records and recommendations and placed them back a grade for "observation" and Bruce, in accelerated Fifth Grade.

Dave's longed-for letters were beginning to arrive regularly.

Three days before school started there was a lunar eclipse which Dave had written about and directed us to watch at Virginia Beach at 5:00 A.M. The children, of course, were anxious to see it and I, too; I wanted to do everything which Dave suggested for enhancement of the children's understanding of their natural world, one of his most ardently pursued interests. I set the alarm for 4:15 A.M. but it was almost four-thirty when I leapt from bed, grabbed the clothes I had laid out, my shoulder bag, stepped into my moccasins and rushed in to awaken Lori, Bruce and Davie: "Just put on your robes and shoes and bring your 'Newfie' blankets" (the four-foot square, red wool, plaid, fringed blankets from Newfoundland always folded at the foot of their beds with their names embroidered in red on the labels, their always wanting their own, for some reason). "Let's hurry; it'll soon be visible."

Fortunately, there was no traffic to the beach at four-thirty in the morning and I exceeded the speed limit a bit. When I got to Dave's stipulated spot, very familiar to us for we had lived close by and romped there often; we dashed from the car, leaving the doors open and ran—as fast as we could in fine sand—to the southeast shore where no trees obscured the low-hanging moon and the children squealed with delight, for the full moon had already moved from the earth's penumbra (partial shadow) and the left side of the moon was in darkness, almost. In half an hour, the eclipse was total and we sat in the sand and watched, the children with their Newfie blankets around them in the cool, pre-dawn, moist air and I, buttoning up my sweater as I handed out the opera glasses. At the height of the eclipse, the moon was still faintly visible to the naked eye, glowing with a dull redness, caused—we learned when we got home—by sunlight refracted in the earth's atmosphere, the slight illumination appearing red because of its passage through the air. When the left edge of the moon began to show brightness, we started back to the car, literally, walking backwards most of the way until Lori touched me on the shoulder and whispered: "Mommy, there're some men!" I spun around and was relieved to see the flashing light of a police car and two policemen inspecting our open-doored—too quickly abandoned vehicle. "Are you

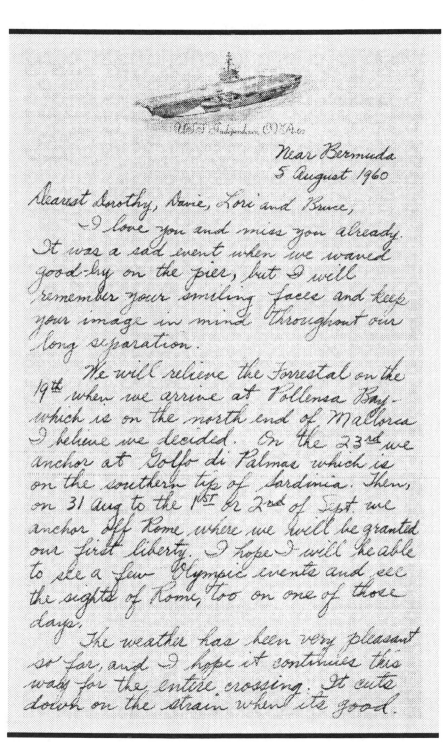

USS Independence (CVA-62)

Near Bermuda
5 August 1960

Dearest Dorothy, Davie, Lori and Bruce,

I love you and miss you already.
It was a sad event when we waved
good-by on the pier, but I will
remember your smiling faces and keep
your image in mind throughout our
long separation.

We will relieve the Forrestal on the
19th when we arrive at Pollensa Bay —
which is on the north end of Mallorca
I believe we decided. On the 23rd we
anchor at Golfo di Palmas which is
on the southern tip of Sardinia. Then,
on 31 Aug to the 1st or 2nd of Sept. we
anchor off Rome, where we will be granted
our first liberty. I hope I will be able
to see a few Olympic events and see
the sights of Rome, too on one of those
days.

The weather has been very pleasant
so far, and I hope it continues this
way for the entire crossing. It cuts
down on the strain when its good.

alright?" one called. "Yes, of course," I responded, "we came out to the beach to watch the lunar eclipse." "The eclipse! You shouldn't be out here *alone* at night," his partner said, gruffly. "Well, I'm not," I pointed to my team, "but thank you for your concern and I'm sorry we startled you." "Policemen are nice," said Davie. "Until they get mad," observed Bruce. "Well, it did look ominous," I admitted, "with the car doors' standing wide-open. I guess they patrol the beach frequently." "I'll bet they didn't even know about the eclipse," speculated Lori, as she nestled under her blanket. "We should have taken the telescope," Bruce said, sleepily. "I wasn't enjoined by your father to do so," I realized that I was talking to myself and wondered if I had ever fallen asleep that quickly, "he knew it would be a last-minute dash without his supervision," I finished and leaned over to lock the doors.

The Haseltons had moved and we missed Polly who had been a happy-natured playmate. LCDR Bob and Lorrain Lichtenberg and Kurt, Lori's age, had bought the house and moved in the first of August. Lorrain was to teach Third Grade at Bayside and we went off together, after my sitter arrived, on August 22, to three days of faculty planning. Mrs. Parkerson appointed me to the Chairmanship of the Faculty, responsible for the monthly meeting and the suggestion of new programs, concepts and goals. She quickly rued my appointment! I saw the need for some changes and articulated them to the faculty at the first meeting, not clearing my thoughts with her first because she had "empowered" me to suggest new concepts. Mine were more specific, however, than the mere verbiage she had theretofore solicited. I was deemed a "heretic" with my first suggestion: "We should be teaching Phonics; the 'look-say' method is obsolete and detrimental to the reading process; it teaches the child to memorize rather than to cerebrate. If the child misses *that* day of new words or clean cards are initiated (he read 'strawberry' if he saw a thumbprint in the lower, left-hand corner), there is a blank in his vocabulary." A few teachers snickered in approval; some stared in disbelief and Mrs. Parkerson did not smile. "Well," she finally smiled, a bit wanly, but reminiscent of her sweet smile, "I didn't anticipate Mrs. Holland would be so *forceful*." So I desisted for that meeting because she had not interfered with my children's grade-placements, each of which had been atypical for the conservative Virginia school system.

I asked her, privately, well in advance of the next meeting, if I might discuss—not curriculum—the library. That seemed innocuous enough and she nodded "Yes."

At the next meeting, I suggested the library was too delimiting, especially since most of the pupils were military and had lived in many locales. "Is it not a responsibility of the school to supply the needs of the students? Our students are sophisticated readers. Why, for example, do we not have Twain's *Huckleberry Finn,* Defoe's *Robinson Crusoe*, and Stowe's *Uncle Tom's Cabin*?" Mrs. Parkerson gasped, "Mrs. Holland!" she moaned, "we can't have *those* books!" I was forever shocking the dear woman but I pressed on: "Why not?" "You will not find those books in Virginia schools; there is a very good reason." "What is it?" She did not reply. Feeling it was my last month as "chairman," of anything, I took a Parthian shot: "Why must we teach *just* Virginia History in our class-rooms? It's rich and wonderful but it isn't enough for the world these children live in. We have NATO, SACLANT and international ships right at our door; one of my students already speaks four languages!" She just shook her head despairingly, at having so misjudged my "professionalism," no doubt, and closed the meeting.

I soon developed my first and only psychosomatic ailment: I developed bursitis in my right shoulder but it only hurt when I raised my hand—which I learned not to do—or when I passed Mrs. Parkerson in the hall, or thought of her. But she had not repressed my children and I was willing, *en revanche*, for her to suppress my recommendations and voice, which so confounded her "philosophy of education" which admitted to no dialogue. We would probably be in another school system in another year; most of their learning took place out of school and always had: one could only *challenge* gifted children; they taught themselves.

Kurt Lichtenberg was a pleasant, attractive youngster, spirited but rather light-headed who played some of the time with Bruce, Davie and Charles but generally played with Richard, who was in High School and lived two houses north with his mother in Warren and Ginny Olney's house which Warren had decided to rent and eventually, retire to. Richard and his mother had moved in during the summer; his father was some-where aboard ship, a Chief, we thought; his mother disdained friendship and stayed in the house; Richard roamed at will, sullen-eyed, hostile, quick-tempered. Our wonderful neighborhood had changed from its original homogeneity and Richard quickly became an anathema to almost everyone. Kurt was an acceptable playmate if Richard was elsewhere but when Richard whistled, Kurt scampered to his side, afraid of the oldest and biggest boy in the neighborhood. But Bruce was not afraid—not of Richard, not of any "bully"; besides, Bruce was a champion runner! Kurt, however, was becoming too much like Richard. One day, Bruce and Kurt were casting their fishing lines in the front yard. Each time they were thrown out and hooked in the sod, Davie was authorized to run up, unhook them and when he was safely out of the way, the lines were reeled in. Kurt cast his one last time, nodded to Davie to go get it and when Davie bent over to extricate the hook, Kurt pulled hard and the weight hit Davie above the right eye, cutting his eyebrow. Kurt professed it was an accident, apologized, hugged Davie and told him how sorry he was. When Bruce and Davie came home, sometime later, I was glad to treat just a superficial cut but suggested perhaps they would prefer not to play with fishlines which were not in the water.

In the fall campaigning of 1960, Presidential candidate John F. Kennedy recommended an exciting concept on the steps of the University of Michigan Union (next to Lacy's Beta House), which he promised to effectuate when he became President. Giving credit to Senate colleague Hubert Humphrey, for the initial idea, John Kennedy proposed the establishment of a "Peace Corps" which would enlist youthful volunteers, with all age groups welcomed, to serve two years in a foreign land. He stated three major goals: to give technical assistance to developing countries; to familiarize countries served with a cross-country sectional understanding of America and to incorporate information from returning volunteers into our understanding of the culture, economies and needs of underdeveloped nations throughout the world.

(In November of 1991, Dave and I were in Ann Arbor for the Michigan-Northwestern football game held during the University's Peace Corps Week commemorating the thirty-first anniversary of the Peace Corps' birth—on the Union steps. David C. Thomas, head of the Peace Corps Recruitment and Selection Division, spoke at Rackham Amphitheater about the exciting plans for Peace Corps initiatives in the deteriorating Soviet Union [dissolved after seventy years of Communism in December 1991] and Baltic States. He expected five hundred volunteers in service in the "Soviet Republics" [the nascent "Commonwealth of Independent States"] by December of 1992. There had been over 130,000 Volunteers in the three decades since 1960, with 5,500 serving in 1991, at least two years in ninety countries, the average age being thirty-two with twelve per cent over fifty years of age; one, aged eighty-one and one, eighty-four!

(I was very proud of my Alma Mater, especially when David Thomas announced a new Peace Corps program at the University of Michigan, and eighteen other universities nationwide, which would send teachers earning their master's degrees into inner-city schools—the best into the least. What a fine beginning to needed renovation of our entire system!

("Ask not what your country can do for you but what *you* can do for your country!" J.F.K.'s ageless epigram was still heeded and both Dave and I felt sanguine about America's youth as we had a "Michigan," for me, club sandwich; "Cornell," for Dave and jasmine tea at Drake's Sandwich Shop on North University, off of State Street, my old campus hangout still filled with ambiance and dark booths, the day before the game—and talked to the fine young scholars. And they gave us miniature Wolverine footballs and Desmond Howard and the team won handily to continual playing of *Hail to the Victors!* on Saturday, November 9, 1991, in the 107,000-seat, newly grass-sodded stadium!)

We did not approve of birthday parties, per se, but Davie had attended so many that he thought he should reciprocate for his friends on November 3, 1960, his Seventh. It was unusually warm and after cake, ice cream, gifts and favors, the boys played in the back yard. Bruce was off with Charles and I had insisted Lori go to her Girl Scout meeting, although she had wanted to stay to "help with Davie's friends." I checked periodically but it was election week and I was watching political news of John F. Kennedy who had just been elected President. The Saturday afternoon party began to lag about four and parents weren't coming until four-thirty, so I took out the croquet set and the boys happily put up the wickets, Davie's assigning colors to his seven friends on his Seventh Birthday Party. I had no sooner returned to the house to listen to the 4:00 o'clock news than Davie came rushing into the house, his face streaming with blood. Grabbing a kitchen towel from the drawer and wetting it, I listened to Davie as I tried to stanch the bleeding. He calmly explained that Jimmy didn't know any rules, that he was standing right beside him when Jimmy suddenly swung back his mallet, without even looking. "I don't like Jimmy anymore," was all that Davie said. A Mother had arrived and was herding the children into the playroom, into their coats and into the front yard. I had Davie on the davenport in the vacated playroom, an ice pack on his eye, the right one again—which Kurt had injured three months before. Lori had come home and, with great composure, began to help. I grabbed my bag and glass case, locked the house but Davie wanted to walk by himself to the car, his head half covered with a white bath towel which Lori had raced upstairs to get—blood-soaked again; I wanted to swoop him up in my arms but his friends and their parents were still in the yard, looking very frightened and helpless, especially Jimmy, who was crying; and my macho little man walked to the car with Lori behind him, sat in the corner and waved to his friends as I backed out of the driveway. Lorrain rushed to the car, asked if she could do anything. I told her Bruce was at Charles' but that I expected to be back because Bruce was staying for supper. "You could call Cathy and tell her to tell Bruce that Davie is going to be fine." "Little Creek?" she called after me. Lori answered, "Yes," and we knew the way.

The doctor took eight stitches; Davie's eyebrow was split open at the inner edge like a plus sign but his eye, apparently, was not damaged. He gave a tetanus shot to Davie, even though I showed him our boosters were up-to-date. He commended Davie for being so brave and gave him a brochure about the eyes and told us where we could buy a science kit which could be put together to produce a large plastic eye, so that Davie could study the components and function of the "marvelous organ." Davie grinned; nothing pleased him so much as to learn something new: "Can we go now?" he urged. "No, dear, it's after five and the stores are closed. We'll drive to school Monday and leave directly from Bayside to get your kit." The kind, young Navy doctor gave me some pills, said we could go to Sunday School tomorrow—if Davie felt like it, requested that we return Monday afternoon, "after you buy your eye kit"—to Davie, and asked me not to change the bandage and "be sure to give him lots of liquids."

Bruce and Charles were sitting by the front door when we drove up and that pleased Davie, mightily. They had not stayed for supper but come right up, picked up the croquet set and hidden it behind the ironing board in the laundry room—after washing off the hated mallet and hosing down the terrace and steps "but we couldn't get the rug clean," Bruce apologized. I hugged them both and thanked them for being so thoughtful and manly. Davie lay down while the boys watched over him and examined the birthday toys. Jimmy had given him a big red fire truck with a pump and hose which Bruce and Charles were asked to demonstrate, in a bucket. Lori opened two cans of Scotch Broth, Davie's favorite, and toasted English muffins. I wanted to clean up the blood in the living room before Davie came up the steps to the kitchen and found that the boys' efforts had been very helpful and thorough.

Davie drank a bowl of soup, a glass of milk, orange juice and water, of course, and began to look less pale. He declined birthday cake but Bruce and Charles accepted and I thought how happily I had baked that ill-fated cake the day before, exactly to Davie's injunctions: a banana with spice, English walnuts, tart lemon filling, marshmallow icing with coconut on top. But he drank a vanilla milk shake and was soon ready for bed, insisting he wanted to go to Sunday School in the morning: "It's my Birthday Sunday and I have to put my money in." Bruce and Charles followed him up the stairs and ran his bath water, Bruce's rushing down again to "get the fire truck." "Bruce, please don't let him stay in long; he's lost a lot of blood and doesn't realize how weak he is. Just in and out, please." "I know, Mama; he won't wash his hair" and hurried back up the stairs. Charles came down. I hugged him again and thanked him for helping us. Lori called Lorrain Lichtenberg for me to tell her the good news about Davie and called Jimmy's parents who had called while we were gone.

I took a pill up to Davie and tucked him in, then dampened his curls and combed out the dried blood. "I hope you can forgive me, Davie, for letting such a dreadful thing happen to you," as I kissed his brow lightly, and his soft cheek. "It wasn't your fault, Mommy," he assured me. "Yes, it was. I was selfish and careless, I should have stayed with you in the back yard; I shouldn't have assumed everyone was intelligent about rules just because you, Bruce and Lori are." "But everyone was," Davie insisted, "except Jimmy!" "Good-night, my sweet, courageous boy," I kissed him again, "we'll go to Sunday School if you feel like it." Bruce came in from his bath to pat Davie gently on the head and tickle his foot and kiss me good night.

After the children were asleep, I sat in the dark living room and watched the moon rise over Lake Smith. I was unsure of myself for the first time; I had failed Dave and I had failed the children. I went upstairs and wrote to Dave—factually; I did not burden him with my remorse; I had been selfish enough for one day, for one lifetime!

Our Thanksgiving came early: Davie's wound was healing quickly, there was no eye damage and the stitches could soon come out! We drove to school all the next week; Davie's teacher let him stay in at recess and Davie let Bruce, Lori and Charles study the physiology of the eye—at home. After each had taken it apart and put it together several times, several days, without interference from the others, Davie carefully glued it in place and I put it on the top shelf of the designated bookcase where it greeted us each time we came in the room.

One afternoon, as we reached the island in front of the Jacobson's, Bruce exclaimed: "Look, there's a truck in our driveway!" I pulled up beside it. "They've got the wrong address; I didn't order firewood." "Oh, it's Mr. Campbell," Lori discovered, as our attractive fence-fixer came smiling through the blue gate. He opened the car door, "How's your foot, Lori?" "It's fine," she dimpled, "what are you doing here?" "I brought some firewood in atonement. What happened to you, Davie?" as our wounded warrior slid out of the car. "I got hit," Davie was tired of telling people; Bruce finished, laconically: "Croquet mallet," and motioned for Davie and Charles and disappeared into the house, after Lori. He smiled at me with his perfect teeth, "How's the fence holding up?" "Oh, it's fine," I said, "but we can't accept your firewood; no one blames you." "I do," he laughed. "It would please me if you would let me help you while your husband's gone." "No thank you, that's very kind but we're fine," I said quickly, "and we even have some firewood!" "Not much," he observed. "I went around to check. Please take it; it came from the farm. I have more than I know what to do with." "Well, just one load," I wanted to get rid of him. "I'll go get the wheelbarrow. Does Nibbles still sleep in it?" he called over his shoulder. What a memory! I said to myself; and I didn't like his easy familiarity. I went inside. After he had deposited a wheelbarrow loadful, I went onto the terrace, thanked him and told him not to leave any more. "But I've got a full load!" he complained. He leaned over to straighten the pile and his cap fell off. I had never seen him without it and almost laughed when I saw how his wavy blond hair had receded. "You've been too generous already," I was able to say, "thank you; I'll have Bruce put up the wheelbarrow," and went back into the house, in dismissal. But he brought another load around and I was about to go out again when he started with empty wheelbarrow for the back garage door. In a few minutes, he knocked on the terrace door and I got up from my paper-grading, not opening the door, the louvers being wide. "I'd like to come again," he smiled, "some evening." And then I did laugh: "Lovely!" I barely managed. "But call before you come—we get awfully busy." He looked pleased and turned to leave. "And don't forget to bring your wife!" I was still laughing at his impudence long after he had closed the gate and roared off down Sunrise Drive.

We had another uninvited guest, as recrudescent as that one apple in a bushel: Richard. He had a miniature plane, not of his construction, inasmuch as his proclivity lay at the opposite end of the continuum, but one on a wire which had kept him confined to his own yard for some weeks. The wire broke one afternoon and Richard's plane flew south—"Onto the Holland's roof," Kurt claimed with mischievous falsity; he had not even been a witness to the solo separation. We had just gotten home from school; the children were changing into playclothes and I was starting a load in the washer and folding one from the dryer.

Bruce and Davie discovered that Kurt had dragged a ladder from his garage and was leaning it against ours and Richard was ascending to our roof. Bruce yelled out my bedroom window for Richard to get off the roof and Kurt to move the ladder. "Make me," Richard was reported to have said and that was challenge enough for intrepid Bruce. After all, Richard was just seven years older than he and Kurt, still on the ground, just two. Bruce got a pan of water and squeezed out through my narrow north bedroom window, Davie's helping, of course, as much as Bruce would permit an injured comrade to participate, tiptoed up the garage and onto the roof, caught Richard by surprise and accurately soaked his head. Bruce got back into the house before Richard could reach him, closed and locked the window, and listened to the descent and the dragging away of the ladder—and waited. Lori had been practicing the piano in the living room and had heard nothing.

Suddenly, we both heard; I, above the roar of the spin-cycle in the laundry room—a splintering, crashing explosion of wood, glass and chain as Richard hurled his football-trained body through the terrace door and galloped up the stairs to tackle Bruce at the top. I was at the bottom of the stairs; Bruce, manfully defending himself, had thrust Davie behind him and Lori had leapt, like a Fury, to her brothers' aid. "*Richard!*" I called and pointed, dramatically: "*Get out of my house!* How . . . Dare . . . You—break down my door and hurt my children!" "He threw water on me," Richard snarled. "You were trespassing," Bruce called. "Do you realize you cannot behave this way in a civilized neighborhood?" I accosted him as he sullenly slouched down the stairs. "What is the matter with you? Tell your Mother to call me. Richard, do you realize you have just committed a criminal act: breaking and entering—look at that door, it was both locked and chained—with the intent to do bodily harm! You are a threat to the entire neighborhood and something has to change. Now, get out of here! Don't you *ever* touch one of my children again or set one foot in my yard. I'm going to take action to see that you don't." I was surprised he had listened. "I'm not afraid of you," he sneered. "It is not *I* you will be dealing with," I called to his retreating, very wet back.

Mr. Gifford, kindly contractor, came that evening to temporarily repair our door and said he'd send one of his men Monday or I could call Mr. Campbell. I said: "Definitely not Mr. Campbell. Please send one of your good workers. Couldn't he put on a stronger lock?"

By Wednesday of the next week, our door had been repaired and we went off to school on the bus in the rain, well-coated, hatted and booted against the predicted snow which the children hoped for. Richard got on in front of his house which still had its shades tightly pulled. We were standing in the aisle being the last few in the bus which serviced both the Grade School and Princess Anne High School. "Hi, Richard," called out Bruce; I said, "Hello, Richard," but he remained mute, standing with his back to us, there being no other place to go. "I hope your Mother isn't ill," I began, with my captive listener. "I've called her—guess the phone is out of order; rung the door bell—guess that's broken—when I knew she was at home, the car was there; and I've written twice. We wanted to settle this in a friendly fashion. Have her call me tonight, I've been very patient, or I'll have to make that phone call tomorrow." I felt sorry for him but *my* children were fatherless, too. I had written to the Mother suggesting she get help for Richard at the High School, gave her a name, and advised help for both of them, at Little Creek. She obstinately preferred enmity to helpfulness. Still, I hated to outwit a child, but so be it: "Lori," I mused, in a theatrical aside—she stood between Richard and me—"do you realize that all three of our family lawyers are *male*? I hope you'll be interested in the law some day. It's fascinating! Breaking and entering, I'm informed, gets ten to twenty—more, with intent to do bodily harm. Good-bye, Richard!" as we evacuated the bus, most of the passengers' crowding behind us into the pouring rain and through the sheltering doors of Bayside Elementary.

Two days later, Bruce announced: "Richard's gone!" "Moved?" "Yes." We concentrated on the Med and the tortoise days ahead.

World Book, Vol. 11

CHAPTER VII

EPISTLES FROM THE U.S.S. *INDEPENDENCE*

Not far from Rota
15 August 1960

Dearest Dorothy, Davie, Lori and Bruce,

It seems like I have been gone for a month, but it has been only 11 days. I love you and miss you. I wish we were together on this long venture.

On Friday, 12 August, we had our first accident. During a landing at night, an A3D caught #3 arresting wire, but it broke on his runout. The pilot had full power on his jet engines, and made a slow bolter. At first we thought he had crashed in the water, but he managed to keep flying speed, even though the bottom of his port engine nacelle and his after fuselage dragged in the water for 300 yards. The pilot flew the plane on to Lajes where the plane was repaired the next day. That plane has flown on to Rota and further repairs will be made there.

Although no one in the plane was injured, 6 men on the flight deck were. Only 1 received serious injuries. One of those injured was injured the last time the cable broke. Needless to say he is rather anxious to get off the flight deck for good.

The next day an A3D came in for a day landing. When he touched down, his gear seemed to collapse. He made a bolter, however, and came around for another landing, even though his port gear registered unsafe. When he caught #4 wire, the port gear collapsed. The plane skidded to the left. Then it went over on its left wing and hung over the side momentarily before it finally dropped in the water upside down. One of the crew got out and was picked up by the helicopter. He has serious internal injuries. The pilot and other crew members were not recovered.

Last night the crew was cheered up a little by a variety show which is being put together in order to trade shows with the Forrestal on the 19th when we relieve them. There were several good performances – one put on by one of my men (Allard) who did the monologue on Khrushchev landing at Idlewild in a jet and being welcomed by Ike. You probably remember it as we saw it on television a few days before I left. There were also the usual musical instrument acts which were good, including one character called Bongo Buston who plays the Bongo drums. Two men in the flight deck crew sang a song they composed about the flight deck boatswain. It was a good show for the first ~~rehearsal~~, rehearsal.

Everybody has sore arms these days from all of the shots we have to take before our first liberty. I'm lucky. I needed only 5 shots. Some of them needed at least 8 shots. I had 3 last week, get another this week and the final one next week. We have to take the immunization cards ashore with us when we go on liberty.

Wednesday morning we form a column of ships and pass through the Straits of Gibraltar. We then become part of the Sixth Fleet and begin the job of policing the Mediterranean area.

When our planes flew into Lajes, Bert Riggs was there to meet each plane as it landed. Our TF flew over twice to deliver and pick up mail.

I am enclosing the receipt for $100 dollars. Add it to the balance if it has not already been added. Today

I am depositing another $275. I won't write any checks for stocks for about 2 weeks-yet, so that we will have enough money to cover it. I shouldn't write many checks, but I do want to keep buying stock. Keep me posted on the bank balance so I don't run you short inadvertently.

I hope to get to see Rome on 31 August. Forrest Merrill and I are going to get two more officers to rent a cab with us and make our tour that way rather than join the large crowd on the bus tour.

I'll soon send you a map of the Med with some of the cities written in. Along with the Nat'l Geographic map it should give you a good idea where places are.

Keep the children well and happy and educate them properly as I ~~know~~ you will. I'll try to write a few educational things myself for the children which you can explain to them.

The mail should go out tomorrow so I'll close now thinking of you and missing you. All my love,

Dave

Figure 100. Olympic Stamps, 1960

Figure 101. Ship Dressed for Port

XVII Olympiad
Rome, Italy
31 August 1960

Dear Mom and Dad,

Early this morning we dropped the hook about 2 miles off the shore at Fiumicino which is on the mouth of the River Tiber about 25 kilometers from Rome. Those of us who had tickets to the Olympics and for tours of Rome were quite anxious to depart on the first boat ashore at 0615. The sea was a little rough, especially near the sea wall where the entrance to the fleet landing is located. Fiumicino is only a small fishing village with little of interest.

The area around Rome is quite dry in the summer, requiring the farmers to irrigate their small plots of crops and vegetables. The farms are very small with many little plots about 12 feet to the side to facilitate the irrigation.

The main highways around Rome are beautifully landscaped with Oleanders and trees similar to the Sycamore (smooth bark). The lanes are narrow, however, since 99 out of 100 cars are the small foreign (to us) type with their little horns which they enjoy blowing. Very few intersections have traffic lights, and at the busy intersections the traffic slows down a little and filters through in all directions. The pedestrian has the right-of-way in Rome.

Rome is quite hilly and the soil is rocky clay. I was dismayed at the lack of individual homes in the outskirts of the part of town I went through. Hundreds of 6 to 8-story apartment buildings were either newly constructed or in the process. The exterior appears to be cement or plaster of various colors. The main difference in the designs was the arrangement of the balconies with each apartment. Otherwise the boxy appearance prevailed. Each balcony contained numerous potted flowers and shrubs, since landscaping and grass was non-existent. Other portions of town may have been better manicured than the section I went through on the way to and from the Olympics

The morning session of the field and track events which I attended was not at all crowded. The bus was late, causing me to miss the shot put qualifications. (I didn't have a ticket for the afternoon session, but the USA placed 1-2-3 in the shot put finals) The oval-shaped stadium could hold about 40,000, but only about 19,000 were in the seats in the morning. In the afternoon it was filled to capacity. I did see some qualification heats for men's 800 meters, women's long jump and women's 100 meter hurdle races. I was a little disappointed, but made the most of the occasion and can now say that I have been to the Olympics.

The different sports were held in various areas around the city. Boxing was in one sports palace across town, basketball in another arena in a different area, canoeing and rowing in a lake up in the mountains south of Rome, equestrian in another area, yachting at Naples, and the pentathlon in most of the sports areas. The Sixth Fleet could obtain tickets only for field and track and for boxing.

After the morning session was over I went into town for lunch with several of the officers from the ship. Five of us crowded into one of the small taxis and placed our lives in the hands of the driver. We found a small restaurant near the center of town. The luncheon was spread out on a center table so you could see what you wanted and order accordingly. I had lasogne (sp.) which, although not warm, was quite good. I also had coke, since there is no milk and the water isn't recommended. That was lunch, except for a few grapes which one of us bought. Most vegetables, fruit and dairy products are not recommended due to method of fertilizing and lack of pasteurization. The children here do look thin, probably from lack of good milk.

There appears to be no "down town" section of Rome, but small stores and hotels throughout. I plan to make a long tour of Rome, when we anchor in Naples which will be frequent between now and Christmas. Our itinerary has been changed several times, eliminating Istanbul and Beirut and adding Athens and more of Naples.

Having seen a little of Rome and a half day of the Olympics, I finally returned to the ship in the afternoon. I am now making plans for a 4-day tour to Paris, starting on 3 September when the ship anchors off Cannes. It is cool in Paris now and it has been rather wet due to cold fronts passing through there regularly for the past month. I hope the rain holds off for my visit.

I hope both of you are enjoying good health and that your numerous activities are not too tiring.

Please send me Charles' address. I would like to send Luanne and Brian some souvenirs of the Olympics.

Love,

Dave

Augusta Bay, Sicily
17 September 1960

Dearest Dorothy, Davie, Bruce and Lori,

I love you and thought about you as hurricane Donna posed a threat to you. I am sure that you and the children weathered the storm in good fashion, since you are a veteran at such things. The only one I've been involved with was the one at Argentia and it wasn't as bad as some you have weathered.

If you did sow the grass when you said you were I imagine that the torrential rain washed it down the gutter and into the lake. I hope you don't have to do it all over again.

I was afraid you might have trouble with the septic tank, but am glad it is fixed now. In the future I will have it cleaned every two years whether it needs it or not!

The termites scare me, too. You might have Bruce crawl under the house and look at the wood for evidence of termites. If there are any small holes & grooves in the wood or any other sign, then I guess you should have an inspection by a termite extermination expert, or you crawl under for an inspection, or wait until I come home. I don't want to shirk any more duties than I have to.

I'm happy to hear that the children's bank accounts are continuing to grow. Have each one write to me how much their balance is and what they would like to do with the money in several more years.

I hope you have sufficient funds in the bank to cover your needs and to pay all the bills. Yesterday I mailed a check to the bank for $300. That should help you until your check is received. I have written the following checks today (the first that I have written):

9/17 1355 WORLD WIDE PHOTO SERVICE, INC. $1.60
9/17 1356 "   "   "   "   "   " $1.60

I'll bet Davie feels pretty important going right into 2nd grade and going to class with you. If he absorbs enough he'll probably skip 5th grade when he gets that far. I'm sure Bruce will benefit greatly from such an outstanding teacher. I think you have passed through your bluffing stage (after all these years) and now speak with great authority (on most all subjects). With your comparatively "small" class you should really be able

to have an excellent class progressing
rapidly on all subjects. Keep up the
good work at your teachers' conferences
and your name will be even more
widely known. I think you have
great courage and that your convictions
merit support from all concerned. I
guess Mrs. Bosserman wanted to be
the principal of the school in which
she taught (or does she teach?). If you
want to start a school I'll be your bus
driver.

I submitted my letter stating I
had read the required publications.
All I have to do now is wait for the
results of the selection board which
met 13 Sept. They will probably take
a month due to the number involved.

About 10% of the 50% of the time
we're supposed to be in port over here
is spent in ports where we can't go
ashore on liberty. These ports are only
one or two days, but they all add up
to make the statistics read the way the
boss wants them to read.

Today I heard Adm Anderson (the
boss) speak on the Sixth's Fleet readiness
posture in the Mediterranean and also
on moral decadence. He is striving

to save the U.S. from decay such as has befallen all great nations in past history - citing the Roman Empire as an example. His theme is that the youth of today have a very low standard of morals. In order to assure our children and grandchildren the heritage of a strong and powerful nation we must all do our part to lift the moral standards higher by proper guidance and counselling of our youth in the Navy. He says this is one of the contributions we can make to our nation in addition to spreading good will in the Med countries and acting as a guardian and deterrent to war. He speaks very well and is very convincing.

I think that you are doing a magnificient job in your own right of educating the youth of today (almost tomorrow, since they are our children) in proper manners, habits and moral character. You are in a commanding position in which to mold the young minds into the proper channels of behavior and sense of responsibility. I am sure you are doing this already in your every-day association with the children at work and at play (where the character of a child

is often revealed in its true light).
At some appropriate time you might
mention this particular goal of the
Sixth Fleet in your own carefully selected
words to your class. You have such a
good command of the English language
that you can be very convincing and can
present impressive inflections in your
words and speech.

I may try to find a particularly
striking stamp or inexpensive souvenir
which I can send to each of your class. If
you have any suggestions let me know.
Also any posters for your projects or
for the library which may be useful.
I know you have probably already
studied the history of this part of the
world, but you may have some theme
which I could exploit for you.

The ship has just departed Augusta
Bay which is the only deep water port in
the Med (so I am told) which can accommodate a large portion of the Sixth Fleet
inside of its breakwaters. This port is
located just south of Catania on the
east side of Sicily if you can find it on
your map. It is just around the point on
the south end of the bay on which Catania
is situated.

From the 20th to 28th we participate in some eastern Med NATO exercises and put into Athens on the 29th. I hope I can find some marble objects in Athens which would be useful in the home and maybe as **gifts** for our *families*.

I'll send a few souvenirs to the children within the next few days. I really don't have much for them, but then as I have told you I didn't have much time for shopping. (I see that I have the duty on Thursday and Saturday in Athens which leaves only Friday for shopping. I hope I get off early enough to do some good.)

Keep up the good work on the home front. I miss you and need you.

All my love,

Dave

Replenishing in the Aegean Sea
27 September 1960

Dearest Dorothy, Lori, Bruce and Davie,

After several days of joint operations with NATO forces we are now replenishing – fuel, ammunition, dry provisions and fresh and frozen provisions. We started about 1730 and will be going until midnight, having pulled alongside 4 different supply ships to complete the job. Replenishment is one of the logistic requirements of keeping the mobile forces afloat going. It is quite an accomplishment to steam alongside another ship at 100 feet in the dark and highlining across the supplies with only red lights showing. The sea room in the Aegean is limited so speed of handling the goods is important. Usually, three destroyers will have come and gone on the other side of the ship while we replenish on the opposite side of the cargo ship.

The weather has been amazingly in our favor for these first two months in the Med, and relatively few flights have been cancelled due to bad weather. I hope we have pleasant weather for visiting Athens for four days beginning on 29th of September.

I have bought a ticket for a four-hour tour of Athens and hope to get some pictures of the Acropolis, the Olympic Stadium, the Attalus Arcade and many other sites rich in historical significance. I also hope to do some shopping for objects made of marble, for which Athens is well known.

Of course you are right about not buying a car. We don't really need one. And I was thinking in a selfish manner, again. I am thankful that you can keep a level head with logical thinking when it comes to deciding such matters. I am a truly lucky man to have you for my wife and for the mother of my children. You say you sound like Mrs. Parkerson, but you sound right to me no matter how you say it. Knowing how much we like to travel together, we should save our money for a really worthwhile venture such as a tour of Europe some summer in the future. It would be one of the greatest thrills of our lifetime.

I hope you can burn the wood from the torn-down fort, as termites may have infested it, too. I don't want an unsightly pile of wood on our terrace again.

Do you have any plans for getting the white front and trim on the house painted? You had made one or two calls about it before I departed. Or do you want to wait until I get home to have it done?

I hope your finances are adequate what with Lori's big initial expense. I have retained some of the money so I won't have to cash any checks if possible. Keep me advised.

In order to apply for Contingency Option I must have a copy of all dependents' birth certificates which means I need a copy of yours as well as the children's. Will you please send me copies as soon as possible? I must apply before 2 December in order to get the option.

Ask Dad if Davie's bonds are coming to the house. I hope the change went through all right. What names now appear on the bonds?

Notice the clipping. And right after I sent in my last requirement!

I am proud of you all and love you so much. All my love,
Dave.

Phaleron Bay off
Piraeus (port of Athens,
2 October 1960

Dearest Dorothy, Bruce, Davie and Lori,

I arrived in Athens on Thursday but was unable to visit the city until Friday afternoon. I was planning to take a tour of the surrounding area Friday morning, but had to remain on board to take care of some postal matters.

Phaleron Bay is fairly well protected except for southwest to south winds. So far the winds have been light and boating has been good. The Fleet Landing and Officers' Landing at Piraeus are in little coves and well protected. Piraeus is a fairly large commercial center with plenty of smoke which, combined with early morning high humidity, reduces visibility in the early morning hours until the sea breeze sets in.

The setting for Athens is not impressive, due mainly I think to the lack of green trees and other colors of vegetation. Only 16 inches of rain falls each year on about 20 to 30 days while the remaining days are devoted to sunshine. Therefore, you can see that it is very dry here which greatly affects the economy — not only of Athens, but of the entire country. The economy is very poor. Someone mentioned that the per capita earnings amounted to about $250-300 per year. In comparison ours is about 10 times as much — and climbing.

Athens is continuing to grow, however, as new capital is made available. Since 1951, its main attraction is the tourist trade. The most famous site in Athens, of course, is the ~~Acropolis~~

Acropolis, the elevated section of the ancient city. The Acropolis is not only the pride of Athens and of all Greece, but it is also the center of attraction for educated people throughout the world. Of the many buildings which comprised the Acropolis only a few have survived, in part, the ravages of war. The best known is the Parthenon (Temple of Virgin Athena) and it is the symbol of classical beauty. Situated high on a hill away from the noise of the city, the Acropolis is quite impressive. The Parthenon took 15 years to build – 447 to 432 B.C. Many years were required to build the entire city within a city and now most of it is in ruins with marble blocks strewn about.

Nearby is the Hill of the Muses which commands a clear view of Phaleron Bay where the ships are anchored. In another part of the city is the Olympic Stadium built some time ago but since relined with new marble. The Olympic games were revived there in 1896. The third Olympics was held in St. Louis in 1904.

Many ruins of historical significance are found throughout Greece. One such is found at Corinth where a canal has been cut through the Isthmus to Peloponnesus. The rock was cut down almost vertically 300 feet before reaching the water level.

The people are very friendly in Athens, and I have noticed that more people speak English here than in most other cities I have visited.

I bought two vases or urns which I had shipped to you. I hope they are unbroken when you receive them. Use them for dry flowers, etc. since they won't hold water too well. I wanted to get a really big one but it was too expensive. I bought a doll for Lori and some things for the boys, too – also some stamps.

I am glad to hear that all of you are doing good work in school. I'll have to study, too, to keep up with you.   All my love, Dave

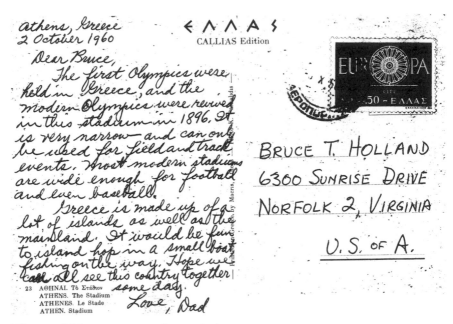

Athens, Greece
2 October 1960

Dear Bruce,
    The first Olympics were held in Greece, and the modern Olympics were revived in this stadium in 1896. It is very narrow—and can only be used for field and track events. Most modern stadiums are wide enough for football and even baseball.
    Greece is made up of a lot of islands as well as the mainland. It would be fun to island hop in a small boat fishing on the way. Hope we can all see this country together some day.
                    Love, Dad

23 AΘHNAI. Τὸ Στάδιον
ATHENS. The Stadium
ATHENES. Le Stade
ATHEN. Stadium

ΕΛΛΑΣ
CALLIAS Edition

BRUCE T. HOLLAND
6300 SUNRISE DRIVE
NORFOLK 2, VIRGINIA
        U.S. OF A.

Figure 102. To Bruce from Athens

Figure 103. Narrow Competition

Ionian Sea
4 October 1960

Dearest Dorothy, Davie, Lori and Bruce,

Whenever I visit a city new to me,
I wish more than ever that all of you
could be with me. I love you so
much and miss you terribly.

I revisited the Acropolis late Sunday
afternoon and took a few more pictures.
I also visited the Tower of Winds in
the ruins at the foot of the Acropolis.
It has eight sides, one for each point
of the compass. Near the top on each side
is a figure carved in the marble which
is supposed to illustrate in some fashion
the weather associated with the wind
from that direction. On the north side, is
supposed to be a man shivering in the
cold; on the east, a man with a basket
of fruit to depict bounty with rain I
presume. I couldn't make out any of
the other figures (and they almost looked
alike to me).

I spent my last few hours ashore
in the USO, writing letters and post cards
to the family (Mom & Dad, Mother H, Ken, Bob,
etc.). I try to send stamps of each country,
as I know they like to receive mail
from a foreign country.

I'll send Charles a cuckoo clock if

you will send me his address. I haven't been able to write them for lack of it.

I bought some more painted vases, or urns, which I will keep in my room until I arrive home. When you receive the vases I mailed to you, be sure to open them in the presence of the postal clerk at the Post Office, or the mailman at home. This is necessary to make a claim if they are damaged. Look for cracks, chips, etc.

I hesitate to send any boxes through the mail, since I have worked in the Post Office and have seen the condition some of them are in when they arrive. Wooden boxes are the only solution, and even they get broken up at times.

I think Davies' printing is outstanding and I am very proud of them.

Have Bruce and Lori practice making D's. They both half print and half write them, e.g., D. Show them — D, D, D — or something similar. I don't like to criticize, but feel I should try to help them. Lori's I's need help, too. I, I, I, should be written — I, I. Misspelled words: Bruce — thers for there's and Tigger for Tiger. Lori — mind for mine.

I am happy to know that Lori plans to save her $211 for college. The boys forgot to tell me how much they have

I'm glad to know that you have the neighborhood situation well in hand. I am sure that I _would_ help if I were there.

LCDR Kouse is the Flight Deck Officer, or will be when Bith Tilghman leaves. LTJG Banman is the Administrative Officer and, as such, works directly for the Executive Officer.

You won't have to worry about my vote this year. I haven't registered yet and, to vote, have to register at least 90 days prior to the election. Next time I'll register prior to the deadline.

Election time reminds me of football. I wish you and I could see the Navy - Southern Methodist game at Norfolk on 8 October.

If you think of anything you want, or the children want from a foreign country, let me know. Also, if you have any ideas for the entire class.

I did pick up a few pieces of marble at the Acropolis for the children's rock collection.

I miss you very much and am thinking of you constantly. I feel lost without you and am eagerly looking forward to the moment when we meet again.

All my love,
Dave

Figure 104. Urgent Mission

Figure 105. Launch of Rawinsonde to Measure Winds Aloft

Somewhere in the
Tyrrhenian Sea

9 November 1960

Dearest Dorothy, Lori, Bruce and David,

I concede — that I love you. You always win — my heart. Those are my election return sentiments. I still love you, anyway. The popular vote was very close from the information I have received. My vote is for you, since you are very close to me and popular, too. (Wish we were real close.)

Another result you will be proud of is the result of my promotion physical which I passed without any trouble. A cardiogram of the heart is now a part of physicals for all officers. I have heard nothing from the doctor concerning mine, so it must be favorable. I have been told that no advancements to Commander have been made since 1 July. That being the case, I may be promoted soon with a date of rank in September or October. That would really be a pleasant surprise. I want to have a wetting down party before I leave the ship, but I would like to have you there also. However, if it happens here in the Med, I will have a special party for you when I get home.

I thought that someone would give the good news to you before I could, since communications are quite slow here. Another name I miss on the list is Jack Sands. I thought he and Bob Born would surely be selected.

The Jenkins' house on Odessa must have been too small. Is that the reason they rented on Sunrise? The Chilton is over here in the Med somewhere. We have been receiving messages from her. Haven't received any lately, though.

I'm glad the children liked seeing Capt. Kangaroo. I wish I could have been there. Try to start places on time!!

I hope my present for David's birthday arrived in time. Let me know how long it takes to receive the air mail packages.

We didn't have any trick or treaters for Halloween on the ship, but we did have a few decorations on dinner table and candy and nuts.

As I said previously - don't pay any insurance premiums. I owe Kenneth nothing. I may take your advice about not sending anything home for Christmas. It may get lost or broken on the way.

I may try to find something small
that won't break, but I know that
you won't be disappointed if I don't
send you anything but my love.
Please don't send me anything, either.
I know Mother and Dad will make
your Christmas very enjoyable.

I will try to remember to send
the gloves as soon as possible. Be sure
to send me your glove size — I mean really.
Do you or Lori need any sweaters?

Go ahead and send presents for
the cousins from there. I have not found
anything suitable.

I'm glad that Bruce won an
election — and President, too. That is very
fine. I am truly proud of him.

I am happy for you, too, that
Kennedy won.

If I don't receive the birth
certificate by tomorrow I will go ahead
and apply for the Contingency Option and
send them in later. I don't want to
miss it.

Stay eager, alert and well, for
I love you best of all.

All my love,
Dave.

USS Independence CVA-62

Tyrrhenian Sea
30 Nov 1960

Dearest Dorothy, Lori, Bruce and Davie,

I hope the remaining 3 months pass quickly, for I miss you very much. I dream of you every night and visualize our being together again, playing and working together, and sleeping. To myself I make vows of being a better father and a better and more devoted husband, for I do want to be a success in all that I do.

Dorothy, we have been together most of our married life and have taken for granted many things. This makes the last two years seem to be rough as it is always tough to be away from those you love. I think we will benefit, though, by being able to see our shortcomings and will want to do better to improve ourselves and our family relations. I want to spend as much time as possible, in the future, with you and the children. There are so many things to teach the children and to teach each other! I know that you have made a better man of me, a better father and a better husband, but I also know that I have plenty of room for improvement. With your loving care and tenderness I shall exceed your expectations of me.

I am shocked to hear of Bruce's misadventure. I hope he is all right and is not injured. Is this the Richard whose last name I have never known, or is it a new Richard in the neighborhood. He must border on the juvenile delinquent side to break into a house as he did. I wish I could have been there to help. If you think it will do any good to use my name, go ahead

United Shikumbra (CVL) ...

and see it. I don't want Bruce to be in jeopardy again if it can be stopped. Where were you at the time?

It seems to me that Kurt needs a little discipline, too. In fact it sounds like he provoked the incident by making a false statement about the plane, by allowing somebody to use his ladder to climb our house and then not trying to stop him when Richard came barging into the house. I think the Lichtenbergs neglect to teach their children the things they ought to know.

Someone else must sense it, too, for Bob Lichtenberg was passed over for Commander. Some of our other friends were passed over also, the following for the second time: Winford Higgins (whom we knew in Argentia), Larry Herst and John Murray (Orleans), Aaron "Zak" Zakarian (Kodiak), Ken Wilzer (now at Norfolk) and Melvin Jasper (both at PG School), Arch "Ill" Gilchrist and Joe Hadley (whom Charles and I both knew at Saipan), and Brady R. "Piggy" Gay from the ship (now transferred to NAS Glynco, Ga.)

Besides Bob Lichtenberg the following have been passed over once: Ray Thompkins, Jack Sands, Bob Born, Harry Wagner and Jerome Nickerson and Charles Woolums (all ██ PG School), John Humphrey (San Diego squadron), Dick Zitter (ships), and Don Miskill (the other, or third, 1530 in year group 45-2 of which I am a member). Two of the three of us were selected.

Was Charles visiting Norfolk again? I will send the cuckoo clock this week for sure.

USS Shangri-La (CVA-38)

The last day in Palermo I went in to take a few pictures and happened to team up with the Catholic Chaplain, Cdr. Burke. He took me to see several very beautiful churches. One was decorated entirely in mosaics, colored glass with a gold background. It was magnificent, and showed the three different religions from the floor to the ceiling. From bottom to top - Moslems, Byzantine and Nordic.

Another church was Nordic and was decorated in marble and wood carvings. The pillars or columns were inlaid marble with figures of children (boys I think) throughout in relief. Both were unbelievable, and date from the 12th Century.

Father Burke also dragged me to the catacombs which I didn't want to see. They date back to the 1700's with latest about 1920. Very gruesome. A cemetery nearby was reserved for rich people who could afford to buy tombs above ground.

Also the last day we were unfortunate in that one of the ship's men fell about 150 feet while mountain climbing and was killed. With the man from a squadron who was lost overboard by a jet blast and the boy who was killed in Naples, we haven't been doing too well here in the Mediterranean. Another boy was injured in a hangar deck accident and may lose his leg. Next to destroyers, aircraft carriers are reported

United States, U.S.S. ...

to have the most dangerous working conditions and have the most accidents.

The children were given their grades in all fairness, I am sure. They did very well, but there is still room for improvement. I am proud of them and will do my best to help them even more when I get home.

How nice of David to earn a Bible. Now all of the children have Bibles. I am glad they are taking an interest in Sunday School.

Mildred's address again, in case you didn't get it, is:

1919 Pagebrook Road
Silver Spring, Maryland.

They will move to Cornell University in Ithaca, N.Y., soon.

It was nice that you could visit with Mr. Campbell. He is such a nice man and a hard worker. It was ~~nice~~ thoughtful of him to bring you the wood. I hope you use some of it. After his visit it will probably be hard for you to think of me.

But I love you anyway! I still regard you as my wife as well as the mother of my children. I'll worry about you as long as the door is not fixed, but then I worry about you when you're out of my sight, for I want nothing to happen to you. Take care of yourself and the children. All my love, Dave.

Figure 106. Dave Accepts Appointment as Commander

Figure 107. In Full Commander's Regalia

Straits near Elba
5 December 1960

Dearest Dorothy, Bruce, Davie and Lori,

I love you very much as I think of you at home tonight. Even though the ship is moving toward a different post which I have not visited, and should find exciting, I find myself wishing it were Norfolk and home.

Tomorrow we arrive at Genoa, and I have predicted rain. I hope I miss this forecast, but Genoa has a bad reputation for rain and rough seas which prohibit boating. Since we left Palermo we have had excellent weather as we have had all during our at-sea periods here in the Med. Now, however, the weather pattern is changing – for the worse I am afraid. The Captain says he is lucky, so we'll see if tomorrow is one of the times he is using his luck.

I have bought a ticket for a tour of Florence and Pisa which are 100–120 miles southeast of here. It will be a two-day trip, and I hope it will be interesting. I thought about going to Venice, but the three-day trip was longer than I can stay away in this port. And besides, I want to save some of the cities for our trip to Europe.

Yesterday we experienced our 20,000th arrested landing. It was made by LT Feltham of VA-72, flying an A4D. He is the pilot of the plane whose light I saw fall into the water one night when he bailed out ahead of the ship when we were south of Cherry Point the first part of this year. Today we had a cake cutting ceremony on the hangar deck, along with a few skits put on by the other squadrons as well as VA-72. The cake was a huge carrier, weighing 500 pounds. Other sheet cakes were cut to serve the hundreds who could attend. Rear Admiral Needham said of the occasion that our ship had come of age. The Captain said on TV tonight that now that we are almost 2 years old, like the 2-year old fillies at the races, we can now run with the best of them.

So far this fiscal year we have completed many of our competitive exercises with high scores, so we have an excellent chance of winning the "E." Although I won't be around at the end of the fiscal year on this ship, I hope they give me recognition at that time of having contributed to the overall effort. Each day, almost, some of the plank owners receive their orders. Forrest Merrill has orders to VAW-12 at Quonset Pt., flying as a radar observer in WF aircraft. We have some assigned to our ship. As you know he lost his wings a few months ago due to poor eye sight. He isn't too happy with his orders.

No doubt you have heard of plans for a Norfolk Christmas party for the children. I am not sure of the location, but it may be on one of the ships there now. I sent the children's names in to the committee, so you should receive a call from them concerning the details.

I get homesick for you whenever I hear Christmas carols. I know you will have a nice Christmas with mother and Dad there. I wish I could be there to visit with them and to learn to know them much more closely than I do now.

My duties as Postal Officer have been keeping me busy in what little spare time that I have. We now have a Second Class Post Office in which we sort and distribute the huge volume of parcel post, papers and magazines that we receive. Several days ago when we were refueling we received 145 bags of this type of mail from the oiler. There is a constant shuffle of mail to and from the ship. Every time we send off mail on a plane or by ship to Naples more mail piles up. We got rid of 20 bags of mail (all classes) today and by tomorrow night we will have 15 bags more to go. The majority consists of packages being sent home, but a lot of letters fit into one bag, also.

Of course, I enjoy receiving mail from you as it brightens the day so much. And then, I like to hear you say "I love you"; for it speeds up the time when I'll return, and I can adequately say it to you and show my appreciation for your wonderful care of the children and of yourself.

Yesterday I went to church for the second consecutive Sunday. It has given me that inner glow which comes to you when you are closer to God. Chaplain Campbell has given some excellent sermons and conducts a very good service.

Recently I graced the local TV audience with my presence by presenting a short commentary on the TIROS weather satellite. TIROS stands for Television Infra-Red Observation Satellite. I showed a drawing of what it looks like, what it does and how we get the weather data on the ship. A TIROS facsimile chart, showing areas of cloud cover came in on our receiver just a few minutes prior to TV time which made the show more interesting. It was a presentation that I thought of only an hour before show time, and after being given the go-ahead I rushed and got the material together. I thought of it from an instructor's viewpoint which is something I seem to like to do.

Rota, Spain, is being mentioned as a possible stop for autos on the way home. Nothing firm on this yet. Maybe I'll get to see Len and Jill, but we may be there only a few hours.

Have you received the gloves, yet, which I sent by Len Shea? He should be in Norfolk by now. If not give his wife a call to see if he has returned yet.

Take care of yourself and the children, for I will need you when I return home. All my love,
Dave.

**Figure 108.   Preparing   Ship's   TV
Weather Broadcast**

Naples, Italy,
15 January, 1961

Dearest Dorothy, Bruce, Lori, and Davie,

Here I am back in Naples again. Charlie Wilcox and I flew the TF here yesterday, so that it could be checked where the facilities were adequate. I guess it is a 30-hr check on the engines. We will fly back to Nice tomorrow. As you know the Independence pulled into Cannes yesterday, and we use the airport at Nice to base the TF.

I had no reason to fly down here, but offered to come when a second pilot was difficult to find. Charlie, who is attached to the staff, has his wife and children in an apartment here in Naples. The children are in school, and he says they can't afford to follow him from port to port. So he tries to get every flight possible, coming to Naples.

As usual it has been raining in Naples. While operating at sea last week, however, we enjoyed our usual good weather.

We did suffer quite a tragedy, though, when two pilots flew into the water at night on 7 January. You have probably heard about it by now. Cdr Shuff had trouble with his navigation aide and was making an approach to the carrier on the wing of LCDR Thayer. At 4 miles on final Thayer broke off and Shuff continued his approach but flew into the water about a mile astern. Thayer reported down wind, but seemed intent on his skipper and he, too, flew into the water. It was a very dark night with no horizon and with a ceiling about 1800 feet. It certainly was a blow to VA-86 and with only a short time to go.

After we leave Cannes on the 25th we have only 16 days more operations. On 28 January we pull into Barcelona, out on the 3rd, back in on the 6th out on the 8th, then operate for 10 days until we are finally relieved on the 20th. We will go into Rota on the 22nd and out the same day, arriving in Norfolk on the 2nd. I hope everything goes well until then and that we arrive on schedule.

When we return to Norfolk, I will be assigned to CDO duties, which I am unable to stand while deployed, since I am an AEDO and cannot succeed to command at sea. Cdr Powell has already assigned me the duty on the first Sunday after we return. I will want you and the children to come to dinner that night and I will see if I can arrange for a good movie.

I think Lori ought to start taking art lessons, soon. Individual intruction would probably be best if an instructor could be found. She needs to start practicing line drawings, proportions, heads and faces, bodies, arms, legs, etc., until she is quite proficient. Then she can start on structures, landscapes and other forms. By following a specified schedule I think she will be able to draw much better and learn more quickly than she is now by copying pictures and drawings.

We ought to think about musical instruments for the boys, too, and see if we can intrest them in drums or piano or something. They would all be the life of the party if they could play the piano. But the important thing is appreciation of music and self satisfaction.

I wish that tomorrow was 2 March, for I love you and miss you so much. All of you keep well and happy. I'll soon be home. All my love,

Dave.

Iberian Sea
3 February 1961

Dearest Dorothy, Lori, Bruce and Davie,

I love you and am sorry I haven't written to you for a week. One month from today and I'll be home. What a joyous thought.

One sobering thought, though. It is almost certain now that I will have the duty the first day in port. However, I hope I can be flown onto the beach the day before and then meet the ship at the pier.

I hope you have had some snow for the children to play in. They really love it, especially when it keeps them home from school. I hope you went to at least one day of the meetings. You shouldn't try to excuse your way out of everything unpleasant.

The cartoon you sent was indeed applicable. The only difference being that our picture window does not face the street side of the house.

Maybe our home in Washington, D.C., will have that arrangement.

Last night I met Ambassador Lodge at a reception at the Ritz Hotel. Many high ranking military officers were there as well as the high ranking consulate and embassy. I went up to John and introduced myself and had a pleasant chat with him. He mentioned his brother Henry and something about an election back in the States. He is very pleasant and handsome. Towers above everyone, except Adm Anderson and one other gent.

Today all of these people came on board for an air demonstration and tours. I was one of the guides. We put out to sea at 0900 and returned at 1700. Rather windy, but otherwise excellent weather. I'm a little tired this evening from the ups and downs of the tour to many of our spaces. Guess the guests are too.

I mentioned Washington earlier, so I guess I better explain after keeping you in suspense for a minute or two. I finally received a letter from Cdr Brehan at the Naval Weather Service Office. He said I was promoted right out of a job in the Norfolk area. He nominated (to BuPers who writes the orders) me for the billet of Plans and Programs in the Office of Naval Weather Service. I don't know exactly what the job entails but will find out as soon as I can.

I relieve Cdr Bob Livingston in June, but will receive orders to be detached sometime in April. It looks like we will have the school problem unless I'm detached late in April, and you stay in Norfolk for one month.

I guess we'll also have to start thinking about selling the house. I hate to move, but maybe its for the best. All my love, Dave

Figure 109. Turning into the Wind for Launch

Figure 110. Ready on the Left. . . .

Figure 111. Catapult Not Needed

Figure 112. Ready on the Right. . . .

Figure 113. Jets Climbing for Altitude

Figure 114. Hold Your Fire... Wait for Us

Figure 115. A3Ds Lead A4Ds in Flyover with F8U Streamers

EJERCICIOS AERONAVALES NORTEAMERICANOS

A bordo del portaviones «Independence», el ministro de Marina, almirante Abárzuza, con el vicealmirante Anderson, Jr., jefe de la VI Flota de los Estados Unidos en el Mediterráneo, y otros altos jefes y oficiales de ambos países presencian los ejercicios tácticos efectuados por las unidades aéreas norteamericanas

(Más información gráfica en la doble página central)

Figure 116.   Dave, Beneath Captain and Admiral's Bridges, Pointing to. . .

Figure 117. ...A Bombing Demonstration, Off Spain

Figure 118. Squadron Skipper Folds Wings

Figure 119. Dressing Ship for Return to Port

Western Med.
Enroute to Gibraltar
20 February 1961

Dearest Dorothy, Lori, Bruce and Davie,

As I head westward nearer to you my love for you swells inside of me, waiting to burst forth when we meet again. These last few days are almost unbearable, and two stops will slow our progress.

On Wednesday will be stop at Gibraltar for a few hours in order to load a few cars there, and to give the men a chance to see Gibraltar, the big rock. Then, on Thursday we stop at Rota to load some more cars and some gear belonging to VF-84, the F8U squadron who flew aboard today. They have been based ashore at Rota most of our cruise. All of them know Len and Jill Welch, especially Jill who is always so friendly. We now have all of our planes aboard and do not expect to do any more flying.

Today everyone has been busy tying down everything that can

move, getting ready for heavy weather, just in case we run into some on the big pond on the way back. It appears from the weather map that we should not have too rough a crossing.

I have no word on my new job yet, but I know it will be challenging to say the least. The children will love Washington as much as you and I will. I'm certainly going to try to get all of you in to see President Kennedy and his lovely wife. Then, too, Davie, will get to see many bones in all of the museums there. We might even take a two or three day trip to New York to see the UN and all of the museums in which Bruce will find many rocks and precious stones.

I think the Valentines were simply marvelous. You children are so thoughtful and enterprising to make such nice cards.

I have a wonderful surprise for Lori and for the boys, too,

when I return. You know I love you, too, Dorothy and have something for you.

I told Cdr Howell that I didn't want to fly in on 2 March, for personal reasons. He said he may give me the duty on Saturday in a switch with Cdr Cockrell who has to be aboard Friday during the day as off-loading coordinator. So, I don't know yet whether I will have it on Friday the 3rd, or Saturday the 4th. In any case — I think it would be nice if you would meet the ship when it comes in about 0930 on Friday the 3rd. Then, too, to have dinner with me when I have the duty. I'll still call you the night of the 1st if I can get through by radio telephone.

Our reunion is so near yet so far - about 3000 miles.

All my love,

Dave.

Gibraltar
The Rock
22 February 1961

Dearest Dorothy, Bruce, Davie and Lori;

Just a note to let you know I am now at Gibraltar and hope to get ashore late this afternoon to mail this letter from a British post office. Tomorrow we go to Rota to be relieved by the Roosevelt.

A few minutes ago the new, big luxury liner, Leonardo da Vinci, built by Italy, departed from Gibraltar. It is almost (if not) as big as the Independence.

The ship will follow Optimum Track Ship Routing as forecast by the Fleet Weather Facility at Norfolk. For our progress (if you want to know, but it will be classified) call Al Dodson at the F.W.F. I'll call you on eve of 1 March if possible.

Only a few short days now and I'll be in your arms. I love you.

All my love, Dave.

CHAPTER VIII

WASHINGTON MARVELS AND MUSEUMS

It was June of 1961 and we were in Washington, D.C. We had made our first visit three years before, when Davie was almost four, and had gotten caught in the traffic around the Tidal Basin. Davie had asked, as we slowed to a stop—bumper-to-bumper: "Why aren't we moving?" "It's rush hour," explained Dave. "Then," exclaimed Davie, "why aren't we *rushing*?" Nothing had changed except the "rush hour" was all day; Dwight D. Eisenhower was living at his farm in Gettysburg; John F. Kennedy was President and CDR David B. Holland had moved his family to the nation's Capital to reside at 7611 Arbroath Drive, Dorchester Estates, Clinton, Maryland, and our new adventure had begun.

We had bought a brick, split-level house which had just been completed in a Maryland suburb, south and slightly east from Washington, D.C., in Prince Georges County, southwest and five minutes away from Andrews Air Force Base but well out of its flight pattern. We lived in the Surrattsville School District, passing the boardinghouse of Mary E. Surratts with its historical marker explaining that John Wilkes Booth had conspired to assassinate Lincoln therein but without the knowledge or assistance of the owner, each time we drove to Surrattsville Elementary and Surrattsville Jr. High. We had chosen to live in Maryland rather than in Virginia because of Maryland's superior school system, Prince Georges County being second in the state to Montgomery County, which was first in the nation but inaccessible to Dave's work at the Naval Weather Service Headquarters, Washington Navy Yard, on the Anacostia River. Dave flew out of Anacostia Naval Air Station, south, across the river. We had reluctantly abandoned The Old Dominion, Virginia, where we had spent five happy years on Lake Smith, Bayside, which was soon annexed by Virginia Beach.

Dave had returned from the Med, his stateroom a repository for Greek marble, alabaster, pottery urns, brass scales; Italian leather handbags, sweaters, gloves, brief cases; Toledo, Spain, hammered-steel cuff links, bracelets, tie clips; French perfume; dolls from each country visited; Olympic flags; and on and on, as he had shopped for gifts for all the families. When I looked askance at the packages and boxes, mounting to the ceiling and wondered where he had slept, he laughed: "Well, I didn't bring back a foreign car—and I wanted to!"

Dave stayed with the *Independence* until May 1, 1961, having extended six months and the Skipper, CAPT Harvey P. Lanham, hated to see the *Independence*'s first Weatherman leave the ship. At Dave's farewell party, at the Norfolk Naval Base O-Club, CAPT Lanham, sitting by me, marveled about Dave's accurate predictions and his promptness: "It doesn't matter what time of night or day it is or how long he's been on duty, when he's needed, he's on the bridge—and always freshly showered, shaved and smelling like a rose!" He leaned over to me: "What aftershave does he use?" I laughed, delightedly, and told him I thought he mixed his own!

Dave had found everything in order upon his return to Lake Smith, except that the weeping willow in the back yard had been dislodged by hurricane Donna, in September of 1960, and looked "like the leaning tower of Pisa"; ailanthus trees were down all along the upper slope of the Lake but the fence, remarkably, was still intact, together with the swing and slide set. He decided to paint all the window frames inside and out, inasmuch as it had flooded in horizontally through each window, despite the children's efforts and mine throughout that long, memorable night.

When the hurricane had first hit, it poured water through the north and east windows which we prevented from damaging the walls with bath towels, sponges and a bucket brigade. After the eye passed, during which we had half-an-hour respite, we emptied the linen closet of the remaining towels and placed them in the south and west windows, knowing the hurricane would hit us from the opposite direction and, with white walls throughout our bright house, we worked frenetically hoping to prevent water streaks or, at least, crumbling plaster. Fortunately, I told Dave, the electricity stayed on and we were able to work efficiently and quickly and washed and dried towels preparatory to the next deluge.

And it rained for the next two days but no more water came in, yet we left dry towels in place throughout the house when we went off to school the following day shocked to see trees uprooted in almost every yard and apprehensive lest Donna, in the Atlantic, gain strength and veer back to scourge land again. It had been the children's first experiential hurricane—they had forgotten the Alaskan "williwaws"—and they had been too busy to see any of it which was impossible, except in the eye, because water, pounding torrentially from the blackness, obscured the violence; but they had remarked, with excited satisfaction, the prolonged roar, the brief stillness, then the incredible repetition of the howling, hammering elements of wind and water.

Dave had the white siding and blue shutters painted, the garage door, front doors—in fact, everything that was not brick, and then put the house up for sale. We experienced, for the first time as house owners, a moil of contradictory activity: the early-morning preparation before school to leave the house in a viewable condition for the realtor and prospective buyer and the packing of books and essentials we intended to transport ourselves to Washington, in the evenings. Dave left for Washington the last of May and "camped out" in our Maryland abode, coming back for us when Alan B. Shepard, Jr. was greeted at Andrews Air Force Base by President Kennedy and we were permitted to witness the ceremony in the hangar—it was pouring rain—to honor Navy flyer Shepard for his fifteen-minute, suborbital flight in U.S. *Freedom 7*—our first American in space! By June 9, we had finished school at Bayside Elementary; the packers had come; and we began our sojourn in an Air Force neighborhood, the hospitable wife of the LCOL across the street inviting us to supper upon our arrival.

As we were establishing *our* Washington domicile, Mildred, Hub, Susan, Nancy and Bill were leaving theirs in Silver Spring, Maryland, for Ithaca, New York. Hub had accepted a July 1, 1961, appointment as Director of the Plant, Soil and Nutrition Laboratory, administered by the Department of Agriculture on the Cornell University Campus.

Hub also had discovered a ten-acre site for his retirement home, complete with woods and lake for fishing, for the studying of natural decay and replenishment and facilitating cross-country skiing. And there were lakes everywhere for Mildred and Susan, who were sailors; Nancy, a champion, ribbon-winning swimmer and Bill, an accomplished baseball player, following in the steps of his father, a college star on the diamond.

Lori, Bruce and Davie were sorry to see their learned scientist-uncle leave Washington and Beltsville Experimental Lab just as they arrived but reasoned that Ithaca was not far away. We all busied ourselves in our new Maryland environment; the children had much to discover on their own.

Our new house, with a bay window in the living room and a fireplace, in which I placed white birch logs and never used, faced north with the dining room and kitchen on the same level, a carport on the west. Built into a decided slope from west to east, the lower level accommodated the family room which was paneled but was not dark, being on the south and having a sliding door and two windows overlooking the back yard and terrace. The corner fireplace, which drew beautifully, had a mantel and was bricked to the ceiling. A half bath, a long laundry-storage room—the latter on the north, completed the level with a shallow basement, leading from the family room, which became damp when it rained and we soon ceased to use. Upstairs were three bedrooms; a nicely floored attic rising up finished hardwood steps from the boys' room, with a door at the bottom; and two baths.

The entire house and yard sat upon a lot somewhat the size of our Lake Smith front yard, south of the driveway, but I doubted that we would do much gardening since

Figure 120. Lori and Patches Survey New Neighborhood

Dave would be eligible for retirement in 1963 and I intended to teach again, having a new school district to investigate. We did plant roses on the south, between the upper terrace, upon which the sliding doors in the dining room opened, down the slope to the family-room terrace; with climbing roses on the carport and a small perennial garden next to the kitchen.

Our new house was commodious and necessitated no additional furniture but had cost considerably more than our house in Virginia which we declined to rent. We finally sold it in late October, taking a loss but not considering it such after five wonderful years in our first house, built to our desires—and on a lake.

LCOL Jim Soderberg and Jan, with two teen daughters, lived on the slope across the street in our gently hilled neighborhood with winding streets, brick homes of individual but harmonious design, and a few old, red oak trees left intact. We were in the middle of the block and the slope to the east and were proud of our restraint in not buying our contractor's largest, most expensive house at the top, west end of Arbroath Drive. We were thinking of resale and had learned that the costliest house in the area did not command commensurate resale value; it went for the average of comparably sized houses; location and "extras" were luxuries for the original owner. Since our tenure would probably be just two years, we bought the average in a highly overpriced market (Washington, D.C. was the most expensive city in the world in which to live; I was surprised to note that Ann Arbor was the second). We anticipated taking a slight loss when selling but wanted none in lifestyle.

West of us lived an Air Force COL and wife, their children departed to marriage and college; east, a LCOL, a widower, with sons younger than ours who bought his new house for his forthcoming remarriage. Touching back yards, south, was another LCOL, with wife and three children, an affable, droll flyer named Charlie who used to laughingly claim: "If the Russians don't get you, we will!" He referred to his Church, with twinkling eyes. His wife and he played good bridge. Navy and Air Force flyers related famously.

The children adjusted resourcefully to their reduced yard by moving up the Arbroath slope to the vacant lot and the small "polluted lake," as Davie dubbed it. We had been ensconced three days, when we were awakened early by the sound of construction close by and wondered, because all of the houses were completed in our immediate vicinity. Dave called from our window overlooking the back yard: "Bruce, what are you doing?" "Building an ark," sailed forth the answer. "Where did you get all that wood?" I was aghast at the huge pile. "Asked." I could envision a lumber shortage in the next block and the sudden cessation of house construction; how neat those half-finished edifices must look with no loose boards or nails littering the ground. "I'll go check," Dave volunteered.

It was Saturday and I soon heard distant hammering. Dave came back from consulting with our building crew. "Bruce and Davie help Mr. Jensen clean up. They've just got odd pieces of plywood and three-inch nails. I've been invited to the launching!" "I hope so," I approved. "We're going up now to arrange for the truck. I'll see if he wants any of this back. French toast and sausage in forty-five minutes?" I nodded on the way to the coffee pot. Lori, we discovered at breakfast, had been all set to make a canoe from a log but Davie didn't think she'd fit, "so I'm doing a 'Huck Finn' raft; they might need rescuing."

Bruce, Davie and company pounded all week end on their craft and Lori, on hers—not nearly so complete because her plans had been drawn for a canoe and she was given wood the ark-makers discarded which even Huck Finn would have scoffed at—but she was artistic and undeterred. Late Monday afternoon, Dave borrowed Mr. Jensen's truck which was generously loaned to anyone in the neighborhood and the ark was loaded. Davie was skeptical and thought it would sink quite rapidly "and no one will ever find it in the polluted lake." Bruce didn't predict but I noticed he carried a long rope. Well, so shipbuilding wasn't their forte!

They turned from sailsmen to salesmen. I returned from the Commissary at Andrews Wednesday afternoon and noticed a sign in our front yard: "Live bullfrogs—10¢ a leg or 25¢ whole." And there were Bruce and Davie, seated on camp stools behind a packing barrel which held a big, white, enamel pail which had originally served to soak Davie's diapers having been purchased in Monterey, November of 1953, and subsequent home to a progression of biological treasures. I parked in the carport, lifted two sacks from the back seat and approached the business-men. "Hi, Mommy," I was greeted. "Want frog for supper?" Davie wondered. "If you think I can afford them," as I peered into the white pail at the ugly critters. "Where's George?" I puzzled. "In the wash tub—without water," Bruce hastened to assure me. Bruce and Davie looked pleased, the latter's making computations on a clipboard and Bruce's fingering a few coins in a little box. "Mrs. Soderberg is going to buy eight!" Bruce briskly announced. "As soon as Lori gets back," Davie added. "She operates—when we can find her," and pointed to another bucket on the ground and my old chopping board on a wooden stool.

I learned later that Davie and Bruce had ill-advisedly *named* their frogs and, after sitting together in the hot sun all afternoon, an attachment had developed. It was hard to part with their favorites, any part, but they decided to sell baby frogs, whole. They sold two to the Den Mother's boys across the street and down one house: Kerry and Dirk. We heard of that sale at dinner—not of frog legs, business looked too promising. Kerry, aged six, had "accidentally" impaled his baby frog with a stick and then rearranged its anatomy with a rock. The Den Mother then clamorously demanded, from across the street, another frog for poor Kerry or his two cents. Bruce and Davie refused. It was not salubrious for business, or frogs. Surreptitiously, they gave Dirk, aged nine, one of their favorites with the provision that he not tell Kerry and that he agree to keep it at our house. He was allowed visitation privileges but had to go home to eat.

After the frog market collapsed, green snakes and tadpoles were offered. That promised poorly but invigorated Patches, drinking from the fish-flavored bucket when night descended upon all in the laundry room—and she produced her six healthiest kittens. That diverted us all and I was glad school was starting—but, "Dave," I moaned, "I want to quit teaching sometime; this makes sixteen!"

At the family council, it was agreed that Patches would not be psychologically damaged to be spayed and that I could find suitable homes for the last six kittens in my Second Grade at Surrattsville Elementary. "But Patches has to stay inside—until the kittens are older. Please, don't *any-body* let her out of the house!" I pleaded, unable to restrain my laughter which Bruce immediately took advantage of. "I think Patches should get to keep one kitten. Couldn't she have just one?" And we compromised on one.

Since Patches would be house-confined, we assigned duties and agreed to leave closet doors slightly open for a week so that Mama Cat could hide her family in a different place each night. A preference for Dave's shoes had been exhibited in the past and he was directed to leave shoetrees out of his oldest pairs and Davie promised not to put his rock collection or marbles in his.

By the time school opened in late August, the kittens—five of them—would be ready for distribution. What Second Grader would not be thrilled, with parents' written permission, to own an adorable calico kitten of distinguished Old Dominion parentage!

In early July, as I was reading *Time* in the family room, I heard scratching in the laundry room which sounded like a cat in a bucket. It was. Patches, having early reached the stage of ennui with her kittens, was in with George—now restored to the white pail. I alerted Lori to see about George, her Christmas chameleon, purchased by her two brothers who had been accompanied by Daddy Frank and Mommy Tom to the Norfolk pet shop, their having driven from Kansas City to be with a lonely family at holiday-time.

Bruce and Davie unceasingly manifested love for all animal life, especially that which Lori would care for—hers seemed to last longer. George was just an ordinary chameleon, his spectrum being limited to brown and green, but he was much loved. He spent most of his day beneath a croton leaf but occasionally ventured forth to lick a sliver of apple or crawl in and out of the Chinese pagoda from Davie's turtle bowl, no longer needed. His movements were always lethargic—until Patches leapt in. She completely covered George and his entire habitat, including live spiders, pine twigs, swimming pools and playground of vermiculite. Lori quickly routed Patches and chided her while the boys demurred. They maintained that Patches and George were friends and while they were on the subject, Davie challenged: "I don't think George is really a George!"

Patches had democratically accepted all the children's wildlife: the fish, frogs, tadpoles, turtles, guinea pigs, snakes, birds—without the least vestige of jealousy. She became particularly attached to the baby rabbit Bruce found in the Gettysburg National Military Park just as we were leaving after an all-day study of the battle sites; monuments and markers—outnumbering all other U.S. shrines; bust of Lincoln in the cemetery, "the only memorial to a speech in the world"; and the Gettysburg Cyclorama, an enormous graphic depiction of the three-day battle, July 1-3, 1863, and General Robert E. Lee's retreat, July 4. We had studied our *World Book, National Geographics, Encyclopædia Britannica,* and *We Were There* and so fortified, drove to Gettysburg on July 1, 1961, not waiting for the One Hundred Year Celebration being planned for 1963, July 1 through July 4, since we disliked crowds of that magnitude and might not, then, even be residing in Washington. We were anxious to see the memorial in the National Cemetery to the Gettysburg Address because the famous address had not been made in Gettysburg, the cemetery being located in the Cumberland Township which bordered the Borough of Gettysburg. (Lincoln had come by train from Washington to the old Western Maryland Railway Depot on Carlisle Street in the little town of Gettysburg, Pennsylvania, to dedicate the Soldiers' National Cemetery, November 18, 1863. He had ridden a horse in the procession from the Wills House to the Cemetery a mile away in the Cumberland Township, the following day, November 19, 1863, when he delivered his immemorial words. The Soldiers' National Monument, a gray granite shaft sixty feet high, was erected on the spot where President Lincoln spoke, his words inscribed on a tablet in front of the monument, both surrounded by Union grave markers. [No Confederate dead lay in the Soldiers' National Cemetery—they were removed after the war to Southern cemeteries].)

After a long, wearying day of battlefields, fortifications, cannons and markers, each one important, we started home with Bruce's trophy, Dave's taking a different road from the one we had traversed very early in the morning. "Why are we going this way?" wondered Davie, as he surveyed the heavily forested hills and boulder-strewn vales. By that time, we had bumped onto a dirt road that the Pilgrims might have plodded. "I thought we'd like to have new scenery," explained Dave, pleased with his discovery. "It doesn't look very new to me," scoffed Dave's youngest momus who handed me the box of rabbit from the lap of Bruce who was cozily pillowed on Lori's shoulder, yawned in commentary on the present scenery and lay down across his brother's knees.

"Do cats eat rabbits?" I anticipated. "Probably," laughed Dave but precluded temptation with the recommendation that the baby rabbit be put in a deep plastic storage box and kept in the family-room bathroom with the door closed at all times when Patches was at large. And that worked well for three days while the rabbit grew surprisingly strong and active, outleaping its confines and investigating everything, to the children's amusement and delight. And Patches sniffed, pushed and circled it and seemed friendly, almost protective. Alas, its natural propensity was its undoing: on the fourth night, it leapt from its cozy bed into the commode, someone's having left the lid up and then carefully closing the bathroom door. Poor Patches! The next specimen she did not feel *any* affection for.

Davie and Bruce found a baby bat in the woods beyond the polluted lake. They kept it overnight in a box in the basement. There had been some difficulty in getting it into the house. It was such a minute rodent, one would not have thought it could fly with such unexpected skill—and suddenness. The body was no bigger than a thumb but it suddenly produced a wing span of six inches and flew in swift, teasing, low circles around the family room. The children were gleeful but I was skeptical and Dave was in Paris. We got out all of our mammal books, bird books, encyclopedias, Scout manuals and Department of Agriculture Yearbooks. From perusal of those, it seemed safe to keep a baby bat as long as it was not handled in such a way that the children would be bitten—and they were practiced animal-handlers. I called several vets who thought it was alright to keep a baby bat. The children insisted they should keep it to study because it was the only *flying* mammal, a *Chiroptera*, having wings modified from forelimbs and hands, with strange nocturnal habits which they were eager to stay up all night to record. But, despite the baby animal's eerie, anatomical appeal, I was still perturbed about hazards for the children. I called the Smithsonian Natural History Museum and asked to speak to an ornithologist. The learned gentleman was adamant and advised us to return the bat to the woods at *once*. "They are frequent carriers of rabies; don't take a chance!"

When Dave got home from his NATO Meteorological Subcommittee meeting, he donned his long, heavy leather Arctic flight gloves (to please me), gently grasped the baby bat, put it back in its box, taping the lid, accompanied the boys to the woods to return it to its natural habitat, commended their interest in wildlife but urged them to bring home no more bats. "Don't even pick one up again—it's too risky."

At dinner, Dave attempted to disabuse his children of the conviction that their love for, and enthusiastic study of, all wildlife was an antidote, a shield against harm. And then we made plans for Fourth of July at the Washington Monument where the finale was to be President Kennedy's portrait created by fireworks followed by a replica of the American Flag. "We'll go early tomorrow—about five," Dave offered, "maybe we can take a picnic supper and beach chairs; there'll be a mob and we'll have far to walk." "Let's just take beach towels or blankets," suggested Lori. "I'll carry the thermos jug," Bruce offered. "May we have fried chicken?" Davie requested. I smiled in approval. "Do you think they can take sparklers?" I asked Dave. "Yes, but I doubt if they'll use them; the display starts at dark." "Let's save them," Bruce decided.

And so the bat, which Patches had the good sense to run from, was forgotten and attention was turned to fireworks—from which I thought everyone should run but Dave had bought the children, with their eager assistance, of course, a few packages of lady fingers, snakes, cherry bombs, slightly larger firecrackers, sparklers and a few bottle rockets, saying they needed to learn; they had been allowed only sparklers in Virginia.

We spent most week ends at the Smithsonian. I had read an article which stated that if one minute was spent viewing each item on display, it would necessitate seventy-five years, without time to eat or sleep, so I reasoned we should squander no minutes since we had but two years. The Smithsonian Institution had been founded by a British scientist who had never been in America. James Smithson died in Genoa, Italy, in 1829, during Andrew Jackson's administration. It was discovered six years later that Smithson had left his fortune, *not* to the Royal Society of London, which was his original intention. When that esteemed body failed to publish one of his papers, he changed his will and left his entire estate "to the United States of America to found at Washington, under the name of the Smithsonian Institution, an establishment for the increase and the diffusion of knowledge among men." ("The Smithsonian, Magnet on the Mall," *National Geographic,* June 1960, p. 800.)

President Jackson accepted the original bequest of $508,318.46. The many-towered and turreted red stone, Norman structure was conceived by James Renwick who had designed St. Patrick's Cathedral in New York City. Congress formally established the Smithsonian Institution in 1846, the building was completed in the 1850s and James Smithson's remains were buried inside the main entrance in 1904. The old red building housed administrative offices and part of the 800,000 volume Smithsonian Library—the most complete scientific library in America.

Most of the exhibits were in the Old National Museum, the Arts and Industries Building, built in 1881 next to the Smithsonian, which preserved all of the Government's scientific, historical, industrial and artistic objects. Hung from the lofty ceiling was COL Charles A. Lindbergh's "Spirit of St. Louis." The first nonstop flight from New York to Paris was accomplished May 20 and 21, 1927. We always stopped to look up and admire that "Missouri plane," every time we entered the building. It was probably the country's best-remembered vehicle. Near by was the first plane purchased from the Wright Brothers by the Government in 1908 and in front of Lindbergh's plane was the most fascinating of all: "The Original Wright Brothers' Aeroplane, 1903," complete with Orville Wright in a black suit, white shirt, tie and cuff links, on his stomach, at the controls of the "Flyer," flown in that epochal first flight at Kitty Hawk, North Carolina. It was our favorite exhibit from pre-*Independence* days.

It was amazing what could be discovered at the Smithsonian which was an umbrella for: Old National Museum, New National Museum, Museum of Natural History (which was being expanded with two new wings), Museum Of History and Technology (to be completed in 1962), National Air Museum (almost complete, the old one still in use), National Gallery of Art, Freer Gallery of Art, National Collection of Fine Arts, National Zoological Park, Bureau of American Ethnology, Astrophysical Observatory, Canal Zone Biological Area and the International Exchange Service. If we wanted to see, and we did, a horned dinosaur, an antique car, a shrunken head, a meteorite, or the original nugget that started the gold rush to California in 1849, it was there.

We could study all manner of transportation from oxcarts, shays, sleighs, fire engines and "John Bull," the oldest complete locomotive in North America, 1831, to the first automobile and Alan Shepard's *Freedom 7* capsule, flown May 5, 1961, and just placed on display outside the National Air Museum. There were scale models of ships; of special interest to us: models of the World War II carrier U.S.S. *Yorktown* and the U.S.S. *Pennsylvania* on which Eugene Ely made the first airplane landing on a ship, in 1911.

We saw inaugural gowns of all the First Ladies from Martha Washington to Jacqueline Kennedy and the Hope Diamond, the world's largest blue diamond weighing 44½ carats which, legend declared, had brought tragedy to all its owners since it was smuggled out of India in the

1640s. We spent much time in the geology, paleontology and natural history exhibits. We also visited, but once only, a Medical Museum which displayed Abel, our first space dog; preserved human parts, pathologically rare, in especial an enormous leg, encased in a huge column of liquid which slightly floated the hair and lightened the toenails of an elephantiasis victim.

Perhaps the most provocative display was the Star-Spangled Banner which had flown over Fort McHenry in Baltimore during the War of 1812. It was larger than a house and hung with the field of blue at the upper left touching the ceiling with its red and white stripes almost touching the floor, with six of its fifteen stripes folded under because of the limitations of the display case. Originally forty-two feet long by twenty-nine feet in width, it contained about four hundred yards of bunting. It was made by Mary Pickersgill whose mother, Rebecca Young, had made the first flag of the Revolution, under Washington's direction. Widow Pickersgill's most serious problem was space, according to Neil H. Swanson's *The Perilous Fight*:

> Four hundred yards of stout goods would be bulky and heavy to carry, but that could be managed. . . . Thirty-six feet (Mrs. Pickersgill's rough estimate of the length) . . . there wasn't a room in the house where even the short upper stripes of a flag like that could be laid out for basting. A warehouse, perhaps . . . there might be one with an empty attic . . . but the warehouses were gorged with goods that couldn't be shipped. Or a sail loft . . . inches deep in dust, as likely as not . . . and a sail loft right under the roof, in this awful heat . . . one of the wharf sheds . . . the mud smelled bad when the tide was out . . . and the rats. . . . Mary Pickersgill found her work room in Clagett's brewery just up the street, across from Charles Carroll's fine house. The brewery's malthouse was ample and cool; they gave her permission to use it. The cutting, however, was done in the "second front room" at home.
>
> Day after day and night after night through the hot midsummer weather, the Widow Pickersgill knelt on the brewery floor, basting and stitching the endless rolls, crawling over the blue field—itself as big as a carpet—to lay the fifteen great stars in their rows of three. At night, while the candles did what they could to keep the darkness pushed into the corners, it was like crawling over the sky itself by the light of a clouded moon. "I remember," (daughter Caroline) "seeing my mother down on her knees placing the stars in position and sewing them fast." It was like having a hand in creation.

Night after night it was twelve o'clock when mother and daughter rolled up the unfinished flag and walked down the silent street past the Carroll house to their own. They were tired. It was painstaking, wearisome business: every seam must be as strong as the seams of a frigate's mainsail to bear the sheer weight of the cloth. Tomorrow would be another seam. They had a "given time" in which to finish their work, but they did not know how much time Baltimore had been given. Tomorrow . . . day after tomorrow . . . next week . . . or the next there might be no malthouse at Clagett's, no Carroll mansion, no home. The Clagetts themselves might be dead, the neighbor and the kinsmen who had ordered the flag might be dead. (One Clagett would be killed at McHenry, under the flag. Another would go down, wounded, in Godly Wood. Joshua Barney, relative, would be wounded at Bladensburg, Maryland. It was he, a Commodore, and another relative of the Widow, General John Stricker and neighbor Will McDonald who had ordered the enormous flag.) Mary Pickersgill and her daughter Caroline would never know that their aching fingers had given a nation its anthem. (pp. 266-268.)

Congress did not pass the bill declaring *The Star-Spangled Banner* the national anthem until March 3, 1931.

We were all intrigued with Fort McHenry on the tip of Whetstone Point, two miles southeast of Baltimore on the Patapsco River. It was anachronistic, rather like a medieval walled city which functioned solely for survival, its artillery concentrated for permanent defense. But yet it was more than a fort; it boasted a village green with four long, story-and-a-half red brick houses and a stable, with a gambrel roof, also of brick just inside the walls which formed a pentagon. As Dave drove toward Fort McHenry from higher ground we could see the large five-pointed star with the corners resembling blunt arrowheads and when we walked up to the star-fort, we were surprised to discover that the walls were not solid masonry but only banks of earth faced, both front and back, with brick. It was easy to envision Mary Pickersgill's gigantic flag's flying (I doubted that it could really "stream") over the "ramparts" on September 13 and 14, 1814, during the British bombardment. And the American flag, though much smaller, still flew over Fort McHenry—twenty-four hours a day, one of the few places in the country so privileged: the Capitol; Flag House Square and Francis Scott Key's grave, both in Baltimore; the Marine Corps Memorial (Iwo Jima Statue), Arlington, Virginia.

Francis Scott Key, a young Washington lawyer, district attorney and amateur poet, had gone out to the British ships, under a flag of truce, seeking the release of his friend Dr. Beanes who had been summarily captured and taken aboard ship after having graciously provided shelter for British officers. Key was placed with his friend aboard a cartel ship and made notes during the bombardment on the back of an envelope. Nota bene: "bomb-bursting" is a noun, *not* bombs' bursting, a verb and a gerund, as it is invariably sung—incorrectly!

When the new, tremendous Museum of History and Technology was opened in 1962, the Star-Spangled Banner was unfurled from the ceiling in its full, unfolded glory, the whilom forty-two-foot length, at its 1814 creation, a bit shortened by the attrition of age and perhaps, humans. An inexplicable appliqued red *V* on the first full-length white stripe from the field of blue—which had been turned under in the old museum's display—was visible for the first time. I speculated it was " *V* for Victory" but there had been no historical evidence for its meaning. The wonderful old flag hung behind the viewing balcony for "Old Glory" and the Foucault Pendulum which enabled us to see the earth turn.

Seeming to stand still, we were convinced via the Pendulum, that we revolved with our planet. Each day, the pointer, which also could be observed on the floor, was set along the path being swung by the 240-pound bob, hung from the ceiling on a 73-foot cable. As time passed, the bob's path appeared to turn clockwise. In reality, the pointer was being moved counterclockwise by the earth's rotation, under the Foucault Pendulum's arc. (Pictured in "Washington: The City Freedom Built," *National Geographic*, December 1964, p. 742.) It was an excellent environment for the timely display of our grand American flag.

Washington, D.C., abounded in American flags from the fifty which surrounded the base of the Washington Monument, to the White House and the President's limousine where a smaller American flag fluttered on the right front, the President's flag of navy blue with the eagle symbol—on the left, to the perpetual-flying American flag over the nation's Capitol. (President Harry S. Truman had not changed the flag but he had the nation's symbol: until his administration, the bald eagle had looked to its left, to the thunderbolts clutched in its left talons, signifying warring might. He changed the eagle's steadfast gaze to the right, to the clutched green olive branch, a signification of peace.)

The children wanted an American flag—we had many of sundry sizes—which would always be significant, so we purchased one from the

O say can you see ~~through~~ by the dawn's early light,
What so proudly we hail'd at the twilight's last gleaming,
Whose broad stripes & bright stars through the perilous fight
O'er the ramparts we watch'd, were so gallantly streaming?
    And the rocket's red glare, the bomb bursting in air
    Gave proof through the night that our flag was still there,
O say does that star-spangled banner yet wave
O'er the land of the free & the home of the brave?

On the shore dimly seen through the mists of the deep,
Where the foe's haughty host in dread silence reposes,
What is that which the breeze, o'er the towering steep,
As it fitfully blows, half conceals, half discloses?
    Now it catches the gleam of the morning's first beam,
    In full glory reflected now shines in the stream,
'Tis the star-spangled banner — O long may it wave
O'er the land of the free & the home of the brave!

And where is that band who so vauntingly swore,
That the havoc of war & the battle's confusion
A home & a Country should leave us no more?
~~Their blood~~
    Their blood has wash'd out their foul footstep's pollution,
No refuge could save the hireling & slave
From the terror of flight or the gloom of the grave,
And the star-spangled banner in triumph doth wave
O'er the land of the free & the home of the brave,

O thus be it ever when freemen shall stand
Between their lov'd home & the war's desolation!
Blest with vict'ry & peace may the heav'n rescued land
Praise the power that hath made & preserv'd us a nation!
    Then conquer we must, when our cause it is just,
    And this be our motto — "In God is our trust,"
And the Star-spangled banner in triumph shall wave
O'er the land of the free & the home of the brave. —

Stationery Store of the Capitol and took it to the office of Stuart Symington, Democratic Senator of Missouri, our permanent address being Kansas City, Missouri, who had it flown over the Capitol of the United States of America and mailed it to Dad's, our address throughout Dave's Navy stint. When we flew the American flag on every sanctioned occasion, the children—with their father's instructive observation—ran it up briskly, lowered it slowly and reverently, and folded it with precise, military nicety, the field of blue on top with three stars centered and three stars on the tucked-in flap, in a compact triangle. Dad mailed our three-by-five "Capitol flag," as the children called it, back to Washington and we continued to avail ourselves of the privileges of being Missouri voters.

We frequented the Capitol building; savored the Senate Restaurant's famous bean soup and hot apple pie; requested visitors' passes for the Senate gallery from Stuart Symington when the Eighty-seventh Congress had a rare Saturday session and during the summer, and Congressman William J. Randall of

Figure 121. Visitor's Pass to Senate

Figure 122. Visitor's Pass to House

Missouri for House of Representative passes and tours of the White House, both before and after Jacqueline Kennedy's redecoration of the historic public rooms.

We felt the excitement of living in Washington during the vitality of John F. Kennedy's administration; the old town was no longer staid. His energy was electrifying and his courageous innovativeness, immediately apparent. He inspired his country's youth with his Peace Corps, the world of science with his Space Program, the intellectual world with his brilliance and humor, the political world with youthful daring and unexpected wisdom and strength. Mother wrote of their response in a letter, January 21, 1961.

Since Mother and Dad continued to be devotees of J.F.K., I wrote enthusiastically, with much frequency, my observations and sent articles and editorials from the *Washington Post*, a thorough, ofttimes, Kennedy-honorific newspaper. I even saved the 1960-61 Washington, D.C., phone book which listed Senator John F. Kennedy at his Georgetown, Virginia, address; the new '61 phone books coming out in July without any listing.

Later in the year, in November, we attended the Army-Navy football classic in Philadelphia which President Kennedy attended, sitting with that wonderful mane of hair, uncovered—(to satisfy hat manufacturers, he often carried a hat but never wore it); first, on the Navy side of the field, then crossed it at the half (with a man suddenly leaping from the stands to run after him whom the FBI immediately tackled; the *Post*, on a back page, announcing him to be an excited admirer), to sit on the Army side. The Navy won the game, much to the President's "impartial" delight, and a Naval Midshipman gave Davie the little American flag all the "Middies" had twirled, with a prolonged hum, whenever their classmates scored. Both the Navy and Army had stood and cheered with fervent vigor throughout the game but the children had been more excited by the rambunctious Navy goat with its gold horns, tended by the low man in the class; the Army mule and the Navy cannon which was fired after each touchdown.

In late February 1962, we sat on a wall of the Senate Office Building on the corner of Constitution Avenue, which faced the turn into the East Portico of the Capitol, when President and Mrs. Kennedy drove in an open limousine with John H. Glenn, Jr. and his wife Annie, the long parade's honoring Glenn's February 20, 1962, four-hour-and-fifty-six-minute flight in U.S. *Friendship 7*—the first U.S. manned orbital mission, which completed three orbits of the earth.

Saturday, snow

Dearest Family,

Well, midst all the snow, cold
and confusion we got a wonderful
new President inaugurated and it
was all very wonderful and is.
I was so proud of the Kennedys
through out and to hope you got
to see some of the festivities —
The Parade was interesting and
flags, color of bands etc beautiful
in color. Dad watched all of it
and was tearful in explaining
about how good Mr. Kennedy's
speech was. Parts of which I heard
and all I read and we will be
seeing quoted many times. The
Star editorial begins (will part of
it today. The Star has come out
so boldly in support of so much
Kennedy stands for. Everything
we they said of their

speech. The note of courage, hope, of confidence was the dominant theme, also in sort of "idealism" could not be accomplished in 100 days, in 1000 days, perhaps not in a life time. Then the star added "It was a short dynamic call for collective action on all world fronts, but the most distinctive feature of J.M. Kennedy's address was the fact that it breathed the spirit of responsible, reverent - yet supremely confident - youth." As one of 3 year old chief speaker said," I do not shrink from this responsibility. I welcome it." Of course they began the Editorial with his quotes "Let the word go forth from this time & place to friend and foe alike, that the torch has been passed to a new generation of Americans born in this century best of my war etc --- and the glow from the can truly light the world." It was thrilling and will go down in

> history as one of the greatest speech
> Somewhere I read that he wrote
> all of his speech and is saving
> the penciled draft of it with the
> written corrections for the archives—
> That's what makes it so thrilling
> he feels and supports all the final
> decision he has. We missed for you
> yesterday afternoon. I went to

All schools were dismissed and government offices closed for a Washington parade in which the President participated; school children, happily waving flags, adults, too, on both sides of Pennsylvania Avenue from Fifteenth Street to the bottom of the Capitol and up the long hill of Constitution Avenue. It was a very exuberant and joyous parade with the other six Astronauts and wives following President Kennedy and John Glenn, all of them looking very young, very boyish and very heroic—all *eight* of them.

Mother had reminded me to tell Bruce and Davie "President Kennedy is the first Boy Scout President, having only had Scouting this century"—and, indeed, all Boy Scouts found an exemplar that day in their young, athletic, Boy Scout, Navy-hero President and his seven courageous Astronauts' providing a prototype of brave daring and skill, which had inspired the entire country. It was an exhilarating, unforgettable time, viewing those eight at the height of their splendid manhood, superbly trained, eagerly confident, presaging new perimeters for the entire human experience.

John F. Kennedy's *Profiles In Courage* had been published in 1955 and had received the Pulitzer Prize for biography in 1957. I had purchased the book at Ship's Service, Argentia, Newfoundland, Naval Base—the Navy intensely proud of its World War II hero, serving his Government still in his capacity of Senator from Massachusetts. I had read it with avidity and was delighted with the announcement that our Thirty-Fifth

President had since abridged his *Profiles In Courage* for a "Young Readers Edition," which was available for the children shortly after we moved to Washington. There were deletions, only to insure narrative attention, with ten dramatic, "action-filled" drawings; a special letter from J.F.K. to his young readers; the 1961 edition, as well as the 1955 and 1956, dedicated: "To My Wife." There was a Proem, although it was not so labeled:

> "He well knows what snares are spread about his path, from personal animosity . . . and possibly from popular delusion. But he has put to hazard his ease, his security, his interest, his power, even his . . . popularity . . . He is traduced and abused for his supposed motives. He will remember that obloquy is a necessary ingredient in the composition of all true glory: he will remember . . . that calumny and abuse are essential parts of triumph . . . He may live long, he may do much. But here is the summit. He never can exceed what he does this day."

> Edmund Burke's eulogy of Charles James Fox for his attack upon the tyranny of the East India Company—House of Commons, December 1, 1783.

And from President Kennedy's letter in the Preface:

> Since first reading—long before I entered the Senate—an account of John Quincy Adams and his struggle with the Federalist party, I have been interested in the problems of political courage in the face of constituent pressures, and the light shed on those problems by the lives of past statesmen. A long period of hospitalization and convalescence following a spinal operation in October, 1954, gave me my first opportunity to do the reading and research necessary for this project.

From "Courage And Politics," also part of the Preface:

> This is a book about that most admirable of human virtues—courage. "Grace under pressure," Ernest Hemingway defined it. And these are the stories of the pressures experienced by eight United States Senators and the grace with which they endured them—the risks to their careers, the unpopularity of their courses, the defamation of their characters, and sometimes, but sadly only sometimes, the vindication of their reputations and their principles.

> A nation which has forgotten the quality of courage which in the past has been brought to public life is not as likely to insist upon or

reward that quality in its chosen leaders today—and in fact we have forgotten. . . .

From the last chapter, "The Meaning of Courage":

Finally, this book is not intended to disparage democratic government and popular rule. The examples of constituent passions unfairly condemning a man of principle are not unanswerable arguments against permitting the widest participation in the electoral process. The stories of men who accomplished good in the face of cruel calumnies from the public are not final proof that we should at all times ignore the feelings of the voters on national issues. For, as Winston Churchill has said, "Democracy is the worst form of government—except all those other forms that have been tried from time to time. . . ." For, in a democracy every citizen, regardless of his interest in politics, "holds office"; every one of us is in a position of responsibility; and, in the final analysis, the kind of government we get depends upon how we fulfill those responsibilities. We, the people, are the boss, and we will get the kind of political leadership, be it good or bad, that we demand and deserve.

These problems do not even concern politics alone—for the same basic choice of courage or compliance continually faces us all, whether we fear the anger of constituents, friends, a board of directors or our union, whenever we stand against the flow of opinion on strongly contested issues. For without belittling the courage with which men have died, we should not forget those acts of courage with which men—such as the subjects of this book—have *lived*. The courage of life is often a less dramatic spectacle than the courage of a final moment; but it is no less a magnificent mixture of triumph and tragedy. A man does what he must—in spite of personal consequences, in spite of obstacles and dangers and pressures—and that is the basis of all human morality.

To be courageous, these stories make clear, requires no exceptional qualifications, no magic formula, no special combination of time, place and circumstance. It is an opportunity that sooner or later is presented to us all. Politics merely furnishes one arena which imposes special tests of courage. In whatever arena of life one may meet the challenge of courage, whatever may be the sacrifices he faces if he follows his conscience—the loss of his friends, his fortune, his contentment, even the esteem of his fellow men—each man must decide for himself the course he will follow. The stories of past courage can define that ingredient—they can teach, they can offer hope, they can provide inspiration.

But they cannot supply courage itself. For this each man must look into his own soul.

My cousin Madge came in August; she was living and working in Florida. Interested in seeing D.C. and the Naval installations, Madge was more knowledgeable by far than I about military life, having served in France in World War II as LT Madge Lacy, Army Nurse. The children loved Madge's soft voice and soothing ways and I listened to her discussion of President Kennedy's back problems and his medication, with amazement. Madge could detect which medication had been prescribed by looking at the puffiness, or lack of it, of J.F.K.'s face. I learned to observe the President's face to understand how much pain his back caused him—when he appeared on television or when we saw him in a parade. He suffered more than the country realized.

The next time we saw Madge was in a picture with adorable baby Roxanna. It was years before Dave and I visited Madge, Foy, Roxanna and Timothy in Tampa.

Beth and Tom Keane and handsome family were hosts to us early in our Washington stay when we enjoyed a warm evening in their enclosed, Colonial garden court—and reminisced.

Figure 123. Roxanna and Madge Lacy Guilford

In the early fall of 1961, Robert J. Donovan published his fascinating *PT 109*, "John F. Kennedy in World War II," with an introductory letter from President Kennedy. It told one of the war's most amazing, heroic adventures involving the skipper of a PT boat, "a skinny, handsome, boyish lieutenant (jg) from Boston named John Fitzgerald Kennedy," his courage, his prodigious swimming feat and a coconut.

Dave's first memory connected with President Kennedy recalled Dave's last month aboard the *Independence*, April of 1961, when the ship was off the coast of Jacksonville, Florida, awaiting President Kennedy's visit aboard his, as Commander in Chief, largest and newest aircraft carrier, "The Latest and the Greatest." The plan was for the President to fly in Air Force I to Mayport Naval Air Station and take a helicopter to the *Independence* for an overnight visit. At the last minute, the President's arrangements were canceled and the Ship was ordered immediately to sail to the Caribbean Sea and stand by, south of Cuba. The calamitous Bay of Pigs Exercise had interrupted the President's felicitous plans to visit his Navy.

As soon as the *Independence* was in place, a force of anti-Castro Cubans, trained by the CIA, staged an invasion of the island, hostilely held by the dictator Fidel Castro. Immediately upon a beachhead's being established by the loyal Cubans, the *Independence* could have been legally requested to provide protective air cover and assistance to a beleaguered country. But the beachhead was never established and the anti-Castro force was decimated, due, Dave speculated many years later, to a lack of secrecy.

The *Independence*'s Photo-Recon planes overhead witnessed the disaster and the Fighter-Bombers sat loaded, on the Carrier's flight deck, ready for launching but unable to assist. Although the crew of the *Independence* received medals for the aborted mission, it was a sad, dispiriting loss of life and opportunity—for the Ship, the loyal Cubans, the country and the President. (Ironically, another "near-miss" of combat has just occurred at the writing of this phase of the chronicle, January 21, 1991—thirty years to the day of President Kennedy's Inauguration as our country's Thirty-Fifth President on January 21, 1961. The U.S.S. *Independence* was the first American ship to arrive in the Persian Gulf when Iraq invaded Kuwait in August of 1990. It was ordered by President George Bush to proceed immediately from its patrol duty in the Indian Ocean to the Persian Gulf for the protection of Saudi Arabia which had requested American assistance, fearing imminent invasion. The *Independence* remained in the Persian Gulf in armed readiness until late December 1990, when it was relieved by the U.S.S. *Saratoga* and returned to San Diego. President Bush ordered missiles fired and planes launched from the *Saratoga* in a massive air attack on Saddam Hussein and militant Iraq, January 16, 1991.)

A more pleasurable memory for Dave concerned August of 1962, when a member of the production crew for the movie version of *PT 109* was directed to contact Dave at the Naval Weather Service Headquarters, Washington, for the prediction of weather in August, in the Bahamas, where Cliff Robertson, as J.F.K., and company were filming the acclaimed adventure of the war-hero President. Dave was able to advise positively, and accurately, that tropical storms and hurricanes would develop farther south and go inland from the Gulf of Mexico—west of the Florida peninsula. He laughed about his contribution and said he should be listed as "Weather Consultant" in the credits. (We forgot to look when we saw the exciting movie, concerned, instead, about hustling the children through the mob at the Washington opening.) Dave and I were pleased with results of Bahamian weather and Cliff Robertson's performance, both as actor and swimmer; the children enjoyed the fierce battle scenes and the coconut.

August was a busy, happy, investigatory month when I took the children to swim and take lessons at the O-Club at Andrews but more often to the small, never-crowded O-Pool at the Navy Yard where Dave joined us after work. Early evenings found us in paddle boats on the Tidal Basin. Bruce pumped with me while Dave, Lori and Davie followed—or usually overtook—us, Davie's pointing when we passed the Jefferson Memorial:"There's 'Old Baldy,'" he would laugh, remembering his four-year-old designation.

We loved the concerts provided nightly by the United States Army, Navy or Marine Corps (the oldest military band) or the Air Force; the children always eager to go to the Watergate on the Potomac in a rented rowboat. Sometimes we sat on the embankment steps above the river or on the grass and listened to the water-borne musicians play from the Watergate barge moored down the slope from the Lincoln Memorial. There was a certain soothing and romantic resonance to music, be it classical, popular or martial, when it was played over water but we enjoyed summer concerts, as well, sitting on the steps of the Capitol's East Portico with one of the marvelous military bands, resplendent in dress uniform, down below.

From autumn through winter, we occasionally went to the National Gallery of Art for a Sunday afternoon of uplifting strolling, a leisurely supper, and an evening's entertainment by orchestra in the East Garden Court amid the fishtail palms, figs, ferns and azaleas, with an elegant fountain's plashing in the center. The children preferred the music to standing in line for hours to see the Mona Lisa, on loan from the Louvre, or the King Tut Exhibit, the Egyptian King Tutankhamen, circa 1358 B.C., of the XVIIIth dynasty—despite all of his golden splendor.

Washington was a wondrous juxtaposition of primeval forest, river and swamp—the State Department built on the drained Foggy Bottom; the

Washington Monument—on a filled swamp; its ascendance to "the-most-beautiful-city-in-the-world" status, less a miracle than an attesting to the perspicacity of the planner, Major Pierre C. L'Enfant, a French architect and engineer, who had come to America with Lafayette—both ardent supporters of the American struggle for freedom. During the Revolutionary War when the seat of government was the Continental Congress in Philadelphia, it was felt that an entirely new, specially planned city should be created for the National Capital of the new nation. Seven years after the end of the American War for Independence and the signing of the Treaty of Versailles in 1783, three years after the drafting of our remarkable Constitution and one year after the inauguration of President George Washington in New York, April 30, 1789; Congress passed a bill in 1790, creating the District of Columbia on the Potomac River as the site for our new Federal City.

President Washington, familiar with all the terrain of the Potomac, as a Virginia plantation owner, surveyor and General of American Revolutionary Forces, was authorized to select a site on the Potomac River between the Anacostia River and the Conococheague Creek, sixty-five miles to the northwest and to appoint three commissioners to make surveys (Thomas Jefferson and Dr. David Stuart of Virginia, Daniel Carroll of Maryland). Accommodations were to be made for the Congress by December 1800.

President George Washington, on horseback, rode along the bank of the river—so well-known and loved by him—and after surveying it carefully, chose the present site of the District of Columbia which was to bear his name but not his presence as our first President (1789 to 1797). Washington's high regard for Major Pierre Charles L'Enfant prompted the sending of the designer-officer-architect to the "Federal City," as Washington modestly referred to the District, to select sites for major buildings. The *Weekly Ledger* of Georgetown announced the selection, March 12, 1791:

"Major Longfont (sic), a French gentleman, employed by the President of the United States, (has arrived) to survey the lands contiguous to Georgetown where the federal city is to be built." In the rainy, snowy winter of 1791, L'Enfant enthusiastically explored the hilly forest and swampy lowlands on horseback, communicating his plans to Washington, Jefferson and Hamilton, the latter's having helped decide upon the Potomac as the main boundary.

It was interesting that L'Enfant's *L*-shaped relationship which he established between the eminence of the Capitol Building, facing east (the rising sun being a symbol of looking toward the future) and the lower-lying White House, looking south over the Ellipse Park to the Washington Monument, the point of intersection with the length of the *L*, the Mall from the Capitol—was probably inspired by the placement of two French royal houses at Versailles: the Palace and the Grand Trianon. According to architectural historian Fiske Kimball in *The White House*: "L'Enfant's father had been a landscape painter at Versailles, and the young man knew well the great park with its splendid houses and broad avenues" (p. 14). Moreover, his love and knowledge of Paris was further reflected as he laid out the city's streets at right angles to each other, adding diagonal avenues to be named for the original states, and at most intersections, providing for a park-like square or circle where a statue of a famous American could be placed which would name the circle or square—or where an uprising, such as those of the French Revolution, could be controlled from any direction.

Whatever his inspiration, Pierre Charles L'Enfant planned a magnificent Washington, D.C., on such a scale, he wrote, "as to leave room for that aggrandizement and embellishment which the increase of the wealth of the nation will permit it to pursue at any period, however remote." (Joseph Leeming, *The Washington Story*, p. 5.) The District of Columbia belatedly honored its brilliant young designer with L'Enfant Square on the southeast edge of its territory at the intersection of Minnesota and Pennsylvania, three blocks beyond the John Philip Sousa Bridge which crossed the Anacostia River; it lay well beyond L'Enfant's original "ten-mile square" city plan.

The other young Frenchman, who played such a prominent role in the American Revolution and became a lifelong friend of George Washington, was more appropriately—and conspicuously—honored in Lafayette Square which faced the White House on the north. Marquis de La Fayette, Marie Joseph Paul Yves Roch Gilbert Du Motier, upon hearing that the colonies in America had declared their independence from England determined to offer his assistance: "On first news of this Quarrel," he wrote later in his memoirs, "my heart was enrolled in it." The young nobleman, only nineteen years of age and speaking no English, arranged with the American agent in Paris, Silas Deane, to enter the American army as a major general, December 7, 1776. At his own expense he fitted out a ship at Bordeaux, was arrested and detained by his king,

Louis XVI, escaped custody in disguise and joined his ship in Spain and learned English on the voyage to Georgetown, South Carolina.

General La Fayette alternately commanded in America, winning plaudits from Congress, and served his king in France—England's declaring war on France in 1778, when France signed an alliance of defense and treaty of commerce with the colonists. He named his eldest son for his American friend: Georges Washington Motier de La Fayette and became a leader of the French Revolution for freedom, proposing in 1789—the year Washington became President—a declaration of rights to the newly formed French National Assembly which was based upon Jefferson's 1776 Declaration of Independence. The statue atop the ornate monument to the daring, romantic young French general and statesman was grandiose and Lafayette Park became the site of demonstrations for every conceivable type of "freedom," the lofty Lafayette (La Fayette), often misconstrued as the "patron saint of every grievance."

In 1783, the Continental Congress voted that a statue be erected to General George Washington. Eight years later, when the site for the capital was decided upon and Major L'Enfant made the memorial to Washington the focal point of the District of Columbia, nothing was done because the designated location was a vast swamp. Fifty years later the Librarian of Congress proposed that something should be done; in another fifteen years, Congress granted permission for the memorial to be erected and a cornerstone was laid July 4, 1848, in the presence of President Polk.

According to *The Washington Story* by Joseph Leeming: "In 1856, when the monument had reached a height of 174 feet, the work stopped, and nothing was done for twenty years. After the Civil War, work was resumed in 1876, when it was found that the monument had tilted and needed a new foundation. It was 1880 before the shaft began to rise once more. Finally, on December 6, 1884, the capstone, a pyramid of gleaming aluminum, was put in place. Visitors can still see the line in the masonry that marks the place where construction work was suspended for 24 years from 1856 to 1880. Below the line is Massachusetts marble, and above it Maryland marble of a slightly different shade" (p. 22).

We walked to the top of the 555-foot Washington Monument, described as the "tallest structure of stone and masonry in the world," and looked out over L'Enfant's perfect *L*—from the Capitol to the monument and the monument to the White House and marveled at the forested beauty surrounding the gorgeous marble buildings far below, amazed by L'Enfant's masterful plan. All of us decided that the hundred years from conception to completion of the monument to our Founding Father had not been unfruitful. Walking down was slower than walking expectantly upward. We took time, especially Dave and I, to study memorial stones to forty states, a number of cities and countries, and historical fragments from Vesuvius, the Parthenon and Napoleon's Tomb on St. Helena.

Our second car was purchased in late August and began our hand-me-down program, for no car was ever turned in on a new one—it came first to me and then to Lori and from Lori to Bruce so that our two-toned blue Olds, which I inherited and drove to Surrattsville Elementary for two years, in time became Lori's car for UMKC and then, Bruce's for KU, which he made all his own by painting it a bright orange. Dave took such excellent care of vehicles—and everything else—that it was many years before one wore out and since we were never addicted to "fashion," we enjoyed them until that happened.

By Labor Day week, we were heading out each morning in opposite directions. Dave, north to the District, across the Anacostia River—in his new, dark blue '98 Olds; the children and I, southbound, past Mary E. Surratts' modest frame boardinghouse, still lived in, to Surrattsville Grade School and Jr. High, three blocks beyond. Lori and Beth Gary, four houses east and across the street, soon started riding the Jr. High bus, their being best friends and independent Eighth Graders. Bruce, in Sixth, and Davie, in Third, were glad to have service from door to door and drove with me, my being "demoted" to Second Grade—and in an annex, which I found ideal.

Our military-impacted school had outgrown its building and two lower-grade annexes had been added, just a step or two from the east exit, parallel to the Second Grade wing and screened, by the southeast offices, from displaying temporariness. I loved my isolation and perpetuated it. My principal, female again, was impersonal, humorless and efficient and somewhat of an anomaly: in the college-rich area, she was "normal-school trained," but working on her Masters.

Thus once again, we were happily ensconced in school. The children were on accelerated tracks; I applauded the curriculum in Prince Georges County which was progressive, if not innovative and we all had time to continue our study of Washington, D.C.

Even Dave's duties seemed lighter and he was home every night with the exception of week-long absences with the Meteorological Subcommittee, NATO, which took him to Naples, Paris and London.

Dave and I spent an occasional evening with the Meteorological Subcommittee officers, from the various NATO countries, three from England and COL Robert Taylor, no relation to the Hollywood hero; U.S. Air Force, rather. One of the English officers and I had a favorite novel in common: Jane Austen's *Pride and Prejudice* and discovered we each read it yearly. We were being entertained at a cocktail party aboard an English carrier (no liquor was ever served aboard an American ship, not even wine) when the English officer began to entertain me with a demonstration of the highly stylized bows Mr. Darcy had made to Elizabeth, the message the bows imparted and Elizabeth's response with her fan, understood and practiced by all aristocrats in Georgian England. He was attractive, graceful and as droll as Mr. Bennet, Elizabeth's father, and agreed with me that it was the arrogant, titled, wealthy Mr. Darcy who exhibited the "prejudice" against the less aristocratic, impecunious Bennet family; Elizabeth's demonstrating defensive "pride" in her loyalty to her father, her sisters and her giddy mother. I was so surprised and pleased, since all readers of *Pride and Prejudice* of my acquaintance had inferred the opposite, that I invited him and the other ten NATO weathermen to dinner, and promised I'd get out my Austen.

Alas, the following Friday arrived and I discovered that we had unpacked only the children's classic having agreed to leave two large boxes of books packed in the storage room during our brief, two-year stay in Washington.

When my Austen friend arrived at the front door with his fellow Englishmen, who had laughed at his demonstration and my enthusiasm, I greeted all three with the distressful announcement: "All I can offer you is a condensed virgin!" My waggish friend said, "That will do," and kissed my hand and doubled with laughter, as did we all—especially Dave. But that was not my only faux pas—or maybe the next one was Dave's.

We had iced soft drinks and beer, as well, which neither of us drank and knew little about. There were cocktails, if they preferred, before the shrimp jambalaya with Chesapeake Bay oysters was to be served. The Englishmen had said they would drink beer when we asked their preference on the English carrier but neither Dave nor I realized that they only drank it, room temperature, and we had packed twenty-four cans of beer in ice. Fortunately, they were not dependent upon it—but agreed to take it all when they left—and I was glad because the children, before whom we never drank, the cocktail hour and habit not a part of our lifestyle, were joining us for dinner and had promised to show our international friends

Die luft ist Kuhl und
es dunkelt,
Und ruhig fliesst
der Rhein,
Der gipfel des Berges
funkelt,
Im abend sonnen-
Schein,

To Mrs. Holllinck Geurs,
with best wishes

Robert Taylor

$SH = \zeta$ $C = C$ $\zeta = CH$

Ben Albay Göksavan. Türk
Askeri Temsil Heyetinde çalışı-
yorum.

A B C Ç D E F G H I İ J K
L M N O Ö P R S Ş T U Ü
Y Z T

I am colonel Goksavan. I work
in Turkish Military Mission.

Il mio soggiorno a Washington
è stato delizioso. — Porterò con
me in Italia un ricordo incancel_
labile. — Ho trovato dovunque una
accoglienza molto cordiale. — Ho
apprezzato in particolare la gentilezza
con la quale la popolazione america_
na accoglie gli stranieri. —
   Ho fra gli americani molti amici
e spero che un giorno molti di
essi avranno l'occasione di visitare
l'Italia. — Potrò così ricambiare
le loro affettuose cortesie

                    Lt. Cl. Lamberto Larminato
                       Italian Air Force

Kuch parwa nahin (Hindustan)
Puste mos. (Welsh)
Tink nultin oout bidd.

Ghotī

(Satu Ampat Jalan (Malay).
    1   4   Road

TOTI
EMUL
ESTO Caesar. Agrippa

what to do with a California artichoke, if any of them showed dubiety. Lori and Bruce also wanted autographs, as well as a sentence or two—for school.

All of the officers, with the exception of the Air Force COL Taylor were vociferously impressed by our house and two cars; of the lot, only the Frenchman owned a car. Our English friends, particularly, were amazed at the discrepancy in living standards, vowing they couldn't "even afford the petrol" for a car. In response to "Why?" they admitted they were at the top of the heap, "except for the peerage," but the English income taxes were exorbitant and they could not even aspire to owning a car if they educated their boys, who left home at fifteen if they were intelligent enough to pass rigid entrance exams for public school (private college, in our terminology); girls, usually, were not educated beyond the age of fifteen, even if they were brilliant. In fact, choices in England between a trade-school education and public school had to be made at age eight, if the child was a boy. They seemed most surprised, however, at the accomplishments and opportunities of Lori, Bruce and Davie. It was a delightful and enlightening evening—thanks to Jane Austen, a literary English meteorologist—and fine young men of the world military.

Rather than opening and searching through the book boxes stored at the bottom of a formidable stack, I took a few minutes from our Saturday-Smithsonian study to buy a copy of *Pride and Prejudice*, with illustrations, too, at a Washington used-book store and laughed at, and read aloud, Mr. Bennet's drollery while we awaited our bean soup at the Capitol restaurant. We all felt lucky and blessed to be Americans and to be privileged to live in the nation's Capital for two wondrous years of education and historical adventuring.

After our hot apple pie à la mode, we strolled about the Capitol (from the Latin, "Capitolium," referring to the central shrine of the Roman Republic, the temple of Jupiter, as opposed to Capital from the Latin word "Capital," meaning "head" or the "chief" city), as was our wont, to investigate a different section—every wall, pilaster, arch and ceiling ennobled by the artistry of one Constantino Brumidi who must have had the fortitude of a dozen. Brumidi, an Italian guardsman, had fled to the United States in 1848, having refused to fire upon the rebels in his own land. Middle-aged when he arrived, he devoted the remainder of his incredible energy to adorning "the Capitol of the one country on earth in which there is liberty." ("Under the Dome of Freedom," *National Geographic*, Jan. 1964, p. 18.) He completed the interior of the 183-foot height of the Rotunda dome, enormous figures of thirteen Classical deities representing the original states and symbolizing the Republic's growth. George Washington, the central figure, sat in immortal splendor, his right hand extended in openness and peace; his left, grasping an unsheathed but unthreatening sword.

At the age of seventy-two, Brumidi began the Rotunda frieze, a series of fresco scenes which looked like sculpture, 300 feet in circumference, 9 feet high and 75 feet above the floor. Before he had completed the frieze, he slipped on the scaffold and dangled helplessly a quarter of an hour, 58 feet above the floor, before he was rescued. He died soon after the terrifying accident, much weakened by the shock, but his devoted pupil, Filippo Costaggini, completed the magnificent project.

In Statuary Hall, south of the Rotunda through the South Small Rotunda, had been placed statues of our most distinguished political leaders. Each state was allowed two choices; after installation of the statue, Congressional action was required to make a substitution, none of which had ever been made. New Mexico, Alaska and Hawaii had yet to deliver their first statues but no more could be placed in Statuary Hall, some having already been moved to other parts of the Capitol—the combined weight of the assembled statuary threatening the safety of the floor.

In the historic Hall, the House of Representatives had met from 1811 until the new House extension was completed in 1857. In the former, tireless John Quincy Adams, who had served as a diplomat, Senator, Secretary of State, and President of the United States, had spent the last seventeen years of his life as a Representative from Massachusetts and there—suffered a fatal stroke. Being a Congressman had satisfied Adams most: "My election as President . . . was not half so gratifying to my inmost soul," he commented upon learning he had been a successful candidate for the House of Representatives from the Bay State. "No election or appointment . . . ever gave me so much pleasure." ("Under the Dome of Freedom," *National Geographic*, Jan. 1964, p. 14.) On a cold February morning in 1848, when John Quincy Adams was eighty-one years old, he rose from his seat, with a bundle of petitions in his hand, and called out, "Mr. Speaker!" and immediately collapsed and fell to the floor (the spot was marked by a bronze circle; Robert E. Lee's statue later placed near by). The Speaker, at once, adjourned the House. An hour later, it was recorded, the grand old gentleman recovered enough to whisper: "This is the last of earth. I am content." He died shortly thereafter.

In 1864 the House voted to make a National Statuary Hall out of their Assembly Hall which had been notorious for its poor acoustics, secret plans constantly wafted over to the opposing party. Capitol guides invariably demonstrated that, by standing at the brass plate in the floor, they could send a "ssh" to the listening group by the wall, forty-five feet away which would be inaudible to the group in between. And it was so; the children delighted in their own experiment, at each Capitol visit. The solemnly impressive, marvelously rich edifice, probably the most famous building in the world, was not without a humorous lightness: Oklahoma chose to honor Will Rogers who wanted to be where he could "keep an eye on Congress!" And there stood he!

We walked down the steps of the East Portico where twenty-four Presidents had been inaugurated and I thought of the snowy January past when President Kennedy had given his memorable, and hatless, address and how I had worried about his health but more about Robert Frost's luxuriantly maned white head buffeted by the blizzard winds which crumpled the paper of his poem he was attempting to read—which he finally stuffed in his overcoat pocket with the comment: "I know it anyhow," and recited it flawlessly, having of course written it for the occasion.

High overhead, far above Brumidi's interior mural, stood the huge, bronze Statue of Freedom on the towering marble dome, looking eastward—at fewer slums and more Government buildings than on our first visit to Washington. We had been struck, by the dissimilitude of the immediate environs to Capitol Hill, its physical and symbolical loftiness tarnished in the area of highest crime, lowest income and most shameful housing. Even during our short residency, we had begun to remark, with satisfaction and pride in our city, the welcome deracination of the slum buildings which had not only detracted from the homogeneous beauty of the District but had implied hypocrisy to the nation's claim of fairness and freedom from want.

Federal buildings were supplanting the ramshackle dwellings and handsome low-cost housing units were rising farther east. The Sam Rayburn House Office Building which dwarfed the Cannon and Longworth House Buildings, contiguous to it on Independence Avenue, south of the Capitol—was almost complete at the bottom of the Hill and did much to enhance the area. Our magnificent District of Columbia and young, vigorous, new President Kennedy radiated a sense of exuberance, strength and viability—and we felt part of it all.

Deciding to get tickets for an early Christmas tour of the White House, we went in a ground-level door of the North Wing of the Capitol and took the Senate subway to the Senate Office Building and were quickly accommodated with White House passes from Senator Symington's office, returning by the rapid underground subway, in just minutes, to the Senate wing (the only part of the Capitol completed by 1800 which both Houses, the Supreme Court and the Library of Congress used initially).

The original North Wing had been witness to halting completion of Dr. William Thornton's grand design. Dr. Thornton, a physician and amateur architect born in the West Indies (remarkable, how internationally eclectic our Capital City was in its planning and construction), won the 1792 competition for the Capitol design. President George Washington laid the cornerstone on September 18, 1793, but did not live to see the completion of the North Wing; he did visit the nearly complete White House in 1799, a few months before his death.

How apropos that the only object from the original occupancy of the White House by John and Abigail Adams, in 1800, was the portrait of George Washington by Gilbert Stuart which had hung in the East Room—except for one memorable absence. On the day the Capitol, both the North and South Wings, was fired by George III's invading troops, August 24, 1814, and the White House was imminently set afire, Dolley Madison, the third First Lady to live in the "President's House"—wrote to her sister: "Will you believe it, my sister? We have had a battle, or skirmish near Bladensburg, and I am still here within sound of the cannon! Mr. Madison comes not; may God protect him! Two messengers, covered with dust, come to bid me fly; but I wait for him. . . . At this late hour, a wagon has been procured; I have had it filled with the plate and most valuable portable articles belonging to the house; whether it will reach its destination, the Bank of Maryland . . . events must determine" (*The White House*, p. 33). The Declaration of Independence, contrary to legend, was not carried by Dolley Madison; when she finally fled the White House, at the last minute, by carriage, she took the silver. The Declaration of Independence, which must have been deemed an ironical document at the time, rumbled away, in its linen bag, piled with other papers in the hastily procured wagon.

"Our kind friend," continued Mrs. Madison to her sister, "Mr. Carroll, has come to hasten my departure, and is in a very bad humor with me because I insist on waiting until the large picture of Gen. Washington is secured, and it requires to be unscrewed from the wall. This process was found too tedious for these perilous moments; I have ordered the frame to be broken, and the canvas taken out; it is done—and the precious portrait placed in the hands of two gentlemen of New York for safe keeping. And now, dear sister, I must leave this house, or the retreating army will make me a prisoner in it, by filling up the road I am directed to take. When I shall again write to you, or where I shall be tomorrow, I cannot tell!!"

Both the White House and the Capitol Wings escaped total destruction when a violent thunderstorm quenched the fires that night of August 24, 1814. The outer walls of both edifices were thus providentially preserved to be rebuilt in the interiors, with extensions of the original buildings occurring over many years.

Those two most symbolic buildings of our nation were connected with the diagonal ray of the Avenue, Pennsylvania—the state where our government was born—wedding the White House to the towering Capitol, sun-facing each new day. Washington, D.C., irradiated poetry! Modern culture, which appeared totally prosaic in comparison to the inspired Georgian America, at least appreciated, preserved and honored its heritage; and then, with unabashed verve, consonant with its own ambi-tion—planned and created beyond!

Lori's piano teacher was a retired musician from the Washington Symphony who grew pomegranates in his front yard, which blossomed a deep orange in the spring and looked like frangipani or cyclamen; cherries and prize-winning roses, in the back. He gave us cherries, which the boys and I picked while Lori played and learned, slips from his roses to be planted in sand, under jars, and was so affable with fascinating tales of early Washington that soon he had four Holland students: Lori, Bruce, Davie and Dave and then came to our house—for most of the afternoon and evening. None of his effort produced a concert pianist but it was wonderful history and entertainment and led us to the purchase of a second piano, which even I was able to master—a player-piano.

CDR M.O. Erwin, "Moe," to his Naval Weather Service friends, had entertained Dave and me at dinner one night and played brilliantly, his piano rolls. A friend of his, a Washington dentist, was a collector of the old players which he bought in New England "for a song," repaired, with dental wire I always postulated, and sold from his garage for a Yankee profit, and we were one of his willing victims. Fortunately we did not make our "Moe" discovery until the spring of '63, thus giving the music lessons a chance of miraculous success and the family-room floor only a two-month, two-piano strain test. And so we all learned how to play piano in Washington, D.C.!

Not remembering that they had ever traveled by train, and Davie hadn't, the children requested to journey by one to Kansas City at Christmastime. Since our plans were to spend our last before-retirement Christmas in Washington and New York, 1961 would be our best time for an extended rail trip for our poor, neglected children who knew all about airplanes, gut-boats, ferries and sleighs, trolleys, horse-drawn carriages, canoes, sailboats, launches, MSTS ships, Coast Guard Cutters, submarines and carriers; canal barges, underground subways, rowboats and paddle boats—but no manifest knowledge of trains. So off we went to Mommy Tom and Daddy Frank's by train, in a drawing room with two upper berths, which Lori, Bruce and Davie democratically agreed to "take turns in," two lowers and one single—which I was happy to be assigned due to my notoriety as a berth head-bumper.

Just to be in the Union Station, which was northeast of the Capitol, Louisiana and Massachusetts Avenues' leading into its classic immensity, was an edification. Because it was an important part of the Capital, built jointly in 1907 by the United States, the District of Columbia and the Pennsylvania and Baltimore & Ohio Railroads, superlatives were needed to describe it. Being the gateway to the Capital, it seemed appropriate that the handsome, circular plaza in front of the station, commemorated Christopher Columbus and the facade of the world's largest concourse welcomed travelers through triumphal Roman arches, the grandiose central arches suggesting those of the Emperor Constantine. I read later that the 760-foot concourse approximated the combined areas of New York's Grand Central and Pennsylvania Stations and that the enormous waiting room was modeled after the central hall in the Baths of Diocletian at Rome; with the eastern end, the State Waiting Room for the President and high officials.

The children were less awed by Union Station, even though it was larger than the Capitol, covering twenty-five acres, than with the train and comforts of the drawing room which boasted two bathrooms and two closets and plush chairs and couches so that all could be next to the windows. But they wanted their Daddy to escort them in their first investigation: the location of the Dining Car.

Since it was late afternoon when we boarded, they had not long to wait before the chimes were played by the porter, hands were washed and we were being seated in the Diner, a red rose in silver vase on our table and a grinning waiter pushing in our chairs. Lori ordered baked chicken; Davie, chicken pie; Dave, salmon steak; Bruce, scalloped oysters; and I, crab. Bruce asked, "Mommy, what are scalloped oysters?" We all laughed with him. Bruce and I were the food adventurers and if there was a dish unknown to us, that was what we ordered. "They'll be larger than the oysters I put in shrimp jambalaya, in a rich white sauce, probably with buttered bread crumbs on the top, maybe a few mushrooms, and you'll love them." And he did, eating all after the one he generously insisted I sample. It was an elegant meal for each and the finger bowls were no mystery, the children having been tutored in polite dining aboard the *Independence* and in the O-Clubs.

When we returned to our drawing room, the beds were made, covers turned diagonally back and a *Mad Magazine*, on the two upper bunks. I asked the porter about them. He grinned, saying he thought the boys would like reading them. Our children did not read comic books and those appeared not only inappropriate, but well-handled, so I thanked him and returned them and the children did not demur. They each had a book in addition to travel games, Rook and bridge cards; besides, they were train travelers and intended a full measure of enjoyment.

After a while, we retired—Bruce and Davie to the upper berths the first night, Lori and Dave's having to wait their turn on the morrow; the room was darkened; reading lights checked, and rechecked, and—then, the excitement of watching a train whisk by with intermittent brightness streaking from windows, absolute blackness and, occasionally, dim illumination from a small town with streets deserted and train signal lights flashing on the black-and-white-striped barrier.

We were up early for breakfast, its being our favorite meal—until lunchtime, and hurried to the Dining Car to sit in the winter sunshine slanting in obliquely and brokenly as trees and sun-obstructions flashed by. The same broadly grinning, white-jacketed waiter served us: French toast, waffles, sausage, hot syrup and juice, lots of coffee with chicory, steaming and fragrant. I had learned to prefer strong Southern coffee with chicory in Norfolk and drank that exclusively, feeling somewhat disloyal to Kansas City's coffee company (the vice president a family friend) but suspected a return to loyalty, after retirement.

It was a relaxing way to travel and the children were pleased with the experience, investigating the length of the train with Dave and sitting part of the day in the Observation Car. The kaleidoscopic scenes were snowy all the trip, for we had an inordinately wet, frigid commencement of winter. My fur coat had felt comfortable when we left and we were all booted and equipped with snow clothes for the weather we invariably, but happily, traveled in when homeward-bound to the Midwest. December 1961, provided special joy because the Christmas before, Dave had been in The Med and Mother and Dad had lovingly come to Norfolk; next Christmas we would experience on the East Coast and the following year at Yuletime, we would be in our own home. Thus we were "going home to Grandmother and Grandfather's" for the last time, in the denotative sense.

Lori, Bruce and Davie were swiftly approaching the confluence of childhood and adolescence and Dave and I felt they needed to live in a permanent community to establish school and church ties, cement friendships and be close to their grandparents, aunts, uncles and cousins. Dave would not be up for Captain for several years; to be considered would probably necessitate an overseas billet, and while we would all delight in that, we felt the children's accelerated schooling would be slowed, if not damaged, by further peripatetic education. Maryland was providing an excellent foundation and we knew a superior school system to which they would move next—and permanently—was essential.

Dave had discussed with me a possibility if he prolonged his Naval career beyond twenty years and did not retire in 1963: President Kennedy was trying to build a stronger relationship with South America and was soliciting suggestions for enhancement of such a program. Dave saw the need for the establishment of a Joint Fleet Weather Central which would provide oceanographic data for fleets' maneuvering in or transiting the waters of South America and would have been willing to volunteer to effectuate the plan. And that would have been a wonderful adventure, if he had sought approval—and if we did not have three precocious children. So as we journeyed westward, Dave and I were somewhat more scrutinizing and less nostalgic because the Midwest might soon become our home land. We no doubt gravitated to that soil because it was our own but overtly preferred its mores and values to all others we had encountered.

Mother and Dad met our train and it was Christmas at once—just to be with them again. Our Kansas City Union Station, so uncluttered and open in its spaciousness, without booths and obstacles in the middle of the concourse and waiting room, that it remained, without contest, our favorite. It was snowing fluffy, fat flakes as Dad pulled up the car and the children and Mommy Tom talked altogether, in a jubilant chorus. Dad drove us home through the Plaza and the children thought they had never seen anything more beautiful: constellations of many-colored lights streaking through the falling snow. Said Daddy Frank, chuckling: "I'll get out the old Flexible Flyers if you'll help me shovel!" We volunteered with alacritous glee.

Early in our Washington sojourn, Dave had suggested to me: "Dad is seventy-one now; what do you think of my retiring after twenty and working with him? That way he could gradually retire and still keep the business in the family." "Why Dave—that would be wonderful!" I exclaimed and went over to kiss him soundly. "Wouldn't that just *thrill* them!" And so I wrote to Mother . . . and it did! Thus our homecoming was a double happiness for there was an exciting, new nexus to be planned and celebrated. We had not told the children of the probability that Kansas City would be their next home; we wanted Mother and Dad to have that privilege—Dad, with his twinkling drollery; Mother, with her exuberant joyfulness.

Christmas was memorable and festive and beautiful and bountiful with the gustatory delights of turkey, Mother's inimitable sage dressing, sweet potato à la orange, fruitcake and Dad's luscious ambrosia. Charles, Barbara, Luanne and Brian were with us and all were overjoyed with our impending return; Charles was particularly delighted with Dad and Dave's plans. Dad insisted we drive his blue Olds to Lincoln—all of his cars were blue, but none as blue as his eyes—which Dave was glad to do since we would be there only briefly. Our Kansas City time was Dave's main chance to plan strategy with Dad and learn something about becoming a manufacturers' representative before his retirement in the summer of 1963.

Mother H was elated at the prospect of having her youngest close to home again; Kenneth, Naomi, Kenny, Johnny and Jane seemed pleased and invited us to come our first summer home to their lake cottage and sail in their new boat. And the children had playtime with Ricky, Robert and Viola's youngest, who had not appeared in family seasonal sittings until after 1955. (He grew up posthaste to become Dr. Rick, Limnologist, and to marry beautiful Dietitian Kathy.)

Figure 124. Ricky

We sped back home by train, our heads whirling with wondrous plans and expectations for Dave's retirement. President Kennedy would just have to be content with a Naval Weather Central in Panama to service entire Latin and South America.

We talked about all we had yet to do and see in Washington, New York and New England and Dave suggested that after he retired, we should drive around the Gaspé Peninsula before heading to the Midwest. "And maybe we can find agates on the beach of New Brunswick," he added, "and see the world's highest tides in the Bay of Fundy!" "Where's Fundy?" the chorus came. "That's between Nova Scotia and New Brunswick—touches a tip of Maine, too, which is contiguous to New Brunswick." "Will it be like Newfoundland?" Lori queried. "Yes, very much," Dave affirmed. "They were all joined in the glacial age."

But Bruce and Davie were more interested in the prevailing snow and ice of West Virginia. "Look," Bruce pointed, as the train slowed for a deep curve, "there's the engine . . . and the caboose!" "And there's another tunnel," Davie exulted. "Turn out the lights—quick!" "There's no caboose," Lori corrected, in the dark of the tunnel. "Well, the end of the train," Bruce agreed. "I like to say 'caboose' too," supported Davie. "I know," Bruce, defending masculine intelligence, "cabooses are only on freight trains; it takes too long to say 'observation car' or 'end of the train.'" "Right!" sanctioned his partner.

"I'm sorry our train doesn't go through the tunnel beneath Capitol Hill," I mused. "Why doesn't it?" asked Davie. "Only trains coming in from the South use the tunnel." "Why couldn't *we* come in from the South?" persisted our youngest. "I don't know of any direct Southern train route from Kansas City," interjected Dave—to Davie's satisfaction, as suitcases were closed and arranged, with nautical nicety, near the door. There was still deep snow on the ground, so we donned boots; it was less to carry and we had brought only what we could manage; Dad would ship the Christmas collection—in his expert, prompt packaging and we had only a maroon and gray-striped knitted hat of Davie's to recover from Kenneth's basement, Davie being very precise as to its location and description as I wrote a card from the train, the first day out.

The weather remained unusually cold in Washington and we almost envied Dave's trip to Naples on his NATO, Meteorological duty. After Dave's return, we began our Washington study again in the "Federal Triangle," the Government buildings in the triangle formed by the Mall and Pennsylvania Avenue, northeast of the Washington Monument—most of the splendid marble structures erected in a ten-year period from 1928 to 1938.

One of our favorites was the National Archives Building with its marvelous Corinthian columns, the classical frieze on the pediment and, gracing the front of the building, on Pennsylvania Avenue, two sculptured figures on large pedestals of granite. Proving that twentieth-century architects and artists were as idealistic and as aesthetic as eighteenth-century, the male figure represented the Past with an injunction from Confucius: "Study the Past"; the female figure, symbolic of the Future, with the words of Shakespeare's Antonia in *The Tempest*: "What is Past is Prologue." Because the Federal Triangle area was a marsh, the Archives Building was placed on five-foot-thick concrete slabs supported by five thousand concrete piles.

We wondered why George Washington chose a penultimate, nearly impossible site for his city. It was certainly on his beloved Potomac River but it must also have been an extraordinary challenge to his indomitable spirit. Much as the Egyptian phoenix of legend arose from its own ashes, Washington, D.C. sprang from the malarial swamps discarded by Virginia and Maryland and, imbued with freshness and life by Washington and the indefatigable Major L'Enfant, it became emblematic of immortality . . . of undying freedom.

The most remarkable feature of the Archives Building was its dyadic structure, one building inside of and, like a giant toadstool, projecting above the other. The inner was of steel and concrete, in effect—a fireproof vault, inasmuch as our most valuable and precious documents were enshrined there, in the Exhibition Hall: the Declaration of Independence, the Constitution of the United States, and the Bill of Rights. Always guarded, they could be lowered mechanically into yet another vault.

The Department of Commerce Building, the west base of the triangle, had been the world's largest office building until the Pentagon was built—capable of berthing three ocean liners in its basement, and wet enough too, initially. Covering eight acres of marshland, it was built on eighty miles of concrete piling with much of the basement floor three feet thick to combat the water pressure of Tiber Creek, flowing beneath the mammoth structure. The Census Bureau boasted a huge chart of constantly changing Vital Statistics inside the main entrance, which was attention-holding and provocative; but of more interest to the children was the display of models in the Patent Office, some hilariously funny, others, amazingly complicated; and in the basement—which had been fraught with and had fought against water—was an incredible amount of it. In the Commerce Department's "down under," the U.S. Bureau of Fisheries had an Aquarium filled with all the fish native to the United States! Remarkable what you could learn from your Government!

When it rained more than an hour or two, we had our own aquarium potential in our family-room terrace. The children didn't want it disturbed, its being a perfect habitat for tadpoles, frogs and ice-skating, but when it rose more than six inches it necessitated keeping the sliding doors closed, turning back the rug, tucking up the drapes and plying wet mops and sponges. And it did not always rain torrentially when I was at home. Our contractor kindly responded to my SOS and heightened the brick edging to an effective dam barrier which not only provided a lovely brick wall to sit upon in the sunshine—Patches and kitten thought it was created especially for them—it forced the rain floods to flow on down the hill and detour around the family room.

Bordering the Department of Commerce on the west was the Ellipse, the large park south of the White House where the Nation's Christmas Tree was always placed—star-topped usually by the wife of the Vice President, which boasted a fascinating marker: the Zero Milestone. In 1920, Congress authorized the Secretary of War to erect the stone: "Point For The Measurement Of Distances From Washington On Highways Of The United States," latitude 38 degrees, longitude 77 degrees, elevation of 28.65 feet above sea level. I wondered if all cities had a zero milestone and Dave theorized that cartographers probably used the city limits to compute mileage. "Bruce, let's write to Daddy Frank and see if Kansas City has one," Davie suggested, knowing that Daddy Frank would know everything about everything.

Bruce and Davie agitated to visit the FBI in the Department of Justice Building which Director J. Edgar Hoover and his "G-men" had made famous. Although Agent Thomas Keane, my cousin Beth's husband, was there, we decided just to visit the shooting range that day to watch the amazing marksmanship of the FBI agents as they shot at life-sized torsos and heads, with unvarying precision. Bruce and Davie were presented one of the black-torso and white-background charts, bullet holes neatly piercing the heart and brain. We were through for the day; they rushed home and taped it to their bedroom wall. I believed it was their most prized memento of their entire Washington experience. I was glad they hung it between their beds and that the heartless, mindless shadow didn't leer at me whenever I looked in my boys' room.

The snow was gone by late February for the many parades in the Capital City. By mid-March the cherry tree buds were swelling. We checked the Tidal Basin every few days to see if any of the blossoms had opened on the Japanese cherry trees, Tokyo's gift to the United States in

1912, and to look at the reflection of the matchless Jefferson Memorial, Davie's "Old Baldy" and still his favorite, in the mirroring water.

The Jefferson Memorial commanded the most magnificent setting of all the Washington monuments; its aspect was ethereal when viewed across the Tidal Basin through the fully opened boughs of low-hanging white cherry blossoms. On the south shore of the Tidal Basin, it was dedicated by President Franklin D. Roosevelt on April 13, 1943, on the two hundredth anniversary of Thomas Jefferson's birth and was an imposing tribute to the author of the Declaration of Independence. In the center of the marble-lined circular chamber beneath the great domed ceiling, a bronze, heroic-sized statue of Thomas Jefferson stood in majestic dignity, with the frieze of the entablature encircling the hall proclaiming his immortal words: "I have sworn on the altar of God eternal hostility to every form of tyranny over the mind of man." It was my favorite monument, too, and I always felt Jefferson would have loved the Greek Pantheon which commemorated his brilliant intellect and versatility. He was not only our first Secretary of State and Third President, he was the devotee of Greek architecture who had insisted upon its use in the Capital City which he helped Washington and L'Enfant plan—being a Greek scholar, architect and engineer, as well as a philosopher, writer, diplomat, statesman, and educator.

We laughed when we thought of how all the land below the Capitol was *filled in* with rock, soil and cement and how Capitol Hill, high and dry, was dug into and *burrowed through*—with tunnels. The Library of Congress was one of our choice institutions at the top of the Hill, the Main Reading Room of which any adult could use, with inconceivable treasures—such as the Gutenberg Bible, the best of three extant; Thomas Edison's first copyrighted motion picture; other rarities in the Library of Congress Annex . . . reachable through a tunnel. In addition to the train tunnel deep under Capitol Hill and the tunnels from the House Office Buildings and from the opposite direction, the Senate Office Buildings; the Government Printing Office (naturally, the world's largest printing office at work twenty-four hours a day, using well over 1,000 carloads of paper and 30,000 miles of sewing thread and binding wire each year and easily printing every word uttered on the floors and in committees of Congress: the overnight *Congressional Record*—ready for early morning distribution), with its huge output, expedited its printed materials directly to the Washington, D.C. Post Office, with a conveyor belt, under the street, through a tunnel. We wondered if the fill down the hill came from the labyrinthine tunnels.

The nation's literary, philosophical, constitutional, scientific, religious and legal wealth was concentrated in the Library of Congress which was established by an Act of Congress, April 24, 1800, but housed for nearly a century in the Capitol. The British troops used the first collection of books to fire both Capitol Wings on August 24, 1814, but the Library was reestablished five months later by the purchase of Thomas Jefferson's library for $25,000 on January 30, 1815. The Library was burned again in 1851, when two-thirds of its 55,000 volumes were destroyed but neither the War of 1812 nor the Civil War could submerge the American zeal for knowledge and the preservation of its heritage. After Congressional appropriations and many private gifts, the Library, having outgrown its old quarters in the Capitol Building, moved into its ornate, domed granite building—which covered three and a half acres—in 1897. The Copyright Office, an important part of the Library, alone received more than 250,000 books, pamphlets, prints and maps each year. I always wanted to get lost in the Library which had some slight appeal for me, but I was invariably found; it remained my chief regret, however, about leaving Washington after just two years; but I knew we'd return, after Dave's next retirement—when we were old and gray but still cerebral and sentient.

The Supreme Court Building, the most elegant of all the District buildings, in my judgment, faced the Capitol with broad stairways, graceful Corinthian columns and sculptured pediment on the west portico depicting Liberty enthroned, with the Scales of Justice on her lap; the main entrance, flanked by two sculptured representations: on the left, the female "Contemplation of Justice" and the male figure on the right, "Authority of the Law." The children preferred the east portico, its pediment showing three ancient men of law: Moses, Confucius and Solon and also the Fable of the Tortoise and the Hare, denoting that law and justice might sometimes be slow and not always won by the swift. I suspected there was a tunnel from the Supreme Court to the Library of Congress but we had no occasion to investigate and spent very little time there, the Court's session being from the first Monday in October to the last week of May—which we had just missed.

So we crossed the street, East Capitol, to the Folger Shakespeare Library, next to the Library of Congress Annex. That, too, was a superlative-requiring institution: it was the largest, and also the most valuable, collection of Shakespeareana in the world, endowed by Henry Clay Folger of the Standard Oil Company and left in trust to Amherst College which administered Mr. Folger's gift to his country, gathered over the years by the oil-company president and his wife. That was another of my destinations for sedentary years for I had loved and read Shakespeare from earliest awareness—and laughed at myself, with Puck, when we passed his fountain in the west garden: "Lord, what fools these mortals be!" Puck and *Midsummer Night's Dream* had introduced me to frivolity and profundity, Shakespeare style.

After resting a few minutes in Puck's garden in the afternoon sunshine of early June, Davie wondered: "Aren't we ever going to eat?" "Yes, right now," soothed his Dad; and Bruce pointed across the Capitol Plaza to the Senate Wing: "Bean soup?" Davie, mopping his forehead, "I think I'll just have a hamburger . . . it's hot!" "I'm having soup and apple pie," Lori determined. "I, too," I agreed; "you can order for me while I get a *Congressional Record*." "Are you worried about Khrushchev's missiles?" Dave surmised. "Yes," I admitted. "Jackson (Washington State Democrat, Head of Armed Forces Committee in the Senate) held a hearing yesterday; they're convinced Russian missiles are being shipped to Castro. I just wanted to read the minutes." "May I take it to school?" Davie requested. "Yes, of course," I smiled, pleased that he wanted to. "We're studying missiles and *Friendship 7;* it's coming to Washington." "To the Space Museum," Bruce added. "Was that in your *Weekly Reader?*" Lori asked, and Bruce nodded affirmatively, as we were hurried along by Davie and Dave.

It was almost 3:30 P.M. when we left the Capitol by the East Portico—the West facade was being cleaned and "face-lifted," and was closed off by scaffolding—to hurry again, down the Hill to the Botanical Garden at the southwest foot. It was a large conservatory of aluminum and glass which provided all the cut flowers and plants for Congress and the White House, displaying rare plants from all over the world—cedars of Lebanon, breadfruit, tapioca trees, the Peace Oak which celebrated the end of the Civil War—but what was of interest to us that day, before the Garden closed at four, was a mundane annual: a climbing nasturtium!

In April we had been appreciative of the dramatic beauty of the simple nasturtium twisting its round, apple-green leaves and spurred blooms of orange, yellow and red upward on tall, white Greek columns which bordered the brick path; and cascaded down from pillared urns in the main greenroom. They were still fresh and beautiful and had covered the height of the columns. We inquired and determined they were not a special hybrid, just a climbing nasturtium offered by Sterns which should be planted outside no later than March 1. That we planned to do when we had our first Kansas City garden!

On the way home, just after we left Suitland Parkway and drove uphill on Branch Avenue, we stopped left of the steep slope, our car leaning precariously in front of the finest doughnut bakery—in the world. We replenished our supply of long johns, honey buns, French crullers, and my favorite: blueberry cake, moist and rich with a delicate glaze. It was the only time I became a doughnut fancier—those were irresistible. They would be our supper with fruit and cheese, for Sunday night. And then we would study with a one-hour TV break and I would transcribe my shorthand notes of the week's activity. Only one more week of school; but only one more year in D.C.!

The alarm went off at 5:00 A.M., Monday, July 23, 1962. I awakened at once and stifled the sound. "Dave, let's get up." He arose with a sailor's swiftness. We had two weeks to do with as we pleased. We were not traveling across a continent or an ocean or racing Santa to the Midwest. It was the first time we would just "take a trip." Dave had plotted a course through New England and I had added innumerable byways without which, I argued, our trip would be meaningless.

While Dave shaved and showered, I laid out my travel clothes and started the bacon and melted butter in the double boiler for the scrambled eggs. I made four cups of coffee but doubted I'd have time for the second. I fixed no orange juice because Bruce seldom traveled well in the early morning with it; besides, we had none in the freezer. Dave awakened the boys, who were instantly eager to dress—"We'll bathe tonight," Bruce promised—and count their money again. They had been supplied with spending dollars by Mommy Tom and Daddy Frank, dimes and pennies from their own provident return of soft-drink bottles. As I called from the bottom of the stairs to enlist Lori's aid in table-setting and awaited a response, I heard Bruce ask Davie: "Which pocket are you putting your billfold in?" "In my right-side pocket," replied Davie, not in the least surprised by the question. "Well, don't put it in your back pocket!" advised Bruce, "we're going to New York." Davie had apparently already considered the exigencies of visiting the big city for he was indignant: "Don't you think I know *anything!*"

Lori finally emerged from the bathroom, fresh and sweet as a primrose, just as I was serving the eggs. We ate rather leisurely and I almost finished a half-cup of coffee before putting the dishes into the dishwasher. Dave and the boys packed the trunk of the car with everything from beach wear and fishing tackle to warm jackets and Arctics. Patches and new family were assembled at the vets—to whom we hadn't gotten her in time. The children had worried about too much light in her cage since the kittens' eyes had just opened. The vet assured them the danger had passed. We were confident that Patches would know how to deal with her kittens' sensitivity; we just hoped the vet would deal with hers.

We were soon ensconced in Dave's Olds, seat belts buckled, ten-dollar sunglasses donned—except for Dave's precision flight glasses—and we were off on our New England adventure. Everything went well the first block. As soon as Dave turned the second, the children chirruped: "You're going the wrong way!" Dave assured them there were other ways out of town than past the White House and they lapsed into two minutes of tolerant silence. But the tenor had been set and Dave was not without advice and assistance throughout the trip.

Sometimes it was quiet. Lori had wanted to bring her ukulele, which she and the boys were learning to play, but she restrained—as did I. I did not bring a single book! I decided to spend my time methodically writing impressions, and in that labor, assuage my sense of guilt. I had always known I should not only pen a few words each day about the children's antics and achievements but that I should keep them in logical order in carefully labeled notebooks rather than on envelopes, church bulletins, scraps of any available paper, deposited—here and there.

"Hey, Daddy, you're going over 60!" Bruce stayed awake long enough to read the instruments. "Turnpike says 60!" Dave slowed a notch and turned on the radio, softly, for the 7:00 o'clock news and weather report: hot and sunny, good motel-swimming weather.

Halfway to Annapolis, I heard Davie recounting his money. He had entrusted forty-two cents to me in an envelope. That he had carefully sealed, notated and initialed, as well as inscribing "DAVIE" in two-inch letters on both sides. The money he was so conscientiously caressing came from the billfold in his right-side pocket. The billfold was an ostentatious artifact wrought by a leather-working "gob" aboard the *Independence*. On the front was an impressive horse's head, on the back the owner's name was emblazoned. Any self-respecting pickpocket named "Davie" would treasure that receptacle nigh as much as its contents.

Lori and Bruce were blissfully asleep and they both carried more money than Davie. They awakened, however, as we approached the Chesapeake Bay Bridge at Annapolis. It was stunningly beautiful in the morning sunlight, curving brilliantly like a long moon slice. A graceful, lengthy bridge, the children clocked it at three and three-tenths of a mile. Rather breathlessly, I looked back at the distance we had come. It seemed fantastic that man could engineer such a fragile-looking but secure structure so high above the Bay. Traffic flashed along unconcernedly; car occupants, when we slowed, were amused at my obvious wonderment. Lori and Bruce returned to the arms of Morpheus and Davie tallied his money again. He finally surrendered his entire hoard to me, pillowed his head on Bruce's back which was lodged across Lori's knees, conveniently in the center, and composed himself to slumber.

Soon after we crossed the Delaware Bay Bridge, Davie, who was always more curious than sleepy, began to notice "tall toadstools." Those appeared at intervals along the New Jersey Turnpike, accentuating well-advertised, low-lying motels. I recorded that Davie counted nine toadstools in all; he concluded that we had seen something "top secret." We were too far from our first day's destination to stay at one of those clandestine lodges—and investigate. Davie agreed that we should continue onward, maybe check it on the way home and started counting non-New York license plates.

Dave had called ahead to New York seeking reservations at two of the better-known motels but had received negative responses. With one eye on the scenery and the other seeking a respectable motel, Dave slowed our pace. Several appeared as we approached the Holland Tunnel: "Look, it's named for us!" Davie laughed, pleased with the unanticipated welcome. "How did that happen?" "New York was settled by Dutch colonists," Dave explained; "it used to be called New Netherland." "Then why is it called New York?" Davie needed to know. "Because," I continued, "the Duke of York, who became King James II of England, gave the land to two English colonists and it was later named for him. Jamestown, you remember, was named for King James I. Isn't it fun to study a bit of history as we travel!" And Davie agreed: "Just like Georgetown was named for King George!" "That's right—for George III who, at first, was a hero to the colonies; he lost them in the Revolutionary War because he became oppressive, curbed their freedom. There have been six King Georges; Queen Elizabeth's father was the last one. When King George VI died in 1952, she became Queen and was crowned Queen Elizabeth II, in 1953."

"Mother says we saw her Coronation on TV, Davie; Bruce and I, before you were born," Lori and Bruce were finally awake. "I don't remember it either, Davie," Bruce admitted. "*But*," he had a fact to contribute, "Georgia was named for one of the Georges (George II, I interjected) but it was settled by prisoners brought over by Oglethorpe." "I'd rather have the tunnel," Davie decided. "Wouldn't it have been funny if they'd named it Oglethorpe!" Bruce giggled. "Look, Daddy," he pointed, "there's one with a swimming pool!" We suddenly sniffed fumes from factories and animals under final utilization. Declared Davie: "I'd rather sleep in town . . . even without a swimming pool!" Dave and passengers concurred.

Coming out of the Holland Tunnel—which we decided to claim after all—we saw our first sight of New York! The formation must have been forty-five years old. She was encased in a short, flaming pink sheath and topped with a superabundance of teased blue hair. Awed and agape, we drove on and missed an opportunity. For a few pennies, or peanuts, we might have had a picture. There she was, standing on the corner . . . without hose.

Driving uptown, Dave located a first-class motel off Times Square. It was just three blocks from the motels he had called and it was three dollars cheaper. For twenty-five dollars, we were made comfortable in a large room with two double beds, a single bed, TV and a deluxe bathroom. Our only problem was the elevator. Our room was on the third floor and there were only two elevators. They were of the self-service type and always in use. We finally got the children out—by shouting and pushing buttons; then they ran down the steps of the garden court to the first floor and started their ride again. Guess they'd been confined in the car too long—they were behaving just like other people's children! It was certainly peaceful and quiet in the room; they made each meal; they didn't care there wasn't a swimming pool—but I didn't think we'd be invited back again.

Our first investigation was the United Nations Headquarters located between 42nd and 48th Streets, the East River and Franklin D. Roosevelt Drive: the low, domed General Assembly Building, the towering glass and marble Secretariat, the long, rectangular conference chambers on the river, and south and west—the Library. Of immediate interest was the Fountain in front of the Secretariat which had been a gift from the schoolchildren of the United States and its territories. A beautiful, big, round pool, it had a fascinating pattern of black pebbles formed into sharp, running waves on the white marble floor. We had read that the pebbles had been gathered by women and children from beaches on the Greek Island of Rhodes (and Dave had produced his Med maps of the Greek Islands) and presented to the United Nations. What an appropriate reminder by the "world capital of man" that children were the font, the source, the aim—of all his endeavor. And to reinforce that conviction, and to include children at once in man's scheme, a playground occupied the north end of the United Nations Complex—swings and seesaws for the children of the neighborhood—and the world.

Near by in the Plaza was the lofty Biblical (Isaiah 2:4) injunction engraved in marble: "They Shall Beat Their Swords Into Plowshares, And Their Spears Into Pruning Hooks; Nation Shall Not Lift Up Sword Against Nation, Neither Shall They Learn War Any More."

The site of the United Nations Headquarters was owned by the United Nations, for which they paid—nothing, and it was international territory. Formerly an area of slums, slaughter houses and breweries, John D. Rockefeller, Jr., offered to buy the East River site as a permanent home for the United Nations. The General Assembly had been considering Westchester, N. Y., and Connecticut areas, as well as San Francisco, but accepted the Rockefeller proposal within thirty-six hours, in December 1946. The Secretariat Building was ready for occupancy in 1950; the General Assembly met in its Building in the autumn of 1952, its famous white logo: the world seen from the North Pole, embraced by olive branches—dramatic against a pale orange background rising above the President and Secretary-General's raised table. The rooms were enormous in size, vivid with color, modern and functional in design and furniture.

The room which impressed us the most was the Economic and Social Council Chamber in the Conference Building. The entire wall behind the horseshoe-shaped conference table was covered with a handmade jute drape, weighing seven hundred pounds, which had been made in Sweden in colors of the northern lights, with a design of giant mussel shells—streaks of blues, tangerine and white softening the stark walls, furniture and exposed pipes and ducts overhead. The Chamber was decorated by the Swedish Government. We sat in the plushly cushioned spectator chairs, donned headphones and listened to the official languages of the United Nations: Chinese, English, French, Russian and Spanish; the working languages being English, French and Spanish. The room seemed to reflect the straightforwardness and dignity of the Swedish Secretary-General Dag Hammarskjold who had completed one five-year term and had been elected to another terminating in 1963.

We went downstairs to the Publications Store and the Gift Shop, the Library Building was not completed, and returned to the motel for one elevator ride apiece—they preferred to pilot the contraption alone—dinner and Shakespeare's *Tempest* in Central Park. But when we arrived at the Shakespeare Garden, a light rain began to fall and the *Tempest* in the Park was canceled for a natural version.

"Let's rent a hansom and see Central Park at night," I suggested. "I get to drive the horse," Lori demanded. But, alas, driver and horse refused separation so we clambered into an open carriage, the rain's having stopped abruptly, with a garrulous ex-pugilist at the reins—or so he appeared—and off we ambled. I looked up at the Tudor-style apartment houses with their tall, slender turrets and flowered points and gestured: "Look, children, don't those pinnacles look garish!" "They look like asparagus to me," Davie commented drily, and with ennui, turning his attention to the victoria drawing alongside. "Why that looks like Daniel Webster. It *is* Daniel Webster!" I exclaimed, elated at having identified one statue in the Park. "You know why they put him up there?" asked the friendly driver. "No, why did they put him up there?" thinking I'd learn an effortless historical fact. "'Cause they couldn't get him in the dictionary!" We all laughed appreciatively at that and I shook my head at the children—any one of whom might retort that Daniel was the statesman and Noah, the lexicographer, an especial favorite of Mommy Tom, Davie's and mine.

"Aw, go on," our man motioned to the victoria whip. "Shaddup, Johnson—let's have a little less arguin' and a little better drivin'." "You stop short like that again and you'll have a horseless carriage," Johnson, turning to us for more laughter. The blonde in back, in a yellow dress, stuck out her head and cocktail glass each time Johnson passed Mickey, our equestrian critic: "Wanta race?" Then, "'East side, west side . . . all around the town,'" sang Mickey. "I think he's drunker than the passengers," snorted Johnson, whipping Old Dobbin until we surged ahead. But they passed and challenged us three more times, singing their invitation and the children loved it. We felt we had enjoyed a Central Park-at-night initiation into innocuous levity. The moon flirted with the dissipating clouds and I wrote my notes in a flicker as we trotted and loped around Central Park and through the Sheep Meadow to circle The Lake and then be delivered to our car by the jovial Johnson, who beamed and flourished his topper as he pocketed Dave's tip.

Early the next morning, we were at the New York Stock Exchange and the pretty tour guide singled Davie out of her large group: "What's your company?" as she demonstrated the ticker tape. "The Holland Company," Davie grinned; unhesitatingly, "we make missiles!"

After Davie was awarded the ticker tape which our group checked as it emerged slowly on a large screen overhead, we assembled on a narrow balcony to watch the confusing commotion down below on the floor of the Stock Exchange, our guide's explaining basic elements of the famous, frenetic scene. Davie proudly placed his personalized ticker tape in his horse's-head billfold, proclaiming: "I'm going to take this to school in September!" Our cordial young guide smilingly shook Davie's hand, "Good luck with your missile company," and shook hands with Bruce and Lori, too. We thanked her warmly for the edifying experience; Dave's praising her for the lucid, intelligible presentation.

Having taken the subway to Broad and Wall Streets—the latter so named because the wall had been the protective southern extremity of New Netherland in pre-Revolutionary War days—we walked the few blocks to Battery Park and awaited the ferry to Liberty Island. We were anxious to see "Liberty Enlightening the World," or the Statue of Liberty, given to the United States by France in 1884, as symbol of the two countries' friendship; the pedestal on which it stood, costing more than the statue itself, was given by the people of the United States. It was a mammoth structure which we began to study as the ferry approached the tiny island. Figuring from our guide book, it was about one hundred feet shorter than the Washington monument, the pedestal being slightly over half the height to the crown, with the right arm and lofty torch's extending the welcome beacon to ships and planes—to produce a very etherized lighthouse. The French sculptor, Frédéric Auguste Bartholdi, in a process called "repoussé," shaped thin sheets of copper over a steel framework made by Gustave Eiffel, who was the designer of the Eiffel Tower in Paris.

As we disembarked, I told the children to look for the broken shackle at the base of the feet which represented the break from a tyrannical king—freedom the United States and France had helped each other achieve. To further the poetry of the Statue, it had been presented to our country on July 4 (1884), and the tablet in the left hand bore the date of the Declaration of Independence: July 4, 1776, which had been the chief instrument of freedom for *both* nations.

We rode the elevator to the top of the pedestal and walked around the observation balcony, enjoying the harbor, boats and ferries but failing

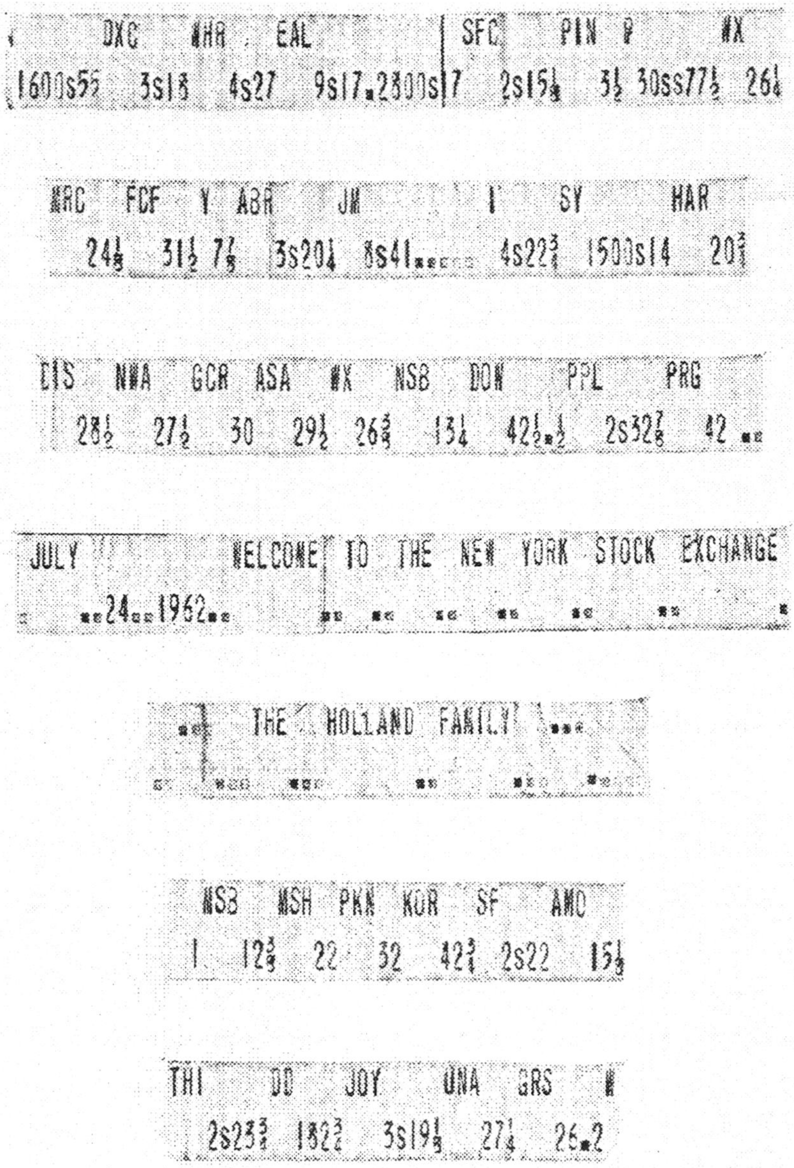
DXC WHR EAL SFC PIN P WX
1600s55 3s18 4s27 9s17 2300s17 2s15 3½ 30ss77½ 26¼
WRC FCF Y ABR JM I SY HAR
24⅛ 31½ 7⅞ 3s20¼ 8s41 4s22¾ 1500s14 20¾
EIS NWA GCR ASA WX NSB DOW PPL PRG
28½ 27½ 30 29½ 26⅜ 13¼ 42½ ½ 2s32⅞ 42
JULY WELCOME TO THE NEW YORK STOCK EXCHANGE
24 1962
THE HOLLAND FAMILY
NSB MSH PKN KOR SF AMO
1 12⅜ 22 32 42¾ 2s22 15⅛
THI DD JOY UNA GRS W
2s23¾ 1s22¾ 3s19⅛ 27¼ 26 2

to see the broken shackle which the base of the Statue precluded. Undaunted, we walked the spiraling stairsteps to the crown—thankfully none of us were subject to vertigo—and emerged, breathlessly, at the celestial windows which revealed a thrilling panorama of harbor and cities and barges. From our eyrie, only the heavy folds of Liberty's Grecian robe were visible and while no severed shackle was discovered, Staten Island was. Dave pointed out the ferries' slithering east of the Statue from our departure point, Battery Park, to the north; twice the distance beyond us, southward, to Staten Island, transporting passengers, cars and trucks. "I've looked enough," proclaimed Bruce, who had an affinity for ferries, "let's go!"

Fortunately, the ladder to the torch was blocked off to the public and we descended, Bruce's advising those, laboriously ascending: "You can't see her feet!" which only we, I suspected, had gone on high to view. Dave and the children were, obligingly, willing to sit a few minutes outside while the poem inscribed on a tablet in the pedestal ("The New Colossus" by Emma Lazarus) was transferred to shorthand:

> Not like the brazen giant of Greek fame,
> With conquering limbs astride from land to land;
> Here at our sea-washed, sunset gates shall stand
> A mighty woman with a torch, whose flame
> Is the imprisoned lightning, and her name
> Mother of Exiles. From her beacon-hand
> Glows world-wide welcome; her mild eyes command
> The air-bridged harbor that twin cities frame.
> "Keep ancient lands, your storied pomp!" cries she
> With silent lips. "Give me your tired, your poor,
> Your huddled masses yearning to breathe free,
> The wretched refuse of your teeming shore.
> Send these, the homeless, tempest-tost to me,
> I lift my lamp beside the golden door!"

The children laughed approvingly as we boarded the Staten Island ferry for a nickel apiece—the greatest bargain of our New England adventure; we paid our nickels again and embarked on another ferry (they ran every ten to fifteen minutes), debarking at the Battery and taking the Broad and Wall subway back to Times Square and our motel.

I examined the children who were examining their Statue of Liberty souvenir, marked "made in Japan." "Davie," I concluded, "we just can't spot-remove your face any longer. You're going to have to take a bath." "Lori," Davie admonished in turn, "don't rub Bruce's face, you're getting him all streaked!" So after everyone had bathed the grime and soot from our pedestrian investigation, the children's checking out the elevator while Dave and I prepared for politer dining, we drove south to Greenwich Village, near NYU and Washington Square, between Broadway and the Hudson River. We had reservations at Albert French's in Greenwich Village, the artists' demesne of New York City, reminiscent of Georgetown but lacking its elegance and élan.

While we awaited our New York strip steaks and Dave and Bruce sampled the Manhattan chowder, I asked the children: "What have you done so far that you've enjoyed most?" "Breathe!" commented Davie, to our ready laughter. "Ridden in the hansom cab," decided Lori. "Eating," demonstrated Bruce, whose capacity was bold and bottomless. Dave reminded Lori: "Yesterday you said, 'The thing I like best about traveling is the gift shop!'" "I've changed my mind," Lori dimpled; "besides, everything's made in Japan!"

"These delivery trucks are terrible," observed Dave as we left the restaurant in the late afternoon and drove south on Broadway, "they dominate the city—together with the taxis," he added as one attempted to crowd in front; not challenging advisedly, a sure-handed, depth-perceptive flyer. The children hooted as Dave forced him back into his own lane. "Most of them don't own their vehicles," Dave explained, "and bent fenders mean nothing to them; I haven't seen a truck or taxi yet which wasn't heavily damaged." "I wouldn't want to live *here*," Lori was convinced; "people are nicer in Washington." "But there are more American flags here," Davie noticed, as we entered the Avenue of the Americas—a lovely, broad street, flag-bordered. And, surprisingly, flags *were* more prominent in New York than in Washington, especially in the Financial District, into which the Americas led, Fifth Avenue and Madison Avenue.

We wanted to cross the Brooklyn Bridge before dark and drive through the Brooklyn Naval Shipyard where our Coast Guard cutter had docked when it returned us to the States from Argentia, Newfoundland. "You've been here before," Dave reminded the children, "but you probably don't remember it." "I might remember tunnels," Bruce suggested, "if we went through some more," nudging Davie, gleefully. So Dave drove us back to Manhattan via the Brooklyn-Battery Tunnel and north along the West Side Express Highway, which edged the Hudson River and through the Lincoln Tunnel to Union City, New Jersey, and south a short distance to Jersey City where we took our Holland Tunnel—and thence to Manhattan at night which had become less bustling. Even Broadway was almost deserted, with cars in every parking space along the streets, apartment dwellers apparently staying home at night after fighting humanity all day. We continued north toward Central Park, enjoying the elaborate apartment-building entrances and hotel interiors—the Vanderbilt, the Hotel Plaza, with chandelier and candlelight's gleaming along Park Avenue.

The next morning, July 25, we awakened to the melodizing Davie and Lori's a cappella strains of "Happy birthday to you . . . happy birthday . . . dear Brucie, happy birthday to you!" Our beaming twelve-year-old selected the Zoo in Central Park and the Empire State Building to be first visited on his birthday, in reverse order. The sky was cloudless and the early morning, already warm as we gazed from the world's highest building over Manhattan, Long Island, and New Jersey, the glistening waters and minute, tinted taxi cabs.

Then we were ready for a walk through the Zoo and a race, part way, to the statues of Hans Christian Andersen, Alice in Wonderland and the Mad Hatter—and a rest on the park bench, for Dave and me, while the children fed the squirrels and pigeons and the ASPCA watered the horses of the hansoms, surreys and victorias from a white covered wagon and a small truck.

Staying on Fifth Avenue, we drove to the Guggenheim Museum, the gorgeous cylindrical building designed by Frank Lloyd Wright, which housed modern art—prompting us to a rapid-ramp departure: "Let's go back to see the blue whale," Davie urged and Dave drove us back to the Children's Zoo.

We walked north on Fifth Avenue along the Park to the Metropolitan Museum of Art, the world's largest, of course, which the children had been to years before. Limiting our choices to Bruce's, we examined Medieval armaments and armour, for both horse and man and Egyptian burial pyramids complete with ancient sarcophagi—and mummies! Then we had lunch in the huge garden court, its high ceiling's billowing with cloud-like draperies and its fountain's bubbling a cascading tune. Dave secured us a choice table and we carried our trays to the water's edge and the children tossed pennies at the dolphins and nymphs. In honor of Bruce, we ate fruit in cantaloupe, chicken chow mein and caramel cream birthday cake!

Leaving New York City, we drove north, paralleling the Hudson River, to Irvington and "Sunnyside," Washington Irving's home. I had been enamoured of Irving's tales since early years and attributed my ocular difficulties to the day I devoured "Rip Van Winkle" in bed, in a darkened room, when I had high fever and the measles and was supposedly "resting my eyes and not reading"—but I could not resist. "Rip Van Winkle" had been the posthumous! writing of Diedrich Knickerbocker, the old Dutch historian who wrote *Knickerbocker's History of New York—From the Beginning of the World to the End of the Dutch Dynasty* and inspired many a prestigious and aristocratic New Yorker to claim descent from the lionized Diedrich Knickerbocker . . . who, unfortunately, never existed.

It was 1809 when the first great work of imaginative literature, *A History of New York*, was created by a native New Yorker—the eleventh child of a merchant family who chose George Washington for a namesake. Washington Irving was the first professional writer of the new American Republic. He immortalized his state, particularly with "The Legend of Sleepy Hollow" and Ichabod Crane; his America; and his president: *Life of Washington*, in five volumes. For drollery, wit and irony, Washington Irving became the American genius of fabulistic exploits elevated to the satiric heights of the English Jonathan Swift, in especial "A Modest Proposal" and Laurence Sterne's *Tristram Shandy.*

We toured the charming house and were impressed with the sunny, book-lined study—he had been a lawyer, ambassador to Spain, world traveler but had never married. The children romped briefly in the woods of Sunnyside on the bluffs of the Hudson while I bought a volume of Washington Irving which included Rip, Ichabod and the unabridged *Knickerbocker History* for I intended to read aloud from the latter as we traveled up the Hudson River to West Point.

I chose the discovery of the island of "Mannahata": "Bruce," I began, "this episode in American history started on the twenty-fifth day of the month!"

In the ever-memorable year of our Lord, 1609, on a Saturday morning, the five-and-twentieth day of March,. . . Master Henry Hudson (Hendrick, the Dutch called him) set sail from Holland in a stout vessel called the Half-Moon, being employed by the Dutch East India Company, to seek northwest passage to China.

The children chortled in unison and I wisely skipped a few pages:

Suffice it to say, the voyage was prosperous and tranquil; the crew, being a patient people, much given to slumber and vacuity, and but little troubled with the disease of thinking—a malady of the mind, which is the sure breeder of discontent. Hudson had laid in abundance of gin and sourkrout, and every man was allowed to sleep quietly at his post unless the wind blew.

There, Dave howled, the children lay down to sleep and I, hysterical with laughter, read valiantly on:

He acted, moreover, in direct contradiction to that ancient and sage rule of the Dutch navigators, who always took in sail at night, put the helm a-port, and turned in—by which precaution they had a good night's rest, were sure of knowing where they were the next morning, and stood but little chance of running down a continent in the dark . . . being under the especial guidance of Providence, the ship was safely conducted to the coast of America; where . . . she at length, on the fourth day of September, entered that majestic bay which at this day expands its ample bosom before the city of New York, and which had never before been visited by any European.

It has been traditionary in our family, that when the great navigator was first blessed with a view of this enchanting island, he was observed, for the first and only time in his life, to exhibit strong symptoms of astonishment and admiration. He is said to have turned to master Juet, and uttered these remarkable words, while he pointed towards this paradise of the new world—"See! there!"

After tarrying a few days in the bay . . . our voyagers weighed anchor, to explore a mighty river which emptied in to the bay . . . little doubting but it would turn out to be the much looked-for passage to China! . . . After sailing, however, above an hundred miles up the river, he (Hendrick) found the watery world around him began to grow more shallow and confined, the current more rapid, and perfectly fresh—phenomena not uncommon in the ascent of rivers, but which puzzled the honest Dutchman prodigiously. A consultation was therefore called, and having deliberated full six hours, they were brought to a determination by the ship's running aground—whereupon they unanimously concluded, that there was but little chance of getting to China in this direction . . . he forthwith recrossed the sea to Holland, where he was received with great welcome by the honorable East India Company, who were very much rejoiced to see him come back safe—with their ship; and at a large and respectable meeting of first merchants and burgomasters of Amsterdam, it was unanimously determined, that, as a munificent reward for the eminent services . . . and the important discovery he had made, the great river . . . should be called after his name!—and it continues to be called Hudson river unto this very day.

"Did he ever get to China?" queried Davie, whom Irving had not been able to lull to sleep. "No, he died shortly after he returned to Holland," I remembered, "but his discovery of Manhattan Island and the Hudson River was of greater wealth to the world." "And, of course, he explored the Arctic," Dave added. "Hudson Bay and Hudson Strait in Canada are named for him; that Hudson Bay blanket on Bruce's bed—the heavy one, white with red, black and yellow stripes—came from the Arctic. I visited Canada with my brothers, sister and parents when I was about your age." "Are we going that far north next summer?" Bruce had heard his name. Dave laughed: "Didn't you have enough cool weather in Newfoundland? It's about like that. We'll be south and east—in the Gulf of St. Lawrence and the Bay of Fundy." "I can hardly wait!" interposed Lori. "Oh, look!" she gasped, "how far down the Hudson is!"

We had crossed the river at Tarrytown, north of Irving's Sunnyside, and taken the Tappan Zee Bridge to the west bank and had arrived at the West Point Military Academy, strategically perched high above the Hudson River. We drove through, inspected cannons positioned on the bluffs, were informed they would shortly be fired and walked back the recommended distance—the boys more excited than I had ever seen them, wide-eyed and grinning broadly. The brisk cadets, crisp in their summer uniforms despite the heat, completed their preparations and the cannons boomed rapidly over the banks, the smoke's hanging in small clouds and then drifting back towards us. The reverberations were not as loud as I had anticipated but satisfactorily and martially resonant for the boys—all three!

It was five o'clock and too early for dinner; besides, we were not dressed for the Officer's Club and any other investigation, after the cherished cannonade, would have been anticlimactic. Dave checked the map and we decided to attempt Hyde Park and Roosevelt's home before it closed. "Would they have been as friendly if you were in uniform?" Lori asked. "Maybe not," Dave chuckled. "We beat them last year." "Let's go back and tell them who you are!" our ever-ready, elder son schemed. "No need," laughed his Dad, "we're friends—except at football games."

We arrived at the home of Franklin D. Roosevelt at Hyde Park in time to revisit the atmospheric mansion (I could always envision President Roosevelt's stately Mother presiding with stern grace over the household when her son was there); the children were interested in the ramps and conveniences for the crippled President. In the Museum, the children discovered much Navy memorabilia (he had been Assistant Secretary of the Navy from 1913 to 1920 as well as a private sailor at the summer home in Campobello, Maine), including his famous lined Navy cape which he had worn at the Yalta Conference in February 1945, where he discussed peace terms and the postwar world with Winston Churchill and Joseph Stalin—his last major meeting before his death at Warm Springs, Georgia, April 12, 1945, just one month before Germany's surrender.

Eleanor Roosevelt had continued her husband's humanitarian policies as an original delegate to the United Nations (1945-1952) and had served a second time in 1961 and 1962 as one of the framers of the U.N.'s Declaration of Human Rights.

The children were touched by Franklin Roosevelt's love for his little black scotty, "Fala," and spent pensive minutes at the graves of the two in the Rose Garden.

We bought the *Autobiography of Fala* and an unframed picture of F.D.R. just as the gift shop was closing.

Enroute to Newport, Rhode Island, the next day, we decided to take the Jamestown ferry to save time. "Oh, I remember this turn," I suddenly realized. "I took the wheel here while you pulled on your uniform. Remember?" But Dave did not remember. "When was that?" Lori inquired. "The summer of 1948," Dave remembered that much. "When did we leave New York City?" Lori was making entries in a small notebook. "On my birthday, July 25, at 2:30 P.M." Bruce was precise and accurate.

"This is Rhode Island where Lori was born! Isn't this exciting!" I thrilled. "How long did it take us?" Lori pondered. "Nine months," wondering about the question. "No-o-o," Lori giggled, "I mean—how long from New York!" "It's your turn to keep the log tomorrow, Bruce," Davie decided, "then I'll do it on the 28th." I looked around as we approached the Jamestown ferry landing. "I don't remember going over on the ferry!" I puzzled. "We didn't," Dave stated; "we didn't have much money then."

As we awaited the arrival of the ferry, the children escaped from the car to investigate the beach, finding four live starfish before the cumbersome vehicle docked. Dave eased the car onto the ferry and we had four extra passengers—but one less Bruce. "Bruce left his Japanese popgun by the fifth starfish," Davie was not alarmed, "the one he didn't get to bring." "This one's growing a new leg; see, Mother!" Lori attempted to distract me from anxiety as the ferry bumped and seemed to move. I was not unaccustomed to the situation: Bruce had always had an uncanny proclivity to do the wrong thing at the least convenient moment. Just as the last two cars had lurched aboard, Bruce tore around the corner and squeezed down to the car. In flew the popgun and Bruce disappeared—his next escapade, no doubt, fermenting. As Dave braked forward to drive off the ferry, Bruce and the fifth starfish reappeared, just in time for the entire family to drive to the Viking Hotel where Dave and I had spent our first night in Rhode Island fourteen years before. And little had changed in the quaint town, except the Viking had a swank new Motor Inn and an Olympic-sized swimming pool, both readied for our eager three. "But you can't take in the starfish!" I anticipated. "Why not?" Bruce moaned, "I've washed them." "In the ice bucket," Lori warned Dave—halfway to the door with that receptacle in hand. "Swim an hour," Dave looked at his watch, "then we'll see where Lori was born, go to 'The Breakers' and have dinner." "Alright, Daddy," agreed his progeny, meekly. "Better count the starfish!" I urged Dave.

I wrote Mother and Dad two cards from Hyannis, Massachusetts, and one from Hyannis Port, mailing the third in the little frame post office near a small store—just yards from the famous summer "Kennedy Compound," on the windy Massachusetts Nantucket Sound. Both postmaster and storekeeper spoke with warmth and pride in J.F.K. whom they had known from his childhood, the storekeeper's adding: "He still comes all the time bringing his nieces and nephews for ice cream; he hasn't changed a bit and we all love him!" I asked her what souvenir I should take home: "I want something indigenous, not 'made in Japan.'" "You want to buy candles," she declared at once. "It's Hyannis Port's only 'industry'" and gave Dave the directions to the picturesque white frame factory where we acquired bayberry candles and additional Kennedy lore.

> Friday morn, 7:45. Stayed in Hyannis at motel with swimming pool, boats and fishing; ready to go rowing before checkout. Drove past K. house; guards cut off access. Hyannis like Va. Beach. Beautiful town, lovely shops, swarms of people, high prices. Had to send a card with postmark, Hyannis Port. This picture reminds me of Lacy. He would have been one of the bright young men. Love DBH[3], L&B.

We left Hyannis and the Rainbow Motel, Bruce's claiming: "The boats were more fun than the elevators"; and Davie: "I liked the ferries best." "The hansom ride was the most fun for me," Lori was consistent. Passing the Pancake Man, Bruce exclaimed: "Boy, I'll miss that!" savoring the memory of cranberry pancakes, Swedish with lingonberry butter, quahog (fresh chopped quahog clams), bacon cakes (strip bacon in buttermilk batter), three little pigs in blankets and ten silver dollars—each free to sample others' orders. Lori laughed and pointed to the Green Harbor Village which advertised "Pool 3000 miles wide" and Bruce shook his head: "No boats," still content with the Rainbow.

Dave took Highway 28 to Cranberry Village, east around the cove from Hyannis. "Some fall I hope we can see the cranberry harvest but I'll probably be in Paris this year. At least we can see the bogs and the vines today." "Do you remember what the only native American fruit is?" I asked. "Cranberries!" sang three. "We learned that at your Scout camp; I still have the history and recipes," recalled Lori. "Can you remember picking wild cranberries in Kodiak?" Dave wondered. "I don't think so," Lori was dubious but Bruce was not and shook his head negatively. "They grew on bushes there, low-bush and high-bush but here the commercial cranberries grow on vines which they flood in winter. They stay green under the ice. When they are harvested, the bogs are flooded again, the cranberries float to the top and are scooped up by machines."

We stopped at the Cranberry Village, inspected the evergreen vines with their minute leaves, smaller than boxwood, and noted the sandy, acid soil which reminded us of Virginia Beach. "The principal cranberry-growing area in the world is here!" Davie read the sign. "And those were the best cranberry pancakes!" Bruce claimed. "But not as good as Mommy's cranberry bread," remonstrated loyal Lori, "and I have her recipe in my Girl Scout notebook!"

Dave continued along Nantucket Sound so that the children could sight the lighthouse. "The tallest is at Cape Hatteras," Bruce asserted. "Down by Kitty Hawk," Davie remembered that fact, too. "I don't think I'd like living in a lighthouse," Lori sighed, relievedly. "No one does now," Dave reminded her; "the Coast Guard operates them automatically, by electricity. But not too long ago, they were manned around the clock; a couple often lived in them, and sometimes—children." Leaving the slow scenic route, Dave crossed over to Highway 6 and drove north along the Cape Cod National Seashore with Cape Cod Bay to our left. The landscape was sand—sand dunes and blowing sea grasses. He stopped at Truro Beach for the children to slide down the dunes, romp through the tall grasses and place their starfish—still miraculously alive—at the water's edge.

Davie pointed as he slid down his dune, "Look at all those cars—isn't it terrific!" Bruce looked, "No, it's traffic!" he guffawed. "Quick!" Dave directed us to the car, "dump your shoes and socks and let's go." The one highway was suddenly alive with vehicles and the dinner hour was approaching. "We'll eat first and then go to the Pilgrim monument; it'll be five when we get to Provincetown," Dave declared. "But let's not go to a motel coffee shop; we need atmosphere—something authentic," I hoped.

Dave found a parking space, expertly wheeling the buggy in and we strung along the narrow sidewalk of the incomparable oceanic town, curiously timeless and styleless in its confinement and isolation but bohemian in its frontier flavor rather than rugged and self-sufficing. We discovered a small clapboard cafe up two cement steps, with the oxymoronic name, "Plain and Fancy." It boasted four tables, the one in the bay window was empty, the napery was immaculate and we were smilingly invited to stay. And it was an excellent Cape Cod meal! Collectively we enjoyed: shrimp bisque, clam chowder, of quahogs, fried clams, seafood platter, pork chops, tossed salad, lyonnaise potatoes, beets, strawberry mousse and mocha pudding. I meant to ask about the clams because New England clam chowder was generally made with soft-shell or long-neck rather than quahogs which they had used in Hyannis as well, but—Bruce, Davie and Lori, satiated, were clamoring to leave, having spotted a gift shop from the bay of Plain and Fancy.

Even the air was expensive in Cape Cod! The gift shop would sell us a can for ninety cents but we laughed and desisted, buying only twelve large clam shells for Mother to bake deviled crab in—at bridge-luncheon time. We saw the Monument to the second wave of Pilgrims who arrived on the *Mayflower*, the captain of which had been unsuccessful in locating the mouth of the Hudson River and anchored instead in Provincetown Harbor, November 21, 1620. "Why didn't any of them know where they were sailing?" Davie wondered. "Navigational equipment was very primitive," Dave explained, "and map-making was worse. It's a wonder they got here at all!" "How did they discover Plymouth Rock?" Bruce asked. "Because that's straight across Cape Cod Bay to the west," Dave pointed. "I guess it's a little south—on the mainland; we'll see it before dark if we get started." "They didn't get there until almost Christmas," Lori announced; "sailboats are certainly slow." "I believe they stayed anchored awhile and sent out a small boat to find a better place to settle," I speculated.

"We can get to Plymouth Rock in two hours; that'll be a little after eight. We'll stop once more for a few minutes at E. Sandwich, on the beach, right before we leave the Cape." "Does that mean we eat again?" Bruce looked a bit pained and was glad to see his father shake his head and laugh: "No, that's the name of the town! We'll stop at E. Sandwich Beach before we get to Sandwich." "Is there a Hamburger too?" snickered Davie. "Well, there's a Hamburg in New York, New Jersey, Iowa and Pennsylvania—and in Germany," his father chuckled; "names are funny things, aren't they!" Time for a bit of background I decided: "'Sandwich' is an English family name; the food was invented in the eighteenth century by the Earl of Sandwich who didn't want to leave the table where he was playing cards, or some sort of a game. He asked to be brought meat between two slices of bread and served at his gaming table." "He must have been winning," Bruce thought. "Or lazy," Davie added. "And wealthy," nodded Lori. "Or maybe," Dave extrapolated, "he was losing so badly he couldn't afford to stop—to go to the dinner table!" ."Anyhow," said Bruce, "I *like* him!"

The children piled out at E. Sandwich, ran and dug on the beach, found a few choice clam shells and bade good-bye to Cape Cod Bay as we crossed the Canal at Sandwich, taking Highway 3 to Plymouth Rock. The Rock proved a disappointment to our threesome despite the neatly chiseled "1620" on its surface which was too small to provoke images of a hundred cold, weary Pilgrims' stepping ashore with its insignificant support. Although the large concrete-roofed monument overhead added importance to the spot of history, the children voted to only inspect "Plimoth Plantation," the reconstructed village, briefly—with its nineteen, mostly thatched, cottages, all of which were replicas. They had seen the "Lost Colony" site of the 1587 settlement on Roanoke Island, North Carolina, and the splendid 1607 Jamestown re-creation, the first permanent English settlement, visited repeatedly during five years in Norfolk, so the last daylight-inspection time was concentrated on the *Mayflower*, anchored east of Plymouth Rock. It was similar to, and somewhat larger than, the *Sarah Constant, Goodspeed* and *Discovery* at Jamestown.

We were replete with Massachusetts history when we stopped for the night in Boston at the Fenwick Motor Court—and very sandy.

The next morning was spent at Harvard, Harvard Square, and MIT, the latter impressing the children most with its perpetual pendulum—much like the one at the Smithsonian and the enormous, beautiful-eyed owl, his head turning almost completely around, his eyes steady, as he watched the children move back and forth, checking his coordination and comparing his fat, fluffy body to the stuffed owl of the same size, its pitiful body—sans feathers—hilariously, unbelievably thin. But the MIT Observatory was the most thrilling of all; the lecture and demonstration of the heavenly splendors, far too brief.

It was the Boston Market Place for lunch at the notorious Durgin-Park Restaurant which accepted no reservations, not even from the President of the United States! Everyone awaited turn on the bare wooden steps, to be served at food-smeared, red-and-white-checked tablecloths by insulting waitresses, who would just as soon spill the food on you as to set it in front of you. From the line, the food was seen, your orders given and paid for and you were unceremoniously seated at the first evacuated table where you hoped to find enough clean napkins for each, piled in the center of the splattered cloth. I used three extras to cover the wet stains beneath the children's plates, and no one demurred—just shouted for more napkins to be delivered by the sullen waitress.

The food, served with speed, in overwhelmingly large proportions which slopped over the plates, was delicious and inexpensive. We ate approvingly of: apple juice, short ribs, chicken pot pie, whipped potatoes, cornbread, Boston baked beans, apple pan dowdy and baked Indian pudding, flooding its bowl and vanilla ice cream melting on top, but, oh! what a treat! We were able to buy a Durgin-Park bean pot, for a sole dollar, before we were pushed back downstairs!

Walden Pond provided exercise in the afternoon and the literary charms of Concord offered the Minuteman Bridge which we all raced across to the Old Manse, my lingering within and the children's returning with Dave to study the first-shot site of the Revolutionary War.

But I read no poetry until that night when we had dinner at Longfellow's Wayside Inn, in South Sudbury. We had returned to the motel for cleansing and Sunday attire for our 8:00 o'clock dinner, reservations mandatory which Dave had made from Hyannis. We had arrived at seven-thirty to tour the historic old Inn, restored by the Ford Foundation, visit the mill and water wheel and the gift shop long enough for me to buy Longfellow's *Tales of a Wayside Inn*.

As we were escorted to a candlelit table for five, Bruce took his seat, looked around solemnly and asked loudly: "Mother does this place have atmosphere?" I assured him it did but I wasn't sure how friendly! But the hostess laughed and we did too. I read several pages, quietly, then asked Lori to inscribe it with date and location and she read "Paul Revere's Ride" so that we would be prepared to visit the North Church, Cemetery and ride the swanboats in Boston Commons on the morrow.

It was an elegant meal: roast Long Island duckling, crab Newburg, prime rib, fruit shrub, cantaloupe with lime, fruit cup with sherbet, potatoes, peas and squash. Bruce looked at the dessert menu and wondered: "Mother, what would I like for dessert?" I was a taster and Bruce knew I liked a variety, five preferably, but Lori's was always so delicious that it was gone before I remembered to sample it, Davie's was usually vanilla ice cream, Dave's—covered with chocolate and unrecognizable but Bruce's, I could always count on, for his satiety, with lobster, crab, clams and duck, made any after-fare, extraneous. We ventured boldly! I chose Norwegian cream cake for Bruce, crème de menthe pie for me. Lori ordered pecan pie, Dave wanted to compare their Indian pudding to Durgin-Park's and Davie's eye was caught by "Deep Dish

Apple Pie with Spiced Whipped Cream." Cocking his head and putting one hand to his stomach, Davie murmured unhappily: "I just wish it wasn't so *deep!*"

As I wrote Mother from the Wayside Inn so that it could be mailed in Sudbury: "We're reeking with history!" We had more Sunday morning, July 28, with Paul Revere and the lanterns in the belfry of the Old North Church: "two if by sea," prompting the Longfellow-immortalized ride which sparked the Revolutionary War. After riding the swanboats in Boston Commons, we drove to Bunker Hill on the bustling Boston thoroughfare, the grassy knoll and tall obelisk's dividing the traffic and minimizing the significance of that heroic defeat which had strengthened the colonists' resolve after the first major encounter with the British, June 17, 1775.

The old frigate *Constitution* in the Boston Naval Yard, preserved and ennobled by Oliver Wendell Holmes' poem "Old Ironsides," was boarded before we left the historic town's vestiges of our two wars with the mother country.

My next card to Mother pictured the "House of Seven Gables" in Salem, Massachusetts:

Mon. noon. Stayed in Pine Pt., Me. right on the windy beach. Children found sand dollars before breakfast after a 2-mile hike up the lovely beach. They made me go too. We're loaded with shells & sea urchins etc. This is claimed to be *the* house but it probably is not. Hawthorne's birth house had been moved down in back. We saw Walden Pond, Old Manse, Emerson's home, L.M. Alcott. Love DB³L&B.

Lori dated our new blue copy of *House of Seven Gables*, July 29, 1962, read us a bit about Hawthorne's life and packed it away with Longfellow's *Tales* -- and Irving's *The History* --.

Maine we planned to visit again next summer, so the White Mountains of New Hampshire and Robert Frost country drew our attention as we packed our sand dollars and headed northwest. Twice we had been to Mt. Washington and the third Dave was determined we would ride the first mountain-climbing cog railroad in the world, which backed up the mountain, its boiler lying nose down to ride level on the slope. It was the highest point in the Northeast and was manned the year-round by NOAA (National Oceanographic and Atmospheric Administration) which had recorded the greatest gust of wind on earth: 231 miles an hour, April of 1934 on Mt. Washington.

The children loved New Hampshire from its antique-seeming cog railroad, covered bridges and aura of Robert Frost, Lori's favored poet, to the high-rising, many-staired waterfalls of the Flume in Franconia Notch State Park and the Old Man of the Mountain.

Vermont provided white cheddar cheese, maple candy and the Green Mountain Boys who captured Fort Ticonderoga by stealth under the command of Ethan Allen, in 1775, during the early days of the Revolution. We stayed at the Ticonderoga Inn near the sturdy old stone Fort on the New York shore of Lake Champlain. Imagination soared as we had dinner in the historic old Inn and inspected the ramparts of the Fort with the Green Mountain Boys in uniform—to answer all queries and pose for pictures. There was just something about cannons which appealed instantly to the boys, and Lori too, each of whom was somewhat of an expert after Jamestown, Williamsburg, Fort McHenry, Gettysburg and West Point, Concord and Lexington.

Dave drove us south down the Adirondacks to Lake George where we had a delightful but brief visit with CAPT Bob Livingston and Jean at their summer lake cottage in the thick woods. They urged us to stay but there was another compulsion: Lake George Battlefield and Fort and south of Glens Falls, the Saratoga National Historic Park. We were curious about the Saratoga Springs Race Track, as well, where The Belmont was annually held, the third race of the "Triple Crown," having seen the second run—The Preakness—in Baltimore, in the balmy spring-time.

The children had been entertained by more than horses at The Preakness when they discovered that the victory floral blanket was composed of yellow daisies with black shoe-polish eyes' masquerading as the rudbeckia or black-eyed susan, the Maryland state flower, which did not bloom until July, and which was more native to the Midwest than to the Atlantic Seaboard. Before the famous race was run, Pimlico presented early arrivals with a harness race reminiscent of Will Rogers in the classic *State Fair* movie—a race we all preferred because it was perceivable: each beautiful horse, each brightly colored driver in satin adroitly maneuvering the drawn sulky, a two-wheeled carriage sitting very low to the track. We chose favorites, very unscientifically, by color or name, and cheered wildly in both races, staying to enjoy the painting of The Preakness' victory colors on the horse-and-jockey weather vane high above the Winner's Circle.

The Hudson River trickled into existence in the lower Adirondacks and we envisioned "Hendrick's" concluding he was not in China and laughed at his fortuitous success. Paralleling the Hudson to Albany for a brief tour of the history-rich river city with an almost vertical governmental center gleaming new and white in the August sun, we crossed the "Dutch" river and aimed southeast for Pittsfield, Massachusetts, through green ski trails, to the home of Oliver Wendell Holmes, the literary contemporary of Washington Irving—not Oliver Wendell Holmes, jurist, who served on the Supreme Court thirty years, until 1932, the senior Holmes' distinguished son and namesake.

I had been introduced early by Mother to *Autocrat of the Breakfast Table* and admired the witty essays of the elder Holmes as well as his early Americana poetry. One of the savants of the Harvard-Concord-Emerson milieu, he held supremacy as a conversationalist and lecturer. Dr. Holmes, as a professor of medicine at Harvard, was sent exhausted students at the end of the day because he alone could keep them awake—with his humorously sparkling lectures on anatomy, in which he occupied "not a chair, but a settee" because his instruction was demanded in kindred departments. Being thus in the Berkshire Hills, we stayed overnight at Lenox after attending an evening performance outdoors at Tanglewood of the Boston Symphony Orchestra directed by Eugene Ormandy in a gloriously idyllic, pastoral setting, lyrical without a note's being played. The many gems of Massachusetts and so few hours to study them!

With Lori's ascendancy into the amorphous world of the "teenager," and Bruce's joining her shortly after Dave's retirement, we were conscious of the imminence of college and canvassed New England's distinguished universities, mostly via Dave's camera. Robert was soon to arrive in Northampton, Massachusetts, as Chief of Staff of the V.A. Hospital and Head of Psychiatry, so Dave drove due east to that beautiful town to view Smith College, and in the area: Mt. Holyoke; Amherst College and Emily Dickinson's birthplace at Amherst; and the University of Massachusetts, eventually chosen by one of Robert's progeny. (Robert and Viola's eldest, Joan, had chosen Trinity in San Antonio and Boston College, for her Master's, teaching English at Chapel Hill, University of North Carolina. Patti was loyal to the University of Massachusetts; Bobby to my archrival, Michigan State and Ricky to the University of Nebraska.)

Continuing straight south to Hartford, at which we contrived to arrive at dinner time, we furthered our culinary survey at the Honiss' Oyster House. The molluscan cuisine was excellent, and the atmosphere quaintly unassuming—the children's ranking both slightly below Boston's Durgin-Park and Wayside Inn at South Sudbury but comparable to the Old Meeting House Inn at Little Compton, Rhode Island, and Twombly's Tavern at Peterborough, New Hampshire, and Locke-Ober's in Boston but none touching the piquant heights of savor and site of Ruth Wakefield's Toll House at Whitman, Massachusetts, still famous for her 1930 cookie-creation.

Surfeited and sleepy—Dave concluded activity at New Haven Harbor—we trooped into a luxurious, residential motel close to the University, the children's not even reconnoitering the swimming pool. The next morning we saw the walled splendors of Yale, the country's third oldest educational institution, by our calculations. Established in 1701, Yale was next to the College of William and Mary (1693) at Williamsburg, Virginia; with Harvard University, foremost, at Cambridge, Massachusetts (1636). Princeton (1746) educated many of the early American statesmen and literati in Princeton, New Jersey; as well as Columbia University, New York City (1754), Aunt Beth's school; Brown in Providence, Rhode Island (1764), eventually selected by Lori's Nebraska cousin and chief competitor in age—John (later, Dr. Holland).

Feeling New England had been as educatory as time and inclination permitted, we left Connecticut and proceeded to Coney Island to frolic and swim and, while I foundered on the beach, Dave and the children fished, having used their gear just twice—at Hyannis and in Maine. We arrived at our hotel in downtown Philadelphia in late afternoon with ample time for repast preparations, arriving at Old Original Bookbinder's, down by the Delaware River. That marvelous landmark, all-famous since 1865 and even extolled—much later—in the *Congressional Record*, was considered by the children as important to their culinary experience as the Toll House. There was a full tank of lobsters, from which we chose our dinner—much easier than choosing from pet frogs—and a long counter where chefs prepared clams in special steamers which extracted the sand. We relished snapper soup while our clams steamed and our lobsters broiled, and, later, shared a mandatory dessert: Bookbinder's cheesecake with cherries, not intending to eat royally the next day when we would be homeward-bound.

After a light breakfast, we strolled Independence Square in the old city were Jefferson's Declaration of Independence had been adopted, the

Continental Congress and Constitutional Convention of 1787 had met and our Government had sat from 1790 to 1800, and of course—we saw the Liberty Bell and the petite brick house of Betsy Ross's early, not first, flag.

As we piled into the car, Dave inquired: "Do you want to spend the day at Atlantic City and drive on home tonight or do you want to stay out another day and go back through Gettysburg?" "What about our salt-water taffy?" worried Bruce, "don't we get any?" "We'll go just long enough for that," promised sweet-toothed Dave, who had recollected—audibly—that delicacy from his childhood's travels. "Maybe we'll find another baby rabbit," planned Davie, mentally enroute to the battlefield. "And eat again at the Dutch Cupboard!" appended Lori, dimpling in anticipation. I applauded her reverie, musing about the Pennsylvania Dutch to whose culture—and kitchens—we seemed to gravitate when at leisure.

Shortly after school abandoned us, we had hurried off to Gettysburg, forgetting the sage Pennsylvania Dutch axiom, which so titillated us the first time we saw it: "The hurrier I go, the behinder I get!" I recognized myself and tried to get a little ahead as I wrote a card of summer freedom to Mother from the Dutch Cupboard:

> Sat. afternoon, Gettysburg, June 23, 1962. Having Schnitz Un Knepp, Sauerbraten, Shoofly pie at this quaint little restaurant. We're getting ready to relive another battle. Children got excellent reports. Lori made all A's except B in gym. We're enjoying our leisure. It's good to read again—and cook. Had swiss steak and rice last night (like old-time Sat. night) and fresh green beans; a fresh blackberry pie. Love, DB³L&B

Dave took the Atlantic City Expressway southeast of wonderful Philadelphia and we were sauntering the Boardwalk very shortly, glorying in the ocean again and not anxious to depart. But after a long walk through the throngs, Brooklyn accents prominent, and boxes of salt-water taffy from three shops—Dave conveniently unsure of the source of his boyhood confection—we straggled docilely to the car; jaws rhythmical.

No one was hungry at Valley Forge, where Washington had wintered his troops, and where we visited the new, impressive American Baptist Convention Headquarters which Mother and Dad had recommended we show the children.

Taking the Pennsylvania Turnpike to Adamstown, Dave drove us southwest through exquisite Pennsylvania Dutch farmland, geometrically green and gold-squared on the rolling hills of the brisk Conestoga Creek in Lancaster County. The barns, contrasting the fields, with fresh brick-red paint, were invariably adorned with vivid round "hex signs" on a white ground which we could not interpret until we stopped at the Lancaster Fair where we glimpsed the perfection of their famed produce, bought hex signs and a book explaining that the Pennsylvania Dutch were German. Our new book identified both bottle-stopper hex signs and Mennonites, whom we saw at the Fair and in somber attire in wagons along the highway. They lived and farmed principally in Lancaster County, we read. After over-sampling our taffy, the large, hot, doughy, soft, salty pretzels—with a soft drink—were welcomed by all as a surcease from sweetness.

But we were only half through our candy-spree: Hershey was northwest and Dave, magnetically on track, pulled us and the car to that irresistible town. The factory was closed when we arrived; I was outvoted and we stayed at the Hershey Hotel, a very old and imposing resort on a green height overlooking a magnificent rose garden, mulched with redolent cacao-bean hulls.

Strolling the gardens in the last sunshine, we recorded the ones we "needed" to plant when we returned to the Midwest. Almost reeling from deliciousness of old roses, and chocolate, our appetites returned with a verve amid speculation that there might be a Hershey dessert—or two—on the menu. But first, thorough lavation for each after a sandy, sticky, doughy day.

The boys even donned white shirts from Dave's suitcase; ties, from mine—and jackets; leaving theirs, crammed with fishing tackle, socks and sand dollars, safely closed. Lori's bag, housing the souvenirs, offered one last, clean dining outfit. Tomorrow, fortunately, we could "slum."

We broke our fast early and accompanied the first tour of the Hershey Plant, the grounds artistically landscaped by the Hershey Nursery and aromatic with cacao mulch—which we bought for our roses. Only one bag could be squeezed into the trunk which had accumulated a few boxes of rare old volumes discovered in the ubiquitous New England antique shops which undervalued books and overvalued objects. The children, gleefully accepting lagniappes'—tasting sweeter than purchased candy, contented themselves at gift-shop departure time with Hershey Kisses.

Crossing the Susquehanna at Harrisburg, we traveled slightly southwest to the familiar terrain of Gettysburg and drove to the boulders and cannons where the baby rabbit had been found—the year before.

Satisfied that no orphans needed a home, we returned to the favorite site: the Dutch Cupboard, and ordered lunch.

South through the Catoctin Mountains to Frederick, Maryland, I read for the first time since we left Philadelphia when I noted the information that Henry Hudson discovered Delaware Bay before he blundered into the New York river. Now I was ready with a poem from my new, dusty volume of John Greenleaf Whittier. "We're going to visit the home of Barbara Frietchie, a Civil War heroine made famous by Whittier—in fact, he *created* her from a composite of brave women he had read about." "But why are we going to a house named for a poem?" demurred Davie, the realist. "Because it shows the power of the pen!" I suggested. "Many myths, especially of wars, are so popular they're indistinguishable from fact. Don't you think that's interesting?" I asked my youngest. "*No!*" responded four, emphatically. "You have to be informed of the universal fiction in order to refute it, do you not?" I persisted. "Go ahead, Mother," decided Bruce, the mediator, "we'll listen." "You children read the poem to us; I'll just read the introduction."

Davie volunteered to start as I handed back the book. He looked it over. "I'll be narrator," he decided; "Lori—you be Barbara; Bruce—you read Stonewall. 'Barbara Frietchie,'" he announced:

> Up from the meadows rich with corn,
> Clear in the cool September morn,
> The clustered spires of Frederick stand
> Green-walled by the hills of Maryland.
> Round about them orchards sweep,
> Apple and peach tree fruited deep,
> Fair as the garden of the Lord
> To the eyes of the famished rebel horde,
> On that pleasant morn of the early fall
> When Lee marched over the mountain wall;
> Over the mountains winding down,
> Horse and foot, into Frederick Town.
> Forty flags with their silver stars,
> Forty flags with their crimson bars,
> Flapped in the morning wind: the sun
> Of noon looked down, and saw not one.
> Up rose old Barbara Frietchie then,
> Bowed with her fourscore years and ten;

"Gee, she was old!" expostulated Davie. "I didn't think they lived that long," Lori agreed. "*Read*!" demanded Bruce. "My line's coming."

> Bravest of all in Frederick town,
> She took up the flag the men hauled down;
> In her attic window the staff she set,
> To show that one heart was loyal yet.
> Up the street came the rebel tread,
> Stonewall Jackson riding ahead.

"Alright!" approved Bruce. "Two words?" he remonstrated, poking Davie.

> Under his slouched hat left and right
> He glanced; the old flag met his sight.
> "Halt!" (shouted Bruce, and it was a good thing Dave was)
>   —the dust-brown ranks stood fast,
> "Fire!" (thundered Bruce, frightening all in the parking lot)
>   —out blazed the rifle-blast.
> It shivered the window, pane and sash;
> It rent the banner with seam and gash.
> Quick as it fell, from the broken staff
> Dame Barbara snatched the silken scarf.
> She leaned far out on the window-sill,
> And shook it forth with a royal will.

"Go, Lori," prodded Davie; and Lori, in her best superannuated, lachry-mose wail:

> "Shoot, if you must, this old gray head,
> But spare your country's flag," she said.
> A shade of sadness, a blush of shame,
> Over the face of the leader came;
> The nobler nature within him stirred
> To life at the woman's deed and word;

Bruce whipped out his sword and waved it threateningly, commanding in the voice of a martinet; lips, snarling; jaw—outthrust:

> "Who touches a hair of yon gray head
> Dies like a dog! March on!" he said.

All day long through Frederick street
Sounded the tread of marching feet:
All day long that free flag tossed
Over the heads of the rebel host.
Ever its torn folds rose and fell
On the loyal winds that loved it well;
And through the hill-gaps sunset light
Shone over it with a warm good-night.
Barbara Frietchie's work is o'er
And the Rebel rides on his raids no more.
Honor to her! and let a tear
Fall, for her sake, on Stonewall's bier.
Over Barbara Frietchie's grave,
Flag of Freedom and Union, wave!
Peace and order and beauty draw
Round thy symbol of light and law;
And ever the stars above look down
On thy stars below in Frederick town!

"Let's go see where she might have lived," concluded Davie. "And tell everyone she didn't," planned Bruce. "It's as small as Betsy Ross's house," Lori observed and turned to me: "was *she* fictional, too?" "No, she lived," I assured her, "although historians believe that the first flag of the Revolution was made by Rebecca Young of Philadelphia, not Elizabeth Ross of Philadelphia. General Washington was supposed to have requested the flag and professional flag-maker Becky Young was commissioned to make it in the fall of 1775—almost a year before Betsy Ross was supposedly approached." "Did it look like this?" wondered Davie, pointing to "Barbara Frietchie's" flag. "No, it had the same thirteen stripes but the field of blue held intersecting red and white crosses of St. George and St. Andrew." "Who were they?" Davie was never content with just a rudimentary answer. "The St. George cross is used in the Union Jack, the English flag; it's a Greek cross, red on a white ground. St. Andrews is a town in Scotland—has one of the oldest golf courses in the world, guess golf originated in that area (Dave nodded in apparent affirmation, though I'd seen that nod before, during a prolix explication); it looks like a white X on a blue ground. It was called the Grand Union flag and Betsy Ross couldn't have made it. Why not?" I checked to ascertain if I had any listeners. "Because Betsy Ross had five-pointed stars on hers," Bruce was still with me. "We didn't have stars on our flags until almost a year after the Declaration of Independence; it was the middle of June 1777. They took out the crosses, put thirteen stars in a circle on the field of blue and called it 'a new constellation.'"

We walked through the tiny house; the children alerted the few they met to the facts of history and were frowned upon by the proprietress. As we moved out the front door, Lori looked up to the flag suspended from an attic window: "How many stars should there be, Mother?" "Thirty-four: four rows of seven and a middle row of only six." "Uh, oh!" came the indictment as three index digits pointed aloft. I smiled at the lady who had followed, or chased us to the entrance. "I'm teaching them history," I laughed. She didn't, and closed the door.

"Now let's see if we can find the birthplace of Francis Scott Key; he was born in Frederick County and practiced law here in Frederick. It should be close by," I was convinced. "Let's go ask the lady," Bruce sniggered. "Leave the poor woman alone," Dave laughed, "she's probably gone after her dogs! If it's not on the map in red, it no longer exists." Lori thought it ironic, after searching and not finding Key's birthplace on the map, that a fictional female was converted into a national heroine and an actual hero was unacknowledged in his place of birth. "Well, he's a hero in Baltimore," Davie consoled us, "and the flag always flies over his grave." "That's right, Davie," his Dad applauded, "what greater honor could any American earn!"

"Isn't it fascinating," I ruminated, "that a mother and daughter made the most important flag in each of our two wars with England! The British forced Rebecca Young and family, including little daughter Mary, to escape to Baltimore during the Revolutionary War and then Mary (Pickersgill) grew up, married and was helped by her daughter to make the Star-Spangled Banner from which the *British* retreated!" "Did Rebecca see the Star-Spangled Banner?" asked Bruce. "Yes, she was apparently there part of the time while it was being made but didn't help; she was quite old." "That had just fifteen stars, didn't it?" Lori was trying to remember from our Smithsonian visit, "and fifteen stripes?" "Very good!"

"Aren't we going to Antietam?" Davie agitated. "We're turning onto ALT 40 now—it's red on your map—to Boonsboro; that's about 10 miles. Watch for 34; we take it south to Sharpsburg," Dave preferred his progeny navigate rather than I—who was sometimes busy writing notes or "plotting" an unplanned excursion. "It's only 7 miles!" discovered a pleased Davie, whispering over the napping Bruce and Lori. "Shouldn't we have gone to Harper's Ferry?" I wondered quietly to Davie and Dave, "that incident could have started the war." "No!" my D-Team was firm. "We'll come back that way—there's a little backroad through Mount Briar and Gapland through the forest . . . or, we can parallel the Potomac east and south through the village of Antietam—Harper's Ferry is on the junction of the Potomac and Shenandoah." "Is there a ferry?" Davie hoped. "No, there's a bridge and it's high above the rivers." "Good! let's go along the Potomac," Davie decided.

At the National Battlefield on Antietam Creek, close to Sharpsburg, Maryland, we discovered the two-day battle, September 17 and 18, 1862, was the bloodiest of the Civil War and prevented General Robert E. Lee's first attempt to invade the North. Over 12,000 Union troops, led by General George B. McClellan, were dead by the end of the second day and 10,000 of the Confederates—who then retreated. Lee withdrew his forces to Fredericksburg, Virginia, to the high bluffs south of the Rappahannock River. "And General Lee was victorious there," volunteered Davie, our Civil War expert. "He defeated General Burnside overwhelmingly," Davie chuckled, "then Lincoln took the Potomac command away from Burnside." "Lee was your favorite, wasn't he, Davie?" verified Bruce. "He was the best," Davie nodded. "Both sides tried to get him!" "The pamphlet says Lincoln finally had enough of a victory at Antietam that he could issue the unpopular Emancipation Proclamation," Lori informed us. "'Five days later,'" Lori read, "'on September 22, President Lincoln announced that all slaves in states still in rebellion would be freed in one hundred days. He formally issued the Emancipation Proclamation, January 1, 1863.'"

"Now let's go to Harper's Ferry where John Brown's efforts to free the slaves, in 1859, probably sparked the Civil War." "We know all about him from school," Bruce asserted. "That's wonderful!" I commended, "that's the only note I made on Harper's Ferry—didn't think we'd get this far." "He probably was crazy," Bruce began. "He hated slavery and decided he'd march through the South and free them. And with only twenty-one men; some of them were his sons." "What happened?" Davie was receptive, "we haven't gotten that far in my class." "They needed weapons and captured a federal arsenal at Harper's Ferry. Then the militia from Maryland and Virginia surrounded them. Killed most of his men, but he escaped to some brick building." "Why was it bad to free slaves?" inquired his young brother, "Lincoln did it." "It wasn't," interjected Lori, "but John Brown was fanatical and violent. He'd moved to Kansas which was neither proslavery nor a free state and killed some innocent people in Osawatomie. Northern abolitionists supported him but he was terrorizing slaveowners. We've been to Osawatomie."

"Guess who captured him!" Bruce teased. "One of his good sons?" "COL Robert E. Lee of Virginia led some United States Marines—and they got him!" "Good! did they kill him?" "No," interposed Dave, in the defense of military justice, "He was tried in Virginia for insurrection, murder and treason. He was convicted and hanged at Charlestown, Virginia; it's now Charles Town, West Virginia."

Harper's Ferry, with its infamous distinction, was a steep, heavily wooded, slumberous town on the edge of the Appalachian Trail; the views of the Shenandoah and Potomac Rivers far beneath were spectacular. It was almost inconceivable that violence could have occurred on those serene bluffs but Dave drove us up, and up, to find the sturdy brick firehouse where John Brown had hidden, having taken sixty residents prisoner from the peaceful community to be used as hostages. As we eased back down the narrow streets, Dave remembered the song popularized by Northern abolitionists about the West Virginia episode:

"John Brown's body lies a-mouldering in the grave,
But his soul goes marching on."

We were all singing as we headed down the Potomac for home. "We have to get Patches," reminded Bruce. "Lori and I can hold the kittens," Davie offered, Lori being disinterestedly asleep. "We better stop for milk, eggs and fruit; and doughnuts would be nice, if they're open." Dave nodded. "I'll go to the Commissary tomorrow," I suggested, "although, I might not. We have a pork pie in the freezer and I probably should wash and iron and—I have a book or two," I was forced to admit, as Dave's grin widened and his eyebrow lifted.

School would not start until September 4, when Bruce, as a Seventh Grader, would join Lori in her last year, Ninth Grade, in Junior High. Davie, a fourth Grader, would return with me to Surrattsville Elementary where I had requested the "Trailer" Second. We had almost a month left for Washington study, swimming and cat-keeping. Patches was happy with our children and hers—her last, the Vet assured us, and I urged the caretakers not to name them for the fat, cuddly kittens would soon belong to Second Graders.

When Bruce began to demur, I reminded him of the last kitten he'd kept and of its demise under the wheel of a car as COL Soderberg's guests departed late one night, and noisily enough to awaken Davie, Lori and him—all three of whom witnessed Patches' scurrying from under the car as the engine started, the commotion over the kitten—which didn't, and the tossing of the carcass into our front yard by COL S., with accompanying expletives. After a sad service the next morning, and no Polly to sing the Brownie Smile Song, we decided kittens were safe only in fenced yards—not following an insatiably curious mother.

For some reason, though neither the Soderbergs nor I mentioned the incident, my respect and liking for him was tarnished and the cordial bridge suppers we had frequently exchanged, ceased; my greeting, though polite, was perfunctory. However, as a pilot for Air Force II, COL Soderberg was increasingly away—Vice President Johnson being a tireless traveler—and wifely coffee supplanted the bridge foursome. Bridge was relegated to Charlie on the south, Joy and Jack Hinkleman and the Moe Erwins.

We kept social activities as minimal as possible as the children's demand upon our parental time increased. Dave and I attended the mandatory cocktail and dinner parties, usually held at the sprawling Army-Navy Country Club but preferred the smaller, intimate evenings at the Navy Yard O-Club. Our best times were with Lori, Bruce and Davie, studying, experimenting, playing and cooking at home.

Dave flew to Paris for his NATO meeting in late September. Since his Meteorological Subcommittee documents were classified, I knew naught of the agenda but I had long ago become inured to military "secrets," which I schooled myself to consider—unintriguing.

I was more concerned about the probability of Russian missiles in Cuba, which was becoming less and less of a secret, and I was more and more glad that Dave was not on the *Independence*. There were rumors in Washington that a Naval "quarantine" of Cuba was contemplated by President Kennedy. Moscow had finally admitted that Communist weapons and "technical advisers" were being shipped to Cuba to help a friendly power, in the face of "threats," defend itself from the United States—thinly veiled as "aggressive imperialist quarters." The President countered by asking Congress for the standby authority to mobilize 150,000 reservists as he had done in the Berlin crisis, the year before.

At a televised press conference, at the time Dave left for Paris, the President stated: "If at any time the Communist buildup in Cuba were to endanger or interfere with our security in any way . . . then this country will do whatever must be done to protect its own security and that of its allies." The situation was still smoldering when Dave returned from Paris but I knew he could confide nothing so I continued to rely upon television, the "Ev and Jerry Show" (Everett Dirksen, Senator; Gerald Ford, Congressman; both Republicans who supported stern measures against Khrushchev), the *Washington Post,* the *New York Times,* the *Kansas City Star, Time* and the *Congressional Record.*

On October 22, 1962—Dave was at home and we would always remember the date—President Kennedy acted, broadcasting an ominous message throughout the world, and taking most of it by surprise: Despite denials by Khrushchev, the U.S.S.R. had established weapons in Cuba which were capable of launching a nuclear attack upon the United States. Our government would hold the Soviet Union, not Cuba, responsible; any attack from the island of Cuba would be met with "a full retaliatory response" against Russia itself. President Kennedy *demanded* the U.S.S.R. immediately dismantle and withdraw their offensive matériel from Cuba. He then announced he had already ordered a Naval quarantine of all Cuba-bound shipping. He displayed U.S. aerial reconnaissance photographs which revealed the Soviet offensive missiles, on the ground, fully assembled. President Kennedy utilized the U.N., NATO, International forums throughout the world in the most sweeping propaganda barrage the United States had ever undertaken. Huge photographs of the Soviet missile installations in Cuba were displayed in cities worldwide and J.F.K.'s speech broadcast over and over again for twenty-four hours, in English and thirty-seven other languages. And our courageous, young President was successful!

Khrushchev was silent the first day but, on the second, he wrote a public letter to the aging British philosopher, Lord Russell, proposing a summit conference and promising no reckless behavior if the United States would "display reserve and stay the execution of its piratical threats"! After that ludicrous beginning, he then offered to pull out of Cuba if we dismantled bases in Turkey. The next day, October 28, Khrushchev announced that in "the interests of peace" the Kremlin would destroy the Cuban rocket installations and ship the missiles back to the U.S.S.R. President Kennedy immediately responded and praised the "statesmanlike decision," while ignoring Khrushchev's suggestion of a guarantee against invasion of Cuba. The incredible crisis was averted. Had it not been, there, most likely, would have been no record of it.

Eleanor Roosevelt lived to see the young Kennedy triumph over the wily Khrushchev and the United Nations vigorously champion and support the American President. "The first lady of the world" had been named by President Kennedy as one of the U.S. representatives to the fifteenth session of the U.N. General Assembly in 1961, and was serving in that capacity at the time of her death, November 7, 1962.

Anna Eleanor Roosevelt, born in New York City, October 11, 1884, was the niece of Theodore Roosevelt and the fifth cousin of Franklin Delano Roosevelt whom she married in 1905. Her time consumed with the rearing of her six children, she had no interest in political involvement until her husband was stricken with polio in 1921; later, her help was supplicated to persuade Franklin to run for New York Governor in 1928, and for his reelection to the Governorship. As F.D.R.'s personal political representative, she became almost as controversial as he by the time he was elected the country's thirty-second president, in 1932.

Eleanor's "My Day" syndicated column, begun in 1936, read eagerly by Mother and me, reached almost as widely as Franklin's "Fireside Chats," launched in 1933, to forward his New Deal. A remarkable woman of tremendous moral stature and courage, in my estimation; she worked unceasingly for world peace, improved race relations, education and women's rights and even joined a labor union: the American Newspaper Guild.

Her hands fascinated me! They were large and strong but graceful and as eloquent as her quietly spoken, lyrical prose. I loved watching her in newsreels when she headed the Commission on Human Rights, as President Truman's delegate to the First U.N. General Assembly in 1945, serving until 1952. And who knew more about human rights and human conditions than Mrs. Roosevelt! She had traveled the world for her husband, visiting American troops during the war—both as a concerned citizen and as the Assistant Director of Defense to which she was appointed in 1941; visited the Allied Countries and was guest of King George VI and Queen Elizabeth and traveled constantly when home.

Mother and Mrs. Roosevelt—my paradigms of self-actualizing Womanhood! I thought of an old Chinese proverb: "Woman is the root of man's tree; it grows only as strong or as high." As a woman, I applauded the stature of Anna Eleanor Roosevelt.

Dave informed us at Thanksgiving time that he had been destined for the Antarctic but here he was in Washington instead—he knew not why. "Don't ask!" Davie advised. "Good heavens!" I exclaimed, aghast, "from shipboard duty in the Med to Antarctica?" "Well, I had certain qualifications plus my Ice Reconnaissance Training that were rather persuasive and the billet was open," explained Dave. "Did you want to go?" asked Bruce. "Not really," came the unsatisfying response. "All those letters from the Med," I teased, "some—I'll never let anybody see! And all the time . . . you were *requesting* to get farther away!" "No!" Dave chortled. "I'm innocent! I didn't request it—I didn't even want to *think* about it!" "Who went?" I was only mildly curious, knowing he wouldn't be among our best friends. "Jim King." "Was he a Commander?" "Yes, a bit senior to me—might have been why he went." "Daddy was just needed here in Washington," Lori was convinced. "I agree," and I bussed our essential man on the back of the neck.

"Hasn't it been wonderful here in Washington! How lucky we've been!" expatiating to all the family. "What else was a close call?" Bruce probed. "Did I tell you?" questioned Dave, "that I thought I was Korea-bound but my orders were cut for Kodiak." "My goodness—you were secretive!" I was amazed, again. "I didn't know *that!*" "That's precisely why I didn't tell you either time," Dave laughed at my consternation. "You would have been alarmed—needlessly; rumors abound when orders are due!" "I thought only the wives were gossips," shaking my finger at his maleness. "I've never put credence in scuttlebutt and never repeated it," and Dave successfully defended his honor. I saluted him with a right joyful hug and thanked him for his thoughtfulness, *mirating*: "How wise you are—for one so young!"

"Are you old, Mommy?" Davie worried. "Not yet!" Laughing, I kissed him too. "You're all so good to me!" moving happily around the table to thank Bruce and Lori as well. "Do we get whipped cream on the pumpkin pie?" suggested Bruce. "Would you prefer it at suppertime?" I thought. "With a cold turkey sandwich and a glass of milk," requested the head of the house. "And tetrazzini tomorrow?" hoped Lori. "With lots of cheese and mushrooms like Mommy Tom's," added Davie, "and artichoke hearts!" It was a joy to have my culinary skills—and Mommy Tom's—appreciated on our last Thanksgiving away from home.

The waning autumnal days were mild enough to visit the National Zoo and kick through the gold and red leaf-strewn trails of Rock Creek Park, most of the trees already spectral. It was a gorgeous city in every season, its native forests and streams zealously preserved. Davie reminded us, as we stopped to peer at the tropical birds, that we had seen most of the Civil War battlefields in the East but hadn't gone to Manassas. "You prefer cannons to polar bears?" queried his Dad, unnecessarily. "We can see those in Kansas City," came Davie's rejoinder. "There're a few battlefields in Missouri, too," Lori remarked. "Missouri was one of the most important slavery states; even after the Emancipation, slavery was permitted in Missouri and Kentucky." "And Maryland and Delaware," contributed Bruce. "Why?" asked Davie, glad to benefit from the advanced knowledge of his brother and sister. "Because," Lori began the elucidation, "those border states refused to sell their slaves to the Government which wanted to free them and Lincoln was afraid they might join the Confederacy." "So--o--o," continued Bruce, with a flourish of his 'presidential' chapeau, "Lincoln only banned slavery in the South." "That wasn't right," opined Davie, heading for the car, "may we go to Manassas now?" "Wouldn't you like to go home for lunch?" I proposed. "No!" from the battlefield foursome—which surprised me . . . not at all. When a decision was made, we acted—with military expedition!

Dave crossed the Potomac at the Lincoln Monument and took the George Washington Memorial Parkway west to the Dolley Madison Highway and the Capital Beltway south to Highway 66 and drove southwest to the Bull Run Creek. The Union forces called both battles "Bull Run" but the South referred to them as the battles of Manassas for the small Virginia village near by. In juxtaposition to Bull Run was our objective: the Manassas National Battlefield Park where we had lunch and studied the brochures, my having no reference materials because they wouldn't let me go home. I suspected General Robert E. Lee's involvement if I read aright Davie's enthusiasm and proceeded to read the document which I shared with Lori. We were informed that the first Bull Run battle, July 21, 1861, was the initial major conflict of the Civil War. The Union forces were commanded by General Irvin McDowell; the Confederate, by Generals Johnston and Beauregard. The Federal troops at first seemed victorious, routing the Southern line along Bull Run but Stonewall Jackson (of "Barbara Frietchie" fame) turned disaster into a Confederate triumph.

I noticed Davie wasn't reading his folders and saved time and eyesight by just asking him about the second Bull Run, aware that all of our *National Geographic*s dealing with the Civil War had been identified "Davie Holland" in ink on the top and taken to school, from Second Grade at Bayside upward, for show and exposition. His teacher at Bayside had confided in me that while her other Second Graders brought pet turtles and barbie dolls, Davie lectured on Civil War pictures and maps! "What happened, Davie?" Lori, too, decided to listen. "It was a year after the first battle," Davie was pleased to accommodate, "Stonewall had more men and destroyed Union stockpiles at Manassas and then it was easy. General Lee joined him and another general. . . ." "Longstreet," read Bruce, "and

Pope was the Union general . . . everybody was a General!" "Well," continued Davie, "Pope had to retreat—back to Washington, I guess; Stonewall, Lee and Longstreet naturally won and headed north to Antietam Creek. Pretty smart, weren't they: defending a creek, a hill or a river bluff!"

"It was a disgraceful and horrible war," I remonstrated. "The South lost everything. Maybe, if Jackson and Lee had lost both Bull Runs it would have been better; the war might have ended then." "No," Davie shook his head at such heresy; "they wouldn't have given up." "He's right," agreed his Dad, "the honor of the South was challenged; there was too much at stake to have a short war; besides, we've always been a bellicose nation, settling all conflicts with physical force." "So that's why I like to fight!" Bruce put up his 'dukes' and grinned, challengingly. "Pugnacity should be a last resort," I was sententious; "it emits no intelligence to become belligerent." "No, but it's fun!" "I believe in self-defense; I'm delighted my boys are accomplished in the art of pugilism—and Lori too; but I deplore inane, cowardly aggression; it lacks mental discipline—it's an affirmation of weakness." "*You're* a fierce fighter, Mother," Bruce looked at me merrily, "we've seen *you* in action!" "But not physically! Richard?" Nods and grins. "But you're right, I know how—to defend my family. I believe verbal defense, and at times offense, is almost always—efficacious." "Why don't women fight wars?" Davie thought Lori and I could acquit ourselves. "Too dangerous!" laughed Dave; "it's true! Women would be too vicious—too unrestrained if their home or loved ones were threatened." "Well, let's go see *this* battlefield," Lori suggested, deciding two females should extricate themselves from a masculine discussion . . . before we lost it!

In early December we visited the National Cathedral, begun in 1907; the estimated completion date was 1990. The Cathedral of St. Peter and St. Paul, or the Washington Cathedral, was America's Westminster Abbey and was comparable in its dimensions to the imposing English cathedrals and realized L'Enfant's Plan: a great church "for national purposes, such as public prayer and thanksgiving." And it was, in truth, a national building having been financed by every state in the nation. Of fourteenth-century Gothic architecture, it was designed to form a cross; its apse, the longer section, pointing to the spot on the horizon where the sun had risen on Ascension Day. According to *The Washington Story* (p. 43) the turreted central bell tower, when completed, would rise 133 feet higher above the Potomac River than the 555-foot Washington Monument due to the Cathedral's location on Mount St. Alban, in the northwest corner of the District. The children, treasure-hunting in the "basement" to discover the many, ornate Russian icons, most of them egg-shaped, also found the tombs of Woodrow Wilson and Admiral George Dewey, the "hero of Manila."

Dave told us about the Admiral's acclaimed capture of the enemy fleet in the Manila Bay of the Philippine Islands during the Spanish-American War of 1898. He was outnumbered almost two-to-one but lost not a single American sailor nor ship and although he was named Admiral of the Navy—a rank higher than Admiral—and the only American to be thus honored, he was best remembered for his command to the captain of the *Olympia*: "You may fire when you are ready, Gridley."

Outside, we walked down terraced gardens framed with fragrant boxwood, reminiscent of Monticello and Mount Vernon, some enclosing late herbs—redolent and ready for drying. "When we go home," I told Dave, "I want to take three or four English boxwoods. I bet I can grow them in the Midwest." "If you can get them in that greenhouse car!" Dave's skepticism was no dissuader. "Oh, I'll just take small ones," I promised.

"Shall we go to see the new airport?" Dave offered, as we all gathered at the car. "We can have lunch there." Both ideas had instant appeal, so Dave took the Beltway to Arlington and from thence, westward to the New Dulles International Airport, a massive facility which had just opened. As we approached, having driven about half an hour from Arlington, we saw what appeared to be a huge hammock of concrete with enormous windowpanes slung beneath, gleaming in the late fall sun like an extra-terrestrial space station. Davie, Bruce, et al were immensely impressed. "Alright!" was the young-male consensus. When we got inside, there were miles and miles to walk but escalators helped us along our wonder-struck way—in the midst of so much modernity and efficiency. Dave was interested in the control tower and was informed the multi-tiered tower, with what looked to be a dark box and ball atop, contained a radome—in the "ball," I assumed—which swept the runways and skies sixty times a minute, in all directions. Bruce was quizzical: "Would you ever land here, Dad?" Dave shook his head: "Only in an emergency." "Would you like to—just on a routine flight?" "Yes, I would!" "Why does it have to be so large?" Davie's interest needed satisfying. We had read it was two-thirds the size of Manhattan—to which we were heading again, shortly. "It was built purposefully for jets," Dave pointed out. "National was built when we only had prop planes; the jet runways are dangerously short; the Potomac restricts access. There's just no more space for expansion; but small jets can use it safely." "Is Anacostia safe for you?" asked Lori, with a little, worried frown. "Yes," laughed Dave, putting his arm around her, "props can take off and land almost anyplace. You've seen me at Oceana—and I can always divert to Andrews, if necessary. As a matter of fact, I'll soon be flying out of Andrews, exclusively, because they're closing Anacostia to air traffic." Anticipating Davie's query, Dave grinned at his namesake: "Because there are so many flights out of Anacostia Naval Air, and National is just across the river, there's increased stacking-up—of both military and commercial planes, especially in foggy weather. So it will save both time and money to close it and use Andrews." Reassured that all was well, we found a bright, brand-new restaurant and studied the menu—with hungry assiduity.

The following Saturday found us at the Pentagon, before Davie asked us why we hadn't gone. Dave had offered to take us several times but *somebody's* plans always seemed to interfere! We had sailed past it on the highway many times, especially Dave and I as we attended a function at the Army-Navy Country Club, but today it was top of the agenda. I read statistics to the family as Dave took Suitland Parkway, crossed the Anacostia River and paralleled the Washington Channel—we always delighted in the yachts and marina and deciding which seafood establishment to sample next—to the George Mason Memorial Bridge, named for the statesman who had drafted the declaration of the rights of man, in 1776, which influenced Jefferson's Declaration of Independence.

"How does it happen we have a free Saturday?" Dave quirked. I looked at him with innocent mien, "What do you mean, sir?" "Run out of places to go?" "She likes to walk!" my school-partner defended me. "It's better than Dulles," Dave promised. "Are you glad you're not stationed there?" Lori surmised. "Yes, I go there enough. There's a lot of ground to cover—but it's efficiently arranged."

I returned to my role of background informer: "The Pentagon is the largest office building in the world, 'it covers 29 acres . . . has room for more than 30,000 workers . . . contains 16½ miles of corridors . . . and has parking space for 8,000 cars. There is no other building of its unique design in the world. It is composed of five five-sided rings. . . .'" "Being five stories high," yawned our driver, "with no elevators. There're ramps and escalators." "I like escalators," Davie approved. "Well, don't stop them," Bruce advised, "or they'll throw you in the brig." "I'll just look," Davie assured him, accustomed to reminders of his infantile escapade.

Inside the Pentagon, already metonymical for military power of the United States, Dave showed us the directory. I pointed, laughingly, at the ramp designations and showed Lori: "*A, B, C, D* and *E*. Now isn't that typical of the prosaic male! What an opportunity wasted! Think of all the military heroes—or battles that shaped our nation!" "Look at the names of the floors," Lori put her finger under the first. "Colors?" I choked on a cackle. "Takes too long to say names or places," Dave defended his military, amused at my amusement. "Right!" nodded Bruce. "I like those colors," sided Davie, "at least there's a 'Dutch' blue." "But Blue, Gray, Red, Green and Brown!" challenged Lori, "sounds like a nursery school!" "It's just simple," hazarded Dave. "It certainly is," Lori and I agreed, laughing together. "Be careful!" Dave warned, "you might get hungry." So we started walking along the Dutch Blue corridor—Lori and I—and tried to behave ourselves, watching the mostly slender, uniformed men pass hurriedly, but politely. We strode solemnly up each alphabetical ramp and inspected the color of each floor and saw many military VIPS—or so they impressed us. And it was a reassuring experience! Our military looked very fit, businesslike, and capable of great and noble deeds. Our pride in our country swelled; we patted Dave on the back for his contributions.

"Shall we go see CAPT Livingston's office?" suggested Dave. "Is it a different color?" Davie elicited. Dave had to laugh: "No, it's battleship gray." "We've just seen him," Bruce remembered quickly, "at Lake George." "He's probably at lunch anyway," agreed Dave. We went back down by escalator which had well-concealed manual stops, Davie informed us. Going out into the interior Pentagon court, we found springtime warmth; trim, austere, landscaping and box lunches enjoyed on benches. Walking us around two sides of the five, Dave knew just where the car was. Lori and I had earned gold stars for subsequent behavior and we were all taken to lunch across the Rochambeau Memorial, the northwest-bound bridge named for the French marshal who aided the Patriots to victory at Yorktown, in 1781. "Do you want seafood?" Dave inquired, "or do you want to go downtown to Luigi's for lasagne?" "Seafood!" was unanimous and Dave stopped on Channel Street opposite the Capital Yacht Club.

After shrimp cocktails, crab Mornay and fried oysters, Dave proposed to make the day completely military to which we assented with alacrity. Driving two blocks west on Maine Avenue, Dave took U.S. 1

around "Old Baldy"; Ohio Drive, northwest along the Potomac—looking increasingly polluted and muddied—to cross, at the Lincoln Memorial, on the Arlington Memorial Bridge, into the hilly and wooded Arlington National Cemetery. Dave turned left on First Drive East, north on McClellan Drive to Roosevelt—slowly passing the steps to the Tomb of the Unknown Soldier and circled the Memorial Amphitheater, the elegant Athenian theater where our war dead were honored on Decoration Day.

Cautioning the children not to run, Dave led us around the Amphitheater to the Tomb of Unknowns where soldiers from World War I, World War II and Korea were buried. Bruce and Davie were impressed by the perpetual guarding of the Tomb and the briskness and precision with which they moved when the honor guards were changed. "But it seems to me," Davie observed, "there should be an American flag close by." Dave nodded, "I'll show you the best flag and war memorial in Washington: Marines on Iwo Jima; we'll go there last—it's north of the Cemetery." "First, Davie, I thought you'd like to see where General Lee lived." "Yes, sir!" grinned Davie, "let's go."

We twisted through gorgeous Virginia terrain on Wilson Drive, north to Lee Drive and the beautifully classic Lee Mansion, high on a slope overlooking the Potomac to the east and Washington, D.C. The mansion, built by George Washington Parke Custis, grandson of Martha Washington, was eventually occupied by his daughter and her husband, General Robert E. Lee—the house, the site and the occupants epitomizing gracious Southern living. "Davie, it's better than Mount Vernon," Bruce approved, "except for the cemetery." "The Lees were certainly a wealthy family," Lori was impressed, "this is a lot of land!" "When did it become a cemetery?" Davie asked. "Very soon after Lee left," I answered. "I was telling my class about it the other day." Davie figured: "Well, Lee refused command of the Union forces and took command of Virginia's in 1861." "Yes, and the Union Army took over the house for their headquarters and the land for a camp. The house later became a hospital; they began burying soldiers here in 1864 but it was almost twenty years before the Government bought the property from General Lee's son. Now, there are over four hundred acres; soldiers from every war, even a few from the Revolutionary War, lie here. It's sad to contemplate, isn't it?" as we walked back to the car. "But the honor and courage make it beautiful; the setting is peaceful—somehow, it's restorative."

Dave wound us down Sherman Drive and out of the National Cemetery onto Ridge Road, north a bit to the intersection of Jefferson

Davis Highway where he took the entrance to the hill of the Iwo Jima Marine Corps Memorial. Based upon the famous photograph by Joe Rosenthal, the monumental bronze sculpture captured the moment when five Marines and a Sailor raised the American flag on Mount Suribachi during World War II. It was an impressive moment, just at dusk, as we walked around, looking up at the massive, heroic figures' anchoring the angled American flag—brilliant with floodlights and stretched out by the wintry wind. "The flag flies here twenty-four hours a day," Dave reminded his family. Across the Potomac, the Lincoln Memorial, bright for the night; the Washington Monument, gleaming beyond; and dominating the horizon, the Capitol on its pinnacle, its eminence supreme, presented a panorama for poets.

The Protestant Chapel at Andrews provided our religious program. We generally attended church services as a family unit since Sunday School was held concurrently. The children had loved their five years of Sunday School at Little Creek and looked forward to the permanency of First Baptist Church with Mommy Tom and Daddy Frank, within the next year. Frequently, we had gone on an excursion early Sunday morning and missed chapel but we were neither superstitious nor fanatical about church and related activities. Morality was important; structuring our lives to impress others—was not; teaching our children—uppermost.

Tschaikovsky's *Nutcracker Suite* ballet was presented at Constitution Hall the week before Christmas. We attended Friday evening, December 21, and there was enough rambunctious, militant dancing in the Nutcracker's battle with the mice; beauty and grace of snowflakes and flowers; symbolism and mysticism to please each taste. It would become a tradition, together with Dickens' *A Christmas Carol*, for both evoked reflection on family; each distinct interpretation kept values visible.

The Ellipse was beautiful with blue-lighted trees alternating with green to form the evergreen cross south of the White House. Mrs. Lyndon Johnson placed the star atop the lofty red spruce, flanked by arms of blue and green and the season's Pageant of Peace was opened by President Kennedy's Yule message and lighting of the National Christmas Tree—which suddenly shimmered gold against the night's blackness. The White House was adorned with huge window wreaths of fresh green and the ceiling-high tree in the Blue Room sparkled with crystal white; the ornaments, bright miniature toys, trumpets, dolls and soldiers—for children lived in the White House: Caroline and John Jr.

The third Washington Christmas Tree we visited—not putting one up, we vicariously enjoyed several—was in the lobby of the Mayflower Hotel where a creative housewife, whose mother was Pennsylvania Dutch, decorated a fifteen-foot tree with large, saucy animals and storybook characters, flamboyantly attired, which were edible! Her name was Louise LaGorce and we arrived as she was hanging her cookies. Since her own children were grown, she preserved her cookie-ornaments for several years in layers of tissue paper. She showed us how she baked in the hanger—a thick length of fuzzy jute—which would not pull out from the heavy, over-dressed creation. I had saved the picture from the magazine section of the *Washington Post,* Sunday, December 17, 1961, and was elated she had put up her tree a second year. She told us: "I was asked to do it in 1958 and have done it every year since." Then she laughed: "And some of the characters are that old!" I praised her ingenuity vociferously and bought her recipe and pattern book; for Lori, of course, and the royalty went to charity. The boys decided, as we walked to the car, that they would be too young in 1963 for their cookie-tree characters to be preserved. I laughed: "I'll bake you fresh, unhandled ones painted with eggyolk colors whenever you wish, and gingerbread too." "Tomorrow?" they wished.

After a day of baking, and assembling of suits, dresses, shirts and ties, we left early Christmas-Eve morning for New York. It would be a swift visit and we were lightly packed but warmly dressed because the children wanted to try out their new ice skates on the outdoor rink at Rockefeller Plaza. Our downtown hotel had been recommended for its proximity to Rockefeller Center but with strong, moist wind—snow was predicted—and heavy skates, Dave decided to drop us off at the sunken rink, deposit our bags in our room and hope to find a place closer than the hotel to park. "But," he warned, "all of us walk in the morning." Heads were nodded in accord and the children and I tumbled out, pointing ecstatically to the Christmas tree—tintinnabulous with twisting, colliding, large, gold metal disks. Zephyr had never played so melodious a tune! The immense green tree, hung with hoards of flat, giant coins, was lighted in gold and was in perfect harmony with prodigious golden god Prometheus, stretched out below. Dangling their skates, the children inspected the wondrous tree—and captured two gold plates which blew from the tree to tumble down the steps. It was a wild wind and most skaters had gone inside but mine naturally wanted to make an attempt. I was glad Dave had arrived for I anticipated the skating demonstration would be short-lived. The few skaters were propelled without effort, if their backs were to the wind; Davie had trouble getting on his feet and Lori lasted the longest.

When the snow began, with no diminution of wind, appetites were recalled and our troop desisted to tramp into Ye Olde English Pub for lunch, at a rink-side table. Sated and warmed to sightseeing determination, we took skates to the car and walked down Fifth Avenue to marvel at the lofty, modern buildings—when we could look up—and appreciate the Christmasy adornments. Returning to the festive Promenade between La Maison Francaise, where I wanted to have dinner and the comparably high, British Empire Building, where we lunched; we passed Prometheus and his towering, twirling, gold tree to enter the RCA Building, the centerpiece of Rockefeller Plaza.

The children were curious about a television studio, having forgotten their brief activity in Monterey, prior to Davie's membership in the family, so we joined an NBC tour group. Lori, Bruce and Davie and Dave smirked, in turn, for the TV camera while we watched each fleeting face on the near-by screen, then we all followed our girl-guide from one machinery-packed room to another to be finally deposited in a small studio where *What's My Line* was about to begin. Steve Allen and Jayne Meadows were absent but Kitty Carlisle was charming and we enjoyed the half-hour show, although the boys would have preferred "more action." We rode to the top of the seventy-storied building, peering briefly from the roof at the Hudson River and Fifth Avenue, then descended to inspect murals and paintings; and in the lowest level, small shops and eating establishments. It appeared that everything one could want was available in the RCA Tower.

The next morning, Christmas Day, we were at the Radio City Music Hall at 6:00 A.M. and the line was only a block long! We had come to New York to see the renowned Christmas Show of elaborate tableaux of the traditional Biblical story, with choirs, and the precision dancing of the famous Rockettes, afterwards. That would be followed by a movie, if anyone was interested, or still awake, our having arisen at four. As we waited, and the line moved quite swiftly, we breakfasted on cookies and apples—after we had caught our breath. Dave had walked us almost at a run, from the hotel. Advance tickets had been denied us but Moe Erwin had given us good advice: "Go early to the 7:00 A.M. show; it's impossible at 2:00 P.M. and 7:00."

Somebody remembered it was Christmas and "Ho! Ho!" rang out; I had a dozen miniature candy canes which the children distributed; we followed along with affable New York families; most, with children—some of whom were sucking candy canes from the Capital.

It was a wonderful telling of the Christmas story on the massive stage where angel choirs sang high above from billowing clouds and one tableau immediately followed another, in disparate character and location. The ensuing performance of the Rockettes seemed inappropriate but they began with *Parade of the Wooden Soldiers* and immediately won our attention—and no one slept. It was a very merry morning; we brunched at Trenton; and opened Christmas packages before our own fire in the early evening, the Rockefeller disks' gleaming gold in the gloaming.

January 1, 1963, Dad's seventy-second birthday, dawned bright, cold and beautiful. At our New Year's Day breakfast, we unhurriedly enjoyed scrambled eggs, sausage and Alaskan Christmas coffee cake, belatedly made, and discussed our remaining six months in Washington. "We need to spend more time at the Natural History Museum," suggested Lori; "I'd like to study mammals, early man, fossils and rocks." "We haven't been to New Technology enough," Bruce reminded us. "How about Space?" prompted Davie, "haven't even seen *Friendship 7* and it's been in all the papers." "We missed the Embassy Tours last spring," I added. "I hope we can go to a few in April."

"What would you like to do, Dad?" invited Bruce. "Take you to the David Taylor Model Basin where the Navy tests designs for new ships; they make their own waves to test for strain and endurance; it's very interesting. It's not open to the public but I'll make arrangements. Then, I'd like to take you to the Naval Observatory, and spend more time at the Naval Academy." "I checked the Observatory," I interrupted, "they want children to be at least eleven. It might be best to wait on that until the last week." "Don't worry, Davie," soothed big brother, "they'll get you in." "We certainly will," Dave promised. "Wait until they hear what an astronomer you are!" "Are you interested in the Wax Museum?" I inquired. "Not much," I was told. "Maybe, just quickly," Lori, vaguely interested, "if we're down that way."

President Kennedy's back, injured initially in World War II and again in 1961, at a tree-planting ceremony in Canada, was causing him increasing discomfort and creating national concern—and a demand for old-fashioned cane rocking chairs. Dr. Janet Travell, the first woman to be named official physician to a president, had prescribed a stiff-backed rocking chair to ease the President's back pains. That unglamorous item was in sudden demand at furniture stores and antique shops, having been confined for generations to Southern front porches and Northern attics and basements. His secretary, Evelyn Lincoln, and press spokesman, Pierre Salinger, were asked almost as many questions about his preference for rocking chairs as about the state of the Union and plans of the day! The intellectual, saturnine Salinger was not visibly amused by continual inquiry about the relative merits of wooden rockers and the subject soon received no press coverage, but it came to be as much identified with the youthful President as the walking stick and jaunty hat symbolized Harry S. Truman.

Before Dave flew to London for his NATO Meteorological session, I asked him not to bring anything home. I had enough French perfume, Italian leather gloves and handbags, and the children enough souvenirs, to last beyond a lifetime. But I knew it was futile when he said: "I thought I'd just go to the Silver Vaults, one last time. Don't you need *anything?*" And I spoke dithyrambs about what I had—and loved—and what I didn't need, or want. I had been successful before, about silver; but those had not been the final trip. "Maybe I'll just look," he almost compromised. "I love you *anyway!*" he teased, kissing me good-bye and the children, in turn. "Remember," I called after him, as he started his car, "we're too rich—for more," and blew him a kiss.

After Dave's return from London in early springtime with only silver candelabra "for Mother's teas and luncheons," he said quickly, and cleverly, "and only this one slender vase for you," we began a systematic appreciation of the Smithsonian again. Borrowing Davie's guidebook, we spent each Saturday and Sunday at one of the Smithsonian buildings except for one Saturday when I inveigled them to take me on the Embassy Tour. After having our picture taken by the *Washington Post* at the Vietnam embassy, which would appear on Monday, April 15, 1963, and prove that they had gone, the children and Dave declined a second day on Embassy Row but agreed to the Pan-American Union Building. (That was as close as my boys got to Vietnam but Lori's future husband, Terry Walters, served in the Army during that conflict and Dr. Ken Holland, Jr., D.D.S.—a stint in the Navy.)

Considered one of the most beautiful public buildings in the world, the children were more impressed with the Aztec garden behind it and the macaws inside, which screeched at and preened for their rapt admirers. The

Pan-American was usually closed on Sunday, so the day was a bonanza and it was not half gone.

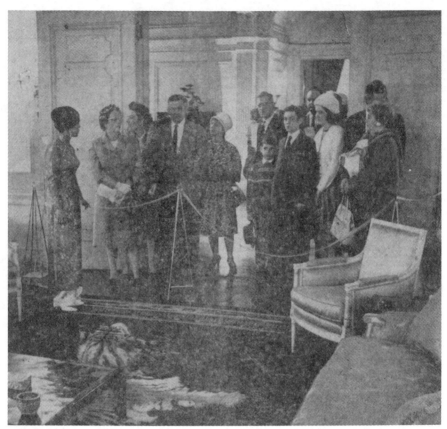

Figure 125. Embassy Row: Davie, Bruce, Dave, Lori, and Tip of a Hat

Since we were not far from the Wax Museum we visited that, which the children found rather distasteful in its graphicness. Nothing was said but I sensed they were disturbed by the realistic figures of "The 4 Heroic Chaplains of World War II" who gave up their lifevests to soldiers and were shown singing and praying, one's helping a soldier in lifevest over the rail, on the slanting deck of the battered ship. Dave, aware of the quieted children, suggested paddle boats on the Tidal Basin. "After lunch at Luigi's?" And everyone was happy and talkative again about who paddled with whom and which boat would win.

All of our objectives were accomplished in Washington. As Dave wrote Dad, we even attended a tobacco auction barn, Upper Marlboro,

6 Jun 1963

Dear Dad,

Upon my retirement I am required to file with the Department of the Navy a Statement of Employment furnishing information concerning my employment activities. This is necessary to avoid any possible conflict between private interests and my former official duties.

The following are the specific questions I wish you would answer for me so that I can complete the form:

1. <u>My employer's name and address:</u> (If you consider that I will be representing all the manufacturers you now represent, then all names and addresses should be listed. If, however, you consider that I will be ~~not~~ employed by you then I will list your name and address.)

2

2. <u>My employer (s) sells, or offers</u>
<u>for sale, to agencies of the Department</u>
<u>of Defense, the Coast Guard, the Coast</u>
<u>and Geodetic Survey, or the Public</u>
<u>Health Service, the following types of</u>
<u>products or services</u>:

    (It appears to me that if you
sell only to jobbers then you don't
sell to any of the above directly.
However, if you have any OEM
accounts direct to above agencies
you should describe those products.)

3. <u>My position title</u>:

4. <u>My duties are, briefly</u> (a
<u>complete description of your job, a</u>
<u>copy of your employment contract,</u>
<u>or any other pertinent information,</u>
<u>may be attached</u>):

3

It does not appear to me that I will be violating any conflict of interest regulations. Those former regular Navy officers now retired and employed by firms that deal directly in government contracts are the ones that have to worry.

I know this is your busy season. I am anxious to start learning all of the facets of the business so that I can take a big load off of your shoulders and so you won't have to travel so much.

Although I haven't heard from Charlie Simmons yet, I have requested that I come to Philadelphia to visit Mulconry on Thursday, 13 June. My schedule this last month is getting to be a little tight now, so I hope that date is acceptable.

Memorial Day Dorothy, the children, and I went to a tobacco auction at Upper Marlboro. In addition to "hog's head" (a very large cylindrical container made of wood) packing for the market in Baltimore we saw the steaming process for overseas shipment. A lot of migrant workers made up the work force. I made a recording of one of the auctioneers. Came out very clearly as it was recorded in the Office after the real thing. Lot of interesting background material included.

Last Friday night the Duty Officer at the David Taylor Model Basin gave us a private tour through the facilities there. We saw various stages of construction of ship hull models made of wood and wax. The tank is 3/5 of a mile long and some of the rigs pulling the models get up to 60 mph along the tracks along the basin. Another "square tank, called an "instant ocean" can generate random waves for testing purposes. Another smaller circular tank tests submarine hulls. Other areas test the strength of materials, such as steel and aluminum. They also have three small wind tunnels for testing various aspects of aviation. Tours are not given while tests are being conducted, although they may have run demonstrations for Armed Forces Day (when we were at Pimlico).

Visited the Naval Academy Sunday and had dinner at the Officers Club.

Hope to tour the Naval Observatory on the night of 2 July—if we're not too tired—as the packers pick up our household effects that day.

Dorothy and I have been looking at house plans in case we build, but circumstances may cause us to buy. Looking forward to seeing you in August.
Love,
Dave, Dot, L, B, D

Maryland, which Dave recorded so that the children could take it to school, back in the Midwest. The Naval Academy at Annapolis was not neglected. We dined there, saw a regatta from the captain's gig on the Severn and inspected the new paint of Tecumseh to see what the graduating class of '63 had done to the antique ship's figurehead. We wished we could see All-American quarterback Roger Staubach beat Army again his last year at the Academy but knew President John F. Kennedy would be in Philadelphia to cheer on his Navy—and his Army, too, of course.

Driving past the Maryland State House, we walked back to read its plaque announcing it was the oldest in the nation still in legislative use, where "General George Washington resigned his commission before the Continental Congress December 23, 1783.... Congress ratified the Treaty of Paris to end the Revolutionary War, January 14, 1784.... Capitol of the United States, November 26, 1783 - August 13, 1784." And Dave took us slowly through the campus of prestigious St. John's College which based its entire curriculum upon the Great Books of the Western World and produced doctors, lawyers and scientists, as well as philosophers!

Our late June 1963 agenda dictated one last, all-day-Saturday activity before leaving Washington and we bought tickets for the slowest of travel modes: a mule-drawn barge trip on the Chesapeake and Ohio Canal. The historic waterway, linking Washington with Cumberland, Maryland, had once handled five hundred boats and barges a day; the mule path, well-worn and wide, breaking the verdant confines of the mirror-calm canal. The roofed, many seated barge was drawn by one mule which, without apparent strain, plodded along accompanied by two pipe-smoking attendants, conversing with the bargeman, intermittently. Our C. and O. barge trip had commenced in Georgetown with its quaintly fashionable, and exceedingly expensive, brick row houses. The oldest section of the nation's Capital, Georgetown and its Georgian architecture, was an area of Historic Preservation, both by law and the pride of its residents. Usually,

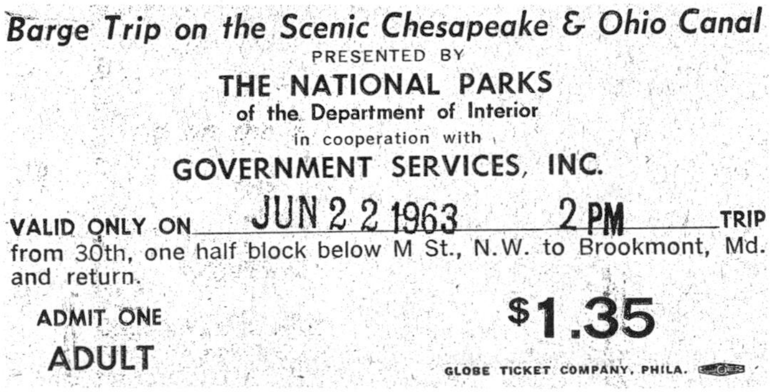

Barge Trip on the Scenic Chesapeake & Ohio Canal

PRESENTED BY

THE NATIONAL PARKS

of the Department of Interior

in cooperation with

GOVERNMENT SERVICES, INC.

VALID ONLY ON   JUN 2 2 1963   2 PM   TRIP

from 30th, one half block below M St., N.W. to Brookmont, Md. and return.

ADMIT ONE

ADULT   **$1.35**

GLOBE TICKET COMPANY, PHILA.

Figure 126. C & O Barge Ticket

the brick houses were very narrow, the width of one room, and three stories high; built steps away from the limited Colonial street—yards and gardens in the back, very similar to row houses in Williamsburg.

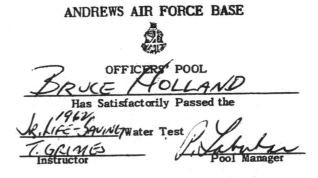

ANDREWS AIR FORCE BASE

OFFICERS' POOL

Bruce Holland

Has Satisfactorily Passed the

1962

Jr. Life-Saving Water Test

T. Grimes
Instructor

P. Labula
Pool Manager

Figure 127. Bruce's Jr. Lifesaving Card

We had bought our barge tickets a week in advance, encountering a little difficulty when informed that children under ten were not permitted to take the trip—they wanted no accidents "at sea," the Canal being six feet deep! We returned the next day armed with proof that Davie, nine and a half, was an Intermediate swimmer and the rest of the Nautical Family—Lifesavers, and purchased our five tickets for the following Saturday.

George Washington, when the Federal City was being planned by Pierre L'Enfant, had dreamed of a great natural waterway to the west which the Potomac River was incapable of providing due to the presence of the Great Falls northwest of the District. The Chesapeake and Ohio Canal was thus conceived; built in the 1820's, it was 184 miles long and 68 feet wide and transported coal from the Cumberland region of the Allegheny Mountains to Washington. Built north of the Potomac, the Canal skirted the river's Great Falls by a series of locks which slowly lifted the barge upward—to the vast enjoyment of the children. We added the Great Falls of the Potomac to our next day's list and visited them by car and footbridge, still appreciating the mule's long tug.

Our first Peace rose graced Dave's beautiful silver bud vase from London as we planned what verdure I could take home to Kansas City. I would drive the plants; and Dave, the children. I had already dug the mint which Mother had given me from her garden years ago, which had grown for five years in Virginia Beach and two in Washington and yearned for the Midwest. I planned to take two small camellias, *japonica*; two gardenias; the philodendron from both mantels and the four petite English boxwoods which we had just bought. If there was room, I wanted hostas from Mildred and Hub's yard in Ithaca to which my plants would be temporary companions as we drove Dave's car around the Gaspé peninsula.

Our last night in Washington, D.C., nine-and-a-half-year-old Davie Holland, all gear packed and Patches on *its* way to Daddy Frank's, took his family to see the amazing splendors of the heavens at the U.S. Naval Observatory!

We had prevailed in our determination to attend the lecture, star and moon observing at the official U.S. time station, my offering to submit Davie's report cards and "scientific papers" to prove his maturity. But they accepted us on faith (and Dave's status) and our excited astronomers were thrilled and enriched.

The United States Naval Observatory was established in 1842 under the jurisdiction of the CNO (Chief of Naval Operations) to study stars and magnetism and provide official time signals to regulate clocks throughout the country, territories, planes in the air and ships at sea.

American standard time was determined, not by the famous 26-inch telescope which surveyed the skies, but by a telescope forever fixed in a vertical position to record the moment selected stars crossed the zenith. The PZT (Photographic Zenith Tube) enabled Naval scientists to "keep their own master clock (and the broadcast time signals it controls) in time with the spinning earth to within one tenth of a second. The master clock, operated by the vibrations of cesium atoms, divides the 24 hours between PZT sightings into intervals that are accurate to one millionth of a second a day" (*Time*, Life Science Library, p. 101).

We were permitted to see the Time Room where countless clocks were being tested but the special standard clocks were kept in an underground vault, free from dirt and vibration, which no one ever entered except the repairman; the clocks were read through a periscope.

Inquiring about Greenwich time, Davie was informed the Observatory's master clock was set to Universal (Greenwich Mean) Time. Researching via the *World Book* before the packers came, Davie discovered the Greenwich Observatory, ordered built on the Thames River, London, by Charles II in 1675, was designated the prime meridian of the earth at a conference of astronomers in Washington in 1884. The earth was divided into 24 time zones, 15° longitude wide, with 0° longitude at Greenwich. (When the Observatory was moved southeast to a castle in Sussex, the prime meridian remained fixed, British astronomers' deducting a minute and a quarter from their reading to determine Greenwich time.)

That Capital-culminating, astronomical occasion was a timely termination of Dave's marvelous Naval Career!

CHAPTER IX

EL MONTE ON A KANSAS PRAIRIE

We left Washington at the dawning of July 3, 1963, sadly joyous; sometimes, ambivalence was unavoidable.

At our last Washington, D.C., dinner, we were served a soft, sharp, yellow cheese which, like the dill pickles of Dave's searching, I was never able to duplicate. CDR Ed Scully, whom I considered Dave's most brilliant, fascinating, impatient and arrogant friend who tolerated few but flew with and felt close to Dave—joined us. Photography was one of Ed's hobbies and he insisted upon taking a family picture on the Navy Yard O-Club patio, in the heat, without jackets, before our eight o'clock invitation

Figure 128. Washington Farewell

to the Observatory. Ed would miss Dave who reciprocated both his friendship and respect but I knew they would correspond; and Ed promised to visit us in Kansas City.

Much as I deplored scrutiny by camera—I

Figure 129. Midwest in Store

had not changed since our multi-tree honeymoon—I did not demur. It was the end of Dave's Naval career—he had enlisted December 2, 1942, with active duty dating from April 15, 1943, and extending to midnight June 30, 1963, when he became a youthful civilian. Ed was serious and stern and we *all* cooperated—and I forsook my cheese query.

School had been successful for four; we had been entertained and bade adieu by the neighborhood, friends and Navy; and our house had sold to an Air Force Colonel; our furniture, enroute to the warehouse, NAS, Olathe, Kansas.

The plants and I followed Dave and the children to Ithaca, New York. Dave was so familiar with the path and I so cautious of my companions, we almost parted company when our cars careened around back country roads in the cool hills to have supper with Mildred and Hub at their utopian wooded home, and lake acreage. Hub was a smoker of pipes, a modest, philosophical intellectual, a soil scientist, an environmentalist, world lecturer, and fisherman—without peer. Mildred was the Perle Mesta, Republican style, of the campus and Ithaca, tireless in accomplishment, hostess to hoards of family and friends, and inimitable fryer of Hub's fish. So there we were, knocking at their door—not only with five to feed and bed for the night but with a carload of greens, and the car itself, to tend for a fortnight. How much we had depended and imposed upon Mildred and Hub—throughout Dave's eastern tours!

The next morning we breakfasted early on fried bass from Hub's lake and cinnamon rolls from Mildred's famed oven. What a repast! The children were invited by Hub to a day of fishing and woods-exploration upon our return from Canada while Mildred offered to escort Lori and all to Corning for the study of glass making, the next day. Delighted with the prospect of both, we apologized—for burdening them with our plants and set our sights for Niagara Falls.

Leaving gorgeous Lake Cayuga, site of Cornell University, founded in 1865, and member of the distinguished Ivy League: Brown, Columbia, Cornell, Dartmouth, Harvard, Princeton, the University of Pennsylvania and Yale; Dave took Highway 20 west to Buffalo, and the Peace Bridge to Fort Erie, Ontario, Canada. Paralleling the Niagara River which connected Lake Erie and Lake Ontario, 326 feet below, and received water from all the Great Lakes except, of course, the low-lying Ontario; we felt compelled to study the amazingly short, about thirty-five miles, important waterway.

Dave found us a motel on Niagara Parkway right on the bank of Niagara River West and across from Grand Island which caused the first separation of the river. The Island and Niagara River East were both in the United States. Within sight of our motel was the Navy Island, which belonged to Canada, upon which a barge had gone aground. Bruce and Davie thought we should rent a rowboat and go at once to investigate but Dave diverted their zeal by discovering their little cache of firecrackers and suggesting they had time to discharge a few on the riverbank while he made dinner reservations.

The first thing the children wanted to do after we finished our lunch at an open-air dining room looking south to the American Falls and the Canadian Falls, north to the International Bridge where, midway, a Canadian flag faced the American flag, was to ride the *Maid of the Mist* and investigate the Cave of the Winds. We could see tiers of steps, drenched by blowing spray, which descended to the Cave where, the folder said, we could view the Falls from the inside. It was the first time I had ever seen the children eager to wear raincoats and they were not disappointed after they bundled into them. We were in the U.S. when in the Cave of the Winds but I inferred the small steamboat *Maid of the Mist* was jointly operated because it had landings in both countries, a felicitous sea venture.

There was time to inspect the Welland Canal and its four locks which enabled shipping to enter at Port Colborne on Lake Erie or Chippawa on Niagara River West, navigating the Welland River straight west to the Canal—and avoiding the nine miles of Falls and rapids—to be dropped down to Lake Ontario at Port Weller. Canals and locks! How much time we spent over the years at canals and locks!

Returning to our motel and the beached barge which so distressed the boys—no doubt remembering their own erewhile efforts to launch a seaworthy craft—we made our ablutions and changed for dinner, the children's rushing to light more firecrackers to toss over the famous river.

The Canadian Niagara Falls had a large International Shop with elegantly displayed, expensive and tempting items which were custom-free. I had contrived to allow Dave and threesome just half an hour to walk through the sparkling store, the children's having become resistant by that time, even to high quality items, but Dave, with his flyer's vision and extravagant preferences, missed nothing.

It was not my fault because Dave showed them to me: a huge cluster of marble grapes, Concord purple, on a two-inch thick gnarled and twisted grapevine, most artfully arranged. The perfect centerpiece for my antique cream French Provincial dining-room table, which I did not have, in our new Midwestern abode, of like amorphous condition. It took Dave ten minutes to order, give Dad's address, and pay for my new Italian marble cluster of grapes which they promised would fade gradually from deep purple to Wedgewood blue, to its natural marble with shades of grey and gold. "I like the swan better," said Davie, referring to our other purple-blue, needed non-essential: the crystal swan from France, of Dave's collecting, the spread litmus wings a lovely blue in dry weather; blue-purple, with increasing humidity, to predict precipitation and deep pink during rain or snowfall.

Hungry for food and fireworks, we drove to Seagram's Tower, opposite the Falls, for our eight o'clock dinner in the lofty glass-encased restaurant overlooking the lighted Canadian horseshoe, roaring and splashing silver far below, and the higher but narrower, American waters, gushing in two foaming torrents. After we had finished shrimp cocktail at our window table, the blackened night across the river erupted suddenly with Fourth of July aerial rainbows over the American Falls and restaurant lights dimmed to accompanying "oh's" and "ah's" from all of us. "Guess they're shooting them at the Washington Monument about now," Lori remembered our Fourth nights the last two years. "Wonder if they'll do President Kennedy again," mused Bruce. We dined in a sky of gems!

The next morning we surveyed the Hydroelectric Canal and Power Plants: Sir Adam Beck's, Canadian side; Robert Moses, American; and the gigantic, and accurate, floral clock on the Canadian Niagara Parkway, near by. Dave took the short Garden City Skyway over the Welland Canal to The Queen Elizabeth Way around the southwest shore of Lake Ontario. We spent the night on a high Toronto hill overlooking a maze of traffic-laden freeways below and felt we had never left the States, Toronto being more American than Canadian. Continuing north around the Lake, we arrived at Kingston and entered the St. Lawrence Islands National Parks taking the Thousand Islands tour by speedboat at Gananoque. What an enchanted boat ride! Dave had remembered it from boyhood. A multiplicity of islands, some just large enough for one summer home of the wealthy Canadians and Americans; they must easily have exceeded a thousand. There were luxurious homes but their waterfront privacy was invaded from June through October and we surmised that many had been abandoned. "I'd rather live on Lake Smith!" declared Davie, our reliable conclusion-drawer, provoking nods of affirmation and smiles of remembrance.

An informational short movie provided us with a knowledge of the St. Lawrence Seaway adequate to comprehend the magnitude of the joint Canadian-American project. Designed to make ocean seaports of lake cities, our country and Canada had built a deep channel from Lake Superior to the Atlantic Ocean by way of the Saint Lawrence River which had required dredging from Kingston, Ontario, to Montreal, Quebec. A remarkably complicated and continuing program, it projected, and was in the process of building: hydroelectric power plants, much like the ones at Niagara Falls; canals; locks; dams and bypasses. All but the largest of ocean vessels had been using it successfully for many years. The operation of the locks was the most fascinating aspect for us and we spent most of our time in that observation. "A bit different from the mule-drawn barge on the C & O," laughed Lori.

I asked Dave and children if they were ready to go to Ottawa to see the Capital of Canada and the Parliament buildings; and maybe, the changing of the guards. And northwestward we went. The July 1963, *National Geographic* just happened to have an article entitled "Canada's Dynamic Heartland: Ontario" and the yellow-edged cover bore "Davie Holland" affixed to the upper left, the lead articles being "Gettysburg and Vicksburg: Just a Hundred Years Ago and The Battle Towns Today."

Davie kindly imparted salient facts about Ontario as we neared the Capital: "'Back in 1857,'" Davie nudged both Bruce and Lori to be alert, "'Queen Victoria . . . looked at the still largely empty map of Canada and chose a site on the Ottawa River, 100 miles west of Montreal, as the capital. It wasn't a popular choice.' Oh boy!" Davie made a discovery. "Are we going now to Parliament Hill?" he queried and Dave affirmed. "Well, there're lots of little locks and a Rideau Canal right by Parliament!" Bruce looked: "The 'Ri-dow' runs into the Ottawa and the buildings look like castles on a mountain—with green roofs!" he laughed. "'Eau' is pronounced 'long *o*'" came from linguist Lori. "Maybe we'll see some Mounties," Davie hoped. "I remember them from Newfoundland!" Bruce claimed.

Lori had the *Geographic* now: "The mayor of Ottawa is a woman, Charlotte Whitton, who wears a black tri-cornered hat, a scarlet cape with a front of fur and a heavy gold chain of office and the ex-Governor-General of Canada is Vincent Massey. He's the brother of Raymond Massey who always plays Lincoln!" "He played in one of Mother's favorite movies with Cary Grant," Bruce noted, voice deepening, "he looked like Boris Karloff!" "That was *Arsenic and Old Lace*, Bruce. What a memory!" I exclaimed. "I'd forgotten that Raymond Massey was a Canadian." "And his brother," added Davie, always logical.

When we arrived in Ottawa, fecund with facts and fancies, it was too late to see the changing of the scarlet-coated guards, hot in their tall black bear hats which all but covered their eyes—but we reconnoitered Parliament Hill and its castle-like Gothic buildings, Peace Tower with Big Ben-type clock and the quaint staircase locks of the Rideau Canal before going to our hotel and discovering an atmospheric establishment for dinner. We learned the guards would have their colorful changing at 10:00 A.M. in front of Parliament and concentrated on our dinner menu written in both English and French, read with expertness by Lori.

The Parliamentary Honor Guards were changed with fanfare and impressive precision the next morning, their bear hats less uncomfortable under cloudy skies. We even saw a group of Mounties with their sensible World War I campaign hats, and astride well-disciplined horses, directing traffic and adding to the romance of the scene. Since the museum was close by, we hastened to check dinosaurian and paleontological exhibits but, being Smithsonian-spoiled, found them unremarkable. The spectacle we had eagerly awaited: the changing of the Commonwealth Guards and the presence of the Royal Canadian Mounted Police had thrilled us all.

Dave bought silver maple leaves to be added to charm bracelets and we left Ottawa. It had seemed a happy blend, although our inspection was very fleeting, of both French and English cultures. The Capital of Canada lacked the modernity of Toronto, the capital city of Ontario Province, but appeared enriched by its aura of antiquity and the fairy-tale beauty of its surroundings.

"It would be interesting to see Queen Elizabeth open Parliament," commented Dave, as he drove us across the Ottawa River into Quebec. "Why does the Queen of England still open Parliament in Canada?" asked Lori, "when they have equal status in the Commonwealth." "It's just a tradition of respect for the symbolic monarch; she opens the English Parliament but has no power there either," intoned Dave. "Pays well, though," Davie reminded us. "Why don't they just stop supporting the royal family?" Bruce wondered, "and make them work like everyone else." "When I was there this spring," recalled Dave, "there was some agitation for that. But they'll never do it. The English are traditionalists; besides, Prince Charles is very popular."

We had seen the Gatineau Hills in Quebec from Parliament and decided to cross over to Hull, towering over the convergence of the Gatineau and Ottawa Rivers—and look back, and down, upon the picture-card kingdom of Canada. And there was a mythic, almost an apocryphal, essence to the scene which stifled speech.

Not wishing to go as far as Gatineau Park, we followed the river bank a bit westward, on the wooded south side of the river, winding far below, and discovered a mostly round, mostly glass lookout which happened to be an elegant provincial restaurant. Sitting well back from the road, native stone steps led to it and from it, down terraced, flowered borders to the Gatineau River.

We all suddenly realized we were famished: Dave, Lori and I for food; the boys, to shoot the rest of their firecrackers in an appropriately isolated setting. Dave and I kept them in their dining chairs by the windows, which displayed the glorious rhododendrons and pines, long enough to order black bass and river trout and enjoy their meal with sufficient refinement—just barely! Lori, too, had a cache of crackers and Dave paid the bill, quickly, while I lauded the hostess on the beauty and excellence of the facility and asked questions about the Province of Quebec, hoping to distract concern at the sound of the first bang. But Dave's long legs had carried him, Lori and the boys, whom he interrupted, far on down the steps to a sound-buffering clump of mountain laurel. Bruce engineered the saving of a small hoard "just in case we need them later" and we returned, after a while, to wash hands and be smiled at approvingly by the hostess, impressed by the entire family's study of Canadian dendrology and horticulture!

Backtracking to the St. Lawrence Seaway, we followed it to Cornwall to view the hydroelectric developments there and at Massena, New York, which had created Lake St. Lawrence. Before water had been released into the man-made lake, entire towns and villages had been evacuated, some families' having to leave homes built by ancestors in the eighteenth century—but such was the modern need for electrical power. We watched a foreign freighter, Norwegian, Dave said, leave the Eisenhower Lock and asked questions about the huge dam. It was called the Moses-Saunders Powerdam, the Robert Moses installation on the American side and built by the United States, while the Robert Saunders was Canadian in location and construction.

Back on the highway, Dave pointed to a sign which advertised "The World's Only Lacrosse Factory" and the car was automatically drawn to the Chisholm Lacrosse Manufacturing Company of Cornwall, Ontario, where three "De Luxe Special, Hand Made" rackets were immediately purchased. We had seen lacrosse informally played on the Washington Mall, at Harvard and the Naval Academy, thus the children were experts in the game and needed sticks, so Dave bought the top of the line. Almost four feet long, of hickory, the "crosse" looked like a shepherd's crook before the basket network of narrow leather thongs, gut and heavy cord was intricately knotted into the "face," which served the same purpose as the pocket of a baseball glove. The ball was about the size of a baseball but more deadly—it was hard rubber. The owner of the unique factory laughed: "That's why lacrosse players don't have any teeth!" Dave bought four balls despite the agitated movement of my head, which Lori noted: "We'll be careful, Mother."

Dave chose a flat spot backed by woods, with a rustic cabin on the side, for our Quebec lacrosse court, outside of Montreal, where we were able to lose the first ball. When it became too dark to play their new Indian game, Dave and the children abandoned themselves to sightseeing and we drove into "Mount Royal" and up the Mountain Royal to view the great lighted cross on the summit which had named the city; the marker, placed there three centuries before when the new settlement was saved from flood. Montreal was conspicuously French Canadian and even though menus were printed in English and French, for the first time, we heard more French spoken than English but everyone selling—knew American.

Everywhere in Canada, we had been met with friendly interest and polite informativeness; they had been unhurried and gracious in direction-giving and in amplifying what little we knew about their land and customs.

We left the St. Lawrence Lowlands south of the city of Quebec. The Lowlands were just a finger extended from the Great Central Plain of North America and broken by Mount Royal and several other volcanic hills backed against the Laurentian Shield and Plateau, west and north. The Algonquin Indian word for "the place where the river narrows" had been retained by the French founder of Canada, Samuel de Champlain, at his settlement of "Quebec," in 1608. As the oldest and strongest province in Canada, Quebec played much the same part as our original thirteen colonies but the emphasis was upon French, rather than English, culture.

The farther we got from Niagara Falls and Toronto, the more archaic, picturesque, simple and charming became the Old World communities and methods; inhabitants, almost exclusively now, French

Canadian in language and Roman Catholic in religion. And Dave remembered Quebec well as he found us a hotel away from the Old City and made dinner reservations for us at the castle-hotel on the high bluffs of the St. Lawrence River, the Château Frontenac.

Close enough to stroll to dinner, we entered the towered and turreted stone Saint Louis Gate into Old Quebec City with its narrow brick streets constricted by row houses and shops which would have looked like New Orleans' French Quarter . . . except it was straight uphill. We saw the Norman splendors of the Château Frontenac from the heights of the Citadel, the ancient French fortification lost by General Montcalm to the British General Wolfe in the final defeat of the French aspiration for an empire in the New World: the Battle of Quebec in 1759, which was why Americans spoke English and not French. The Citadel, still in use as a Canadian military school, was memorable for the Holland siblings because it boasted a gold-horned goat which they got to pat, its reminding them of the Navy mascot.

"It's another finger-bowl place," declared Davie as we were seated in the center of the ornate and sedate dining room for which we, fortunately, were appropriately attired. "The hotel hasn't changed," Dave observed. We ordered cups of bouillabaisse, while the Daves' wild duck was prepared; baked chicken for Lori; trout Meuniere for Bruce, and I, curious to sample, ordered stuffed stomach of calf.

"We came here in the summer of 1936," Dave began to reminisce. "My Mother was one of the national officers of the Alpha Gamma Delta Sorority and they held their national convention here." "Did you stay here at the Frontenac?" asked Lori, looking around at its grandness. "No, but we all had dinner together here one night; there were some other families, too." "Did you camp out and fish?" Bruce hoped. "No, there were six of us: Mother, Dad, Robert, Mildred, Ken and I and Mother had to bring her nicest clothes. The convention lasted five days, so we rented a house. It was a row house and belonged to a retired Canadian General." "Did he tell you about being a general?" wondered Davie. "No, he was on vacation in the States." "That's funny!" laughed Bruce, "you traded places; anyone a general in your family?" "Not quite," his Dad admitted.

"And it's a good thing he wasn't there. One day while Mother was at her meeting, the rest of us went sightseeing. When we came back, the police were there waiting for us!" "Wow!" exclaimed Bruce, his eyes widening in anticipation. "What'd you do?" Dave shook his head, chuckling: "It's what we didn't do!" "You forgot to pay the rent," Lori posited. Dave denied that. "You didn't drive on the right side of the street!" Davie knew. "No," laughed Dave, "you'll never guess!" "They thought you were lost 'cause you didn't report in"—Bruce had it. "Negative." "Aren't you guessing, Mother?" invited Lori. "I know," I admitted. "Let him tell you; you'll never get it—if you guess from here to Kansas City!" Dinner was arriving and Bruce took the last stab: "You didn't pay customs!" "Wrong!" Dave chortled. "Are you ready?" he teased. "Yes!" pleaded three in eager accord.

"Wel--l," the duck looked savory and Dave felt hunger, "we forgot to turn off the green beans . . ." three groans of disappointed reproof . . . "the water boiled away, the pot caught fire and smoke poured out the window." "Why didn't they send for the fire department?" Davie remonstrated. "They sent for a lot of help," his Dad confessed, "but they were all gone when we got there—except for the police. There wasn't much damage but it was embarrassing. But I learned a new song." "About burned beans?" Bruce and Davie laughed together, and guessed again. Lori was intent upon her baked chicken which the hovering waiter had already attempted to remove, each time she put her fork down.

After a while, Dave resumed: "We had a record player in the den which we used in the evenings. Our favorite was *The Prune Song.* "A song about prunes?" Lori stopped masticating to laugh quizzically. "Sing it," requested Bruce. Dave looked around at the quiet diners, motioned us to put our heads together, and softly warbled:

> Now -a -days
> We often gaze
> At women over fifty
> Without the slightest trace
> Of wrinkles on their face.
>
> The doctors go
> And take their dough
> To make them young and nifty.
>
> But doctors I defy
> To tell me just why . . .
>
> No matter how young a prune may be
> It's always full of wrinkles.

We may get them on our face.
Prunes get them every place!

In the kingdom of the fruit
Prunes are snubbed by others.
The only friends they may have
Are their sisters and their brothers.

Dave sat back in his chair: "End of memory," he declared. "How did you remember that much?" Bruce was vastly impressed. "Oh, I taught it to my best friend and we used to sing it together; that's Marv Hendrix." Davie looked askance at his Dad: "I thought Mommy was your best friend!" Dave smiled reassuringly at both of us. "She is and was! But that was ten years before I met her.

"Marv was my neighborhood friend; we played together; walked to school together; we even delivered papers together. On Sundays, real early in the morning, we used to push my Dad's big old Buick out of the garage and down the driveway and west half a

block in neutral, going downhill; then we'd both jump in and I'd start it and we'd deliver our papers in a hurry and then take a drive out in the country." "Why Dave!" I tried to look shocked for the children's benefit. "How old were you?" Bruce was taking lessons, I feared. "I *think* I was sixteen," Dave smirked. "Uh oh!" Lori surmised a lecture on morality was forthcoming—or a change of topic. "Dave, you must have been sixteen; that was the year your father died, wasn't it?" "Yes, you're right," Dave recalled, "it was 1939; Dad died on Easter Day." The thought saddened the children but the answer relieved us all.

"I learned to drive by watching my older brothers and sister; I used to hang over the driver's seat and just observe what they did. On short trips,

Figure 130.   "Star" of Starr Street; Dave at Sixteen

before I could drive, I used to say: 'Pops on the front by the side' so I could see out of the window. Then on long trips, I always sat in the middle, up front, between Dad and Mother. When Dad parked the car for a few minutes and we all stayed in it, I'd move over to the driver's seat and start it for him. One time we were in a parking lot in Washington, D.C., and I started it and it was in gear and we shot backwards . . . fortunately, we were on the end . . . that cured me for a while!" "Why Dave!" I could envision it all. "What a bold boy you were—and are!" "There's no one like Daddy!" approved Davie. "Thank goodness!" I appended.

"How was the calf's stomach?" Dave thought his exoneration from his youthful escapades warranted withdrawal. "Delicious, but too bountiful," I invited him to taste, "it's really just Pennsylvania Dutch: ham, potatoes and onions inside of the stomach which is like crackling with a thin lining of soft veal. I thought it would be more highly seasoned; it's quite bland, but very good." "No dessert," Davie groaned, "just let them bring the finger bowls." We all nodded and so Dave did.

We left Quebec early the following morn and I looked back at the marvelous loft of the Château Frontenac and theorized that the intrepid Frenchmen, Jacques Cartier in the sixteenth century and Samuel de Champlain in the early seventeenth, must have landed there in desperation. The inhospitable heights of the cliffs, towering sheer above the St. Lawrence River—frozen almost half of the year—would have precluded approach, it seemed to me, by all but the most undaunted survivors.

But Quebec Province, west of the St. Lawrence, was paradisiacal

when compared to the spartan fishing settlements and bleak topography of the eastern Gaspé Peninsula. Yet there were both charm and dignity in the sturdy stone cottages, colorfully roofed wood abodes, the friendly fisherfolk and dog-cart conveyances.

Low, igloo-shaped stone ovens—some with planked A-frame protections—provided us with the most wonderfully crusty, rounded French breads removed from the ovens with long, flat, wooden spades to be coupled with cheddar cheeses for our Heidi lunches on the rocky coast. That was the best of the entire Gaspé experience although it paled, or rather, odoriferously exacerbated as days passed, for I had purchased—the first morning on the Peninsula—a medium-sized paper tub of port wine cheddar which began to ooze and declare its identity in the hot summer sun. And no one would help me eat it. Both of us became increasingly unpopular, although I encased the cheddar in multiple plastic bags, inside of multiple boxes, inside of paper sacks—but we both held on, Dave's relegating one of us to the trunk between Heidi-times.

Before we left the southeastern coast of the Gaspé, we stopped at a little shop to inspect the wood carvings which we had seen around the Peninsula. Depicting the culture and mode of life—they certainly were not "made in Japan"—most were small figures, unpainted, the names of the artists inconspicuously placed, if at all. We chose three bird book-clips, the wood cleverly split to the top to hold back pages and only the bird painted on the front. They were painstakingly carved and accurately painted: a gull, robin and cardinal plus a hollowed-out birch stump in which to hold them; painted, too, with a yellowish-green, black-tailed bird, on the bole. Dave and the boys found a fisherman whose methodology struck home—his hook was caught in the derrière of his trousers. Lori liked book ends: a wishing well with a Quebec male figure, on the right; an outdoor oven, with frame protection, long lifting paddle and woman, for the left book end. The male and female were in French peasant dress, their features weathered with age and climatic conditions; the fisherman, in darker wood, grimaced in pain—his mouth a round *o* of shock; and there was a loaf of French bread in the oven. The carving was remarkably detailed for such small figures.

Our wood carvings from St. Roch Des Aulnail's, Quebec, were very carefully wrapped and we bade good-bye to the delightful shopkeepers, the principal wood carvers, and to the fascinatingly divergent Province of Quebec, Canada.

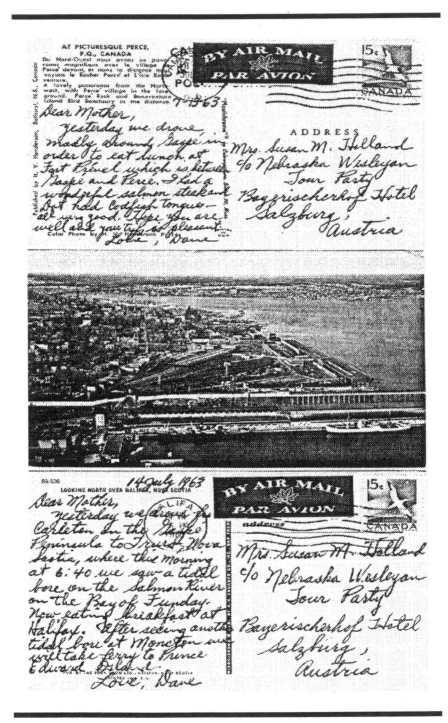

Lobster traps in stacks periodically dotted the coast of New Brunswick and our expert, Dave, together with his students, soon discerned that New Brunswick lobster was as excellent as its famous Maine cousin. What seafood feasts we had enjoyed on the long, happy coastal investigation of a glistening watery cloak, a panoply of Poseidon!

As we crossed the border of New Brunswick and Nova Scotia, bag pipes were heard and Scottish kilts and plaids, blowing from the shoulder, with knee socks protecting marching legs, came into view. We certainly were cognizant of the acculturation there and New Scotland welcomed us with fanfare. Having seen Scotsmen parade and play in Washington, the children were over their merriment—and questions—and appreciated the music and welcome, without quandary or bemused comment.

The tidal bores at Truro, Nova Scotia—on the world-famous Bay of Fundy where the highest tides known to man were registered at the top of the funnel in Cobequid Bay at fifty-three feet—were the compelling attractions of our journey to the Northeast. Staying at a motel in Truro, not far from the bridge at Cobequid Bay which we "checked out" before checking in, we supped and retired early.

At 6:40 A.M., we were on the bridge with the mud flats below at a distance, which we investigated with flashlights before moving back to the bridge lookout; and, precisely on time, the thundering roar began. With the power of buffaloes herded into a constrictive ravine, it threatened and bellowed, roared and roiled, foamed and boiled until—suddenly, the torrent subsided, just under our feet, and on the other side of the bridge, it looked to be no more than a swiftly moving river.

Nova Scotia, New Brunswick, Prince Edward Island and New-foundland were the eastern maritime provinces of Canada and were referred to as the Acadian Region, being a continuation of the Appalachian Mountains which paralleled the Atlantic Coast of the States. Nova Scotia was named for the Scottish settlements attempted in the 1600's on Cape Breton Island, while New Brunswick was named, but not the same time, for the royal family of England, the Brunswick-Lüneberg, or the Hanovers—English loyalists' moving north from the thirteen colonies after the Revolutionary War. Prince Edward Island, the smallest province of all Canada, was named for Prince Edward, the father of Queen Victoria. Called the "Garden of the Gulf" (St. Lawrence), it was more mild than the mainland, with red, sandy soil which permitted agricultural and orchard success. Newfoundland had the most ancient history, I reminded the children, having been discovered by John Cabot, the Venetian navigator who had sailed, in pay of England, 1497, to discover North America.

"The Land of Evangeline," as Nova Scotia was called, had been made famous by Henry Wadsworth Longfellow when he wrote of the Acadians, the French colonists exiled from New France after refusing to swear loyalty to England upon their victory in Quebec. Longfellow had written "Evangeline. A Tale of Acadie" in 1847:

> This is the forest primeval. The murmuring pines and the hemlocks,
> Bearded with moss, and in garments green, indistinct in the twilight.
> Stand like Druids of eld, with voices sad and prophetic,
> Stand like harpers hoar, with beards that rest on their bosoms.
> Loud from its rocky caverns, the deep-voiced neighboring ocean
> Speaks, and in accents disconsolate answers the wail of the forest.

> This is the forest primeval; but where are the hearts that beneath it
> Leaped like the roe, when he hears in the woodland the voice of the
>   huntsman?
> Where is the thatch-roofed village, the home of Acadian farmers,-- . .

> Somewhat apart from the village, and nearer the Basin of Minas,
> Benedict Bellefontaine, the wealthiest farmer of Grand-Pré,
> Dwelt on his goodly acres; and with him, directing his house-hold,
> Gentle Evangeline lived, his child, and pride of the village. . . .

> Fair was she to behold, that maiden of seventeen summers. . . . .

After breakfast at the Hotel Halifax, which was very cosmopolitan and displayed yachting trophies and paraphernalia of the sport, we drove around the mast-filled harbor. Every odd year, as was the year of '63, the Boston Yacht Club and the Royal Nova Scotia Yacht Squadron sponsored the Marblehead, Massachusetts, to Halifax Race while the Newport-Bermuda Race, sailed in even years, was supported by the Cruising Club of America and the Royal Bermuda Yacht Club. Halifax, the largest and most sophisticated city of the maritime, was alertly awake, even at an early hour; yachtsmen, as well as tidal-bore watchers, rising before bird-call. We enjoyed the nautical mystique, the jaunty attire, the beautiful, billowing sails and felt we were back in Newport which, most likely, was not new to many of the assembled craft.

Halifax closed the last gap in our knowledge of the Eastern Coast of North America which extended for me, only from Havana to Newfoundland; Dave's stretched through Goose Bay, Labrador, across Baffin Bay and eastward to Greenland. Our western geographic understanding was similar: from Mexico, Dave's taking Mother, Lori and me in 1972, to Alaska; with Dave's skills taking him onward to the Bering Strait and Little Diomede Island (stopping short of Big Diomede, U.S.S.R.), through the Arctic Circle and north to Point Barrow and the Beaufort Sea.

Crossing back into New Brunswick, we watched, with the same thrill, the early evening tidal bore at Moncton on the Shepody-Bay arm of the Bay of Fundy which roared its immediate inundation into the Petitcodiac River. Seconds before, it had been a mud channel with small, isolated pools of seaweed and sea animals, a starfish or two, it appeared from a distance, but there had been no time to investigate and signs warned against such an attempt. We were ever respectful of water and its power.

A ferry northeast of Moncton at Cape Tormentine took us across the Northumberland Strait to Port Borden, Prince Edward Island, where Canadian "1" delivered us to the capital, Charlottetown. Before anyone asked, I volunteered: "Charlotte was the niece of Prince Edward and granddaughter of George III and the only legitimate heir to the British throne, after her father, the Prince Regent, who became King George IV in 1820. I suspect the capital was named for her rather than for Queen Charlotte, King George III's wife, because Queen Victoria, under whom Canada was consolidated into one union in 1840 and flourished with her support, would never have become Queen if heiress Charlotte had not died in 1817. That threw the House of Hanover into turmoil: old George III had been irreversibly insane since 1811; the Prince Regent was ruling under the Regency Bill but was already fifty-five; and then his daughter Charlotte died in childbirth.

"Out of thirteen sons and daughters of George III and Queen Charlotte, only one legal heir, Charlotte, had been produced and her legitimacy had been questioned." "Well, why do you like the Georgian Period so much?" Lori challenged. "It sounds dissolute." "Actually, it wasn't," I claimed. "George III had a very long reign; he ruled from 1760 to 1811, dying in 1820, and he and the Queen lived an exemplary family life; he was a good king for England; but insanity began to surface . . ." Four laughed; I, too. "Is it always hereditary?" Bruce asked. "Usually. So, watch out!" I riposted.

"Well . . . back to Victoria and Charlotte. Three of George III's sons, all middle-aged, married the next year and got busy. The elder of the three produced two sons, both dying in infancy; the youngest had a son—the Duke of Cambridge, Victoria's only first cousin, but since his father, also the Duke of Cambridge, was younger than Edward, Duke of Kent—Victoria became the heir-apparent and Queen in 1837, at the age of eighteen. She was England's longest reigning monarch: for sixty-four years, four years longer than poor old George III and Queen Elizabeth was third, with forty-five years." "Gee, that's too long!" Davie declared. "I'm glad we've just got presidents! Look!" he suddenly pointed, "they've got shuffleboard; let's go there!" And Dave drove up the gentle slope of a very modern motel which boasted television in the rooms and shuffleboards on the terrace. Our stay on P.E.I. would be just overnight; we had come to buy a book but it was Sunday afternoon on the small agricultural island and all stores, even gift shops, were closed.

Anne of Green Gables, which Mark Twain had called: "The sweetest creation of child life yet written," had been published in 1908, in London. Lucy Maud Montgomery had been born on Prince Edward Island, growing up on her grandparents' farm at Cavendish on the north central coast, to create the semi-autobiographical "Anne of Avonlea," a motherless girl who lived happily and industriously on idyllic acres close to the sea—a book as important to American girls as Louisa May Alcott's *Little Women*. So the Holland women needed a copy from the island home of L. M. Montgomery plus Prince Edward bracelet charms—after an afternoon and evening of exploration and shuffleboard.

The island was green and floriferous and red of soil; iron ore, Dave said, with beaches—the first we had seen in the Acadian Forest, which grew thick with fir and pine, spruce and hemlock to drop its rocky cliffs abruptly into the sea. It was a hospitable land and the beaches invited but we did not even have time to go northward to the Prince Edward Island National Park near Cavendish which included "Anne's" farm where Mrs. Montgomery had lived with her grandparents and described so lovingly as "Avonlea," by the sea.

We looked for agates, formed in cavities of ancient lavas and igneous rocks, rock-hound Davie informed us, when we returned to New Brunswick and drove along the southeast coast from Hopewell Cape on Shepody Bay to the Fundy National Park. We found no agates on the Bay of Fundy but many interesting rocks in the Park which Dave said we could not keep but pointed to the rock shop in a long "wild-western" wooden

Hope my cards are reaching you

Rock formation at Hopewell Cape near
MONCTON, N.B., CANADA

7-15-63

Dear Mother,

We spent the night in Charlottetown on Prince Edward Island and are now at the Magnetic Hill near Moncton. Later will visit these rocks when tide goes out. We plan to return to Mildred's on Wed. 17th to see if we have been accepted for trip to San Juan. We have driven over 3000 miles since leaving Washington. Keep well and have fun

Love, Anne

AIR MAIL
PAR AVION

15¢

CANADA

POST CARD

Mrs. Susan M. Holland
c/o Nebraska Wesleyan
Tour Party
Bayerischerhof Hotel
Salzburg,
Austria

building, well back from the shore. There, all needs were satisfied and Dave discovered two sets of cuff links for me: a large, elliptical black obsidian; and an oval mother-of-pearl, also large, with a carved, sky-blue tortoise in the center. I demurred at his extravagance, but without much ardency.

Soon the Acadian Forest of the Maritime Provinces of Canada became the Acadia National Park of Maine, U.S.A., and we bypassed Campobello Island, Roosevelt's summer home in Canadian waters at the southern tip of the Bay of Fundy—the Roosevelt Campobello International Park—to hurry through the Forest, thicker, taller conifers intermingled with deciduous oak, beech and maple, toward Mildred and Hub's. We followed the rocky, indented shores of poetry-provoking Acadia to Bar Harbor to discover that sand dollars were on the beach and the ledges of wet boulders guarding them were knife-edged. After the left knee of geologist Davie, with trophy attained, received stitches from the resort doctor of the wooded town, we discussed our "finds" over delicious Maine lobster on the balcony of the small frame hotel perched on a knoll of verdure and flowers.

From Bangor, we took Highway 95, south to Boston and the Massachusetts Turnpike, west to Albany, arriving in Ithaca on July 17, eager to enjoy the sylvan beauties at Mildred and Hub's. Excited, Bruce and Davie were ready to go fishing as soon as they leapt from the car. What a gorgeous, peaceful spot of universe—we had not seen anything as lovely in our orbit of two weeks! Rocks and shells were exhibited and discussed, conifer fruit and hardwood leaves identified by Hub and Mildred and Davie's knee received a new dressing. "We had bass in Quebec," Bruce volunteered to Hub, "but it wasn't as good as yours!" We knew fishing in Hub's lake would soon be underway.

It was early afternoon and we all strolled to the lake, Mildred's identifying wild plants and Hub's indicating how much, or how little, decay had taken place in a fallen tree, how long it had been down, how much a seedling had grown, a newly sprung lichen or moss. But the tug of fishing was great and youthful anglers were ready to discuss bait. The woods were beautiful with swatches of sun—ferns everywhere and fragrant pine. Mildred took Dave and me on the cross-country ski trail—not very far—but their woods were extensive and full of riches. What unsurpassed treasure! "Evangeline" enjoyed far less in Acadie. To have both woods and lake! We had enjoyed that once, in Norfolk, but we would soon be confined to suburbia and a few perennials and roses. But we would not be moving in another year and a half—we would be home! We could plan for the future, a stationary one—one neighborhood, one church, one school system! Mildred and Hub had worked unceasingly to have their Arcady in Ithaca, to develop it, study it, watch its growth and changes. But it was not only a laboratory . . . it was a life . . . and a haven.

"You can't leave Ithaca without going to Corning." Mildred asserted at the breakfast table. "What's at Corning?" Davie grinned, hoping it was a battlefield or a beach. "A glass factory," smiled Mildred. "Oh," chorused Davie and Bruce, politely. The Navy had no space on the sailing, about which Dave had inquired, to Puerto Rico, thus we were on a relaxed schedule for the first time since leaving Washington. "Is that where they make Steuben?" Lori inquired. Mildred nodded in the affirmative. "Mother H has told us about it and shown us her pieces. We'd love to go," I added, "if you have the time. Wouldn't you prefer we just leave now and see it on the way?" "No!" Mildred was emphatic, "I want to go with you." She turned to Bruce and Davie: "Corning made the giant mirror for the telescope on Mount Palomar. You can see the first casting!" "Wow!" Bruce and Davie were impressed, the latter asking Hub: "Will you come, too?" Hub smiled and shook his head, "No I have classes this morning but I'll have the bait ready when you get back."

"Plan to stay over," Mildred urged us, "it takes two hours to go through the Glass Center, an hour each way and an hour for lunch; it'll be 2:00 o'clock before we get back and then they have to fish." Dave readily agreed: "If you'll let us take you out to dinner." Four negatives came swiftly: "We have to cook the fish!" "Maybe you won't catch any," contended Lori. "Yes, we will!" "Don't worry," Hub reassured the boys, "I've got some frozen—just in case. But before we fry them, I'll show you Cornell and where I teach." "Oh, that's wonderful!" I exclaimed, "you have everything—right here! You live in a pastoral Nirvana, a bucolic Greek Arcady, and over the hill is Ivy League and a cosmopolitan town. Don't ever leave!" "We bought it for our retirement home," Hub assured us. "Well, we were really lucky to find it," Mildred added, "we love it here." "And the children do, too," said Hub, "maybe one of you will come to school here," he smiled. "Bill and Nancy are doing well at Cornell; Susan is finishing at Duke." "That's another reason you have to stay over," remarked Mildred, "the children will all be home tonight." "Thank you," I hugged her, "we're so anxious to see them!"

The Corning Glass Center at Corning, New York, southwest of Ithaca, instructed and surprised us. In the lobby of the Glass Center, the children, Dave and I were dazed by the stupendous, golden glass disk, standing seventeen feet high and weighing twenty tons which was the first casting of the two-hundred-inch mirror of the Hale telescope. Dave and I had seen the telescope on Mount Palomar a few years before—the first sight he had shown me during our first, San Diego, residence. The children had been only to the observatory at MIT and the Naval Observatory, and the Hale telescope, the world's largest, was high on our post-retirement agenda.

We discovered that the disk had been made of a special pyrex glass with very high silica content and possessed a low coefficient of expansion which prevented the position of the focus from changing as much, with change of temperature, as it would—had the mirror been made of plate glass. In addition, the pyrex disk had annealed in ten months; ordinary plate glass required nine years for the annealing process! The wondrous, largest mirror, circa 1930, was contrasted to one of the oldest-wrought, glass vessels in the world, circa 1400 B.C.—a four-inch-high Egyptian *amphoriskos* of cobalt blue glass, elaborately beaded with wavy lines of white, gold and light blue. It had probably been used for milady's cosmetics but looked like a miniature Greek urn with a narrow neck, without handles.

The children thought they were back in the Smithsonian as they examined the wonders of the Corning Museum of Glass and the Hall of Science and Industry. In the latter, we examined a large block of cullet, scrap glass—a very hard, solid object which weighed over seven hundred pounds. We learned that it was not a solid at all; indeed, glass did not fit into any of the three states of matter: gases, liquids and solids; gases cooling into liquids, which cooled into solids. Molecules of water, when cooled, rearranged into a crystalline pattern and became ice. But not so with glass, our little hard-backed book, *The Corning Glass Center*, told us. Glass never became a true solid because "it never reaches a crystalline state at low temperatures. . . . It is a kind of fourth state of matter, a 'super-cooled liquid.'" We were also informed that glass, a fusion which looked and behaved like a solid, was made "with varying combinations of nearly all the one hundred and two elements in the earth's surface." So our three amateur chemists, who had already planned their lab in their new basement—because they knew they would have a real one, like Daddy Frank's, for the first time in their lives—were enthralled with the properties, and diversification, of glass.

In the Steuben Factory, named for the county where Corning was located and pronounced *Steu-ben´*, where the finest modern glass was crafted, we watched each of the hand processes which dated back to methods of the Romans over two thousand years ago. "It's just like Jamestown!" Davie observed. "Remember that thick green glass." "They blew it on pipes just like those," Bruce pointed. We walked back to Lori at the melting furnace; she was studying the book. "Listen to this: 'Into a melting furnace goes a dry batch, along with crystal glass cullet.' It's 'silica sand, potash, and lead oxide . . . of exceptionally high purity . . . with no chemical decolorizers that might dull the glass. Fused at temperatures as high as 2500° F., the end-product is an absolutely clear, colorless, transparent, crystal glass.'" "Guess we won't do it with a Bunsen burner," Bruce decided. "Do you realize that glass making at Jamestown was America's first industry? And look how much we have progressed in technology!" I enthused. "Yes," Davie concurred, "but the best is still made by hand!" "Right!" seconded Bruce. "Look! They use the same seat and bench as Jamestown's!" Bruce and Davie watched a craftsman trim excess glass from a vase he was shaping, turning it steadily on its long rod. "Wonder if he'd give us a sample," Bruce wished. I shook my head and Lori joined us: "It's a secret formula," she advised. "Yeah," Davie conceded, "just like the Bureau of Printing and Engraving—no samples, not even a scrap!" "We'll buy a vase," I consoled them. "Not the same," Bruce moved ahead, catching up with Mildred and Dave who were watching an engraver execute a design with various-sized copper wheels fitted into a lathe—the artist's design on his work table.

It was a fascinating factory. I would have enjoyed spending the rest of the day watching the creation of the exquisite crystal but for the pressing need to go fishing—which the boys were soon indicating. Working swiftly through the gorgeous temptations in the Steuben Gift Shop, we ordered a large floral bowl for Mother and tall vase for me; a taller, for Lori.

Fishing was successful for all the men of the two families, except Bill, who lacked his father's dedication to the sport; the entrée was cleaned and proudly presented. While Mildred, Susan and Nancy prepared dinner, Hub escorted us "high above Cayuga's waters" to Cornell University.

We left Ithaca early the next morning, after a delicious Mildred-breakfast complete with fresh cinnamon rolls, having packed my car with the Washington plants and Allaway hostas the night before and leaving the windows down. Planning to head southwest around Lake Erie to

Cleveland, our caravan departed with two reluctant boys—who would have stayed "at Hub's" forever. It had been a wonderful reunion with Mildred, Hub, the energetic, multi-talented Susan, Nancy and Bill and we promised to return while exacting their commitment to "visit our new house—soon." And we knew they would, for the Midwest was their *real* home and they came as frequently as five full schedules permitted.

From Ithaca we drove to Davenport, Iowa, and down the west side of the Mississippi River to Hannibal, Missouri, to Tom Sawyer's home town. Mark Twain was born Samuel Langhorne Clemens in Florida, Missouri, November 30, 1835; his father, a lawyer, moved his family northeast to Hannibal when his youngest, and last of five, was four years old. Samuel, named for his grandfather, spent his youth in Hannibal until 1853, absorbing the lore of the Mississippi River upon which he based his Every-Boy tales: *The Adventures of Tom Sawyer, The Adventures of Huckleberry Finn, The Tragedy of Pudd'nhead Wilson. Life on the Mississippi* related his adventures as a riverboat pilot, from 1857 to 1861, when the War Between the States precluded commercial river traffic.

Mark Twain was Samuel Clemens' pseudonym adopted at the death of another Mississippi River pilot, Isaiah Sellers, who signed articles for a New Orleans newspaper with that pen name. "Mark Twain" was the river pilot's call which meant "two fathoms deep."

Our being acclimated to calls of the deep, Mark Twain, probably the most widely read American writer, drew the children, Dave and me to Hannibal and the whitewashed fence. Tom Sawyer, who did not like painting, inveigled his friends, with adroit Missouri psychology, to do the job by beginning it himself with great fervor: "Well, I don't see why I oughtn't to like it. Does a boy get a chance to whitewash a fence every day?" We visited McDougal's Cave which Injun Joe frequented and there was buried and the Becky Thatcher Book Shop where we bought a deluxe, Norman Rockwell-illustrated book of Tom Sawyer and Huckleberry Finn "In the home of Tom Sawyer's Boyhood Sweetheart."

Mark Twain, whose drollery was reflected in Will Roger's wit and acerbic irony in H. L. Mencken's iconoclasm, was adulated as both a writer and brilliant conversationalist. He lived to the age of seventy-five and when told of a rumor he had died, intoned his legendary assertion: "The rumors of my death are greatly exaggerated."

Due to Dave's expert driving and his flyer's precision in judging distance and time—he, in effect, drove both vehicles—we made every signal light, stop sign and intersection, together, and not a car got between us from New York to Missouri. Not a one—until we got to St. Louis! And then a Missourian—heaven forbid!—rudely whipped out from a parallel-parking space and would have crushed my right front fender but I had abruptly braked my two-toned blue buggy and "sat on my horn," while he crossed in front of me to turn left! My plants were so tightly packed, they didn't move . . . but *I* did—and shook my fist at him out of the window. He looked astonished at my reaction—which I was glad to see—but my "record" was broken. The children were laughing and pointing to the importunate car, which had slowed down, at least, as Dave awaited me across the intersection. Dave gave me a "thumbs up" and off we sailed on the straight stretch to Kansas City and Home!

We were in the driveway at Mother and Dad's by mid-afternoon, July 21, 1963, and they were out to greet us before we could turn off the engines. "Shell out!" Dad called to the children and, like peas in the pod, they did—and there was Patches! It was our very happiest homecoming! Mother and Dad were well—and Patches, too, who hadn't forgotten the children and it had been three weeks! After hugs and kisses, Mother praised Patches to the children: "She's the cleanest kitty; her box was as sweet and dry when Daddy Frank and I picked her up at the airport as when you put her on the plane! We've loved having her!" Dad hugged and kissed me: "Were you a good tail?" he chuckled. "Yes," I laughed, "they couldn't shake me—I'm a bold persistency! It's wonderful to be home, Dad." Mother and the children were already inside . . . making joyous plans . . . and all talking at once, I knew.

It was Sunday evening before Dad and Dave were able to work briefly on their job plans. Charles, Barbara, Luanne and Brian had come for a quick, happy hello. Both Charles and Barbara urged us, as had Mother and Dad, to buy in Johnson County, Kansas. The Shawnee Mission School District was vastly superior to the Kansas City, Missouri, schools which I knew was true, having studied the rankings in Washington, yet I was loath to abandon Kansas City—proud of the public-school education I had received there. "We know how you feel," Charles soothed, "we felt the same way." "There are no accelerated programs in Kansas City to compare to Shawnee Mission's," I admitted, "in fact, K.C. does not—*track* yet. I want to check Red Bridge and Center Districts tomorrow—they might be more flexible. We like the looks of the homes in Verona Hills," I motioned to the Sunday Real Estate section of the *Star*, and laughed: "Dad won't have to mail that to us anymore! Oh, it's grand to be home!" And I hugged my "little" brother and Barbara. "It's wonderful to have you back, hon, and Dave and Lori, Bruce and Davie," and I got a squeeze, a kiss on the cheek and a pat on the back. "Mommy Tom and Daddy Frank have been so excited!" Barbara laughed. "I don't think they could have lasted until August 1—good thing you didn't go to Puerto Rico." "Yes," I nodded, "we were going MSTS out of Brooklyn and would have waited for the next sailing but we were anxious about schools; and Dave wanted to get started with Dad. I'm glad we came on."

Bruce and Davie were displaying their miniature Canadian flags from each province and their lacrosse sticks, which I made them take to the back yard. Brian and Luanne were not too interested in the unwieldy things but the boys were suddenly enthusiastic, having forgotten them for two weeks. I rushed to hide the hard balls, envisioning broken windows, a crippled Patches and toothless grins. "Have Daddy Frank give you tennis balls from the basement," I urged.

"Look, Mother!" Lori, all smiles, was bringing her trophy to show us, "my alabaster horse from Niagara! Isn't it beautiful!" Mother called from the dining room where she was preparing to serve dessert: "Sis, have you seen your grapes?" Barbara and I got up to look. "They're absolutely beautiful," Mother showed us the deep purple, big, marble grapes with the thick, bent, grapevine stem reposing in the center of her long mahogany buffet. "I think I better keep them," she cocked her head to laugh at me, "they're just the thing to pick up my blue!" "Do!" I kissed her sweet cheek, "they'll fade to Wedgewood blue but they're lovely in here now—and purple is *your* color." I turned to Barbara: "Guess how much we paid for these in Niagara Falls." "They're beautiful," Barbara smiled. "Knowing Dave, it must have been a pretty penny!" "Neither of us could believe the price tag; they were in the elegant International Gift Shop. They cost us seven dollars and fifty cents!" I effused. "They're Italian marble—dramatic, aren't they?"

We had surprises for all—after the car trunks were excavated. The big boys came up from Dad's office; we gathered the young ones and girls and sat down, with such happiness, at the familiar, massive dining-room table to hear Dad's prayer of gratitude for all of our many blessings and for our loving families; and to be replenished by each, plus Mother's moist applesauce cake with caramel icing.

Dad would not hear of Dave's starting out with him, not even to work in town, until we had located a house and decided on schools for the children. So we started out the next morning to search the new-housing areas in the southern extremities of Kansas City. The development of

Verona Hills, not far from the Blue Hills Country Club where Charles played golf, was a lovely rolling terrain with three and four-bedroom houses being built in the Center School District which I learned was somewhat superior to the Kansas City mainstream schools. We saw several houses which had elements of appeal but not one which had all we wanted—or rather, lacked the features we did not want.

We did not want a split-level, a house at the bottom of the hill, sliding-glass doors, two lavatories in one bathroom, an entrance hall which looked into the dining room or the kitchen, or revealed every nook of the family room, a fireplace without mantel and bookshelves, a fireplace in the living room, an outdoor entrance to the basement and, because we intended to garden with a variety of plants, we did not want an eastern or a northern exposure; our garage was not to sit on the plane of the facade of the house but back like Dad's, nor was the driveway to be circular. We wanted a tight, well-constructed house, as water free and draft free as possible, facing west—as had our Virginia purchase—with a back yard for play, gardening and outdoor living. We were prepared to build but hoped we would not have to do so.

With the assistance of J. C. Nichols, we found our house in a new Nichols' development in Johnson County, Kansas, which had been a nursery a year and a half before and, north of that, a corn field at the edge of which, Corinth Hills had been the southern residential area of Prairie Village. Charles and Barbara lived at 8141 Rosewood Drive, Corinth Hills, and our last visit to their new house, Christmas of 1961, revealed that they were on the extremity of humanity! There was nothing beyond but plowed ground. "Prairie land with hedge-apple rows!" Barbara described it with succinct accuracy.

Swiftly, in the summer of '63, contractors were building south to 95th Street, and grade schools, junior high and senior high schools were already in place for the Shawnee Mission School District.

"Randy" knew exactly what we wanted by the third day and drove us to Kenilworth to a corner of El Monte—the flattest "mountain" we'd ever seen. Aesthetically and ingeniously utilizing the large corner lot, the builder, M. David Evans, had constructed a zigzag-shaped, one and a half-story house of old brick and heavy cedar shakes of sage green, with trim on garage and cupola, shutters and over-sized door, of olive. It was just being completed; trucks were in the slightly curved driveway—but it wasn't in front of the house—landscaping was underway and the yard was being graded for sod; workmen were coming and going but Mr. Evans had approved our seeing the house which was not yet "on the market." The entrance hall, of dark green Italian marble, had light cream wallpaper and louvered closet doors, baseboards and ceiling molding of cream finish. It led into a family room of white ash with a heavily timbered, vaulted ceiling and a pegged, hardwood floor; the fireplace of old brick had a bookcase on the left with a white-ash cabinet below, a ceiling timber stretching high—across both bookcases and fireplace to three corner windows with southern exposure. From a cubicle beyond the windows, a door led to the patio and another, to the full-sized, very dry basement with copper pipes and tubing.

When we came back upstairs, we knew we had found our house, Dave's even checking to see where the children's chemical lab could be set up and the gas piped to the Bunsen burner. The rest of the house was a bonus. It was expensively and tightly built and rooms were small and cozy, except for the bathrooms and kitchen-breakfast room which was paneled in walnut up to the chair-rail with generous walnut cabinets under and above white countertops. The breakfast room was papered with vertical garlands of grapevines, fruits and flowers tinted sage green with touches of burnt orange. The dining room with north bay window was finished in cream from the louvered doors to the ceiling molding, elegant grass paper from the baseboard to the chair-rail. The separate, cream-treated, living room—with picture window, of course—was at a right angle to the dining room and opened into the hall. "I'd want a chandelier here," I told Dave and Randy, back in the dining room; "this fixture is too Early American for our furniture and we need overhead lights in the family room and a mantel over the fireplace."

"Let's go see the bedrooms," Dave suggested, as Randy made notes, "you might want some changes there, too." There were four bedrooms, three downstairs, the smallest of which we decided would be the library, with a duofold for overflow guests plus the duofold in the family room. The library would be Dave's office as well but we would have the shelves, desks and counters built in later, after Dave decided what he needed. Our bedroom on the southeast, with full bath, had two commodious closets and two windows, as did Lori's, on the southwest. The guest bathroom was partially paneled in walnut, with walnut cabinet and drawers beneath the long counter of small white and gold-streaked tiles; one white lavatory; white wall paper, patterned in alternating rows of gold fleurs-de-lis; brass-shaded sconces on either side of a very large, rectangular mirror with a heavy, ornate gold frame antiqued with white. The floor was gold, marbled and glossy, ending at the white-tiled bathtub area, separated by white louvered doors.

The stairs, half open to the family room with a handsomely turned newel post of solid white ash, golden oak finish of the family room on post, handrail and decorative spindles—led to the boys' hideaway, up and on the east. It was even finished in blue; the other bedrooms, cream, except for the delicate blue pattern in Lori's wallpaper; there was a full bath; a large walk-in closet with attic beyond; their windows overlooked the back yard and patio which wrapped part way around the family room and connected to the south end of the kitchen with a covered porch.

I turned to Randy: "We'll need a small counter and cabinet below built in the boys' bathroom—finished in the same blue." And Dave added: "I want two more shelves in the utility area, behind the louvered doors in the kitchen, and a dryer vent; also a humidifier in the furnace." Randy nodded, "I'm sure Mr. Evans will do it; we'll write it in the contract." I became more specific about the family-room lights: "We'd like the star-shaped lights with the clear glass, brass-edged, which we saw at the last house in Verona Hills. We need plenty of light for the children to study." "Right!" Randy understood, "those are from a local distributor. There's Dave Evans now—I'll go get him." We were introduced and he agreed to everything we wanted, even to my exchanging his informal light fixture in the dining room, which was brass, for a chandelier with a more formal effect (which several years later we upgraded to Swedish crystal).

We signed the contract August 1, and with proof in hand, I bought swimming patches for the Prairie Village Pool for the family and took the children daily to swim while I went to our house and watered the sod. My, but it was a large yard! We had all of our lot plus an additional ten feet of the next lot which allowed for a utility-line easement between our house and the M. David Evans house next door, owned by a delightful older couple who had fenced in their back yard, no fences permitted in front, for their huge dog, which Patches loved to tease, we quickly discovered.

Davie was enrolled in Fifth Grade at Trailwood; Bruce in Eighth Grade at Nallwood Jr. High and Lori, a Sophomore at Shawnee Mission East High School and I signed up to substitute, Elementary-Secondary levels in the much-touted Shawnee Mission School District. We moved in August 22, and school began Monday, August 26. The children rode three different buses which stopped close by; they were each placed in accelerated classes; Lori taking all "honors," at East, and approving of most of her teachers, and classmates, the majority of whom were a year older but she was both tall and mature. I substituted at Nallwood and East; once in a while, at North—the original high school—and was impressed with what I observed. I decided I'd apply to teach the succeeding year, 1965-66, preferably at Nallwood where Davie would be in Seventh and then at the new Shawnee Mission South High School which was to be completed by the fall semester of 1966.

Our engineers, Dad and Charles, inspected our choice before we signed the contract and enthusiastically approved it, as did Barbara and Mother; the latter, though, wishing the living and dining rooms were larger or, at least, positioned so they "could be thrown together" to serve a large party. "No . . . thank you, Mother," I laughed, kissing her cheek, "no Mommy-Tom luncheons and dinner parties here! I finished my mandatory entertaining in the Navy; just family from now on, and a few friends." I looked around the dining room, "Dad, don't you think I can get twelve around the table?" I called. "Of course!" he grinned, "if no one gains any weight!" Barbara, with a merry peal, tucked in her tummy and held up her hands: "I'm innocent; I even lost three pounds!"

We sent for our furniture and Dave concentrated on his new career with Dad as a manufacturers' representative of industrial hardware. The Navy had teased him about ball valves and male and female couplings and had thought that a "far cry" from flying. He thought he might buy a small plane and do both but Dad had said distances between customers weren't great enough to warrant the expense.

I planted orange gladioli bulbs on the south side of the house for fall color, as soon as we signed the contract. How exciting it was to plan our permanent yard and garden! We were told there would be a red maple boulevard tree on the west and a white ash on the north but that we could choose four other trees, in addition, to be planted in early autumn. We studied their lists, J.C. Nichols', and our Department of Agriculture and college texts on Dendrology, and chose a Chinese elm for the middle of the front yard (later uprooted by tornadic winds and replaced by a male ginkgo), an Austrian pine, southeast of the house for morning shade, coupled with a red oak. (The oak we sadly removed in 1977, when I resigned from teaching Advanced-Placement and Senior English, reading and grading of papers becoming increasingly onerous after retinal surgery in both eyes, in 1971; right eye again, in 1972. I developed a dizziness aggravated by left-to-right eye movement, called "benign paroxysmal postural vertigo" for which there was no medication but I controlled by sleeping on three pillows, not turning to the right with my eyes—but like an owl—with head only, and not reading. So I reluctantly resigned from the Shawnee Mission School District and Shawnee Mission South's Advanced-Placement English which I had initiated and loved teaching—those wonderfully gifted, challenging youngsters—to garden, crochet, knit, cook and play bridge, where I could limit my eye movement to straight ahead and from right-to-left.

(Thus the gorgeous, tall red oak had to come down to provide sunlight for my expanding outdoor gardens and the glass and shake-roofed sunroom with solar panels which Dave had built with a southern exposure, from the family room, in a long *L* around the kitchen—to accommodate my reviviscence of gardening.

(For over ten years I did not read—except for editorials, growing orchids in the sunroom with gardenias, jasmine, bougainvillea, and perennials from seed watered by the splatter from the goose-boy fountain;

Figure 131. Dave Checks Orchids, Bougainvillea, Macramé

and learned how to crochet and knit from picture books. With my usual conceit, deeming the chore had to merit my untested—but predictable ability, I skipped over "For Beginners" and undertook only the most complex patterns, remembering the flawless knits produced by uneducated women in the back country of Newfoundland and the Gaspé Peninsula.

(My family soon rued my "proficiency," I speculated—too late—for I veritably inundated them with afghans and knits. At one full-family gathering with Mother; Erica and Bruce; Agnes, Erica's Mother; Nana, Erica's Grandmother; Carol and John, Erica's sister and brother-in-law; Lori; Dave and me and, most important of all, Erica's announced expectancy, they were not only forced to "oh and ah" about my Christmas turkey and trimmings but also about my crocheted coat-hanger tree trimmed with sweaters for each, except for the baby-to-be who received a full blue set: sweater, hat and scarf. Since I had put myself thus in charge of the day, I became totally exhibitionistic and in each water-filled napkin ring-orchid vial, I deposited a cymbidium of green, gold or maroon.

(I "blamed," positively, my sister-in-law Barbara for my orchid-raising. A year before my eye problems, she had called Dave: "They have *Cymbidium* orchids at Milgram's on 95th—it's the whole plant and there's just one left. I think you should get it for Dorothy!" So Dave took ten minutes from his office work at home and bought my first orchid plant—large white and cream orchids with a blush labellum which I used

Figure 132. Lori's Orchids and Jasmine

years later in Lori's 1984, bridal bouquet. It was a very large plant with cascades of strap-like foliage and three long stems of bloom, thirteen to fifteen, four-inch *Cymbidiums* per stem. I placed it, in the winter, in the south and east corner windows of the family room, putting the tall, broad standard, not miniature, orchid plant outside in full sun two-thirds of the day from May until August 1, when I dropped the temperature twenty degrees by placing it in the cool basement sunlight and icing it twice a day for two months.

(When the sunroom was completed we had eight, over-sized bakers' racks built with expanded metal shelves for quick drainage, the fancy, wrought-iron, scrolled construction finished a water-proof Wedgewood blue to match our blue house and sunroom, with blue slate floors; and we soon filled them with orchids from Tegucigalpa, Honduras, to Maui, Hawaii. And we owed it all to Barbara—for her intuitiveness! She knew I *needed* that first orchid for happy years of study, new friends, unanticipated adventures.

("Look how long it's kept you out of trouble!" applauded Dave. "Yes," I admitted laughing at his mocking encouragement, "and it's a good thing we don't yearn to travel anymore! Our orchids are true individuals: each wants a different treatment at a different time. If I were smart, I'd grow just *Cymbidiums* or *Cattleyas,* or *Phalaenopsis or Paphiopedilums* but I love *Miltonias* and can't give up on them and *Dendrobiums* might be my favorite, especially the *nobiles.* And look at the *Oncidium varicosum, rogersii* and the *Dendrobium aggregatum;* I've got an *Odontoglossum grande* and a *crispum* I'm going to treat like a standard *Cymbidium* and I know I can get them to bloom. And this *Epidendrum radicans,* why that's your favorite; and this *Catasetum* "Jack of Diamonds," it's so waxy and beautiful—and it's deciduous—I put it back out of the light and don't water it for four months. I am determined to bloom this blue *Vanda* and the *Brassavola nodosa* but that *digbyana* just defies me. Do I sound committed—or trapped? They're like misunderstood children; I know there's a way to make them, by patient inducement, into *blossoms . . .* so I can't quit!")

Our fourth tree was a swamp white oak which was my choice of trees, in the deciduous classification. We placed that in the middle of the back yard, due east of the kitchen; it had large, dark green, very glossy leaves of slight sinuation in the true oak pattern. The boys and Dave added an American elm on the southeast border of the back yard which appeared in the springtime of 1964, under the dining-room bay, next to the topiary court. A sweet gum, two dogwoods, soft maple, Chinese pistachio and redbuds completed the plan.

One of the rewards of being home was a permanent church affiliation. We went with Mother and Dad to the Red Bridge Branch of the First Baptist Church of Kansas City, Missouri. I was still a member and Dave had joined when we married. Our historic, home church at Linwood and Park was very far north of most of the congregation, therefore a second building was erected at 100 West Red Bridge Road (with an eventual Heritage Room created by Gene and Mary Jean Brown to grandly preserve the Church's past and present). It was a beautiful, sprawling white Colonial with native stone, set atop, and into, a gently rolling hill, looking very much like a charmingly inviting, New England conventicle such as Robert Frost described in his New Hampshire landscapes. Lori, Bruce and Davie, after study in the new members' class, were the third, fourth and fifth to be baptized in the first Baptismal, Palm Sunday, 1964. Mother's Palm Sunday procession and program was on a much smaller scale than the earlier morning presentation at Linwood and Park but was memorably inspiring in the new sanctuary, with its white pews, red cushions and carpeting, elevated pulpit, and arch of clear glass behind the baptistry to embrace the green, blue and fleece of white from without. Dr. Robert Middleton (Dr. Robert I. Wilson's having re- tired—our wonderful family friend) hailed the coming of the palms with mellifluous voice—Mother's approving, by her smile, of his youthful verve and eloquence—and later baptized the children in the ever-impressive ceremony. We felt, then, we were fully . . . home.

At 2:00 P.M., Friday, November 22, 1963, I finished dusting our bedroom and hurried to the kitchen to fix my fruit and cottage cheese salad and finish reading *Time*. I was in the family room, dust cloth still in hand, when the phone rang. Thinking it was Dave, soliciting advice about Christmas cards—he and Mother had gone downtown to Demaree's to select both business and personal cards—I sat down at the kitchen desk, pulling up a pad and pen and turning on the light. It was Barbara: "Are you watching television?" "No, taking a break from house-cleaning." "Well, I knew you wouldn't be; are you sitting down?" And I told her where I was. "The President's just been shot, in Dallas; go turn it on," she said, all at once. I automatically thanked her for calling me and hurried the few steps to the television in the family room to turn on Channel 4 and there was Frank McGee—calm, voice steady, cuff links showing as he held a phone to his left ear and made notes with his right hand . . . and then freed his hands to face the camera with the horrifying news that the President had been wounded by gunshot and was just then being wheeled into the hospital! It was too astounding for comprehension! But the pandemonium behind strong, gentle Frank McGee suddenly ceased and the whole world quieted . . . and remained so. Dave returned; but he didn't speak. We just listened. But it was silence . . . perpetuating itself.

Dave told me later that he and Mother were having lunch at Wolferman's on the balcony when they heard the news. They left immediately. Everyone went home directly that afternoon; there was nothing else they could do. The children came from school . . . and did not want to believe . . . they had seen him too often, in Washington, run down the steps of the North Portico; straightening the imagined waywardness of his tie with quick fingers of his right hand, smoothing it inside his buttoned jacket; brushing back his famous mop of hair, at the same time, which was as unruffled as his tie—to smilingly greet his public; welcome a dignitary; or tuck his tall frame into his limousine. The next day an old-fashioned, cane rocking chair, the back pillow embossed with the Presidential seal, was removed from the White House. The world would miss J.F.K.

In the winter of 1964, schools consumed the children's time and interest, and research at home was continual, as my notes reflected: "February 1, 1964. I got back rather late from the Commissary (Richards-Gebaur) and noticed Lori busied in the kitchen. Pans were steaming away on the range and containers awaiting the aromatic results on the counter. I beamed with pride and laughed joyfully with surprised glee—she was beginning to benefit from my innuendoes. Or was it my constant berating? Dinner was being prepared by Lori! What a consummate luxury!

"I brought in the last of the seven bags, took off my gloves and coat and tantalizingly emptied the first bag of groceries before I peeked in a pan. Leaves for dinner? 'Lori! what are you cooking?' My gratefulness was wilting before the pangs of a teased palate. 'Geranium leaves,' came the matter-of-fact reply from the recesses of the bedroom-laboratory. 'I'm going to take the chlorophyll out of them.'

"Dave was out of town and the children and I had an opened-and-dumped supper: chili, but I was strangely hungry for spinach, kale, mustard greens, even dandelions.

"February 3. Davie is growing molds. His fourteen foods have reached the stage where he examines while I spray. But I've finally gotten them off the kitchen counter. The last two weeks, I'd bustle in to prepare a meal and suddenly lose my appetite. I didn't feel like cooking with tomatoes, apples, oranges, potatoes, carrots, bread, cheese, mushrooms, chestnuts, avocados, whipped cream, blueberries, cottage cheese or eggs. Mommy Tom provided us with scent-proof jars, firmly lidded, so the furry fourteen are now floored in the pantry.

"February 6. Lori is to debate 'Whether or not Puerto Rico should become our fifty-first state.' She has written to these decision-making men: The Honorable Robert Taft Jr., Charles A. Halleck, Everett Dirksen, Carl Albert, Hubert H. Humphrey, Stuart Symington, The U.S. House Subcommittee on Insular Affairs, Victor L. Anfusco and the President of the United States, Lyndon B. Johnson.

'February 5, 1964

The Honorable Everett Dirksen
United States Senate
Washington, D.C.

Dear Senator,

My name is Lori Holland. This year I am a sophomore at Shawnee Mission East High School and I take debate. A group of four of us will be debating, very shortly, whether Puerto Rico should become the 51st state of the United States of America. I would appreciate it if you would make known to me your views (and reasons why you think thus) on this proposition.

I am sincerely grateful to you for taking time to read and answer my letter.

Yours truly,

Lori Holland

P.S. Any information about Puerto Rico will be welcome.'

"Saturday, February 22. We went to see *Tom Jones* acted by Albert Finney. It was superb. A favorite novel of mine, next to *Pride and Prejudice*. Magnificently filmed, it was full of the ribaldry, tongue-in-cheek jesting at exuberant 18th-century English morals and manners.

One of the few books not destroyed by movieland. Of course, this was an English film which invariably was a recommendation. 'Was that Georgian England?' Davie inquired as we left. I admitted it was, 'Robust and raucous, wasn't it?' 'Tom was always in trouble—just like real boys; I liked it!' Davie decided. 'Good!' pleased with his perspicacity. 'Henry Fielding was the master portrayer of the lovable rogue. That was the first novel ever written—in 1749, and it's the cleverest, in my estimation. The title is academic and sounds like a case study: *The History of Tom Jones, a Foundling.* It's always listed among the ten greatest novels in the world!' 'Do we have all of them?' Lori wondered. 'Yes, and you've each read some of them.' I laughed at the memory, '*Pride and Prejudice* is one of them!' 'How about *Huckleberry Finn?*' suggested Bruce. 'No, usually not, but it's high. Herman Melville is the only American on most lists of the ten best—*Moby Dick.*' 'Good!' came the approval. '*Wuthering Heights* by Emily Bronte.' 'I've read that,' from Lori. '*David Copperfield*—you've all read that, at least, the junior version; there's always one by Charles Dickens; he probably would have recommended *Old Curiosity Shop*—Little Nell was his favorite character. *Old Man Goriot* by *Honore de Balzac.* We have all of Dickens and all the works of Balzac. Two more I read frequently are *The Red and the Black* by Stendhal—his first name was Marie—(giggles) and *The Brothers Karamazov.* We also have most of Fyodor Dostoyevsky, of which I prefer *The Idiot* to *Crime and Punishment* which makes some lists.' 'Whose list are you giving us?' asked Bruce. 'An Englishman's: W. Somerset Maugham's but it's pretty standard.' 'Two more,' counted Dave. '*Madame Bovary* by Gustave Flaubert is on everyone's list as is Leo Tolstoy's *War and Peace.*'

"February 20. I have to repeat each thing I say to Dave at least twice: he is either reading the paper, listening to TV or suddenly out of the room. I was watering the flowers and beginning my monologue which I thought he might be heeding since he was with me in the library, at his desk—without newspaper or TV. 'What did you say?' he asked. I had to laugh at my own insignificant prolixity. 'I don't know,' I admitted, 'why should *I* listen when you don't!' He agreed I had a case. 'But next time,' I wiggled my finger-held watering can at him, 'if I have something important to say, I'm going to hit you in the ear with my flapper!' And he roared with laughter. I had often threatened to treat him like one of the learned men inhabiting the flying island of Laputa in Jonathan Swift's *Gulliver's Travels.* They were so brilliant they were oblivious of mundane behavior, concerning themselves with abstruse thought, mathematics, globes, spheres, musical instruments, the zenith—towards which one of their eyes was permanently turned, the other—inward, and had to be reminded when it was time to listen or to speak. Each was followed about by a servant called a 'flapper' (the king had two), who carried a short stick with a little bladder filled with pebbles fastened to the end, with which the mouth was gently struck when the great man of thought should speak and when it was deemed desirous that he listen, he was hit lightly on the right ear. Once in a while, they were flapped in the eyes, when in danger of falling, but that didn't do much good. When Gulliver didn't need a flapper, the Laputans concluded he was very limited in intelligence. Dave, of course, was brilliant—and might soon get flapped!

"February 27. Bruce is busy making crystals. Davie is finishing his fungi project with the supervision of Dave for the Science Fair. Lori is writing a short story for the Lit Contest entitled 'The Pilaster'—have no idea what it is about. I just discovered Patches' exploring the china cabinet in the kitchen. Someone must have left the door open; glad we have a dishwasher.

"February 28. Lunchtime. I am substituting in Second Grade at Brookwood today. I have developed an ambivalence about substitute teaching. I don't want to be called—don't want to disturb my serene indolence at home—yet I'm dismayed because I am not called more often. 'Teachers in Johnson County,' I told Dave at breakfast, 'are chosen by their appeal to the eye. Those very young, refreshingly inexperienced female aspirants, whose knees are not unseemly, find a ready class for their pedagogy and petticoats.' 'Good thing you still qualify!' chuckled Dave, waiting to be thanked or chided. But I couldn't decide: 'Do you mean knees—or inexperience?' I try to conceal both. Last week a youngster looked at my skirt, slightly below my knees, and asked: 'Mrs. Holland, why do you wear your skirt so long?' Before I could respond, another young wit answered: 'Because her legs don't go up that far!' Pretty clever for before-school humor but they were Seniors.

"March 10. Substituting in Fourth, these answers appeared on exam devised by regular teacher: 'flying buttress is the lady of the castle.' 'A participle is the thing that holds the petals together.' 'Oasis means more than one.' 'The capital of Portugal has many stories—rooms. It is made of white marvel. It has been up for many years.' I decided I should prepare to teach on a permanent basis, ad infinitum.

"March 19. Lori today is delivering a speech to her English class entitled: 'My First One Million Years As a Fossil!' Davie gets up at six each morn to do research on salt. He reminded me this day at 6:30 A.M. when my eyes were just beginning to fully ope that the word 'salary' comes from salt in which payment for services rendered was made in old Roman days.

"Bruce is engrossed in the intricacies of the stock market. They have set up a sham market at school in their Unified Studies class and he has been selected as one of the brokers, not so much, I suspect, from any financial acuity he may have displayed as for the availability of eight-o'clock and five-o'clock transportation.

"Davie is growing molds again. Woe is me! I washed seventeen of the egregious collection last Friday. It was a somewhat distasteful chore. On Monday Davie asked: 'Where are my molds, Mother? I have to go to the Greater Kansas City Science Fair after all.' 'Can you do it again in time?' I hoped after confessing to destruction. 'Yes,' he assured me, 'and I'll do more this time!'

"Lori won third place in her Science Fair. She lectured on her findings of the effects of ultraviolet light on legumes. Next year she plans to pump mice full of amino acids, inject certain enzymes not yet discovered by man—or Lori—into the creatures, and lo, they will live underwater without air! She is currently freezing goldfish with liquid nitrogen and plans to bring them back to life her Senior year.

"Bruce is growing more crystals . . . sensible boy!

"March 31. Dave went down to Tip Top Plumbing to select our sixth, and last, lavatory for the master bath. Mr. Ladd said he would break open three crates and Dave could have his pick—but that was to be our *final* choice. How stern the man is! I adore having a new lavatory put in every month! I began to 'threaten' Dave of dire consequences if he made the wrong choice. 'Be sure to take Comet and a wet cloth and wash out each lavatory. The first time I scrubbed the next to last one, most of the enamel came off. Why don't you take a flashlight and a magnifying glass, too,' I urged. 'I will if you'll come along and carry everything!' Dave agreed.

"By the time he got to the car he had been, rather forcefully, persuaded to take a small can of Comet, a dripping rag in a baggie and a neatly folded piece of cheesecloth—his own contribution. As he backed out, Bruce tossed a pair of blue socks and brown socks in the car window. These had nothing to do with the selection of the lavatory. I had discovered a small hole in Dave's black socks and sent Bruce scurrying to get another pair. I just said 'black' once to Bruce so I really didn't expect other than blue or brown. I did wish I had had the foresight to say 'brown and blue' once. When I shouted to Dave what he was to do with the socks, he berated me saying the hole was my fault and that he intended to wear any of the socks placed in his sock drawer despite the condition. I thought this was sound reasoning and readily admitted my shortcomings but I did feel it was poor planning, psychologically, to ask for the sixth lavatory with a hole in his sock. I worried for fifteen minutes for fear the holey sock would produce a holey lavatory. Then I smelled my coffee, beginning to perk for the third time, I with just half a cup enjoyed. Spying Samuel Richardson's *Clarissa*, who was dying, I gave my attention to more important matters.

"Dave came back an hour later, having scrubbed his first three lavatories—ever. His choice was made and the die cast as I hoped this one was—and baked a bit too. Alas, this was our last! I began to feel a bit forsaken at the prospect of no more plumbers in the house. I had gotten attached to all five of them. I think I liked the sixth one best though . . . he was the one who replaced the bathtub in the guest bath. Now *that* was a job!

"April 1. Mother called at 7:30 this morn to wish us 'Happy April Fools' Day' which I probably would have forgotten. I was in the basement looking for bald eagles for Davie. He remembered at the last minute, as usual, that his class was doing a bulletin board on the national emblem. Whenever there is a class project, he felt it was mandatory for him to supply the resource material. After I had looked at the Table of Contents of fifty-six *National Geographics*—fortunately the T. of C. is found on the cover page, I found an article replete with bald eagles in every stage of existence in the Everglades National Park. This, together with *All About Birds*, where a particularly bellicose carnivore grasped a shrinking rodent in its four talons, comprised the day's offering. I was almost glad I didn't have time to go through my still-packed Elementary file because I felt the teacher herself should be responsible for the information she always expects Davie to supply.

"Lori's goldfish look appealingly at me when I go down to wash clothes, the chemistry corner being contiguous to the laundry area. She soaks them first in DMSO to preserve their cells—thoughtful girl. I know nothing about anything these children do in their corner—just grateful they're brilliant like their Dad! The house still stands.

"Davie brought home a new friend from school. After we were introduced, they went to the basement and Davie left the door open. Now he was methodical, just like his father and Daddy Frank, so I did not close the door but, wondering, listened a bit. Davie's instructions to his classmate were graphic and concise: 'Now, hold out your hand,' he was saying, 'here's a piece of aluminum foil and a drop of potassium permanganate. Now walk slowly up the stairs, we're going outdoors, and *don't squeeze the aluminum foil*.' Boom! Never had child been so instantly punished for disobedience! Davie (who was a gentle Daddy Frank) raised his voice a bit: 'I *told* you not to squeeze it!' We soaked the fist in ice water; they ate cookies and went on about their play—outside, in the dirt. The father, irate, called me that night and said I should have taken his son to the doctor immediately. I explained there was no burn, no broken skin, no redness even and gave him the name of the chemical—which Davie assured me was harmless, ergo it was—and told him it was innocuous. He, comprehending nothing, said he would sue me. 'That's not wise,' I advised, 'we have lawyers in the family, you know,' neglecting to tell him they were in Washington, Florida and Mississippi." (But it proved to be prophetic: Lori's third degree would be in law; first, French-English-Education; second, English.)

Dave loved his work with Dad; they were grand partners—both of the same happy temperament and Boy Scout morality, tireless in efforts to serve customers, precise and thorough in record-keeping and report-making and always warmly greeted by the busy men they called upon. "Everyone knows Dad," Dave told us, at our family Easter gathering. "That's because I'm the only man they know with two first names," chuckled Dad. Then he became serious, "I'm proud to have Dave as my partner." Charles, a Vice President of Butler Manufacturing Company and never considered by Dad as a possible "heir" of his business, patted Dave on the back, "It's great to be able to keep the business in the family, Dave." Mother was effusive in her praise and we were all grateful for our good fortune and familial togetherness.

Spring burst forth in Kansas and Missouri and at breakfast the appropriate morning, I produced my *Kansas City Times* article of Saturday, April 6, 1957, which Mother had sent to me marked: "Sis, this is about the *state of your birth*!" It was entitled "William Allen White Sang of Spring and Redbud Trees in Kansas" and had passages from the sage of Kansas who made the Emporia *Gazette* and his state world-known. It seemed très apropos to read the paragraphs recommended by Mother: "Read this to the children." "This." And "This," in our first springtime in Kansas:

The blue grass and the dandelions are running a race, and the lawns look fresh and green, with the dandelions flecking them. . . . The first spring rain—the kind that comes gently and soothingly down from the south, mistily drenching the cold earth with penetrating and comforting warmth; reaching with placid fingers in under shrubbery. . . Its warmth informs the sleeping root tendrils that life is on its way back to the earth.

The robins have been tapping the ground for worms for weeks. Forsythias are cascading their golden flood upon the lawns. . . .

The wheat is thumb high. The iris is inching its pale nose out of the earth. The brown buds of the elm trees are thickening the shadows on the lawn. The ice has melted in the shady places, along the creeks. Now and then in the sunny spots, a <u>turtle</u> (underlining, Mother's) trails its bubbles on the surface. The fish are beginning to bite. The voice of the candidate is twittering in the brush. . . . Pancakes don't taste quite as well as they did. . . . The <u>bees</u> (Mother's line) are buzzing around in that slow, go-as-you-please gait. . . .The lisping tattle of slow moving feet in the late twilight tells the tale of the ever-recurring mystery of love. And the politicians are looking around for a candidate for county commissioner.

If, when and as you get to Heaven, sometime, sitting on a pink cloud, you will ask wistfully, "What is it that this reminds me of? Where did I experience all the gentle joy before?"

And if memory has not left you, you will snap your fingers and say: "Oh yes—this is Kansas in the spring."

We had our last late spring snowfall overnight on a Saturday. My notes read: "Dave has taken pictures; fed the birds; heated their bath. Bruce is cooking sulphur in the basement at his chemistry corner preparatory to painting the snow. Lori is drawing large geometric designs and Davie is magnifying his molds 300 times and drawing them under the bright sunlight."

And we were busy those warming days. Davie was finishing his last year as a Cub Scout; I, as Den Mother; Dave, as weather and knots and spacecraft teacher—and merit-badge counselor for same as well as Assistant Scoutmaster for Bruce's Scout Troop. Bruce was winning blue ribbons for the "440" at Spring Track Meets for Nallwood Jr. High and both he and Davie were pitchers on their "3-2" baseball teams which played at night on beautifully kept fields, contiguous to Shawnee Mission Park. We had discontinued piano lessons although we had a piano in the

Figure 133. Unpainted Back Yard

Figure 134. Bird Food Welcomed

living room and the player in the family room which we soon moved to the basement play area; the piano, neglected, in that space—science and sports, the children's forte; instrumental music, not. Dave and I took over the planning for Palm Sunday at the Red Bridge Branch, to help Mother; I taught Sunday School; Dave was asked to become a Deacon; the boys soon following as Junior Deacons; and Lori gave the sermon from the pulpit, the following Youth Sunday.

I worked on my Master's in English at the University of Missouri, Kansas City, taking only enough courses in Education to satisfy the Kansas State requirements for certification, the school year of 1964-65.

Bruce's poetic potential was manifested in the autumn when he read his poem "Never More" at our family dinner on what we called Armistice

---

Never More

It's all over now.

No longer do the birds sing

Nor the trees grow.

No more laughing children;

Even the waves are still.

There will be no more wars,

No more fights or disagreements.

The dead now have their peace.

There will be no more debts

For we all have paid.

We no longer have to fear it;

It is gone, and so are we.

Only time still lives...

God has seven days.

                                    Bruce Holland
                                    11 Nov 1965

Day (changed to Veterans' Day in 1954). For a fifteen-year-old, it was provocative poetry about nuclear war and we ate in a prolonged silence.

Dave asked our "lay Preacher" Bruce to write the prayer for the Thanksgiving family gathering of the eleven. Bruce produced sanguine sentiments in short minutes at the old Royal portable.

THANKSGIVING PRAYER

Thank you, Lord, for all this food

  And all the things we own.

Bless the families gathered here

  And bless our lovely homes.

Help us live the ways we should

  And watch the things we say.

Thank you, Lord, for all these things

  And especially for this day.

                          Bruce Holland
                          25 November 1965

(After several years in the family business, Bruce's concern for fellow man and the environment necessitated his effort to reduce waste and want [precipitated by his attending the World Food Conference at Iowa State]. He discovered encroaching mounds of supplies and equipment discarded by business and industry and needed by schools, churches and charitable groups unable to afford them. He initiated his non-profit reutilization company in his garage to collect, repair and redistribute. Grown to two warehouses, in 1992, Bruce's company "demanufactures" what cannot be reused; recycles component metals, plastics, woods; remanufactures "new" items; and reduces remnants to scrap. His efforts provoke national attention.)

Lori, too, was inspired by Euterpe and wrote and published poetry, highly symbolic and often, obfuscating to her prosaic parents. Davie's genre was the short story and Dave threatened to write fiction but business reports monopolized. I tried to keep head above water and learn what I had neglected for many years. They finally promoted me to Junior High School!

In 1965-66, I taught Ninth Grade at Nallwood where Davie was in Seventh. Watching from my second-floor windows, I encouraged the completion of Shawnee Mission South High School, towering atop its hill a mile south, where I would teach English, 1966-67. Bruce would be a Junior there, having gone his Sophomore Year to Shawnee Mission East where Lori was a Senior.

Finishing my Capstone Seminar at night school in the spring of 1966, I wrote my thesis on "The Imperfect Person: Man's Imperfections Viewed as Stimuli to Achievement and Explicated Through Etymology, Ethics, Economics, Philosophy, Biology, Theology, Architecture and Poetry."

In early afternoon in mid-April 1966, Dave took pictures of a tornado from our front porch which Davie and I witnessed through the wide western windows of Nallwood Jr. High. Bruce and Lori followed it two miles northeast. It was a perfectly formed tornado; and it was watched "by Dorothy in Kansas," as one of the witty teachers observed.

We learned at evening news time the horrendous devastation it had caused several miles to the west where a school had been damaged and blocks of homes leveled without any loss of life, fortunately. Kansas City had long been the National Severe Storms Center and had skillfully warned residents when to take cover. With that

Figure 135. "Dorothy's" Tornado

invaluable service, basements in most homes and tornado cellars in the country, the area had experienced few casualties over the years. Still, it was a relief to welcome every excited member home from school and to discover Dave had delayed his trip to Iowa, after studying the turbulence aloft and noting tornadic potential in the cold front.

The tornado was not the only memorable event of the springtime: we had a sweet, girl graduate.

Lori graduated from East thinking she would major in French or Archaeopaleontology. All three siblings had been fascinated by fossils and rocks, influenced, of course, by Daddy Frank's picks and hammers, knowledge and library, his having taught Geology at Mississippi State (then A.&M.) and discovered oil in the fields of New Mexico, Wyoming, and Montana before the needs of Mother and Fatherhood dictated city existence. Lori decided to stay at home the first year and attend UMKC and make a determination about her major. She was not undetermined about a sorority, however, and pledged Chi Omega which pleased me mightily—and surprised her, later, for I was surreptitiously included in the ceremony.

Bruce ran cross-country at South and played football as a defensive back, until he broke his ankle, and then it was back to the chemistry corner. He built a large contraption, which was an air filter, I was told, and placed it in the back yard, keeping data and records for a long time as he hobbled about on crutches. He collected his findings in a technical paper: "The Determination of Sulfate in Atmospheric-Suspended Particulates, Under Various Conditions, by Turbidimetric Methods." Entering a local Science Fair: Ranchmart, Prairie Village, Bruce won first place, a trophy and a trip to Chicago to tour the Industrial Museum.

The Greater Kansas City Science Fair had become a tradition for all three children, so Bruce entered his air filter and paper and won the Second Grand Award, a large, handsome trophy and the interest of the Missouri Research Institute which gave him a slide rule and requested he come to see them when he got his degree in Chemical Engineering.

Dave did not seem to miss flying which I thought he might. Each activity fully interested and occupied him, as learning a new business certainly did, as well as his Scouting and Church activities on week ends. We often attended air shows at the Olathe Naval Air Station and the Richards-Gebaur Air Force Base when the Blue Angels or Thunderbirds flew.

Christmas of 1966 and New Year's Eve were celebrated at Mother and Dad's. Christmas Day summoned the Thomas brood, all eleven; and New Year's Eve, the Dozen Club when Barbara officiated at the dessert of Dad's traditional ambrosia in his coconut bowls and Mother's fruitcake.

Barbara and Charles entertained the family at Dad's seventy-sixth birthday dinner the next evening, January 1, 1967, in their new house a few blocks south of ours in Kenilworth South, Overland Park, Kansas. (Johnson County had many towns and townships: we lived in Kenilworth

North, Prairie Village, and our mail was routed through the Shawnee Mission, Kansas, Post Office, but there was a town of Shawnee and a town of Mission. It was no wonder Americans east of the Mississippi thought only Indians lived in the Midwest on a confused reservation. Bruce and Erica would live in Shawnee, Kansas, still in the Shawnee Mission School District, but Lori, practicing law in her office in Kansas City, Missouri, and Terry, would stay across the state line, with their family.)

Figure 136. **Barbara and Ambrosial Delight**

Dad wished us all seventy-six long, happy, healthy years of life such as he had enjoyed and praised his family for all the blessings they had conferred upon him. It was a very joyous beginning to a New Year!

But we lost our strong, gentle Dad on June 27, 1967, as he and Mother prepared to leave Swope Park, having escorted Bible School youngsters on an outing. Mother was alone for the first time in her life; but she, too, was strong—and independent. Lori put her arms around Mother: "Don't worry, Mommy Tom, I'm going to stay at UMKC and come to live with you." Mother hugged and kissed her, "No, Lori, you have your own young life to live; I'll be just fine—I'm used to being here alone when Dad's on the road. Why, I'm even going to learn how to drive again and use Dad's new car!" And she did, at age seventy-five. (Seven years later, after Lori had a B.S. at KU, an M.A. from MU, had taught Senior and Advanced-Placement English at Shawnee Mission North and bought her first horse, she moved to Mother's—for which we were all thankful. Even our active, self-sufficing Mommy Tom was grateful to have Lori there—beginning her J.D. at UMKC.)

It was June 1, 1968, and, twenty years later, we were heading to California again—Dave and I, together in the front seat of an Olds, with three rapidly maturing, very sentient beings in the back seat . . . when

Bruce or Lori didn't supplant us in the driver's seat. There were even more *mirabilia* than in 1948 with five to view, to complement and to share!

We had enjoyed Davie's drumlins, oval, glacial hills of lush grasses but completely treeless—his identifying topography and rock formations throughout the trip for us, while Bruce or Lori drove, or looked quickly and asked questions, or slept. The drumlins of Kansas were unique and looked more like buffalo country (Dave collected buffaloes made of every conceivable material—I even did a requested counted, cross-stitch wall hanging to go under my Plains Indian, in crewel, for his office) than a landscape from the Dorothy-country of *Wizard of Oz*, for there were no farm houses or fields of graceful wheat.

After visiting Bruce's good friend, Bob Kirby, in Arvada, a suburb of Denver, we drove northwest to Boulder to the fashionable hillside home of Jack and Joy Hinkleman for nostalgic hours and a subsequent conducted tour of NCAR, the National Center for Atmospheric Research. The NCAR Laboratory, looking like a massive, red, Pueblo construction, had been designed by I. M. Pei and completed in the fall of 1966, having been initiated in 1960, under the sponsorship of the National Science Foundation, by the University Corporation for Atmospheric Research: twenty-four universities with graduate programs in the atmospheric sciences.

Jack had joined the illustrious group after retirement from the Navy and was an important member of NCAR's Research Aviation Facility, flying a jet equipped with special instrumentation for high-altitude sampling of the atmosphere and measuring of its properties. Jack praised Bruce for his research and awards and recommended he not only major in Chemical Engineering but look into the atmospheric sciences as well. We were shown about the long structure, set atop a mesa at the foot of the Front Range of the Rocky Mountains, with its two five-story towers and a two-story center section interconnected by enclosed bridges, courtyards and basements and providing very bright, multi-level privacy for clusters of offices and laboratories. I thought I was on the sky-island of Laputa surrounded by mad scientists, except the present learned eyes could look, not only to the zenith and through thunderstorms, but also, straight ahead and down to the earth.

Enroute to the southwest corner of Colorado, we stopped first at the Royal Gorge, west of Pueblo, where the Currant and Arkansas Rivers intersected 1,053 feet below—slightly north of the Grape's joining the two. What a wondrous panorama of fruity water!

The children wanted to romp on the Great Sand Dunes before dark so Dave drove west to Salida and Poncha Springs, following the San Luis River south on 285 to Mineral Hot Springs, 17 to Mosca, east past the San Luis Lakes to the amazingly beautiful Great Sand Dunes National Monument. On huge hills of sand, finer than sugar, Lori, Bruce, Davie—et al—ran, jumped and slid. In the woods near by, a campground invited and it was the one time we missed having camp gear to enjoy the tranquillity and quietude of a place. But as we left and drove westward into the late afternoon sky, we soon experienced a magnificent sunset flirting with low stratus clouds and widening contrails.

Coming down the Wolf Creek Pass to Pagosa Springs, as we crossed the San Juan River in the dusk, a car blocked Dave's slowed, downhill progress, and driving cautiously around it—there, captured by the headlights of the car ahead of us were two deer and a fawn in the middle of the road. The deer delighted us and occupants of both cars watched until they ambled across the highway. I almost forgot, in my enjoyment of the family scene, how their cousins had savored my calla lilies and fuchsias on our Monterey hill.

Davie had been instructing us for two days on the marvels and enigmas of Mesa Verde and correcting our pronunciation of *verde* when necessary. He was our Indian-lore expert and Spanish linguist and told us that *mesa verde* meant "green table" and referred to the long, flat mountains covered with scrub evergreens.

Hauling out *America's Wonderlands*, the *National Geographic*'s book on the national parks, in our Durango motel after dinner, Davie informed us we should concentrate on Mesa Verde's largest village. "Let's spend most of our time at Cliff Palace. 'Beneath its sandstone roof are 200 family rooms and 23 kivas!'" "What's a kiva?" Bruce questioned our leader. "Where ceremonies are held." "What kind?" "Don't know. Like Stonehenge, they can't figure it out." Davie looked further: "They lived in the twelfth century; by the end of the thirteenth their culture was in trouble. They used stone-age methods." "That's a job for me," Lori asseverated, "*that's* where I'll start!" "Yeah," Bruce encouraged, "we should know about our own Indians before digging in Africa." "Right!" Davie concurred.

"Daddy Frank would have known about the rock strata—he spent years in this area," Lori reflected. "He gave his entire library to Linda Hall Library," I advised Lori. "Mommy Tom has only a few extraneous texts." "I know," Lori smiled. "Daddy Frank told me; I used to go over there when I was at UMKC; I saw some of them." "That's one of the best science libraries in the country!" Bruce claimed. "I did some of my research there. Boy! we're lucky to have it." "Dad took me when I did fungi," said Davie. "It's an impressive library," added Dave, "it helps the entire community."

"Bruce," I called, as he headed for the shower, "are you working with Youthpower this summer?" "Yes, I gave them Mommy Tom's number; she'll take my job calls; they know I won't be back until the 15th." "Wish Mommy Tom had come," Davie frowned. I leaned over and kissed him on the back of the neck. "She would have loved to have come but she was too busy—has programs to plan for both the Church and the Browning. Besides, this was their terrain which they loved wandering together after Dad resigned his professorship; it might have made her sad. You see, they spent nine happy years out here in the field, from 1918 to 1927. After World War I, the country needed new sources of oil, so Daddy Frank who was a Petroleum Geologist as well as a Civil Engineer—he was Colonel in the Army Engineers—came West with his 'Southern belle.' Both Mommy Tom and Daddy Frank, you remember, had been born, reared and educated in Mississippi but they loved the vastness and beauty and color of these states." "She could have told us a lot," Davie reasoned. "Yes, she has wonderful stories; I've written them down. I should have brought them! She met the wife of 'Buffalo Bill,' Mrs. William Cody, on the train and once had to hire a car and driver to go out into the field after Dad, late at night. She knew his big old touring car which he carried his equipment in must have broken down; there were no roads where he was surveying but she knew exactly where he would be and how to get there because he drew her a map and indicated each morning where he would work and when he would get home. And if he didn't arrive on time, she was to wait two hours and then go after him—and that's what she did." "Did he discover much oil?" "Yes, he did."

After Mesa Verde, where we would have enjoyed a week's stay, we traveled south to the Petrified Forest which satisfied the penchant for rock-hounding but precluded collecting since it was a National Park; the Painted Desert; and southwest a short distance to the tremendous hole in the earth, the Meteor Crater, dug 25,000 years ago. Grand Canyon was next, where Dave and I had honeymooned a week in January of 1948, and on to the Hoover Dam, Lake Mead and Las Vegas.

I, too, wrote a card to Mother about Las Vegas: "Friday, June 7, 1968. We are leaving Anaheim and Disneyland. Children loved it—took

Figure 137. Youth Power

all day. We have been so dismayed and angered by R.F.K.'s death. Just incredible! We have watched television—indeed, saw it happen Tues. night as we watched victory speech, in Las Vegas. It was so unbelievable—so horribly ironic. We are enroute to Monterey—have crowded much in. Hope you are fine. Love, DB³L&B."

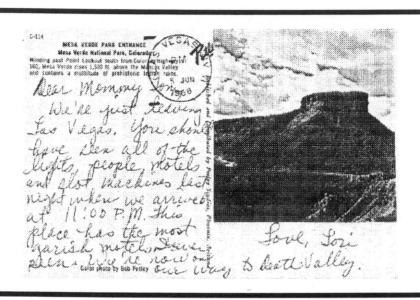

Wednesday we had driven across Death Valley, listening to the radio as the wounded Robert Kennedy clung to life. The symbolism escaped none of us. Tourists were not crowding the road, all having left May 1. It was a hot day, much above 100° in "North America's basement," the lowest spot—minus 282 feet—in the Western Hemisphere; but not yet 134° which July and August would record. Not a car or truck, and certainly not the twenty-mule team hauling borax, was seen during the slow, blistering trek. We wondered how any of the Forty-Niners had survived. Our car heated up and the water in the radiator boiled but didn't overflow. "It's because of the very low altitude," Dave assured us, "we're way below sea level. There's no danger of our car's breaking down but I've turned off air-conditioning to avoid straining the engine." "Down scope!" called Bruce and we window-sitters pushed our buttons and down went the glass. "Water!" Bruce gasped, clutching his throat. Davie snickered, prodding Bruce with his left elbow, "We're last. Driver and Navigator first; I'll ration it but no cookies—only fruit."

We took our progeny to see where Davie was born, Fort Ord Army Base, and then wound up the hillside in Monterey to our post-Kodiak dwelling at 1336 Castro Court. A high hedge concealed the front yard, the house visible only through the break of the walk which I thought sad because the hilltop prominence was not being enjoyed and the valley rim of the old Spanish Mission would no longer be visible from the living room, front bedroom and kitchen. No one was at home and we did not trespass but saw the high terrace, where I had actually enjoyed out-door ironing and the steeply sloping side yard, from the car, and then Dave, ever anticipatory, drove around the cul-de-sac once more and slowly eased by our happy memories again.

After enjoying avocado-burgers, guacamole on ground round, we directed our attention to Yosemite and the rustic cabin we had reserved, stopping along the way to gather gigantic sugar pine cones on steep banks and cones of every size to identify before we got to the National Park; I gathered wild flowers for we had brought that book, too. Yosemite was always inspiring and overwhelming with too much to see but our cabin in a pungent, pine-needled grove expedited our excursions and study.

The Wawona Tree, "Yosemite's living tunnel," was closed to automobile passage but we had verbal attestation at least, if we couldn't find the picture, to having driven through a decade and a half ago.

Lori and I prepared Heidi lunches for our daytime hikes but our breakfast and evening meals were enjoyed at the long, timbered lodge which served simple, excellent foods with enterprising college students' attending to our needs and Davie, always quick to keep my coffee cup full, morning and night.

We were reluctant to leave but the Great Salt Lake Desert beckoned and its sands had to be compared to approaches of the Great Sand Dunes, a sample of which Lori had collected in our first family champagne bottle—from our elaborate, candlelit dinner at the Air Force Academy Officers' Club, in Colorado Springs, courtesy of the Air Force to the Navy! We also had a sample from Death Valley.

What a marvelously diverse country was ours, both in topography and history! We did not want to depart when once we stopped to examine. From Salt Lake City, Utah, Dave drove due north to Idaho's Snake River, the Upper Snake leading us to Jackson Hole in the Wyoming Rockies—the Tetons rising precipitously from the valley-hole of multitudinous, minute, blue-sky reflecting lakes. There was still snow on the three tallest peaks: South, Middle and Grand. The aspect was dramatic for the Teton

Mountains had no foothills; they rose without prelude to the clouds—to 14,000 feet, Davie announced, via the book—and, from a distance, looked bluer than the heavens. Dave had pointed out herds of elk as we drove in a parallel study and stopping on the shoulder of the grassy embankment, the sharp-eyed children and he showed me white streaks of swimming beaver. They were visible without binoculars, once my naturalists told me where and at what to look. A splendid picture: meadows, lakes, animals, forests, river, and sudden mountains—all on one gloriously colored canvas.

But Yellowstone, squared into the northwest corner of the Wyoming rectangle, where Mother and Dad had spent much adventure-time, and now the third generation was *mirating*—was the quintessential experience. Its intrigue was in its chemistry and geology and proximity rather than in its spectacular emissions of water and steam. The children were close enough to bend over and examine. We pulled on boots and chose unfrequented gravel paths, which were clearly marked, however, and on which we carefully stayed, to cross shallow, clear streams for on-knee scrutiny and photography of minuscule, gurgling, Lilliputian eruptions of mud. "Look!" Davie exclaimed, farther up the path, "here are *all four stages* of the volcano I built!" Lori and Bruce stood up quickly. "Move carefully!" Dave warned, conscious of the exact placement of his own large *pedes.*

Bruce's olfactory awareness led us to sulphur, steaming naturally and coloring rocks and pebbles—or *yellowing stones.* "And *I* had to use a Bunsen burner!" he laughed. "Wish I could have *this* in the yard." "Take another picture; no samples," I teased. "Remember—Lori's working with Judge Bundschu again this summer: we have to be on good report; I, especially!" "Mother!" Davie admonished me for my levity, "we're *Scouts!* Bruce's making Eagle next month!" "I know, dear," hugging him, "I'm so proud of you both, and Lori, too; if all young people were as honorable as you three, there'd be no problems in the whole, wide world!" Bruce tooted a tantara and bowed from his perch, "Thank you!" Lori and Dave were almost out of sight and we scampered to catch up with them.

I wrote Mother. "Thurs. morn"—as we left Yellowstone.

The children felt they knew all about Devils Tower in the northeastern corner of Wyoming where the Black Hills from North Dakota leveled into plains. Lacy, at the age of eighteen months, had been photographed by Dad in the foreground of the massive, ribbed pillar and a framed enlargement hung on the "Rogues'-Gallery" wall of the family room.

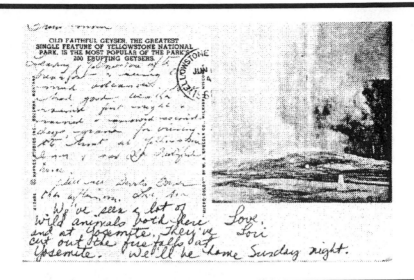

We drove across the top of the state through threatening weather most of the morning, then the sun shone brightly as we stopped for lunch. By mid-afternoon, the sky suddenly darkened to night, crackled with vertical lightning and reverberated with barreling thunder. We were soon the only car on the road but how magnificent the storm was! Dave pulled off the road several times during the heaviest sheets of zero-visibility inundation but it subsided in an hour and he quickly pointed out the anvil top of the storm, angry clouds' roiling with turbulence beneath the spreading canopy. "How high is the top?" Lori asked. "About thirty thousand feet," judged Dave. "Why is it in front of us when we're going east?" questioned Davie. "And winds blow from west to east," added Bruce. "Because it's in the jet stream; upper clouds are blowing the anvil much faster—ahead of the main thunderstorm." "How fast is that going?" Lori wanted to understand. "About thirty miles an hour over the surface of the ground." "And how fast is the jet stream?" she persisted. "Fifty to two hundred—but two hundred is mostly observed in winter."

By 7:00 o'clock we were at Devils Tower but it was light enough, with lifting clouds, to see. It looked like a tree stump of Gargantua's, ridged on the sides like uneven rivulets of tallow, rounded gently on the top, treeless—except at the very base—and fossilized all over. Dave took pictures of the children, about where we thought Lacy's had been taken, and we wound back downhill on the hairpin turn through the ponderosa pines which seemed to collar the entire majestic tower, to feed thrown crumbs to prairie dogs on the plain beyond.

There were acres of the busy creatures, scurrying from mound to mound, disappearing into holes, popping up tiny heads to look jerkily around and dropping instantly out of sight. We observed the prairie dogs until the skies lowered with darkness of night and inclemency—and Davie announced that was the last of the cookies. Crossing into South Dakota, we were glad we had guaranteed reservations at Rapid City, close by.

At our hurried breakfast the next morning, preparatory to seeing Mount Rushmore, I asked the boys when they were going to Camp Naish. "July 20 to the 27th—just a week," Bruce answered. "Dad's going too," Davie beamed. "The whole troop is going this year," reported their Dad. "Lloyd Pope and I'll take them out." "You flyers!" I teased, "you always seem to become Scoutmasters!" "It's the uniform!" Lori giggled. "Myron Chaffee's in insurance," Dave laughed. "Yes," I nodded, "and I've never seen a more dedicated Scoutmaster!" "Right!" my three Scout boys were in vigorous agreement. "Well, I'm glad you're all going and it's early enough for Bruce to get back for fraternity rush. Just think, Davie—Bruce and Lori will skip out in August and then you and I will head for S.M. South!" "Glad we have Jasper!" Davie laughed toward his siblings. (Jasper, our black male Persian had replaced Patches, reposing beneath the Crimson Glories.)

The southeastern face of the Black Hills' Mount Rushmore presented leviathan heads of four of America's greatest Presidents: George Washington, completed first; Thomas Jefferson emerged from slightly behind the first President and to the right; Abraham Lincoln balanced the semicircle, directly across from Washington but lower than both Washington and Jefferson; and Theodore Roosevelt was in the curve of granite, to the right of Jefferson and less elevated. The likenesses were history-book perfect and amazed us to momentary, reverential speechlessness.

"How close can we get?" inquired Davie. "This is the best perspective," artist Lori explained. "Look at their eyes! They *see* four different vistas. That's remarkable!" Lori had the book: "They were sculpted by Idaho-born Gutzon Borglum. It took him fourteen summers. Calvin Coolidge commissioned the project in 1927." Asked Bruce: "How tall are the faces?" "As high as a five-story building—sixty feet!"

Davie borrowed the book. "Listen to this," he grinned. "When Borglum learned this granite erodes an inch in 100,000 years, he added a foot to Washington's nose. 'It will give him another million years!'" We all laughed, and looked at Washington's nose again and went inside the glass-enclosed viewing area, restaurant and gift shop which exhibited pride in America. Nothing was tawdry, nor "made in Japan."

Bruce and Davie combined finances and bought *The New Indians* by Stan Steiner—"The first full-scale report of the gathering 'Red Power' movement . . . a revolt against the white man's culture and its debasement of the tribal way," which mapped all tribes in front and back endpapers and was autographed to "Bruce Holland" by "Yonnie Kocee Couch, ¼ Sioux Indian of Pine Ridge." Dave enhanced his buffalo collection with a golden keyring. "Does that mean we'll stop eating those luscious buffalo roasts and steaks?" "No, no," he told me, "we have to help them keep their herds to a manageable size!" One tall, Sioux pottery urn with geometric symbols on bands of black, green and cobalt for forsythia, pussy willow, redbud or sumac was added.

When we came back outside to again view the Presidents across the canyon, Davie was interviewing an Indian in full regalia and making notes. Dave asked to take their picture and they sat, side by side, American brothers, shoulders touching! (I noticed when the picture was developed that Davie's left cheek was swollen and that his benign nasal angio-fibroma must have grown again which had been removed three times since his eleventh birthday. A few days after his first surgery the nurse had asked why he was so brave and uncomplaining. "I have to take care of the little ones!" he explained. "They cry." I was allowed to stay with him in his room until nine o'clock at night and then I was sent home by the lovely young night nurse: "We like to take care of him, too," she smiled. "We don't get many like Davie!" But when they found him, in the middle of the night, in a room down the hall, comforting a crying, frightened child; they agreed I could stay with him at night, too. They permitted my staying with Davie each time—except at Mayo's.)

Making one final perusal of Mount Rushmore's great men, Davie swept his arm across the distant Presidential faces. "None of this would have been possible without Theodore Roosevelt—that's one reason he's my favorite President. I read last night that Devils Tower was the first National Monument; Theodore Roosevelt designated that in 1906, when he created the Antiquities Act. By proclamation, he could declare a national monument and that place would be preserved. About half the National Park System was established that way. It started when they needed to protect the Indian ruins at—Mesa Verde; all the southwestern

Figure 138. Proud Scouts: Bruce Behind Davie; Dave Behind Both

Indians." We all immediately looked, and more appreciatively, at Theodore Roosevelt. "Yes, he looks scholarly—even omniscient!" agreed Lori. "And look at his glasses!" prompted Bruce, "he's not missing a thing that's done in his National Park!" "Good choice, Davie," his Dad patted his youngest on the back.

At Sioux City, Iowa, we visited with Dave's vigorous Uncle Larry Holland and his lovely musician-wife, Mona. Larry was the last sibling of Dave's father. Larry and Mona were a pleasure to be with but we had to hurry southward, down the "wide Missouri" to Kansas City, Mommy Tom and home.

We had completed a twenty-year circle of joyous experience of family and country. Our eldest two would be college-bound and Davie, in high school. It had been a wonderful twenty years! We had so much to be thankful for!

The boys soon left for their Kansas Scout Camp, Naish; I loved seeing them all in the same uniform: my three handsome brunet males! Lori and I were invited one night for the family-attended bonfire, songs and skits—our threesome always excelling as clowns; and they and Lori, unlike I, could sing, on key.

Lori returned to her "legal" summer work with Bundschu, Bailey and Disney; the latter, a younger nephew of Kansas City's famous Walt Disney, who was also named Walt. Davie would earn his "project money" cutting yards in the neighborhood and Bruce would have time for a few Youthpower jobs between KU rush parties and college-clothing and equipment gathering.

The Sunday after the boys' return, Bruce and Davie were in the first group of six to receive their God and Country Award, initiated and counseled by Dave and several Scout fathers, Jerry Hill, Dave Davis and LeRoy Heggy, of the First Baptist Church at Red Bridge. Parents were invited to participate in the simple, impressive ceremony during the Morning Service. Dave and I stood behind Bruce, our Eagle Scout, in his Explorer uniform; and Davie, our Star. Dave squeezed my hand and held it in his firm, strong, galvanic clasp—communicating his pride in our sons, Lori, families; our Church; and our vast, enriching, challenging America.

AFTERWARD

NEW FAMILIES

John Carol Agnes   Erica Bruce Dorothy Lori Dave
          Fredrickson   Holland
     Handelin   Holland

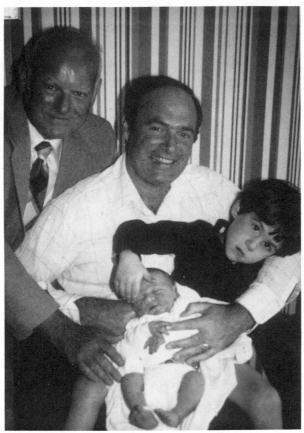

Figure 140. And Then There Were Four Handy Holland Males: Dave, Bruce, David Charles, Steven Michael

Figure 141. Andrea Marie and Steven Holland

Figure 142. Andrea

Rick Bonnie Erica Lori Terry CAPT Dan Beckie Bruce
Walters   Holland   Walters Holland
       Payne   Walters

Figure 144. Grandave and Coreen Ashley
Walters' Yule Visit Next Door
Recorded by June

Figure 145. Corey and Skyler Cody Walters

BIBLIOGRAPHY

Aikman, Lonnelle. "The United States Capitol. Under the Dome of Freedom," *National Geographic*, Jan. 1964, 4-59.

America's Wonderlands: The Scenic National Parks and Monuments of the United States, ed. M. Serey. Nat'l Geo. Book Service. Washington, D.C., 1959.

Bowie, Beverley M. "New England, a Modern Pilgrim's Pride," *Nat'l Geo.*, Washington, D.C., Jun. 1955, 733-796.

Brief Guide to the Smithsonian Institution. Washington, D.C., n.d.

Browning, Elizabeth Barrett. "Sonnets from the Portuguese," *The Poetical Works of Elizabeth Barrett Browning.* London, 1932.

Browning, Elizabeth Barrett. *Sonnets from the Portuguese (1845-6).* London and Glasgow, 1969.

Browning, Robert, Elizabeth Barrett Barrett. *The Letters of Robert Browning and Elizabeth Barrett Barrett.* 2 vols. New York, 1899.

Bullock, Helen. *The Williamsburg Art of Cookery or Accomplished Gentlewoman's Companion.* Williamsburg, 1955.

Campbell, Marjorie Wilkins. "Canada's Dynamic Heartland: Ontario," *Nat'l Geo.*, July 1963, 58-97.

"Canyons and Mesas," *The American Wilderness*, by Jerome Doolittle and the editors of Time-Life Books. New York, 1974.

Carmichael, Leonard. "The Smithsonian, Magnet on the Mall," *Nat'l Geo.*, June 1960, 796-845.

Carroll, Lewis. "Jabberwocky," *The Golden Treasury of Poetry.* Selected by Louis Untermeyer. New York, 1959.

Carson, Rachel L. *The Sea Around Us.* New York, 1951.

Clemens, Samuel L. *The Adventures of Tom Sawyer. The Adventures of Huckleberry Finn.* New York, 1936 and 1940.

Corning Glass Center, The. Corning, NY, 1958.

De Roos, Robert. "New England's 'Lively Experiment,' Rhode Island," *Nat'l Geo*, Sept. 1968.

Dodge, Natt N. *100 Roadside Wildflowers of Southwest Uplands.* Globe, AZ, 1967.

Donovan, Robert J. *PT109: John F. Kennedy in World War II.* New York, 1961.

Dulles, Foster Rhea. *The United States Since 1865.* The Univ. of Michigan History of the Modern World, Vol II. Ann Arbor, MI, 1959.

Emerson, Ralph Waldo. *Compensation.* New York, n.d.

Emerson, Ralph Waldo. "Concord Hymn," *The Romantic Triumph, American Literature from 1830 to 1860,* ed. T. McDowell. New York, 1933.

Encyclopædia Britannica. 24 vols. Chicago, 1957.

Fischer, David Hackett. *Albion's Seed.* New York, Oxford, 1989.

Frost, Robert. "Birches," *Complete Poems of Robert Frost.* New York, 1961.

Glossary of Meteorology, ed. Ralph E. Huschke. Am. Meteorology Soc. Boston, MA, 1959.

Goudsmit, Samuel A. and Robert Claiborne. *Time, Life Science Library.* New York, 1966.

Grant, Ulysses S., 3rd, Maj. Gen., U.S.A. (Ret.). "The Civil War," *Nat'l Geo.,* April 1961, 437-451.

Harrington, J.C. *Glassmaking at Jamestown: America's First Industry.* Richmond, VA, 1952.

Hawthorne, Nathaniel. *The House of the Seven Gables.* Cambridge, MA, 1932.

Hawthorne, Nathaniel. "The Old Manse," *Mosses from an Old Manse.* New York, n.d.

Hawthorne, Nathaniel. "From 'Passages from the American Note-Books,'" *The Romantic Triumph, American Literature from 1830 to 1860,* ed. T. McDowell. New York, 1933.

Höhn, Reinhardt with Johannes Petermann. *Curiosities of the Plant Kingdom,* trans. Herbert Liebscher. New York, 1980.

Holmes, Oliver Wendell. "The Autocrat of the Breakfast-Table," *The Romantic Triumph, American Literature from 1830 to 1860,* ed. T. McDowell. New York, 1933.

Indians of the Americas, ed. Matthews W. Sterling, et al. A Volume in the Nat'l Geo. Soc. Story of Man library. Washington, D.C., 1958.

Irving, Washington. "A History of New York," *Selected Writings from Washington Irving,* ed. S. Commins. New York, 1945.

Johnson, Florence Ridgely. *Welcome Aboard: A Service Manual for the Naval Officer's Wife.* Annapolis, MD, 1951.

Judge, Joseph. "Williamsburg, City for All Seasons," *Nat'l Geo.,* Dec. 1968, 812, 818.

Kennedy, John F. *Profiles in Courage.* New York, 1961.

Kocher, A. Lawrence and Howard Dearstyne. *Colonial Williamsburg: Its Buildings and Gardens.* Williamsburg, 1949.

Kraus, Michael. *The United States to 1865.* The Univ. of Michigan History of the Modern World, Vol. I. Ann Arbor, MI, 1959.

Leeming, Joseph. *The Washington Story: Pictorial Guide to Washington, D.C.* Buffalo, NY, 1961.

Longfellow, Henry Wadsworth. "Evangeline," *The Poems of Henry Wadsworth Longfellow.* Roslyn, NY, 1932.

Longfellow, Henry Wadsworth. *Tales of a Wayside Inn.* New York, 1961.

Lunt, W.E. *History of England.* New York, 1938.

Montgomery, L.M. *Anne of Green Gables.* Toronto, 1962.

"Northeast Coast, The," *The American Wilderness,* by Maitland A. Edey and the editors of Time-Life Books. New York, 1972.

Patterson, Carolyn Bennett. "Date Line: United Nations New York," *Nat'l Geo.,* Sept. 1961, 304-331.

Peterson, Roger Tory. *A Field Guide to the Birds.* Boston, 1947.

Sanderson, Ivan T. *The Continent We Live On.* New York and Toronto, 1961.

Selection of Williamsburg Restoration Reproductions, from the Craft House. Williamsburg, 1958.

Steiner, Stan. *The New Indians.* New York, 1968.

Stevenson, Robert Louis. *Treasure Island.* New York, 1948.

Swanson, Neil H. *The Perilous Fight.* New York, 1945.

Swift, Jonathan. "Gulliver's Travels," *Great Books of the Western World,* Britannica vol. 36, ed. in ch. R.M. Hutchins. Chicago, 1952.

Thoreau, Henry David. "Walden: Where I Lived, and What I Lived For," *The Romantic Triumph: American Literature from 1830 to 1860,* ed. T. McDowell. New York, 1933.

Time magazine, Dec. 30, 1991, 31.

Trees: The Yearbook of Agriculture, 1949. GPO. Washington, D.C.

U.S.S. *Independence* (CVA-62). *Cruise Book: Commissioning and Shakedown Cruise.* 1959-1960.

U.S.S. *Independence* (CVA-62). *Cruise Book: Profile of Mediterranean Cruise.* 1960-1961.

When the Ice Worms Nest Again. Sung by Montana Slim. RCA Victor 45RPM Record No. 48-0139-A. Camden, NJ, n.d.

White House: An Historical Guide. White House Historical Assn. Washington, D.C., 1962.

Whittier, John Greenleaf. "Barbara Frietchie," *The Golden Treasury of Poetry.* Selected by Louis Untermeyer. New York, 1959.

Wolfe, Thomas. *Of Time and the River.* New York, 1944.

World Book Encyclopedia. 18 vols. Chicago, 1957.

World In Your Garden. Nat'l Geo. Soc. Washington, D.C., 1957.

Your United Nations: The Official Guide Book. New York, 1961.

INDEX